ENCYCLOPEDIA of the
MIND

ENCYCLOPEDIA of the
MIND

Volume
TWO

Editor-in-Chief

Harold Pashler

University of California, San Diego

⑤SAGE reference

Los Angeles | London | New Delhi
Singapore | Washington DC

Los Angeles | London | New Delhi
Singapore | Washington DC

FOR INFORMATION:

SAGE Publications, Inc.
2455 Teller Road
Thousand Oaks, California 91320
E-mail: order@sagepub.com

SAGE Publications Ltd.
1 Oliver's Yard
55 City Road
London, EC1Y 1SP
United Kingdom

SAGE Publications India Pvt. Ltd.
B 1/I 1 Mohan Cooperative Industrial Area
Mathura Road, New Delhi 110 044
India

SAGE Publications Asia-Pacific Pte. Ltd.
3 Church Street
#10–04 Samsung Hub
Singapore 049483

Publisher: Rolf A. Janke
Assistant to the Publisher: Michele Thompson
Acquisitions Editor: Jim Brace-Thompson
Developmental Editor: Diana E. Axelsen
Production Editor: Jane Haenel
Reference Systems Manager: Leticia Gutierrez
Reference Systems Coordinator: Laura Notton
Copy Editors: Colleen Brennan, Kimberly Hill,
    Karin Rathert
Typesetter: Hurix Systems Pvt. Ltd.
Proofreaders: Jeff Bryant, Annie Lubinsky,
    Susan Schon
Indexer: David Luljak
Cover Designer: Gail Buschman
Marketing Manager: Carmel Schrire

Copyright © 2013 by SAGE Publications, Inc.

Printed in the United States of America.

Library of Congress Cataloging-in-Publication Data

Encyclopedia of the mind / Edited by Harold Pashler, University of California at San Diego.

pages cm
Includes bibliographical references and index.

ISBN 978-1-4129-5057-2 (cloth)

1. Thought and thinking. I. Pashler, Harold E., editor.

BF441.E53 2013
150—dc23   2012031251

SFI Certified Sourcing
www.sfiprogram.org
SFI-00453

13 14 15 16 17 10 9 8 7 6 5 4 3 2 1

Contents

List of Entries

Reader's Guide

Action and Motor Control

Computational Perspectives

Layered Control Architectures
Natural Action Selection, Modeling

Development

Motor System, Development of

Disorders and Pathology

Apraxia

Neural Basis

Apraxia
Common Coding
Desire
Mirror Neurons
Preconscious Free Will

Philosophical Perspectives

Action and Bodily Movement
Collective Action
Desire
Explanation of Action
Freedom of Action
Joint or Collective Intention
Know-How, Philosophical Perspectives
Mental Action
Phenomenology of Action
Philosophy of Action
Preconscious Free Will
Teleology

Psychological Research

Action Slips
Attention and Action
Common Coding
Motor System, Development of
Multitasking and Human Performance
Optic Flow

Preconscious Free Will
Psychological Refractory Period
Voluntary Action, Illusion of

Attention

Computational Perspectives

Attention and Emotions, Computational
 Perspectives

Evolutionary Perspectives

Attention, Evolutionary Perspectives

Neural Basis

Attention, Evolutionary Perspectives
Attention, Neuroimaging Studies of
Inhibition of Return
Mental Effort
Neurodynamics of Visual Search

Philosophical Perspectives

Attention and Consciousness

Psychological Research

Attention, Resource Models
Attention and Action
Attention and Emotion
Attentional Blink Effect
Automaticity
Change Blindness
Divided Attention and Memory
Inattentional Blindness
Inhibition of Return
Mental Effort
Multitasking and Human Performance
Neurodynamics of Visual Search
Perceptual Consciousness and Attention
Psychological Refractory Period
Stroop Effect
Visual Search

JEALOUSY

Jealousy is a subjectively unpleasant emotion that occurs when one perceives that an important aspect of one's relationship with another, or the relationship itself, is being threatened by a third person. Hence, jealousy requires the involvement of three individuals (a "love triangle"): the self, the loved one (partner), and the rival. Jealousy can occur in romantic relationships over acts such as infidelity. It also occurs in other forms of relationships such as when children feel upset over a parent showering attention on a new sibling, or when a person feels distress due to being excluded by friends who are socializing together. The proposed function of jealousy is to motivate behaviors that will protect or maintain the relationship between the self and the partner and reduce the threatening bond between the partner and rival.

Although jealousy may lead to desirable outcomes such as redirecting a loved one's attention to the self and reestablishing bonds, it can also have serious negative consequences. For example, jealousy is often implicated as a cause of spousal abuse and is the third or fourth most common motive in non-accidental homicides across cultures. This entry discusses theories of jealousy, including conceptual debates about its origin and definition, and presents research on the development of jealousy and individual differences in jealousy.

Theories

Theorists agree that jealousy involves unpleasant feelings, but there is no unanimity on the precise nature of the distress. One possibility is that the feelings commonly referred to as jealousy may be a blend of other emotions such as anger, fear, and sadness. There are two routes by which this could occur: (1) People may simultaneously experience several emotions during a jealous episode, or (2) they may experience a series of different emotions over the course of a single jealousy episode. In the latter case, the emotion felt at any given moment would depend on the aspect of the situation on which the person focused. For example, contemplating the loss of the relationship might elicit sadness, whereas thinking about the partner's dishonesty might elicit anger. It is also possible that jealousy is a unique emotional state that produces its own distinct feelings and behaviors that differ from other emotions such as fear and anger.

Development

Signs of jealousy have been found in children as young as 6 months when their mothers directed attention to what appeared to be another baby. This suggests that at least some primitive forms of jealousy can be elicited without complex thoughts. However, with cognitive development, the triggers for jealousy become more sophisticated. For example, one study found that 4-year-old children showed more jealousy when their mothers interacted with a similar-aged peer than when she interacted with an infant. Jealousy in younger infants was not affected by the rival's age. Thus, it appears that over the course of development, an individual's appraisals of the nature and meaning of the interactions between the rival and the loved one become increasingly important in the elicitation of jealousy.

Social-cognitive theorists have focused on two general factors that cause a loved one's involvement with another to be particularly upsetting: (a) when it reduces benefits obtained from the primary relationship, and (b) when it threatens some aspect of a person's self-concept or self-esteem. People ponder the meaning and ramifications of their loved one's relationship to the rival—"Will my partner stop giving me time and attention?" and "What does this mean about me? Am I unattractive or unlovable?" Conclusions that people draw from such questions affect the intensity and nature of their jealousy.

Individual Differences

Attachment Styles

According to attachment theory, people's experiences, beginning in infancy, lead them to form mental models of relationships that include beliefs about others and the self. People who have a secure attachment style readily trust others and are comfortable with intimacy. Research suggests that differences in attachment style may play an important role in jealous reactions. For example, one study found that securely attached individuals reported that a past jealousy experience brought them closer to their partners—an effect not experienced by individuals with insecure attachment styles.

Gender

There is controversy over whether men and women are jealous over different things. The jealousy as a specific module view hypothesizes that women should feel more jealous over emotional betrayal and men over sexual betrayal because the two genders face different reproductive threats. (The basic tenet of modern evolutionary theory is that we inherited our psychological and/or physical traits from the ancestral people who reproduced the most, i.e., had higher inclusive fitness.) Because fertilization occurs internally within women, men could never know for certain whether an offspring was biologically their own. Therefore, men should be particularly concerned about a mate's sexual infidelity because it could lead to the man expending valuable resources (food) on offspring that were not genetically his own, which would be costly to his inclusive fitness. Ancestral woman faced a different threat; she needed to ensure that her mate did not give his resources to other women and their children, which could decrease the likelihood of the woman's own children surviving. Thus, present-day women should be particularly jealous over emotional infidelity. Inherent in this is the assumption that a man's emotional involvement is a proxy for his spending resources on another.

This hypothesis drew apparent support from early work that found when forced to predict whether a partner's sexual or emotional infidelity would be more upsetting, more women than men picked emotional infidelity. However, several lines of new research with other measures and with participants who have actually experienced a loved one's betrayal have not found consistent gender differences in reactions to sexual and emotional infidelity. For example, one study found that men and women, regardless of sexual orientation, focused more on the emotional aspects of their partner's actual betrayal relative to the sexual aspects.

This begs the question of why men and women have similar jealousy reactions. One possibility is there may have been no need for sexually dimorphic jealousy mechanisms—a more general jealousy process may have addressed the inclusive fitness risks faced by either gender. Flirting behaviors (increased eye contact, smiling) usually occur well before having sex or falling in love. Because the same behaviors can signal the beginnings of emotional interest, sexual interest, or both, attention to these common early warning signs could enable both men and women to prevent their partners from engaging in either form of infidelity, without the need for sexual dimorphic mechanisms.

Christine R. Harris and
Ryan S. Darby

See also Emotion Regulation; Envy; Rationality of Emotion; Relationships, Development of

Further Readings

Harris, C. R. (2004). The evolution of jealousy. *American Scientist, 92,* 62–71.

Salovey, P. (Ed.). (1991). *The psychology of jealousy and envy.* New York, NY: Guilford Press.

Joint or Collective Intention

Among those attitudes of individual human beings that have attracted the attention of philosophers are their intentions. The branch of philosophy that deals with such personal intentions is generally referred to as *action theory.* This may itself be considered a part of the philosophy of mind. In everyday speech, people talk not only of what "I" intend but also of what "we" intend. This suggests that there are not only *personal* intentions, that is, intentions of an individual person, but also *joint* or *collective* or *shared* intentions, that is, intentions of two or more individual people. The present discussion offers an introduction to contemporary philosophical discussions of joint intention, discussions that have been of interest to social scientists and others in a variety of fields, including social and developmental psychology and cognitive science.

Joint Intentions With Regard to the Future Versus Joint Intentions in Acting

Theorists of personal intentions commonly divide these into the following two kinds: intentions with respect to the future and intentions in acting. Personal intentions in acting are an important aspect of much human behavior. Indeed, a large class of words that are applied to such behavior in everyday life depend for their applicability on the presence of a certain intention. Thus, suppose someone's arm rises; this rising of the person's arm will only properly be described as his or her *raising* it, if he or she intends to raise it.

Although not all personal intentions with respect to the future would naturally be referred to as *plans,* one with a plan thereby has a personal intention with respect to the future. Such intentions bring an important element of organization into the personal lives of individual human beings.

Joint intentions can also be divided into intentions with regard to the future and intentions in acting. This discussion focuses on the former kind of joint intention.

Questions About Joint Intention

On what is probably the most natural reading of sentences of the form "We intend . . ." in English, they are not elliptical for sentences of the form "We both intend . . ." or "We all intend . . ." Rather, they ascribe an intention to *us*—a joint intention.

The question arises: What is a joint intention? Is there, indeed, such a thing as a joint intention? Is it really the case that two or more people, as opposed to each of a number of people, can have an intention? Some may think that this cannot be, as it suggests that, in addition to the minds of individual human beings, there are minds of another kind—group minds, if you like. And that may seem impossible. Since the late 1980s, there has been a fair amount of discussion of these questions by philosophers working in the Anglo-American analytic tradition.

Generally, these philosophers do not doubt that an intention can truly be ascribed to *us* as opposed to *me* on the one hand and *you* on the other. There is disagreement, however, on what *our* having an intention amounts to.

Some of the main issues that have emerged include the following: What is the relationship, if any, of a joint intention to the personal intentions of the participants? More broadly, what is the relationship of a joint intention to specific psychological states of the participants? Can joint intention be understood in terms of the attitudes of the participants at a given time without reference to their past history? Does there need to have been some form of communication between the parties? These and related questions concern the *nature* or *constitution* of shared intention.

Other questions relate to *reasoning from a joint intention.* If the participants in a joint intention wish to act appropriately, in the absence of other pertinent considerations, must their actions respect the shared intention? For instance, in the absence of other pertinent considerations, if we intend to fly to France from London tomorrow morning, is it incumbent on me not to buy tickets for a flight to France that leaves London in the evening?

Given that this is the case, am I also obligated to the others to respect the joint intention? That is, does each participant owe the others such respect? What if the intention is to do something bad? Alternatively, what if one party comes to participate in the shared intention only because he or she is coerced into doing so by the other party?

Schools of Thought on Joint Intention

As to the relationship of a joint intention to specific psychological states of the participants, there are several schools of thought. This entry distinguishes between what might be called "correlated personal intentions," "subjective we-intentions," and "joint commitment" accounts, and makes note of the advantages and disadvantages of each.

Personal Intentions Accounts

A popular perspective on the matter centrally invokes appropriately correlated personal intentions of the participants. Such intentions are expressible with "I intend" and other similar expressions. One advantage of personal intentions accounts is that the idea of a personal intention is already familiar from action theory.

The personal intentions invoked in correlated personal intentions accounts have a variety of contents. Thus, Michael Bratman invokes personal intentions *that we do such-and-such*. More fully, Bratman's earliest account of a joint intention to J posits a set of "interlocking" personal intentions and runs roughly as follows: I intend that we J; you intend that we J; I intend that we J by virtue of both my intention that we J and your intention that we J; and you intend likewise. Finally, it is *common knowledge* between the participants that they have these personal intentions. That means, roughly, that each knows of these intentions of each, and each knows this. In later work, Bratman added various further clauses.

One might also propose that a joint intention involves not personal intentions that we J, but rather personal intentions on the part of each to act as best he or she can to achieve their J-ing, given the actions of the other party. This is roughly in the spirit of work on the topic by Raimo Tuomela and Kaarlo Miller, among others.

Subjective We-Intentions Accounts

Rather than invoking a personal intention expressible with the words "I intend," some philosophers,

notably Wilfrid Sellars and, later, John Searle, have proposed that, on the contrary, our intending to do something is a matter of each of us being in a special psychological state, expressible by the words "We intend . . . ." The author may give the psychological state a special label, such as "we-intending."

One problem with this proposal is that it is relatively obscure. It says little more than that those to whom a joint intention can correctly be ascribed are in a special psychological state, a state appropriate specifically to those who participate in a joint intention. Presumably this state involves some understanding of who "we" are, whether by description or by enumeration. Other than that, it is not clear what it amounts to. At the end of the day, the move from the question "What is a joint intention?" to "What is a we-intention?" does not take us very far. The negative point made by those who advocate an account in terms of we-intentions as opposed to personal intentions, however, appears to be sound. There are significant problems with personal intentions accounts of joint intentions.

Problems With Personal Intentions Accounts

One problem with personal intentions accounts is that a joint intention to paint the house together soon, for instance, does not appear necessarily to involve personal intentions of the type to which personal intentions theorists appeal. One reason for saying this is as follows.

It seems that those who have *agreed* to paint a house together can immediately and truly say, "We intend to paint the house together," simply by virtue of this agreement. And it is at least not obvious that those who have agreed to paint a house together tomorrow must each personally intend that they paint the house together tomorrow, or personally intend to do his or her part in their painting the house together, or something of that sort. Indeed, it is not obvious that each must have any particular personal intentions with respect to what "we" intend. One or more of them may have such intentions, of course, but the fact that they made the agreement in question does not seem to entail that they have such intentions. If no such personal intentions must be present when there is a joint intention, then clearly no personal intentions account will work.

Another problem with a personal intentions account is that those who participate in a given joint intention tend to think and act as if, by virtue of one's participation in a joint intention, one owes the other participants actions that respect the shared intention. This is indicated by the kinds of rebukes and demands on one another in which participants engage. So one might say to another, in a rebuking tone, "Why did you buy tickets for an evening flight? Our plan was to go in the morning." Accounts of joint intention in terms of personal intentions have difficulty explaining such reactions, which appear to be based on the very existence of the joint intention or plan.

A further problem is the fact that participants in a joint intention understand themselves and the other parties not to be free to unilaterally alter or cancel the joint intention, absent special background understandings. Thus, a participant might appropriately respond to a rebuke such as the one mentioned in the previous paragraph with "Oh, I forgot" but not "Oh, I changed our plan!" To the latter response, the first party might object "But you can't change our plan, not just like that!" Because one can alter one's personal intention, just like that, this aspect of joint intentions may be impossible for a personal intentions account to capture.

Joint Commitment Accounts

An account of joint intention that provides an alternative to both personal intentions and subjective we-intentions accounts has been proposed by Margaret Gilbert. It appeals to more than the subjective states of the participants, as the we-intentions accounts do, and does not require personal intentions in favor of the joint intention, as the personal intentions accounts do. Gilbert has argued that when people have a joint intention, they owe each other conforming actions and are open to rebukes for nonconformity and demands for conformity.

Using the example of painting the house together, Gilbert's account runs roughly as follows: Two or more people have a joint intention to paint the house together if and only if they are *jointly committed* to intend as a body that the house be painted by virtue of the coordinated activity of the two of them. It is understood that, in order that such a joint commitment be established, each has communicated to the other his or her readiness jointly to commit them all to emulate as far as possible a single creature that intends that the house be so painted. "Communication" is understood here in a broad sense. It can take place without face-to-face interaction.

In a special kind of case, the parties are jointly committed to accept decisions of a given person or body as to what they are jointly committed to intend as a body. The initial joint commitment establishes the person or body in question as having the authority to establish joint intentions for the parties.

What of joint intentions to do something bad and joint intentions such that one party or more of the parties have been coerced into participating in the joint intention? Gilbert argues that given such factors, the parties may well be able to argue that it is not appropriate to act in accordance with the shared intention, all things considered. Nonetheless, they can still be said to owe each other such action, in a particular sense of "owe."

People owe one another actions in accordance with any joint commitment insofar as by jointly committing one another they have together imposed a constraint on each other, with respect to what they may appropriately do. To that extent they may together be said to have "put their dibs" on the action of each. So each may rebuke any other with respect to action that is not appropriate to the shared intention, in the name of them all.

Gilbert labels any set of jointly committed persons a "plural subject." In using this label, she does not mean to imply that there is a group consciousness, or subjective state, distinct from the consciousness of each individual person. Hence, her account respects an important constraint that other theorists of joint intention have insisted on.

Her account also allows that those with a joint intention will appropriately form, where necessary, personal intentions that will support the joint intention, as when someone forms the personal intention to drive to the store for paint, in light of a joint intention to paint the house with another person, whom, he or she knows, will be buying other necessary items. Yet such personal intentions need not be present in every case where there is a joint commitment of the kind in question here. This respects the point made earlier as to the apparent nonnecessity of such personal intentions to the existence of a joint intention.

Margaret Gilbert

See also Action and Bodily Movement; Collective Action; Philosophy of Action

Further Readings

Bratman, M. (1999). *Faces of intention.* Cambridge, UK: Cambridge University Press.

Clark, A. (1994). Beliefs and desires incorporated. *Journal of Philosophy, 91,* 404–425.

Gilbert, M. (2000). *Sociality and responsibility: New essays in plural subject theory.* Lanham, MD: Rowman & Littlefield.

Gilbert, M. (2009). Shared intentions and personal intentions. *Philosophical Studies, 144,* 167–187.

Searle, J. (1990). Collective intentions and actions. In P. R. Cohen, J. Morgan, & M. E. Pollack (Eds.), *Intentions in communication.* Cambridge, MA: MIT Press.

Sellars, W. (1963). Imperatives, intentions, and the logic of "ought." In G. Nakhnikian & H.-N. Castaneda (Eds.), *Morality and the language of conduct.* Detroit, MI: Wayne State University Press.

Tuomela, R., & Miller, K. (1988). We-intentions. *Philosophical Studies, 53,* 115–137.

Velleman, D. (1997). How to share an intention. *Philosophy and Phenomenological Research, 57,* 29–50.

Know-How, Philosophical Perspectives

Any philosophical entry on know-how must begin with Gilbert Ryle, who was responsible for the modern distinction between *knowledge-how* and *knowledge-that*. Having set out the distinction, this entry will examine the use to which Ryle puts it in his critique of René Descartes, before considering the role it plays in contemporary philosophy, particularly in the debate over physicalism.

Knowledge-How Versus Knowledge-That—Ryle's Distinction

To a first approximation, the distinction we inherit from Ryle is between what might be termed *intellectual* knowledge-that, which is *propositional* in nature, and *practical* knowledge-how, which may be understood in terms of having *abilities to do* certain things. Consider a project to learn all about bicycles. There is a lot of knowledge-that to be gained about bicycles: One can learn *that* bicycles have two wheels, *that* they balance along their longest axis, *that* one must pedal while remaining balanced to keep the bicycle upright, and so on. (The phrases after each *that* in the previous sentence express facts or *propositions*—hence, knowledge-that is propositional knowledge, knowledge of propositions.) But still, it is fairly obvious to most that even someone who has learned all the propositions there are to know about bicycles will not thereby be gifted with the *ability to ride* a bicycle. We might expect such a cycling know-it-all to fall flat on his face when attempting his first unaided ride. What the know-it-all lacks, the story goes, is *know-how:* He does not know *how* to ride a bicycle. Alternatively, we might say that having learned academically all about bicycles, this learner has yet to acquire the practical ability to ride bicycles. Further, whereas time in the classroom arguably suffices for acquiring all the knowledge-that about bicycles that our student has come to possess, we know that acquiring, in addition, the knowledge how to ride a bicycle will require some first-hand experience—some practice in bike riding on the student's part.

Ryle's Critique of Descartes

Ryle introduced the previously described distinction in his important book *The Concept of Mind*, as part of his campaign against the then (Ryle is writing at the start of the 1950s) orthodoxy of a Cartesian conception of mind and mentality. René Descartes had proposed his dualism: the idea that the mind is a nonphysical object separate from, though connected to, the physical body and, consequently, not observable or measurable using conventional scientific methods. Ryle strongly objected to the notion that mental processes go on *in secret:* hidden and unobservable as a matter of principle. He posed the following dilemma for what he labeled Descartes' "intellectualist legend," the doctrine that all intelligent bodily action (as opposed to mere reflex) is preceded by rational thought—the consideration of a relevant proposition—that effectively plans the next move for the body. Ryle observes that planning a bodily movement, considering propositions, is itself an operation, an action of sorts. Now if the act of proposition-consideration itself were unintelligent, it would be hard to see how it could confer intelligence on the bodily movement that it preceded. So clearly, the act of considering the relevant proposition prior to originating an intelligent bodily action had itself better be intelligent. But what is it to be an intelligent act according to Ryle's Cartesian intellectualist legend? It is to be preceded by a mental operation of considering a relevant proposition. In which case the mental planning procedure that originated the bodily action in this case itself needs to be preceded by a mental act of planning, an act which, in turn, must be intelligent and thus preceded by a further contemplative act, and so on. The dilemma that arises for the Cartesian, then, is this: Either an intelligent action can never get started, for it must always be preceded by a further mental act of planning, or some actions are intelligent without being preceded by mental operations, operations Ryle considers appallingly occult on Descartes' conception of mind and its processes. This reasoning led Ryle to posit a distinct, nonintellectual, practical genre of knowledge, that is, knowledge-how, knowledge, in some sense, *of the body*.

Know-How Versus Know-That in Modern Philosophy

The know-how/know-that distinction as proposed by Ryle is of philosophical interest in its own right, as well as for the part it plays in the Rylean critique of Descartes. Nowadays the distinction is more familiar to philosophers because of its employment in another controversy concerning the philosophy of mind. Frank Jackson tries to disprove physicalism—the doctrine that all that exists is physical matter and its combinations—with an argument that centers on an omniscient color scientist, Mary. Mary knows all the scientific facts relating to human color vision, despite never having seen color. Living her life hitherto in a monochrome laboratory, Mary has extensively studied red-seeing subjects in the outside world, thus accumulating her stock of scientific knowledge. One day, Mary is shown a red rose. Jackson invites us to agree that Mary learns something important in this encounter: the fact of what an experience of redness is like, qualitatively, for the person undergoing it. In which case Mary's

prior stock of physical-factual knowledge concerning color vision was incomplete, and it follows, claims Jackson, that physicalism is false. There are some nonphysical features of the world to be learned about.

One of the first and most enduring replies to this provocative argument draws on Ryle's distinction. David Lewis, following Lawrence Nemirow, asserts that what Mary learns when she sees red is not any new fact, but a set of new abilities—in other words, she gains no knowledge-that, only knowledge-how. Specifically, Lewis proposes that Mary acquires the abilities to *recognize, remember,* and *imagine* the experience of redness through her meeting with the rose. However, because Mary learns no new fact, as there is no new proposition that Mary now knows, Lewis claims, physicalism is not threatened by Mary's increase in knowledge. She learns how to do some new things, but there is no new—and so nonphysical—fact that she discovers.

Lewis's argument has brought renewed attention on Ryle's distinction, mostly in the service of discussions concerning mind, but also independently. Some remain dubious about the distinction. An article by Jason Stanley and Timothy Williamson makes a good case for the assimilation of knowledge-how to knowledge-that. But Stanley and Williamson's thesis, that knowing how to ride a bicycle (for example) is really knowing, of some manner of riding a bicycle, *that* this is a way to ride a bicycle, is itself widely rejected. Thus, the controversy rumbles on. Sam Coleman is also sympathetic to the view that know-how, or ability knowledge, might reduce to knowledge of fact. He notes that abilities, such as the ability to ride a bicycle, depend on knowing what certain sensations feel like—in the case of cycling, the would-be rider must, crucially, become well acquainted with the sensation of balancing on her bicycle in order to gain the ability. But if knowing what sensations feel like is factual knowledge—as Jackson suggests—then know-how/ability knowledge will be partly constituted by knowledge-that. If this is so, then Ryle's distinction may collapse, and with it Lewis's popular objection to Jackson's "knowledge argument."

Sam Coleman

See also Knowledge by Acquaintance; Mind-Body Problem; Physicalism; Reductive Physicalism

Further Readings

Coleman, S. (2008). Why the ability hypothesis is best forgotten. *Journal of Consciousness Studies, 16*(2–3), 74–97.

Jackson, F. (1982). Epiphenomenal qualia. *Philosophical Quarterly, 32,* 127–136.

Lewis, D. (2004). What experience teaches. In P. Ludlow, Y. Nagasawa, & D. Stoljar (Eds.), *There's something about Mary: Essays on Frank Jackson's knowledge argument against physicalism* (pp. 77–103). Cambridge MA: MIT Press.

Nemirow, L. (1980). Review of Nagel's *Mortal Questions. Philosophical Review, 89,* 473–477.

Nemirow, L. (2007). So *this* is what it's like: A defense of the ability hypothesis. In T. Alter & S. Walter (Eds.), *Phenomenal concepts and phenomenal knowledge. New essays on consciousness and physicalism* (pp. 32–51). Oxford, UK: Oxford University Press.

Ryle, G. (1949). *The concept of mind.* London, UK: Hutchinson.

Stanley, J., & Williamson, T. (2001). Knowing how. *Journal of Philosophy, 98*(8), 411–444.

KNOWLEDGE ACQUISITION IN DEVELOPMENT

Childhood is a period of remarkable knowledge acquisition—unparalleled in human learning. In the first five years of life, children are transformed from helpless infants with virtually no understanding of the world around them to articulate students with a rich understanding of time, space, and number; an ability to organize objects and animals into category hierarchies; a capacity to infer cause and effect; and sensitivity to the emotional states of others. In the next dozen years, children are further transformed, as they engage in complex reasoning in domains including politics, art, history, moral judgments, and science. As impressive as these intellectual achievements are, they are tempered by the observation that children's knowledge acquisition is also shaped and constrained by pervasive reasoning biases. Children find certain kinds of concepts difficult to acquire and easy to misunderstand (such as evolutionary theory, fractions, or irony), they hold firm misconceptions in nearly every domain studied, and they insufficiently consider the available evidence when making decisions. These two themes (remarkable learning and persistent biases) may at first seem contradictory, but they are not. Remarkable learning often occurs because of early biases.

The study of knowledge acquisition sheds light on several classic theoretical debates in psychology, including the following: What is the interplay between innate capacities and environmental experiences? What is the role of domain-general processes and processes specific to particular domains of knowledge? How much continuity or discontinuity is found across development? What are the forces (evolutionary, social, neurological) that contribute to developing conceptual systems? Although each of these topics remains the focus of active debate, research over the past 50 years provides rich insights into these core questions.

This entry discusses four questions that have been a focus in studying knowledge acquisition in development. Traditionally, scholars have focused on three primary aspects: process (what are the mechanisms that enable learning to take place), content (what do children know), and structure (how is knowledge organized). More recently, researchers have emphasized a fourth aspect: the role of context and culture (how is learning influenced by the social and cultural context in which it takes place). Each of these approaches has theoretical, practical, and educational significance. For example, understanding the process of how children encode, retain, and retrieve memories has implications for improving learning skills as well as establishing procedures for child witness interviews. Determining the content of children's knowledge about illness can help when counseling a child with a seriously ill sibling. Discovering the structure of children's knowledge of causality has theoretical significance for understanding whether scientific reasoning is continuous or undergoes considerable restructuring over development. Finally, examining the contextual effects of parent-child conversations on a child's language and conceptual development has important implications for administering advice and interventions to parents.

Knowledge Acquisition as an Active, Constructive Process

Theories of knowledge acquisition have historically distinguished *empiricist* from *nativist* views. Empiricists suggest that children enter the world as "blank slates," without any innate mental structures beyond basic sensory capacities and domain-general learning mechanisms. Thus, knowledge is viewed as built up primarily from experience. In contrast, nativists suggest that infants are endowed with innate knowledge and abilities that unfold over time. In contrast to both of these views, a *constructivist* approach (epitomized by Jean Piaget) proposes that children actively construct their knowledge. On this view, children enter the world with basic capacities to organize information in the world into mental structures and then elaborate on these structures as new information is encountered. In this way, children are like scientists, forming theory-like representations of the world and interpreting new information in light of existing theories.

Piaget suggested that knowledge development involves *qualitative* change, with children proceeding through four developmental stages marked by distinct modes of thinking: sensorimotor (birth to roughly age 2 years), pre-operational (roughly 2–6 years of age), concrete operational (roughly 7–12 years of age), and formal operational (roughly 12 years on). However, it is now widely acknowledged that a strict stage view of knowledge development is incorrect, as it underestimates children's early capacities and overestimates the rationality of adolescents and adults. Early knowledge is much richer than previously thought. Young children understand certain concepts before they can demonstrate them (also known as a competence-performance gap). For example, infants younger than 9 months of age fail to search for an object that is covered with a cloth, seeming to indicate an implicit belief that "out of sight is out of mind." However, careful experiments that track infants' gaze and reaching behaviors indicate awareness of hidden objects as young as 3 to 4 months of age. Contemporary researchers have developed numerous other implicit and subtle measures (e.g., rate at which infants suck a pacifier as a measure of interest in a stimulus, sequential order of manual object exploration as a measure of categorization, neuroimaging techniques as measures of the role of attention and control in cognitive tasks), which reveal that basic cognitive capacities are in place early in development.

There are several contemporary views of cognitive development that differ from Piaget's view but build on his insights. For example, *information-processing theories* emphasize that development involves domain-general changes, such as increased processing speed or working memory capacity. On this view, developing brain capacities and increasing knowledge of the world (expertise) contribute to general developments in capacity, reasoning strategies, and performance. *Structural theories* posit that development involves acquiring the ability to reflect on early representations, with knowledge proceeding from largely procedural and unconscious to more explicit and deliberate. *Theory theories* suggest that children are born with innate, albeit rudimentary, knowledge about the world that constrains how they process and interpret information they encounter, but that important reorganizations of knowledge take place with development. For example, preschoolers distinguish between material and immaterial entities (e.g., objects vs. thoughts) and understand some principles about material substance (e.g., that matter occupies physical space), but, between ages 4 and 12, their concept of "matter" undergoes considerable reorganization as they incorporate more complex principles (e.g., that all matter has weight, regardless of its size or density).

Content and Structure of Early Knowledge

Children's naïve "theories" about the world differ from scientific theories but are similar in the following respects: They presume a domain-specific ontology (e.g., "objects" are units in naïve physics; "animals" are units in naïve biology); they are constructed from evidence; they generate predictions and causal explanations; they posit unobservable theoretical entities (e.g., gravity) to account for observable phenomena (e.g., objects falling); they are coherent; and they are defeasible in the face of counterevidence. Three foundational domains in which children construct causal theories include physics, psychology, and biology. In each of these domains, there are impressive early capacities as well as considerable changes across development.

Fundamental elements of a naïve theory of physics are evident early in infancy. Infants represent objects as solid, bounded entities whose behavior accords with certain physical regularities. They expect objects to continue to exist when out of sight, and they expect them to move lawfully (e.g., not through obstructions). With age, children acquire richer understandings of physical and mechanical principles. For example, they are not born with an understanding that objects obey the laws of gravity, but begin to develop expectations about gravity by about 2 years of age. Further changes in physical understanding take place even into adulthood, as adults struggle to overcome an intuitive physics in which they have pre-Newtonian beliefs about the physics of everyday objects (e.g., incorrectly predicting that a ball rolling out of a curved tube will continue on a curvilinear, rather than a linear, trajectory).

A naïve theory of psychology, also known as a "theory of mind," also has precursors in infancy. By 5 months, infants interpret behaviors of animate entities as goal directed and distinguish between intentional and accidental actions. By preschool age, children distinguish between mental and physical entities (e.g., thoughts vs. actual objects), link perception with knowledge, and see people as having beliefs and desires that are linked to their actions. Richer understandings of the links among beliefs, desires, and actions emerge across development. For example, not until age 6 do children appreciate that differences in preexisting expectations differentially influence how people interpret ambiguous events.

Knowledge of the biological world entails classifying living things and reasoning about biological processes, such as growth and reproduction. There is debate about whether children's biological knowledge constitutes a theory; however, at the very least, by preschool age, children exhibit certain key understandings. For example, they distinguish between biological and inanimate entities and appreciate that biological processes only occur with the former. Less is known about biological knowledge in younger children; however, infants expect animate objects to exhibit self-initiated movement and inanimate objects to require external force, which is a likely precursor to a naïve biological theory.

As children construct knowledge systems, they also reveal systematic biases in how they interpret and incorporate new information. These include an essentialist bias (assuming that categories have an underlying reality), a teleological bias (assuming that all entities and events have a purpose), and causal determinism (assuming that all entities and events have a cause), among others. These biases are particularly evident in early childhood, but they may also persist into adulthood.

Context and Culture

Until recently, the focus in cognitive development was primarily on characterizing children's knowledge, and relatively little attention was paid to the contextual nature of the input. For example, Piaget provided the example of a child discovering basic principles of mathematics by rearranging and re-counting a set of pebbles. However, learning is not entirely a solitary act; instead, it is embedded in social and cultural understandings. Much of children's knowledge is derived not from their direct interactions with the environment but rather from the testimony of knowledgeable others. Studies of theory of mind tell us that learning often requires attending to others as a crucial source of information. Social transmission is also a mechanism for transmitting scientific concepts (germs, shape of the earth), natural categories (tomatoes are fruit), social concepts (ethnicity, personality traits), and supernatural concepts (God, witchcraft). The typically developing child interprets and evaluates the surrounding social input, and disruptions to these capacities can be devastating (as with autism). Cultural factors also play a key role. In a long tradition influenced by Lev Vygotsky, cultural psychologists have concluded that cultural contexts significantly influence children's learning. Finally, comparative studies with humans and nonhuman species suggest that certain forms of social learning—imitative learning, instructed learning, and collaborative learning—may be unique to humans (or if not unique, then at least particularly well developed). Humans are the preeminent species that create culture and cultural artifacts. Thus, human knowledge development is uniquely influenced by social and cultural factors.

Conclusions

The study of knowledge development in childhood provides a particularly fruitful approach to understanding human intelligence. Much of what makes our species distinctive is our capacity to acquire information (from observing the world and learning from others), to organize that information into explanatory and predictive theories, and to reorganize knowledge in the face of new and unexpected evidence. These capacities are rooted in fundamental processes that are evident early in infancy and continue to grow and flourish with maturity and experience.

Elizabeth A. Ware and Susan A. Gelman

See also Concepts, Development of; Folk Psychology; Language Development; Representations, Development of; Social Cognition

Further Readings

Carey, S. (1985). *Conceptual change in childhood.* Cambridge, MA: MIT Press.

Gelman, S. A. (2003). *The essential child: Origins of essentialism in everyday thought.* New York, NY: Oxford University Press.

Gopnik, A., Meltzoff, A. N., & Kuhl, P. K. (2000). *The scientist in the crib: What early learning tells us about the mind.* New York, NY: HarperCollins.

Keil, F. C. (1989). *Concepts, kinds, and cognitive development.* Cambridge, MA: MIT Press.

Piaget, J. (1936). *The origins of intelligence in children.* New York, NY: Norton.

Siegler, R. S. (1996). *Emerging minds: The process of change in children's thinking.* New York, NY: Oxford University Press.

Spelke, E. S. (2000). Core knowledge. *American Psychologist, 55,* 1233–1243.

Tomasello, M. (1999). *The cultural origins of human cognition.* Cambridge, MA: Harvard University Press.

Vygotsky, L. (1978). *Mind in society: The development of higher psychological processes.* Cambridge, MA: Harvard University Press.

Wellman, H. M., & Gelman, S. A. (1992). Cognitive development: Foundational theories of core domains. *Annual Review of Psychology, 43,* 337–375.

KNOWLEDGE BY ACQUAINTANCE

Knowledge by acquaintance is knowledge of an object that depends solely on one's acquaintance with the object. By contrast, *knowledge by description* is knowledge of an object that depends on one's knowledge of descriptive truths about the object. The distinction between knowledge by acquaintance and knowledge by description played an important role in the philosophy of Bertrand Russell, and it continues to inform much contemporary work in epistemology and the philosophy of language and mind. This entry is divided into four sections: (a) the acquaintance relation, (b) the objects of acquaintance, (c) the role of acquaintance, and (d) contemporary work on acquaintance.

The Acquaintance Relation

Acquaintance is a relation that holds between subjects and the objects of their acquaintance. But what kind of relation is it? It is sometimes said that the nature of acquaintance cannot be known by description, but only by acquaintance—in other words, one must be acquainted with acquaintance in order to know what it is.

Acquaintance with an object is usually defined as a conscious state of direct and unmediated awareness of an object. This follows Russell's (1912) definition: "We shall say that we have *acquaintance* with anything of which we are directly aware, without the intermediary of any process of inference or any knowledge of truth" (p. 25).

According to Russell, there are various different forms of acquaintance, including not only perception, but also memory, introspection, and conceptual awareness of universals. Nevertheless, perception is the least controversial example: In perception, we are acquainted with objects. But what are the objects of our perceptual acquaintance?

The Objects of Acquaintance

According to common sense, we are acquainted in perception with ordinary physical objects, including tables, chairs, and other people. According to Russell, however, when I see a table, I am not directly acquainted with the table, but rather with mental objects, which he calls *sense data*. Therefore, I do not know the table by acquaintance, but merely by description, as "the physical object which causes such-and-such sense data." On this view, expressions used to refer to physical objects, including demonstratives and proper names, are really descriptions in disguise.

Russell uses a version of the *argument from illusion* to support his view. He argues that, when I view a tilted coin and seem to see an elliptical object, there is in fact an elliptical object that I am seeing. However, this object is not the coin, which is circular, but rather a mental sense datum. Critics of the argument deny that, in cases of illusion, if it seems that I am seeing an object that has certain properties, there is in fact an object that I am seeing, which has the relevant properties. Thus, there is no elliptical object that I am seeing; rather, I am seeing the circular coin, but its apparently elliptical shape is illusory. However, the problem of giving an adequate account of illusion remains one of the central problems in contemporary philosophy of perception.

The Role of Acquaintance

Acquaintance is central to Russell's theory of knowledge and his theory of conceptual thought. He draws a distinction between knowledge of things and knowledge of truths, which is best understood in terms of the distinction between our conceptual ability to think about things and our epistemic ability to know truths about those things. According to Russell (1912), acquaintance plays a foundational role in explaining each of these abilities: "All our knowledge, both knowledge of things and knowledge of truths, rests on acquaintance as its foundation" (p. 48).

First, acquaintance plays a foundational role in Russell's theory of knowledge. He argues that all of our knowledge of truths depends ultimately on acquaintance, which is foundational in the sense that it does not itself depend on any knowledge of truths. Acquaintance with an object enables us to know descriptive truths about the object, but this descriptive knowledge depends on acquaintance, rather than vice versa.

Second, acquaintance plays a foundational role in Russell's theory of conceptual thought. He argues that we can think about an object only if we know which object we are thinking about. Either we know the object by acquaintance or we know it by description, in which case we must be acquainted with the properties in terms of which it is described. This is the rationale for Russell's (1912) principle of acquaintance, which states: "Every proposition which we can understand must be composed wholly of constituents with which we are acquainted" (p. 58).

Contemporary Work on Acquaintance

Few contemporary philosophers endorse all aspects of Russell's philosophy, but many follow his example in finding an important role for acquaintance in the theory of knowledge and conceptual thought. A common strategy is to identify conscious states that play the role of Russell's notion of acquaintance in grounding our conceptual and epistemic abilities. For example, John Campbell argues that conscious visual attention to an object enables one to grasp demonstrative concepts of the object and to know truths about its visible properties. Similarly, David Chalmers argues that introspective attention enables one to grasp phenomenal concepts and to know truths about the phenomenal properties of one's phenomenally conscious mental states.

Since Russell, there has been widespread agreement on the importance of a distinction between thinking of an object by description and thinking of an object in a more direct way that exploits a descriptively unmediated relation to the object. Indeed, the term *acquaintance* is sometimes used as a mere placeholder for whatever relation it is that enables one to think nondescriptive thoughts about an object. From this perspective, however, it is a substantive question whether Russell was entitled to assume that the role of acquaintance could be played only by states of conscious awareness.

For example, Gareth Evans introduces a category of information-based thought, which exploits information that is causally derived from an object. According to Evans, the role of Russell's notion of acquaintance is played by the information link with an object that is provided in perception, memory, and testimony. However, it is a focus of contemporary debate whether the information provided by perception, memory, and testimony must be conscious to play the role of Russell's notion of acquaintance.

In sum, Russell's work on acquaintance raises important questions about the role of consciousness in grounding our conceptual and epistemic abilities. These questions are central to much current work in epistemology and the philosophy of language and mind.

Declan Smithies

See also Descriptive Thought; Know-How, Philosophical Perspectives; Object-Dependent Thought

Further Readings

Campbell, J. (2002). *Reference and consciousness*. Oxford, UK: Oxford University Press.

Chalmers, D. (2003). The content and epistemology of phenomenal belief. In Q. Smith & A. Jokic (Eds.), *Consciousness: New philosophical perspectives* (pp. 55–62). New York, NY: Oxford University Press.

Evans, G. (1982). *The varieties of reference*. Oxford, UK: Oxford University Press.

Russell, B. (1912). *Problems of philosophy*. London, UK: Oxford University Press.

Smithies, D. (2011). What is the role of consciousness in demonstrative thought? *Journal of Philosophy, 108*(1), 5–34.

LANGUAGE DEVELOPMENT

Language development is the process by which children come to understand and produce language. This entry focuses on the period between birth and 5 years of age. The entry presents theoretical perspectives on language development, followed by a review of the biological basis of language. The language acquisition process is then described for various components of language, with a focus on typically developing children learning one first language; brief sections also discuss bilingualism and atypical language development.

Historical and Theoretical Perspectives on Language Development

In the first half of the 20th century, the field of language development was dominated by studies documenting the normative course of language acquisition. In the late 1950s and 1960s, the linguist Noam Chomsky published several works that took the field in different directions. The first was a review of B. F. Skinner's book *Verbal Behavior*. Skinner applied behaviorist theory to language development, arguing that it results from processes such as imitation and reinforcement. Chomsky's review was a rebuttal of the application of behaviorism to language and suggested that language development is much more complex. Chomsky followed with his theory of innate linguistic knowledge in which he claimed that there is a language acquisition device in the human brain that contains innate knowledge of the structure of language, also known as universal grammar.

Chomsky's theory is a nativist view of language development as it claims that children have preexisting knowledge of language, whereas Skinner's behaviorist approach is an empiricist view that all knowledge of language comes from experience. The extreme empiricist view is not popular today. The interactionist perspective provides a more moderate approach to language learning by highlighting the importance of experience in language development while acknowledging the existence of brain structures that support language development. The main difference in the nativist versus interactionist perspectives lies in the importance they place on experience. Further, in their emphasis on experience, interactionists tend to see the child as playing more of an active role in language development than do nativists, who see the development of language more as something that happens to the child in a predetermined way. Although much has been learned over the past 50 years about child language development, there are still many unanswered questions.

Biological Basis of Language

Almost all humans learn to talk. From birth, human beings are biologically prepared for language. A specialized vocal tract helps humans produce language, and the position of the larynx and properties of the lips and tongue make rapid sounds easy to produce. Upright teeth, while not necessary for eating, allow for the production of certain sounds such as /s/ and /f/. These characteristics are unique to humans. The vocal tract is not the only human characteristic that makes language production possible; specific parts of the brain work in tandem with the vocal tract to produce language. For 85% of the population, the left hemisphere is dominant for language processing. This is known as functional asymmetry, in which one hemisphere in the brain plays a different or larger role than the other for a specified function.

The classical model of lateralization argued that specific regions of the left hemisphere are particularly important for language functions. Based on symptoms of Broca's aphasia, Broca's area was originally thought to be responsible for language production; however, the underlying disorder is now thought to involve grammar and phonology in both comprehension and production. Similarly, lesions to Wernicke's area, a left-hemisphere area originally thought to be involved in written and spoken language comprehension, are now thought to underlie semantic and conceptual deficits in both production and comprehension. While the right hemisphere can comprehend some language, it is especially involved in aspects of pragmatics, prosody, and discourse comprehension. Both hemispheres are involved in semantic processing, but in different ways. For instance, there is evidence that the left hemisphere activates the main meaning of a word in a particular context, while the right hemisphere activates a broader range of meanings. The role of each hemisphere in language processing, and how the hemispheres interact, is still being examined.

The human brain also appears to be quite plastic in terms of language acquisition and development. If left-hemispheric injury occurs early in life, the right hemisphere sometimes compensates by taking on the injured area's functions; the ability of the right hemisphere to take over may decline with puberty. Researchers take this finding to argue for a critical period, or a time (often before age 8–13) during which language is more readily learned.

Development of Pragmatic, Phonological, Lexical, and Grammatical Skills

Language can be broken down into several components that develop concurrently in the child: pragmatics, phonology, lexicon, and grammar. The following sections provide the typical developmental progression within each component across early childhood.

Pragmatics

Pragmatic development refers to the understanding of how to use language appropriately and to serve different communicative functions and intents (e.g., to direct someone's attention or ask a question). Children can understand and express communicative intents before they can use spoken language productively. One way they do this is through communicative gestures such as pointing. For example, a 1-year-old who wants an object that is out of reach might request the object by pointing to it and then looking at an adult. Alternatively, if an adult is taking an object away from an infant, the child might protest by getting upset and shaking the head to mean "no." These early communicative behaviors suggest that the child has developed intentionality, which, in this context, is the ability to communicate intent (e.g., in the previous cases, to make a request and to protest). Intentionality is found to develop in preverbal infants around 10 months of age. Detailed studies of children's early pragmatic development suggest that 1-year-olds have a repertoire of between 5 and 30 communicative intents, whereas 2-year-olds have a repertoire of between 50 and 90 intents. Thus, as children increase in their formal abilities to use language productively, they also increase in the communicative purposes for which they can use language.

Pragmatic development continues across childhood and encompasses the development of conversational skill. Although young children can use language for many communicative acts by age 2, the ability to engage in conversation requires skills that often do not develop until years later. For example, children need to understand the conversational rules of turn taking and topic relevance. Understanding culturally relevant rules of politeness also falls under the realm of pragmatics.

Phonology

Phonological development involves understanding how to distinguish between, and produce, the sounds of the adult language. Phonemes are the meaningfully different sounds in a given language, such as /g/ and /d/ in English. From birth, infants can distinguish between phonemes when they are presented in isolation using habituation/dishabituation procedures such as the high amplitude sucking paradigm. In this paradigm, infants will slow down their pacifier sucking once they are bored with a stimulus (e.g., the sound "pa"). If the infant's sucking then increases on presentation of a new phoneme (e.g., "da"), it is an indication that the infant detects the difference in sounds. Interestingly, after about 9 months of age, infants have a harder time distinguishing between phonemes in languages other than their own. Thus, language experience influences language perception, as it is easier for infants to perceive differences in phonemes they hear regularly.

The first sounds infants produce are vegetative sounds such as crying and burping. Around 6 to 8 weeks, infants begin cooing or producing long drawn-out vowel-like sounds of contentment. Between 4 and 7 months, babies engage in vocal play and increase their repertoire of sounds. Vowels are produced first because they are easiest to produce physiologically, followed by consonants formed in the back of the mouth (/g/), and then by consonants formed in the front of the mouth (/m/). Between 6 and 9 months, children start babbling, first by producing reduplication of true syllables from their language, also known as canonical babbling (e.g., /nana/), and later by working in a larger range of phonemes. During this period, children also produce jargon where they string together sounds with the melody and intonation of their language. Indeed, studies have found that parents exaggerate their intonation when talking to infants as compared with talking to adults. As is found with perception of sounds, after 6 months of age, the sounds infants produce start to resemble the sounds of the language(s) they are exposed to rather than other languages.

Children's first words often have a simple syllable structure. During the second year of life, when children are limited in their repertoire of phonemes, they find creative ways to transform sounds to make them easier to produce. For example, they use what is called reduplication of syllables to transform bottle to /baba/ or delete syllables in words, such as transforming banana to /nana/. They often mispronounce words during this period as well. By age 3 years, speech is more intelligible, and by age 7, children sound adultlike in their phonology. Children show some signs of phonological awareness—that is, awareness of their phonological abilities—as early as age 2, when they play with sounds and appreciate rhyme. As children get older, this awareness grows and they can correctly answer questions such as "say

cat without the /c/ sound." Phonological awareness is an important precursor for learning to read.

Lexicon

Words are difficult to learn because they are arbitrary symbols with no inherent relation to their referents. The ability to map a word to its referent (e.g., to know that when they hear "dog," it is referring to the four-legged animal) is crucial to lexical development. How children do this is a topic of much debate. Nativists would argue that children are born with knowledge of how words work. Other psychologists explain the mapping problem using a variety of constraints. For example, the whole object constraint suggests that children first assume words to refer to a whole object, rather than its parts. Social-cognitive psychologists assert that children solve the mapping problem by focusing on the intentions of others and the meanings they are trying to convey. Finally, researchers with more of a domain general perspective would argue that other cognitive processes, such as attention and memory, can help explain word learning. Thus, the process of word learning is less clear-cut than the facts of word learning at different ages.

As with other aspects of language, comprehension precedes production in lexical development. Children tend to recognize their own name by 5 months, and by 10 months they can comprehend between 10 and 150 words as well as simple phrases, yet they do not often produce their first words until they are 10 to 15 months old. Children reach a productive vocabulary of 50 words between 15 and 20 months. In children learning English as well as many other languages, on average approximately half of the first 50 words produced are nouns (e.g., *ball*, *mama*), yet there is variation across children. However, in some languages such as Mandarin, there is less of a noun bias in children's early lexicons. Differences across languages may be due to the structure of the languages themselves in how nouns and verbs are used, and to cultural differences in parenting practices such as labeling objects.

By age 2, children can produce between 50 and 550 words. Some of these large individual differences in vocabulary development can be explained by phonological memory as well as environmental factors. For example, studies consistently find a positive relation between the variety of vocabulary words parents use with children and children's vocabulary size. As toddlers, children often produce unconventional word-meaning mappings. Overextensions refer to using a word more broadly than is appropriate such as using "dog" to refer to all four-legged animals, whereas underextensions refer to using a word more narrowly, such as using "dog" to refer only to German shepherds but not to collies.

As children's vocabulary size increases during early childhood, so does the depth of their vocabulary in that they gain greater understanding about specific words and their meanings and appropriate uses. Vocabulary acquisition is by no means complete at age 5. In fact, school-age children have been shown to increase their vocabularies by approximately 3,000 words per year.

Grammar

Grammatical development includes an understanding of morphology and syntax. Morphology consists of the rules for combining morphemes to create words. Morphemes are the smallest unit of meaning in language. Free morphemes are words that stand alone (e.g., *dog*) whereas bound morphemes cannot stand alone (e.g., plural *s*). Morphemes can be combined by (a) compounding, or combining two or more free morphemes (e.g., *houseboat*); (b) derivation, or combining a bound and free morpheme to change the meaning (e.g., *teacher*); or (c) inflection, or combining a bound and free morpheme without changing the meaning or grammatical category of the word (e.g., *dogs*).

Evidence that children acquire morphological rules comes from observing children's productive errors (e.g., *falled*) as well as from experimental studies. A famous early study in 1958 by Jean Berko used nonsense words to test children's morphological development. An experimenter first presented children with a picture and labeled it with a nonsense word such as *wug*. The experimenter then presented children with another picture and said, "Now there is another one, there are two of them, there are two __?" If children could correctly answer "wugs," this was evidence that they had learned the morphological rules because they had never heard the word *wugs* before in their language. The preschoolers in her study (the youngest subjects) performed well on these tasks. Another measure of children's early productive morphological development is a count of the mean length of utterance (MLU) measured in morphemes. Roger Brown developed stages of grammatical development based on the MLU of children he was observing longitudinally. He transcribed all their utterances, counted how many morphemes were in each utterance, and then averaged the total utterance length per child at each age. On average, children between 16 and 31 months are shown to have MLUs between 1.0 and 2.0. MLUs increase to between 2.0 and 3.0 for children between 21 and 41 months, and MLUs of 4.0 or more are reached by children around 3 years old or older.

Syntax is the component of grammar that governs the ordering of words in sentences. Studies show that as early as 16 to 18 months, children can comprehend meaning carried in word order. As children begin to produce language, they go through phases of syntactic development, which becomes increasingly complex with age. In the two-word phase of productive grammatical development, children tend to use the same words in different combinations to express possessives such as "my chair" and "my book" and descriptives such as "pretty doll" and "pretty dress." Three-word speech combinations tend to be telegraphic at first in that they omit morphemes (e.g., "put it table"); at around 2 to 3 years, children fill in these obligatory morphemes. At around 3.5 years, when children reach an MLU of 3.0 to 4.0, they also start to produce passives as well as complex sentences. However, some more complex aspects of syntax such as anaphora, or the understanding of how pronouns refer to their referents in a sentence, are not mastered until middle childhood.

Bilingual Language Acquisition

Recent estimates suggest that almost 50% of the world's population is bilingual, and by 2030, 40% of American school-aged children will be English-language learners. The study of bilingualism is important given these social circumstances, as well as to learn about how bilingualism develops and varies across children. Bilingualism develops either sequentially, when one language is introduced after the acquisition of the first language, or simultaneously, when both languages are learned in tandem.

Although monolinguals and bilinguals learn language in some similar ways, bilingualism has been shown to slightly alter the course of development of certain linguistic and cognitive processes. Children in both monolingual and bilingual environments begin canonical babbling at approximately the same time. Bilinguals, however, have smaller vocabularies in each language than their monolingual peers;

lexical knowledge appears to be distributed across the two languages. Bilinguals, however, are found to show greater metalinguistic awareness, phonological awareness, grammatical awareness, and cognitive control. Proficiency in second language learning depends on several factors. First, individuals who are exposed to a second language earlier in childhood are better able to speak without an accent and ultimately master certain grammatical structures, because they have more opportunities to speak. However, receptive vocabulary, translation, and story comprehension seem to be skills that are better honed when second language acquisition occurs at an older age.

Atypical Language Development

Studying children with atypical trajectories of linguistic development is important for understanding how various abilities contribute to language acquisition as well as to help develop new interventions for language disorders. Typical language development relies on exposure to linguistic models in the environment. Deaf children born to hearing parents are not exposed to these models and must use alternative ways to acquire language and communicate with others. Approximately 1 in 1,000 children are born with severe hearing loss, yet if they are exposed to sign language from birth, deaf children demonstrate a typical linguistic progression using sign. These children typically babble manually rather than vocally, and they produce their first sign before or at the same time as typically developing children produce their first words.

Studying language disorders can also help researchers better understand typical language development, specifically with regard to the extent to which language and other cognitive processes are interrelated. For example, children with Down syndrome show general cognitive defects and are also late to babble and begin talking; they produce toddler-like phonological patterns into adulthood. Thus, cases of Down syndrome provide some evidence that linguistic and cognitive processes operate in tandem, as both are delayed in these children. On the other hand, some children who have impaired cognitive development do not have impaired language development. This provides evidence that cognitive and linguistic functioning may be separate processes. Individuals with Williams syndrome, for example, have IQs that are similar to those with Down syndrome but have stronger language

abilities. In contrast, children with another language disorder, specific language impairment (SLI), do not display cognitive deficits. SLI usually results in language production 1 year behind and comprehension 6 months behind typically developing children. SLI seems to be hereditary, as 20% of children with SLI have relatives with language difficulties.

Children with autism spectrum disorders (ASD) provide an example of the social nature of language development. Lower functioning children with ASD show delayed linguistic development, and some of these children never acquire language. Higher functioning children with ASD, however, display similar syntactic abilities to typically developing children but struggle with communicative competence. Toddlers with ASD show little interest in others, do not initiate joint attention, and rarely produce pointing gestures. Later, pragmatic development is also impaired in children across the autism spectrum.

In sum, in the first 5 years of life, children make great gains in oral language skills. These abilities are found to contribute to the acquisition of reading and writing during school. Further, language development is by no means complete when children enter school; rather, it is a lifelong process, as even adults continue to build their vocabularies and gain greater understanding of language over time.

Meredith L. Rowe and Kathryn A. Leech

See also Bilingual Language Processing; Bilingualism, Cognitive Benefits of; Dyslexia, Developmental; Gesture and Language Processing; Heritage Language and Second Language Learning; Innateness and Parameter Setting; Language Development, Overregulation in; Word Learning

Further Readings

Berko Gleason, J., & Berstein Ratner, N. (2009). *The development of language* (7th ed.). Boston, MA: Pearson.

Bloom, P. (2000). *How children learn the meanings of words*. Cambridge, MA: MIT Press.

Hoff, E. (2009). *Language development* (4th ed.). Belmont, CA: Wadsworth.

Hoff, E., & Shatz, M. (Eds.). (2007). *Handbook of language development*. Malden, MA: Blackwell.

Lust, B., & Foley, C. (Eds.). (2004). *First language acquisition: The essential readings*. Malden, MA: Blackwell.

Pinker, S. (1994). *The language instinct*. New York, NY: Morrow.

Poeppel, D., & Hickok, G. (2004). Towards a new functional anatomy of language. *Cognition, 92,* 1–12.

Tomasello, M. (1995). Language is not an instinct [Review of the book *The language instinct,* by S. Pinker]. *Cognitive Development, 10,* 131–156.

LANGUAGE DEVELOPMENT, OVERREGULATION IN

The study of language development has revealed many interesting findings and has contributed to the field of language acquisition and, more generally, to linguistics and psychology. Of particular importance is the emergence of certain intriguing patterns that are characteristic of early language development. This entry will discuss one particular feature of language development, namely, overregulation. Overregulation in language development occurs when children apply linguistic generalizations in contexts where that would not be deemed appropriate for adult speakers.

Linguistic Background: The Case of the Past Tense

For instance, in English, verbs can be classified into two main types: regular and irregular. Regular verbs are so-called as their past tense forms are created by the addition of the suffix -ed to the stem (e.g., *walk—walked*). On the other hand, the irregular verbs cannot be summarized under one "rule" as can be done for the regular verbs. As such, the relationship between the stem and the past tense form is more arbitrary (e.g., *go—went*).

Properties of Overregulation

U-Shaped Curve

At some point during language development (around the age of 2 years), children begin acquiring past tense formations. Although they produce both regulars and irregulars more or less accurately in the early stage of past tense acquisition, as they begin to acquire more verbs, they start producing errors, especially with regard to irregular formation. It is at this point during language development when children incorrectly inflect irregular verbs in a regular manner. For example, they may produce **goed* instead of *went*, or **thinked* instead of *thought*

(an asterisk indicates ungrammatical forms). This developmental pattern is commonly referred to as a U-shaped learning curve. The irregular past tense forms are said to undergo this U-shaped learning curve because, during early acquisition of the irregular past tense, children produce inflected irregulars correctly. They then go through a phase where they overgeneralize the regular formation in which -ed is simply added to the verb stem. This overregulation of the regular formation to irregular verbs results in irregulars being produced incorrectly. In the final phase of the learning curve, children's performance on irregulars increases as they learn to associate the correct irregular past tense form with its stem.

Explaining Overregulation

It is worth examining why this phenomenon occurs. Recall that the past tense can be inflected regularly or irregularly. In English, many irregular verbs are highly frequent (i.e., they occur quite often). This could explain why the irregular forms are produced accurately at first. However, although individual tokens of irregular verbs are high in frequency, there are many more regular verbs then irregular verbs in English. This difference in type frequency (such as more regular verb types than irregular verb types) may play a role in the overregulation. Therefore, because children come across many more regular verbs than irregular verbs, they overapply the regular rule.

On the other hand, it has also been argued that overregulation occurs because children make use of a grammatical rule (i.e., add -ed to a verb stem), which acts as the default rule. Hence, in cases where no irregular form can be retrieved, the default rule is applied. In German, the regular participle (-t) has a smaller type frequency than the irregular participle (-n) but exhibits overregulation in the same way as the English regular past tense. From this point of view, overregulations are argued to show evidence for symbolic or rule-based representations.

Overregulation in Other Linguistic Phenomena

Although the primary example used here is the past tense, evidence of overregulation can also be found in the development of plural formation. In this case, the regular plural marker in English, -s, is overapplied incorrectly to nouns that would normally undergo an irregular plural inflection (e.g., *mouse—*mouses*). In addition, children are also known to produce incorrect comparative and superlative forms of adjectives. In English, the comparative form of an adjective is created by adding the suffix *-er* to the adjective (e.g., *high—higher*), and the superlative form is created by the addition of the suffix *-est* (e.g., *high—highest*). A common error in comparative formations occurs with the adjective *good* where children incorrectly produce **gooder* as the comparative form. Likewise, **goodest* may be produced as the superlative form. Finally, irregular inflections themselves may be used as stems allowing for concatenation with a regular affix (e.g., for the past tense, *come—*camed*; for plurals, *mouse—*mices*; and for superlatives, *good—*bestest*).

Theoretical Implications

Overregulations in language development have been argued to provide evidence for nativist views of language acquisition (generally, views that language-specific innate processes play a large role in language acquisition). This view is predicated on the finding that overgeneralizations are attested implying that children do not simply acquire language based on input alone, as adults do not normally produce these errors and therefore there are no such errors in the input. Non-nativists, on the other hand, would argue that there are models of language acquisition which use error-free input that can simulate the U-shaped curve representative of past tense acquisition.

Although overregulation may not occur very frequently in language development, it nevertheless provides valuable insight into the mechanisms and processes that children make use of during language acquisition.

Renita Silva

See also Language Development; Language Production, Agreement in; Syntactic Production, Agreement in; Word Learning

Further Readings

Clahsen, H., Hadler, M., & Weyerts, H. (2004). Speeded production of inflected words in children and adults. *Journal of Child Language, 31*, 683–712.

Kuczaj, S. A., II. (1977). The acquisition of regular and irregular past tense forms. *Journal of Verbal Learning and Verbal Behavior, 16*, 589–600.

Marcus, G. F., Pinker, S., Ullman, M., Hollander, M., Rosen, T. J., & Xu, F. (1992). Overregularization in language acquisition. *Monographs of the Society for Research in Child Development, 57*(4, Serial No. 228).

LANGUAGE PRODUCTION, AGREEMENT IN

Agreement refers to the correspondence of some formal feature (person, gender, number) between an agreement controller (e.g., the subject noun) and syntactically related words in the sentence (e.g., the verb). Being syntactic in essence, this phenomenon provides a privileged window on the processes involved in grammatical encoding. This entry summarizes two major lines of research on agreement that have been pursued in psycholinguistics. The first line explores the influence of semantic and phonological factors in agreement to shed light on the issue of modularity in language production. The second line addresses agreement deficits in the production of specific populations.

Semantic and Phonological Factors in Agreement Production

In the early 1990s, Kathryn Bock initiated what became a whole research program on agreement production. She showed that so-called attraction errors by which an element with agreement features interferes in the realization of agreement (e.g., *cabinets* in **The key to the cabinets are on the table; * = ungrammatical sentence) can be reproduced and boosted in the laboratory by asking participants to complete sentences under time constraints. Experimental research showed that interference is primarily guided by the syntactic features of the "attracting" element, independently of the representation of these features at the conceptual level (e.g., plurality) and at the morphophonological level (i.e., in the form of the word, like the final *s* on English nouns). Nevertheless, agreement turns out to be under the partial guidance of conceptual and morphophonological features of the agreement controller. For example, the grammar of English allows plural verbs to occur with grammatically singular but conceptually plural collective head nouns (e.g., the faculty *are* threatening to protest). Along these lines, experimental research on attraction errors across languages showed that erroneous plural verbs are more frequent with collective subject head nouns (e.g., the fleet) than with nouns referring to individual entities (e.g., the ship), or with distributive subjects (e.g., the label on the bottles, in which one has to assume a multiplicity of labels) than with nondistributive subjects (e.g., the baby on the blankets). Research on antecedent-pronoun agreement showed that pronouns (reflexive and tag) are also prone to conceptual agreement and this to a larger extent than verbs. Studies of subject-predicative adjective gender agreement in Romance languages also revealed sensitivity to the conceptual features of the agreement controller. For example, gender attraction is reduced when the subject noun's gender has a conceptual feature, as is the case for biological gender (e.g., the girl) as compared to when it has strictly grammatical gender, not represented conceptually (e.g., the table, which is grammatically feminine in these languages). Research showed that the manifestation of agreement features in the morphological form of the controller also modulates attraction. For example, attraction in number and gender is significantly reduced when the subject expresses number or gender morphologically (e.g., in Italian, nouns ending in o are typically masculine) as compared to when it fails to express it (nouns ending in e may be masculine or feminine). Similarly, the presence of case markers (i.e., markers that indicate the grammatical function of a noun, e.g., as a subject or object) was also found to reduce error rates as compared to ambiguous case marking. More generally, morphophonological influences were found to vary cross-linguistically as a function of the validity of the morphophonological marker in the language.

Different interpretations of conceptual and morphophonological effects on agreement have been proposed. Gabriella Vigliocco and colleagues interpreted them within an interactive framework in which grammatical encoding is maximally influenced by nongrammatical information. In the marking and morphing model developed by Bock and colleagues, nongrammatical influences are restricted to two specific stages of agreement production: Conceptual influences arise at the marking stage of sentence production when features from the message level are transmitted to the syntax, whereas morphophonological influences arise subsequently at the level of morphing when features are transmitted to structurally controlled elements (like verbs) and morphophonologically specified. Finally, Julie

Franck and colleagues proposed that both conceptual and morphophonological influences arise at a stage of lexical selection during which the controller's features are being selected within the functional lexicon (i.e., the lexicon for grammatical morphemes like nominal or verbal inflections), whereas these features are copied at a stage operating on the basis of syntactic principles, following characteristics of modular systems.

Agreement in Specific Populations

Children produce agreement markers on nouns (such as the final s in English) before they produce verbal or adjectival agreement morphology. Initial productions (of nouns as well as agreeing particles like verbs or adjectives) are characterized by a tendency of the child to produce unmarked forms (singular, masculine). Nevertheless, from early on, children also produce occasional plural and feminine forms and this consistently in the context of plural or feminine agreement controllers. This systematicity attests that even though young children tend to simplify their productions, they do so in virtue of grammatical constraints in agreement and not by chance. Across languages, children with specific language impairment usually show difficulties with inflectional morphology, with an overuse of default agreement forms. Difficulties with agreement production are also commonly reported in children with developmental dyslexia. Nevertheless, evidence is accumulating in favor of the hypothesis that the observed impairment with agreement in these populations does not result from a deficit in the syntactic machinery per se, but rather of impoverished processing and memory systems involved operating at the interface with syntax in language production. (For example, these populations show optional production of agreement markers, production in consistent contexts, and preserved sensitivity to agreement in comprehension.)

Similar profiles of agreement deficits are found in agrammatic speech in individuals with Broca's aphasia, commonly described as involving a general breakdown in the production of grammatical morphemes. However, recent studies based on a finer grained approach to syntactic production in these patients have shown that, across languages, agreement morphemes are often either intact or better preserved than other inflectional morphemes like tense. The tree pruning hypothesis accounts for the patterns of impairments in people with agrammatism by assuming that higher projections of the syntactic tree are pruned, following the hierarchical order of functional categories. Under this account, agreement production by individuals with Broca's aphasia is conceived of as a grammar-based phenomenon but driven by processing or working memory limitations.

Julie Franck

See also Aphasia; Planning in Language Production; Production of Language; Syntactic Production, Agreement in

Further Readings

Bock, J. K., Eberhard, K. M., Cutting, J. C., Meyer, A. S., & Schriefers, H. (2001). Some attractions of verb agreement. *Cognitive Psychology, 43*, 83–128.

Franck, J., Vigliocco, G., Antón-Méndez, I., Collina, S., & Frauenfelder, U. H. (2008). The interplay of syntax and form in language production: A cross-linguistic study of form effects on agreement. *Language and Cognitive Processes, 23*(3), 329–374.

Friedmann, N. (2006). Speech production in Broca's agrammatic aphasia: Syntactic tree pruning. In Y. Grodzinsky & K. Amunts (Eds.), *Broca's region* (pp. 63–82). Oxford, UK: Oxford University Press.

Jakubowicz, C. (2011). Measuring derivational complexity: New evidence from typically-developing and SLI learners of L1-French. *Lingua, 21*(3), 399–351.

Vigliocco, G., & Harsuiker, R. J. (2002). The interplay of meaning, sound, and syntax in sentence production. *Psychological Bulletin, 128*, 442–472.

LANGUAGE PRODUCTION, INCREMENTAL PROCESSING IN

Language production involves the generation of several successive levels of representation. These representations map between the thought to be expressed and the motor commands that articulate it. Current models of language production are in broad agreement about the nature of these representations. Speaking begins with the construction of a conceptual representation of the meaning to be expressed. This representation triggers grammatical encoding processes, which select the appropriate words from the mental lexicon and generate a syntactic structure to fix their linear order. Phonological encoding processes then generate the abstract sound structure of the utterance prior to articulation.

Models of language production agree that speakers need not generate all levels of representation for an entire utterance before beginning to speak. They propose that fluent speech output is accomplished by *incremental* processing, so that the articulation of early parts of an utterance occurs in parallel with the planning of upcoming segments. However, exactly how processing at different levels is coordinated remains a matter of dispute. In particular, there is disagreement about how much of an utterance must be generated at a particular level of representation before processing at the next level can begin.

This entry will introduce different proposals about the degree of incrementality operating during speech production. It will discuss the relevant findings for processes involved in the generation of grammatical and phonological structure.

Generating Grammatical Structure

There is conflicting evidence about how much of an utterance must be grammatically encoded prior to articulation. Some theories claim that the verb of a sentence must be retrieved before the generation of syntactic structure can commence. Verbs control the structure of clauses and there is evidence that the clause operates as a planning unit during speech production. Planning pauses in speech have been shown to occur more frequently between clauses than clause internally. Speech error data have been used to claim that the words for a whole clause are retrieved prior to speech onset. Word exchange errors such as "put the drawer in the cloth" suggest that the exchanging words *drawer* and *cloth* are retrieved in parallel. However, it is also proposed that these effects could occur during conceptual, rather than grammatical, processing.

Experimental evidence exists for tightly incremental planning. In recent years, eye-tracking studies have recorded the gaze patterns of speakers while they describe pictured scenes. These experiments demonstrate that speakers almost always fixate on pictured objects in their order of mention and rarely look ahead at objects to be named later (although some peripheral processing of immediately adjacent objects can occur). The time spent looking at an object is a function of the ease with which it can be identified, as well as of the ease with which the phonological form of its name can be retrieved. These findings suggest that we plan speech word-by-word with planning progressing only slightly ahead of articulation. However, these experiments usually involved the production of one sentence structure to one fixed pattern of pictures. It is possible, therefore, that the observed visual and linguistic processing patterns are strategic rather than typical.

Evidence from reaction time experiments in which speakers produce more varied utterances is consistent with the first phrase as a planning unit. Sentence onset latencies (i.e., the time it takes to begin sentences) have been shown to increase as the complexity of the sentence initial phrase increases. In contrast, priming the retrieval of the verb in subject-verb sentences does not speed sentence production. For example, exposure to a verb (e.g., brushing) does not speed the production onset of a sentence with a semantically related verb (e.g., the woman is combing her hair). This finding suggests that the verb need not be accessed before speech onset.

It is possible that there is some flexibility in the degree of incrementality that speakers can adopt. However, there are also minimum planning units that must be employed due to grammatical dependencies. In many languages, grammatical agreement must occur between the elements of a sentence and the lower limit of advance planning will differ depending on the scope of the dependencies in a given language. For example, in many languages, the form of a determiner (e.g., *the*) is dependent on the gender of the noun it refers to (e.g., *das rote auto*, the red car).

Generating Phonological Structure

Generating the sound form of an utterance does not simply involve the retrieval of the stored phonological representation for each word, because the exact sound structure of a word is dependent on the context in which it is produced. Willem Levelt argued that prior to articulation, we construct a complete phonological word—a prosodic unit with one stressed syllable that can comprise several words. For example, the five words in the utterance, *I gave it to her,* can form one phonological word, I-*ga*-vi-ter.

A number of experiments provide support for this hypothesis. The time to begin to produce a word has been shown to increase with its number of syllables, suggesting that all syllables of a word are encoded prior to articulation. Moreover, sentence onset latency has been shown to be a function of the length of the initial phonological word, even when

that unit comprises more than one lexical item (e.g., I-like-to).

However, the syllable latency effect has proved difficult to replicate. Moreover, it has been demonstrated using the picture-word interference task that priming may be limited to the initial syllable of disyllabic words in some two-word utterances. For example, naming a picture of a colored object (e.g., purple ball) is speeded by hearing the first syllable of the adjective (i.e., *pur*) but not the second syllable (i.e., *ple*). It is possible, therefore, that although the phonological word may be the preferred unit of phonological encoding, it may not constitute the *minimal* unit of phonological encoding.

As with grammatical encoding, it is possible that the degree of incrementality employed by speakers may vary across different speaking contexts. Similarly, there remains the issue of cross-linguistic differences in the scope across which dependencies operate during the generation of phonological structure.

Linda R. Wheeldon

See also Language Production, Agreement in; Production of Language; Prosody in Production

Further Readings

Levelt, W. J. M. (1989). *Speaking: From intention to articulation.* Cambridge, MA: MIT Press.

Meyer, A. S., Sleiderink, A. M., & Levelt, W. J. M. (1998). Viewing and naming objects: Eye movements during noun phrase production. *Cognition, 66,* B25–B33.

Schriefers, H., Teruel, E., & Meinshausen, R. M. (1998). Producing simple sentences: Results from picture-word interference experiments. *Journal of Memory and Language, 39,* 609–632.

Wheeldon, L. R., & Lahiri, A. (1997). Prosodic units in speech production. *Journal of Memory and Language, 37,* 356–381.

LAYERED CONTROL ARCHITECTURES

A layered control architecture is one in which there are multiple levels of control at which the sensing apparatus is interfaced with the motor system. It is distinguished from hierarchical control by the constraint that the architecture should exhibit *dissociations*, such that the lower levels still operate, and exhibit some sort of behavioral competence, in the absence (through damage or removal) of the higher layers but *not* vice versa. A substantial body of the neuroscience literature can be interpreted as demonstrating layered control systems in the vertebrate brain; layering is also an important theme in the design of artificial control systems, for instance, for autonomous robots.

Layered Control in the Vertebrate Brain

In many ways, the notion of layering is a common, often unspoken, assumption in neuroscience; however, the implications of the layered nature of the brain are not always acknowledged in a field often dominated by the study of the mammalian cortex. The idea of the brain as a layered architecture can be traced to the views of John Hughlings Jackson, a 19th-century neurologist inspired by the Darwinian revolution. According to Jackson, the various anatomical levels of the brain implement multiple functional levels of sensorimotor competence with higher centers supporting the same sort of "sensorimotor coordinations" as those below, but in a more complex fashion. This view contrasted with that of many of Jackson's contemporaries for whom the highest levels of the brain, particularly the frontal lobes, were considered to be the seats of understanding and consciousness. Jackson strongly asserted that, although the frontal lobes may play a role in these more refined functions, the brain is a product of evolution and, therefore, all of its levels must be involved, in some way, with the coordination of sensing with action. Jackson also popularized the idea of *dissociation*; he argued that a breakdown at a higher layer should cause a reversion to the next highest layer of control. Discoveries of such dissociations between the vertical layers of the vertebrate nervous system were among the first findings of neuroscience. For instance, removing the cortex from a cat or a rat eliminates many major sensory, motor, and cognitive centers but leaves intact the ability to generate basic motivated behavior. That is, the animal still shivers when cold, escapes or fights when attacked, searches for food and drink, stops eating when sated, and so on. When most of the forebrain is removed, integrated behaviors can no longer be generated, but the capacity for elementary actions

(walking, grooming, eating, etc.) is spared. With all but the hindbrain and spinal cord removed, the animal cannot coordinate the movements required for these actions; however, most of the component movements that make up the actions are still possible. The notion of a layered architecture is now being mapped out in more detail in the context of specific types of behavior. For instance, as illustrated in Figure 1, the vertebrate defense system—the control system that protects the body from physical harm—can be viewed as being instantiated in multiple layers from the spinal cord (reflexes), through the hindbrain (potentiated reflexes), midbrain (coordinated responses to species-specific stimuli), forebrain (coordinated responses to conditioned stimuli), and cortex (modification of responses according to context). In this system, the higher layers generally operate by modulating (suppressing, potentiating, or modifying) responses generated by the lower layers.

Layered Control in Robots

Although many control architectures for artificial agents include elements of layered control, the *subsumption architecture,* proposed by Rodney Brooks, illustrates the idea in perhaps its purest form. The principle of the subsumption architecture is that control systems are built incrementally, one layer at a time, with each new layer fully tested and debugged before another is added (emulating, perhaps, the process of natural evolution). New layers operate primarily by injecting their signals into lower layers thereby "subsuming" the lower level functionality. A key idea is that the system as whole does not construct integrated representations of the world; rather, sensory signals are processed differently at each level to implement relatively direct and behavior-specific mappings between sense data and the motor signals required to control the robot's actuators. Robots built according to the principles of the subsumption architecture can operate in cluttered real-world settings, despite having relatively simple control systems, and show rapid responsiveness together with robustness to breakdown or damage (if higher levels become inoperable, the lower level system should still function). Arguably, however, the principles of subsumption have failed to scale to allow the control of robots with many actuators and multiple goals, that is, where the system is faced with particularly difficult problems of action selection.

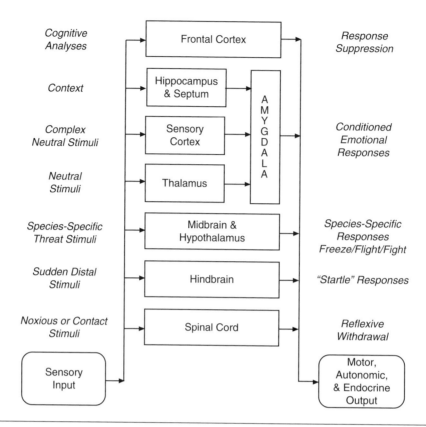

Figure I   Layered organization of neural mechanisms for defense in the vertebrate brain

Source: Prescott, T. J., Redgrave, P., and Gurney, K. (1999). Layered control architectures in robots and vertebrates. *Adaptive Behavior, 7,* 99–127.

Note: The nature of the sensory input, the principal brain structures involved, and the nature of the defense reaction are indicated for each level. The output of all layers appears to be relayed to a relatively restricted set of motor, autonomic, and hormonal effector systems.

Other Dimensions of Brain Organization

The nervous system is an intricately complex structure. Thus, although the vertebrate brain shows clear evidence of layered control, there will likely be other important governing principles in its organization. Indeed, a system that works by the principles of layered control alone may be too rigid to exhibit the intelligent, flexible behavior that vertebrate animals are clearly capable of (and currently far exceeds that achievable by robots). One proposal is of a centralized, or *centrencephalic,* organizing principle whereby a group of central, subcortical brain structures serves to coordinate and integrate the activity of both higher level and lower level neural systems. Although the notion of centrencephalic organization appears to oppose that of layered control, it is possible that the brain, although fundamentally layered, uses central integrative systems to manage and coordinate activity across the different levels. A better understanding of this full hybrid control architecture remains an important goal for the sciences of mind.

Tony J. Prescott

See also Common Coding; Decision Making, Neural Underpinnings; Natural Action Selection, Modeling

Further Readings

Brooks, R. A. (1991). New approaches to robotics. *Science, 253,* 1227–1232.

Gallistel, C. R. (1980). *The organization of action: A new synthesis.* Hillsdale, NJ: Erlbaum.

Prescott, T. J., Redgrave, P., & Gurney, K. (1999). Layered control architectures in robots and vertebrates. *Adaptive Behavior, 7,* 99–127.

Thompson, R. (1993). Centrencephalic theory, the general learning system, and subcortical dementia. *Annals of the New York Academy of Sciences, 702,* 197–223.

LEARNING STYLES

Theories of *learning styles* suggest that learning varies across individuals, based on how the person perceives material (e.g., visually vs. auditorily) or how the person thinks about it (e.g., trying to solve a problem sequentially vs. trying to think about it globally). This entry describes what learning styles theories predict about human learning and discusses the lack of evidence supporting these predictions.

Definition of Learning Styles

The key prediction of learning styles theories is that learning and thinking ought to be faster and more effective if a person thinks about the material in a way that matches his or her style than if there is a mismatch. This preference is predicted to be stable and thus observable across time and with different learning tasks.

A few particulars of this definition require elaboration. First, learning styles are specific. The claim is not that "everyone learns differently" but that there is a limited number of styles. Second, learning styles reflect performance, not just preference. A sequential learner not only likes doing tasks sequentially rather than globally, he or she also performs tasks better that way. Third, learning styles occur on a continuum. It is usually assumed that a few people will show extreme preferences but that most will be somewhere in the middle. Fourth, learning styles are distinct from abilities. It is always better to have more ability than less, but styles are meant to be value neutral. There is nothing inherently better about being a visual learner or an auditory learner.

Different researchers have proposed different bases for learning styles. Some have suggested that a style is a relatively fixed part of one's cognitive makeup, built into the mind. Others have suggested that learning styles actually reflect more broadly based personality types; the theoretical distinctions are meant to capture not only learning but also how one interacts with other people, for example. Still other theorists have suggested that learning styles are somewhat open to change, based on experience and on the moment-to-moment demands of the environment.

Examples of Learning Styles Theories

Testable theories of learning styles began to be proposed in earnest in the 1940s and 1950s. Since that

Table 1   Examples of learning styles theories

Species	Description
Visual/auditory/ kinesthetic	Learning is more effective if the material is perceived in the preferred modality
Converging/ diverging	A preference for deductive thinking or for broad, associational thinking
Serialist/holist	A tendency to work through problems incrementally versus globally
Verbalize/ visualize	A tendency to use words or to use mental pictures when thinking and reasoning
Field dependent/ field independent	A tendency to see and think about related objects as a whole, versus separating an object from its surrounding context

time, dozens of theories have been proposed, many of which are rather complex. Some that may be described simply are shown in Table 1.

Styles are most often assessed through self-report questionnaires, which typically ask about the types of activities the respondent enjoys ("I like cross-word puzzles and anagrams"), behaviors ("I often find myself humming a tune or tapping in time to music"), or beliefs about styles of thought ("I prefer a concrete, step-by-step solution to problems, rather than trying to come up with a shortcut"). Assessment may also include completion of some tasks and an interview.

Researchers have used two important criteria to evaluate learning styles theories: reliability and predictive validity. Reliability means that the assessment of a person's style should be consistent. One should be able to administer two or more tests of style and always get the same classification. Predictive validity means that the people with different styles should show meaningful differences in how they think and learn when confronted with real-world tasks. By these two criteria, learning styles theories are not well supported.

Lack of Evidence Supporting Learning Styles

Researchers have developed testing instruments of reasonable reliability for a few theories, but for most theories, there is not a reliable way to evaluate an individual person's style. This failing renders the theory untestable because, if one cannot say with certainty what a person's style is, there is no way of testing whether the style influences how that person thinks and learns. There are reliable methods of classifying learning styles for a few theories, but for these, validity is a problem. In other words, people with one learning style or another do not think and learn as the theory predicts they should.

Rather than thinking or learning in accordance with a particular style, individuals seem much more flexible, adapting their approach based on the demands of the task. Learning styles theories have been tested in a variety of situations, for example, how children learn basic print concepts, how college undergraduates study and understand complex material, and how children with learning disabilities learn to read. Learning styles theories are unsupported across these different people and tasks.

Despite the lack of scientific support, learning styles theories are widely believed to be accurate by educators, business people, and the general public. The bedrock of the idea is certainly optimistic. Educators hope to help struggling students, and business people hope to maximize efficiency. It would be a huge step forward if these goals could be better met through relatively minor changes in how information is presented or how people are encouraged to think about it. Unfortunately, the theory describing individual styles that could provide the basis for such changes has remained elusive.

Daniel T. Willingham

See also Metacognition and Education; Multiple Intelligences Theory

Further Readings

Coffield, F., Moseley, D., Hall, E., & Ecclestone, K. (2004). *Should we be using learning styles? What research has to say to practice.* London, UK: Learning and Skills Research Centre.

Sharp, J. G., Bowker, R., & Byrne, J. (2008). VAK or VAKuous? Towards the trivialization of learning and the death of scholarship. *Research Papers in Education, 23,* 293–314.

LEGAL REASONING, PSYCHOLOGICAL PERSPECTIVES

Legal reasoning typically refers to the reasoning of judges deciding cases in trial or appellate courts. (Trial court judges decide cases; appellate court judges decide cases and more general legal or constitutional issues.) This entry describes the two main types of legal reasoning, the debates among legal scholars about the nature of legal reasoning, and the major differences between legal reasoning and scientific reasoning.

Legal reasoning includes both deductive and analogical (case-based) reasoning. In deductive reasoning, the decision maker is presented with a set of facts, searches statutes and legal precedents to discover the law that covers these facts, and reaches a verdict according to the law. The reasoning is syllogistic, with the law the major premise, the facts the minor premise, and the verdict the conclusion. In analogical reasoning, the decision maker examines the similarities and differences between the current case and earlier related cases and chooses the verdict that corresponds to the holdings of the cases it most resembles. Such case-based reasoning requires the ability to identify relevant prior cases, to discern their factual and legal similarities and dissimilarities to the present case, and to recognize which similarities and dissimilarities are relevant (e.g., the defendant's state of mind) and which are not (e.g., the defendant's name).

In practice, both methods require the resolution of various ambiguities. Usually the judge is not given a single set of facts, but two contradictory accounts, each suggesting the inevitability of a different legal outcome. In applying deductive reasoning, the judge may find several statutes or precedents that could be relevant, and the legal language may suggest more than one interpretation. In applying case-based reasoning, the judge must define the universe of possibly applicable cases and decide which are most like the current case and which, although apparently similar, are actually irrelevant. In both kinds of reasoning, the significance of a particular fact depends on its legal significance, and the significance of a particular law or previous case depends on the particular fact pattern of the current case.

Legal Formalism and Legal Realism

Legal formalism was a form of deductive legal reasoning promulgated by Christopher Columbus Langdell, who became dean of the Harvard Law School in 1870 and who transformed legal education from apprenticeship to professional education. According to formalism, the law is hierarchically organized with a few highly abstract principles at the top, from which a larger number of mid-level rules are derived, and finally a very large number of specific legal rules and case precedents, rather like the taxonomic system of Linnaeus (phyla, genera, species). Like the explorer who discovers a new species, the judge confronted with a new case could find its exact place in the ordered structure by comparing it with the low-level exemplars. Langdell promoted law as a logical, deductive science.

Formalism was sharply criticized by Oliver Wendell Holmes Jr. and later critics such as Roscoe Pound, Karl Llewellyn, and Benjamin Cardozo, who argued that application of legal rules does not yield definite answers in any but the easiest cases. Judges do not *discover* the defining distinction between one case and another by logical analysis; the boundaries are often fuzzy and overlapping, and what judges do is *create* the defining distinction. The fundamental principles and legal rules are important and provide guidance, but in many cases, are insufficient to determine the outcome.

In the 20th century, these criticisms were further developed in the *legal realism* movement. Its adherents were an eclectic group of political activists, admirers of the rapidly growing social sciences, and legal scholars who believed that the purpose of the law was as important as the letter of the law. The unifying theme was a rejection of formalism and a belief that legal doctrine played a limited role in actual legal decision making. They focused on the political, social, cultural, and psychological forces that influence legal decisions and on how legal decision makers *actually* reason, rather than how they justify their decisions. Legal realism has largely been absorbed into legal education, and consideration of the social context, purposes, and policy implications of the law is common. Few people still believe in strict Langdellian formalism, although many law courses are a blend of formalism and the considerations raised by the legal realists, and judicial opinions are often written in formalist language, describing the decision as unequivocally constrained by the law.

Differences Between Legal Reasoning and Scientific Reasoning

Scientists are more concerned with discovering valid generalizations than with specific cases. Legal reasoning is more like early psychiatry, in that individual cases are central. Excellence in legal reasoning involves finding factors that distinguish among apparently similar cases and general rules that unite apparently disparate cases.

When scientists are trying to decide among multiple competing hypotheses, they can design and carry out empirical research to generate new information. Judges do not have this power. Judges must work with the information given to them, and that information consists of what other people have said (attorneys, witnesses) or written (attorneys, judges, legal scholars) and their own background knowledge.

Scientists can also postpone making any decision at all. They can look at the evidence available and decide that it is inconclusive. Trial court judges have to make a decision on the basis of the evidence before them, even if it is ambiguous. Usually they have to decide for one party or the other. Appellate court judges have to make a decision based on the briefs and oral arguments. Their decisions have precedential force, defining the law for years to come, whether the case was close or clear. A 5-to-4 decision from the Supreme Court is as final as a unanimous decision. In science, no decision is reached when scientists are closely divided on an issue. Judicial decisions are always supposed to be final; scientific decisions never are.

Scientists think of variables like sanity or parental fitness or maturity as matters of degree, but legal decision makers are forced to draw bright lines and make categorical decisions: A 17-year-old is a child; an 18-year-old is an adult.

Ideas of free will and free choice are fundamental to legal thinking, and this creates a tension between law and the social sciences, which are, to varying degrees, deterministic. The judge's task is to assign responsibility, which implies the assumption that people are personally accountable for their actions.

Some conditions can reduce responsibility, but free will is the starting point.

Finally, just as methodological rigor is central to science, adherence to the rules of law is central to legal decision making. Every decision that has precedential value must be justified by explicit discussion of the applicable law. Whether or not the rules actually determine the outcome, the judge must always provide a legal reason for the decision.

Phoebe C. Ellsworth

See also Analogical Mapping and Reasoning; Case-Based Reasoning, Computational Perspectives; Deductive Reasoning; Scientific Reasoning

Further Readings

Burton, S. J. (1995). *An introduction to law and legal reasoning* (2nd ed.). Boston, MA: Little, Brown.

Ellsworth, P. C. (2005). Legal reasoning. In K. J. Holyoak & R. G. Morrison (Eds.), *Cambridge handbook of thinking and reasoning* (pp. 685–704). New York, NY: Cambridge University Press.

Horwitz, M. (1992). *The transformation of American law, 1870–1960: The crisis of legal orthodoxy*. New York, NY: Oxford University Press.

LIE DETECTION

Most educated people understand that the link between body and mind makes plausible the physiological detection of deception. However, in the absence of a physiological response unique to lying, developing a valid lie detector has been both challenging and controversial. Modern lie detection relies on polygraph tests—collections of interrogation techniques assisted by physiological recording that are intended to detect criminal offenders, screen out dishonest job applicants, and identify personnel who pose security risks. Despite the widespread use of polygraphy in the United States, mostly by government agencies, the scientific community remains skeptical that polygraphy could have the high accuracy claimed by polygraph practitioners.

Relevant-Irrelevant Technique

Modern polygraph testing is computerized and involves obtaining digital representations of autonomic nervous system activity associated with palmar sweating, respiration, and blood pressure while individuals are asked different types of questions. The first broadly used polygraph techniques became known as relevant-irrelevant tests (RIT). The RIT includes a relevant or "did you do it" question (e.g., in the case of a woman's rape, "Did you place your finger in Glenda's vagina?"). The physiological reaction to relevant questions is compared to the response to truthfully answered irrelevant questions dealing with simple facts (e.g., "Is your name John?"). Guilt is inferred if the relevant question elicits the stronger response. The problem with the RIT is that the accusatory relevant question can be emotionally arousing even when answered truthfully, thus ensuring that it will elicit a strong physiological reaction, often much stronger than the response to the innocuous irrelevant question. Recognized for this bias against the innocent, the RIT has been largely replaced by the control or comparison question test (CQT).

Control (Comparison) Question Technique

The CQT, first introduced in the 1940s, is typically used in forensic applications. Like the RIT, the CQT includes relevant questions. However, the reactions to the relevant questions are compared to those from "control" questions that are thematically related to the content to the relevant question. Control questions, which are answered "no," are believed to tap a "probable lie" based on the expectation that people typically engage in misbehaviors that are covered by the question. An example of a control question appropriate for an interrogation concerning a sex crime would be "Have you ever committed a sex act you were ashamed of?" CQT theory assumes that innocent individuals will be disturbed more by their denial to the control than to the relevant question because only the control question is likely to elicit a lie. By contrast, guilty individuals are expected to respond more to the relevant question because, for them, this question elicits a more important lie.

Regrettably, for the innocent, the significance of the accusation contained in the relevant and control questions is not equivalent. Only the relevant question deals with the criminal allegation, and only the response to this question can lead to consequences such as prosecution or public embarrassment. Just as is the case for the RIT, the CQT is biased against the innocent because only the relevant question deals with a consequential allegation. Hence, the accuracy of failed CQTs is suspect. But can passed tests be trusted? Unfortunately, research has shown that liars can augment their physiological reactions to the control questions by lightly biting their tongue or doing stressful mental exercises, thereby beating a CQT. Neither failed nor passed CQTs can be trusted.

Screening Techniques

The most common applications of polygraphy occur with screening of law enforcement job applicants and of government employees with security clearances. Applicant screening tests deal with the of integrity of prospective employees by, for instance, asking if they told the truth in response to hundreds of questions on their job application dealing with their trustworthiness on previous jobs, use of drugs and alcohol, meeting financial obligations, and so forth. Employees who already have jobs can be queried regarding their adherence to protocols designed to protect classified information entrusted to them. Screening test formats vary across settings, but many of the tests resemble an RIT with many relevant questions. Any relevant questions eliciting stronger responses than others are likely to become a basis for interrogation by the polygraph operator. If the examinee cannot explain the reactions to the satisfaction of the examiner, the test is failed. Although accurate statistics regarding the rate at which these tests are failed is lacking, anecdotal evidence indicates that preemployment tests are somewhat frequently failed whereas postemployment tests are rarely failed. This pattern is generally believed to reflect the examiner's understanding that the cost of erroneously failing a qualified but untrained prospective employee is considerably less than that associated with failing a highly trained and thoroughly vetted current employee.

Evaluation of the Scientific Foundation for Lie Detection Techniques

Proponents of polygraph tests typically claim near infallibility for their techniques, especially for the CQT. Scientists at arm's length from the polygraph profession have repeatedly evaluated the evidence in support of these claims and have concluded consistently that they are unfounded. The most recent and thoroughgoing evaluation of polygraph testing was carried out by a panel of more than a dozen scientists for the National Academy of Sciences. The panel held public hearings, had access to classified government documents and data on polygraph testing, and systematically evaluated the world literature on test validity. They concluded that the weak theory underlying polygraph tests renders implausible high accuracy claims, the generally poor quality of research on polygraph testing leads to overestimates of accuracy, the precise accuracy of polygraph tests is indeterminate, and there is no evidence that polygraph tests provide information about truthfulness that cannot be achieved by other methods.

An important question becomes why polygraph tests are used if they have such a weak scientific foundation. Polygraph tests are typically administered under circumstances where having the truth is important but difficult to obtain. Examiners are skilled interrogators adept at using the test occasion to leverage information from the examinee. Under the circumstances, important admissions and even confessions to otherwise unsolvable crimes are obtained. That anecdotal evidence indicates that such discovery frequently occurs speaks to the utility, not the accuracy, of polygraph tests. Indeed, the fastest growing application of polygraph testing involves their use with convicted sex offenders whose treatment progress and compliance with rules governing their release are difficult to monitor. Challenged to be truthful during their polygraph tests, sex offenders often divulge information about deviant sexual behavior and fantasies that monitoring programs use to help manage their rehabilitation.

Probing Memory: The Guilty (Concealed) Knowledge Test

Although conventional lie detection methods have, at best, a weak scientific foundation, there are memory-based detection methods that have a strong scientific rationale. The best known of these, introduced by David Lykken in 1959, is called the guilty knowledge test (GKT; sometimes referred to as the concealed information test). It is well established that a physiological response accompanies brain recognition of personally important information. The GKT is based on the principle that the perpetrator of a crime can be detected if bodily responses are recorded while being presented with crime-relevant memorial information that only the guilty and the police possess. For instance, in a case of rape, GKT questions such as the following might be asked while recording a suspect's physiological activity:

"If you sexually assaulted Glenda, then you would know what weapon was used to force her compliance. Was it (a) a box cutter, (b) a baseball bat, (c) a hammer, (d) an ice pick? . . . In what room in her house did the crime take place? Was it (a) the pantry, (b) the attic, (c) the bathroom, (d) the garage?" Knowing that he grabbed an ice pick off the tool bench and assaulted her in the garage, the rapist would be expected to give the strongest response to these relevant items. An innocent suspect, not knowing the correct answers, would respond randomly to the multiple choice options. If enough questions are asked, there is little likelihood of an innocent person failing a GKT by chance. Likewise, if a recognition response is evident to almost all the correct alternatives, the likelihood of guilt is high. As one might expect, given the sensible rationale underlying the GKT, research has shown its potential to be highly accurate, with errors identifying the innocent as guilty especially unlikely.

However, there are several reasons why the GKT is seldom used in real-world applications. Basic research is needed to determine what criminals remember from their crimes. Without such knowledge, it is difficult to know how much confidence to place in a passed GKT because it is possible that the items do not deal with crime facts the perpetrator remembers. In addition, GKT item development requires considerable investigative work to identify material likely to be readily recognized by the perpetrator that is not likely to be known to other suspects in the case. Because the CQT, the main polygraph technique used by law enforcement, does not have these limitations, is believed by polygraph proponents to be very accurate, and has proven utility, the police see little advantage to substituting the GKT for the CQT.

Looking to the Future

Historically, lie detection has employed autonomic nervous system measures from peripheral body sites. Advances in neuroscience methodology now make relatively straightforward the recording of activity in the brain using techniques such as the dense array electroencephalogram and functional magnetic resonance imaging. These methods offer promise for the future, but how well they improve on autonomic measures has not been established. More important, research with these measures depends on the use of questioning formats that are similar to those already in use and thus are vulnerable to the well-known criticisms already leveled at existing lie detection techniques.

Conclusion

In conclusion, notwithstanding more than a half century of experience with conventional lie detection techniques, there are no generally accepted methods for detecting lying or identifying liars. Despite long-standing criticism that polygraphic interrogation is without scientific foundation, polygraph testing in the United States remains commonplace, and government agencies administer tens of thousands of these tests every year. This common usage points to the utility of the polygraph, the belief that polygraphic interrogation provides an effective vehicle for obtaining information from criminals and untrustworthy personnel that likely would be undiscoverable otherwise. As the National Academy of Sciences report noted, unlike other fields of scientific inquiry, polygraph research has not progressed over time, thus failing to strengthen its scientific underpinnings in any significant manner. Hence, it is unlikely that polygraph testing will be substantially improved or gain acceptance in the scientific community as valid. Memory-based methods, such as the GKT, that have sound scientific underpinnings, may profit from further refinement and appraisal.

William G. Iacono

See also Deception, Linguistic Cues to; Emotion, Psychophysiology of; Eyewitness Memory

Further Readings

Ben-Shakhar, G., & Elaad, E. (2003). The validity of psychophysiological detection of information with the guilty knowledge test: A meta-analytic review. *Journal of Applied Psychology, 88*(1), 131–151.

Honts, C. R., Raskin, D. C., & Kircher, J. C. (2006). The case for polygraph tests. In D. L. Faigman, D. H. Kaye, M. J. Saks, J. Sanders, & E. K. Cheng (Eds.), *Modern scientific evidence: The law and science of expert testimony: Vol. 4. Forensics* (pp. 787–831). Eagan, MN: Thomson West.

Iacono, W. G. (2008). Effective policing: Understanding how polygraph tests work and are used. *Criminal Justice and Behavior, 35*, 1295–1308.

Iacono, W. G., & Lykken, D. T. (2006). The case against polygraph tests. In D. L. Faigman, D. H. Kaye, M. J. Saks, J. Sanders, & E. K. Cheng (Eds.), *Modern scientific evidence: The law and science of expert testimony: Vol. 4. Forensics* (pp. 831–895). Eagan, MN: Thomson West.

National Research Council. (2003). *The polygraph and lie detection.* Washington, DC: National Academies Press.

LOVE

Love has the potential to make people both very happy and very unhappy. Yet, there seems to be no easy and unambiguous answer to questions as to what love is and how people fall in love. This entry will address some major areas of psychological research on love. First, taxonomies of love will be introduced. Then, the biological foundations of love will be explored. Finally, applications of the findings will be considered.

Theories

Taxonomies

Taxonomies are used to try to shed light on the different styles and kinds of love that may exist.

Romantic Love Styles

John Alan Lee proposed that there are three primary styles of love—*eros, ludus,* and *storge*—and three secondary styles of love that result from mixtures of the three primary styles—*pragma, mania,* and *agape. Eros* is an erotic kind of love that comes with strong passionate emotions and physical attraction. *Ludus* is a game-playing love that is uncommitted and tends to realize itself with a variety of partners. *Storge* is a friendship kind of love that does not come with emotions as strong as those of eros; in contrast to eros, it is relatively calm and unobtrusive. *Pragma* is a kind of calculating love that sees the partner in terms of attributes that are desired (or not desired) in a relationship. *Mania* is a highly emotional secondary style of love that alternates between euphoria and desperation or even agony. The third secondary love style is *agape,* which is a kind of communal and altruistic love that is very giving and compassionate but that usually does not appear in a pure form in romantic relationships.

Susan Hendrick and Clyde Hendrick used these love styles as the basis for their research program and suggested that those six love styles can be depicted in a six-dimensional matrix in which every person gets assigned a certain point on all of the six love styles to describe the "amount" of each love style. These styles are largely independent of each other. People can be especially high on one style or moderately high on several of them. Also, it is possible to experience different love styles with different partners. The love styles, therefore, are dependent not only on the individual but also on the partner, as well as on demographic factors like age, life stage, and so forth.

The Duplex Theory of Love

The duplex theory of love, developed by Robert J. Sternberg, has two parts. One part specifies the structure of love, the other part, how this structure comes to be. The two parts are called the triangular subtheory and the subtheory of love as a story.

The Triangular Subtheory of Love. The triangular theory of love holds that love can be understood in terms of three components that together can be viewed as forming the vertices of a triangle. These three components are intimacy, passion, and decision/commitment. *Intimacy* refers to feelings of closeness, connectedness, and bondedness in loving relationships. It thus includes within its purview those feelings that give rise to the experience of warmth in a loving relationship. *Passion* refers to the drives that lead to romance, physical attraction, sexual consummation, and related phenomena in loving relationships. *Decision/commitment* refers, in the short term, to the decision that one loves a certain other and, in the long term, to one's commitment to maintain that love.

The three components of love generate eight possible limiting cases when considered in combination. Each of these cases gives rise to a different kind of love. It is important to realize that these kinds of love are limiting cases: No relationship is likely to be a pure case of any of them.

Nonlove refers simply to the absence of all three components of love. *Liking* results when one experiences only the intimacy component of love in the absence of the passion and decision/commitment components. *Infatuated love* results from the experiencing of the passion component in the absence of the other components of love. *Empty love* emanates from the decision that one loves another and is committed to that love in the absence of both the intimacy and passion components of love. *Romantic love* derives from a combination of the intimacy and passion components. *Companionate love* derives from a combination of the intimacy and decision/commitment components of love. *Fatuous love* results from the combination of the passion and decision/commitment components in the absence of the intimacy component. *Consummate love,* or *complete love,* results from the full combination of all three components. Most loves are "impure" examples of these various kinds: They partake of all three vertices of the triangle, but in different amounts.

The Subtheory of Love as a Story. The kind of love triangles discussed in the previous section emanate from stories. The interaction of our personal attributes with the environment—the latter of which we, in part, create—leads to the development of stories about love that we then seek to fulfill, to the extent possible, in our lives. Various potential partners fit these stories to greater or lesser degrees, and we are more likely to succeed in close relationships with people whose stories more closely match our own. Although the stories we create are our own, they draw on our experience of living in the world. There is a potentially infinite number of stories, and the stories may contain some overlap.

Examples of stories are

1. *Addiction.* Strong anxious attachment; clinging behavior; anxiety at thought of losing partner.
2. *Art.* Love of partner for physical attractiveness; importance to person of partner's always looking good.
3. *Business.* Relationships as business propositions; money is power; partners in close relationships as business partners.

The most common conception is of love as a travel story, or a journey that two people take together, trying to stay on the same path.

We may have multiple stories represented hierarchically, so that the stories are likely to vary in salience for us. In other words, we will prefer some stories over others, so that we may find partners differentially satisfying as a function of the extent to which they match our more salient stories.

Prototype Theory

Eleanor Rosch suggested that there are many concepts in everyday life that can be best described by means of prototypes. Prototypes are members of a category that represent the essence and typical features of the category members in a particularly good way. Other members of a category may differ in that some of their features are more or less prototypical of the category than others.

Beverley Fehr used the prototype approach to examine people's conceptions of love. She found that people regarded characteristics of companionate love, such as caring and respect, as more prototypical of love than characteristics of passionate love, which would include features such as passion and sexual desire. Similar to the prototypical features of love, people regarded friendship as more prototypical of love than passionate love. Studies show that couples who had a rather prototypical view of love also felt more love for their partner.

Biological Theories

Biological theories focus on biological and physiological processes as well as knowledge of evolution to explain psychological phenomena.

Love as a Decision Bias

Douglas Kenrick and his colleagues view love as a system of decision biases that evolved over time. Human beings, similar to members of other species, have to make many decisions over the course of their day. In the domain of love, potential questions are: Who is the best person to mate with, how do I attract potential mates, and how do I retain them over a longer period of time? People often do not make decisions on an objective basis but rather have an (often unconscious) inclination toward one or the other action alternative. Kenrick suggests that their decisions are biased because there are some inborn decision biases that have evolved over the course of human history and development. The decision biases take the form of if-then rules where "if" refers to a certain condition in the environment and "then" constitutes a response that is designed to adapt to the environment. For example, when men are looking for potential partners, they tend to pay relatively more attention than women to physical features like beauty and young age, which indicate fertility.

Different social situations necessitate different decision biases, which interact in dynamic ways with each other. These decision biases are the basis of all human behavior, so that although there may be cultural variations due to ecological differences, human behavior cannot be seen as a completely blank slate because the decision biases provide a certain framework.

Love as a Means to Commitment

David Buss suggests that love is primarily a device to achieve commitment—a means that helps bind people together through better or worse. He starts his explanation with changes that occurred when humans started diverging from their primate ancestors: Women's ovulation was concealed, so that men could not recognize when would be the best time to have intercourse with, and impregnate, them. This is one of the reasons men and women started to be engaged in long-term bonding. Buss has suggested that love evolved as a means to help people stay committed to each other even in difficult circumstances, for example, when they get sick or meet some other, more attractive potential mate.

Research has shown, for example, that when people feel love for their partner, they can better suppress thoughts of alternative attractive mates.

Love From an Attachment Point of View

Phillip Shaver and his colleagues applied the conceptual framework of attachment theory to adults. They suggest that for every behavior that is exhibited in attachment relationships of young children to their caregivers, there is also a parallel behavior in adult relationships. Shaver and colleagues suggest that three attachment styles exist in adults, just as in children.

A *secure* attachment style leads to people being comfortable being close to their close others, without any great fear of being abandoned or others getting too close to them. An *anxious-ambivalent* attachment style leads people to cling to their loved ones and to be afraid of losing them. An *avoidant* attachment style leads people to avoid closeness to others and to become anxious once those others seek proximity.

In addition to the attachment system, there are two other behavioral systems that may play a role in romantic love—the caregiving system and the sexual system. The caregiving system is triggered by others' expressions of needs and attachment. Its goal is to help others in need and to reduce their misery. The sexual system is activated by the presence of a potential attractive and fertile partner. Its goal is to engage in sexual intercourse and, ultimately, to pass on one's genes to the next generation.

Applications

A feature of research on love is that it has applications to people's everyday lives. For example, people can assess their own love triangles or love stories or attachment styles. Assessing such patterns can help people better understand how they love and also what they are looking for in a partner. Partners can also assess the extent to which they are looking for the same things in a relationship.

Individuals and partners can also use theories of love to enhance their relationships. For example, people who have an anxious-ambivalent style of loving may have difficulties in their relationships and may wish to work on this style—either on their own or, preferably, in the context of psychotherapy—if it is causing them problems in their life. People first need to understand what their issues are in relationships. Theories of love can help them find out what these issues are. Then they can decide whether they want to resolve them, and how.

Summary

Theories of love address questions such as what love is, how it develops, how it can be assessed, and how it can be enhanced. We have considered several approaches, including taxonomic, prototypic, and biological ones. These theories differ in both the assumptions and assertions they make; however, they have in common that they attempt to provide plausible and empirically supported accounts of the nature of love.

Because the theories deal with somewhat different aspects of the phenomenon of love, they are not necessarily mutually exclusive. There may be elements of many theories that, in combination, help us understand the mysterious nature of love.

Robert J. Sternberg and Karin Sternberg

See also Attraction; Jealousy; Relationships, Development of

Further Readings

Buss, D. M. (2007). The evolution of human mating strategies: Consequences for conflict and cooperation. In S. W. Gangestad & J. A. Simpson (Eds.), *The evolution of mind: Fundamental questions and controversies* (pp. 375–382). New York, NY: Guilford Press.

Fehr, B. (1988). Prototype analysis of the concepts of love and commitment. *Journal of Personality and Social Psychology, 55,* 557–579.

Fisher, H. (2004). *Why we love: The nature and chemistry of romantic love.* New York, NY: Henry Holt.

Hatfield, E., & Rapson, R. L. (1996). *Love and sex: Cross-cultural perspectives.* Needham Heights, MA: Allyn & Bacon.

Hendrick, S. S., & Hendrick, C. (2008). Satisfaction, love, and respect in the initiation of romantic relationships. In S. Sprecher, A. Wenzel, & J. Harvey (Eds.), *Handbook of relationship initiation* (pp. 337–351). New York, NY: Psychology Press.

Kenrick, D. T., Sadalla, E. K., & Keefe, R. C. (1998). Evolutionary cognitive psychology: The missing heart of modern cognitive science. In C. Crawford & D. L. Krebs (Eds.), *Handbook of evolutionary psychology* (pp. 485–514). Mahwah, NJ: Erlbaum.

Shaver, P. R., & Mikulincer, M. (2006). A behavioral systems approach to romantic love relationships: Attachment, caregiving, and sex. In R. J. Sternberg & K. Weis (Eds.), *The new psychology of love* (pp. 35–64). New Haven, CT: Yale University Press.

Sternberg, R. J. (1998). *Cupid's arrow.* New York, NY: Cambridge University Press.

Sternberg, R. J., & Weis, K. (Eds.). (2006). *The new psychology of love.* New Haven, CT: Yale University Press.

M

MACHINE SPEECH RECOGNITION

Speech represents the most natural means of human communication. Machine speech recognition, often called automatic speech recognition, is the automatic process performed by machine or computer to transform a speech utterance into a text consisting of a string of words. The term *machine* aims at making the distinction between machine speech recognition and human speech recognition (human speech perception). Machine speech recognition is also different from machine speaker recognition, which is the automatic process performed by machine to identify a speaker or to verify the identity of a speaker based on his or her voice. After a brief overview of the general steps involved in machine speech recognition, this entry introduces two of the most prominent machine speech recognition techniques.

There are different techniques for machine speech recognition, but generally speaking, they consist of a common series of steps. First, the acoustic waves of pressure corresponding to the speech utterances are transformed into electric signals by a microphone. These electric signals are then transformed into a string of feature vectors, usually called acoustic feature vectors. The feature vectors are representations of the spectrum and energy of the speech signal over short periods. Then, the extracted string of acoustic feature vectors is matched against previously stored models of sentences, words, syllables, or phonemes. The text string of words that best matches the incoming string of acoustic feature vectors is presented at the output of the machine speech recognition. Based on the type of input utterances, machine speech recognition can be classified as isolated word recognition or continuous speech recognition. Based on the generality of the models, machine speech recognition can be classified as speaker dependent or speaker independent. Based on the size of the vocabulary, machine speech recognition can be classified as small vocabulary (up to 100 words), medium vocabulary (up to 1,000 words), or large vocabulary (up to hundreds of thousands of words). Applications of machine speech recognition include voice dialing (e.g., digit recognition), command and control, form filling (e.g., data entry), web search by voice, and dictation (e.g., speech-to-text word processing).

Dynamic Time Warping

One of the most successful early techniques for machine speech recognition is called dynamic time warping (DTW) and is based on a combination of template matching and dynamic programming. Dynamic programming is a mathematical optimization process of finding the best (optimal) decisions in a recursive manner. A string of acoustic feature vectors corresponding to the input test utterance is matched consecutively against each stored reference template of feature vectors corresponding to training utterances. The test string of vectors and the stored string of vectors corresponding to each reference template form a search grid on which DTW finds an optimum path. The test feature vectors are warped nonlinearly in time (compressed or expanded) with the feature vectors of the stored templates. A matching score or distance is then computed between the test utterance and each stored reference template. The input test utterance is recognized to be the utterance corresponding to the stored reference template that provides the highest score or lowest distance to the test utterance. The first DTW approaches used isolated words to create templates. Later, this technique was extended to connected speech by creating sentence templates made of concatenated word templates.

Hidden Markov Models

The most prominent modern technique for machine speech recognition is called hidden Markov models (HMM). In this technique, each stored model (e.g., a word or a phoneme) is characterized by a set of model parameters that consists of a sequence of states, an initial state probability vector, a state transition probability matrix, and an observation probability density function corresponding to each state. The initial state probability vector defines the probability of each of the states to be the entering state of the model. The state transition probability matrix defines the transition probability between each state and all other states, including itself. The observation probability density function defines the multivariate probability distribution of the feature vectors. The observations consist of acoustic feature vectors, which most commonly are in the form of mel frequency cepstral coefficients. These coefficients represent the spectrum of speech using the cosine transform of the logarithm of the spectrum on the mel frequency scale (a perceptual scale of pitch). The HMM technique consists of two phases: training and recognition. The training phase focuses on estimating the model parameters given multiple training utterances (observation sequences). The recognition phase focuses on searching for the hidden, most likely sequence of words and usually employs one of two kinds of algorithms—the A* algorithm (stack decoder) or the Viterbi algorithm (based on dynamic programming). For a given test utterance, the HMM provides the hidden sequence of states within sentences, words, and phonemes and its corresponding likelihood. The recognition process involves acoustic models (which characterize how words and phonemes are acoustically pronounced) and language models (which characterize the rules of combining different words into sentences). Both types of models are created from large numbers of training utterances and sentences for a given language.

Performance

The dream of machines capable of recognizing speech attracted many researchers during the past 6 decades. Many commercial products today claim accuracies between 95% and 99% for large-vocabulary continuous speech recognition in clean conditions and when models were adapted to the voice of the speaker. Yet, in spite of intensive research efforts, the performance of machine speech recognition is far behind the performance of human speech recognition. Some research studies show that the word error rate of humans is still about an order of magnitude lower than that of machines performing the same speech recognition tasks. There are many factors that make machine speech recognition a difficult problem. One is represented by the large acoustic variability and pronunciation variability both within speakers and across speakers. Another factor is the linguistic complexity of the task, which is due to the fact that words can be combined to form an infinite number of different sentences. Yet another challenge is the deterioration of speech signal due to environmental acoustic noise or channel noise.

Sorin Dusan

See also Cohort Model of Auditory Word Recognition; Speech Perception; Word Recognition, Auditory

Further Readings

Deller, J. R., Hansen, J. H. L., & Proakis, J. G. (2000). *Discrete-time processing of speech signals.* New York, NY: IEEE Press.

Jelinek, F. (1997). *Statistical methods for speech recognition.* Cambridge, MA: MIT Press.

Jurafsky, D., & Martin, J. H. (2000). *Speech and language processing: An introduction to natural language processing, computational linguistics, and speech recognition.* Upper Saddle River, NJ: Prentice Hall.

Rabiner, L. R. (1989). A tutorial on hidden Markov models and selected applications in speech recognition. *Proceedings of the IEEE, 77*(2), 257–286.

Rabiner, L. R., & Juang, B. (1993). *Fundamentals of speech recognition.* Englewood Cliffs, NJ: Prentice Hall.

McCollough Effect

All of us have experienced visual adaptation in some form or another. Stare at a bright red light for half a minute, look away and you will see a green spot on your retina before it fades away quickly. You just adapted to the (red) light and, as a result, saw a (green) color that is opposite or complementary to the original. In general, persistent exposure to a stimulus causes the neural circuitry responsive to the stimulus to adapt. The adaptation results in afterimages or aftereffects, namely, percepts that are dissimilar from the actual stimulus. Aftereffects are generally negative insofar as the feature value perceived following the adaptation is opposite that of the adapter (the stimulus that causes the adaptation), as in the preceding example.

Celeste McCollough's discovery of an aftereffect that was contingent on a feature of the adapting pattern radically altered the study of adaptation. The aftereffect, known as the McCollough effect, has since been extensively replicated in other laboratories. It arises from the alternating presentation of stripes (gratings) of perpendicular (orthogonal) orientations of complementary colors for a modest time period (5–10 minutes). Figure 1 illustrates the adapting stimuli, which consist of red, horizontal and green, vertical gratings. Subsequent to the adaptation, achromatic (i.e., black and white) horizontal gratings appear greenish and achromatic vertical gratings pinkish, opposite to the colors shown

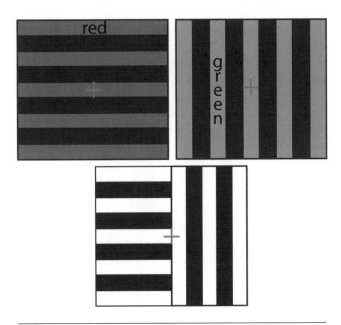

Figure I   McCollough effect

Note: A typical sequence of stimuli used to elicit the McCollough effect. To obtain an effect, the stimuli are not in grayscale, as shown, but colored.

during adaptation. Thus, similar to the overwhelming majority of aftereffects, the McCollough effect is a negative aftereffect.

The McCollough effect is a dramatic departure from other negative aftereffects, however. In contrast to simple aftereffects that do not require a test stimulus for the misperception to be evident, the McCollough effect is a contingent aftereffect that is created by relatively brief experimentally induced correlations between stimuli that are usually uncorrelated in the real world. The aftereffect is different depending on whether the test stimulus is horizontal or vertical in the previous example. Also, in contrast to simple aftereffects that last a few seconds, the McCollough effect is stable for weeks, or even months.

There are at least two other fascinating aspects of the McCollough effect. The observer does not have to maintain fixation on a point on the adapter; in fact, the observer can let the eyes wander over the pattern, and the resulting aftereffect will be largely unaffected. Second, the effect does not transfer interocularly: If adaptation is limited to one eye, no discernible negative aftereffect is observed in the non-adapted eye. Given that the McCollough effect is contingent on adapter orientation, that orientation selectivity does not emerge before primary visual cortex (or V1), and that orientation-tuned cells in V1 typically have binocular responses, one would expect the McCollough effect to transfer to the non-adapted eye. That it does not is surprising, and suggests a subcortical locus, where information from the two eyes is segregated.

Stemming from the McCollough effect, research has expanded into investigations into mechanisms or theories to explain the McCollough effect, explorations of aftereffects on other visual dimensions, and discoveries of positive contingent aftereffects.

Mechanisms and Models

It has been proposed that the McCollough effect be thought of as an instantiation of classical or Pavlovian conditioning. Others have proposed a neuroecological interpretation: The visual system is always calibrating its neutral point, and a strong correlation between a specific color and specific orientation is unusual enough to warrant a new neutral point, that is, the negative aftereffect. These studies, although critically placing the McCollough effect within a wider scientific milieu, do not claim to offer a biologically plausible model. In this regard, McCollough originally proposed that cells that were sensitive to both color and orientation, which lie in visual cortex, adapted. A more recent and influential neural network model by Stephen Grossberg and colleagues accounts for the spectrum of empirical findings related to the McCollough effect and is based on known mechanisms in biological vision.

Contingent Aftereffects

In addition to inspiring models and theories of learning and visual function, the discovery of the McCollough effect spawned a veritable cottage industry of contingent aftereffects. A number of aftereffects that are contingent on color have been found by pairing color with visual dimensions such as movement and spatial frequency. Complementary to the McCollough effect, which is a color aftereffect contingent on orientation, a tilt aftereffect that is contingent on color has been found. Contingent aftereffects with visual dimensions other than color have also been obtained. For example, aftereffects that are contingent on the direction of stimulus motion have been reported in a number of studies. Motion aftereffects that are contingent on stimulus luminance, size, direction of gaze, binocular disparity, the orientation of a stationary grating superimposed on a moving textured surface, and even the color or pattern of a stationary area surrounding the moving stimulus have been reported. Negative aftereffects that are contingent jointly on two different dimensions of a stimulus have also been reported. Finally, a long-lasting contingent aftereffect has been observed in the auditory system.

Positive and Double Negative Aftereffects

Not all contingent aftereffects are negative. There have been reports of a *positive* aftereffect; that is, the test color perceived following the adaptation is the same as the color of the oriented adapter. In another study, observers simultaneously viewed alternating orthogonally oriented achromatic gratings in one eye and alternating red and green homogeneous textureless fields in the other eye. When the eye that adapted to the color fields viewed achromatic test gratings later, observers reported a classical negative aftereffect, but when the eye that adapted to the oriented gratings viewed the same gratings, observers reported a positive color aftereffect. More recently, a double negative aftereffect has been reported. Binocular or monocular exposure to alternating

red and achromatic horizontal gratings for equal durations leads to an aftereffect of at least 24 hours duration in which test achromatic horizontal gratings appear reddish, that is, the color that is paired with the adapter orientation. The effect, termed the anti-McCollough effect, transfers 100% to the non-adapted eye, suggesting a neural locus on a higher level than that of the classical McCollough effect. One interpretation of the finding is that the neurons in a lower order area adapted to the stimulus, and neurons in a higher order area downstream adapted to the signal from the lower order area, giving rise to a negative aftereffect of the classical negative aftereffect. The findings are in accord with the idea that signals from higher order areas have greater access to visual awareness than those from lower order areas. Finally, studies have used contingent aftereffects to distinguish fast, preconscious from slow, conscious color processing by demonstrating that McCollough aftereffects can be induced at frame rates at which conscious perception fails.

The discovery of the McCollough effect in 1965 revolutionized the area of sensory adaptation, but its inner workings still remain somewhat of a mystery. Nevertheless, contingent aftereffects, in general, can be promising tools for understanding how the brain perceives.

Bhavin R. Sheth

See also Face Perception; Reinforcement Learning, Psychological Perspectives; Stereopsis

Further Readings

Coltheart, M. (1973). Letter: Colour-specificity and monocularity in the visual cortex. *Vision Research, 13*(12), 2595–2598.

MacKay, D. M., & MacKay, V. (1973). Orientation-sensitive after-effects or dichoptically presented colour and form. *Nature, 242*(5398), 477–479.

McCollough, C. (1965). Color adaptation of edge detectors in the human visual system. *Science, 149,* 1115–1116.

Sheth, B. R., & Shimojo, S. (2008). Adapting to an aftereffect. *Journal of Vision, 8*(3), 1–10.

MEMORY, INTERFERENCE WITH

There are two types of memory interference: proactive interference and retroactive interference. *Proactive interference* occurs during memory retrieval when a later memory trace is hindered by a highly similar earlier memory trace. *Retroactive interference* can occur during both memory retrieval and memory consolidation (strengthening). It occurs during retrieval when an earlier memory trace is hindered by a highly similar, later memory trace. Retroactive interference with consolidation occurs when the consolidation of a recently acquired memory trace is hindered by further cognitive activity, drugs, brain lesions, or seizures. Memory interference theory differs from another theory of forgetting, decay theory, in that it attributes forgetting to interference rather than to the sole passage of time.

Retroactive Interference

Retroactive Interference With Memory Consolidation

Retroactive Interference by Further Cognitive Activity

The notion that forgetting might occur due to memory interference was first put forward in 1900 by the German psychologist Georg Müller and medical student Alfons Pilzecker. They noted during their early experimental work on healthy participants that recently learned material often seemed to "pop into consciousness" in an unwilled manner, especially when their participants were not engaged in any mentally effortful activity following new learning. Müller and Pilzecker hypothesized that this "perseveration" of recently learned material reflected a transiently continued activity of learning-related physiological processes that served the "consolidation," that is, the strengthening of new memory traces.

They posited that the consolidation of a recently acquired memory trace could be hindered by subsequent cognitive activity; they called this effect "retroactive interference." Their work showed that, indeed, more nonsense syllables were forgotten by their participants when the learning of such nonsense syllables was followed by the learning of further nonsense syllables (filled delay) than when it was followed by a period of rest (unfilled delay). This retroactive interference effect was also apparent when the interpolated material was not similar to the earlier material, that is, when the learning of nonsense syllables was followed by a picture description task; this result indicated that this interference effect was nonspecific. Further evidence for such nonspecific effects comes from John Jenkins and Karl Dallenbach, whose much-cited study demonstrated that more nonsense syllables were forgotten

when the learning phase was followed by routine daily activities as opposed to a period of sleep.

In an attempt to explain how (nonspecific) cognitive activity might impede the consolidation of an earlier memory trace, the psychologist John Wixted argues that any cognitive activity engages the consolidation system to allow for the retention of this activity and its associated material. Moreover, he hypothesizes that consolidation resources are not unlimited. Therefore, according to Wixted, post-learning cognitive activity impedes the consolidation of an earlier memory trace because it actively deprives the earlier memory trace of limited consolidation resources.

However, the magnitude of this interference effect is not constant over time. Indeed, the most important and influential finding to have emerged from Müller and Pilzecker's as well as Ernest Burton Skaggs's early memory research is that of a temporally graded effect of further activity on early memory traces: Retroactive interference is largest when further activity occurs immediately following the learning of early material, and it decreases with increasing delay in the onset of further activity. This temporal gradient of retroactive interference indicates that memory traces are initially highly fragile and vulnerable to interference but that they consolidate and become less susceptible to interference over time.

Increased Retroactive Interference by Further Cognitive Activity in Patients With Amnesia

Recent neuropsychological work on amnesic patients by Nelson Cowan, Sergio Della Sala, Michaela Dewar, and their colleagues has shown substantially augmented effects of post-learning activity on recent memory traces in some patients with anterograde amnesia, indicating that these patients are especially vulnerable to retroactive interference. In line with the consolidation theory, the research has revealed a steep temporal gradient of retroactive interference in at least some amnesic patients. This gradient demonstrates that, even in amnesic patients, memory traces can consolidate over time, provided that this time is devoid of further activity.

Retroactive Interference by Brain Lesions

It is not only further cognitive activity that differentially interferes with older and newer memory traces. Around the same time as Müller and Pilzecker were investigating consolidation and retroactive interference in healthy participants, the French psychologist Théodule-Armand Ribot noted that certain types of pathological damage to the brain had a more detrimental effect on recent pre-morbid than remote pre-morbid memories, implying that earlier memories are less vulnerable to pathological brain damage than are later memories. This effect, which has been widely reported and is known now as "temporally graded retrograde amnesia," is in line with Müller and Pilzecker's consolidation theory, in that it is strongly suggestive of a gradual strengthening of memories over time.

Retroactive Interference by Drugs

Pharmacological animal work has shown that memory consolidation can also be hindered by certain drugs such as protein synthesis inhibitors, which are toxins or antibiotics. This work usually involves the learning of a response such as shock avoidance, followed by the injection of a protein synthesis inhibitor, and subsequent memory testing. As with retroactive interference by further cognitive activity, protein synthesis inhibitors have a temporally graded interference effect on new memory traces. They are most detrimental to a new memory trace when injection occurs immediately following learning, and they become less effective with augmenting delay between learning and injection.

Retroactive Interference With Memory Retrieval

Interpolated cognitive activity not only interferes with memory consolidation of an earlier memory trace; it can also interfere with the retrieval of an earlier memory trace, provided that the memory trace resulting from the interpolated cognitive activity is highly similar to the earlier memory trace. Similarity can take various forms: Two or more memory traces can be similar in type, that is, visually, phonologically, or semantically, or they can be similar because of a mutual association with a retrieval cue. For example, a computer login screen might cue one's private as well as one's work computer password.

One of the classic early experimental psychology paradigms to demonstrate a similarity effect of retroactive interference was that by the psychologists John McGeoch and William MacDonald. They showed that the magnitude of forgetting of new verbal material was closely related to the degree of similarity between the early and interpolated later material. Forgetting of a list of adjectives was lowest following relatively dissimilar interpolated material (the reading of jokes, referred to as "rest" by the authors), and it increased progressively from interpolated three-figure numbers to interpolated

nonsense syllables to interpolated antonyms and finally to interpolated synonyms.

Retrieval-based retroactive interference theory continues to dominate psychological memory interference research, and most current psychology textbook definitions of retroactive interference refer solely to retrieval, not consolidation.

The general consensus is that the attempted retrieval of a particular memory trace also activates those memory traces that are highly similar to the to-be-retrieved memory trace, or which are associated with the same retrieval cue. Such activation of multiple memory traces is said to lead to competition for retrieval and, thus, to interference. According to this theory, retroactive interference arises if the attempted retrieval of an early memory trace also activates a later acquired and currently stronger memory trace. For example, when asked to verify one's previous phone number it is likely that one's new phone number will be activated and indeed initially retrieved.

In the laboratory, such retrieval retroactive interference can be reliably produced via paired associate learning paradigms (AB-AC paradigms). These paradigms consist of the learning of a list of word pairs, each comprising a cue word and an associated word, for example, *dog-train*. List 1 learning is then followed by the learning of a second list of word pairs, which consist of the same cue words and new associated words, for example, *dog-sun*. This interpolated list tends to interfere during the subsequent cued recall of List 1 (i.e., dog-?). It has still not been established conclusively whether the interpolated memory trace is (transiently) stronger than the older trace or whether it might actually weaken the old trace within memory storage, for example, as a result of the active inhibition of the old trace during learning of the new trace.

Proactive Interference

One of the first explicit references to proactive interference comes from the 19th-century German psychologist Hugo Münsterberg, who always carried his pocket watch in a particular pocket. He noticed that after changing pockets he continued to automatically reach to the old pocket watch location. Such instances of proactive interference are believed to occur because a cue (in this particular example the intention to check the time) is associated with both an old, established memory trace and a new memory trace. Given the greater strength of the old memory trace, the cue results in the retrieval of the old memory trace. Similar situations can arise when one changes one's computer password or one's address, or when a woman marries and takes on her husband's surname.

Early Experimental Work on Proactive Interference

In the 1950s, the psychologist Benton Underwood went as far as to propose that most forgetting could be accounted for by such proactive interference as opposed to by retroactive interference. He argued that the then-prominent retrieval retroactive interference theory could not explain why some participants showed extensive forgetting of nonsense syllables over a period of 24 hours when this period was not filled with any similar material (i.e., when it was spent engaged in everyday activities at home). Having examined various studies, he noted that the amount of forgetting over 24 hours was in fact closely related to the number of study lists learned *prior* to the learning of the to-be-recalled list.

Importantly, however, this relationship was only present in studies in which the learning of prior lists was massed. The amount of forgetting was unrelated to the number of prior lists when these were spread over a longer time frame, as tends to be the case outside the laboratory. Proactive interference theory also appeared to be unable to explain the benefit of *interpolated* sleep that was demonstrated by Jenkins and Dallenbach. Underwood's claims that proactive interference was a major source of forgetting could thus not be sustained for very long.

Increased Proactive Interference in Patients With Executive Impairment

Even though no longer in the top list of forgetting causes, proactive interference does of course produce some forgetting as evinced in the Münsterberg example presented earlier. It is especially often observed in the laboratory in patients with damage to the executive system who have difficulties in the inhibition of irrelevant stimuli and distracters. In the aforementioned AB-AC paradigm, for example, dysexecutive patients often continue to recall AB associations during the AC learning trials. These patients are also often reported to show increased levels of retroactive interference with retrieval. It is hypothesized that such increased levels of experimentally induced retrieval interference are the result of the patients' general impairment in the inhibition of irrelevant, in this case competing, stimuli.

Michaela Dewar and Sergio Della Sala

See also Amnesia; Memory, Neural Basis; Memory Recall, Dynamics

Further Readings

Cowan, N., Beschin, N., & Della Sala, S. (2004). Verbal recall in amnesic patients under conditions of diminished retroactive interference. *Brain, 27,* 825–834.

Dewar, M. T., Cowan, N., & Della Sala, S. (2007). Forgetting due to retroactive interference: A fusion of Müller and Pilzecker's (1900) early insights into forgetting and recent research on anterograde amnesia. *Cortex, 43,* 616–634.

Dewar, M., Fernandez Garcia, Y., Cowan, N., & Della Sala, S. (2009). Delaying interference enhances memory consolidation in amnesic patients. *Neuropsychology, 23,* 627–634.

McGeoch, J. A., & McDonald, W. T. (1931). Meaningful relation and retroactive inhibition. *American Journal of Psychology, 43,* 579–588.

Müller, G. E., & Pilzecker, A. (1900). Experimentelle Beiträge zur Lehre vom Gedächtnis [Experimental contributions to the theory of memory]. *Zeitschrift für Psychologie. Ergänzungsband, 1,* 1–300.

Wixted, J. T. (2004). The psychology and neuroscience of forgetting. *Annual Review of Psychology, 55,* 235–269.

MEMORY, NEURAL BASIS

The ability to learn new information, and subsequently remember it, is critical to all animals. Whether it is apparent in response changes to repeated stimuli by an invertebrate, or by the collection of events in one's personal past that shapes the complex behavior of a human, memory allows an organism to effectively adapt to the environment. The study of memory processes has been arguably the most exciting and productive area of behavioral neuroscience in the past 50 years. Because learning is ubiquitous across animals, it has been possible to study its biological mechanisms in animal models in a way not possible for most other human cognitive capacities. This work has allowed researchers to understand neural mechanisms of memory at multiple levels of analysis, including molecular interactions, plasticity in circuits, and the roles of different anatomical systems. In this entry, the critical contributions at each of these levels of analysis will be discussed. Findings from human amnesic patients are described in terms of how these studies led to the idea that there are different brain systems that support different kinds of memory. In subsequent sections, studies at the circuit level are described which focus on how associations are formed in the brain. Finally, the entry outlines work examining the molecular mechanisms of long-term plasticity using brain slices.

Memory and Neural Systems

Most modern discussions of memory and the brain begin with the case of Henry Molaison, who was known as patient H. M. to most psychologists and neuroscientists until his death in 2008. Molaison had suffered from serious epileptic seizures starting in childhood, and he underwent bilateral surgical removal of the medial temporal lobe in 1953 in order to remove the epileptic foci. While this surgery was effective in that the frequency of seizures decreased substantially, it resulted in a severe impairment in memory. Molaison was virtually unable to retain any

new information, such as the names of new people he met. What was surprising at the time was that this profound memory impairment occurred with a background of normal intellectual functioning. H. M. was able to perceive, reason, and use language relatively normally. Thus, it appeared that memory could be selectively affected by a lesion, demonstrating that a distinct neural system supports memory processing. Although memory impairment had been reported before as the result of brain injury or neurological disease, such as Alzheimer's disease, these cases typically involved more widespread cognitive impairment. The careful study of patient Henry Molaison, and of other amnesic patients that followed, promoted the view that memory can be localized in the human brain.

The brain structures that are often damaged in amnesia include the hippocampus and cortical regions in the medial temporal lobe that surround this structure. This medial temporal lobe system is organized in a hierarchical fashion. The hippocampus receives and sends projections to the entorhinal cortex, which is interconnected with the parahippocampal and perirhinal cortices (Figure 1).

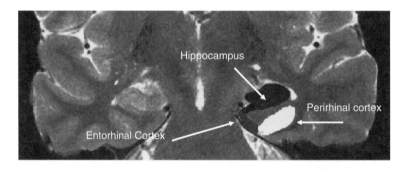

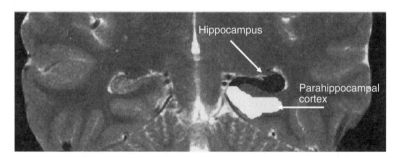

Figure I   Magnetic resonance images of the human brain, showing regions that are damaged in medial temporal lobe amnesia

Note: The panels show frontal sections, with the top of the figure representing the top of the head, and the image being in the plane of the face. The top panel is more anterior (closer to the face) than the bottom panel. The hippocampus is shown in black on the right side in both images. The entorhinal cortex is shown in dark gray and the perirhinal cortex is shown in white in the anterior image. These structures do not extend to the posterior section. The parahippocampal cortex appears in more posterior sections and is shown in white in the lower panel. These brain structures can be seen as on the left side as they appear in the magnetic resonance image.

These regions are, in turn, interconnected with a wide range of high-level association cortical areas, including frontal, temporal, and parietal regions. With this architecture, the hippocampus is positioned to receive highly processed input from all over the brain. This is consistent with the idea that memory representations are complex and multimodal. Amnesia can also result from damage to structures in the diencephalon that are connected to the hippocampus via the fornix.

While much focus has been on the hippocampus, it is clear that the surrounding cortices make additional contributions above and beyond their role as conduits for information. While damage restricted to the hippocampus results in a significant memory impairment, a far more significant and profound impairment results when these cortical regions are damaged as well, as in the case of Henry Molaison. These results suggest that these regions play a role in memory processing, particularly in the primate brain in which these cortical areas are well developed and provide the major input into the hippocampus. A currently unresolved question is whether the hippocampus and these cortical areas play similar or slightly different roles in memory.

A second major insight gained from the study of amnesic patients is the fact that the eventual storage site of memories is not in the medial temporal lobe. Patients with medial temporal lobe damage are impaired at learning new information, but memories from the remote past are intact. Thus, Henry Molaison's knowledge of facts about the world and vocabulary from before his surgery remained intact, although he was unable to acquire much in the way of new facts, and words that were invented after his surgery did not enter his vocabulary for the most part. These findings indicate that remote memories are stored in regions that are intact in amnesic patients. A likely site is the cerebral cortex. Cortical regions outside the medial temporal lobe, particularly the lateral and inferior temporal lobe, are likely candidates. These regions receive output from medial temporal lobe cortices, and enduring memory traces may be set up here. By another view, the medial temporal lobe structures remain important for retrieving memories about events, even those that were learned remotely. By this view, individual elements of memories may be stored in cortex, but medial temporal lobe structures are needed to bind together these traces to reexperience all elements of an episode.

Some support for the idea that remotely learned information is stored in temporal cortex comes from the study of patients with semantic dementia. Semantic dementia is a progressive neurological disease that involves degeneration of temporal lobe cortex. These patients lose knowledge of the world, and appear to have lost older memories, but new memories can still be formed, at least as long as medial temporal lobe regions are not affected by the disease.

Whereas remote memories are preserved even after extensive medial temporal lobe damage, more recently learned information can be vulnerable. Damage to the medial temporal lobe can result in amnesia for information learned before the injury, a phenomenon known as retrograde amnesia. In some cases, the extent of retrograde amnesia can be fairly brief (a few days), but in other cases, it may extend for many years. A primary factor in the duration of retrograde amnesia is the extent of damage to the medial temporal lobe memory system. Those patients with complete damage to the hippocampus may have difficulty remembering information for several weeks or months before their lesion, whereas patients with extensive damage to medial temporal lobe cortices as well as hippocampus may have retrograde amnesia extending throughout most of their adult lives.

The existence of retrograde amnesia indicates that, for some time after initial encoding, the medial temporal lobe is necessary for memories to be retrieved. This finding suggests that a kind of "consolidation" takes place, with memory traces changing gradually across time. These changes would lead to a gradual independence of these memory traces from the medial temporal lobe. One possibility is that memory traces are set up in the cortical areas, but that for an extended time, the medial temporal lobe is needed to access them. As noted earlier, it is also possible that the medial temporal lobe is always needed for retrieving detailed contextual memories.

The Declarative/Nondeclarative Distinction

In addition to the importance of the medial temporal lobe in memory functioning, another major lesson learned from the study of Henry Molaison is that there are multiple forms of memory that depend on different brain regions. Amnesic patients show impairments in memory for events and facts, known as declarative memory. Declarative memories share the property that one can "declare" them; that is, they are verbalizable. Despite impaired declarative memory, amnesic patients are able to show learning in different domains. Skill learning has been one of the most widely studied forms of intact learning in amnesic patients. These patients are able to learn to perform new motor skills at the same rate as neurologically intact subjects. One of the visuomotor skill tasks commonly used in the laboratory to assess performance of amnesic patients is the rotor-pursuit task. In this task, subjects attempt to keep a stylus in contact with a rotating disk. At first, it is difficult to keep the stylus in contact, but it becomes easier with practice. Although an amnesic patient may have difficulty in remembering the testing episode from one day to the next, he or she would show absolutely normal performance as measured by the decrease in errors over trials.

Another visuomotor task in which amnesic patients show normal performance is the serial reaction time task. In this task, an asterisk prompt appears in one of four locations, and subjects press a key corresponding to the position as soon as it appears. The asterisks appear according to a complex sequence that is not readily apparent to the subjects. Nevertheless, subjects react more quickly to each prompt with practice. It also appears that they have learned the sequence, because if the asterisks begin to appear randomly, performance slows down. Amnesic patients show normal learning of this sequence despite their poor memory for the testing episode.

The motor skills tested in the laboratory are similar to the more complex skills learned in daily life in that what is learned is often difficult to verbalize. While most of us learn to ride a bicycle with practice, we generally have a great deal of difficulty telling someone how to do it. Another example is learning to drive a car with a manual transmission. One must learn by doing, and not through verbal instructions. This characteristic of skill learning sets it apart from the kind of learning that is impaired in amnesic patients that is dependent on medial temporal lobe structures. The distinction between our declarative memory for facts and events, which we can verbally describe and which we are aware of learning, and non-verbalizable knowledge that we acquire in a motor skill learning task is fundamental to differentiating between the roles of different brain systems in memory.

Another memory domain in which performance of amnesic patients is intact is perceptual priming. When people see a stimulus, such as a word or picture, they can process it a little more effectively (faster and more accurately) if they had been presented with it previously. It appears as if the initial presentation leaves some sort of trace that allows more efficient processing when it is presented again. This facilitation does not depend on remembering that the primed stimulus had been presented. In fact, amnesic patients who are unable to remember that stimuli had been presented at all nevertheless exhibit normal priming. This finding demonstrates that the neural changes that support priming are independent of the medial temporal lobe memory system.

Priming and motor skill learning share the property that neither requires conscious awareness of what has been learned. However, in other ways, these two kinds of learning are different. Skills are generally learned gradually and incrementally. Priming, on the other hand, occurs rapidly, even after a single exposure to a stimulus. These two forms of memory also depend on different brain systems. Motor skill learning depends on the striatum and its interaction with the cerebral cortex, primarily the frontal lobes. Patients with neurological diseases that affect the striatum, including Huntington's disease and Parkinson's disease, show impaired ability to learn new motor skills in addition to their difficulties in motor performance. Neuroimaging findings also show activation in the striatum that is related to motor skill learning.

Priming appears to involve changes in the sensory cortex that processes the primed stimuli. Most of the work in this area has been done in the visual modality. The second viewing of a stimulus is generally accompanied by less activity in the extrastriate visual cortex than the first viewing as measured by neuroimaging techniques such as functional magnetic resonance imaging. This finding is consistent with the idea that the initial exposure makes it easier to process subsequent exposures, and thus less blood flow is needed to the neural region representing the item. This efficiency may be realized by the representation becoming more tuned to the task at hand. For example, if one is identifying objects, the second time around, those elements of the representation that are key for identification will be more activated, and those elements that are not critical will be activated less, thus resulting in behavioral priming (faster identification) and neural priming (less blood flow to the region).

The most compelling evidence for separate memory systems comes from double dissociations in memory performance observed in neuropsychological patients. Whereas amnesic patients exhibit normal skill learning and impaired declarative learning, the opposite pattern is observed in patients with basal ganglia dysfunction, such as those suffering from Parkinson's disease, who are able to remember training episodes but who exhibit impaired skill learning. A double dissociation has also been reported between declarative memory and perceptual priming. A few patients with lesions in extrastriate visual areas have been described who show deficits in perceptual priming despite normal declarative memory for the same items. These double dissociations are important in that they demonstrate that skill learning and priming are not simply easier than declarative learning, as one could argue based solely on the intact results from amnesic patients, but rather rely on independent brain systems.

Neural Circuits in Associative Memory

In the quest to describe how the brain contributes to memory processes, a particularly fruitful approach has been to study relatively simple forms of learning in animal models. For example, in Pavlovian conditioning paradigms, what is learned is an association between a conditional and an unconditional stimulus (CS and US). A tractable approach is to identify the neural circuits that process the CS and US and sites of their convergence. These convergence areas would be likely candidates for sites of plasticity and thus could be targeted for physiological investigations.

This approach has been applied to discover the neural substrates of Pavlovian conditioning of the eyeblink response in the rabbit. Rabbits have a nictitating membrane, or third eyelid, that moves in response to an unconditional stimulus, such as a puff of air to the cornea. If this unconditional stimulus is consistently paired with a neutral conditional stimulus, such as a tone, a conditional response will gradually develop in response to the tone alone. Early work showed that animals retained the conditional response even after the removal of the forebrain. These results strongly implicate the cerebellum, which receives sensory input from the brain stem and plays an important role in precisely timed behaviors. The conditioned eyeblink response is timed optimally so that the nictitating membrane is maximally closed when the unconditional response onset is expected. That is, if a rabbit is trained with the airpuff occurring 500 milliseconds after the onset

of a tone, the rabbit's conditioned eyeblink response will peak at 500 milliseconds after the tone onset.

The main input to the cerebellum is from sensory nuclei in the brain stem. Through a series of lesion studies, the pathways that are necessary and sufficient for this learning have been mapped out. The lateral pontine nucleus sends information about auditory conditional stimuli to the cerebellum. Information about the unconditional stimulus is conveyed via the climbing fibers from the inferior olivary nucleus. Lesioning or inactivating this nucleus in a well-trained rabbit does not abolish the conditional response. Rather, the conditional response is gradually extinguished over trials. This outcome arises because the input of the unconditional response is removed from the learning circuit. It is as if the air puff is no longer being presented.

Input from the conditional and unconditional stimuli converge on cerebellar Purkinje cells. These are remarkable neurons with extensive arbors. Based on the anatomy of the cerebellum, David Marr developed a model in 1969 in which convergent inputs could become associated by impinging on the Purkinje cells with close temporal proximity. When both climbing fibers and the conditional stimulus inputs are activated, long-term changes occur in the synapses. Although the conditional stimulus inputs are initially weak, they are strengthened through pairing with the much stronger climbing fiber inputs. After training, presentation of the conditional stimulus alone becomes adequate to affect the Purkinje cells. In these neurons, the strengthened synapses are actually inhibitory, so these cells have reduced output in response to the conditional stimulus compared to the level before learning. This reduced output ultimately modulates motor regions of the brain, resulting in a conditional response. The immediate output of the Purkinje cells is the deep nuclei of the cerebellum. Input from the conditional and unconditional stimuli also converge in this region, so the deep nuclei may work together with the Purkinje cells in the cerebellar cortex to produce optimally timed learned responses.

By studying this simple form of learning, it has been possible to identify the essential site of the memory, or the "engram." A similar approach has been taken to study the circuit supporting the conditioning of an emotional response. One procedure that has been studied in detail is conditional fear in the rat. As rats are prey animals, they have evolved robust neural mechanisms that support defensive behaviors. For example, rats will freeze, or become motionless except for breathing, when presented with a stimulus, such as a tone, that had been paired with a painful unconditional stimulus, such as a foot shock. This conditional emotional response is thought to reflect an acquired fear of a previously neutral stimulus. Information about the conditional and unconditional stimuli converge in the amygdala, which has been shown to be important for the acquisition and expression of fear. Unlike in the case of eyeblink conditioning, in which a discrete motor response is learned, learned fear activates a number of different responses—freezing, as well as effects on heart rate, respiration, and digestion. The amygdala orchestrates this system through its outputs to brain stem structures. Like the cerebellum, the amygdala is not necessary for declarative learning, but rather these two structures are key elements of two different nondeclarative memory circuits.

Molecular Mechanisms of Learning

The hippocampus, cerebellum, and amygdala are critical structures supporting different types of learning as shown primarily through lesion studies. Each of these structures has been the subject of intense scrutiny in terms of the changes that are occurring at the level of the synapse to support learning. Many of these studies are done using in vitro techniques in which a slice of brain is removed and kept alive in an oxygenated bath. This preparation allows access to individual neurons and their inputs.

The most popular in vitro preparation in the past several years has been the hippocampal slice. Using this preparation, one can record neural activity in the different hippocampal regions, including the dentate gyrus. While responses can be recorded from single neurons, researchers often measure the population spike—the result of a population of action potentials in response to stimulation of the input to this region. By stimulating the perforant path in the slice, a clear population spike can be recorded in the dentate gyrus. An exciting development in cellular neuroscience was the finding of long-term potentiation (LTP) in the dentate gyrus. After an intense stimulation of the perforant path (called a tetanus), a small stimulus now elicits a much larger population spike than the same stimulus did before the tetanus. This potentiation of neural activity can last many hours, as long as

the slice remains viable. LTP has been often touted as a neural model of memory—a strong or salient input gives rise to a long-lasting change in a structure that is known to be critical for memory processing. Although LTP is readily measured in the hippocampus, it is by no means confined to there, as long-term plasticity (either potentiation or depression of activity) has been measured in cortex, striatum, and cerebellum.

The tetanus results in LTP because the rapid frequency of pulses means that neurotransmitter continues to be released even when the postsynaptic neuron is already depolarized. This situation also occurs when a weak input is paired with a strong input that depolarizes the cell. A weak input is as effective as a tetanus in causing LTP if the postsynaptic cell is simultaneously depolarized. These conditions would occur naturally when a weak and strong stimulus occur together—whereas the weak stimulus alone cannot cause the neuron to fire, when it is paired with a strong stimulus it gains strength to the point in which it can subsequently cause the neuron to fire on its own. This idea, that temporal proximity of firing of a weak and a strong input leads to a change in synaptic strength of the weak input, was promoted by Donald Hebb in 1949 as a means for associative learning in the nervous system.

LTP has been a popular model system to study possible cellular and molecular bases for learning. The N-methyl-D-aspartate (NMDA) receptor that is abundant in the hippocampus appears to be critical for the activity-dependent plasticity that leads to LTP. This receptor is activated by the neurotransmitter glutamate, which is the primary excitatory neurotransmitter in the brain. When the neuron is at rest, this receptor is blocked by a positively charged magnesium ion, which prevents glutamate from activating the receptor. However, when the postsynaptic cell is depolarized, and thus becomes more positively charged, the magnesium ion moves away, and glutamate released from a cell conveying a weak input can now bind to this receptor. Activation of the NMDA receptor results in a cascade of events in the cell that do not occur after activation of other types of glutamate receptors. The results of NMDA-receptor activation include the synthesis of new proteins that change the structure of the synapse, making it more efficient, and the release of nitric oxide that travels back to the presynaptic neuron and facilitates the subsequent release of neurotransmitter. Both of these mechanisms may underlie learning in the intact mammalian brain. Interfering with the NMDA receptor with drugs such as MK-801 severely disrupts memory formation, suggesting that there is a link between this receptor and memory function.

Future Directions

Progress in understanding the neural basis of memory has proceeded in parallel at several levels of analysis: the level of the anatomical structures, of neural circuits within those structures, of changes in neurons, and of the molecules involved. Although progress at each of these levels has been immense over the past few decades, there is much work to be done in bridging between the levels. For example, it is unclear whether the same principles that apply to neural changes for simple conditioned responses also apply to declarative learning. Whereas the site of plasticity for simple conditioned responses is usually localized, it appears that the storage of declarative memories is more distributed in the cortex. Also, while the mechanisms underlying long-term potentiation have been studied extensively in the laboratory, these may not be identical to changes that occur under physiological circumstances. Questions such as these are likely to feature prominently in behavioral neuroscience in the next decade.

Barbara Knowlton

See also Amnesia; Implicit Memory; Reinforcement Learning, Psychological Perspectives

Further Readings

Aggleton, J. P., & Brown, M. W. (1999). Episodic memory, amnesia, and the hippocampal-anterior thalamic axis. *Behavioral and Brain Sciences, 22*, 425–444.

Barrionuevo, G., & Brown, T. H. (1983). Associative long-term potentiation in hippocampal slices. *Proceedings of the National Academy of Sciences, 80*, 7347–7351.

Bliss, T. V., & Collingridge, G. L. (1993). A synaptic model of memory: Long-term potentiation in the hippocampus. *Nature, 361*, 31–39.

Corkin, S. (2002). What's new with the amnesic patient H. M.? *Nature Reviews Neuroscience, 3*, 153–160.

Fanselow, M. S., & Poulos, A. M. (2005). The neuroscience of mammalian associative learning. *Annual Review of Psychology, 56*, 207–234.

Knowlton, B. J., Mangels, J. A., & Squire, L. R. (1996). A neostriatal habit learning system in humans. *Science, 273*, 1399–1402.

Malenka, R. C., & Bear, M. F. (2004). LTP and LTD: An embarrassment of riches. *Neuron, 44*, 5–21.

McCormick, D. A., Steinmetz, J. E., & Thompson, R. F. (1985). Lesions of the inferior olivary complex cause extinction of the classically conditioned eyeblink response. *Brain Research, 359*, 120–130.

Schacter, D. L. (1985). Priming of old and new knowledge in amnesic patients and normal subjects. *Annals of the New York Academy of Sciences, 444*, 41–53.

Squire, L. R. (1992). Memory and the hippocampus: A synthesis from findings with rats, monkeys, and humans. *Psychological Review, 99*, 195–231.

Squire, L. R., Clark, R. E., & Knowlton, B. J. (2001). Retrograde amnesia. *Hippocampus, 11*, 50–55.

Squire, L. R., & Zola-Morgan, S. (1991). The medial temporal lobe memory system. *Science, 253*, 1380–1386.

Thompson, R. F., & Steinmetz, J. E. (2009). The role of the cerebellum in classical conditioning of discrete behavioral responses. *Neuroscience, 162*, 732–755.

Wiggs, C. L., & Martin, A. (1998). Properties and mechanisms of perceptual priming. *Current Opinion in Neurobiology, 8*, 227–233.

MEMORY AND KNOWLEDGE

One important strand of psychological research on memory has been concerned with uncovering ways in which human memory can be unreliable, misleading, or even involve complete fabrication. In apparent contrast to this line of research, philosophical discussions of memory typically seek to give it a central, indispensable role in knowledge. This entry will review some of the accounts philosophers have given of the epistemology of memory, before briefly returning to the question as to the potential relevance of empirical research in psychology for such accounts.

What Role(s) Does Memory Play in Knowledge?

To bring out one way in which memory may be thought to be central to knowledge, consider the following argument attacking the so-called myth of the given. Its target is a position in epistemology known as classical foundationalism, according to which empirical knowledge must ultimately rest on a set of "basic beliefs" whose epistemic status does not, in turn, depend on that of other beliefs. Traditionally, foundationalists' favorite candidates for such basic beliefs have been beliefs about our own sensations. Suppose you have a certain visual experience on the basis of which you form the belief "There is a ripe tomato in front of me." Arguably, the epistemic status of that belief turns on whether you are right to believe that things actually are as they visually appear to you. Yet, the foundationalist would claim that there is another belief you can form in this situation, whose epistemic status does not seem to turn on that of other beliefs, namely, the belief that you are, at any rate, having a red sensation.

Implicit in this line of thought is the idea that the mere having of a sensation, by itself, can put you into a position to have a belief about it—and this is what has been criticized as the "myth of the given." Your having the belief "a red sensation is occurring" or even just "this type of sensation is occurring" seems to require that you can think of your current sensation as being of one type *rather than some other,* which, in turn, seems to require drawing on memory. If you can't remember (and thus have beliefs about) any other sensations you could have instead, your putative beliefs about your current sensation will be devoid of content—there will be nothing in them that can distinguish that sensation from any other sensation. Thus, it looks as though not even beliefs about our own sensations can serve as "basic beliefs" in the foundationalist's sense.

It is often said that, without memory, we would know very little, because any knowledge we might have through sensory experience would only last as long as the experience itself. The preceding example suggests that this statement might not go far enough in acknowledging the epistemic centrality of memory. Rather, if the kind of attack against the "myth of the given" sketched is along the right lines, memory plays a key role in our very ability to gain knowledge from experience. At the same time, however, there is of course also a sense in which memory, in turn, depends on a capacity for experience (or other capacities for acquiring knowledge). Memory is not itself a faculty for coming to know something; it is dependent on there being other such faculties. As it is sometimes put, memory is not a source of knowledge, or, if it is, it is a *preservative,* rather than a *generative,* source.

Memory and Justification

Many epistemological theories focus primarily on generative sources of knowledge, and, as a

consequence, at least some of them have difficulties accounting for the distinctive epistemological significance of memory. For instance, there is an influential tradition in epistemology that is centered on the notion of *justification,* often associated with the thought that justification is a necessary condition for knowledge (as opposed to, say, mere true belief). Following this tradition, it is sometimes assumed that questions about the epistemological significance of memory are best approached by asking in virtue of what beliefs retrieved from memory (henceforth: *memory beliefs*) might count as beliefs the subject is justified in holding. On closer inspection, however, it is not obvious that this latter question best captures the role memory plays in knowledge.

Consider one possible answer to the question as to what justifies memory beliefs: that remembering that *p* is itself a source of justification for the belief that *p.* In effect, the strategy behind this answer is to downplay the epistemological significance of the generative/preservative distinction: Memory may be preservative with respect to *content*—that is, it preserves beliefs acquired by some other means— but it is generative with respect to *justification.* This latter idea is typically spelled out in terms of the thought that there is a specific phenomenology attached to retrieving beliefs from memory (as opposed to, say, just guessing). There is an *experience of recall,* which can serve as a justification for believing that *p.*

One problem for this view is that it is by no means clear how exactly invoking the idea of a distinctive phenomenology of retrieval might help flesh out the idea that remembering is itself a source of justification. It is perhaps tempting to think that such experiences can play a similar role in the justification of memory beliefs as, say, visual experiences play in the justification of visually based beliefs. Yet, intuitively, the epistemic role of perceptual experiences has something to do with the fact that there is a sense in which those experiences directly present us with the very things our beliefs are about. In particular, it is the specific perceptual experience I have which makes it rational for me to form the specific beliefs I do. By contrast, the putative epistemic role of memory beliefs, on the view we have been considering, would have to be rather different. Insofar as there is a distinctive experience of recall, it seems to be the same experience that accompanies different instances of memory retrieval, no matter what beliefs are being retrieved.

An alternative answer to the question of what justifies memory beliefs turns on the idea that memory is preservative not just with respect to the content of beliefs but also with respect to their justification. As normally understood, the suggestion here is not that, to be justified in believing that *p* (where the belief that *p* is a memory belief), I need to be able to remember the circumstances under which that belief was acquired and thus be in a position to rehearse my original justification for acquiring the belief. This would make all but a fraction of our beliefs epistemically problematic. Rather, as it is normally understood, the view at issue here is that beliefs held in memory in fact retain the justification with which they were originally acquired, even if the subject herself is no longer able to remember how she acquired the belief.

This view faces the problem that it is not obvious what exactly the idea of a belief's retaining its justification comes to. This idea seems to presuppose that justification is something akin to a property of beliefs, that is, *states* (of believing that *p*, or *q*, etc.) that a subject is in over time. Yet, when the notion of justification is explicated in the epistemological literature, it is typically by means of examples in which a subject acquires a belief for the first time, or holds on to a belief in the presence of countervailing evidence. That is, the notion of justification is attached to aspects of the subject's cognitive *activity*, something the subject does at a time.

As already indicated, perhaps the most basic worry about both of the views outlined previously is whether it is right to assume that the epistemic significance of memory is best framed in terms of the notion of justification. As against this assumption, some authors have held that it is actually more intuitive to think of the role that memory plays in knowledge in terms of the idea that memory *frees* the subject from the need to seek justification for certain of her beliefs. Any sort of sustained rational inquiry seems to presuppose that we can normally rely on beliefs we acquired earlier without constantly having to establish their epistemic credentials anew. Thus, it might be thought that there is a sense in which memory has a more fundamental epistemic role to play than can be explained by invoking the idea of memory generating or preserving justification for individual beliefs held in memory. Rather, on this view, the epistemic significance of memory needs to be seen within its wider role of making it possible for us to acquire extended bodies of knowledge.

"False Memories" and the Epistemology of Episodic Memory

The previously discussed considerations are all concerned (at least primarily) with *factual* or *semantic memory*, that is, the ability to retain knowledge of facts, concepts, or meanings that we learned about in the past, but not necessarily knowledge about the past itself. Yet, perhaps the first thing to come to mind when the issue of the relation between memory and knowledge is raised is the idea that memory plays a role specifically in our *knowledge about the past*. Philosophical discussion of this idea has centered primarily on the epistemology of *event* or *episodic memory*, that is, the type of memory for particular past events that we might express, for example, by saying "I remember seeing/doing *x*." In particular, theorists have tried to reconcile two intuitions about this type of memory: that it plays a fundamental role in our knowledge of the past, and that it involves the having of memory images.

The idea of a memory image is meant to capture a sense in which recollecting specific events from one's past life involves something akin to reexperiencing them. Yet, it has been argued that the having of a memory image—that is, a present occurrence—cannot constitute our most fundamental way of knowing about the past. The thought has been that if we did not have a more fundamental way of knowing about the past, not involving imagery, we would never come to connect present memory images with the past. This argument, though, seems to assume that the only role imagery might play in knowledge about the past is by serving as *evidence* on the basis of which we make judgments about the past. It can be avoided if we can make sense of an alternative way of viewing the epistemic role of memory images. Specifically, it has been suggested that, in the case of episodic memory, the subject's ability to call up a memory image is itself the specific *form* her knowledge of the past takes.

It is in this context, in particular, that empirical work on the reliability of memory might be thought to raise challenges for the epistemology of memory. Space prohibits a proper review of the large variety of empirical studies in this area. However, very broadly, a general theme that emerges from much of this research is that subjects' memories about past events are susceptible to interference from information received some time after the relevant events took place. At the extreme, entirely false apparent memories can be "planted" in subjects by giving them misleading information. This clearly raises a general challenge for epistemologists to provide grounds for thinking that, by and large, we can nevertheless regard memory as reliable. More specifically, though, the intuition that episodic memory has a distinctive epistemological role to play seems to trade on the idea that there is an essential difference between simply remembering facts *about* a past event and recollecting the event itself, that is, having some more direct access to the past through having witnessed it. It is this idea, which is arguably a key ingredient of our commonsense understanding of memory, that might be seen to be under threat once it is clear just how much what we seem to remember having experienced can actually be the result of post-event construction.

Christoph Hoerl

See also Knowledge by Acquaintance; Memory, Interference With; Objects of Memory

Further Readings

Huemer, M. (1999). The problem of memory knowledge. *Pacific Philosophical Quarterly, 80,* 346–357.

Loftus, E. F. (2005). Planting misinformation in the human mind: A 30-year investigation of the malleability of memory. *Learning & Memory, 12,* 361–366.

Martin, M. G. F. (2001). Episodic recall as retained acquaintance. In C. Hoerl & T. McCormack (Eds.), *Time and memory: Issues in philosophy and psychology* (pp. 257–284). Oxford, UK: Clarendon Press.

Neisser, U. (1981). John Dean's memory: A case study. *Cognition, 9,* 1–22.

Owens, D. (1999). The authority of memory. *European Journal of Philosophy, 7,* 312–29.

Soteriou, M. (2008). The epistemological role of episodic recollection. *Philosophy and Phenomenological Research, 77,* 472–492.

MEMORY RECALL, DYNAMICS

How do we search our memories to recall information that occurred in a given temporal context? In the laboratory, this basic question concerning human memory is addressed by asking people to study a sequence of individually presented items (typically words) and then to try to recall all of the items they can remember in any order. This task, first introduced by E. A. Kirkpatrick in 1894, is termed *free recall.*

By analyzing the order in which participants freely recall list items, one can gain considerable insight into the nature of the recall process. The analysis of recall dynamics in free recall reveals several striking regularities. This entry first reviews five major phenomena that govern the way people search their memories: the effects of recency, primacy, contiguity, forward asymmetry, and semantic proximity. Subsequent sections discuss how these phenomena occur both in the patterns of correct recalls and recall errors, as well as in the latencies measured between successively recalled items. This entry closes with a brief discussion of the theoretical implications of these phenomena.

Recency

In immediate free recall, participants are far more likely to begin recall with the final list item than with an item from any other list position (Figure 1A). This tendency persists for the first several responses, after which recalls tend to come from more distributed list positions. Participants' tendency to begin recall at the end of the list has been strongly linked to the well-known *recency effect*—the increased probability of recalling items from the end of the list. The striking recency effect seen in the data (Figure 1B) is greatly reduced when participants are asked to perform an unrelated cognitive task, such as mental arithmetic, in between list presentation and the recall period (delayed recall). Although the recency effect is easily disrupted in delayed free recall, other manipulations that influence overall recall performance have little effect on the recency effect.

Dissociations between recency and pre-recency effects in recall have led some theorists to argue for a fundamental distinction between short-term and long-term memory. In this view, recency arises due to retrieval from a limited capacity short-term store (STS) whose contents are easily displaced by new information. In contrast, recall of pre-recency items arises from a search of associative memory, where associations between items reflect both newly formed associations between items that were together in STS

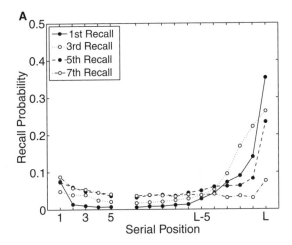

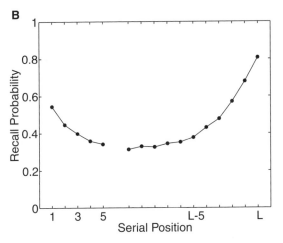

Figure I Serial position effects. (A) The probability of recalling a list item from each list position in output positions 1, 3, 5, and 7. (B) The probability of recalling list items in any output position (the serial position curve) for data from the same immediate free recall studies.

Note: "L" represents the last serial position of a list (thus, "L-5" is the fifth to last serial position). The *x*-axis is not continuous because the studies analyzed differ in the number of items presented per list, though all were between 15 and 30 items.

and long-standing associative knowledge concerning the items themselves. If, however, recency depends exclusively on the operation of STS, then one would not expect to find recency in continual distracter free recall—a task where participants perform a distracting task (e.g., mental arithmetic) after every list item, including the last one. According to the STS account of recency, the final distracter should greatly attenuate the recency effect, as in delayed free recall. However, in continual-distracter free recall, one

observes a strong recency effect and participants are nearly as likely to initiate recall with the final list item as in immediate free recall. This "long-term recency" has been taken to support the view that recency reflects a more general forgetting process that operates at both short and long time scales.

Primacy

In addition to the recency effect, one also observes a *primacy effect* in free recall, whereby the first few list items are remembered better than items from the middle of the list. This is seen both in the overall probability of recalling list items and in an increased tendency to initiate recall with the first list item (Figure 1). The primacy effect is largely attenuated when participants are discouraged from rehearsing list items throughout list presentation. This is because early list items tend to be rehearsed more frequently than other items (they have more rehearsal opportunities), and they also tend to be rehearsed throughout the input sequence, thus giving them a recency advantage. Unlike the recency effect, the primacy effect is not reduced in delayed free recall.

Contiguity

Because in free recall the order of recall reflects the order in which items come to mind, recall transitions reveal the organization of memory for the list items. Consider, for example, that a participant has just recalled an item from serial position i and that the next recall is from serial position j. To examine the effects of the temporal organization of the list on free recall transitions, one can measure the relation between recall probability and the *lag* between i and j, defined as $j - i$. This measure is called *the conditional-response probability as a function of lag*, or *lag-CRP*.

Given that the participant has just recalled the item from serial position i, the lag-CRP indicates the probability that the next item recalled comes from serial position $i + $ lag given the possibility of making a transition to that serial position. Lag-CRP analyses have shown that the *contiguity effect*, a tendency for participants to recall items from nearby in the list to the just-recalled item, and the *asymmetry effect*, a tendency for participants to recall items in the forward direction, are extremely robust properties of free recall.

Figure 2A illustrates these phenomena. Positive values of lag = $(j - i)$ correspond to forward recalls; negative values of lag correspond to backward recalls. Large absolute values of lag correspond to words spaced widely in the list; small absolute values correspond to words spaced closely together in the list. The *contiguity effect* seen in these data also appears in the form of shorter interresponse times (IRTs) between recall of items from neighboring list positions. This can be seen in the conditional-response latency (lag-CRL) function shown in Figure 2B.

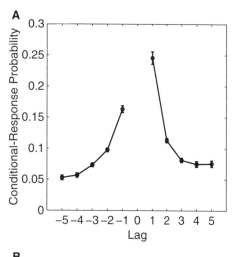

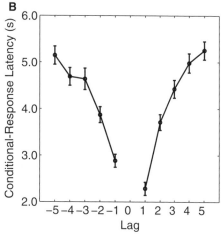

Figure 2 Temporal contiguity effect. (A) The conditional-response probability as a function of lag (or lag-CRP) shows the probability of recalling an item from serial position i + lag immediately following an item from serial position i. (B) Conditional-response latency (CRL) functions. Interresponse time between recall of items from serial positions i and i + lag.

Note: Error bars represent Loftus-Mason corrected error.

The contiguity effect in free recall is also related to participant's overall ability to recall list items. For example, older adults, who recall significantly fewer correct items than do younger adults, exhibit significantly reduced contiguity effects. Moreover, the magnitude of each participant's contiguity effect is positively correlated with that participant's recall performance.

Associative Asymmetry

An interesting feature of the contiguity effect, as seen in Figure 2, is the strong forward asymmetry, with recall transitions being nearly twice as likely in the forward than in the backward direction. This tendency to make forward transitions is also seen in serial recall (where it is more pronounced) and in the pattern of errors observed in probed recall of serial lists. However, the forward asymmetry effect in free recall contrasts with the finding that recall of words studied in pairs (e.g., *BOY–TREE*, *SHOE–CAR*, etc.) is almost perfectly symmetrical, with participants exhibiting nearly identical rates of forward and backward recall (*BOY* retrieves *TREE* just as easily as *TREE* retrieves *BOY*), and with forward and backward recall being highly correlated at the level of individual pairs. It may be that temporally segregated word pairs (as in paired associate memory tasks) are more likely to be encoded as distinct experiences than neighboring words in a list. Associative symmetry may thus be a property of well-integrated pairs that is broken by interference among items from different list positions.

Semantic Proximity

Whereas the contiguity effect illustrates the temporal organization of memories, it is also well known that participants also make use of preexisting semantic associations among list items. This can be seen in people's tendency to make recall transitions among semantically related items, even in random word lists that lack obvious semantic associates. This *semantic proximity* effect can be seen in Figure 3A, which shows how the probability of making a recall transition among two items increases with their semantic relatedness. Not only are people more likely to make recall transitions among semantically related items, but they also make those transitions more quickly than transitions among less strongly related items (Figure 3B). Both of these effects are evident even at low levels of semantic similarity (e.g., NUMBER and JOURNAL have a latent semantic analysis [LSA] similarity of 0.11, whereas PONY and FOREHEAD have an LSA similarity of 0.21). Analyses of recall dynamics reveal how even modest semantic relations can exhibit a powerful influence on the way people search their memories. Even when lists lack any strong associates or any obvious categorical organization, recall transitions are driven by the relative semantic strengths among the stored items.

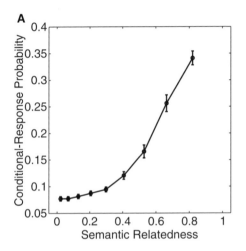

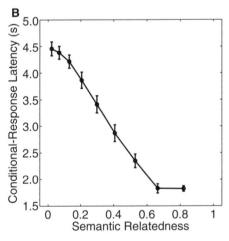

Figure 3 Semantic proximity effect. (A) Conditional-response probability as a function of semantic relatedness. (B) Conditional-response latency as a function of semantic relatedness.

Note: Semantic relatedness is determined using latent semantic analysis (LSA), which derives relatedness from the co-occurrence statistics of words that appear in a large corpus of text. Error bars represent Loftus-Mason corrected error.

Recall Errors

Temporal contiguity and semantic proximity not only dictate the dynamics of correct responses in free recall; they also influence the kinds of recall errors people make. When recalling a list of words, participants occasionally recall items that were not on the target list. By examining the dynamics of recall, one can show that these intrusion errors exhibit the same three basic properties described earlier. First, they tend to be items that were studied on recent lists. Second, they tend to be semantically related to the just recalled (correct) item. Third, when participants commit two intrusions from the same prior list, they tend to be items that were studied in neighboring list positions. This latter result is another manifestation of the contiguity effect. Thus, the same three principles that govern the dynamics of correct recalls also help to explain the kinds of recall errors that people commit.

Source Clustering

One can also show that people exhibit clustering as a function of encoding task. Sean Polyn and colleagues asked participants to make either size or animacy judgments on different list items. During free recall, participants not only exhibited temporal and semantic clustering effects; they also exhibited clustering of responses based on the task in which the words were studied. That is, following recall of an item that was given a size judgment at encoding, participants were more likely to recall another item that was given a size judgment. Furthermore, this task clustering effect interacted with temporal clustering, being greater for items presented at neighboring list positions.

One may wonder whether the entire recall process can be described as a sequence of probabilistic draws influenced by temporal contiguity and semantic clustering effects, or whether there are changes in the dynamics of recall process over the course of the retrieval period. In immediate free recall, the contiguity effect is larger and the semantic proximity effect is smaller for the first few responses and then increases/decreases to a stable state for subsequent recalls. In delayed free recall, however, the contiguity effect and semantic proximity effect are relatively stable throughout the recall period.

Interresponse Times

In 1970, Ben Murdock and Ron Okada showed that interresponse times between successive recalls increase steadily throughout the recall period, growing as an exponential function of the number of items recalled. This increase in IRTs is highly predictive of recall termination—following an IRT of greater than 10 seconds, people rarely recall further items. The dynamics of recall also appear to be significantly affected by recall errors. Following intrusions or repetitions of already recalled items, people have a significantly increased tendency to either commit further errors or terminate recall, a pattern that is true at all stages of the recall process. Although the exponential increase in IRTs during the recall period has been argued to support a model of recall in which items are randomly sampled with replacement from a set of available responses, this account is falsified by the strong dependencies in sequences of responses, including the temporal and semantic clustering effects, as reviewed earlier.

Retrieved Context Theory

Whereas the contiguity effect can be easily accommodated within the view that neighboring items become associated when they co-occupy a short-term buffer (or working memory system) several studies are hard to reconcile with this classic information processing account. For example, Marc Howard and Michael Kahana found that separating items by an unrelated distractor task (mental arithmetic) did not disrupt the relative tendency to make transitions to neighboring items. This finding was further extended in 2008 by Marc Howard and colleagues who asked participants to free recall items from 48 previously studied word lists. Under these conditions, participants exhibited a significant contiguity effect even when making recall transitions among items that occurred on different lists. For instance, following recall of an item from list 5, participants were more likely to recall an item from lists 4 or 6 than from lists 3 or 7, and so forth. In 2008, Orin Davis and colleagues also found that in recalling lists of paired associates, recall errors exhibited a strong contiguity effect, extending across several intervening pairs. Because interpair rehearsal would be a major source of interference in this task, it is unlikely that the contiguity effect can be entirely explained on the basis of rehearsal strategies. Even in item recognition of lists of pictures, participants exhibit contiguity effects in which recognizing a picture makes it easier to subsequently recognize a picture studied in a nearby list position. On the basis of these results, the contiguity effect may be seen as reflecting a kind of mental time travel undertaken during memory search and retrieval. In recalling an item, the participant "travels back" to the time of its presentation, making it more likely that subsequent recalls will come from neighboring list positions. According to this view, contiguity arises due to a contextual retrieval process in which recalling an item reinstates its associated temporal contexts, which, in turn, serve as a cue for neighboring items.

Summary

By analyzing the dynamics of memory retrieval in free recall, one can see how the search of episodic memories is a highly cue-dependent process. Five major principles govern the way people recall lists of studied items. First, people tend to initiate recall with recently studied items. Subsequent responses continue to show a bias toward recent items, but this recency effect rapidly dissipates over the course of retrieval (Figure 1). Second, recall of a given item tends to be followed by recall of an item from a neighboring (contiguous) list position—a phenomenon known as the contiguity effect (Figure 2). Third, the contiguity effect exhibits a strong forward asymmetry effect, with forward transitions being approximately twice as common as backward transitions (Figure 2). Fourth, recall of a given item tends to be followed by recall of a semantically related item (Figure 3). These principles not only govern correct responses; they also govern the errors people make during recall. A fifth principle is the tendency to make transitions to early list items, as seen in the primacy effect. Because primacy is not always observed and largely reflects people's use of rehearsal strategies, this principle may be considered secondary to the first four major phenomena described earlier. By studying the order of recall responses, and not just whether or not items are recalled, one can observe the striking effects of temporal contiguity and semantic similarity on the accuracy and timing of both correct recalls and recall errors. The study of recall dynamics thus allows us to characterize the basic associative processes operating in recall and to test theories of these associative mechanisms.

Michael Kahana and Jonathan Miller

See also Rehearsal and Memory; Semantic Memory; Semantic Memory, Computational Perspectives; Sequential Memory, Computational Perspectives; Serial Order Memory, Computational Perspectives; Similarity

Further Readings

Davis, O. C., Geller, A. S., Rizzuto, D. S., & Kahana, M. J. (2008). Temporal associative processes revealed by intrusions in paired-associate recall. *Psychonomic Bulletin & Review, 15*(1), 64–69.

Howard, M. W., & Kahana, M. J. (1999). Contextual variability and serial position effects in free recall. *Journal of Experimental Psychology: Learning, Memory, and Cognition, 25*, 923–941.

Howard, M. W., Youker, T. E., & Venkatadass, V. (2008). The persistence of memory: Contiguity effects across several minutes. *Psychonomic Bulletin & Review, 15*, 58–63.

Kahana, M. J., Howard, M. W., & Polyn, S. M. (2008). Associative retrieval processes in episodic memory. In H. L. Roediger III, *Learning and memory: A comprehensive reference: Vol. 2. Cognitive psychology of memory* (J. Byrne, Vol. Ed.). Oxford, UK: Elsevier.

Landauer, T. K., & Dumais, S. T. (1997). Solution to Plato's problem: The latent semantic analysis theory of acquisition, induction, and representation of knowledge. *Psychological Review, 104*, 211–240.

Murdock, B. B., & Okada, R. (1970). Interresponse times in single-trial free recall. *Journal of Verbal Learning and Verbal Behavior, 86*, 263–267.

Polyn, S. M., & Kahana, M. J. (2008). Memory search and the neural representation of context. *Trends in Cognitive Sciences, 12*, 24–30.

Polyn, S. M., Norman, K. A., & Kahana, M. J. (2009). A context maintenance and retrieval model of organizational processes in free recall. *Psychological Review, 116* (1), 129–156.

Romney, A. K., Brewer, D. D., & Batchelder, W. H. (1993). Predicting clustering from semantic structure. *Psychological Science, 4*, 28–34.

Schwartz, G., Howard, M. W., Jing, B., & Kahana, M. J. (2005). Shadows of the past: Temporal retrieval effects in recognition memory. *Psychological Science, 16*, 898–904.

Sederberg, P. B., Miller, J. F., Howard, W. H., & Kahana, M. J. (2010). The temporal contiguity effect predicts episodic memory performance. *Memory & Cognition, 38*(6), 689–699.

MENTAL ACTION

One central concern in the philosophy of action is to provide an account of what it is that distinguishes the things that merely happen to people—events they undergo—from the things they genuinely do, where these latter events are *actions* of an agent. For example, there is a difference between an event of one's arm moving that is due to an involuntary twitch, and the event of one intentionally raising one's arm. When one intentionally raises one's arm, the bodily movement involved is not simply a mere happening that one undergoes, but a bodily action one performs. It has been argued that the same sort of distinction can be marked in the mental domain: Some mental events are not simply mental occurrences that subjects undergo, but are, rather, mental actions they perform.

Some philosophers argue that acknowledging that the perspective one has on one's mental life can be that of its agent may have significant implications for the epistemology, metaphysics, and phenomenology of mind. However, there is disagreement over the question of which aspects of our mental lives should be regarded as mental actions. For example, while some hold that our mental actions include judgings and decidings, as well as calculatings, reasonings, and tryings, others have argued that although there is such a thing as mental action, most of our thoughts, including our decisions, just happen. This entry will briefly explore these issues.

The Scope of Mental Action

Thinking about something involves the occurrence of mental acts that are individuated by their propositional contents. For example, when one makes a conscious judgment, one judges *that such and such is the case*. What one judges to be the case is a content that is propositional in form that distinguishes that act of judging from other mental acts. Some argue that such mental acts can be mental actions only if the particular contents that individuate them are ones that one intends to think. However, in the case of many such mental acts, it seems that the content of the mental act cannot figure in the content of one's prior intention. For example, having judged that *p*, one might choose to assert that *p*, and having formed the intention to F, one might choose to express that intention, but the mental acts of judging that p and deciding to F cannot themselves be intended.

One response to this line of thought is to claim that when one is engaged in directed thinking, such as trying to figure out an arithmetical problem, although one does not intend to think a thought with the content that p, intention may still have a significant role to play in one's mental activity, for one's intention may be to think a thought that stands in a certain relation to other thoughts or contents. Although one does not decide to judge *that p*, and one does not decide to decide *to F*, one may be able to decide to determine (or attempt to determine) *whether p*, and one may be able to decide to decide (or attempt to decide) *whether to F*. The conclusion that some draw from this is that although mental acts like judging and deciding are not themselves mental actions, mental action may sometimes play an important role in explaining their occurrence.

An alternative response is to reject the assumption that a mental event can only be a mental action if the content of the mental event is intended. For example, according to Christopher Peacocke, for a mental event to be a mental action, it must consist of an event that either is, or constitutively involves, a trying, and Peacocke has argued that tryings should be distinguished from prior intentions. Peacocke argues that conscious events of deciding and judging can be caused by such events of trying, and so can be mental actions. He has suggested that such mental actions have the phenomenology of doing something, rather than involving the phenomenology of being presented with something as being the case, as in perception, or as something occurring to one, as in unintended imagination.

Mental Action and Self-Knowledge

For Peacocke, knowing what one is consciously thinking will often involve knowing what mental actions one is performing. Peacocke's account of how we standardly know our own actions appeals to the occurrence of events of action-awareness that are not beliefs and that have a first-personal, present tensed content of the form "I am doing such-and-such now"—for example, "I am judging that p now." This action-awareness is standardly brought about by an event of trying that causes the action that the action-awareness represents. According to Peacocke, the distinctive way in which a subject comes to know of his own actions is by taking such an apparent action-awareness at face value. He argues that this distinctive action-awareness exists for mental actions, as well as for bodily actions.

Other accounts of how one knows what one is doing when performing an action appeal to the idea that our intentions can embody a form of self-knowledge—practical knowledge of our intended actions. According to this view, intended action is behavior that realizes the agent's knowledge of it. The suggestion is that this can accommodate the intuition that one does not normally need to find out by observation or inference what one is doing when performing an intentional action, for performing the action was one's own idea to begin with. On this view, one's knowledge of what one is thinking may sometimes be explained, in part, by the distinctive epistemic role of one's intentions in thinking.

Mental Action and Wakeful Consciousness

Brian O'Shaughnessy appeals to the idea that there is a distinctive form of self-knowledge that accompanies one's mental actions in arguing for the claim that mental action has a crucial role to play in an account of the state of wakeful consciousness in the self-conscious. He argues that the progression of the stream of conscious thought and imagination is, in the awake self-conscious subject, distinctive. The respect in which it is distinctive is connected with the variety of self-knowledge that accompanies it, and the relevant form of self-knowledge is linked with the idea that the "mental will" is operative. According to O'Shaughnessy, the awake self-conscious subject (as opposed to one who is dreaming) is able to make sense of what is happening in a certain domain of his mental life insofar as he is able to make sense of what he is up to, and the variety of self-knowledge involved is importantly linked with the idea that the perspective he has on this aspect of his mental life is that of its agent.

Matthew Soteriou

See also Action and Bodily Movement; Philosophy of Action; Self-Knowledge

Further Readings

O'Brien, L., & Soteriou, M. (2009). *Mental actions*. Oxford, UK: Oxford University Press.

O'Shaughnessy, B. (2000). *Consciousness and the world* (chaps. 5, 6, 14). Oxford, UK: Clarendon Press.

Peacocke, C. (2008). *Truly understood* (chap. 7). Oxford, UK: Oxford University Press.

Soteriou, M. (2005). Mental action and the epistemology of mind. *Nous*, 39(1), 83–105.

Straswon, G. (2003). Mental ballistics or the involuntariness of spontaneity. *Proceedings of the Aristotelian Society*, 103(3), 227–256.

MENTAL CAUSATION

Mental causation is the causation of physical effects by mental causes. The paradigm case of mental causation is the causation of someone's bodily movement by a mental state or event of hers. The belief that mental causation exists is deeply rooted in common sense. It seems uncontroversial to say, for instance, that a sudden pain caused Jones to wince, or that Smith's thirst caused him to have a drink. Nevertheless, explaining how the mind can have physical effects has proven a challenge for philosophers of mind. For physical effects already have physical causes, which threatens the claim that they also have mental causes. The problem is most pressing for positions according to which the mind is not itself physical. However, recent decades have also seen a debate over whether the view that the mind is physical can adequately explain mental causation.

History

The existence of mental causation was generally considered uncontroversial by ancient philosophers. For instance, both Plato and Aristotle, although differing in their views about the nature of the mind, held that agents' mental states need to be invoked in order to give causal explanations of some of their bodily movements.

The modern debate about mental causation can be traced back to René Descartes and the controversy about his theory of the mind. Descartes held that minds and bodies are two radically different kinds of substance: Minds are substances that are thinking and not spatially extended, whereas bodies are substances that are spatially extended and not thinking. (By a substance in general, Descartes understood something that exists and whose existence does not depend on anything else.) In correspondence, Princess Elizabeth of Bohemia complained

to Descartes that she found it unintelligible how his theory could allow minds to cause the motion of bodies. She held that bodies could only be moved by things in spatial contact with them, which ruled out minds as causes of bodily movements because they lacked the required spatial attributes. Although he never resolved the dispute with Princess Elizabeth, Descartes later developed a theory that identified the pineal gland as the locus of mind-body interaction. By moving the pineal gland, he claimed, the mind affects the motion of our animal spirits (an air-like kind of matter), which communicate the impulse to our muscles via the nerves.

Gottfried Wilhelm Leibniz criticized Descartes' position for being at odds with physics. He held that the law of conservation of momentum was violated if minds affected the motion of bodies in the way envisaged by Descartes. Leibniz's own position denied mind-body interaction altogether. According to his view, different substances never interact, but God created them so that their histories unfold independently in perfect, preestablished harmony.

The Argument From the Causal Completeness of the Physical

In the 21st century, virtually no one endorses Leibniz's doctrine of preestablished harmony or Princess Elizabeth's conception of the motion of bodies. Still, most contemporary philosophers share the spirit of their objections to Descartes, which demands that mental causation fit into our picture of the physical world. One element of this picture is the principle of the causal completeness of the physical, which says that every physical effect has a physical cause (this principle is also called "causal closure of the physical"):

Completeness: Every physical event that has a cause has a physical cause.

Completeness is the starting point for an influential argument about mental causation. It seems that if an event has a physical cause, this cause is sufficient to bring the event about, which rules out that any nonphysical causes are involved. This idea is expressed by the following principle:

Non-redundancy: If an event has a physical cause, it does not have any nonphysical causes.

We may add to our assumptions the commonsensical view that some mental events, such as Jones's pain or Smith's thirst, have physical effects:

Mental causes: Some mental events have physical effects.

From *completeness*, *non-redundancy*, and *mental causes*, it follows that some mental events, namely those that have physical effects, are physical causes and thus are themselves physical events. Because it is implausible that there should be a difference in kind between those mental events that have physical effects and those that do not, the conclusion generalizes to the claim that *all* mental events are physical events.

Objections to the Argument

If one denies the conclusion of the argument from completeness, non-redundancy, and mental causes, one has to reject at least one of its premises. If one rejects mental causes, one has to hold that no mental events have physical effects; this view is called *epiphenomenalism*. Accepting epiphenomenalism comes at a price, as it requires abandoning the intuitively plausible claim that some of our mental events cause bodily movements. This has far-reaching consequences: Given that performing intentional actions requires that intentions and desires cause bodily movements, it follows from epiphenomenalism that we never perform intentional actions.

Whereas completeness seems to have a good standing, some philosophers have taken issue with the assumption of non-redundancy. Defenders of non-redundancy typically reply that giving up non-redundancy means accepting that some physical events are overdetermined by physical and non-physical events; it is implausible, they hold, that overdetermination is so widespread a phenomenon as accounting for all cases of mental causation would require. Whether such widespread overdetermination would be objectionable is a matter of controversy. The issue is complicated by the fact that overdetermination can be read in two ways. It can either simply mean that an effect has two causes, or it can refer to a case with a specific causal structure analogous to the case of a firing squad, where two shots are individually sufficient to bring about the victim's death.

Physicalism

If one accepts the generalized conclusion of the argument from completeness, non-redundancy, and mental causes, one has to accept the claim that all mental events are physical events. This claim can be spelled out in different ways.

Type Identity

According to the type identity theory, every type of mental event is identical to a type of physical event. For instance, a proponent of the type identity theory might hold that pain is identical to a certain type of neural event. The type identity theory has been criticized for reasons independent of mental causation. It seems that mental events are multiply realizable. For instance, for some animals, pain may coincide with a physical event that is of a different type from the neural event occurring in humans when they are in pain; there might even be possible beings that can be in pain while their physiology differs radically from that of any animals we know. Multiple realizability contradicts the type identity theory. For if pain is identical to a certain type of neural event, pain and this neural event are one and the same type of event, so that, necessarily, if a pain event occurs, so does an event of the neural type.

Token Identity

Instead of accepting the type identity theory, one may opt for the weaker theory that identifies each token mental event, that is, each particular occurrence of a mental event, with a given token physical event. This so-called token identity theory allows for multiple realizability, since the different tokens of pain events, say, may be identical to token physical events of different types.

The most influential token identity theory has been Donald Davidson's theory of anomalous monism. While identifying token mental events with token physical events (hence "monism"), Davidson denies that there are strict laws relating the mental and the physical (hence "anomalous"). He holds that causation requires strict laws, and that token mental events can be causes or effects because they fall under physical descriptions and hence are subject to the strict laws of physics. It has been objected against anomalous monism that, while it allows token mental events to be causes, it does not explain how token mental events can be causally efficacious *by virtue of their mental properties*. It has been argued that because it is only mental events' physical properties that matter for their causal relations, according to anomalous monism, their mental properties, such as the property of being a pain event, are rendered causally irrelevant.

Supervenience

Currently the most common view according to which mental events are physical events is *supervenience physicalism*. In a standard formulation, this view says that whenever a mental event of a certain type occurs, this is by virtue of the occurrence of some type of physical event that necessitates the occurrence of the mental event. Like the token identity theory, supervenience physicalism is compatible with the multiple realizability of mental events. For it is consistent with supervenience physicalism that different occurrences of a certain type of mental event are due to occurrences of different types of physical events, provided that an event of the mental type could not have failed to occur given the occurrence of an event of any of these physical types.

With respect to mental causation, supervenience physicalism faces the so-called exclusion problem. Suppose that a certain mental event occurs. Given supervenience physicalism, this occurrence is due to, and necessitated by, the occurrence of some physical event. It seems that any putative physical effects of the mental event will already be caused by the physical event. This, however, calls the causal efficacy of the mental event into question. The rationale behind the final step of this argument resembles the non-redundancy principle: If a physical effect already has a physical cause, other events simultaneous with this cause seem to be rendered causally irrelevant. Some philosophers accept that the exclusion problem makes mental events causally irrelevant if supervenience physicalism is true. Others contend that, unlike in the case of physical versus nonphysical events, supervenient mental events do not compete with their underlying physical events for causal efficacy. The latter philosophers are often motivated by a desire to prevent generalized epiphenomenalism. For if the exclusion problem is genuine, it generalizes beyond mental events and threatens the causal efficacy of other entities that plausibly supervene on the physical, such as the events and properties described in chemistry and biology.

Content Externalism

A further problem of mental causation arises for the widely held position of content externalism, according to which some mental states and events have contents that depend not merely on what is going on in the subject's head but also on the subject's environment. For instance, a content externalist might hold that the content of Smith's belief that he is holding a glass of water is partly due to the fact that Smith has been in causal contact with water in his environment. It seems desirable to be able to say that contentful mental states and events can have physical effects and that their contents play a role in their causal efficacy. However, on the face of it, it seems that the causes of an agent's bodily movements are internal to the agent and independent of the environmental factors relevant for the content of the agent's thoughts. How content externalism might be reconciled with the causal relevance of mental content is a matter of ongoing controversy among philosophers of mind.

Thomas Kroedel

See also Anomalous Monism; Anti-Individualism About Cognition; Emergence; Mind-Body Problem; Physicalism; Reductive Physicalism

Further Readings

Crane, T. (1995). The mental causation debate. *Supplement to the Proceedings of the Aristotelian Society, 69,* 211–236.

Davidson, D. (1980). Mental events. In *Essays on actions and events* (pp. 207–225). Oxford, UK: Oxford University Press. (Reprinted from *Experience and theory,* pp. 79–101, by L. Foster & J. W. Swanson, Eds., 1970, Amherst: University of Massachusetts Press)

Descartes, R. (1988). The passions of the soul. In J. Cottingham, R. Stoothoff, & D. Murdoch (Eds.), *Descartes: Selected philosophical writings* (pp. 218–238). Cambridge, UK: Cambridge University Press.

Heil, J., & Mele, A. (Eds.). (1993). *Mental causation.* Oxford, UK: Oxford University Press.

Kim, J. (2009). Mental causation. In B. P. McLaughlin, A. Beckermann, & S. Walter (Eds.), *The Oxford handbook of philosophy of mind* (pp. 29–52). Oxford, UK: Oxford University Press.

Kroedel, T. (2008). Mental causation as multiple causation. *Philosophical Studies, 139,* 125–143.

Leibniz, G. W. (1989). Monadology. In R. Ariew & D. Garber (Eds.), *G. W. Leibniz: Philosophical essays* (pp. 213–225). Indianapolis, IN: Hackett.

Yablo, S. (1997). Wide causation. *Philosophical Perspectives, 11,* 251–281.

MENTAL EFFORT

Mental effort refers to the intensity of a person's engagement with a cognitive task. High-effort situations are associated with high load on attention and executive control mechanisms, as distinct from situations in which cognitive processing is more automatic. Committing more effort can improve task performance. Applying effort to a focal task may also detract from performance on secondary tasks. Effort can be associated with a subjective sense of difficulty, strain, or work. Effort also tends to be accompanied by bodily arousal and is sometimes measured via increases in heart rate, pupil diameter, blood pressure, or galvanic skin response.

For most of its history, mental effort has remained an elusive and slippery construct, but the application of modern neuroscientific methods coupled with the development of formal theory promises to lend it greater rigor.

This entry describes the role of mental effort in theories of cognitive function, addresses how people strategically decide whether and how to devote effort to tasks, discusses how people use their experience of mental effort to make other inferences, and reviews relevant findings in neuroscience.

Mental Effort and Its Place in Theories of Cognition

Cognitive Resources and Capacity Mobilization

Traditional, resource-based models regard cognitive performance as dependent on a limited supply of cognitive resources, energy, or channel capacity. Within this framework, devoting more effort to a task involves allocating more general-purpose resources to it. For tasks that are more difficult, successful performance draws more resources away from other ongoing activities. Thus, the amount of effort devoted to a focal task can be measured by the performance decrement on secondary tasks.

In an early, influential treatment of the subject, Daniel Kahneman suggested that mental effort might involve not only resource reallocation but also modulation of the attentional system's total capacity. On this view, mental effort—and the associated physiological arousal—reflects the transient expansion of an elastic pool of available resources.

Viewing effort as capacity recruitment can explain why markers of physiological arousal respond both to cognitive demands and to incentives.

Effects of Effort on Performance

Increased effort can improve performance on a variety of target-detection, memory, problem solving, and decision tasks. This can be demonstrated by showing that performance varies together with task-related incentives. For instance, individuals dividing their attention between simultaneous tasks tend to perform better on the task with the greater incentive.

Some tasks are relatively insensitive to changes in effort (e.g., easy tasks can often be performed well with little commitment of effort). In other cases, effort can even be detrimental. If a task involves well-practiced, automatic physical skills (e.g., golf putting), arousal and focused attention can cause "choking." Effort can impair types of problem solving that depend on associative processing or sudden insight. Additional effort can also be harmful if physiological arousal is already high (e.g., in a test-taking environment), a principle known as the Yerkes-Dodson law.

Self-Regulatory Depletion

Although resource-based frameworks have traditionally emphasized competition among concurrent activities, exertion of mental effort can also impair later performance. Roy Baumeister and colleagues have proposed that the mental resources underlying self-regulation not only are limited but also can be temporarily depleted. For example, if someone initially performs a task in which he or she must override impulses, that person might show reduced self-control or perseverance in a subsequent activity. Such findings have been used to support a "muscle" metaphor, wherein the ability to exert effortful self-control is subject to short-run fatigue.

Controlled Versus Automatic Processing

Mental effort is associated with processes that require executive control, as distinct from more automatic processes. For example, it is effort demanding to maintain information in working memory in the face of interference, or to override automatic responses. Controlled processing is typically assumed to proceed slowly, serially (rather than in parallel), and to facilitate pursuit of goals that are poorly supported by the immediate environment. Tasks that are controlled and effort demanding when they are initially learned, such as searching for a target in a field of distracters, can come to demand less effort after extensive practice.

Research on judgment and decision making similarly recognizes a distinction between two broad categories of decision processes that closely parallels the distinction between automatic and controlled processing: "System 1" processes are relatively fast and automatic, whereas "system 2" processes are slower, more deliberative, and associated with a greater sense of effort.

Effort Costs and Effort Allocation

When physical exertion is involved, people generally choose the least demanding paths to their goals. There is evidence that a similar principle applies to mental effort. For a given activity, people tend to weigh the cost of effort against its expected payoff.

Effort seems to be recruited on an as-needed basis. In psychophysiology experiments, arousal tends to increase as people prepare for moderately difficult tasks (where effort will likely help), but not when they prepare for tasks that are trivially easy or impossibly difficult (where effort is unlikely to change performance substantially). These types of findings suggest that effort allocation involves strategic decisions.

Models of attention and executive control often posit an internal mechanism for monitoring ongoing levels of cognitive demand. This monitoring mechanism regulates the engagement of effort, attention, and control; engagement of these functions is high when needed, and low otherwise. Effortful cognitive control is treated in such models as if it carries a cost, not being engaged unless it is expected to bring gains.

The Nature of Effort Costs

One possible explanation for effort costs is metabolic consumption. If mental effort consumes energy, minimizing effort might help conserve nutritive resources. However, this is a matter of debate; effortful cognitive processing seems to bring about relatively small changes, if any, in the brain's total glucose consumption. Alternatively, effort might be viewed as involving an opportunity cost. If there is a limited capacity for cognitive control, then capacity

devoted to one task cannot be devoted to another. Yet another possibility is interference: Trying to carry out many tasks at once can cause cross-talk in processing and responding. Effort may be the brain's way of limiting the potential for such interference.

Effort and the Selection of Decision Strategies

Tradeoffs between effort and accuracy have been discussed extensively in the field of decision making. When someone making a decision faces many sources of information and possible responses, there are many ways they could integrate the information and arrive at a decision. Simpler strategies might save effort, while reducing the likelihood of making the best possible choice.

There is evidence that decision makers often rely on simplifying heuristics, such as considering only a subset of the relevant information or the available alternatives. Several researchers, including John Payne and colleagues, have proposed that people choose strategies adaptively, rationally evaluating the expected accuracy and effort of each possible strategy. A simplifying decision strategy (e.g., focusing on only a single source of information) might be chosen if it minimizes the costs of effort with only a modest loss of accuracy.

Personality

Individuals differ in their inclination to engage in mentally effortful activities or to process information deeply; for example, people vary on a scale of *need for cognition*. Individuals also vary in measures of cognitive ability, such as general fluid intelligence and working memory span. Both motivation and ability are likely to influence the costs and benefits attributed to mental effort.

Metacognition: Interpreting Effort

How people interpret and evaluate their own mental states is known as metacognition. One form of metacognition is the use of the experience of mental effort as a basis for predictions and factual inferences. This has been studied experimentally by manipulating *disfluency*, the subjective sensation that information requires effort to perceive, remember, or process. Subtle manipulations of disfluency (such as degrading text legibility) can influence a variety of judgments. Disfluency can cause people to judge that products are less valuable, cities are less populous, pictures are less likeable, and that aphorisms are less likely to be true.

In a notable example, Norbert Schwarz and colleagues asked participants to evaluate their own level of assertiveness. Before making this judgment, some participants were asked to recall 12 examples of their own assertive behavior; other participants were asked for 6 examples. Members of the 12-example group then described themselves as less assertive, despite having recalled a greater amount of supportive information. These participants presumably inferred, from the sense of mental effort involved with generating 12 examples, that such examples were scarce.

Experiences of mental effort can also inform judgments of learning. Information might be judged as poorly learned if it takes effort to interpret and recall; as a result, a person might devote additional study time to the material. Conversely, if information feels easy to interpret, a person might conclude (perhaps inaccurately) that it does not need to be studied further.

Mental Effort and the Central Nervous System

As noted earlier, mental effort is often measured using physiological indices of autonomic nervous system activity. Mental effort is also associated with specific patterns of brain activity.

In neuroimaging experiments, tasks that require controlled processing consistently activate a network of brain regions, including lateral prefrontal, anterior cingulate, and parietal cortices. This collection of regions has been referred to variously as the cognitive control, executive attention, or task-positive network. The network responds to numerous manipulations of difficulty, including working memory demands, task novelty, and response override.

A separate network of brain regions, including ventromedial prefrontal and posterior cingulate cortices, often shows activity reductions during tasks that demand effort. This system is sometimes called the default mode or task-negative network. An active hypothesis is that these regions support episodic or self-reflective thoughts, and that such thoughts decline in frequency when individuals commit mental effort to a task.

Mental effort is also associated with specific neuromodulators, including dopamine and norepinephrine. Both of these neurotransmitters are released by brain stem nuclei with diffuse cortical projections, exerting broad influence on cortical dynamics. Dopaminergic modulation influences the executive attention network; dopamine levels relate to incentives, response vigor, physical effort exertion, and control-related cognitive processes such as working memory. Norepinephrine levels influence focused attention and are related to indices of physiological arousal such as pupil diameter.

A neuropsychological case study provides striking evidence linking the cognitive control network to physiological and subjective aspects of mental effort. The patient, reported by Lionel Naccache and colleagues, had a large medial frontal cortical lesion that included anterior cingulate cortex. She could successfully perform demanding cognitive tasks, but these tasks evoked neither their usual physiological response nor any subjective sense of effort. This suggests that the subjective and physiological characteristics of effort can be dissociated from response generation processes.

Joseph T. McGuire,
Jonathan D. Cohen, and
Matthew M. Botvinick

See also Attention, Resource Models; Automaticity; Metacognition and Education; Two System Models of Reasoning; Working Memory

Further Readings

Botvinick, M. M. (2007). Conflict monitoring and decision making: Reconciling two perspectives on anterior cingulate function. *Cognitive, Affective, & Behavioral Neuroscience, 7,* 356–366.

Cacioppo, J. T., Petty, R. E., Feinstein, J. A., Blair, W., & Jarvis, G. (1996). Dispositional differences in cognitive motivation: The life and times of individuals varying in need for cognition. *Psychological Bulletin, 119,* 197–253.

Camerer, C. F., & Hogarth, R. M. (1999). The effects of financial incentives in experiments: A review and capital-labor-production framework. *Journal of Risk and Uncertainty, 19,* 7–42.

Kahneman, D. (1973). *Attention and effort.* Englewood Cliffs, NJ: Prentice Hall.

Kahneman, D. (2003). A perspective on judgment and choice: Mapping bounded rationality. *American Psychologist, 58,* 697–720.

Miller, E. K., & Cohen, J. D. (2001). An integrative theory of prefrontal cortex function. *Annual Review of Neuroscience, 24,* 167–202.

Muraven, M., & Baumeister, R. F. (2000). Self-regulation and depletion of limited resources: Does self-control resemble a muscle? *Psychological Bulletin, 126,* 247–259.

Naccache, L., Dehaene, S., Cohen, L., Habert, M. O., Guichart-Gomez, E., Galanaud, D., & Willer, J.C. (2005). Effortless control: Executive attention and conscious feeling of mental effort are dissociable. *Neuropsychologia, 43,* 1318–1328.

Payne, J. W., Bettman, J. R., & Johnson, E. J. (1993). *The adaptive decision maker.* Cambridge, UK: Cambridge University Press.

Schwarz, N. (2004). Metacognitive experiences in consumer judgment and decision making. *Journal of Consumer Psychology, 14,* 332–348.

META-ANALYSIS

Meta-analysis is the quantitative cumulation of scientific evidence. There has long been pessimism in the younger social, behavioral, educational, and biomedical sciences in that our progress has been slower and less orderly than we would like, at least when compared to the progress of older, more programmatic sciences, such as physics and chemistry. In other words, the more recent work in physics and chemistry seems to build directly on the older work of those sciences, whereas the more recent work of the social, behavioral, educational, and biomedical sciences seems often to be starting from scratch. Those who have looked closely at the issue of cumulation in the physical sciences have pointed out that these disciplines have ample problems of their own. Nonetheless, in the matter of cumulating evidence, the social, behavioral, educational, and biomedical sciences have much to be modest about.

Limited success in the process of cumulation does not seem to be due to lack of replication or to the failure to recognize the need for replication. Indeed, there are many areas of the social, behavioral, educational, and biomedical sciences for which the results of many studies, all addressing essentially the same question, are available. Our summaries of the results of these sets of studies, however, have not been nearly as informative as they might have been, either with respect to summarized significance levels or, more important, with respect to summarized effect sizes, that is, the magnitudes of the effects examined. Even the best reviews of research by the most sophisticated scholars have been primarily qualitative narratives and have rarely told us much more about each study in a set of studies than the direction of the relationship between the variables investigated, and often not even that, and whether or not a given significance level was attained.

This state of affairs is beginning to change, however. More and more reviews of the literature are moving from the traditional literary approach to quantitative approaches to research synthesis described in an increasing number of textbooks of meta-analysis. The goals of these quantitative approaches of meta-analysis are to help us discover what we have learned from the results of the studies conducted and to help us discover what we have not yet learned.

In what follows, this entry defines the concept of "research results," briefly examines the history of meta-analysis, defines the concept of "successful replication," and concludes by comparing a more traditional view of replication success with a newer, probably more useful view.

Defining Research Results

Before we can consider various issues and procedures in the quantitative cumulation of research results, we must become quite explicit about the meaning of the concept "results of a study." It is easiest to begin with what we do not mean. We do not mean the prose *conclusion* drawn by the investigator and reported in the abstract, the results, or the discussion section of the research report. We also do not mean the results of an omnibus F test with $df > 1$ in the numerator or an omnibus χ^2 test with $df > 1$, that is, tests of statistical significance that leave unspecified exactly what differences were found.

What we do mean is the answer to the question: What is the relationship between any variable X and any variable Y? The variables X and Y are chosen with only the constraint that their relationship be of interest to us. The answer to this question should normally come in two parts: (a) the estimate of the magnitude of the relationship (the effect size), and (b) an indication of the accuracy or reliability of the estimated effect size (e.g., as indexed by a confidence interval placed around the effect size estimate). An alternative, or better, an addendum, to the second part of the answer is one not intrinsically more useful, but one more consistent with the existing practices of researchers: the significance level of the difference between the obtained effect size and the effect size expected under the null hypothesis (usually an effect size of zero).

Because a complete reporting of the results of a study requires the report of both the effect size and level of statistical significance, it is useful to make explicit the relationship between these quantities. The general relationship is given by the following:

Significance Test = Effect Size × Study Size

In other words, the larger the study is, in terms of the number of sampling units being studied, the more significant the results will be. This is true unless the size of the effect is truly zero, in which case a larger study will not produce a result that is any more significant than a smaller study. Effect sizes of exactly zero, however, are rarely encountered.

Meta-Analysis: A Historical Note

We are inclined to think of meta-analysis as a recent development, but it is older than the famous *t* test, which dates back a hundred years. We can simultaneously describe the early history of meta-analysis, while providing a classic illustration of the meta-analytic enterprise. In 1904, Karl Pearson collected correlation coefficients (called *r*s); there were six of them, with values of .58, .58, .60, .63, .66, and .77. The weighted (by sample size) mean of these six correlation coefficients was .64, the unweighted mean was .63, and the median was .61. Pearson was collecting correlation coefficients because he wanted to know the degree to which inoculation against smallpox saved lives. His own rough and ready summary of his meta-analysis of six studies was that there was a .6 correlation between inoculation and survival—a truly huge effect. In practical terms, a correlation of that magnitude describes a situation in which inoculation increases the survival rate from 20% to 80%.

When Karl Pearson quantitatively summarized six studies of the effects of smallpox inoculation, a meta-analysis was an unusual thing to do. Recently, however, there has been an explosion of meta-analytic research syntheses such that a rapidly increasing proportion of all reviews of the literature

are in the form of quantitative reviews, that is, meta-analyses. Despite its increasing frequency in the literature, however, meta-analysis is not without controversy and criticism (see Further Readings).

To gain a deeper understanding of meta-analytic procedures, it will be useful to consider the concept of replication. Meta-analysis, after all, involves summarizing or synthesizing studies that are broadly thought of as replications. It is important to note that studies typically included in meta-analyses are not replications in a narrow sense. Rather, they examine the same underlying relationships even if their independent and dependent variables are operationally defined in different ways. For example, in a meta-analysis of the effects of psychotherapy, the independent variables might be behavior therapy versus placebo, or psychodynamic behavior therapy versus placebo, or cognitive behavior therapy versus placebo. The dependent variables might be patients' scores on a standardized paper and pencil measure of psychological health, or the ratings by observers of the effectiveness of patients' interpersonal interactions, or the patients' report of the degree to which they are experiencing an improvement in their enjoyment of life.

Defining Successful Replication

There is a long tradition in psychology of urging replication of each other's research. Although we have been very good at calling for such replications, we have not been very good at deciding when a replication has been successful. The issue we now address is this: When shall a study be deemed successfully replicated? Ordinarily, this is taken to mean that in a new study at time 2, a null hypothesis that has been rejected at time 1 (i.e., was found significant) is rejected again, and with the same direction of outcome. When one study is significant and the other is not, we have a "failure to replicate," but such "failures" may be quite misleading. Let us consider an example.

Pseudo-Failures to Replicate

The Saga of Smith and Jones

Smith has published the results of an experiment in which a certain treatment procedure was predicted to improve performance. She reported results significant at *p* < .05 in the predicted direction. Jones published a rebuttal to Smith, claiming a failure to replicate. Both had an effect size *r* of .24. But Smith had 80 participants and Jones had only 20. In this type of situation, it is often the case that, although the *p* value associated with Smith's results is smaller than Jones's (i.e., more significant), the studies were in quite good agreement as to their estimated sizes of effect as defined by *r*, the correlation (technically, the point biserial correlation), between group membership (coded 0 or 1) and performance score (a more continuous score). Thus, studies labeled as "failure to replicate" may turn out to provide quite strong evidence for the replicability of the claimed effect.

On the Odds Against Replicating Significant Results

A related error often found in the behavioral, educational, biological, and social sciences is the implicit assumption that if an effect is "real," we should expect it to be found significant again on replication. Nothing could be further from the truth.

Suppose there is, in nature, a real effect of treatment with a true magnitude of $r = .24$, equivalent to a difference in success rates of 62% versus 38%. Further suppose an investigator studies this effect with an *N* of 64 participants or so, giving the researcher a level of statistical power of .50, a very common level of power for behavioral researchers of the past 45 years. Even though an *r* of .24 can reflect a very important effect, there is only one chance in four ($p = .25$) that both the original investigator and a replicator will get results significant at the .05 level; that is, the probability (power) for the first study ($p = .50$) is multiplied by the probability for the second study ($p = .50$) to yield $.50 \times .50 = .25$. If there were two replications of the original study, there would be only one chance in eight ($p = .125$) that all three studies would be significant (i.e., $p = .5 \times .5 \times .5 = .125$), even though we know the effect in nature is very real and very important.

Contrasting Views of Replication

The traditional, less useful view of replication success has two primary characteristics: (a) It focuses on significance level as the relevant summary statistic of a study, and (b) it makes its evaluation of whether replication has been successful in a dichotomous fashion. For example, replications are successful if both or neither $p < .05$, and they are unsuccessful if one $p < .05$ and the other $p > .05$. Behavioral researchers' reliance on a dichotomous decision procedure has been well documented. In this dichotomous procedure, differences between *p* levels are all regarded as trivial except the difference between a $p \le .05$ and a $p > .05$, or some other critical level of significance at which we have decided to "reject the null hypothesis." This dichotomous approach to significance testing has been increasingly criticized, for example, by the American Psychological Association's Task Force on Statistical Inference.

The newer, more useful view of replication success has two primary characteristics: (a) a focus on effect size as the more important summary statistic of a study, with a relatively more minor interest in the statistical significance level, and (b) an evaluation of whether replication has been successful made in a continuous, not dichotomous, fashion. For example, two studies are not said to be successful or unsuccessful replicates of each other, but rather the degree of failure to replicate is indexed by the magnitude of difference between the effect sizes (e.g., *r*s) obtained in the two studies.

Robert Rosenthal

Further Readings

Cohen, J. (1988). *Statistical power analysis for the behavioral sciences* (2nd ed.). Hillsdale, NJ: Erlbaum.

Cooper, H., & Hedges, L. V. (Eds.). (1994). *Handbook of research synthesis.* New York, NY: Russell Sage.

Cooper, H., Hedges, L. V., & Valentine, J. C. (Eds.). (2009). *The handbook of research synthesis and meta-analysis* (2nd ed.). New York, NY: Russell Sage.

Glass, G. V, McGaw, B., & Smith, M. L. (1981). *Meta-analysis in social research.* Beverly Hills, CA: Sage.

Hunt, M. (1997). *How science takes stock.* New York, NY: Russell Sage.

Light, R. J., & Pillemer, D. B. (1984). *Summing up: The science of reviewing research.* Cambridge, MA: Harvard University Press.

Rosenthal, R. (1991). *Meta-analytic procedures for social research* (Rev. ed.). Newbury Park, CA: Sage.

Rosenthal, R., & DiMatteo, M. R. (2002). Meta-analysis. In H. Pashler (Ed.), *Stevens' handbook of experimental psychology: Vol. 4. Methodology in experimental psychology* (J. Wixted [Vol. Ed.]), (3rd ed., pp. 391–428). New York, NY: Wiley.

Rosenthal, R., & Rosnow, R. L. (2008). *Essentials of behavioral research* (3rd ed.). New York, NY: McGraw-Hill.

Wilkinson, L., & the Task Force on Statistical Inference. (1999). Statistical methods in psychology journals: Guidelines and explanations. *American Psychologist, 54,* 594–604.

METACOGNITION AND EDUCATION

Lying in bed, Kendall is doing science homework. Kendall usually enjoys science and believes she can succeed on most of her classwork. She is particularly motivated to learn the planets, because her fifth-grade teacher has just discussed the solar system. Kendall repeats every planet name while looking at its picture, and then she decides to cover up each name to test herself. She remembers most of them but forgets Saturn and Venus, so she decides to spend more time memorizing their names.

In this scenario, Kendall is relying on cognitive and metacognitive processes to complete her homework. Cognition refers to mental activities and mental representations, such as Kendall's underlying memories for the planet names. Metacognition refers to people's thoughts (or cognitions) about their cognitions, such as Kendall's understanding that testing herself may help her identify planets that have not been stored in memory. Accordingly, her understanding of cognition (metacognition) may lead her to use effective strategies and, in turn, improve her memory (cognition). This entry discusses the role of metacognition in education.

Components of Metacognition

Metacognition is not a unitary construct; it has three general components: knowledge about cognition, monitoring of cognition, and control of cognition. *Metacognitive knowledge* includes any knowledge or beliefs—whether they are valid or invalid—about how our minds operate. An expert on cognition would have detailed metacognitive knowledge about how the mind operates, whereas many students may have rudimentary knowledge about how the mind operates. For instance, many students do not know how to study most effectively or how to optimally solve problems. *Monitoring* refers to assessing the current state of any cognitive process, such as when Kendall attempted to monitor her progress by testing her memory for each planet. In doing so, she was able to use the outcome of the test—for example,

whether she recalled the correct name and how quickly she recalled it—to infer how well she had learned the planet's name. *Control* refers to regulating any aspect of cognition, such as beginning a new activity, doing the same one in a different manner, or even deciding to continue the current activity. Often, monitoring is used in metacognitive control, such as in the earlier example where Kendall used the outcome of her self-tests (monitoring) to decide which planet names to continue studying (control).

The Role of Metacognition in Learning

Metacognition can contribute to student successes and failures. Students who do not accurately monitor their progress may not spend enough time on activities that they believe they are doing well on but in fact have not been learned well. For instance, if a student believes that he is able to solve algebra equations for a particular variable, he may stop practicing this particular kind of problem even if he still requires further practice to master it. Some students may not monitor their progress, which could limit the effectiveness of problem solving. Alan Schoenfeld had novice and expert mathematicians solve a variety of difficult math problems. The major difference between the two was that the experts continually monitored their progress; if they monitored that one approach was not working, they tried another one. The novices failed to monitor altogether, and hence they spent too much time exploring a single—and usually invalid—solution to a problem.

Given that students must monitor (and do so accurately) to efficiently control their study, a common focus of research on metacognition has been to establish how accurately students can monitor their ongoing progress. Unfortunately, across many domains, students have demonstrated limited skill at accurately monitoring their progress. They are relatively poor at judging how well they have learned to associate pairs of words (e.g., *cheval*—horse); they are relatively poor at evaluating how well they comprehend text materials and often fail to detect inconsistencies in texts that they are reading; they are relatively poor at evaluating how close they are to finding the correct solution for insight problems; and they often have difficulties monitoring the relative effectiveness of a variety of learning strategies. Even though students' monitoring is often unimpressive, they still use monitoring to make decisions on how to study. Put differently, students may use inaccurate monitoring to control study, which can lead to poor student outcomes. In fact, almost every teacher has had students perform poorly on an exam, yet afterward, the students complain that they were sure they knew all the material. In these situations, they likely did not accurately evaluate their learning and prematurely stopped studying.

Fortunately, techniques are being discovered to help students accurately monitor their progress in many domains. Kendall evaluated her learning by first studying each planet and its name and then asking herself, "Can I recall the name from memory?" Students who use this technique right after they study each to-be-learned item show poor accuracy at evaluating which items they have learned well, because the memory for each item would be easily accessed from short-term memory. By contrast, students who first study items and then wait to assess their learning show very high levels of accuracy, because by delaying their monitoring they can assess whether each item has been stored in long-term memory. Thus, simply having students delay their monitoring after study can greatly enhance its accuracy. Although delayed monitoring can help students monitor their learning of simple materials (e.g., associating a picture of Saturn with its name), delayed monitoring per se does not always improve accuracy. For instance, students' evaluation of how well they comprehend text materials does not improve if these evaluations are delayed after reading the texts. Instead, other techniques—such as summarizing each text—may be necessary for achieving accurate evaluations of comprehension.

The Role of Self-Efficacy in Learning

Beyond monitoring-and-control processes, students' beliefs about their own abilities appear to have an influential role in their classroom performance. In our opening scenario, Kendall believed she could successfully learn science materials, and this high self-efficacy will motivate her to persist while learning even difficult science concepts. More generally, academic self-efficacy refers to a student's belief about how well he or she can perform in the classroom. To measure efficacy, students rate themselves on statements such as "I know how to study to perform well on tests." As compared to students with low efficacy, students with higher academic self-efficacy

are expected to persist longer and use better strategies to study and hence should have higher academic achievement. As expected, academic self-efficacy of college students is related to cumulative grade point average, even after controlling for other relevant factors such as academic skills and commitment to college.

Relative to research on cognition, research on metacognition is in its infancy. Even so, over 2 decades of metacognitive research involving education has demonstrated the vital role of accurate metacognition to student performance across many disciplines, including memorizing key concepts in the classroom, problem solving, writing, reading, and mathematics.

Keith W. Thiede and John Dunlosky

See also Implicit Memory; Mental Effort

Further Readings

Dunlosky, J., & Metcalfe, J. (2009). *Metacognition.* Thousand Oaks, CA: Sage.

Hacker, D. J., Dunlosky, J., & Graesser, A. C. (2009). *Handbook of metacognition in education.* New York, NY: Psychology Press.

Schunk, D. H., & Zimmerman, B. J. (2008). *Motivation and self-regulated learning: Theory, research, and applications.* Mahwah, NJ: Erlbaum.

METAPHOR

Metaphors—figurative uses of language in which a word or phrase that ordinarily designates one thing is used to designate another—occur across languages and across uses of language, from ordinary conversation to literary and scientific writings. In spite of the prevalence of metaphors, it has proved surprisingly difficult to characterize precisely how they work. Consider a few examples: "Juliet is the sun," "My surgeon is a butcher," "Vanity is the quicksand of reason." Each of these metaphors brings together otherwise unrelated entities to achieve informative and perhaps insightful effects in a remarkably compact way. Comprehending them requires the hearer (or reader) to draw on the literal meanings of the words used, but broader knowledge about the entities literally denoted by the words in question—the sun, butchers, and quicksand—also seems to be required. This discussion will focus on two questions about metaphor that have received particular attention from philosophers, linguists, and psychologists in recent years. The first question concerns the nature of metaphorical content: What, if anything, does a metaphor mean beyond the literal meanings of its words? The second question concerns how hearers construct metaphorical interpretations: Do they treat metaphors as implicit comparisons or as explicit categorizations?

Metaphorical Content

Although metaphors are notoriously resistant to being paraphrased, there is no doubt that they can provoke extensive and vivid effects. The nature and status of these effects has been a matter of considerable recent debate. Four main positions have been defended regarding the nature of metaphorical content and how that content is related to the literal meanings of the words (or sentence) uttered: a broadly semantic account, a non-cognitivist account, and two pragmatic accounts, one in terms of implicature, the other in terms of direct content.

According to semantic accounts of metaphor, particular words or phrases of the metaphorical sentence are reinterpreted so that the sentence as a whole takes on a new (metaphorical) meaning. Whereas early versions of the semantic account attributed this to an interaction or conflict between the literal meanings of the sentence's subparts, more recent work by Josef Stern posits a metaphor-operator in the sentence's logical form that demands metaphorical instantiation. The metaphor-operator is a covert marker in the underlying structure of the sentence, attaching to the part of the sentence that is interpreted metaphorically and directing the interpretive process toward the generation of a metaphorical, rather than literal, interpretation.

Although semantic accounts give full credit to the centrality and importance of metaphorical language, it remains difficult to defend the idea that metaphor is a matter of semantic, that is, linguistically encoded, meaning, rather than of language use. Early semantic accounts struggled to explain the status of metaphorical meanings in relation to literal meanings; insofar as metaphorical meanings are both novel and contextually sensitive, it's difficult to see why they should count as an aspect of what

the words of the metaphor mean, rather than something that the speaker means (which she manages to convey by uttering those words). Stern's metaphor-operator neatly sidesteps this worry, but at the cost of a substantial increase in the complexity of the general process of semantic interpretation.

Partly in response to worries about early semantic accounts, philosophers such as Donald Davidson have moved to the other extreme, denying that metaphors have *any* determinate content beyond their literal meaning. Although agreeing that a given metaphor may give rise to a wide range of thoughts (or other effects) in its hearer, this "non-cognitivist" view insists that a metaphor does not *express* those thoughts. Instead, the metaphor simply *causes* its hearer to notice a range of thoughts by nudging her to see one thing as another (e.g., to see a certain surgeon as a butcher). The non-cognitivist view thus allows for the full variety of metaphors' effects, its capacity to stir emotions and stimulate vivid mental images or a sense of new insight. Further, the difficulty of paraphrasing metaphors is easily explained: If a metaphor does not have a distinctive metaphorical content, then it is unsurprising that attempts to capture this putative content routinely fail. Nonetheless, the view has been widely criticized for denying that there is anything to get right or wrong when interpreting a metaphor, for we routinely take speakers who utter metaphors to be making truth-evaluable claims and we agree and disagree about both the substance and correctness of those claims.

Intermediate between the semantic and non-cognitivist extremes are two pragmatic accounts of metaphor. Both accounts endorse the idea that metaphors communicate a determinate content but reject the idea that the sentence itself has a metaphorical meaning in addition to its literal one. Instead, metaphorical content is something that the speaker communicates by speaking as she does: It is what *she* means, not what *her words* mean. These positions are distinguished by whether they take the metaphorical content to be communicated to the hearer *directly* or *indirectly*, that is, to constitute something that the speaker asserts or something that she merely implies.

On the *indirect* account, deriving from the work of H. P. Grice and John Searle, the speaker is taken to be saying (or "making as if to say") exactly what her words literally express. Insofar as this literal interpretation is inadequate as a contribution to the ongoing conversation (e.g., it is patently false or irrelevant), the hearer is led to consider the possibility that the speaker is making a more oblique conversational contribution. If someone says, "My lawyer is a shark," she probably isn't intending to assert that her legal representative is a large fish; instead, she should be interpreted as intending to communicate indirectly, describing her lawyer as a shark in order to convey that the lawyer has various qualities typically associated with sharks: perhaps that he is ruthless, vicious, or predatory.

One strength of the indirect pragmatic account is that it shows how metaphorical content might depend on literal meaning without needing to posit metaphorical meanings as well. However, metaphors seem to function much more directly than this view allows: It is perfectly acceptable to answer Romeo's claim that Juliet is the sun by saying "Indeed she is" or "No, she isn't," and these are responses to a claim that Romeo has asserted, not to something he has merely implied. Further, the claim that metaphorical utterances are processed by first computing the sentence's literal meaning has been challenged on empirical grounds. Work by Sam Glucksberg and colleagues has shown that when subjects are asked to judge the literal falsity of sentences, they take longer to reach a decision when the sentence has a plausible metaphorical interpretation. This suggests that people have difficulty ignoring metaphorical interpretations, and more specifically, that those interpretations do not depend on the inappropriateness of a literal alternative.

The final option is to take metaphorical content to be communicated *directly* by the speaker, that is, to be something that the speaker *asserts* by her utterance, by allowing asserted content to extend well beyond sentence meaning. One cognitively oriented example of this position is developed within the framework of relevance theory by Robyn Carston, Dan Sperber, and Deirdre Wilson. According to this account, there is no presumption that speakers aim to use words literally, but only that their utterances will be relevant enough to their hearers to be worth processing, and as relevant as the speakers themselves are willing and able to make them. The hearer thus undertakes to construct an optimally relevant interpretation, employing a single interpretive mechanism in both metaphorical and literal cases. Encoded concepts are replaced as needed by "ad hoc" concepts with broader or narrower

denotations in order to generate an interpretation of the speaker's utterance able to support a range of implications sufficient to achieve optimal relevance. For example, suppose that a speaker utters the sentence "John is a soldier" to say of John (someone who is not literally a soldier) that he is metaphorically a soldier—perhaps that he is steadfast, loyal, and can be counted on in a tight spot. Whereas the encoded concept soldier picks out the set of soldiers, the interpretive process draws on contextually relevant assumptions associated with the encoded concept, such as being steadfast and loyal, to construct a related, ad hoc concept with a broader denotation than that of the encoded concept—a denotation that picks out not just actual soldiers but also other individuals (such as John) who share these associated properties of soldiers. This ad hoc concept is then taken to capture the property the speaker is asserting of John.

This account respects both the directness of metaphorical utterances and the ubiquity and naturalness of their occurrence in ordinary discourse. At the same time, the direct pragmatic account is consistent with psycholinguistic work on both the automaticity and relative effortfulness of metaphor processing. One might ask, though, whether the account reduces the difference between metaphorical and literal cases too much: The interpretation of especially poetic metaphors seems to involve more conscious reflection and explicit appeal to the metaphor's ordinary literal interpretation than the process of ad hoc concept construction looks to allow.

Metaphor Comprehension

Arising in counterpoint to questions about the nature of metaphorical content are questions about how hearers construct metaphorical interpretations. When a metaphor juxtaposes two entities, what sort of connection is the metaphor thereby presenting? Specifically, is the metaphor *comparing* the two concepts in question, or is the metaphor's topic being *categorized* as belonging to a group of which the metaphor's vehicle is a typical or exemplary member? (A metaphor's "topic" is its subject, while its "vehicle" is that thing the topic is compared to or described as being—e.g., Juliet and the sun, respectively.)

Comparison models begin with the idea that metaphors involve feature matching, that they highlight similarities between the metaphor's topic and vehicle. However, there are a number of difficulties with any straightforward feature-matching account. Metaphors routinely highlight correspondences between features that are not literally shared by topic and vehicle. For example, the sun is a source of literal warmth to anyone who feels its rays, but Juliet is not—she is, at most, a source of emotional warmth to Romeo. Further, good metaphors tend to involve new and informative ways of thinking about their topics by allowing us to see how certain properties of the vehicle might be carried over to the topic.

Dedre Gentner and colleagues have developed a more nuanced comparison model based on the idea of "structure mapping." This account models the comprehension process in two steps: First, an alignment process looks for structural correspondences between the two conceptual domains of the metaphor (e.g., the domain of lawyers and the domain of sharks). These correspondences may be indirect, involving relational properties that, although instantiated differently, play similar roles within the two domains. So, although we might say that lawyers and sharks are both predatory, in one case the predation relation is entirely social while in the other it's rather more carnivorous! Further, the model prioritizes matching of interconnected systems of properties over piecemeal matching of individual features. The second step involves projecting unmatched properties within the aligned system of concepts from the vehicle to the topic (e.g., the property of being the center of the solar system is mapped to the property of being at the center of Romeo's life and thoughts). The structure-mapping account thus aims to generate structural and relational resemblances beyond direct feature matching while using projection to explain a metaphor's informativeness.

However, this account does not explain how so-called emergent properties are derived. These are properties not standardly possessed by either topic or vehicle, yet which are central to the metaphorical interpretation. For example, "That surgeon is a butcher" communicates that the surgeon is careless, but carelessness is not a property typically associated with either surgeons or butchers. Further, the structure-mapping account does not explain a striking discrepancy between metaphorical and literal comparisons: Only the former can be transformed into meaningful class-inclusion statements. Whereas "My job is like a jail" can be transformed into "My job is a jail," literal comparisons such as "Emeralds are like sapphires" become nonsense when turned into the categorical "Emeralds are sapphires," suggesting that something other than comparison underlies the metaphorical case.

Sam Glucksberg has taken this discrepancy to show that metaphors really are what they appear to be: categorical statements, rather than implicit comparisons. According to his "category-transfer" account, comprehending a metaphor requires using the metaphor's vehicle to construct a superordinate or abstract category of which that vehicle is a prototypical member—the metaphor asserts that its topic belongs to this category. In the metaphor "My lawyer is a shark," the word *shark* refers not simply to the set of sharks but to the set of predatory creatures more generally—it has *dual* reference. However, because a single vehicle may be used metaphorically to convey more than one meaning (we would mean something quite different were we to say that Achilles, rather than Juliet, is the sun, for example), the metaphor's topic must play a filtering or constraining role in selecting the correct metaphoric category in a given instance.

Assigning the topic a merely "filtering" role may not be sufficient, though: It relegates the topic to a passive role in the interpretive process and might entail unnecessary processing effort by requiring that alternative metaphorical categories be computed. Further, as with the structure-mapping account, the category-transfer account lacks a clear explanation of emergent properties. More generally, the two accounts seem best suited to explaining different kinds of metaphors: Structure mapping looks most plausible for novel metaphors, whereas category transfer more naturally explains more conventionalized cases.

Empirical and theoretical investigations of these questions are increasingly proceeding hand in hand. Both developmental and clinical populations are proving rich sources of data for evaluating the competing models of metaphor discussed here. At the same time, new methods of collecting data, such as neuroimaging, are also being brought to bear, further expanding the range of available evidence.

Catherine Wearing

See also Analogical Mapping and Reasoning; Conversation and Dialogue; Discourse Processing, Models of; Inferences in Language Comprehension

Further Readings

Bowdle, B., & Gentner, D. (2005). The career of metaphor. *Psychological Review, 112*(1), 193–216.

Carston, R. (2002). *Thoughts and utterances.* Oxford, UK: Blackwell.

Davidson, D. (1978). What metaphors mean. *Critical Inquiry, 5,* 31–47.

Gibbs, R. (Ed.). (2008). *The Cambridge handbook of metaphor and thought.* Cambridge, UK: Cambridge University Press.

Glucksberg, S. (2001). *Understanding figurative language.* Oxford, UK: Oxford University Press.

Ortony, A. (Ed.). (1993). *Metaphor and thought* (2nd ed.). Cambridge, UK: Cambridge University Press.

Searle, J. (1993). Metaphor. In A. Ortony (Ed.), *Metaphor and thought* (2nd ed., pp. 83–111). Cambridge, UK: Cambridge University Press.

Sperber, D., & Wilson, D. (2008). A deflationary account of metaphor. In R. Gibbs (Ed.), *The Cambridge handbook of metaphor and thought* (pp. 84–106). Cambridge, UK: Cambridge University Press.

MICROGENESIS OF CONSCIOUSNESS

The purpose of this entry is to suggest how microgenetic theory, a fundamentally new paradigm for understanding the relation between brain and mind, can be used to illuminate one of the oldest and most fundamental problems in psychology and the philosophy of mind—the nature of consciousness. The entry begins with an explanation of microgeny and the structure of the mental state as such (a perception, an action, a feeling), then proceeds to demonstrate how consciousness arises in the transition from one state to another.

The Structure of the Mental State

Microgeny is the process by which a momentary mental state is formed across successive, qualitatively different phases that represent (in a rather literal sense of that term) phases in brain evolution (phylogeny), whereas ontogeny is replicated in the processual aspects of the microgenetic sequence. The clinical observation of cognitive, emotional, and behavioral symptoms in brain-damaged patients provides evidence in support of a process-based approach to the brain/mind problem. Microgenetic theory is contrary in both substance and spirit to much contemporary theorizing in psychology and the neurosciences, still largely dominated by cognitivism and information theory, but it harks back to certain ideas found in older theories from psychology (William James, Sigmund Freud, Gestalt psychology), behavioral neurology (John Hughlings Jackson, Karl Goldstein, Alexander Romanovich Luria) and philosophy of mind (Charles Peirce, Henri Bergson, Alfred North Whitehead).

Microgenetic theory offers a theory of the mind/brain state as such, that is, without reducing mind to brain or brain to mind. Mapping the cortex actually tells us very little about what the brain is, or what it does, because the brain is a four-dimensional object that does what it does precisely by changing and becoming. Microgeny begins with the "reptilian" brain, that is, the brain stem and hypothalamus, the first part of the central nervous system to appear in phylogeny (similar to Plato's thymos and Freud's Id), then moves to the "paleomammalian" brain (the limbic system, the seat of emotion and some aspects of memory), and from there to the cortex. The overall movement, literally and metaphorically, is from an inner core outward to the periphery, from simple wholes to the increasingly detailed parts, where the outside world is not the beginning of the process, but the end.

From a philosophical standpoint, the theory postulates that mental or external objects are not solid or static entities, such as the solid chair out there in the world, but that there is a brief microtemporal history in the mind that is part of their structure. In its journey out from the mind to the world, the chair passes through unconscious stages of form, concept, and meaning relations, in which the figural appearance of the chair, its recognition and category-relations to other similar objects, and to the life experience, are traversed. This means that the chair is not the solid object it appears to be, but is the outcome of a dynamic series of phases.

Consciousness is interpreted in microgenetic theory, then, as the relation across these phases in the mental state, that is, the relation of the empirical self (the subjective center of experience) to images in personal space and/or objects created by the mind/brain in an external space that is the final phase of a subjective process of object and space formation. Specifically, it is a relation across the phases that constitute a single mind/brain state, an epoch of microgenetic time, as depicted in Figure 1.

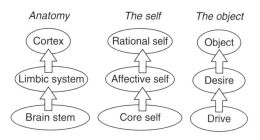

Figure 1   The structure of the mental state

Note: Within the brain, this unfolding proceeds along phylo- and onto-genetic lines, from older, deeper, central structures, progressively upward and outward to the cortex. On the psychic level, the core (instinctual, unconscious) self is derived to the empirical (feeling) self, which in turn leads outward to the perception of objects in the world by the rational (calculating, analyzing) self. There is a corresponding transition from drive through desire to an object perceived as being objectively valuable (or not). The transition from core to world is a continuum; the entire sequence constitutes a momentary mental state or an act of cognition.

Thus, conscious perception is not a passive process of recording what is actually "out there," Kant's *die Dinge an sich*, but rather it places the self in relation to objects that emerge from within, located in a speciously objective space and time grid that is created by the brain/mind, constrained by sensory data only in the last stages of the process to fit with reality. The unconscious self operates with a limited repertoire of instinctive pre-objects and behaviors oriented to survival with no concept of past or future, or any space other than the immediate perceptive field, or any objects other than those recognized there as belonging to a limited set of primitive categories, or any possible actions other than stereotyped reactions to objects or pre-objects that conform to these categories. The limbic system (a cluster of gray-matter nuclei that lie above the brain stem and under the neocortex) imbues objects with the feelings they arouse, pain or pleasure, delight or disgust, amusement or boredom. The neocortex appears last in phylogenesis and is more highly developed in humans than the higher primates (especially the frontal lobes). The neocortex mediates the final phase of object- and action-formation. The developing configurations undergo a final adaptation to the environment through the influence of sensory constraints. The instinctual activity of the core can be contained within the microgenetic epoch, which lasts for milliseconds, but feeling states can be more or less persistent (revived), and thoughts can be maintained (recur more or less

continuously) for a lifetime. In microgenetic theory, the duration of persistence is a function of the iteration or recurrence of the object, while its revival in memory is a recurrence in the present.

Microgeny is an adaptive becoming in which the environment, in the form of sensation, trims or parses away what is maladaptive to the inferred physical surround but does not provide the stuff of which perception is made. Rather, the brain "thinks up" the world it perceives. The perceptible world is the furthermost rim of mind in a rapid transition from inner core to outer surface. The physical world is known indirectly through its model in consciousness; its nature depends on the type of organism and the adequacy of sensory data, but consciousness cannot sustain the world without the constraints of sensation. The degree of approximation to an objective world determines the content of the state, for example, daydream, reverie, fantasy, hallucination, delusion, confabulation, and so forth, all of which are psychic events that actualize at different points in object formation. Without the impact of sensation, especially at the final phase of the microgeny, thinking is dreaming; psychosis is an intermediate phase.

In this "bottom-up" sequence, sense data do not enter the act/object development, but remain external, where they sculpt or constrain what develops. Sense data, even within the sculpting process, are imperceptible: We perceive the effects of sensory parsing in perception but not the assembly of sensory bits. In the transition from limbic memory to neocortical perception, there is a cascade of whole-part or context-item shifts that leads from inner and private to outer and public, from events that are memory-like to those that are perception-like, from past to present, from concept and image to external object, from the archaic to the recent in forebrain anatomy, from unity to diversity, and from the simultaneity of the unconscious to temporal order in conscious recollection and in the world. The sequence recurs in overlapping fashion every fraction of a second. The recursive nature of this process causes the stream of consciousness to appear as overlapping moments in an unsteady, even occasionally chaotic rhythm of repetition and novelty.

Subject and Self, Awareness and Consciousness

A subject is the subjective whole of the organism excluding its external portion. The external portion of that whole is made up of objects, perceived as existing outside the organism and belonging to the physical world. Objects are psychic appearances, literally phenomena ("that which appears" in ancient Greek), which, on reflection, point to entities that putatively exist independently of what we think we know of them. Awareness refers to the relation of subject to object. The conscious self, a segment in the stream of outgoing subjectivity aware of its own priority and subjectivity, arises within a subject that is aware of objects. Consciousness can be conceived as consisting in the relation of a self to inner and outer objects, where the relation is the unidirectional process of becoming through which subject, then object, actualizes. The relation of the self to inner objects is introspection or reflection; to outer objects, exteroception or perception.

The core, an early phase in the epoch, is the seed of personality. In higher mammals and young children, the core shows the first tendency to individuality, expressed in temperament or attachments. Prior to its appearance, behavior seems to be regulated by mechanism: instinctual drive, environmental signal, consummation. The core or unconscious mind is dependent on drive and the immediate occasion. In the evolution of mammals, individuality and awareness show a gradual advance from species to species, as the core becomes more detached from the object world, capable of entering into the binary "I/Thou" relation out of which all subsequent interpersonal relations evolve. Out of the core a conscious self is shaped in relation to beliefs and values and guided to actuality by sense data. The self is conscious of inner and outer objects, fixed in the present by the attention system and short-term memory, yet able to attend to events in the past (long-term, episodic, and semantic memory) and to plan for those in the future (prospective memory, imagination).

As partition continues, object and lexical concepts, images and feelings, punctuate the subjective pole. At the objective pole, value penetrates objects with greater specificity and refinement: The simple archaic category of "edible" is broken down into "tasty" or "not tasty" (essentially "I like it" or "I don't like it"), conditioning later aesthetic judgments of increasing subtlety, while requiring the intervention of a subject, the "I" who does or does not like. There is a parallel articulation of inner and outer. The present encompasses events of greater duration, enfolding a narrative of self and experience. The bodily space of the core expands to the perimeter of the arm's reach, that is, a "manipulation" space,

then beyond this perimeter to an external world that finally "detaches" from the observer. The action space of young infants transforms to the independent space of the conscious adult. We see an analogous transition from the implicit and unconscious to the conscious and explicit in all areas, for example, a word that individuates from a "mental lexicon," a specific recollection from a "memory store." The transition from concept to object, store to item, lexicon to word, unconscious to conscious, is not a transfer of like to like, as if the depth were a mere container. The transition of category to instance or whole to part occurs over a qualitative series of largely hidden internal phases that constrain consciousness to an outcome that delimits a theoretically infinite number of possibilities.

Conclusion

William James regarded consciousness as the central issue in psychology and the duration of the present as the central issue for its understanding. Time and space are specified out of the core: Space as objects grow out of concepts, time as duration is incremented by events. Subjective time develops in a transition from the simultaneity of the core to serial order in the world. Inwardly, time is counted in duration, externally in increments. The duration required for events to be perceived as stable objects is also the basis for the perception of events. The persistence of an object over a minimal duration to be perceived for what it is entails a recurrence within successive nows. All objects are events in which change (recurrence) is imperceptible.

Duration is the "glue" of continuity that carves events out of flux. Time is not a uniform flow but a replacement of changing objects across intervals, themselves changeless, thus nonexistent. The continuity of the self, of inner and outer, and the recognition of sameness or difference, owes to the overlap in a succession of present moments. Specifically, the overlap of the present (now) in the replacement of a categorical self and its objects is the basis for the near-identity of recurrences. The scenario of incessant change with a relative stability of inner and outer events is comprehensible in terms of categories sufficiently flexible to accommodate deviance and sufficiently habitual to cancel brief atypical replications.

Maria Pachalska,
Bruce Duncan MacQueen,
and Jason Walter Brown

See also Consciousness, Comparative Perspectives; Consciousness and Embodiment; Consciousness and the Unconscious; Self-Consciousness; Time Perception

Further Readings

Brown, J. W. (1977). *Mind, brain, and consciousness: The neuropsychology of cognition.* New York, NY: Academic Press.

Brown, J. W. (1988). *Life of the mind.* Hillsdale, NJ: Erlbaum.

Brown, J. W. (2005). *Process and the authentic life* (N. Rescher, J. Seibl, & M. Weber, Eds.). Heusenstamm, Germany: Ontos Verlag.

Brown, J. W. (2010). *Neuropsychological foundations of conscious experience.* Louvain-la-Neuve, Belgium: Chromatika.

Brown, J. W., & Pachalska, M. (2003). The nature of the symptom and its relevance for neuropsychology. *Acta Neuropsychologica, 1*(1), 1–11.

Dennett, D., & Kinsbourne, M. (1992). Time and the observer: The where and when of consciousness in the brain. *Behavioral and Brain Sciences, 15,* 183–247.

James, W. (1890). *Principles of psychology.* New York, NY: Holt.

Pąchalska, M. (2002). The microgenetic revolution: Reflections on a recent essay by Jason Brown. *Journal of Neuropsychoanalysis, 4*(1), 109–117.

Pąchalska, M., & MacQueen, B. D. (2005). Microgenetic theory. A new paradigm for contemporary neuropsychology and neurolinguistics. *Acta Neuropsychologica, 3*(3), 89–106.

MIND-BODY PROBLEM

The mind-body problem is the problem of explaining how the mind and body are related. Put that way, the problem seems singular even if not simple. Is the mind simply the body or some part of it? If it is not, then what is it and how is it related to the body? Most important, if the mind is not the body, how do they interact?

Descartes and Dualism

The most obvious strategy for solving the problem is to insist that minds are bodies or some proper part of the body, perhaps the brain or the central nervous system. This position, the identity theory, claims that minds and brains are identical. René Descartes famously argued that the identity theory must be false. According to Descartes, it is conceivable that minds exist without bodies, and so it is possible that minds exist without bodies, and so minds are not bodies. Now the relationship between what is conceivable and what is possible is tricky and has attracted much attention. It is dubious that Descartes is licensed to move from conceivability to possibility. But what of the move from the notion that it is possible that minds are not bodies to the conclusion that minds are not bodies? That move might seem a nonstarter. Much that is possibly the case is not actually the case. But what Descartes assumes, at least implicitly, is that if minds and brains are identical, then they must share all of their properties in common. Descartes assumes that whatever is identical must be indiscernible: For any two objects, x and y, if x is identical to y, then for any property x has y has, and vice versa. And so if minds are brains, then whatever property the one has the other also has. But it is not possible for brains to exist without brains. And so, if minds are brains, then minds could not exist without brains. Thus, if it is possible for minds to exist without brains, then it follows that minds are not brains.

Descartes' response to the mind-body problem is that minds and bodies are radically different kinds of things; the latter material, the former immaterial. But Descartes' solution, dualism, introduces two new problems. The first challenge is to make intelligible what an immaterial thing might be. The second problem, related to the first, is the problem of mental causation: How do minds causally interact with bodies? This problem for Descartes is especially acute: How do immaterial substances interact with material substances?

The contemporary version of the mind-body problem is not cast in terms of substances and is often cast, instead, in terms of laws, states, properties, or events. In terms of properties, for instance, the mind-body problem is this: How are mental properties related to physical properties? That is, how are mental properties related to the properties of interest to the natural sciences? And the problem of mental causation, in its modern guise, concerns the causal closure of the physical. It is commonly presumed that the laws of physics are causally closed; there are no physical events that are not caused by other physical events. Were this not the case, then there would be, at the explanatory level of physics, miracles: physical events with no physical explanations. But if the instantiations of mental properties are causally efficacious with respect to the physical, if having some mental property is the cause of some behavior, for instance, then we are left with only three possibilities. First, there are physical events that are not physically caused, and so there are physical events without physical causes. Second, whatever the mental causes the physical also causes, and so behavior is causally overdetermined. Third, mental properties are identical to physical properties. The first option is the modern version of Descartes' solution. The third is the modern version of materialism, what is commonly called "physicalism." The second? Well, about that there is much contemporary debate, to which we will return.

Eliminativism

A more radical way to respond to the problem of mental causation, however, is simply to deny that the mental is causally efficacious. One way to do this is to claim that the mental, although it might be caused by the nonmental (e.g., the feeling of pain might be caused by a broken bone) and although it might cause what is mental (e.g., someone's experiencing pain might cause that person to remember being in pain), does not cause anything nonmental (and so the feeling of pain would not cause someone to avoid the cause of that pain in the future). This position, epiphenomenalism, has few contemporary adherents. The problem for the position is that, first, it seems obvious to many that the mental is causally efficacious, and second, if the mental does not cause the physical (if, e.g., it does not cause behavior), it is hard to see why we should believe it to exist.

Early in the 20th century, the more popular response to dualism's troubles was to deny the mental entirely, or at least to deny it any explanatory role. According to psychological behaviorism, what is explanatorily relevant is what is observable, and what is observable with respect to explaining human behavior are environmental stimuli and behavioral outputs. Psychological behaviorism attempts to "solve" the mind-body problem by denying the mental entirely. Another form of behaviorism, logical behaviorism, agrees with psychological behaviorism that what matters is what is observable, but insists that the mental is causally efficacious, or at least that appeals to the mental play an explanatory role. Logical behaviorists attempted to define mental terms in terms of behaviors or dispositions to behave. By comparison, we might think of something's being fragile as its being disposed to shatter if struck. If it shatters when struck, we might say that it shattered partly due to its fragility. But its fragility, it might be thought, just is its being such that it would shatter. There is an explanation, logical behaviorism contends, even though the explanatory circle is small. Logical behaviorism does not deny the mental, per se. Ordinary psychological explanations have a purchase. But, according to logical behaviorism, the mental is not separate from the body. Indeed, logical behaviorism denies that the mental is at all private.

In philosophy, the popularity of both versions of behaviorism went hand in hand with a theory of meaning that was popular during the early part of the 20th century, the verificationist theory of meaning, according to which the meanings of theoretical terms were supposedly the verification conditions for their correct applications. Verificationism and the behaviorist theories following in its train now have few adherents. With better theories of meaning and reference, and especially with better theories with respect to theoretical terms, both philosophy and the behavioral sciences once again began appealing to hidden objects, states, and processes without embarrassment.

Not everyone agreed that these included the mental, however. The latter part of the 20th century introduced new versions of eliminativism. According to defenders of this view, attributions of propositional attitudes (e.g., beliefs and desires) belong to a folk theory for explaining behavior. As a theory, this folk theory is subject to revision and even elimination as better theories are developed. If the best theories for explaining human behavior appeal to neuroscience, and if our folk theories are not reducible to the theories of neuroscience, then, according to these eliminativists, we should conclude that our folk theories of the mind are not simply incomplete, but false.

Functionalism

Another strategy that surfaced during the second half of the 20th century, and that has attracted far more attention, is functionalism. According to this view, someone is in pain, for instance, whenever she is in a state that plays a particular functional role, which is to say whenever she is in that state commonly caused by pain stimuli (e.g., pin pricks) and that commonly produces pain behavior (e.g., moving one's arm quickly away from the pin). Functionalism shares with behaviorism the idea that the meanings of mental predicates are tied with behavior, but it breaks with behaviorism in that, according to functionalism, mental predicates pick out properties and states that not only cause behavior but also cause each other. Pains produce not only behavior but also beliefs and memories. And part of the commonsense explanation for this appeals to the fact that we reflect on our memories, beliefs, and desires and that this reflection results in additional memories, beliefs, and desires.

One version of functionalism, realizer functionalism, is generally thought of as a version of the identity theory. According to realizer functionalism, because mental terms pick out whatever it is that plays a particular functional role, and because it is presumably the job of neuroscience to tell us what that is, mental state terms (at least when used to ascribe mental states to us) pick out neurophysiological states (of us). Thus understood, realizer functionalism solves the problem of mental causation by insisting that mental properties just are certain physical properties, and so there is no threat to the causal closure of the physical and there is no worry about causal overdetermination.

Another version of functionalism, role functionalism, holds that mental terms pick out properties and states at a higher level of abstraction, perhaps those that humans might share with machines having no neurophysiology. As commonly understood, role functionalism holds that mental properties are second-order properties—properties had by properties. Someone is in pain, according to this view, in virtue of having some first-order property (presumably some physical property) the instantiation of which plays the appropriate functional-causal role. So, for instance, if having some neurophysiological property plays the pain role for us, if having that neurophysiological property is typically caused by pin pricks, for example, and typically causes pain behavior, then we are in pain whenever that neurophysiological property is instantiated in us. But that neurophysiological property is not identical to pain. Rather, pain is the having of some property or other (in our case that particular neurophysiological property) that plays the relevant functional-causal role.

Role functionalism is theoretically compatible with both dualism and physicalism about the mind. It is compatible with dualism since it allows that the instantiation of some nonphysical property might play the appropriate functional role. It is compatible with physicalism since, presumably, nothing nonphysical actually plays that role. According to role functionalism, the property of being in pain is not, strictly speaking, a physical property or any particular physical property, and so creatures physically very different than us, and perhaps even machines of the right type, might share the property of being in pain. But assuming that pain is always realized physically, assuming that everything that is in pain has some physical property the instantiation of which plays the functional role of pain for that creature or machine, there is an important sense in which dualism is false.

Exactly how and whether dualism is false and physicalism is true by the lights of role functionalism has itself been an area of intense debate. According to one particularly influential view, token-token physicalism, although mental types (e.g., pain) are not identical to physical or neurophysiological types, particular instances or tokens of the mental (e.g., someone's particular pain at some particular moment) are identical to particular instances or tokens of the physical. By analogy, no one thinks that a particular shade of red, say crimson, is identical to redness, because something can be red but not be crimson. Nonetheless, it might be held, something's being crimson is just its being red.

The Mind-Body Problem Today

Role functionalism was once thought to be a kind of philosophical panacea, a halfway house between a dualism that seems shrouded in mystery and a reductive physicalism that seems counter to common sense, and it continues to be the favored view in the philosophy of mind. But role functionalism faces several objections. According to one objection, being functionally organized in a particular way is insufficient for intentionality. We can imagine, it is thought, a creature or a robot with the right kind of functional organization, but without what we would think of as thoughts or understanding.

It is also challenging to see how functional organization is sufficient for consciousness, but here the problem is seemingly a problem for any theory of the mind, and especially for any physicalist theory. It seems possible, for instance, that someone functionally like me, someone who typically sees blue objects as blue, who typically comes to believe that such objects are blue after seeing them, who typically asserts that such objects are blue when asked, and so forth, might have experiences of blue objects that are qualitatively different than the experiences that I have when I see blue objects. We are functionally the same, she and I, but we are not mentally the same. The problem, the qualia problem, is to explain how functionalism in particular, and physicalism more generally, can explain the qualitative nature of many of our mental states.

Where the qualia problem raises the worry that functionalism cannot avoid all of the problems of physicalism, another problem suggests that role functionalism cannot avoid a perennial problem for dualism. The problem, the problem of mental causation, is that if mental properties are not identical to physical properties, then it would seem that their instantiations would have nothing to do. One version of the problem maintains that any causal explanation of an event excludes all other explanations. The problem, if such there is, would seemingly apply to the properties appealed to by most of the natural sciences. Indeed, it would seem to raise a problem for all of the sciences except for physics since, if the argument were successful, it follows that the lower level causal explanations exclude all other higher level causal explanations. But role functionalism seems to face special challenges in explaining how the mental could, by its lights, be causally efficacious. If a mental property is a second-order property, if it is the having of some property or other that plays a particular functional role, then it would seem to be the first-order property that does the work by definition. And if instances of mental properties are identical to instances of physical properties, if the role functionalist endorses token-token identity, then those instances must play exactly the same causal role. And if they play the same causal role, if instantiations of mental properties never cause anything not caused by instantiations of physical properties, then that would seem a good reason to think either that mental properties do not exist or that they just are those physical properties.

One particularly interesting response to this problem is to think of mental property tokens not as identical to physical tokens, but instead to think of them as proper parts of physical tokens. The position agrees with realizer functionalism that mental properties are not second-order. And it agrees with dualism, but here a dualism about properties and not substances, that instances of mental properties are not identical to instances of physical properties. It also agrees with role functionalism that the mental is physical in virtue of being multiply realizable by the physical. To understand the suggestion, imagine an overly simplified view, a popular philosophical fiction. Imagine that pain in humans is correlated with C-fibers firing and that pain in Martians is correlated with A-Fibers firing. According to traditional role functionalism, if John the human is in pain, then his being in pain is not his having C-fibers fire, although it is true that he wouldn't be in pain if his C-fibers were not firing. His being in pain is his being functionally organized in the appropriate way and, thus, his having something or other that is playing the pain role. Perhaps we might say that his being in pain at this moment is identical to his having C-fibers firing at this moment, but being in pain is not having C-fibers fire. But then it is unclear what causal role there is for pain to play for John since any instance of pain in John just is an instance of C-fibers firing in John.

According to traditional realizer functionalism, if C-fibers firing is the realizer of pain for humans, then it just is pain for humans. And because A-fibers firing just is pain for Martians, it just is pain for them. But then it appears that humans and Martians, although it is true to say of both that they experience pain, actually share nothing in common when they are both in pain.

If we think that pain is multiply realizable, if we agree with the Role Functionalist that humans and Martians have something in common when in pain, then we must also think that the causal powers of C-fibers firing and the causal powers of A-fibers firing are relevantly similar. No doubt they do not share all of their causal features, for otherwise they would not be neurophysiologically distinct, but their causal features must overlap with respect to those features relevant for pain, for otherwise we would not treat them as alike psychologically. Pain, on this view, contributes the set of causal powers that is a proper subset of those powers contributed by both C-fibers firing and A-fibers firing, and so an instance of pain might be thought of as a proper part of any instance of C-fibers (or A-fibers) firing. Whether this strategy will prove successful is as yet a matter of considerable controversy.

Michael Watkins

See also Anomalous Monism; Behaviorism; Consciousness and Embodiment; Eliminative Materialism; Emergence; Explanatory Gap; Mental Causation; Physicalism; Reductive Physicalism

Further Readings

Chalmers, D. (1996). *The conscious mind.* Oxford, UK: Oxford University Press.

Churchland, P. (1979). *Scientific realism and the plasticity of mind.* New York, NY: Cambridge University Press.

Dennett, D. (1991). *Consciousness explained.* Boston, MA: Little, Brown.

Fodor, J. (1974). Special sciences and the disunity of science as a working hypothesis. *Synthese, 28,* 77–115.

Jackson, F. (1982). Epiphenomenal qualia. *Philosophical Quarterly, 32,* 127–136.

Kim, J. (2005). *Physicalism, or something near enough.* Princeton, NJ: Princeton University Press.

Kripke, S. (1972). *Naming and necessity.* Cambridge, MA: Harvard University Press.

Lewis, D. (1966). An argument for the identity theory. *Journal of Philosophy, 63,* 17–25.

Putnam, H. (1975). *Mind, language, and reality.* Cambridge, UK: Cambridge University Press.

Shoemaker, S. (2007). *Physical realization.* Oxford, UK: Oxford University Press.

Yablo, S. (1992). Mental causation. *Philosophical Review, 101,* 245–280.

Mirror Neurons

Our social competence largely depends on the capacity to understand the intentional behavior of others. What are the origins of this capacity? What are its underlying neural mechanisms? This entry will present and discuss a class of neurons originally discovered in the premotor cortex of macaque monkeys that can shed light on these issues: mirror neurons.

Mirror Neurons in Monkeys

In the early 1990s, a new class of premotor neurons, "mirror neurons," was discovered in the anterior sector of the macaque monkey's ventral premotor cortex, known as area F5. Mirror neurons discharge not only when the monkey executes goal-related hand motor acts such as grasping objects, but also when it observes other individuals (monkeys or humans) executing similar motor acts. Neurons with similar properties were subsequently discovered in regions of the posterior parietal cortex reciprocally connected with area F5.

Action observation causes in the observer the automatic activation of the same neural mechanism triggered by action execution. For the first time, a neural mechanism allowing for a direct matching between the visual perception of an action and its execution has been identified. By means of the mirror matching mechanism, the results of the visual analysis of the observed action—which, in principle, has no meaning for the observer—can be translated into an account that the individual is able to understand. It was proposed that this mechanism could underlie a direct form of action understanding. If mirror neurons do in fact mediate action understanding, their activity should reflect the meaning of the observed action, not its visual features.

Two sets of experiments were carried out to verify this hypothesis. The first experiments tested whether the mental representation of an action triggers F5 mirror neurons, the second whether mirror neurons can respond to the sound produced by actions. The results of these experiments answered both questions in the affirmative and showed that what drives mirror neurons' discharge is not the mere visual description of a motor act, but rather its goal.

In the most lateral part of area F5, a class of mirror neurons responding to the execution and observation of mouth actions has been found. The majority of these neurons discharge when the monkey executes and observes mouth-related, object-related motor acts, such as grasping, biting, or licking. However, a small percentage of mouth-related mirror neurons discharge during the observation of communicative facial actions performed by the experimenter in front of the monkey ("communicative mirror neurons"). Macaque monkeys show an initial capacity to control and "voluntarily" emit social signals; this is mediated by the frontal lobe. It is interesting that this capacity develops in a cortical area—area F5—that in humans became Brodmann's area 44, a key area for verbal communication.

More recently, premotor and parietal mirror neurons have been found to have a role in intention understanding. The discharge of mirror neurons during the observation of an act (e.g., grasping an object) is conditioned by the type of subsequent act (e.g., bringing the object to the mouth) that specifies the overall action intention. In addition to recognizing the goal of the observed motor act, mirror neurons allow the observing monkey to predict the agent's next action, and hence its overall basic motor intention. This neural mechanism could provide scaffolding for more sophisticated social cognitive abilities, such as those that characterize the human species.

Mirror Neuron Mechanisms in Humans

Solid evidence, recently also at the single neuron level, demonstrates the existence of a mirror neuron matching mechanism in the human brain as well. Action observation leads to the activation of premotor and posterior parietal cortical areas, the likely human homologue of the monkey areas in which mirror neurons were originally described. Distinct cortical regions within the premotor and posterior parietal cortices are activated by the observation/execution of mouth-, hand-, and foot-related actions.

The mirror neuron mechanism for actions in humans is directly involved in imitation of simple movements and in the imitative learning of complex skills. Furthermore, many interesting phenomena described by social psychologists, such as the "chameleon effect"—the unconscious mimicry by the observer of postures, expressions, and behaviors of her or his social partners—can find a neurophysiological explanation in the mirror mechanism. The premotor cortex, which has the mirror mechanism for action, is also involved in processing action-related words and sentences, suggesting that mirror neurons, along with other parts of the sensory-motor system, could play a role in language processing.

Mirroring mechanisms also underpin our capacity to empathize. When we perceive others expressing a particular emotion such as disgust, the same brain areas are activated as when we experience the same emotion. This, of course, does not imply emotional contagion. In fact, in spite of a common shared activation focus of activation in the anterior insula, no matter whose disgust is at stake, different cortical areas activate when disgust is subjectively experienced as opposed to when it is only observed in the facial expression of someone else. Similar mirror mechanisms have been described for the perception of pain and touch.

Together, these results suggest that our ability to empathize with others is mediated by mechanisms of embodied simulation, that is, by the activation of the same neural circuits that underpin our own emotional and sensory experiences. In this view, empathy is conceived of as the outcome of our natural tendency to experience interpersonal relations at the implicit level of intercorporeity, that is, of the mutual resonance of intentionally meaningful sensory-motor behaviors. Recent studies have suggested that mirror mechanisms could be malfunctioning in individuals affected by autistic spectrum disorders. The discovery of mirror neurons opens exciting new perspectives in a variety of different fields in social cognitive neuroscience, such as our understanding of psychopathological states, language, and aesthetics.

The mainstream view in cognitive science was, and may partly still be, that action, perception, and cognition are to be considered as separate domains. The discovery of mirror neurons challenges this view by showing that such domains are intimately intertwined. It also provides a new empirically based notion of intersubjectivity, which can be viewed first and foremost as intercorporeity, the main basic source of knowledge we directly gather about others.

Vittorio Gallese

See also Common Coding; Consciousness and Embodiment; Emotional Recognition, Neuropsychology of; Facial Expressions, Emotional; Motor System, Development of; Social Cognition

Further Readings

Freedberg, D., & Gallese, V. (2007). Motion, emotion and empathy in esthetic experience. *Trends in Cognitive Sciences, 11,* 197–203.

Gallese, V. (2006). Intentional attunement: A neurophysiological perspective on social cognition and its disruption in autism. *Brain Research, 1079,* 15–24.

Gallese, V. (2007). Before and below "theory of mind": Embodied simulation and the neural correlates of social cognition. *Philosophical Transactions of the Royal Society London B: Biological Sciences, 362,* 659–669.

Gallese, V., & Lakoff, G. (2005). The brain's concepts: The role of the sensory-motor system in reason and language. *Cognitive Neuropsychology, 22,* 455–479.

Rizzolatti, G., & Sinigaglia, C. (2010). The functional role of the parieto-frontal mirror circuit: interpretations and misinterpretations. *Nature Reviews Neuroscience, 11,* 264–274.

MNEMONIC STRATEGIES

This entry reviews mnemonics (memory improvement strategies), describing effective techniques that have been developed over 2,500 years but which have been shown to make a very considerable contribution to the ease of learning disconnected or relatively meaningless material.

Imagery Mnemonics: The Method of Loci

Mnemonics are strategies to improve memory through contrived associations. Their use dates back to classical times. Cicero, writing in 55 BCE, described how, more than 400 years earlier, the Greek poet Simonides discovered the method of loci. Simonides, as the only survivor from a banquet at which the roof collapsed, was able to identify the bodies of the victims by recalling images of the seating arrangements. He realized that location was a powerful cue; if he formed mental images incorporating an image of each item to be remembered with each of several familiar, ordered locations, then the items could be easily recalled by reimagining those locations. From classical times onward, this method of loci (place) was used by orators to remember important points in long speeches, and modern research has confirmed the method's effectiveness at doubling recall.

The method of loci illustrates key features of successful mnemonic methods. The familiar locations provide reliable cues to recall and the images allow the incorporation of otherwise unrelated items into a familiar framework. A mental trip through the locations allows each to cue the image and help recall of the items. Normally, we remember familiar, meaningful, organized, and interesting information without special techniques, but faced with needing to learn apparently meaningless, disorganized, disconnected, and uninteresting information, mnemonic methods help by providing the meaning, organization, and retrieval cues that are lacking.

Imagery Mnemonics: Peg Words

The method of loci has obvious limitations: It requires a known set of ordered locations and is particularly appropriate for serial recall. To create greater flexibility, professional memory experts developed alternative methods that use images to link items to previously memorized peg words, with a separate peg word for each of 100 or more items. For example, the peg word for the 21st item to be remembered might be *net* and for the 22nd might be *nun*. Here, images involving a net or a nun replace the location of the method of loci, and knowing that the 21st peg is *net* cues recall of the relevant image. Different professionals advocate different systems for constructing the pegs, but a commonly used method translates each digit into a consonant sound and then concrete peg words are constructed by inserting vowels. So, in the phonetic mnemonic system, 1 translates as a *t* sound and 2 as an *n* sound—from which the examples of *net* and *nun* were constructed. This translation system not only allows the construction of peg words that can be easily memorized but also enables numbers to be translated into memorable phrases, so aiding, for example, the learning of PIN numbers or dates. (The remaining digits are 3 = m, 4 = r, 5 = l, 6 = j/sh, 7 = k, 8 = f/v, 9 = b/p, 0 = s/z.)

The Linkword Mnemonic

The keyword or linkword mnemonic is a further development of imagery-based mnemonics that has been applied very successfully to the learning of foreign language vocabulary. The sound of each foreign word is converted into an easily imaged word or phrase that sounds similar. The image is linked to the meaning of the word. For example, the Spanish word *perro* sounds like pear and means dog. So an image of a dog eating a pear would cue the meaning (dog) when the word *perro* was encountered.

Imagery mnemonics have been adopted, with varying results, to aid those suffering memory problems caused by brain damage. The benefits are inversely proportional to the degree of deficit. In general, the traditional mnemonic methods are very effective but demand effort and creativity on the part of the learner.

The effectiveness of imagery-based mnemonics derives from the opportunity that the images provide for spatially linking known and to-be-recalled items together when other ways of associating the to-be-recalled items with memory cues may be lacking. Merely forming an image of something to be remembered does not enhance long-term recall. It is only when images are formed that integrate the known (i.e., peg or loci) with the unknown (item to be recalled) that later recall is improved. Any technique that provides cues and a meaningful framework can improve memory. Linking the items to be remembered in a story provides such a meaningful framework and can dramatically improve recall.

Acronyms and Rhymes

Other mnemonics popular with students include acronyms, in which the first letters of words to be remembered are arranged to spell out a meaningful word, and acrostics, in which the first letters of the words become the first letters of words in an easily memorized phrase. For example, the acronym FACE has often been used to remember the notes in the spaces of the treble clef and the acrostic "Every Good Boy Deserves Favor" cues the notes on the treble clef lines. Research has shown such mnemonics can be effective, but primarily as a way of remembering the order of known items rather than for memorizing new information. Rhymes, such as the "Thirty days hath September" rhyme for the lengths of the months, are another technique, and rhymes and rhythm have been shown to help by limiting the possible alternatives during recall.

Applying and Combining Mnemonics

Mnemonics are most effective when the learner combines ability and commitment; when mnemonophobia (fear of using mnemonics) is overcome, they are effective in classroom learning. However, other memory improvement techniques incorporating retrieval practice, such as the name game for learning the names of members of a group, are less demanding on the learner and can be equally effective. Retrieval practice and imagery mnemonics can be combined to achieve even greater memory improvement than when either is used separately. Suitable selection of techniques from among mnemonic and other memory improvement techniques can dramatically ease the burden of memorizing and the embarrassment of memory failure.

Peter Morris

See also Memory Recall, Dynamics; Retrieval Practice (Testing) Effect; Visual Imagery

Further Readings

Fritz, C. O., Morris, P. E., Acton, M., Etkind, R., & Voelkel, A. R. (2007). Comparing and combining retrieval practice and the keyword mnemonic for foreign vocabulary learning. *Applied Cognitive Psychology, 21,* 499–526.

Higbee, K. L. (2001). *Your memory: How it works and how to improve it* (2nd ed.). New York, NY: Marlowe.

Morris, P. E., & Fritz, C. O. (2006). How to . . . improve your memory. *The Psychologist, 19,* 608–611.

Roediger, H. L., III. (1980). The effectiveness of four mnemonics in ordering recall. *Journal of Experimental Psychology: Human Learning and Memory, 6,* 558–567.

MODELING CAUSAL LEARNING

Humans display remarkable ability to acquire causal knowledge. Hume's philosophical analysis of causation set the agenda for discovering how causal relations can be inferred from observable data, including temporal order and covariations among events. Recent computational modeling work on causal learning has made extensive use of formalisms based on directed causal graphs (Figure 1). Within a causal graph, each arrow connects a node representing a cause to an effect node, reflecting core assumptions that a cause precedes its effect and has some power to generate or prevent it. The computational goal is to infer from the observable data the unobservable causal structure conveyed by the graph and the magnitude of the power of each cause to influence its effect.

This entry covers some key issues that arise in modeling human causal learning. Alternative models of causal learning vary depending on the assumptions adopted in the computation, the goal of the computation, and the presentation format of the input data. Understanding models from these perspectives can clarify their commonalities and differences, guide the design of psychological experiments to test the validity of key assumptions, and assess whether models can potentially be extended to

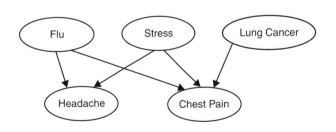

Figure 1   A simple example of a causal graph

real-life problems, such as medical diagnosis and scientific discovery.

Alternative Causal Assumptions

When the causal graph includes multiple potential causes of a single effect, two leading classes of models make different assumptions about the integration rule used to combine causal influences. One class (including the classic delta-P model and the associative Rescorla-Wagner model) assumes a linear integration rule: Each candidate cause changes the probability of the effect by a constant amount regardless of the presence or absence of other causes. A second class is represented by the power PC theory, a theory of causal judgments postulating that learners assume that unobservable causal influences operate independently to produce the effect. Guided by this assumption, causal integration is based on probabilistic versions of various logical operators, such as OR and AND-NOT, chosen to reflect the polarity of causal influence (i.e., whether a cause produces or prevents the occurrence of an effect).

When the causal graph includes multiple effects of a single cause (e.g., flu causes headache and chest pain, as shown in Figure 1), the causal Markov assumption states that the probability of one effect occurring is independent of the probability of other effects occurring, given that its own direct causes are present. Statistical models that examine causal relationships adopt the Markov assumption, which guides exploration of conditional independencies that hold in a body of data, thereby constraining the search space by eliminating highly unlikely cause-effect relations. The extent to which humans employ the causal Markov assumption remains controversial.

When observations are limited, human causal learning relies heavily on some type of prior knowledge. Prior knowledge can be specific to a domain (based on known categories), but it can also include abstract assumptions about properties of a system of cause-effect relations (e.g., preference for causal networks that exhibit various types of simplicity). Use of appropriate prior knowledge can explain the rapid acquisition of causal relations often exhibited by humans.

Alternative Types of Causal Judgments

Causal learning potentially enables two types of judgments: causal *strength* and causal *structure.*

A strength judgment involves a quantitative assessment of a cause-effect relation: What is the probability with which a cause produces (or prevents) an effect? A structure judgment is a more qualitative assessment of cause-effect relations: Does a candidate cause, in fact, produce (or prevent) an effect? In a causal graph, a strength estimate assesses the weight associated with an arrow, whereas a structure estimate assesses the existence of an arrow. Learning causal strength allows a system to anticipate the occurrence of an effect in a new context and respond adaptively. Learning causal structure allows a system to explain events and to choose appropriate actions.

A general model of causal learning needs to achieve both of these computational goals. Although many heuristic models of strength estimation have been proposed, most do not generalize to structure judgments. Within a Bayesian framework, a strength-learning model assumes the learner has some prior guesses about possible values of causal strength and updates beliefs given observed data. A structure-learning model assumes the learner has prior guesses about strength and structure, and computes a score to quantify the support that observed data provide for beliefs about aspects of the structure. Bayes's rule provides the computational engine to update beliefs. A different variant, *constraint-based* models of structure learning, operates in a more bottom-up fashion, computing statistical dependencies in the data and selecting those structures consistent with these dependencies.

Alternative Learning Formats

Formal modeling of causal learning has emphasized acquisition of causal relations from complete statistical data (i.e., a 2 × 2 contingency table tallying frequencies of the four possible combinations of presence versus absence of cause and effect). Some models restrict themselves to predictions based on such idealized data presentation, side-stepping issues related to memory and presentation order.

In many realistic situations, however, such summary data are not available to the learner. Rather, data about cause-effect pairings arrive sequentially with no external record of the events. For nonverbal animals, there is no obvious way to present summarized data; humans also must often learn from sequential data. Because sequential models aim to dynamically integrate prior beliefs with new observations in a trial-by-trial manner, such models are sensitive to order of data presentation. The development of sequential models of causal learning is currently an active research area.

Hongjing Lu

See also Concepts, Development of; Knowledge Acquisition in Development; Reinforcement Learning, Psychological Perspectives

Further Readings

Chater, N., & Oaksford, M. (Eds.). (2008). *The probabilistic mind*. Oxford, UK: Oxford University Press.

Gopnik, A., & Schulz, L. (Eds.). (2007). *Causal learning: Psychology, philosophy, and computation*. Oxford, UK: Oxford University Press.

Shanks, D. R., Holyoak, K. J., & Medin, D. L. (Eds.). (1996). *Causal learning*. San Diego, CA: Academic Press.

MORAL DEVELOPMENT

Morality is a controversial topic and a source of debate in philosophy and psychology. One source of argumentation is due to different perspectives on whether morality is a matter of mind or heart or, to put it differently, reason or emotion. From the point of view of how morality develops in individuals, debates often center on whether children incorporate teachings from adults (representing societal values and standards) or construct ways of thinking about social relationships that entail understandings of issues pertaining to welfare, justice, and rights. Corresponding debates are over whether morality is a matter of habits or processes of reasoning.

The debates over morality parallel debates in psychology, other social sciences, and philosophy regarding the role of reasoning and its connections with emotions in human functioning. On one side are those who presume that, in most realms, people act out of habit or non-rationally. On the other side are approaches presuming that thought and reasoning are central. As succinctly put by the philosopher Martha Nussbaum (1999), "human beings are above all reasoning beings" (p. 71). To say that humans are reasoning beings doesn't, by any means, exclude emotions. Indeed, Nussbaum sees close links in that emotions do not stand alone or overwhelm thought, but are guided by ways of judging social relationships, are part of people's goals in life, and inform their understandings of other people and events. In such a framework, moral judgments include an integration of reasoning and emotions such as sympathy, empathy, compassion, and respect.

This entry focuses on approaches that have examined the development of moral reasoning, as integrated with emotions. First, the entry provides a historical overview describing early and influential theory and research on the development of moral judgments. It then describes research that modified those early theories through findings that young children construct moral judgments about welfare, justice, and rights, which they distinguish from the customs and conventions of society. Finally, the entry considers how moral and other types of social thought are involved in decision making.

Early Research on the Development of Moral Judgments

Jean Piaget presented in 1932 one of the first extensive analyses of the development of morality from such a framework in his classic work, *The Moral Judgment of the Child*. Piaget studied several dimensions of children's thinking about rules and justice. He studied children's judgments about the rules of marble games, lying, causing material damage, and punishments for wrongdoing. Piaget proposed that moral judgments constitute ways of thinking that take one form in early childhood and are transformed into another form of thinking by late childhood and adolescence. Specifically, he proposed that the development of moral judgments proceeds from a *heteronomous* to an *autonomous* level. At the level of heteronomous thinking, children are unable to take the perspectives of others and think in literal ways about rules and authority. They view rules as fixed and sacred and authority as requiring obedience. Heteronomy also involves an inability to distinguish the social from the physical, as well as an inability to take into account intentions or internal psychological states; hence, they judge by consequences rather than intentions. Emotions of fear, sympathy, and respect contribute to the heteronomous way of thinking. In particular, there is what Piaget referred to as unilateral respect for adult authority. A central feature of heteronomous thinking is that children do not distinguish or differentiate moral ideas from adherence to existing rules and customs or from obedience to authority.

According to Piaget, the shift to autonomous thinking involves differentiations of moral concepts pertaining to welfare and justice from existing customs, rules, and adherence to the commands of authorities. For this shift to occur, it is necessary for children to engage more in peer interactions and to focus less on adult-child interactions. Peer relationships promote both a sense of equality and abilities to understand the perspectives of others. At the autonomous level, children develop their own understandings of the purposes of rules and the roles of authority in social relationships entailing fairness, rights, and cooperation. Children are then better able to take the perspectives of others and distinguish moral aims based on welfare and justice from existing rules and customs. Unilateral respect is replaced by mutual respect by which there is concern with reciprocity in social relationships.

Autonomy does not mean that people are individualistic or concerned with the self or independence. Rather, it refers to participation in generating understandings of moral concepts that are applied to decisions as to how people should treat one another. One of the major subsequent contributions to this type of perspective came from Lawrence Kohlberg, who included children, adolescents, and young adults in his research. He proposed modifications in Piaget's propositions through formulations of the development of moral judgments that included six stages grouped into three levels. At the first level (labeled premoral), children are described as making moral judgments first on the basis of punishment (stage 1) and then on the basis of self-interest and prudence (stage 2). At the next level (conventional morality), moral concepts are not differentiated, first, from maintaining good relations and approval of others (stage 3) and then from the rules, conventions, and authority of social systems (stage 4). It is at the third level of postconventional morality, which presumably does not emerge until late adolescence or adulthood, that moral understandings of justice and rights are clearly differentiated from premoral and conventional understandings; moral judgments are based on concepts of social contract and agreement on procedures in application of laws (stage 5) and on moral principles of welfare, justice, and rights separate from particular social systems (stage 6).

Piaget and Kohlberg made some lasting contributions to the study of moral development. They charted a view of the psychology of morality that included substantive definitions of the moral domain. Many philosophers, including Immanuel Kant, John Stuart Mill, John Rawls, Ronald Dworkin, and Martha Nussbaum, have presented analytic formulations of concepts of justice (see especially John Rawls's influential treatise, *A Theory of Justice*), welfare, and rights. Piaget and Kohlberg demonstrated that the study of the psychology of morality could not be adequately conducted in the absence of sound definitions of this domain. They were, therefore, guided in their psychological research by philosophical conceptions as possibly involving the formation of substantive moral concepts (as opposed to research that only looked at psychological variables like learning, internalization of values, and personality traits).

Morality as Distinct From Other Domains

The work of Piaget and Kohlberg also demonstrated that children could be productively posed with problems regarding how people should relate to each other. However, subsequent research shows that the levels they proposed do not accurately capture children's moral judgments because the research tasks used were overly complex. Kohlberg, for instance, presented children with situations entailing conflicts with a number of features to consider. A well-known situation is the story of man who must decide whether to steal a drug he cannot afford to save the life of his wife who has cancer. The situation includes several components in conflict, including the value of life, property rights, law, and obligations in personal relationships. Other research has examined the judgments of children, adolescents, and adults about straightforward issues bearing on physical harm, psychological harm, theft, and fairness. This body of research, conducted by Elliot Turiel, Larry Nucci, Judith Smetana, Melanie Killen, Cecilia Wainryb, and Charles Helwig, first involved studies aimed at determining the criteria that children apply to moral and non-moral issues. In a large number of studies, children were presented with situations describing a transgression identified as part of the moral domain, such as one child physically assaulting another. They evaluated the acts and answered questions ascertaining if they considered the evaluation of the acts to be based on rules (e.g., what if there were no rule about it?), authority (e.g., what if the teacher said it was all right?), and common practice (e.g., what if it was generally accepted in a group or culture?). By 3 or 4 years of age, children's judgments about moral issues are not contingent on rules, authority dictates, or accepted practices. Acts that harm others or involve unequal treatment are evaluated as wrong even if there are no rules or an authority deems them acceptable. In addition, moral prescriptions are judged to generalize across social contexts. These judgments are based on understandings of welfare, justice, and rights. The research shows, however, that young children's concepts are primarily about harm or welfare, whereas older children develop concepts of justice and rights along with concerns with welfare. The development of moral judgments also involves increased capacities to relate concepts of welfare, justice, and rights to other considerations in complex situations.

It is well established that young children differentiate morality from punishment, obedience, authority, and interests of the self. Children distinguish the domain of morality from the domain of social conventions. Social conventions refer to existing regularities in social systems that coordinate social interactions (examples are customary practices about matters like forms of address, modes of dress, eating habits). At all ages, conventions are judged to be contingent on rules, authority, and common practices. Moreover, children form ways of thinking about the personal domain, which pertains to arenas of personal jurisdiction that do not involve impinging on the welfare or rights of others.

Children develop distinct ways of thinking in the moral, conventional, and personal domains. The domains constitute different developmental pathways, with age-related changes within each domain. Observational studies in homes and schools also show that social interactions around moral events differ from interactions around conventional events. Interactions associated with moral events typically do not involve communications about rules or expectations of adults (which do occur for conventional events), but are about feelings and the perspectives of those involved, as well as communications

about harm and fairness. The development of moral judgments is associated with the early emergence of emotions like sympathy, empathy, and respect.

Moral and Social Decision Making

The existence of different domains of social reasoning has implications for explanations of how people make decisions in social situations. In coming to decisions, people take into account different domains, different considerations within the moral domain, and different priorities. Two examples—honesty and rights—illustrate the process of coordinating different considerations in coming to decisions. Honesty is generally considered morally right and necessary to maintain trust. However, in some circumstances, honesty is not necessarily the morally correct course of action. An example discussed in philosophical discourse is a situation in which lying might be necessary to save a life. In this regard, it has been found that physicians judge deception of medical insurance companies acceptable when it is the only means to obtain treatment for a patient with a serious condition. They give priority to preventing harm over honesty. Other studies have shown that adolescents consider it acceptable to defy and deceive parents who direct their offspring to engage in acts considered morally wrong. Deception of parents is also judged acceptable when they direct activities seen as part of adolescents' legitimate personal choices. Similar results of the coordination of honesty and moral or personal considerations have been obtained in research on adults' judgments regarding marital relationships. Similarly, coordination of different considerations is seen in decisions about rights like freedom of speech and religion. Although children and adults endorse rights, in many situations they subordinate rights to matters like preventing harm or promoting community interests.

To understand moral and social decision making, it is necessary to examine the different domains of thought that people apply to social situations. Therefore, the study of moral development requires examination of social and personal domains, as well as the moral domain.

Elliot Turiel

See also Concepts, Development of; Emotion and Moral Judgment; Folk Psychology; Knowledge Acquisition in Development; Social Cognition

Further Readings

Killen, M., & Smetana, J. G. (2006). *Handbook of moral development.* Mahwah, NJ: Erlbaum.

Kohlberg, L. (1984). *Essays on moral development: Vol. 2. The psychology of moral development.* San Francisco, CA: Harper & Row.

Nussbaum, M. C. (1999). *Sex and social justice.* New York, NY: Oxford University Press.

Piaget, J. (1932). *The moral judgment of the child.* London, UK: Routledge & Kegan Paul.

Rawls, J. (1971). *A theory of justice.* Cambridge, MA: Harvard University Press.

Turiel, E. (2002). *The culture of morality: Social development, context, and conflict.* Cambridge, UK: Cambridge University Press.

MOTIVATED THINKING

Once controversial, the notion that people's motivations can influence their thoughts now features prominently within many areas of psychology and plays an important role in current research on memory, reasoning, decision making, and perception. The effects of motivation on cognition can be conceptualized as stemming from three general sources: (a) motivations to use particular types of judgment strategies (e.g., a focus on minimizing missed opportunities versus eliminating mistakes); (b) motivations to achieve broad, content-independent (*nondirectional*) types of judgment outcomes (e.g., decisions as concise and unambiguous, or as accurate as possible); and (c) motivations to achieve narrow, content-dependent (*directional*) types of judgment outcomes (e.g., impressions of oneself as successful or loved). Whereas motivations for judgment strategies primarily affect the quality of cognitive processing that occurs, and motivations for nondirectional judgment outcomes primarily affect the quantity of processing, motivations for directional judgment outcomes often affect both the quality and quantity of processing. Thus, in addition to being "cognitive misers" whose biases result from generally limited cognitive processing capacity, people are also "motivated tacticians" whose biases result from specific changes in cognitive processing that serve their current goals.

Strategy-Motivated Thinking

Motivations for particular judgment strategies can arise from many different concerns, but those most thoroughly examined relate to concerns with attaining growth (*promotion*) or maintaining security (*prevention*). Promotion motivations produce gain-oriented strategies focused on achieving advancement, whereas prevention motivations produce loss-oriented strategies focused on maintaining a satisfactory state. Promotion motivations thus elicit inclusive modes of cognitive processing to identify opportunities for gain, whereas prevention motivations elicit exclusive modes of cognitive processing to minimize losses. For example, when promotion-focused, people consider a broader variety of explanations during causal reasoning, engage in more creative and divergent thinking during problem solving, and attend more to abstract and global properties of a stimulus. In contrast, when prevention-focused, people consider a narrower selection of causal explanations, engage in more analytical and convergent thinking, and attend more to concrete and local stimulus properties. Thus, motivated judgment strategies can influence the quality of cognitive processing that occurs across many domains.

Nondirectional Outcome-Motivated Thinking

Beyond motivations to use particular judgment strategies people may also have motivations to reach particular judgment outcomes. Some types of outcome motivations have been labeled nondirectional because they do not involve specific desired conclusions and focus on more general objectives during judgment. The two most-studied nondirectional outcome motivations are desires for accuracy and desires for *closure* (conciseness, clarity). Because these desires do not concern the specific contents of a judgment, they primarily affect the quantity rather than the quality of cognitive processing that occurs. Whereas desires for accuracy increase how many explanations people consider during causal reasoning, the effort they dedicate to evidence evaluation and information search, and how much information they retrieve from memory, desires for closure have the opposite effect. Accordingly, judgment complexity increases with desires for accuracy and decreases with desires for closure, whereas simple reliance on recently or frequently activated knowledge during judgment increases with desires for closure and decreases with desires for accuracy. However, these processing differences do not always result in more valid conclusions when motivated by accuracy.

Because of limitations in cognitive resources or access to necessary information, biases can remain even when accuracy motivation is active. Thus, desires for accuracy or closure affect the quantity of cognitive processing during judgment more than they affect how good a judgment is made.

Directional Outcome-Motivated Thinking

Other types of motivations for particular judgment outcomes have been labeled directional because they do specify particular desired conclusions. Directional outcome motivations include people's desires to believe they are competent, socially connected, and in control. Whatever the desired conclusion, directional outcome motivations affect cognitive processing in two ways: They alter the quality of cognitive processing in ways that selectively highlight evidence for this conclusion, or they alter the quantity of cognitive processing such that evidence for this conclusion is accepted after only a cursory review but evidence opposing this conclusion is thoroughly scrutinized.

Some examples of quality-related effects are that desires for perceptions of competence encourage explanations that accept responsibility for success but not failure, encoding and activation of knowledge that emphasizes potential for success, and selecting standards of comparison that imply higher levels of ability. Similarly, desires for perceptions of social connection encourage explanations that diminish relationship conflict, encoding and activation of knowledge that emphasizes commonalities with valued others, and selecting standards of comparison that imply higher levels of belonging. Some examples of quantity-related effects are that desires for perceptions of competence encourage more thorough processing of competence-threatening feedback and generation of more hypotheses undermining such feedback. Similarly, desires for perceptions of personal control encourage an extended analysis of evidence that contradicts individuals' basic understanding of how the world works.

Although common and extensive, effects of directional outcome motivations do have limits. Whatever their motives, people still recognize they must meet standards of objectivity while forming judgments. Thus, directional outcome motivations have the strongest influence when the evidence is uncertain or ambiguous, and typically function to intensify judgments that support prior beliefs rather than produce new conclusions.

Influences of motivation on cognition are pervasive, and studying these influences provides important insights into the human mind. Having settled the first-generation question of "Does motivated thinking occur?" research on strategic, nondirectional, and directional motivation is now considering second-generation questions of when and how effects of motivations on cognitive processing arise. Answers to such questions will provide a deeper understanding of the motivation-cognition interface and further advance the field of cognitive science.

Daniel C. Molden and E. Tory Higgins

See also Cognitive Dissonance; Debiasing; Decision Making and Reward, Computational Perspectives; Placebo Effect

Further Readings

Kruglanski, A. W. (1996). Motivated social cognition: Principles of the interface. In E. T. Higgins & A. W. Kruglanski (Eds.), *Social psychology: Handbook of basic principles* (pp. 493–520). New York, NY: Guilford Press.

Kunda, Z. (1990). The case for motivated reasoning. *Psychological Bulletin, 108*, 480–498.

Molden, D. C., & Higgins, E. T. (2005). Motivated thinking. In K. Holyoak & B. Morrison (Eds.), *Handbook of thinking and reasoning* (pp. 295–320). New York, NY: Cambridge University Press.

MOTOR LEARNING, PRACTICAL ASPECTS

Motor skills are an essential part of our lives. From toddlers attempting to walk, children throwing and catching balls, young adults learning to ski, to older adults or those with physical disabilities trying to regain walking and balance capabilities—throughout our lifetime, we learn and perform motor skills. Even though motor skills vary widely in type and complexity, the learning process that individuals go through when acquiring various motor skills is similar. During the first phase (so-called cognitive stage), considerable cognitive activity and attentional capacity is required, and movements tend to be controlled in a relatively conscious manner. The result of using conscious control strategies is that the movement is relatively slow, fragmented, and inefficient and that the outcome is rather inconsistent. The second phase of learning (associative stage) is characterized by subtle movement adjustments. The movement outcome is more reliable, and the performance is more consistent from trial to trial. Inefficient muscular co-contractions are gradually reduced, and the movement becomes more economical. In addition, at least parts of the movement are controlled more automatically. After extensive practice, the performer reaches the autonomous stage, which is characterized by fluent and seemingly effortless motions. Movements are accurate, with few or no errors, consistent, and efficient. The skill is performed largely automatically at this stage, and movement execution requires little or no attention.

How can the learning process be facilitated and individuals' ability to perform or maintain those skills be enhanced? This is a question that interests practitioners (e.g., coaches, physical therapists, athletes, musicians) and theorists alike. Studies have identified a number of factors that influence learning. Yet, the functioning of those factors has been viewed mainly from an information processing perspective. Only recently has it become clear that the learning process is not merely the acquisition of a specific movement pattern that is facilitated by providing learners with the right information at the right time. Learning also encompasses affective reactions, the self-regulation of cognitive processes, and attentional focus to meet task demands. This is particularly relevant in the natural and almost inevitably social context of movement. Thus, both the learner's informational and motivational needs have to be optimized to enhance learning.

To help learners acquire the goal movement pattern and reach a state of automaticity, they are typically provided with *demonstrations, instructions,* and *feedback.* The following sections discuss how the effectiveness of these learning variables can be enhanced by taking into account both their informational and motivational roles. When considering learning, it is important to keep in mind that learning is assumed to reflect a relatively permanent change in a person's capability to perform motor skills. Therefore, in experimental studies, learning is typically assessed in retention or transfer tests (the latter involve a variation of the task), performed under the same conditions for all groups and at a given time interval following practice under different conditions of interest.

Demonstrations

Demonstrations (e.g., live or video presentations of a model) are often used in practical settings to provide the learner with an idea of the goal movement.

Studies have shown that learning through observation is effective, especially if it is combined with physical practice. Observational practice appears to be particularly beneficial for the learning of complex motor skills, and combined observational and physical practice can be more effective than physical practice alone. It has been argued that observation gives learners the unique opportunity to extract important information concerning appropriate coordination patterns or subtle task requirements, or to evaluate the effectiveness of strategies—which would be difficult or impossible to do while executing the movement. From that perspective, observational practice offers the learner a chance to conduct information processing that could not occur while physically practicing.

Demonstrations can involve expert models or another learner (learning model). Observing a learning model can be as effective as observing an expert, particularly when two learners practice in a dyad (pair) and alternate between physical and observational practice. In some studies, dyad practice resulted in more effective learning than individual (physical) practice—even though dyad participants had only half the number of physical practice trials that participants in the individual, physical practice group received. Aside from the information gained by observing another learner, learning benefits of dyad practice are presumably also a result of enhanced motivation, resulting perhaps from competition with the partner, the setting of higher goals, or the loss of self-consciousness as people fulfill interdependent dyadic roles and find another in the same learning boat. It is perhaps not coincidental that participants in collaborative or cooperative learning situations often anecdotally report more enjoyment than they have experienced learning alone.

Thus, interspersing physical practice with demonstrations can make an important contribution to skill learning. Considering the high costs of certain types of training (e.g., pilot training, medical education, physical therapy), the incorporation of demonstrations, dyadic, or collaborative practice, may not only be cost-efficient but can also enhance the effectiveness of training.

Instructions

Focus of Attention

Studies have shown that the wording of instructions has an important impact on performance and learning. Specifically, instructions directing attention to performers' movements (inducing a so-called internal focus) are relatively ineffective. In contrast, directing attention to the effect of their movements on the environment, such as on an implement (inducing an external focus), generally results in more effective performance and learning. For instance, focusing on the swing of a golf club has been demonstrated to lead to greater shot accuracy than focusing on the swing of one's arms. On tasks involving balance, focusing on the movements of the support surface results in greater stability than focusing on the movement of one's feet. The learning advantages of instructions promoting an external focus have been shown for a variety of motor skills, levels of expertise, and populations (including children and persons with motor impairments).

An external focus of attention appears to speed up the learning process, or shorten the first stages of learning, facilitating movement automaticity. In contrast, a focus on one's own movements results in a more conscious type of control that constrains the motor system and disrupts automatic control processes (constrained action hypothesis). Movement efficiency has also been shown to be enhanced by an external focus. The mere mention within the internal focus instructions of the performer's body may act to increase self-consciousness, or self-focus, which, in turn, may lead to self-evaluation and activate implicit or explicit self-regulatory processes in attempts to manage thoughts and affective responses.

Conceptions of Ability

Individuals' beliefs about, or conceptions of, key abilities have been shown to affect the learning of motor skills. Specifically, whether people view their ability as something that is genetically determined (i.e., reflecting a fixed capacity or "talent") versus something that is amenable to change with practice influences their motivation and learning. Even though most adults have certain ability conceptions, these can also be influenced by instructions given in a learning situation. Some researchers have manipulated those conceptions to assess their influence on individuals' motivation and performance of motor skills. In these studies, ability concepts were induced through instructions depicting performance on the task as something that reflected either an inherent ability or an acquirable skill. Learners who viewed the task as an acquirable skill, as opposed to reflecting an inherent capacity, showed greater self-efficacy,

more positive affective self-reactions, greater interest in the task, as well as more effective learning and greater automaticity in movement control.

The construction of a task as something that reveals one's inherent capacity may act as a threat to one's ego. Learners who view a task as a reflection of an inherent ability presumably approach the learning situation with more apprehension than those who see task performance as an acquirable skill. This, in turn, may hinder the learning process compared with a situation that is regarded by the performer simply as a learning opportunity. Similar to other variables (e.g., attentional focus and normative feedback), a person's ability conception appears to affect the extent to which he or she becomes self-conscious—with concomitant effects on motor performance and learning.

Feedback

Frequency of Feedback

Views regarding the role of feedback (knowledge of results, knowledge of performance) in motor learning have changed considerably over the past century. Whereas early researchers believed that feedback should be given frequently and immediately after the movement, this notion changed in 1984 when Alan Salmoni, Richard Schmidt, and Charles Walter proposed the guidance hypothesis. According to this hypothesis, feedback guides the learner to the correct movement pattern, while at the same time carrying the risk that—if provided frequently, immediately after, or even concurrently with, the movement—learners might become dependent on it, thereby failing to develop the capability of detecting and correcting errors themselves. In addition, the learning of a stable movement representation has been assumed to be made more difficult by frequent feedback, due to increased variability in performance in the learner's attempts to correct errors. Numerous subsequent studies have provided support for those assumptions, for example, by showing that reducing the feedback frequency or delaying feedback can be beneficial for learning.

However, recent findings suggest that detrimental effects of frequent or immediate feedback may occur primarily when the feedback induces an internal focus (i.e., directs attention to the body movements). If the feedback promotes an external focus (i.e., directs attention to the desired movement effect), a high frequency has been shown to be more effective than a reduced feedback frequency—presumably because it helps learners maintain an external focus. Even concurrent feedback can be beneficial for learning if it induces an external focus.

Self-Controlled Feedback

Having learners decide after which trials they want, or do not want, to receive feedback has been demonstrated to lead to more effective learning than predetermined feedback schedules. The percentage of practice trials on which self-control learners requested feedback varied widely between studies. Yet, the actual feedback frequency appears less important than the learner's ability to choose, or not to choose, feedback. Self-controlled practice conditions have generally been assumed to lead to a more active involvement of the learner, enhancing motivation and increasing the effort invested in practice. Self-controlled feedback might also produce better correspondence to learners' needs for information about their performance, such as after a strategy change, or allow them to ask for feedback after presumably successful (more motivating) trials.

Positive Feedback

Feedback after "good" trials has been demonstrated to enhance learning compared to feedback after "poor" trials. In studies in which learners were provided with feedback after blocks of trials, groups who received feedback about their best trials in that block (and not about the worst trials) showed superior learning compared to those who received feedback about their worst trials (and not about their best trials). It is interesting that, in studies on self-controlled feedback, learners indicated that they preferred to receive feedback—and chose feedback—more frequently after relatively successful trials. This may be another reason for the learning benefits of self-controlled feedback.

Similarly, positive or negative normative feedback can affect learning. Normative feedback involves norms such as a peer group's actual or bogus average performance scores. Thus, normative feedback, by definition, involves social comparison—a ubiquitous phenomenon in settings that involve the performance and learning of readily observable motor skill or lack thereof. In studies in which learners were provided with a (fabricated) average score of other performers, in addition to their own score, it was found that learning was positively or negatively affected depending on whether learners were led to believe that their performance was above or below average. Specifically, the conviction that one's performance was better than average was associated with more effective skill learning than the belief that one's performance was below average—essentially resulting in a self-fulfilling prophecy.

Positive or negative performance feedback presumably influences the cognitive perception of personal capability (e.g., self-efficacy expectations, perceived competence) and creates positive or negative affect experienced for the self. Self-efficacy expectations, in turn, may influence individuals' goal setting, effort, and attention to task performance. Recent neuroscientific evidence links positive affect to the dopamine processing that supports sequence learning. Negative affect may also dampen, or interfere with, memory processing.

Gabriele Wulf and Rebecca Lewthwaite

See also Automaticity; Skill Learning, Enhancement of

Further Readings

Salmoni, A. W., Schmidt, R. A., & Walter, C. B. (1984). Knowledge of results and motor learning: A review and critical reappraisal. *Psychological Bulletin, 95,* 355–386.

Schmidt, R. A., & Lee, T. D. (2005). *Motor control and learning* (4th ed.). Champaign, IL: Human Kinetics.

Wulf, G. (2007). *Attention and motor skill learning.* Champaign, IL: Human Kinetics.

MOTOR SYSTEM, DEVELOPMENT OF

Motor development involves advances in behavior across the entire body—the eyes and head for looking, the trunk for maintaining a stable postural base, the arms and hands for manual actions, and the limbs for locomotion. Development entails increasing coordination between active muscle forces and passive gravitational and inertial forces. However, there is more to the study of motor development than muscles and biomechanics. Goal-directed movement is inextricably linked with perception, cognition, and social interaction, and motor skill acquisition includes developmental changes in all of these domains. This entry summarizes four critical aspects of motor development: Movement is ubiquitous, prospective, creative, and malleable.

Movement Is Ubiquitous

Movement is the most pervasive and fundamental of all psychological activity. The body is constantly in motion. Some movements occur in the background (breathing, swallowing, postural compensations), some are spontaneous by-products of arousal and brain activity (twitches, shakes, flails), and some are goal-directed (looking, talking, reaching, walking). The massive amounts and variety of children's motor experiences facilitate discovery of new skills and their improvement. New forms of movement also set the stage for changes in other psychological domains by creating new opportunities to explore the environment and engage in social interactions. Movements in the face and throat make possible behaviors that are fundamental for life, such as sucking, chewing, and swallowing; those required to produce speech are among the most sophisticated movements learned by humans.

The first self-produced movements occur prenatally. Fetuses nod and turn their heads, open and close their jaws, yawn, suck, and swallow amniotic fluid. They wrinkle their foreheads, move their lips and tongue, and, after 25 weeks, open and close their eyes. Whole body movements and large movements of the arms and legs peak at 14 to 16 weeks postconception, then decrease as the growing body fills the uterine space. Some fetal movements are not random: Fetuses direct hand movements toward their own faces and bodies, the wall of the uterus, and the umbilical cord.

The sheer amount of movement is staggering. By 3.5 months of age, infants have performed 3 to 6 million eye movements. By 10 months, infants have accumulated enough crawling steps to travel more than half the length of Manhattan. By 12 months, infants have experienced over 110,000 bouts of wiggles, waves, kicks, and flaps of 47 different types of spontaneous stereotypies. At 14 months of age, infants take about 15,000 walking steps per day. Sleep does not quiet newborns' active bodies. While sleeping, they stretch, roll, wave, and twitch.

Actions Are Prospective

For motor actions to be adaptive, they must be controlled prospectively—guided into the future based on perceptual information about the body and environment. Even the simplest movements of the head and limbs require anticipation of disruptions to a stable postural base. Perceptual feedback from just prior movements informs the consequences of future actions.

Infants' earliest actions show inklings of prospectivity. At 1 month of age, infants predict the trajectory of a moving target and smoothly follow it with their eyes, but prospective control is fragile and easily disrupted. The target must be large and slow moving or eye movements will lag behind. The development of prospective looking is protracted over several months. By 4 to 5 months of age, predictive looking is sufficiently stable for infants to track targets moving behind an occluder, so that their eyes wait on the far side to spot the target when it reappears.

As with looking, the development of prehension involves increasing prospectivity. In general, infants demonstrate prospective control of looking before reaching, and once they can reach, they frequently bring objects to their eyes for visual inspection. Newborns are highly motivated to keep their hands in view. In a dim room illuminated with only a narrow shaft of light, newborns move their hand when the light beam moves and slow their arm movements before the hand arrives in the light, rather than after their hand appears. Reaching for stationary objects appears at 12 weeks and intercepting moving objects appears at 18 weeks, but infants' first reaches and catches are jerky and crooked. Infants' arms speed up, slow down, and change directions several times before the hand finally contacts the toy. After a few months, reaches and catches become more adult-like, with one large movement to bring the hand near the target and a subsequent smaller movement to grasp it. Infants reach for glowing objects in the dark at the same age that they reach in the light, suggesting that they can gauge the location and size of the object and use muscle-joint information about arm position to guide the reach. By 9 months, infants pre-orient their hands to grasp in the dark. By 11 months, infants catch moving objects as they appear from behind an occluder.

Prospective control of locomotion also takes months to develop. When approaching a sheer drop-off or steep slope, novice crawlers and walkers plunge right over the edge. After several weeks of locomotor experience, they guide locomotion prospectively by using perceptual information gathered from exploratory looking and touching to decide when cliffs and slopes are safe or risky. With sufficient experience, infants—like adults—can adapt locomotor actions to changes in the environment and in their own bodies and skills. For example, when experimenters load experienced toddlers with lead-weighted shoulder-packs to make their bodies more top-heavy, infants instantly recalibrate their judgments of risky slopes to their new, restricted abilities. They correctly treat the same slopes as risky while wearing lead-filled shoulder-packs and safe while wearing feather-filled shoulder-packs.

The ability to create new possibilities for action with tools also requires prospective control, but before 1 year of age, infants have difficulty planning tool use strategies. For example, 9-month-olds grab a spoon by the bowl-end instead of the handle or hold it with the bowl pointing away from their mouths. They correct grasp errors reactively by switching hands or awkwardly rotating their hand to bring the bowl to their mouth. By 18 months of age, infants know which end of a tool to grasp, how to grasp it, and how to plan their motor actions in advance, but they are still inefficient when using a tool to act on another object (hairbrush on doll) rather than performing an action centered on their own body (hairbrush on self). By 24 months of age, infants prospectively adjust their typical strategies to use tools in a novel way, such as gripping a spoon with a bent handle to scoop food from a bowl.

Solutions Are Creative and Enlist a Variety of Means

The movements of infants (and novices of any age) are notoriously variable and unreliable, whereas movements of adults and experts are smooth and consistent. Over weeks of practice, infants' visual scanning patterns, reaches, and steps become increasingly efficient, reliable, and predictable. However, all infants do not solve the problem of moving their bodies in the same way. More lethargic infants learn to reach by powering up the muscle forces; more lively infants hone reaching skills by dampening down inertial forces from ongoing arm flaps.

Variety in infants' spontaneous exploration provides information about objects and surfaces and about the efficacy of the self in control. Spontaneous leg kicks in 2- to 4-month-olds transform into deliberate one-legged, alternating, or simultaneous two-legged kicks as infants explore the contingencies between their movements and the jiggling of an overhead mobile yoked to their legs. By the second half of the first year, infants explore the sound-making properties of objects and surfaces and eventually bang the hard side of objects against the hard side of a tabletop. Visual, manual, and oral exploration are coordinated into bouts of rotating, fingering, and mouthing objects.

Variable routes to development suggest that individual infants explore multiple solutions before settling on the most efficient solution. For example, prior to crawling on hands and knees, infants display a variety of locomotor strategies. They hitch in a sitting position, crab on their backs, and log roll. Belly crawling is so variable that infants change the configuration of limbs used for support and propulsion and the timing between limbs from cycle to cycle. Infants move ipsilateral limbs together like a camel, move contralateral arms and legs together in a near-trot, lift front then back limbs like a bunny hop, and "swim" with all four limbs lifted into the air at once.

When the constraints of infants' growing bodies and nascent skills preclude adultlike solutions, infants find temporary "placeholder" actions that get the job done. Although 12-month-olds chew well enough to break down food and swallow it, they chew with lateral rather than rotary jaw movements. It takes years before the lips and tongue are involved and cooperating in a planful and deliberate way and before rotary movements are incorporated into the chewing action. Moreover, infants chew the same way for every kind of food, whereas older children flexibly adapt their jaw movements to the food consistency and to the emergence of new teeth and molars. Even habitual actions such as moving the bolus to a consistent "working" side of the mouth take years to develop.

Sometimes infants' ignorance about conventional motor solutions opens up new means for solving motor dilemmas. When challenged to cross narrow bridges with only a wobbly rubber handrail for support, 16-month-olds use a "light touch" strategy, grazing their hands along the rail to generate somatosensory information for controlling posture, and a "heavy touch" strategy, where they exploit the deformability of the handrail to rappel as if mountain climbing or lean back as if wind surfing. When faced with impossibly steep slopes, infants descend in a conventional sitting position but also slide down backward feet first or head first with arms outstretched like Superman.

Development Is Malleable

Traditionally, motor development was described as a universal series of stages with little deviation in order and timing. However, the apparently invariant sequence resulted from ordering normative data by average onset ages. In actuality, infants acquire skills such as rolling, sitting, crawling, cruising, walking, and stair ascent and descent in a large variety of orders, and infants can skip "optional" skills such as crawling and cruising.

Moreover, onset ages are extremely malleable. True experiments with random assignment to treatment and control groups and historical/cultural differences in child-rearing practices show that the age at acquisition of motor skills can be hugely accelerated with practice and delayed with lack of opportunity. For example, 3-month-olds normally lack the motor skill to grasp and manipulate objects. But after practice wearing "sticky mittens" with Velcro-covered palms as they play with Velcro-edged toys, 3-month-olds pick up toys and explore them as well as 5-month-olds who have acquired their manual skills naturally. With a few minutes of daily practice moving their legs in an upright position, infants begin walking at younger ages than infants in a control group who received only passive experiences moving their legs.

"Natural" experiments resulting from differences in how caregivers hold, carry, bathe, dress, exercise, and toilet their infants provide additional evidence for malleability. In some regions of Africa, the Caribbean, and India, caregivers vigorously massage and exercise infants as part of daily bathing routines, stretching infants' limbs, tossing them into the air, and propping them into sitting and walking positions. Infants who receive massage and exercise begin sitting and walking at earlier ages than infants who do not. Infants with stairs in their home learn to ascend stairs at a younger age than children without stairs in their home.

Lack of opportunity to practice movements has the opposite effect. In northern China, the practice of toileting infants by laying them on their backs in sandbags for most of the day delays the onset of sitting, crawling, and walking by several months.

In the United States, the recent practice of putting infants to sleep on their backs rather than their stomachs has resulted in delayed onset of crawling and other prone skills. In cultures that do not encourage crawling (including American infants circa 1900), large proportions of infants skip crawling altogether, either bum-shuffling or proceeding straight to walking.

Karen E. Adolph and Sarah E. Berger

See also Motor Learning, Practical Aspects

Further Readings

Adolph, K. E., & Berger, S. E. (2005). Physical and motor development. In M. H. Bornstein & M. E. Lamb (Eds.), *Developmental science: An advanced textbook* (5th ed., pp. 223–281). Mahwah, NJ: Erlbaum.

Adolph, K. E., & Berger, S. E. (2006). Motor development. In W. Damon & R. Lerner (Eds.), *Handbook of child psychology: Vol. 2. Cognition, perception, and language* (D. Kuhn & R. S. Siegler [Vol. Eds.]) (6th ed., pp. 161–213). New York, NY: Wiley.

Bertenthal, B. I., & Clifton, R. K. (1998). Perception and action. In W. Damon & R. Lerner (Eds.), *Handbook of child psychology: Vol. 2. Cognition, perception, and language* (D. Kuhn & R. S. Siegler [Vol. Eds.]) (5th ed., pp. 51–102). New York, NY: Wiley.

Campos, J. J., Anderson, D. I., Barbu-Roth, M. A., Hubbard, E. M., Hertenstein, M. J., & Witherington, D. C. (2000). Travel broadens the mind. *Infancy, 1,* 149–219.

Gibson, E. J. (1988). Exploratory behavior in the development of perceiving, acting and the acquiring of knowledge. *Annual Review of Psychology, 39,* 1–41.

Gibson, E. J., & Pick, A. D. (2000). *An ecological approach to perceptual learning and development.* New York, NY: Oxford University Press.

Thelen, E., & Smith, L. B. (1994). *A dynamic systems approach to the development of cognition and action.* Cambridge, MA: MIT Press.

von Hofsten, C. (2004). An action perspective on motor development. *Trends in Cognitive Sciences, 8,* 266–272.

MULTIMODAL CONVERSATIONAL SYSTEMS

Multimodal conversational systems are computer systems that engage human users in intelligent conversation through speech and other modalities such as gesture and gaze. These systems are motivated largely by human-human conversation, where nonverbal communication modalities such as hand gestures, body postures, eye gaze, head movements, and facial expressions are used to complement spoken language. Studies have shown that multimodal conversational systems provide more natural and effective human-machine interaction compared to speech-only systems. This entry provides a brief overview of the types of systems, their general architecture, and key components of automated multimodal interpretation and generation in such systems.

Types of Systems

A variety of multimodal conversational systems have been developed in the past 3 decades. They range from multimodal conversational interfaces to embodied conversational agents and to more recent situated dialogue agents. Multimodal conversational interfaces address interaction with interfaces from computers or other devices (e.g., handheld devices). A user can look at the interface, point to regions on the interface, and talk to the system. These types of interfaces are particularly useful for map-based applications. Embodied conversational agents (also called virtual humans) allow users to carry on conversations with virtual embodied agents (often life-size virtual agents) through multiple modalities such as speech, facial expressions, hand gesture, and head movement. These types of systems are often applied in the domain of cultural training, tutoring, and education. Situated dialogue agents represent a new generation of dialogue agents that are co-present with human partners in a shared world, which could be virtual or physical. In situated dialogue (e.g., human-robot dialogue), the perception of the shared environment and the mobility and embodiment of the partners play an important role in success of the dialogue. In these systems, language processing needs to be combined with vision processing, gesture recognition, and situation modeling. Situated dialogue in virtual worlds can be applied in the domains of interactive games, training, and education, while dialogue in the physical world can benefit a range of applications involving human-robot interaction.

System Architecture

Most multimodal dialogue systems share a similar architecture with four major components: multimodal interpreter, dialogue manager, action manager, and multimodal generator, as shown in Figure 1. The multimodal interpreter is responsible for combining different modalities and identifying the semantic meanings of user multimodal input. Based on the understanding of user intent, the dialogue manager decides what to do in response, for example, ask for clarification or provide information requested by the user. Once this decision has been made, the action manager takes charge of any required backend processes, such as retrieving relevant information. The multimodal generator uses the gathered information to produce specific responses such as multimedia presentations on graphical interfaces or multimodal conversational behaviors for embodied agents. Each of these components is critical to the overall performance of a multimodal conversational system. The multimodal interpreter and generator are the two important components unique to multimodal conversational systems in contrast to traditional spoken dialogue systems.

Multimodal Interpretation

The capability to process and identify semantic meanings from user multimodal inputs is one of the most critical components in multimodal conversational systems. A large body of research has focused on how different modalities are aligned, how different modalities and/or shared visual environments can be integrated to derive an overall semantic representation (such as user intent), and how nonverbal modalities may improve spoken language understanding.

When interpreting human input such as speech, the first step is to automatically recognize what has been communicated (e.g., through speech recognition) and to represent this information as several recognition hypotheses. Previous studies by Sharon Oviatt have shown that using complementary modalities such as speech and pen-based gestures can improve selection of the best recognition hypothesis through mutual disambiguation. Many approaches have been developed for integrating different modalities. For example, rule-based methods and finite state machines have been applied to unify semantic structures from individual modalities based on

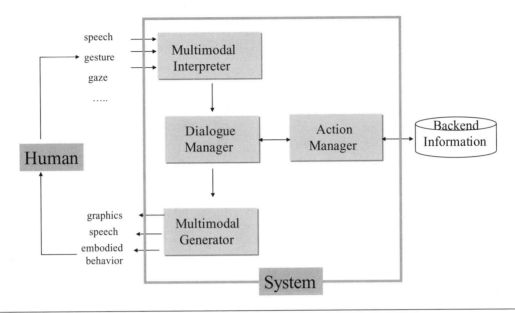

Figure I   A general architecture for multimodal conversational systems

multimodal grammar (e.g., grammar that encodes temporal relationships between pen-based gestures and linguistic units). Probabilistic approaches have been used to merge semantic representations from individual modalities based on constrained optimization (e.g., minimizing or maximizing an objective function based on a set of constraints).

Psycholinguistic studies have shown that human eye gaze reflects attention and engagement. Eye gaze is tightly linked with human language processing. Recent advances in eye tracking technology have made it possible to incorporate human eye gaze during human-computer interaction. Studies have shown that incorporating eye gaze in a conversational interface improves automated language understanding at multiple levels, from speech recognition and reference resolution to automated language acquisition.

Multimodal Generation

Different types of multimodal conversational systems require different capabilities for multimodal generation. In conversational interfaces, graphical visualization is important to provide better access to, and allow better understanding of, the requested information. Thus, multimodal generation is mostly concerned with how to automatically plan, allocate,

coordinate, and present multimedia information, for example, with synchronized graphical and speech output. In systems with embodied conversational agents, automated generation of multimodal behaviors is a major research focus. In addition to natural language generation and speech synthesis, recent work also generates synchronized facial expressions to reflect the different emotional states of an agent, models eye gaze and head nodding to indicate grounding, enables hand gestures to indicate emphasis, and produces shifts in posture to signal the beginning or ending of a conversational turn or segment. The same issues concerning behavior generation are also applied to situated dialogue agents where agents/robots often have physical bodies (e.g., head, face, arms, etc.) which require hardware configurations. To address the challenges of integrating multiple modalities and generating natural interactive behaviors for embodied agents, representation languages (e.g., behavior markup language) are developed to describe behavior elements (e.g., individual modalities such as head, gesture, gaze, speech, etc.) and synchronization of behaviors to control an agent.

In summary, computational models and approaches in multimodal conversational systems are developed based on empirical observations of human-machine interaction and are guided by the cognitive and communicative principles in human-human conversation. Research advances are made possible by contributions from multiple disciplines, including psychology, cognitive science, linguistics, and computer science and engineering. With synergistic collaboration among these disciplines, further technological advancement is anticipated. This will benefit a wide range of applications from information search and task assistance, to training, education, and entertainment.

Joyce Chai

See also Conversation and Dialogue; Gesture and Language Processing; Machine Speech Recognition; Natural Language Generation; Speech Perception

Further Readings

Cassell, J. (2001). Embodied conversational agents: Representation and intelligence in user interface. *AI Magazine, 22*(3), 67–83.

Chai, J., Prasov, Z., & Qu, S. (2006). Cognitive principles in robust multimodal interpretation. *Journal of Artificial Intelligence Research, 27,* 55–83.

Kuppevelt, J., Dybkjaer, L., & Bernsen N. O. (Eds.). (2005). *Advances in natural multimodal dialogue systems.* New York, NY: Springer.

Oviatt, S. L. (2002). Breaking the robustness barrier: Recent progress on the design of robust multimodal systems. *Advances in Computers, 56,* 305–341.

Qu, S., & Chai, J. Y. (2010). Context-based word acquisition for situated dialogue in a virtual world. *Journal of Artificial Intelligence Research, 37,* 347–377.

Traum, D., & Rickel, J. (2002). Embodied agents for multi-party dialogue in immersive virtual world. *Proceedings of the First International Joint Conference on Autonomous Agents and Multi-Agent Systems* (pp. 766–773). New York, NY: Association for Computing Machinery.

MULTINOMIAL MODELING

Multinomial modeling is a formal approach to measuring cognitive processes, such as the capacity to store and retrieve items in memory, or to make inferences and logical deductions, or to discriminate and categorize similar stimuli. Although such processes are not directly observable, theoretically they can be assumed to interact in certain ways to determine observable behaviors. The goal of multinomial modeling is to identify which underlying factors are important in a cognitive task, explain how those processes combine to create observable behavior, and then use experimental data to estimate the relative contributions of the different cognitive factors. In this way, multinomial models can be used as tools to measure unobservable cognitive processes.

This entry is organized as follows. First, the type of data used in multinomial modeling is described, and how these data can be used to develop models of this type is explained. A detailed example of multinomial modeling is provided as an illustration. Next, a number of common aspects of multinomial modeling are discussed, including validation testing, models for complex data structures, and the use of multinomial models to test hypotheses about cognitive processing. Finally, current work and future directions for multinomial modeling are outlined.

Data Structure and Model Development

Multinomial models are developed for categorical data, where each participant's response falls into one and only one of a finite set of observable data categories. These data usually come from a cognitive experiment, where each participant in an experimental group produces a categorical response to each of a series of items; for example, pictures are "recognized" or "not recognized" or letter strings are judged to be "words" or "nonwords." Most data sets for multinomial modeling involve more than two response categories, and in addition there may be more than one type of item, each with its own system of response categories. For example, in a source-monitoring experiment, participants study a list of items from two sources, Source A or Source B (e.g., presented in a male vs. female voice, or presented visually vs. auditorily). Later, participants are given a recognition memory test consisting of three types of items, namely, the two types of old list items and new distracter items, and they must classify each tested item as Source A, Source B, or New. The resulting multinomial data structure consists of three category systems (A, B, or New), each with three response categories (i.e., participants indicate if each item is from Source A, Source B, or is new). If the responses in different category systems are independent and category counts within a system follow a multinomial distribution, the probability of the data structure is given by the product of three multinomial distributions, one for each category system.

To express this more formally, assume that the data structure for an experimental task consists of J categories and N experimental response observations, where n_j observations fall into category C_j, $j = 1, 2, \ldots J$. Then if the observations are independent and identically distributed with probability p_j of falling into category C_j, the category count vector, $\mathbf{D} = (n_1, n_2, \ldots n_J)$, follows the multinomial distribution given by

$$\Pr[\mathbf{D}|\mathbf{p} = (p_1, \ldots, p_J)] = N! \prod_{j=1}^{J} \frac{p_j^{n_j}}{n_j!},$$

where the category probabilities are nonnegative and sum to one.

The key to creating a multinomial model is to take a multinomial data structure such as the one above and express the category probabilities in terms of underlying, cognitively interpretable parameters. One needs to specify a cognitive processing architecture along with formal computational rules that can generate the count data in terms of the parameters. Once the model is constructed and data are collected, standard tools in statistical inference can be used to analyze the data and evaluate the adequacy of the fit of the model to the data. In addition, one can estimate the values of the cognitive parameters that are likely to have created the data. In this way, unobservable cognitive processes can be measured indirectly with the use of the model.

Multinomial models of various types have been used in cognitive psychology since the 1960s; however, in the 1980s and 1990s, a particular approach called multinomial processing tree (MPT) modeling was developed at a general level by William Batchelder, David Riefer, and Xiangen Hu. The central characteristic of MPT models is that they have a particular type of cognitive architecture represented as a rooted tree structure. Such a structure assumes that cognitive processes follow one another, and subsequent processes are conditionally dependent on the success or failure of earlier processes. For example, if a model has parameters for item attention, item storage, and item retrieval, then successful storage depends on successful attention. In turn, successful retrieval depends on successful storage. If any of these processes fail, then responses may be governed by guessing biases corresponding to various states of incomplete information. Each series of processing possibilities leads to different observable responses, and there are usually many of these processing patterns, each represented by the "branches" of the tree architecture.

An Example: Batchelder and Riefer's Pair-Clustering Model

One early example of an MPT model is the pair-clustering model developed by Batchelder and Riefer. Their model was designed to separately measure storage capacity from retrieval capacity in human memory. The data for the model involve a specially designed free-recall task where participants study a list of words one at a time, and then, at a later time, memory is tested by having the participants recall as many of the studied words as they can in any order. The list consists of pairs of exemplars from several categories such as vehicles (taxi, car) or flowers (rose, daisy). Recall of each category pair is scored into one of four categories: (1) both words recalled successively, C_1; (2) both words recalled but not successively, C_2; (3) exactly one word recalled, C_3; and (4) neither word recalled, C_4. The model postulates three parameters each designed to measure a different cognitive process: (i) a storage parameter c representing the probability that a pair of words is "clustered" and stored in memory during study, (ii) a retrieval parameter r representing the probability that a word pair is recalled given that it is stored as a cluster, and (iii) a parameter u for the probability that a word in a pair that was not clustered is recalled as a singleton. Because the parameters refer to probabilities of successful cognitive processes, their values must be between zero and one.

The connection of the parameters to the category probabilities is based on a combination of psychological considerations and reasonable approximations. In particular, it is assumed that both members of a category pair are recalled successively if and only if the words in the pair are clustered and the cluster is retrieved (joint probability cr). Also, if a cluster was stored but not retrieved, then neither word is recalled. In contrast, with probability $(1 - c)$, the words in a pair are not clustered, and in this case each word in the pair is or is not recalled individually with probability u, subject to the condition that if both non-clustered words are recalled, they are not recalled successively. These assumptions can be displayed in the processing tree found in Figure 1.

To briefly turn to the mathematical details, it is easy to use this tree to express the category probabilities, $p_j = \Pr(C_j)$ for $j = 1, 2, 3, 4$, in terms of the parameters. The result expresses each category probability as a sum of the probabilities of the branches that lead to that category as follows: $p_1 = cr$, $p_2 = (1 - c)u^2$, $p_3 = (1 - c)u(1 - u) + (1 - c)(1 - u)u$, and $p_4 = c(1 - r) + (1 - c)(1 - u)^2$. It is a matter of simple algebra to show that if we collect data $\mathbf{D} = (n_1, n_2, n_3, n_4)$ and estimate the category probabilities by relative frequencies, $P_j = n_j/N$, then we can solve the four model equations for parameter estimates (denoted by *) yielding $u^* = 2P_2/(2P_2 + P_3)$, $c^* = 1 - P_2/(u^*)^2$, and $r^* = P_1/c^*$. In order for these equations to yield estimates of the parameters in the interval $(0,1)$, it is necessary that $(P_3)^2 < 4P_2(1 - P_2 - P_3)$.

Common Aspects of Multinomial Modeling

The example of the pair-clustering model illustrates the basic properties of multinomial modeling, which are the tree architecture and the computational rules that tie the cognitive processing parameters to the categorical data. However, the example does not illustrate three aspects typical of most applications of MPT models. First, in the example, there were three parameters representing cognitive processes and only three degrees of freedom in the data structure (as the four category probabilities are required to sum to one). In cases where there are more degrees of freedom in the categorical data than parameters, the system of equations expressing category probabilities in terms of parameters is overdetermined, and standard techniques in mathematical statistics

are used to estimate the parameters. Second, the pair-clustering model involves just one system of categories, but many MPT models are developed for several category systems, each of which is associated with its own processing tree. For example, MPT models for the source monitoring experiment discussed earlier specify three processing trees, one for each item type (Source A, Source B, or New).

Finally, unlike the example of the pair-clustering model, most applications of MPT models involve two or more experimental groups of participants, where the same model with possibly different parameter values is assumed to govern each group's category count data. In this case, MPT models are used to conduct hypothesis tests in an effort to discover which cognitive processes account for differences between the groups. This approach contrasts with the usual approach in experimental psychology for analyzing data from multiple experimental groups, which is to apply standard statistical tools like analysis of variance or linear regression. Although these tools are well developed to detect group differences and associate them with experimental manipulations, they do not allow one to pinpoint the cognitive bases for the differences.

As can be seen, MPT models are simple statistical models that are easy to develop and analyze. However, before an MPT model can be used as a measurement tool, it must be validated. A validated model is one in which the parameters can be shown to represent the cognitive processes they stand for. Establishing validation involves conducting simple cognitive studies where experimental manipulations are designed to affect some parameters and not others. These experiments attempt to dissociate the parameters by showing that they can be independently manipulated in ways that are consistent with established psychological theory. For example, for the pair-clustering model providing retrieval cues during recall should increase the value of the retrieval parameter r but not the value of the cluster storage parameter c. Other manipulations, such as increased study time, should affect the storage parameter but probably not the retrieval parameter.

Current and Future Directions

Since the 1990s, MPT modeling has become an increasingly popular approach to cognitive modeling, and its use has been facilitated by several

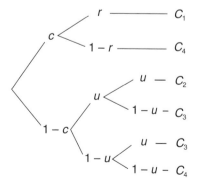

Figure 1   The pair-clustering model

software packages that can perform parameter estimation and hypotheses testing. To date there have been more than 100 examples of the application of MPT modeling. Most of these applications have been in the standard cognitive areas of memory, reasoning, and perception; however, clinical, social, and developmental psychology are also areas where MPT modeling is active. There are also a number of ongoing projects that explore the statistical properties of these models. For example, there has been recent work creating hierarchical MPT models to handle variation in parameter values due to individual differences in the participants, as well as latent class MPT models that can be used to model subgroups of participants with different cognitive abilities.

William H. Batchelder, Xiangen Hu,
and David M. Riefer

See also Memory Recall, Dynamics; Modeling Causal Learning

Further Readings

Batchelder, W. H., & Riefer, D. M. (1986). The statistical analysis of a model for storage and retrieval processes in human memory. *British Journal of Mathematical and Statistical Psychology, 39*, 129–149.

Batchelder, W. H., & Riefer, D. M. (1990). Multinomial processing models of source monitoring. *Psychological Review, 97*, 548–564.

Batchelder, W. H., & Riefer, D. M. (1999). Theoretical and empirical review of multinomial process tree modeling. *Psychonomic Bulletin & Review, 6*, 57–86.

Batchelder, W. H., & Riefer, D. M. (2007). Using multinomial processing tree models to measure cognitive deficits in clinical populations. In R. Neufeld (Ed.), *Advances in clinical cognitive science* (pp. 19–50). Washington, DC: American Psychological Association.

Erdfelder, E., Auer, T.-S., Hilbig, B. E., Aßfalg, A., Moshagen, M., & Nadarevic, L. (2009). Multinomial processing tree models: A review of the literature. *Journal of Psychology, 217*, 108–124.

Hu, X., & Batchelder, W. H. (1994). The statistical analysis of general processing tree models with the EM algorithm. *Psychometrika, 59*, 21–47.

Hu, X., & Phillips, G. A. (1999). GPT.EXE: A powerful tool for the visualization and analysis of general processing tree models. *Behavior Research Methods, Instruments, & Computers, 31*, 220–234.

Klauer, K. C. (2006). Hierarchical multinomial processing tree models: A latent-class approach. *Psychometrika, 71*, 7–31.

Riefer, D. M., & Batchelder, W. H. (1988). Multinomial modeling and the measurement of cognitive processes. *Psychological Review, 95*, 318–339.

MULTIPLE INTELLIGENCES THEORY

Multiple intelligences theory was proposed by psychologist Howard Gardner in 1983 to oppose the narrow meritocracy of *g*, or general intelligence, and to reflect evidence for the possible brain basis of content-specific information processing. Gardner argued that the general intelligence factor *g* should be replaced by seven intelligences: linguistic, musical, logical-mathematical, spatial, bodily-kinesthetic, intrapersonal (sense of self), and interpersonal. Gardner proposed that the intelligences were innate and that each intelligence had its own unique brain mechanism comprised of 50 to 100 micro modules.

Gardner's list and characterization of intelligences changed somewhat over time. In 2000, Gardner proposed an eighth intelligence, naturalist, involving the comprehension of natural things, and suggested that there might be a ninth intelligence, existentialist, involving one's sense of the relation of the self to the cosmos. In 2004, Gardner suggested two additional mental abilities, which he later characterized as profiles. He suggested that creative specialists in the arts, sciences, and trades have more narrowly focused laser-like intelligence and that leaders with high scholastic IQ may have a more broadly scanning mental searchlight.

Multiple Intelligences Theory Was Applied Widely in Education

Multiple intelligences theory was widely disseminated in the field of education, and many teachers and psychologists published articles that described the application of the theory to classroom practice. Theory adherents claimed that successful classroom application validated the existence of multiple intelligences. Educators and theory supporters argued the varied intelligences provided better cognitive skill profiles of typical students, savants, prodigies, and individuals with brain injuries than did the verbal and visual subskill tests of IQ measures.

Moreover, many educators saw multiple intelligences theory as a means to assess children without using culturally biased standard IQ tests. In addition, educators valued Gardner's view that multiple intelligences testing would allow students to be enthusiastic about cognitive assessment. The ideal of multiple intelligences testing was to allow children to solve problems in many different contexts. Standard paper-and-pencil, single-answer tests were thought inappropriate for determining the strengths and weaknesses of the different intelligences, and educators promoted the assessment of multiple intelligences through interesting materials. Teacher observations, student work portfolios, and learning inventories were recommended as a means of assessing the multiple intelligences of a student.

A key corollary of multiple intelligences theory was that assessing all of the intelligences would permit teachers to find each student's strongest intelligences, and students would have the opportunity to find an intelligence in which they might feel a greater competence. Teachers would then be able to avoid the student's weaker intelligences and use the student's stronger intelligences to create learning materials unique to each child. For example, multiple intelligences testing of the naturalist intelligence asked students to play with different natural objects, such as a feather and a stone. Students would be asked to observe the differences and similarities between these objects, describe them in detail, and address why some objects sink and some float. Similarly, musical intelligence was tested by asking students to sing a range of songs from simple to more complex. The assessment recorded whether a student was sensitive to pitch, rhythm, and melody.

Multiple Intelligences Theory Led to the Meme of Many Types of Intelligence

The popularity of Gardner's theory of multiple intelligences led others to theorize individual content-specific intelligences. Six intelligences had currency in different disciplines. Business Intelligence was proposed as skill with processes, trends, tools, and ideas current in business practices. Social Intelligence was hypothesized as four skills: self-awareness, social awareness, positive social beliefs and attitudes, and skill and interest in managing complex social change. Musical Intelligence was characterized as notable sensitivity to pitch, melody, and rhythm. Emotional Intelligence was hypothesized to include perceiving and understanding emotions, using one's own emotions to facilitate problem solving, limiting negative emotions and maintaining positive emo-

tions. Cultural Intelligence was claimed to include four dimensions: emotional resiliency, perceptual acuity, flexibility and openness, and personal autonomy. Spatial Intelligence was identified as the basis for skill in architecture, because this intelligence was proposed to reflect individual ability to move through varied spaces and recall accurate images of those spaces.

These six theorized intelligences and many additional proposals for unique content intelligences invoked Gardner's multiple intelligences theory as valid supporting scientific evidence that the brain was indeed partitioned into many possible intelligences.

Neuroscience Research Has Not Validated Multiple Intelligences Theory

Gardner argued multiple intelligences theory was validated through its basis in cognitive neuroscience research, through its successful classroom application, and through its ability to successfully account for cognitive skill patterns of individuals. Gardner also claimed that neuroscientists were conducting research to explore the specific brain circuits governing each of the multiple intelligences. It is true that neuroscience research has explored brain circuits and systems underpinning human skills. However, researchers such as Lynn Waterhouse have noted that no neuroscience research had tested the theory of multiple intelligences and that neuroscience research had disconfirmed the existence of the putative separate content processing modules in the brain.

Multiple intelligences theory was never a focus for cognitive neuroscience researchers, because even in 1983 when Gardner initially proposed his model, there was evidence that content processing did not occur in separate brain circuits. For example, in 1983, Robert Dykes outlined the division of components of sensorimotor information and the melding of that information with spatial and visual processing. Nearly 20 years later, Dana Strait, Jane Hornickel, and Nina Kraus confirmed that music, reading, and speech processing occurred in the same shared brain circuits.

Neuroscience evidence from the early 1980s to the present confirmed two major interacting brain pathways for information processing. The ventral path computes the nature of an object, while the dorsal path computes where an object is in space. The music we hear, our spatial analysis of an architectural plan, our computations to solve a math problem, and our understanding of people's emotions and the content of what they are saying are all processed through these interacting dorsal and ventral brain pathways.

Neuroscience research accumulated significant and compelling evidence for several large information processing systems, each of which may have undermined the possibility that the brain was organized by multiple intelligences. In addition to the dorsal-ventral system, the brain was found to have a fast, automatic decision-making process and a slow, effortful, consciously monitored decision-making process. Jonathan Power and colleagues outlined evidence for a third large brain system that included self-reflection processing of social, emotional, and self-related information, and externally directed information processing active during calculations, listening to others speak, attending an opera, or navigating a kayak. A fourth large information processing system was identified as the action-observation network. It governs automatic imitation and recognition of motor actions, social gestures, facial expressions, and language production of another person. The evidence for all four brain-wide systems demonstrates various pathways of analytic and collective processing of information that Gardner theorized to be separately processed by the individual multiple intelligences.

The Appeal of Multiple Intelligences Theory

Cognitive neuroscience's disconfirmation of Gardner's claims for discrete content processing in the brain had no effect on the dissemination of multiple intelligences theory. It remained popular with the public and continued to be applied in classrooms around the world. In 2009, Ji-Qie Chen, Seana Moran, and Gardner outlined the use of multiple intelligences in classrooms in Argentina, Australia, China, Columbia, Denmark, Ireland, Norway, the Philippines, Romania, Scotland, South Korea, Turkey, and the United States. Chen and colleagues argued that the central benefit of multiple intelligences theory in the classroom was that it allowed a concept to be viewed from multiple perspectives, thus contributing to deeper learning.

Lynn Waterhouse

See also Intelligence, Neural Basis; Learning Styles

Further Readings

Chen, J.-Q., Moran, S., & Gardner, H. (2009). *Multiple intelligences around the world.* San Francisco, CA: Wiley.

Dykes, R. W. (1983). Parallel processing of somatosensory information: A theory. *Brain Research Reviews, 6*(1), 47–115.

Gardner, H. (1983). *Frames of mind: The theory of multiple intelligences.* New York, NY: Basic Books.

Gardner, H. (2000). A case against spiritual intelligence. *International Journal for the Psychology of Religion, 10*(1), 27–34.

Gardner, H. (2004). Audiences for multiple intelligences. *Teachers College Record, 106*(1), 212–220.

Power, J. D., Cohen, A. L., Nelson, S. M., Wig, G. S., Barnes, K. A., Church, J. A., . . . Petersen, S. E. (2011). Functional network organization of the human brain. *Neuron, 72,* 665–678.

Strait, D. L., Hornickel, J., & Kraus, N. (2011). Subcortical processing of speech regularities underlies reading and music aptitude in children. *Behavioral and Brain Functions, 17*(7), 44.

Waterhouse, L. (2006). Multiple intelligences, the Mozart effect, and emotional intelligence: A critical review. *Educational Psychologist, 4,* 207–225.

MULTITASKING AND HUMAN PERFORMANCE

The pace of modern life places a higher demand on the ability to multitask than at any time in human history. Indeed, today's lifestyle often requires people to manage several concurrent activities and to deal with constant interruptions to ongoing tasks (e.g., ringing phones, e-mail alerts, instant messaging, etc.). Multitasking refers to the concurrent performance of two or more tasks, where each task can be defined as an activity with distinct goals, processes, and representations. For example, it is not uncommon for operators of a motor vehicle to talk on a cell phone or interact with a variety of other electronic devices while driving. In this example, the cognitive operations associated with driving a vehicle (e.g., navigating, maintaining speed and lane position, reacting to both expected and unexpected events, etc.) are independent of the cognitive operations associated with conversing on a cell phone. There is now clear and unequivocal evidence that the current performance of these two activities yields performance on each task that is inferior to the performance of the two tasks when they are performed separately. In fact, the literature is replete with studies that have examined multitasking performance and found patterns of interference indicating that people cannot perform two or more attention-demanding tasks simultaneously without costs. Why are there limits on human ability to multitask?

Types of Processing

There are two general categories of multitasking activity. On the one hand, a person may alternate performance between tasks, switching attention between them in discrete units of time. This creates a form of *serial processing* in which the performance of one task creates a bottleneck, briefly locking out the processing of other tasks. There are obvious decrements in performance associated with this processing bottleneck. An alarming real-world example of attention switching comes when a driver attempts to text message on his or her cellular phone. Here, visual attention can be allocated to driving, or texting, but not both at the same time. This may be an extreme example of a bottleneck that involves both cognitive and structural limitations; however, one can find these limitations separately as well. Another example based on a large body of laboratory research using the psychological refractory period (PRP) paradigm has found that the processing of one task systematically delays the processing of another concurrent task. The processing delay is thought to stem from a central-processing bottleneck in information processing that is stubbornly resistant to practice, and empirical efforts to bypass the bottleneck have largely been unsuccessful. Together, these findings indicate that a fundamental characteristic of the cognitive architecture is a limited ability to perform more than one attention-demanding task at a time.

On the other hand, some multitask combinations may allow *parallel processing,* in which attention is shared between two or more concurrent tasks. In this context, attention has been conceptualized as a resource that can be flexibly shared between concurrently performed tasks. However, given the limited capacity characteristics of attention, there is a reciprocal relationship between the tasks such that as one task prospers, because attention is allocated to its processing, performance on the other task

suffers. In 1984, Christopher Wickens developed a multiple-resource model, suggesting that some dual-task combinations may draw on separate processing resources. This multidimensional framework conceptualizes modalities of input (auditory vs. visual), codes of operation (verbal vs. spatial), and modalities of response (vocal vs. manual) as separable pools of attentional resources, with performance in dual-task situations varying as a function of the overlap in demand for processing resources; the less overlap there is, the more proficient the multitask performance will be. Other researchers have suggested that it may be better to consider multitask performance with regard to the degree of cross-talk between the cognitive operations and mental representations of the separate tasks. Interestingly, the cell phone/driving dual-task combination would seem to represent a fly-in-the-ointment for this class of theories because driving is primarily a visual/spatial/manual task and conversing on a phone is primarily an auditory/verbal/vocal task. That is, even though these two tasks should, in theory, draw on distinct processing resources, they nevertheless produce considerable dual-task interference. It seems then that bottlenecks in performance may still be present even in circumstances where parallel processing can, at least in principle, take place.

Task Switching

In addition to the central-processing bottleneck costs, persistent costs are also observed when attention is switched from one task to another. In this case, switching from one task to another results in a cost in reaction time associated with performing the first trial in a series (i.e., the switch cost), and this cost often persists for several trials following the initial switch. That is, it takes time for performance to settle into a stable state following a switch from one task to another. Here again, the costs of switching are largely resistant to the effects of practice. Taken together, a general characteristic of attention switching is that performance, particularly performance requiring speeded reactions, is not as good in multitasking contexts as it is if the tasks are not performed concurrently.

Processing Duration

Distinguishing between switching and sharing models of multitasking often proves difficult based on empirical data. Indeed, some estimates of rapid switching of attention make virtually indistinguishable predictions from sharing models of attention. Thus, it may be more profitable to think about multitasking in terms of the processing duration of the cognitive operations underlying each task. As the processing duration increases, the evidence for serial processing bottlenecks becomes more compelling (e.g., the text messaging and driving example discussed earlier). Interestingly, one situation where PRP bottlenecks may potentially be bypassed is when the processing demands of the second of two tasks is relatively simple (i.e., with a short processing duration). Moreover, there are suggestions in the literature that practice can improve task efficiency, reducing processing time, and thereby improving multitasking performance. Can practice altogether eliminate the bottleneck in multitasking performance?

Practice and Automatization

Under certain circumstances, practice can result in task performance transitioning from slow, controlled, and effortful to fast, automatic, and effortless. In the conditions where performance can be characterized as automatic, researchers have often questioned whether these routines can be performed in combination with another task without measurable cost (i.e., an example of perfect time-sharing). Some of the early research addressing this topic reported that, with high levels of practice, a few hardy souls could learn to play the piano while shadowing words, or to take dictation while reading aloud, although in both instances error rates were higher in dual-task situations than when each task was performed by itself. One of the most carefully controlled studies on this topic claimed that, after extensive practice, subjects were able to perform two visual search tasks without noticeable deficit after one of the search tasks became automatic; however, even in this study, a careful inspection revealed that the accuracy of detection dropped significantly from single- to dual-task conditions. At the other end of the spectrum are situations where there is inherent unpredictability in the environment, such as in the case of talking on a cell phone (where each conversation is unique) and driving (which often requires reacting to unpredictable events). In these cases, performance cannot become automatic even with

extensive practice. Indeed, in such cases, persistent costs are observed despite years of real-world practice. Thus, despite some claims in the literature of perfect time-sharing, a critical analysis of these findings suggests that perfect time-sharing, if it exists, is an elusive exception rather than the general rule.

As mentioned earlier, a number of researchers have also explored whether practice can eliminate the bottleneck in performance associated with the PRP effect. In the PRP paradigm, two stimuli from different tasks are presented in rapid succession, and the reaction time to the second of the two stimuli systematically increases as the time between the beginning of the stimuli (the *stimulus onset asynchrony*) decreases. In circumstances where both of the tasks require a manual response, the PRP effects are little changed with practice. However, with separate input and output modalities for the two tasks, participants were able to significantly reduce, but not eliminate, the PRP effects. However, others have argued that, even in the best of circumstances, there is virtually no evidence for perfect time-sharing. Thus, the data from the PRP literature suggest that, even with relatively simple tasks and extensive practice, significant dual-task interference is the rule, at least for the majority of individuals.

Neural Mechanisms

There is growing body of neuropsychological evidence that a subregion of the prefrontal cortex, specifically the dorsolateral prefrontal cortex (DLPFC), plays a significant role in maintaining the processing goals for task completion. Switching between tasks places a load on this brain region as one goal, and its related processing operations, is supplanted by another. Moreover, individual differences in the functioning of DLPFC are correlated with differences in multitasking ability. Indeed, a small portion of the population (e.g., 2%–3%) seems to be able to perform complex multitasking operations such as talking on a cell phone while driving with no measurable decrement in performance on either task. Current speculation is that these "supertaskers" use more broadly distributed brain regions to control multitasking performance.

Threaded Cognition

Despite the general lack of evidence supporting perfect time-sharing, people do multitask at performance levels greater than chance (e.g., people do not immediately drive off the road when they talk on a cell phone). What is the mechanism underlying multitasking performance? One group of researchers recently developed an ACT-R based *threaded cognition* model of multitasking in which the task procedures are entered into a queue and processed in the order in which they enter the queue (i.e., least recently processed rule). Given that productions fire one at a time, threaded cognition creates a central processing bottleneck to the extent that the processing of one production locks out the others in the queue. Moreover, as the processing duration of a thread increases, the apparent costs in multitasking become more apparent. Likewise, as practice strengthens a production (thereby speeding its processing), the lockout period for concurrent operations decreases, reducing the overall interference that this production has on multitasking performance.

Implications for Multitasking

It is noteworthy that the distinction between a reduction in dual-task interference and no dual-task interference (i.e., perfect time-sharing) is both practically and theoretically important. The first interpretation suggests that the inherent structure of the cognitive architecture places important, potentially insurmountable, limitations on doing more than one cognitive task at a time. The second interpretation suggests a different structural design such that, with sufficient practice, it may be possible to perform independent cognitive operations simultaneously and without costs. On the whole, the data tend to support the former rather than the latter interpretation for the architecture of mind. Some researchers have speculated that the structural limitations arise from competition for specific brain regions, such as the DLPFC, that are essential for controlling and coordinating cognition and action.

General Principles

Several general principles can be distilled from the literature on multitasking. First, with the exception of a few cases, performance in a multitasking context is worse than when each of the tasks is performed alone. That is, performing two or more attention-demanding tasks at the same time always produces interference. Even though many people believe that they are experts in multitasking, a careful analysis of

their performance would indicate otherwise. Second, practice can improve multitasking performance in situations where performance on one or more of the tasks can be automated. However, practice does not eliminate all sources of interference associated with multitasking. Third, as the complexity of the constituent processes of each task increases, the impairments in multitasking performance will become more pronounced. In sum, despite the ever-increasing demands placed on attention in the modern world, bottlenecks in the cognitive architecture of the mind/brain place significant limits on the ability to multitask, creating tradeoffs between the quality and quantity of processing.

David L. Strayer,
Nathan Medeiros-Ward, and
Joel M. Cooper

See also Attention, Resource Models; Attention and Action; Automaticity; Divided Attention and Memory; Psychological Refractory Period

Further Readings

Kahneman, D. (1973). *Attention and effort*. New York, NY: Prentice Hall.

Navon, D., & Gopher, D. (1979). On the economy of the human-processing system. *Psychological Review, 86,* 214–255.

Pashler, H. (1992). Attentional limitations in doing two tasks at the same time. *Current Directions in Psychological Science, 1,* 44–48.

Salvucci, D. D., & Taatgen, N. A. (2008). Threaded cognition: An integrated theory of concurrent multitasking. *Psychological Review, 115,* 101–130.

Strayer, D. L., & Johnston, W. A. (2001). Driven to distraction: Dual-task studies of simulated driving and conversing on a cellular telephone. *Psychological Science, 12*(6), 462–466.

Tombu, M., & Jolicoeur, P. (2004). Virtually no evidence for virtually perfect time-sharing. *Journal of Experimental Psychology: Human Perception and Performance, 30,* 795–810.

Van Selst, M., Ruthruff, E., & Johnston, J. C. (1999). Can practice eliminate the psychological refractory period effect? *Journal of Experimental Psychology: Human Perception and Performance, 25,* 1268–1283.

Wickens, C. D. (1984). Processing resources in attention. In R. Parasuraman, J. Beatty, & J. Davies (Eds.), *Varieties of attention* (pp. 63–102). New York, NY: Academic Press.

MUSIC AND THE EVOLUTION OF LANGUAGE

The relationship between music and language has inspired discussion and controversy for centuries. Like language, music is a human universal, found in all cultures, and human infants appear to be born with considerable musical abilities. Research on congenital amusia (a severe, heritable form of what is popularly called "tone deafness") reveals that some humans cannot process the relatively fine pitch differences needed for music perception. A capacity to name notes from memory (absolute or "perfect" pitch) also has a heritable component. These facts suggest that music has some genetic basis. However, unlike language, the function of music remains elusive, and Charles Darwin therefore considered music one of our most mysterious cognitive faculties. Darwin resolved the mystery by positing a hypothetical "musical protolanguage": an intermediate form of communication that preceded the evolution of language. This entry explores Darwin's hypothesis and reviews recent data consistent with a close evolutionary link between music and language.

Most contemporary models of language evolution posit some intermediate form of protolanguage. For example, anthropologist Gordon Hewes introduced the term *protolanguage* in the context of a hypothetical gestural protolanguage, where language initially evolved using the visual/manual modality, and speech evolved later. Another model of protolanguage was offered by linguist Derek Bickerton, who hypothesized a vocal protolanguage involving words and simple meanings, but lacking complex syntax. All protolanguage models share the assumption that language is a complex system whose different components evolved during separate evolutionary stages. Such models differ in the order in which these different components evolved and in the sensory modalities involved.

In Darwin's model, prehuman hominids were hypothesized to communicate vocally with a system resembling non-lyrical singing. Musical protolanguage was vocal, learned, and emotionally expressive: Vocal utterances could convey emotions and individual identity and would be used during courtship, rivalry, and group bonding. However, this hypothetical protolanguage lacked the kind of explicit propositional meaning that typifies language. It would not be possible to express specific thoughts (like "the red berries on the tree by the lake are poisonous") in protolanguage, any more than in modern instrumental music. Thus, Darwin's hypothesis suggests that complex vocal control—proto-speech—evolved before meaning. Note that such vocal performances might include speech-like components (e.g., the "eeny meeny miney mo" of children's songs, "bebopalula" of rock and doo-wop, or the meaningless syllables of jazz scat singing): Protolanguage lacked meaningful words but not articulated syllables.

Darwin supported his hypothesis with a number of arguments, many of which are further supported by more recent scientific research. One of Darwin's main inspirations was song in birds. He recognized that many birds learn their song by listening to other birds sing, a characteristic analogous to humans for both song and speech. This similarity is all the more striking given that most mammals and nonhuman primates *do not* learn their vocalizations. Apes and monkeys raised in the absence of vocalization nonetheless produce their species-typical calls in the appropriate circumstances. Furthermore, chimpanzees lack the motor control necessary to master song or speech and, even with intensive training, cannot learn to produce even simple monosyllabic words. Thus, the neural mechanisms allowing flexible, learned vocalization in humans have evolved some time since our divergence from chimpanzees.

In contrast, many bird species, including parrots, mynahs, and mockingbirds, can easily imitate speech, environmental sounds, or the songs of other birds. Darwin suggested that vocal learning in humans evolved prior to language and, by analogy, functioned in a communication system similar to that of birdsong. New comparative data unavailable in Darwin's time support this suggestion: Vocal learning has independently evolved in additional bird species (hummingbirds) and several mammal species (including whales, dolphins, seals, bats, and probably elephants). Although vocal learning allows complex vocalizations to be produced and learned, none of these species use their complex "songs" to communicate propositional information: Vocal learning does not support language, in the human sense. Repeated convergent evolution in many species strongly suggests that a vocal learning capacity can evolve easily, under the right conditions, in vertebrates, and that it often does so in a "song" context, like that of songbirds or whales.

Further support for the musical protolanguage hypothesis comes from computational characteristics shared by music and language. Both are hierarchically structured: Just as words are made up of separate meaningless syllables, musical phrases are built up from meaningless notes. Just as words can be arranged into longer and more complex sentences, musical phrases are typically combined to form larger melodies. Both systems are capable of generating an unlimited diversity of signals, and only some of these are "grammatical," obeying unstated rules of combination. Similar properties would have been present in musical protolanguage.

The main difference between music and language concerns the expression of meaning. In language, propositional meanings can be expressed explicitly with great precision. Music, although ill-suited for expressing explicit propositions, is well suited for expressing dynamic, feeling-laden contours, which can be mapped in continuous fashion onto emotions, movement, or other more abstract cognitive dimensions. Thus, music is often better suited to expressing feelings, or eliciting movements like dance, than is language. This aspect of protolanguage has not disappeared in modern humans, and it remains an important function of music. As predicted by Darwin's hypothesis, spoken language retains a prosodic or "musical" component, and tone of voice, melodic contour, and speech rhythm continue to play an important role in speech (though not the written word) today.

The problem of how propositional meaning came to be associated with protolinguistic utterances has been addressed by linguists Otto Jespersen and (later) Alison Wray with their "holistic" model of protolanguage. In a second evolutionary stage, musical protolanguage was augmented with more specific meanings, but still tied to whole musical performances. Just as "Happy Birthday" signifies birthday celebrations, Jespersen envisioned songs becoming explicit indicators of hunting, gathering, or festivity, or signaling particular individuals or objects. The crucial transformation came when listeners began to detect possible connections between components of propositional meaning and individual subsections of the vocal performance: This was the birth of words as we know them today. Such a process of "analysis" has been demonstrated in computer simulations

by Simon Kirby and his colleagues, and can, over many generations, produce a significant vocabulary.

Interest in Darwin's musical protolanguage hypothesis has undergone a resurgence in recent years; the topic is reviewed by archaeologist Steven Mithen in his book *The Singing Neanderthals*. New data from neuroscience, musicology, and animal communication have augmented Darwin's original arguments, and although all models of protolanguage remain controversial, musical protolanguage is a leading model for the evolution of language in contemporary discussions. Further research comparing the neural and genetic mechanisms underlying music and language offers considerable hope in the coming decades for the resolution of these age-old debates about human cognitive evolution.

W. Tecumseh Fitch

See also Language Development; Music Perception; Speech Perception

Further Readings

Darwin, C. (1871). *The descent of man and selection in relation to sex*. London, UK: John Murray.

Fitch, W. T. (2006). The biology and evolution of music. *Cognition, 100*, 173–215.

Mithen, S. (2005). *The singing Neanderthals*. London, UK: Weidenfeld & Nicolson.

Patel, A. (2008). *Music, language, and the brain*. New York, NY: Oxford University Press:

Wallin, N., Merker, B., & Brown, S. (Eds.). (2000). *The origins of music*. Cambridge, MA: MIT Press.

Music Perception

Most people assume that the world is just as they perceive it to be. But experiments have forced researchers to confront the reality that this is not the case. What we *perceive* represents the end of a chain of mental events that give rise to a mental representation of the physical world. Our brain imposes structure and order on certain sequence of sounds and thereby creates what we call music. Molecules in the air vibrate but do not themselves make a *sound*. Sound—and three of its musical components, pitch, loudness, and timbre—are psychological constructions, present only in the minds of perceivers. Thus, to answer Bishop Berkeley's famous question, if a tree falls in the forest and no one is there to hear it (even if it falls on top of a stack of pianos!), it doesn't make a *sound*, although it may make physical disturbances in the atmosphere. Music perception can thus be defined as those processes undertaken by the human mind in creating music from the physical properties of sound. This entry reviews the components of music, experimental methods for studying music perception, and a few of the most prominent topics in the field, including the neuroanatomy of music (music and the brain), music and emotion, and music and personality.

The focus of research in music perception and cognition encompasses the mental and neural operations underlying music listening, music-making, dancing (moving to music), and composing. The science is interdisciplinary, drawing principally on methods from cognitive psychology, neuroscience, and music theory, as well as from musicology, computer science, linguistics, sociology, genetics, and evolutionary biology. Music processing is a complex, high-level cognitive activity, engaging many areas of the brain and employing many distinct cognitive operations. As such, it is a useful tool for understanding functions of the mind and brain and informing larger issues in cognitive science, such as memory, attention, categorization, and emotion.

The field traces its origins to experimentation with musical instruments in ancient Greece and China. Aristoxenus (364–304 BCE) argued that one must study the *mind* of the listener, not merely the collection of sounds impinging on the ear. In the late 1800s, Hermann von Helmholtz, Gustav Fechner, and Wilhelm Wundt first applied modern scientific methods to study musical experience. Today, music psychology is experiencing a renaissance, with an exponential increase in scholarly activity over the preceding decades. This surge of interest follows increasing communication across scholarly disciplines, the emergence of cognitive psychology in the 1960s, and new technologies that facilitate the preservation, presentation, and manipulation of sound (e.g., magnetic tape, hard disks, computers, digital signal processing).

Building Blocks of Music

Although music can be defined in many ways, most would consider that to be called *music,* more than one tone must be present, creating a sequence of tones. (We reserve the word *note* for a tone that is *notated,* or written on paper.) A sequence of tones spread out over time constitutes a *melody;* simultaneously sounded tones constitute *harmony.* Two pitches define a musical *interval,* and a sequence of intervals define *contour*—the direction of movement of the sequence (up, down, or same) without regard to the size of the intervals. This kind of directional movement also exists in speech where it is known as *prosody.* Contour is especially salient and may be subject to preferential processing—infants attend to it more readily than they do intervals, and contour is more easily remembered by adults learning a new melody than are the precise intervals.

Tones typically are written or performed with different durations, and the sequence of durations gives rise to *rhythm, tempo* (the pace or speed of the piece, loosely related to the temporal interval at which one would tap a foot or snap fingers), and *meter* (the way in which tones are perceived to be temporally grouped or organized, the most common in Western music being groups of two, three, or four). Our brains assemble these fundamental perceptual attributes into higher level concepts such as melody and harmony (just as a painter arranges lines into shapes, contours and forms in creating a cohesive whole). When we listen to music, we are in fact processing these multiple attributes or "dimensions" and their interactions.

Although our subjective experience of music may be seamless and complete, its perceptual components are processed in separate areas in the brain. For example, pitch height—the dimension of pitch perception that is correlated with frequency—is encoded in primary auditory cortex, which contains a tonotopic map: a map of pitches from low to high that mirrors the neuronal pitch map in the cochlea. In addition to relying on absolute pitch information, human appreciation of music relies on pitch relations; in this regard, human music perception may be qualitatively different from that of most animal species.

Melodies are defined by the *pattern* or *relation* of successive pitches across time; most people have little trouble recognizing a melody that has been transposed in pitch. In fact, many melodies do not have a "correct" pitch, but simply float freely in pitch space. "Happy Birthday" is an example of this, typically sung with naïve disregard to whether it is being sung in the same key from one occasion to the next. One way to think about a melody, then, is that it is an auditory object that maintains its identity under certain transformations. So, for example, when we hear a song played louder or slower than we're accustomed to, we can still identify it.

Music and Evolution

Darwin argued that music was an evolutionary adaptation, used for signaling sexual fitness. The past 10 years have seen an increased interest in questions surrounding the evolutionary origins of music and its relation to language evolution: which came first, or to what extent they may have coevolved. Evidence comes from archeological findings (e.g., bone flutes at ancient burial sites), anthropology (the study of contemporary preliterate and preindustrial societies), biology (especially the study of communication among closely related species, such as chimpanzees), and neuroscience (differential activation of brain circuits by music and language, with music tending to activate phylogenetically older structures). Music is characterized by its antiquity and its ubiquity—no known culture now or anytime in the past lacked music. Music has clearly shaped the course of human culture, societies, and history. In addition, specific neurochemical processes accompany musical activities, including the modulation of dopamine levels in response to music listening.

Musicology and Musical Grammar

Each human culture develops its own traditions for the ways in which its music is created. In general, Western music tends to employ duple or triple meter, corresponding to what we would perceive as a simple march or a waltz, respectively, whereas other cultures routinely employ more complex meter in their music. The system of rules or conventions by which sounds are assembled in a given culture can be thought of as the grammar for that music and as reflecting a musical style, syntax, and idiom. Musical phrases are composed of notes, chords, or both, but as in language, these are not randomly ordered, and a reordering of elements produces a different melody. Some musical experiences that we take for granted are in fact culturally dependent. For example, in Western tonal music, minor chords and keys are often associated with sadness and major chords with happiness, although this is not a cross-cultural universal.

Music and Emotion

Music has been called the "language of emotion," but it is unclear whether our ancestors used music in this way. Unlike visual art, such as cave paintings, which left a permanent trace for scientists to study, music made an impression only in the minds of those contemporaries who heard it; music recording has existed for scarcely 100 years. Inferences must be drawn from extant writings about music (some of which date to 6,000 years ago) and from the study of contemporary preliterate and preindustrial cultures. To contemporary humans, music represents a dynamic form of emotion—the conveying of emotion is considered to be the essence, if not the purpose, of music and the reason that most people report spending large amounts of time listening to music. Recent laboratory studies have focused on the biological underpinnings of musical emotion, particularly the involvement of neural reward systems. This has been studied through investigating the chill response, a physical sensation up the spine. It varies from individual to individual and is based on a number of factors, such as structural components and loudness of the music as well as character/personality organization of the listener and his or her musical experience. When people listen to music which they report consistently gives them chills, blood flow increases to centers of the brain that are implicated in reward, emotion, and arousal, regions that modulate dopaminergic levels.

Our emotional reactions to music are believed to be caused in part by the meeting and violating of musical expectations. Listeners track the progression of music over time, noting the pitches and rhythms employed, and form subconscious predictions about what will occur next. A musical piece that we find pleasing strikes the balance between meeting those predictions some of the time and violating them in interesting ways the rest of the time.

Musical Preferences

Measures of personality and individual differences have been shown to correlate with taste in music; the correlations are relatively small but significant and robust. From research using the Big Five personality inventory and a cross-section of songs representing major genres and subgenres of Western tonal music, certain consistencies have emerged. Although such research is still in its early stages, results indicate that extraverted individuals tend to like music that is characterized as energetic and rhythmic. Individuals who rate high on Factor 5, openness to new experience, show no correlation with such music, but rather with music that is described as reflective and complex. Upbeat and conventional music correlates with Factor 2, agreeableness.

Several hypotheses exist as to why musical taste might be related to personality. In some cases, people may prefer and seek out styles of music that reflect and reinforce aspects of their personalities. Personality influences how individuals think, feel, and behave. For example, people with high levels of extraversion may seek out situations that allow them to be talkative and sociable. In contrast, more introverted people tend to seek out environments where they have limited contact with others, especially people they don't know. Just as people seek out and create social environments that reinforce aspects of their personalities, so, too, might people seek out auditory or musical environments that conform to aspects of their personalities. Because music is a component of social identity in contemporary society, people may also seek out music that they believe will create a desirable impression of them.

Adolescents, in particular, use music as a way of communicating their status and affiliation with a particular peer group or style. Individuals of all ages report using music for mood induction. Those who are normally extraverted, for example, may help to maintain their self-identity and typical level of stimulation by listening to energetic music. Some listen to fast-paced or uplifting music to "get going" in the morning. In times of sadness or sensitivity, individuals may listen to an artist who conveys the same kinds of feelings they are going through, in order to feel understood. Music may also maintain a person's mood when it is simply music they enjoy.

Daniel J. Levitin and Anna K. Tirovolas

See also Audition, Neural Basis; Emotion Regulation; Music and the Evolution of Language

Further Readings

Deutsch, D. (Ed.). (1999). *The psychology of music.* San Diego, CA: Academic Press.

Huron, D. (2006). *Sweet anticipation: Music and the psychology of expectation.* Cambridge, MA: MIT Press.

Juslin, P., & Sloboda, J. A. (2001). *Music and emotion.* Oxford, UK: Oxford University Press.

Levitin, D. J. (2008). *The world in six songs: How the musical brain created human nature.* New York, NY: Dutton.

Meyer, L. (1956). *Emotion and meaning in music.* Chicago, IL: University of Chicago Press.

Thompson, W. F. (2008). *Music, thought and feeling.* New York, NY: Oxford University Press.

NAÏVE REALISM

Although the label "naïve realism" has been used for different theories in different contexts, the theories it names tend to be those that play a certain role in a discipline. More specifically, naïve realism tends to be used as a name for a theory that would, within a discipline or subdiscipline, be a starting point—a theory that is motivated by an initial appeal to how things seem to us, pretheoretically speaking. This entry briefly considers naïve realism as it is discussed in cognitive psychology, the philosophy of perception, and metaphysics, and how these different theories are related to one another.

Naïve Realism in Cognitive Psychology

The eminent cognitive psychologist, Ulric Neisser, uses the label naïve realism to name a simplistic view that claims, among other things, that a subject's visual experience "directly mirrors the stimulus pattern; . . . [is] a passive . . . copy of the stimulus," and "begins when the pattern is first exposed and terminates when it is turned off" (p. 16). This naïve view is then taken to be refuted by, for example, evidence that expectancy can alter a subject's visual experience and evidence that the visual experience can persist beyond the extinction of the stimulus.

It is important to note that, although naïve realism is supposed to be a pretheoretic starting point, as Neisser's characterization shows, this does not stop the views so labeled from being theoretically loaded. On the characterization just given, naïve realism goes along with a piece of cognitive psychological doctrine—that visual experiences represent the world. What distinguishes naïve realism from more sophisticated theories within cognitive psychology is the further claim that the representation is both perfectly faithful and passively created.

Naïve Realism in the Philosophy of Perception

This feature of Neisser's characterization of naïve realism actually serves to render it inconsistent with philosophical naïve realist theories of experience. Within the philosophy of perception, naïve realism has been used to name two closely related theses. The first is the view that the things that we perceive are actually *constituents* of the perceptual experiences we have. So, for example, if I see a tugboat, then the tugboat itself—part of the external world—is literally a constituent of my experience. If I merely *seem to see* a tugboat—say, I have a tugboat dream or tugboat hallucination that is completely indistinguishable from my experience of actually seeing one—because there is no suitably situated tugboat in the world, the experience I have when I merely seem to see a tugboat could not be the same kind of experience I have when I actually *see* one. The experience of actually seeing something and merely seeming to see something are experiences of fundamentally different kinds. The second claim differs in virtue of being specifically about *consciousness:* It says that, according to naïve realism, the things that we perceive actually shape the conscious character of our experiences. Thus, according to such a view, the pink color that we are consciously presented with when we see a flamingo just is the flamingo's pinkness. Again, this has the consequence that we could not have such a conscious experience of pinkness without there being some pink thing that we are aware of. Both of these claims are inconsistent with naïve realism as Neisser conceives of it because they deny that visual experiences are representations of the world, claiming instead that they are states or events that actually involve the world in some way.

The major objection to these characterizations of naïve realism turns on the possibility of misleading experiences, such as hallucination or illusion. Consider a case in which a subject sees a tugboat. According to this kind of naïve realist, the tugboat is either a constituent of the subject's visual experience or shapes the contours of the subject's (conscious) visual experience. Yet, the objection goes, Couldn't we have an experience just like this in the case of a suitably convincing hallucination? Because hallucinations just are visual experiences that occur in the absence of appropriate objects of perception, a real-world tugboat could not be a constituent of such an experience nor could it shape the conscious contours of that experience. Yet if this experience is just like the experience of actually seeing a tugboat, then doesn't it show that naïve realism is false: that we can have the kind of experience we have when seeing a tugboat without a tugboat being a constituent of and/or shaping the conscious character of that experience? Defenders of naïve realism therefore need to offer an account of how naïve realism can be made consistent with the possibility of such hallucinations. Similar problems arise when considering the evidence, mentioned above, that the visual experience of a stimulus can persist for a short time after that stimulus is extinguished.

Naïve Realism in Metaphysics

In addition to these theories about visual experience, there is also a metaphysical thesis that does business under the name of naïve realism. This is the position according to which there is a world of physical objects whose existence does not depend on being perceived and that really do possess all the properties—including properties such as color, temperature, texture, taste, and smell—that we perceive them to have (as well as more besides). Although this is a distinct thesis, it is related to the previous two characterizations in as much as, if such claims

were true, then metaphysical naïve realism would have to be true too. Given this, if metaphysical naïve realism were shown to be false, then this would show naïve realism about perceptual experience to be false in turn. And over the years, metaphysical naïve realism has been subject to an important criticism. For instance, note that, while orange juice normally tastes quite sweet, the same juice can actually taste quite bitter if it is preceded by something sugary, such as pancakes with maple syrup, say. This suggests that the property of being sweet is not a property that the orange juice has independently of us but is rather a way we *experience* the orange juice. This kind of contention can also be supported by scientific findings. For example, it has been claimed that empirical research into the workings of our visual systems shows that colors are, so to speak, in the eye of the beholder rather than on the surfaces of objects. Again, then, defenders of naïve realism will also need to show how the scientific world view can be reconciled with a conception of the world as containing such things as colors, textures, smells, and tastes.

William Fish

See also Conscious Thinking; Disjunctive Theory of Perception; Realism and Instrumentalism; Smell, Philosophical Perspectives; Theory of Appearing

Further Readings

Cornman, J. W. (1975). *Perception, common sense, and science.* New Haven, CT: Yale University Press.

Hardin, C. L. (1988). *Color for philosophers: Unweaving the rainbow.* Indianapolis, IN: Hackett.

Martin, M. G. F. (2004). The limits of self-awareness. *Philosophical Studies, 120,* 37–89.

Neisser, U. (1967). *Cognitive psychology.* New York, NY: Appleton-Century-Crofts.

NARCISSISTIC PERSONALITY DISORDER

Narcissistic personality disorder (NPD) is a personality disorder that includes grandiosity, a lack of empathy for others, and a range of behaviors that serve to maintain and increase self-esteem. According to the *Diagnostic and Statistical Manual of Mental Disorders* (4th edition, text revision; *DSM-IV-TR*) of the American Psychiatric Association, to qualify as a personality disorder, the narcissistic emotions, cognitions, and behaviors need to be pervasive (i.e., evident across all aspects of a person's life) and enduring (i.e., part of a person's disposition for an extended period of time, beginning in early adulthood). For a person to be diagnosed with NPD, the individual's personality must "deviate from cultural expectations" in at least two of the following four areas: thought processes (cognition), emotional life (affect), relationships (interpersonal functioning), or self-control (impulsivity). NPD can be related to difficulties in each of these areas (e.g., *cognition:* overconfidence and resistance to accurate feedback; *affect:* anger, depression, anxiety; *interpersonal functioning:* infidelity, aggression, difficulties with commitment; *impulsivity:* problems related to sensation and novelty seeking such as abuse of illegal substances and gambling). A diagnosis of NPD also requires evidence that the personality traits are causing the individual distress or resulting in impairment. Finally, for an NPD diagnosis to be made, other problems and disorders must be ruled out. For example, the abuse of some drugs such as cocaine may lead to grandiosity and lack of empathy. Likewise, manic states can include grandiosity and overconfidence that may be mistaken for NPD. Diagnoses of NPD should be made by a clinical psychologist, psychiatrist, or trained professional. This diagnosis will often entail a structured interview that covers the specific diagnostic criteria for NPD. The use of clinical interview and inclusion of informant reports (i.e., significant others) may be particularly important with NPD because there is evidence that individuals with NPD lack insight into the nature of their traits. This entry describes the features and prevalence of NPD, its relationship with other personality disorders, treatment issues, and some ongoing controversies.

Specific Diagnostic Features and Prevalence

The *DSM-IV-TR* describes nine specific criteria for the diagnosis of NPD. To warrant a diagnosis of NPD, a person must meet five of these nine criteria. These (paraphrased) include

1. grandiose self importance,
2. a preoccupation with grandiose fantasies,
3. a sense of "specialness,"
4. a need for admiration,
5. psychological entitlement,
6. willingness to exploit or take advantage of other people,
7. low levels of empathy for others,
8. envy for others or sense that others envy him or her, and
9. arrogance.

Because a full five of nine of these criteria are needed to diagnose NPD, the prevalence of clinically significant NPD is thought to be somewhat rare. The "point prevalence," or number of people in the general population estimated to currently have NPD in the population, is around 1%. The "lifetime prevalence," or number of people who have ever had NPD, is higher at around 6%. Some have posited that narcissism and NPD are increasing; recent data suggest that individuals in their 20s have a lifetime prevalence of approximately 9%.

Relationship With Other Personality Disorders

Narcissistic personality disorder is located in the Cluster B group of personality disorders (i.e., NPD, borderline personality disorder, antisocial personality disorder, and histrionic personality disorder). NPD shares characteristics with each of these disorders but differs in important ways as well. For instance, relative to narcissistic individuals, borderline individuals are more anxious, depressive, and impulsive. In contrast, antisocial individuals are more likely to be aggressive and impulsive and often manifest cognitive deficits. Finally, histrionic individuals are more likely to be dramatic, shallowly emotional, and inappropriately seductive.

Narcissism is also related to psychopathic personality. Specifically, narcissism is thought to be strongly linked to the interpersonal and affective characteristics of psychopathy but is less strongly related to the socially deviant behaviors and impulsivity-related traits of psychopathy. Overall, the lines between these personality disorders are not bright. They share many features in common, and often an individual will have characteristics consistent with more than one personality disorder.

Treatment

Treatment for NPD is universally described as difficult. Most individuals with NPD avoid treatment because they experience only limited distress and tend to externalize blame for their functional impairment. In addition, much of the suffering caused by NPD is actually experienced by individuals who are in close contact with the narcissistic individual (i.e., romantic partners, parents, children, colleagues).

Even when individuals with NPD enter psychological or psychiatric treatment, the dropout rate is high. Individuals with NPD do not react well to criticism, and feedback given in therapy can lead the individual with NPD to end treatment. In addition, practitioners find it difficult to treat individuals with NPD because of problems in establishing clinical rapport.

There is limited empirical evidence as to which treatments work best for NPD. There are reports that various forms of treatment, including cognitive behavioral, interpersonal, schema based, and psychodynamic, can work in some instances. There is no well-established pharmacological treatment for NPD.

Controversies

The scientific literature on NPD is relatively small, and there are still many controversies and unanswered questions. One prominent question is whether there are multiple forms or types of NPD. The emerging consensus is that there are at least two forms of NPD. The first is a grandiose form that includes a sense of personal dominance, a callous interpersonal style, and the experience of more positively valenced affect and self-esteem. The second is a vulnerable or covert form that includes more paranoia and envy, a similarly callous interpersonal style, and greater negative affect (i.e., depression and anxiety) and low self-esteem. The *DSM-IV* diagnostic criteria for NPD appear to focus entirely or predominantly on the grandiose form, although the descriptive text does reference the vulnerable form. A related issue is whether narcissism is a defense against hidden feelings of low self-worth. The data do not support this view. Individuals with grandiose narcissism do not manifest evidence of hidden low self-esteem and individuals with vulnerable narcissism, who do seem more defensive, are aware of their lower self-esteem.

Finally, the etiology of NPD is unclear. Given the evidence supporting the heritability of general and pathological personality traits, it is safe to assume there are some genetic roots. The specific environmental influences are less well understood. For grandiose narcissism, there may be a small link with permissive parenting and noncontingent praise; in contrast, for vulnerable narcissism, there seems to be an association with cold and controlling parenting and some forms of childhood abuse. More research is needed on NPD and narcissism as there has been an imbalance between theoretical speculation and empiricism.

William Keith Campbell and
Joshua David Miller

See also Borderline Personality Disorder; Emotion and Psychopathology

Further Readings

American Psychiatric Association. (2000). *Diagnostic and statistical manual of mental disorders* (4th ed., text rev.). Washington, DC: Author.

Betan, E., Heim, A. K., Conklin, C. Z., & Westen, D. (2005). Countertransference phenomena and personality pathology in clinical practice: An empirical investigation. *American Journal of Psychiatry, 162,* 890–898.

Cain, N. M., Pincus, A. L., & Ansell, E. B. (2008). Narcissism at the crossroads: Phenotypic description of pathological narcissism across clinical theory, social/personality psychology, and psychiatric diagnosis. *Clinical Psychology Review, 28,* 638–656.

Miller, J. D., Campbell, W. K., & Pilkonis, P. A. (2007). Narcissistic personality disorder: Relations with distress and functional impairment. *Comprehensive Psychiatry, 48,* 170–177.

Levy, K. N., Reynoso, J., Wasserman, R. H., & Clarkin, J. F. (2008). Narcissistic personality disorder. In W. O'Donohue, K. A. Fowler, & S. O. Lillenfeld (Eds.), *Personality disorders: Toward the DSM-V* (pp. 233–277). Thousand Oaks, CA: Sage.

Natural Action Selection, Modeling

Put simply, action selection is the task of deciding what to do next. As a general problem facing all autonomous entities—whether animals or artificial agents—action selection exercises both the sciences concerned with understanding the biological bases of behavior (e.g., ethology, neurobiology, psychology) and those concerned with building artifacts (e.g., artificial intelligence, artificial life, and robotics). The problem has two parts: What constitutes an action, and how are actions selected?

Models of natural action selection allow us to test the coherence of proposed social and biological theories. Although models cannot generate data about nature, they can generate data about theories. Complex theories can therefore be tested by comparing the outcome of simulation models against other theories in their ability to account for data drawn from nature. Each model attempts to account for transitions among different behavioral options. A wide range of modeling methodologies is currently in use. Formal mathematical models have been complemented with larger scale simulations that allow the investigation of systems for which analytical solutions are intractable or unknown. These include models of artificial animals (simulated agents or robots) embedded in simulated worlds, as well as models of underlying neural control systems (computational neuroscience and connectionist approaches). A potential pitfall of more detailed models is that they may trade biological fidelity for comprehensibility.

General challenges facing models of action selection include the following: Is the model sufficiently constrained by biological data that it captures interesting properties of the target natural system? Do manipulations of the model result in similar outcomes to those seen in nature? Does the model make predictions? Is there a simpler model that accounts for the data equally well? Or is the model too abstract? Are its connections to data trivial, making it too obvious to be useful?

Models of natural action selection have delivered new insights in many domains. What follows is a review of several: (a) the relationship between evolved behavior and optimality, (b) biological mechanisms of action selection, (c) whether or not sequencing behavior can require special representations, (d) the role of perception, (e) explanations of disability or disease, and (f) finally individual action selection in a social context.

Action Selection and Optimality

When an animal does one thing rather than another, it is natural to ask *why*? A common explanation is that the action is optimal with respect to some goal.

Assessing behavior from a normative perspective has particular value when observations deviate from predictions, because we are forced to consider the origin of the apparently suboptimal behavior. One approach is via the notion of *ecological rationality*: Cognitive mechanisms fit the demands of particular ecological niches and may deliver predictably suboptimal behavior when operating outside these niches. Models assist this approach by determining the behavioral consequences of hypothesized optimal mechanisms. Modelers can also use automated optimization techniques such as genetic algorithms (a machine learning technique inspired by Darwinian selection) to find mechanisms delivering near optimal behavior in specific contexts.

Neural Substrates

An important open question is whether there are specialized mechanisms for action selection in brains. Arguably, such a mechanism should have properties including (a) inputs that signal internal and external cues relevant to decision making, (b) some calculation of urgency or salience appropriate to each available action, (c) mechanisms enabling resolution of conflicts between competing actions based on their relative salience, and (d) outputs that allow the expression of winning actions while disallowing losers. Recent computational modeling has focused attention on the *basal ganglia* (a group of functionally related structures in the vertebrate midbrain and forebrain) as meeting these criteria. Other large-scale models encompass both cortical and subcortical mechanisms, indicating that in animals there may be a range of selection mechanisms interacting at different levels of the neuraxis.

Behavioral Sequencing

Adaptive action selection requires generating behavioral sequences appropriate to achieve longer term outcomes. Such sequences often appear to have a hierarchical decomposition, with selection taking place at multiple levels of abstraction—from choosing among high-level objectives (e.g., whether to eat, drink, or rest) through to selecting specific movements implementing the same immediate goal (e.g., which grasp to use in picking up a cup). Computational models have explored not only this approach but also the alternative—that apparently hierarchical behavior may be implemented by a framework without a hierarchical decomposition.

Perceptual Selection in Decision Making

Action selection is mediated by perception as much as by motor control. For example, selective attention can guide action by linking specific motor outputs to one among a range of stimuli. Recent models such as the *leaky competing accumulator* show that noisy sensory evidence supporting each of a range of alternatives can be accumulated until one option passes a threshold, triggering an action. This model explains experimental data and is mathematically optimal in some conditions. More generally, action selection is sometimes modeled via competing, nested, sensorimotor loops with no clear decomposition into sensory or motor components.

Disorders of Action Selection

The normal flow of integrated behavior can become disrupted following neurological damage or disease. Models have suggested that conditions including Parkinson's disease, schizophrenia, Huntington's disease, and obsessive-compulsive disorder can be linked to the same corticobasal ganglia circuits that have been identified as possible substrates for action selection. Computational models of these substrates have been used to provide improved explanations for how these disorders arise and to investigate possible avenues for treatment.

Action Selection in Social Contexts

In nature, action selection usually involves a social context. Agent-based models of social action selection explore interactions among individuals mediated both directly and indirectly via, for example, resource consumption. Examples include minimalist models of factors that influence the troop structure of primate species and models of how ants determine when and where to move a colony to a new nest; models can even explore patterns of voting in a democratic society. Modeling also allows examination of evolutionary mechanisms operating on individuals that lead to social outcomes.

Summary

The study of action selection integrates a broad range of topics including, but not limited to, neuroscience, psychology, ecology, ethology, and even political

science. These domains have in common a complexity that benefits from advanced modeling techniques, exemplifying the notion of "understanding by building." These techniques can help answer many important questions such as why animals, including humans, sometimes act irrationally; how damage to neural selection substrates can lead to debilitating neurological disorders; and how action selection by individuals impacts on the organization of societies.

Anil Seth and Joanna J. Bryson

See also Decision Making, Neural Underpinnings; Decision Making and Reward, Computational Perspectives; Layered Control Architectures

Further Readings

Gurney, K., Prescott, T. J., Wickens, J., & Redgrave, P. (2004). Computational models of the basal ganglia: From membranes to robots. *Trends in Neurosciences, 27,* 453–459.

Pratt, S. C., Sumpter, D. J. T., Mallon, E. B., & Franks, N. (2005). An agent-based model of collective nest choice by the ant *Temnothorax albipennis. Animal Behaviour, 70,* 1023–1036.

Prescott, T. J., Bryson, J. J., & Seth, A. K. (Eds.). (2007). Modelling natural action selection [Special issue]. *Philosophical Transactions of the Royal Society B: Biological Sciences 362,* 1519–1529.

Usher, M., & McClelland, J. L. (2001). The time course of perceptual choice: The leaky, competing accumulator model. *Psychological Review, 108,* 550–592.

Natural Language Generation

Natural language generation (NLG) systems are computer software systems that automatically generate texts in a human language (English, French, Chinese, etc.) from nonlinguistic input data, using techniques from computational linguistics and artificial intelligence. This entry gives a brief overview of NLG from the perspective of the choices that NLG systems must make, using examples from the specific NLG task of generating weather forecasts.

A number of NLG systems have been built that automatically generate textual weather forecasts. These systems take as input a set of numbers that predict temperature, precipitation, wind speed, and other meteorological parameters at different locations at various time periods. These numbers are usually produced by a supercomputer that is running a numerical weather simulation model. From this input, the NLG system produces a textual weather forecast that is targeted to the needs of a particular user group; for example, an Arabic text that summarizes marine weather in the Persian Gulf for offshore oil rig workers or an English text that summarizes road icing conditions for local government staff who must decide whether salt and grit should be put on roads.

NLG can largely be regarded as a process of making choices. There are usually thousands if not millions of possible texts that could be produced from a particular data set. For example, consider the temperature prediction data set in Table 1. A number of texts could be generated from this data, including the following:

1. "Tomorrow will be a cool day."

2. "Temperatures increasing from 10 at midnight to 16 at noon, then falling back to 12 at the end the period."

3. "Chilly nighttime temperatures will rise to a comfortable 15 degrees by morning. Temperatures will stay at about this level throughout the day, before falling to 12 degrees in the evening."

Deciding which text to generate requires making several kinds of decisions:

• *Content:* What information should be presented in the text? In the above example, for instance, should the system simply give an overall summary (as in Example 1), or describe how temperature changes throughout the day? In general, an NLG system can communicate only part of the information available to it. Indeed, in some weather applications, the NLG system is expected to generate a few sentences of text from 30 megabytes (!!) of input data. The decision on what to communicate is usually based on a model of what is important and significant to the user and often uses artificial intelligence reasoning techniques such as knowledge-based systems.

• *Structure:* How should the information be structured? In Example 3 above, for instance, should this information be communicated in two sentences (as in the texts shown), or should a single sentence be used? More generally, what order should information be presented in and how should information be grouped into sentences, paragraphs, and other document structures? In theory this can be based on linguistic models of document structure; for example, if the NLG system is producing a story, then it should use a narrative structure (e.g., generally order events by the time they occurred at). But in practice, structure is often determined by the genre; this is usually the case for weather forecasts, for example.

• *Lexical and syntactic choice:* Which words should be used to communicate domain concepts? For example, if temperature is going up, should this be lexicalized as *rising* or *increasing*? Similarly, what syntactic structures should be used; for example, should we use simple active voice sentences (as in Example 1), gerund-based sentences (as in Example 2), or some other structure, such as passive voice? In theory, it would be nice to make many of these choices on the basis of psycholinguistic models of reading comprehension, but unfortunately current psycholinguistic models are often not detailed and robust enough to support this.

• *Reference:* How should domain objects and entities be referred to? For example, should we refer to the time 2100 as *end of period* or *evening*? If referring to a previously mentioned object, should we use a pronoun or a definite noun phrase? NLG researchers have developed a number of algorithms for making reference choices, and these appear to work well in many cases, but many areas are underexplored. For example, we have reasonably good models for deciding when to use pronouns but much less satisfactory models for deciding how to refer to times.

Table 1   Example weather input data for an NLG system

Time	Temperature (°C)
0000	10
0300	11
0600	12
0900	15
1200	16
1500	15
1800	14
2100	12

The above decisions can be made in a number of ways. The most common approach is to manually write decision rules, usually based on a combination of (psycho)linguistic theory, corpus analysis of human-authored texts, and discussions (or more formal knowledge elicitation sessions) with domain experts. However, recently, there has been growing interest in trying to learn decision rules automatically, by using machine learning techniques that automatically analyze large corpora (collections) of human-written texts and attempt to infer from the texts the decision rules used by the human writers who created these texts. Such machine learning approaches have been very successful in other areas of natural language processing, such as machine translation.

A general issue in NLG decision making is whether the system should try to make decisions that imitate what human writers and speakers do or whether it should try to make decisions that lead to texts that are optimal in some sense for human hearers. These strategies lead to different systems, since human speakers of course do not generally produce texts that are optimal for human listeners.

The best current NLG systems can produce short texts (such as weather forecasts) that are regarded by readers as being as good as (or even better than) human-written texts. However, no current NLG system can produce long texts (more than one page) that are as good as human texts. This reflects the fact that our current understanding of low-level syntactic, lexical, and reference choices is much better than our understanding of higher level content and structure choices.

Ehud Reiter

See also Conversation and Dialogue; Discourse Processing, Models of; Multimodal Conversational Systems; Production of Language

Further Readings

ACL Special Interest Group on Natural Language Generation: www.siggen.org

Belz, A. (2008). Automatic generation of weather forecast texts using comprehensive probabilistic generation-space models. *Natural Language Engineering, 14*, 431–455.

Goldberg, E., Driedgar, N., & Kittredge, R. (1994). Using natural-language processing to produce weather forecasts. *IEEE Expert, 9*, 45–53.

Reiter, E., & Dale, R. (2000). *Building natural language generation systems*. Cambridge, UK: Cambridge University Press.

Reiter, E., Sripada, S., & Robertson, R. (2003). Acquiring correct knowledge for natural language generation. *Journal of Artificial Intelligence Research, 18*, 491–516.

NEURAL CORRELATES OF CONSCIOUSNESS

It is widely agreed that some neural activity must correlate very closely with the occurrence of consciousness and, further, that neuroscience has the ability to discover these *neural correlates of consciousness* (NCC). This agreement contrasts with the widespread disagreement about whether neuroscience can ever explain *how* consciousness arises from brain activity.

After defining the NCC, this entry summarizes the two basic approaches to the NCC search, using examples of experimental paradigms. It looks at recent findings and developments and touches on methodological and philosophical controversies.

Definition

Finding the NCC means finding the sufficient neural conditions for the occurrence of consciousness and then narrowing down this set of conditions to the *minimally sufficient* conditions: the neural activity that *most closely* correlates with consciousness. For example, blood supply to the brain is part of the sufficient conditions for consciousness but is not a minimally sufficient condition because it is important for much else besides consciousness. Similarly, certain processes in the cerebellum may influence a given conscious state but may not be closely correlated with it because the state may be able to occur even if the cerebellum processes differ. In contrast, it seems that, normally, activity in the inferior temporal cortex (together with other areas) is needed for some aspects of consciousness, and this therefore seems to belong with the minimally sufficient conditions for consciousness. The NCC is normally not defined in terms of finding the *necessary* conditions for consciousness since it is generally agreed that, at least in principle, different neural states could be sufficient for the same aspect of consciousness. (For example, it should not be ruled out that different neural systems in a developing juvenile brain and an aging brain could correlate with the same type of conscious state.)

Two Basic Approaches to the NCC

The *state*-based approach to the NCC focuses on the contrast between individuals who are in an overall unconscious state versus individuals who are in an overall conscious state (e.g., being in a vegetative state or being anesthetized vs. being awake). One method is to use brain imaging (such as functional magnetic resonance imaging) to reveal the neural activity characteristic of a patient in an unconscious, vegetative state as he or she recovers and regains consciousness. Such studies suggest that a certain thalamocortical pattern of activity may be part of the state NCC. It is important, but also difficult, to match these conditions as closely as possible such that the observed neural activity in the patient is most closely correlated with regaining consciousness rather than with regaining other kinds of nonconscious, cognitive abilities. This methodology is further challenged by intriguing and disturbing studies that arguably show that some patients in vegetative states in fact are conscious.

The *content*-based approach takes individuals who are already in an overall conscious state and focuses on the contrast between specific conscious contents within those individuals (e.g., the conscious experience of a face vs. of a house). It is important, but also difficult, to control conditions such that the neural activity observed when content becomes conscious is not correlated with unconscious content processing of the stimulus. For this reason, bistable perception (e.g., binocular rivalry, in which different stimuli are shown to each eye and conscious perception alternates between them rather than blending them) is widely used in experimental paradigms. This paradigm keeps the physical stimuli constant while varying the conscious contents, such that neural changes should be closely correlated with changes in conscious content; other paradigms include blindsight, inattentional blindness, and masking. In bistable perception, imaging and single-cell studies indicate the importance of activity in the inferior temporal cortex but also in many other areas of the brain, including early visual cortex. This distribution of activity makes interpretation of data difficult since early visual cortex is also active during *un*conscious content processing (unconscious, masked stimuli are processed and can influence behavior, for example). This suggests that qualitatively different *types* of activity in these same cortical areas correlate with conscious and with unconscious contents; neural decoding techniques are being developed that may assist in distinguishing them.

Beyond Mere Correlates

It is clear that the state-based and content-based approaches to the NCC must complement each other, but it is an open question how. Possibly, advances in our understanding of neural interconnectivity and of basic neurocomputational principles (e.g., appealing to the notion of information integration) will help with this question. This kind of development, and others (such as the emerging neural decoding methods), can be seen as attempts at finding systematic rather than merely "brute" NCCs. This could in the future provide hints to the functions of consciousness itself. Though this may not in the end provide a solution to the problem of *how* consciousness as such arises from brain activity, it may significantly improve our understanding of the nature of consciousness and provide insights into its various disorders.

Philosophical and Methodological Issues

In most NCC studies, neural activity is picked out *indirectly* via, for example, fMRI's ability to pick up the blood-oxygen-level-dependent signal, the significance of which is subject to intense technical debate. Likewise, consciousness is picked out indirectly via behavioral responses such as introspective reports. The reliance on introspection is contentious because there is no independent method for verifying such data. Some believe this disqualifies consciousness, and hence the NCC, as an area of proper scientific research, while others believe that we can have sufficient trust in subjective reports. Thus, whereas the NCC search can be pursued in the absence of a solution to the mind-body problem, it is not entirely innocent of traditional philosophical problems at the heart of the very notion of consciousness, concerning its subjective nature and the absence of direct access to other individuals' consciousness.

Introspection and the general *accessibility* of conscious content throughout the cognitive consumer systems (such as introspection, episodic memory, and reasoning systems) in the brain may constitute one notion of consciousness, called *access consciousness*. Another notion may concern the purely subjective, or experiential, aspect of consciousness called *phenomenal consciousness*. Some argue that a clear distinction between these notions is needed such that, for example, introspective awareness can come apart from conscious experience; this implies the controversial claim that in principle there can be phenomenally conscious states that the person having the experience is introspectively unaware of. In that case, neuroscience should expect to find distinct NCCs for access consciousness and for phenomenal consciousness. Experimental paradigms that clearly distinguish these NCCs are yet to be fully developed, and it is unclear how this distinction relates to the distinction between the state-based and the content-based approaches to the NCC search.

Jakob Hohwy

See also Access Consciousness; Anesthesia and Awareness; Blindsight; Consciousness and the Unconscious; Introspection; Sleep and Dreams; Subliminal Perception; Unconscious Perception

Further Readings

Block, N. (2005). Two neural correlates of consciousness. *Trends in Cognitive Sciences, 9*(2), 46–52.

Chalmers, D. (2000). What is a neural correlate of consciousness? In T. Metzinger (Ed.), *Neural correlates of consciousness: Empirical and conceptual issues* (pp. 17–39). Cambridge, MA: MIT Press.

Haynes, J.-D. (2009). Decoding visual consciousness from human brain signals. *Trends in Cognitive Sciences, 13*(5), 194–202.

Hohwy, J. (2009). The neural correlates of consciousness: New experimental approaches needed? *Consciousness and Cognition, 18*(2), 428–438.

Koch, C. (2004). *The quest for consciousness: A neurobiological approach.* Englewood, CO: Roberts.

NEURODYNAMICS OF VISUAL SEARCH

This entry describes the synaptic, neuronal, and cortical mechanisms underlying visual attention. It further discusses how these mechanisms, based on more general principles of competition and cooperation between neurons, underlie the processes involved in visual search.

The Psychophysics of Visual Attention in Search Tasks

The visual system cannot process simultaneously the immense amount of information conveyed in a complex natural scene. To cope with this problem, attentional mechanisms are needed to select relevant scene information. Evidence for attentional mechanisms in

visual processing comes mainly from psychophysical experiments using visual search tasks such as those developed by Anne Treisman. In visual search tasks, subjects examine a display containing randomly positioned items to detect a previously defined target. Items in the display that are different from the target are distracters. The main phenomenology can be understood from the dependence of the measured reaction time on the number of items in the display. There are two main types of search displays: feature search or "pop out" and conjunction or serial search. In a feature search task, the target differs from the distracters on a single feature (e.g., only in its color). In this case, search times are independent of the number of distracters. A typical example of pop-out search is the detection of a red bar within an array of differently tilted green bars. The result can be trivially explained with the activation of only parallel processes, and therefore the unique feature defining the target pops out. In a conjunction search task, the target is defined by a conjunction of features; each distracter shares at least one of those features with the target. Conjunction search experiments show that search time increases linearly with the number of distracters, implying a serial process. An example of conjunction search is the detection of a red vertical bar within a display containing vertical green or tilted red bars as distracters; that is, there is only one item sharing simultaneously (a conjunction of) the two features defining the target, but each distracter shares one feature with the target.

The classical hypothesis accounting for attentional selection in vision is that attention enhances the responses of neurons representing stimuli at a single relevant location in the visual field. This enhancement model is related to Hermann von Helmholtz's spotlight metaphor for focal attention. In this metaphor, a spotlight of attention illuminates part of the visual field; stimuli in the spotlight are processed in higher detail, while information outside the spotlight is filtered out. In this classical view, an object searched for in a cluttered scene is found by rapidly shifting the spotlight from one object to the next until the target is found. In this view, attention is based on explicit serial mechanisms. Based on these concepts, Anne Treisman proposed the so-called *feature integration theory* of visual selective attention. This theory is based on numerous psychophysical experiments on visual search and offers an interpretation of the binding problem, which asks how features detected by different cortical feature maps are assembled into objects. The feature integration theory distinguishes two processing stages. In the first stage, called preattentive, processing done in parallel across the visual field extracts primitive features (e.g., colors, orientation) without integrating them. In the second, attentive, stage information from limited parts of the field is integrated.

The Neurophysiology of Attention

Recent neurophysiological studies, performed mainly in the lab of Robert Desimone, have shown that the effects of the enhancement of attention on neuronal responses can be understood in the context of competition among the stimuli in the visual field. This neurophysiologically more realistic mechanism for selective attention, originally proposed by John Duncan and Robert Desimone, is called the *biased competition* hypothesis. The biased competition hypothesis assumes that populations of neurons encoding different locations and features of the multiple stimuli in the visual field are simultaneously activated and therefore are competing. Attention to a stimulus at a particular location or with a particular feature biases this competition in favor of neurons encoding the location or the features attended. This biased competition leads to an up-modulation of the firing activity of the neuronal populations encoding the attended location or features and to a down-modulation of the activity of the neuronal populations associated with distracting stimuli. The attentional biasing comes through feedback connections from areas outside the visual cortex. In this framework, it is clear that the neurodynamics underlying visual search result from a top-down process biasing the competition between neurons in early visual areas, which selects one stimulus in the visual field. In other words, attention is an emergent property of competitive parallel interactions across the visual field.

Precursors for this type of mechanism include earlier neural network models such as the adaptive resonance model of Steven Grossberg and the interactive activation model of James McClelland.

The Computational Neuroscience of Attention

Let us now see in more detail which kind of cortical architecture is behind visual attention. Figure 1 shows a functional cortical architecture that considers attentional top-down processes interacting with bottom-up processes as proposed by Gustavo Deco and Edmund Rolls. In particular, it schematizes how the dorsal (also called *where*) visual stream (which reaches the posterior parietal cortex [PP]) and the ventral (*what*) visual stream (via V4 to the inferior temporal cortex [IT]) interact in early visual cortical areas (such as V1 and V2), accounting for many aspects of visual attention. This type of architecture implements at the local and global brain area level the principle of biased competition described above. In the original model of Deco and Rolls, the system was composed of six modules (V1 [primary visual cortex], V2–V4, IT, PP, ventral prefrontal cortex v46, and dorsal prefrontal cortex d46), reciprocally connected as schematized in the figure. Information from the retina reaches V1 via the lateral geniculate.

The attentional top-down signal biasing intra- and intercortical competition is assumed to come from prefrontal cortex area 46 (modules d46 and v46). In particular, feedback connections from area v46 to the IT module could specify the target object in a visual search task; feedback connections from area d46 to the PP module could generate the bias to a targeted spatial location created by a spatial attentional cue in an object recognition task. Each brain area consists of mutually coupled neuronal populations whose dynamics are described by conductance-based synaptic and spiking neuronal models. The equations describing the detailed neuronal dynamics can be further reduced using mean-field techniques, which in this case replace the temporally averaged discharge rate of a neuron with the instantaneous ensemble average of the activity of the neuronal population. The dynamical evolution of activity within a cortical area can be simulated in the model by integrating the population activity in the area over space and time.

The computation of a visual search works as follows. An external top-down bias from prefrontal area v46 drives the competition in IT in favor of the population encoding the target object. Then, intermodular back projection attentional modulation pathways from IT–V4–V1 enhance the activity of populations in V4 and V1 encoding the component features of the target. Only locations in V1 matching the back-projected target features are up-regulated. The enhanced firing of the neuronal populations encoding the location of the target in V1 leads to increased activity in the spatially mapped forward pathway from V1 to V2–V4 to PP, resulting in

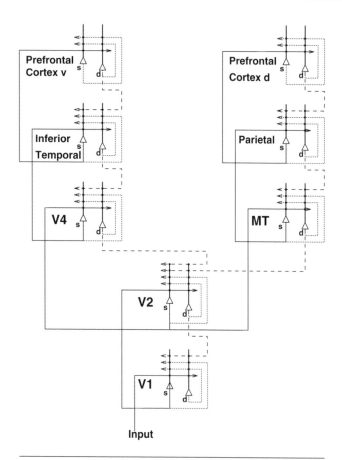

Figure 1 The systems-level architecture of a model of the cortical mechanisms of visual attention and memory

Source: Deco, G., & Rolls, E. T. (2005). Attention, short term memory, and action selection: A unifying theory. *Progress in Neurobiology, 76,* 236–256; reprinted with permission.

Note: The system is essentially composed of six modules that model the two known main visual pathways of the primate visual cortex. Information from the retina via the lateral geniculate nucleus enters the visual cortex through area V1 in the occipital cortex and proceeds into two forward or bottom-up processing streams. The occipital-temporal stream leads ventrally through V2–V4 and IT and is mainly concerned with object recognition. The occipital-parietal stream leads dorsally into PP and is responsible for maintaining a spatial map of an object's location. Both posterior visual pathways send connections to and receive connections from the lateral prefrontal cortex, where short-term memory functions take place. Forward connections are indicated by solid lines; back projections, which could implement top-down processing, by dashed lines; and recurrent connections within an area by dotted lines. The letter *s* = superficial pyramidal cells; *d* = deep pyramidal cells.

increased firing in the PP module in the location corresponding to the target. Consequently, these cascades of biased competition compute the location of the target and are made explicit by the enhanced firing activity of neuronal populations at the location of the target in the spatially organized PP module. This type of cortical model can successfully simulate the neurophysiology and psychophysics underlying feature and conjunction search tasks. Note that the whole simulation is parallel and therefore does not involve a serial moving spotlight process at all. In this model, a conjunction search with more distractors takes longer because the constraints are then more difficult to satisfy and the dynamics of the coupled set of networks show a longer latency to settle. In other words, apparently serial cognitive tasks may in fact be performed by fully parallel processing neuronal networks with realistic dynamics.

Gustavo Deco

See also Attention, Neuroimaging Studies of; Attention and Action; Visual Search

Further Readings

Deco, G., & Rolls, E. T. (2005). Attention, short term memory, and action selection: A unifying theory. *Progress in Neurobiology, 76,* 236–256.

Desimone, R., & Duncan, J. (1995). Neural mechanisms of selective visual attention. *Annual Review of Neuroscience, 18,* 193–222.

Moran, J., & Desimone, R. (1985). Selective attention gates visual processing in the extrastriate cortex. *Science, 229,* 782–784.

Rolls, E. T., & Deco, G. (2002). *Computational neuroscience of vision.* Oxford, UK: Oxford University Press.

NEUROECONOMICS

The study of decision making has occupied researchers in neuroscience, psychology, and economics for centuries. Since the late 1990s a group of scholars have begun to combine theories and methods from these three disciplines, forming the interdisciplinary field of *neuroeconomics.* What these scientists came to believe is that the highly different approaches of the natural and social sciences to the study of decision making could benefit from mutual interaction and constraint. In one direction, theories from economics and psychology could serve to organize the ever-increasing amounts of neurophysiological data into a coherent framework. In the opposite direction, neuroscientific data could provide biological constraints for models of choice behaviors in economics and psychology. A series of papers, meetings, and books has been shaping this field for more than a decade, attracting general public interest but also criticism from scholars in the three parenting disciplines.

Background

The different strategies employed by economics, psychology, and neuroscience in the study of decision making can be thought of as three different levels of abstraction. At the highest level, economists strive to predict human choice behavior based on rigorous mathematical models. These are typically "as if" models, with *as if* meaning that they do not attempt to unravel the actual decision-making mechanism at an algorithmic level and are only concerned with the behavioral accuracy of the predictions they make. This approach has dominated economics at least since the 1940s when the neoclassical school began to dominate economic thought. Paul Samuelson and others developed this approach around the specification of a set of assumptions or axioms from which choice behavior could be mathematically derived. Based on a small number of axioms as simple as "if a person prefers oranges to apples she will not also prefer apples to oranges," John Von Neumann and Oskar Morgenstern developed their model for choice between uncertain outcomes (expected utility), which was extended by Leonard Savage to include subjective estimations of outcome probability (subjective expected utility). Von Neumann and Morgenstern also laid the foundations for game theory, in which decisions are affected by choices made by many players with competing interests. Although these models were meant to describe empirical human behavior, their mathematical construction gave them a more *normative* nature, in the sense that they described how people *should* behave more than how they *do* behave.

At the lowest level of abstraction, neuroscientists aim to reveal the neuronal architecture that underlies the same behavior that economists seek to predict. Traditionally, such research was based on brain lesions in humans and animals and on electrophysiological recordings in anaesthetized animals. Those techniques were very helpful in unraveling the neural circuits for simple sensory and motor functions but were not sufficient for the study of higher cognitive functions. The introduction of electrophysiological recordings in awake behaving animals in the 1960s and of noninvasive imaging methods in humans in the 1980s and 1990s enabled neuroscientists to examine neural activity while humans and other animals were engaged in complex behavior. In turn, those technological advances raised a new challenge: Huge amounts of data could now be easily generated, but these data needed to be sorted out and interpreted in a meaningful way.

The gap between the highest and lowest levels of abstraction is bridged by psychologists, who are interested in the mental states and processes, including thoughts and emotions, that are caused by neural activity and that lead to choice behavior. In the second half of the 20th century, both economics and neuroscience embraced concepts and methods from psychology, two processes that eventually resulted in the birth of neuroeconomics.

On the economics side, in the 1950s economists began to pay attention to cases in which human choices deviate from the normative predictions of the mathematical models. Maurice Allais was the first to describe behavior that violates one of the core axioms of the neoclassical school, a behavior better known as the *Allais paradox*. Allais was followed by Daniel Ellsberg, who described the now famous *Ellsberg paradox* that violated yet another (although admittedly less critical) axiom. By the 1970s and 1980s the psychologists Daniel Kahneman and Amos Tversky had widely extended these early findings by demonstrating that robust axiomatic violations were more common than has been previously suspected. In a series of experiments they revealed a wide range of choice patterns that falsified one or more of the axioms of expected utility theory, leading many economists and psychologists to conclude that economic models could benefit from psychological data and insights. This realization gave rise to the discipline of *behavioral economics,* which lay at the boundary of economics and psychology.

At about the same time that these processes took place in the economic world, neuroscientists began to feel the need to use models of mental processes in designing their experiments and analyzing their data. The ability to record the activity of single neurons in awake behaving animals and to image the activity of populations of neurons in humans allowed more than a simple correlation between neural activation and observed behavior. Using models of cognitive function, neuroscientists could now look for correlates of hidden variables of these models. Studies of this type constituted the new discipline of *cognitive neuroscience,* which lay at the boundary of neuroscience and psychology.

In the mid-1990s these cognitive neuroscientists and behavioral economists who were interested in choice behavior went a step further: Some neuroscientists began to examine economic models and contemplate their use as a normative theory for neurobiological data. At the same time, a few economists considered a further logical reduction of their models, taking into account mechanistic constraints and algorithmic features of the human nervous system. These steps set the stage for the emergence of the new discipline of neuroeconomics.

From Economics to Neuroscience

The first neuroeconomics paper is probably a 1996 review published by Peter Shizgal and Kent Conover in *Current Directions in Psychological Science,* titled "On the Neural Computation of Utility." The paper explicitly employed normative economic theory to describe the neurobiology of choice in rats performing intracranial self-stimulation. Following this paper, in 1999, Michael Platt and Paul Glimcher published their paper "Neural Correlates of Decision Variables in Parietal Cortex" in *Nature.* The authors showed in that paper that neurons in monkey parietal cortex encoded both the probability and the magnitude of reward, a finding compatible with the idea that these neurons played an algorithmic role in decision making closely aligned with the basic models of neoclassical economic theory.

In 2001, the neuroeconomics approach was extended to human studies with the publication of two imaging studies that resulted from collaborations between economists, psychologists, and neuroscientists. In the first of these papers, Peter Shizgal joined Daniel Kahneman, Hans Breiter, and others to map the neural responses to expectation and experience of monetary gains and losses. Breiter and colleagues based their experimental design on two principles from Kahneman and Tversky's prospect theory: that the evaluation of a risky prospect depends on its framing as a gain or a loss and that losses loom larger than gains of equal magnitude. In the second paper, a group of economists, including Kevin McCabe and Vernon Smith, together with MRI specialists, were the first to use game theory in a human neurobiological experiment. Playing either against a human opponent or against a computer, subjects had to decide whether to trust the other player. Results showed that those subjects who tended to trust their opponents had higher neuronal activation in regions of the medial prefrontal cortex while playing against humans compared to playing against computers.

Shortly after the publication of these first papers, Glimcher published a book titled *Decisions, Uncertainty, and the Brain* in which he articulated the need for the use of normative theory in the study of the neurobiology of higher cognitive function. Glimcher proposed that economics could provide such theory and called for neuroscience and economics to join forces in the study of decision making.

In the next few years, a growing number of neurobiological papers on humans and other animals that relied on economic theory in the design and analysis of their experiments have been published. Some examples are papers dealing with the economic value of goods, game theory, the framing effect, loss aversion, intertemporal choice, and ambiguity aversion.

While the contribution of economics to neuroscience is widely recognized in the neuroscience community, many economists maintain that economics does not stand much to gain from neurobiological insights. Nevertheless, several recent papers suggest a potential role for the use of neuroscientific data in developing economic theories.

From Neuroscience to Economics

In 2005, the economists Colin Camerer, George Loewenstein, and Drazen Prelec published a paper in the *Journal of Economic Literature,* in which they made the case for neuroeconomics from the economics side. Camerer and his colleagues argued that understanding the neural mechanism of decision should provide algorithmic insights that will constrain possible economic theories and may direct future studies in economics. In essence, what they proposed was that instead of settling for "as if" models, economists could now use neural data to look for more mechanistic models.

At about the same time, Michael Kosfeld, Ernst Fehr, and colleagues published a paper in *Nature*, which is probably the first to show the potential role neuroscientific data can have in the shaping of economic theory. In that study, subjects played a trust game similar to the one used by McCabe and colleagues described above. Critically in this study, however, in some of the subjects the brain levels of oxytocin, a neuropeptide that is believed to play a role in social attachment, were increased before they made their decision. Kosfeld and colleagues found that those subjects treated with oxytocin were subsequently more trusting compared to a control group.

The next step was taken 2 years later by Glimcher and colleagues, who showed that neurobiological data could be used to falsify existing economic theories. By having subjects make choices between possible gains of different monetary amounts and different times of receipt the authors explored the neural correlates of intertemporal choice. What they found was that the neural architecture underlying this kind of choice process is not compatible with a prominent economic theory of intertemporal choice.

One step further was taken by the neuroscientists Mauricio Delgado and Elizabeth Phelps in collaboration with the economists Andrew Schotter and Erkut Ozbay. In that study, the authors first used neuroimaging to gain insight about the psychological processes that underlie the tendency of most people to overbid in auctions and then used that insight as a basis for behavioral predictions that they tested and confirmed.

Thus, the first attempts to use neurobiological data in the development of economic models have already been made. However, the degree of influence that studies of this sort will have on economic theory remains to be seen. Moreover, there is a strong debate in the economics community not only about whether neurobiological measurements *could* affect economic models but also whether they *should* affect those models. Perhaps the most famous attack

on neuroeconomics was made by Faruk Gul and Wolfgang Pesendorfer in their article "The Case for Mindless Economics." Gul and Pesendorfer argued that the goal of economic theories is to make predictions about behavior and that the actual machinery by which choice is accomplished must remain irrelevant to economists.

An Emerging Field

A major role in the formation of neuroeconomics was played by several meetings and conferences that allowed scientists from different disciplines to interact and to define themselves as neuroeconomists. This series of meetings eventually led to the formation of the Society for Neuroeconomics. The society has been holding annual meetings since 2005, featuring the most recent studies in neuroeconomics, with the number of participants from around the world rising every year. In 2009, the society published a volume titled *Neuroeconomics: Decision-Making and the Brain*, which was edited by Glimcher, Camerer, Russell Poldrack, and Fehr and authored by all the central scholars in the field. This edited volume summarizes nearly all the most recent advances in neuroeconomics and serves both as an introduction to the discipline and as a handbook for researchers in the field.

Recognizing neuroeconomics as an academic discipline, many universities around the world have opened specialized centers for neuroeconomics, offering both some graduate-level training in neuroeconomics and support for independent researchers. These scientists, together with scholars in traditional departments for neuroscience, psychology, and economics, continue to investigate the behavior and neurobiology of decision making.

Ifat Levy and Paul W. Glimcher

See also Allais Paradox; Decision Making, Neural Underpinnings; Decision Making and Reward, Computational Perspectives; Decision Theory, Philosophical Perspectives

Further Readings

Camerer, C., Loewenstein, G., & Prelec, D. (2005). Neuroeconomics: How neuroscience can inform economics. *Journal of Economic Literature, 43,* 9–64.

Glimcher, P. W. (2003). *Decisions, uncertainty, and the brain: The science of neuroeconomics.* Cambridge, MA: MIT Press.

Glimcher, P. W. (2011). *Foundations of neuroeconomic analysis.* New York, NY: Oxford University Press.

Glimcher, P. W., Camerer C., Fehr E., & Poldrack, R. A. (Eds.). (2009). *Neuroeconomics: Decision making and the brain.* London, UK: Elsevier/Academic.

Glimcher, P. W., Kable, J., & Louie, K. (2007). Neuroeconomic studies of impulsivity: Now or just as soon as possible? *American Economic Review, 97,* 142–147.

Kahneman, D., & Tversky, A. (1979). Prospect theory: Analysis of decision under risk. *Econometrica, 47,* 263–291.

Kosfeld, M., Heinrichs, M., Zak, P. J., Fischbacher, U., & Fehr, E. (2005). Oxytocin increases trust in humans. *Nature, 435,* 673–676.

Shizgal, P., & Conover, K. (1996). On the neural computation of utility. *Current Directions in Psychology, 5,* 37–43.

OBJECT-DEPENDENT THOUGHT

Some thoughts are purely general in the sense that they make no reference to specific individual things. *Dogs are descended from wolves*, and *there are infinitely many prime numbers* are both general in this sense. The first makes a statement about concrete spatiotemporal objects but none in particular; the latter, one about abstract objects but again none in particular. Most of our everyday thoughts, however, are singular or object-directed thoughts in that they make reference to particular individual objects, be they concrete or abstract. *Frege was a mathematician; You are not supposed to smoke in here; It is hot over there; That lime tree is tall; This yellow after-image is fading; I am leaving now; 3 is a prime number*: These are all singular thoughts because each involves reference to a particular thing or things. As these examples indicate, singular thoughts (beliefs, judgments) are usually expressed by sentences containing proper names (e.g., *Frege*), indexical expressions (e.g., *you*, *I*, and *now*), demonstrative pronouns (e.g., *that lime tree*, *this yellow after-image*, *here*, *there*), and numeral names (*3*). The debate over the nature of singular thoughts has been largely restricted to thought about concretely existing objects available to perception. This entry will discuss the controversial doctrine that singular thoughts are object dependent. The following two sections expound the doctrine and note some of its allegedly paradoxical consequences. The next two sections sketch the central argument in favor of object dependence and some objections to it coming from rival conceptions of singular thought.

Singular Thought as Object Dependent

Some philosophers maintain that the mental contents of singular thoughts are *object dependent*, meaning by this that the existence and identity of their mental contents depend on the existence and identity of the objects those mental contents are about. For example, consider the thought *that is a lime tree* had by you while looking at a particular tree, where the italicized expression specifies the mental content of your thought. According to the doctrine of object dependence, if, counterfactually, no tree at all had in fact been there to be singled out by you, owing perhaps to a referential illusion or hallucination—call this the "empty possibility"—then there would have been no singular thought content for you to entertain. Consequently, your psychological condition in this situation would be different from what it is in the actual situation. Moreover, if, counterfactually, your thought had instead singled out a qualitatively indistinguishable but numerically different tree—call this the "duplicate possibility"—then the resulting thought would have had a different content from the content it has in the actual situation. Again, your overall psychological state in this duplicate possibility is different from what it actually is.

First-person thoughts expressed with the indexical *I* seem clearly to be object dependent. The thought that you now express with the sentence *I am hot* surely could not exist unless you did. Furthermore, no one else, not even your identical twin, could have had the very same thought. The thesis that singular thoughts expressed with other indexicals, demonstratives, and proper names are object dependent is, however, highly controversial, because of its allegedly paradoxical consequences.

Allegedly Paradoxical Consequences of Object Dependence

It is a consequence of the object-dependent view that a thinker in an empty possibility could suffer the illusion of having a thought when he was not, because his would-be thought failed to pick out an object. But can we really be mistaken about whether we are having a thought? That the answer to this last question is "no" is the very reason why Bertrand Russell notoriously restricted the possibility of genuine singular thought about particulars to those whose existence we cannot be mistaken about—namely, mental entities, such as after-images and other so-called sense data. A person may be mistaken about whether he or she is actually seeing a tree but not about whether he or she is having a visual experience as of a tree. Another allegedly problematic consequence arises when we consider the duplicate possibility. In such a case, everything will seem the same to you: The duplicate object (a qualitatively indistinguishable tree, say) does not appear to affect your conscious awareness in any way differently from how the actual object affects it. Many of those opposed to object dependence, such as so-called internalists about mental content, argue that in order for there to be a genuinely mental difference between the two cases, you must be able to detect the difference.

The Central Argument for Object Dependence

A number of different arguments have been advanced in favor of an object-dependent conception of singular thought. Many of these, especially those of Gareth Evans and John McDowell, involve a synthesis of key ideas of Gottlob Frege and Bertrand Russell. Some of these arguments are unconvincing to their opponents because they rely on questionable epistemic principles as premises. For example, some of Evans's arguments appear to rely on an unacceptably strong reading of Russell's principle that, roughly speaking, to have a singular thought, one must know which object it is that one

is thinking about. Sometimes the debate over object dependence hinges on the role of singular thoughts in action explanation. Here, we shall briefly sketch the strongest argument in favor of object dependence.

The argument has three main premises. The first is a very general claim about the nature of thought content—namely, that it is essentially representational, in that it represents the world as being a certain way. When you have what seems to be a (perceptual demonstrative) singular thought, for example, such as *that lime tree is tall,* your perception-based thought represents the world as being a certain way—namely, that that lime tree (the very one you are seeing) is tall. In other words, there is a certain condition necessarily associated with the thought—the thought's *truth condition*—which is such that, if it is fulfilled, then thought is true, and if it is not fulfilled, then the thought is false. The second premise is specific to the nature of singular thoughts: The truth conditions in question must be genuinely singular. What this means is that when the truth conditions are stated, reference must be made, not just to any object fulfilling certain conditions but to a particular object—namely, the very object of your thought. It will not do, according to the object-dependent theorist, to state the truth conditions for your thought as follows: *That lime tree is tall* is true if and only if there is a lime tree of such-and-such characteristics and it is tall (see the next section for one way of filling out *such-and-such*). Rather, the truth conditions must make reference to the very tree you are seeing: *That lime tree is tall* is true if and only if that lime tree (the very one you are seeing) is tall. The third premise has two parts: (a) in the absence of any object (i.e., in the empty possibility), it is impossible for there to be a singular truth condition; (b) in the presence of a different object (i.e., in the duplicate possibility), the singular truth condition will necessarily be different. From these three premises, the object-dependent theorist infers that singular thoughts are object dependent.

Rival Conceptions

Most parties to the debate accept the first premise. The second premise is challenged by those, such as John Searle, who, influenced by Russell's views, seek to give nonsingular truth conditions based on quantificationally analyzed definite description concepts. A definite description concept is a concept of the form *the such-and-such* that purports to describe something uniquely. According to Russell's quantificational analysis, to say that *the such-and-such is so-and-so* is to say that *there is one, and only one, such-and-such and it is so-and-so.* For example, to say that the present king of France is bald is to say that there is one, and only one, present king of France and he is bald. If there is no such thing as the present king of France (because France is a republic), then the original statement saying that he is bald is not meaningless but simply false because part of what it claims is that there is such a thing and there is not.

We can apply Russell's analysis to our earlier example as follows: The thought *that lime tree is tall* is true if and only if the lime tree causing this very experience is tall—that is, if and only if there is one, and only one, lime tree causing this experience, and it is tall. On this analysis, if you are in an empty possibility, then, contrary to the doctrine of object dependence, you can still have a thought, but your thought will be false. This approach to demonstrative singular thoughts seems problematic, however, for at least two reasons. First, the truth condition in question implausibly overintellectualizes thought content, counterintuitively prohibiting ordinary people, children, and animals, who either do not possess or are not currently exercising the concepts of causation and experience, from having singular thoughts. Second, it assumes without argument the Russellian view that only demonstrative thoughts about mental phenomena (this experience) can be truly singular.

Opponents of object dependence who accept Premise 2 of the main argument, such as Tyler Burge, attack Premise 3. They seek to give genuinely singular but nevertheless object-independent truth conditions by employing a logic free of existence assumptions. Unlike classical logic, such a "free logic" is designed to incorporate non-denoting singular terms, such as *Pegasus*, and accordingly places restrictions on some of the classical rules of inference, prohibiting, for example, the inference (via the rule of existential generalization) of *there exists something that flies* directly from the premise *Pegasus flies.* If such a nonclassical free logic is employed, singular truth conditions for some statements containing non-denoting terms can be formulated. It remains to be seen, however, whether this relatively unexplored rival approach, whose genesis and application lie in formal semantics for natural languages, can be applied to all types of singular thoughts in a psychologically realistic way.

Sean Crawford

See also Anti-Individualism About Cognition; Descriptions; Descriptive Thought; Indexical Thought; Knowledge by Acquaintance

Further Readings

Burge, T. (1974). Truth and singular terms. *Noûs, 8,* 309–325.

Burge, T. (1977). Belief *de re. Journal of Philosophy, 74,* 338–362.

Crawford, S. (1998). In defence of object-dependent thoughts. *Proceedings of the Aristotelian Society, 98*(2), 201–210.

McDowell, J. (1986). Singular thought and the extent of inner space. In J. McDowell & P. Pettit (Eds.), *Subject, thought, and context* (pp. 137–168). Oxford, UK: Clarendon Press.

Searle, J. (1983). *Intentionality.* Cambridge, UK: Cambridge University Press.

OBJECTS OF MEMORY

Memory is a kind of mental state that has an object. Memories are *about* things. But what entities are the objects of memories? Are those entities mental? Are they states of affairs in the world? This entry will examine three different approaches to this issue. The approach will be philosophical (or conceptual) rather than psychological (or empirical).

Two preliminary points are necessary. First, what counts as the object of a mental state? The key characteristic of memories here is their capacity to be accurate or correct. We can think of the object of a memory as that object, property, state of affairs, or event whose presence makes the memory correct and whose absence makes it incorrect. Second, we need to draw a distinction between *experiential* and *propositional* memories. This distinction is drawn in different ways in philosophy and psychology. If you propositionally remember that there is a computer in my office, then you believe that there is such a computer and you believe it because you acquired that belief some time in the past and it has been preserved until now. By contrast, if you experientially remember that there is a computer in my office, then you are in a state wherein my office is presented to you as having contained a computer (you have a sort of "memory image" of the computer) and you are in that state because, sometime in the past, you seemed to perceive the computer. The question that will concern us here is what kinds of entities make our experiential memories correct.

The World as the Object of Memory

At first glance, one would think that the objects of memory are worldly entities. After all, we say things such as, "I remember that you were at the party on Saturday," or "I remember that Jane's car is blue." This way of talking suggests that the objects of my memories are those states of affairs that consist in, respectively, your being at the party on Saturday and Jane's car being blue. Call this the *world-directed* view. The difficulty for it is the following. Suppose I perceive Jane's car as being green, but it is really blue. Days later, I am trying to remember what color it was and I happen to have a memory image of it as being blue. Call this Situation 1. Intuitively enough, we would say that my memory has failed me here. However, the world-directed view commits us to saying that, in Situation 1, I am not misremembering the car.

Sensory Experience as the Object of Memory

One is then inclined to turn to the idea that the objects of memory are one's own past perceptual experiences. This suggests a picture of memory as being similar to introspection. The idea would be that, in both cases, we are attending to our own mental states. In memory, those mental states are past perceptual experiences, whereas, in introspection, they are current mental states. This view, which we may call the *introspective view*, accounts for our intuitions about Situation 1. However, imagine now that your memory experience of Jane's car presents it to you as being green. The car is really blue and your memory image originates in a past perceptual experience of it as being green. Call this Situation 2. The introspective view commits us to saying that your memory experience of Jane's car as being green is correct. But we would not want to say that. If you misperceived the car as being green in the past, how can you be remembering it correctly now when it appears to you as being green? It is hard to see how

a false mental state could have turned into a true mental state just because time has gone by.

Memory Is Its Own Object

According to John Searle's *token-reflexive* view, the object of a memory experience is a causal relation that involves world and mind. The object of a memory experience wherein Jane's car appears to you as having been blue is the following complex event: The car being blue caused a perceptual experience of it as being blue, which in turn caused this very memory experience. This happens neither in Situation 1 nor in Situation 2, so the token-reflexive view accounts for the intuitions that our memories are false in those situations. A concern for this view, however, is that it may build too much into the contents of our memory experiences. What if the car is blue, you have a perceptual experience that presents it as being blue, and it elicits in you a memory experience of it as being blue, but it so happens that your perceptual experience was not caused by the presence of the car? Philosophers disagree on whether these perceptual experiences are true. To the extent that you feel inclined to think that they are, this case is a problem for the token-reflexive view, for it commits us to saying that your memory experience is, in this situation, false.

Conclusion

It seems that we have different notions of what memory is supposed to do, and they pull us in different directions regarding the objects of memory. We think that memory gives us knowledge of the past just like perception gives us knowledge of the present. This pushes us toward the world-directed view. We also think that it should preserve perceptual experiences just like propositional memory preserves beliefs. This pushes us toward the introspective view. Despite the fact that the token-reflexive view seems, at first glance, unnecessarily complicated, it seems that some version of that approach might be the best way to relieve the tension between these seemingly conflicting intuitions about memory.

Jordi Fernández

Author's Note: This research was funded by two grants from the Spanish Ministry of Science and Technology for projects HUM2007-61108 and HUM2006-09923.

See also Causal Theories of Intentionality; Causal Theories of Memory; Intentionality of Bodily Sensation; Intentionality of Emotion; Memory and Knowledge

Further Readings

Bernecker, S. (2008). *The metaphysics of memory.* Dordrecht, Netherlands: Springer.

Searle, J. (1983). *Intentionality: An essay in the philosophy of mind.* Cambridge, UK: Cambridge University Press.

Tulving, E. (1972). Episodic and semantic memory. In W. Donaldson & E. Tulving (Eds.), *Organization of memory* (pp. 381–403). New York, NY: Academic Press.

Von Leyden, W. (1961). *Remembering: A philosophical problem.* London, UK: Duckworth.

OPTIC FLOW

Optic flow refers to the image motion of the environment projected on the retina during our movement in the world. The term was first coined by James J. Gibson and played a key role in the development of the ecological approach to visual perception, an approach that emphasizes studying human perception in the natural environment rather than in a controlled laboratory setting. Ever since Gibson proposed that the optic flow field contains cues for the perception and control of self-motion, much research in cognitive psychology and neuroscience has investigated what specific cues from optic flow people use for the perception and control of self-motion. The major findings are summarized below.

Perception of Self-Motion

The optic flow field is normally represented by a velocity field with each velocity vector depicting the motion of a reference point in the environment. Any optic flow field is composed of two components, a *translational component* of radial flow, which is the pattern of flow due to the observer traveling on a straight path with no eye, head, or body rotation (pure translation, Figure 1A), and a *rotational component* of lamellar flow, which is the pattern of flow due to observer eye, head, or body rotation and/or the observer traveling on a curved path (Figure 1B).

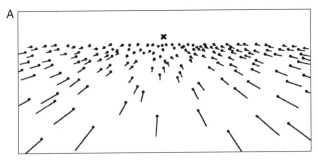

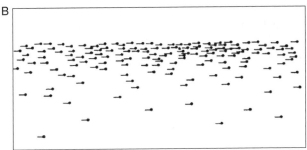

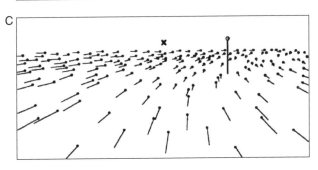

Figure 1 Sample velocity fields for movement over a ground plane. Each line represents a velocity vector depicting the motion of a reference point on the ground. (A) Translational component of radial flow produced by observer translation toward the *x*. (B) Rotational component of lamellar flow produced by eye rotation to the right about a vertical axis. (C) Retinal flow field produced by translating toward the *x* while fixating *o* on top of a post.

Source: Li, L., & Warren, W. H. (2000). Perception of heading during rotation: Sufficiency of dense motion parallax and reference objects. *Vision Research, 40,* 3873–3984. Copyright © 2000 by Elsevier. Reused with permission.

Translation

When traveling on a straight path with no eye, head, or body rotation, the focus of expansion (FOE) in the resulting radial flow (*x* in Figure 1A) indicates one's instantaneous direction of self-motion (heading) and can thus be used for the control of self motion.

To illustrate, to steer toward a target, we keep the FOE on the target; to stay in a lane during driving, we keep the FOE at the center of road; and to steer to avoid an obstacle, we make sure the FOE is not on the obstacle. Research by William Warren and others has shown that humans can indeed use the FOE in optic flow to estimate their heading within 1° of visual angle during simulated translation. Note that good heading performance for pure translation may not involve the perception of self-motion, because the task could be performed by locating the FOE in the 2-D velocity field on the screen without any 3-D interpretation of the velocity field.

Translation and Rotation

When one is traveling on a curved path or is traveling on a straight path but rotating one's eyes to track an object off to one side, the retinal flow pattern is not radial any more. The flow field now contains both translational and rotational components, and the lamellar flow generated by the path or eye rotation (Figure 1B) shifts the FOE in the retinal flow field away from the heading direction (Figure 1C). To recover heading in this case, many mathematical models have been proposed that use information such as global flow rate and motion parallax in the flow field to compensate for the rotation, a computation that has been implemented with neurophysiological models of primate extrastriate visual cortex.

To determine whether humans are capable of recovering heading from combined translational and rotational flow, a number of behavioral studies have examined heading perception during translation with simulated eye movements (the display is generated in such way that the retinal image of the display on a stationary eye is the same as if the eye had moved). While some behavioral studies by Martin Banks and others show that observers need extraretinal information (such as oculomotor signals about eye movement) to remove the rotational component in the flow field for accurate heading estimation at a high eye rotation rate, more studies by James Cutting, Leland Stone, Li Li, and others find that observers can estimate their heading within 2° of visual angle by relying on information solely from optic flow, especially when a large field of view and realistic complex 3-D scenes are provided.

Path Perception

Apart from heading, an equally important feature of self-motion is one's future trajectory of traveling (path). The common locomotion control tasks that can be achieved using heading can be similarly accomplished using path. Heading and path coincide when one travels on a straight path but diverge when one follows a curved path of motion; in the latter case, heading is the tangent to the curved path (Figure 2).

While heading can be perceived from a single 2-D retinal velocity field of optic flow, path recovery requires more. The instantaneous velocity field during translation and rotation is associated with one heading direction but is consistent with a continuum of path scenarios ranging from traveling on a straight path with eye, head, or body rotation to a circular path with no eye, head, or body rotation. This path ambiguity problem can only be solved using information beyond a single retinal velocity field such as the acceleration in the translational flow field, dot motion over an extended amount of time, reference objects in the scene, or extraretinal signals. All these cues can be used to determine whether the rotational component in optic flow is due to eye, head, body,

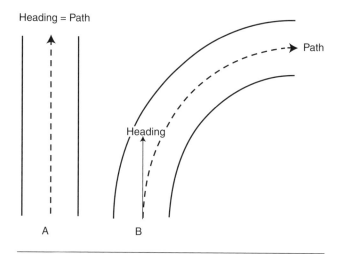

Figure 2 An illustration of the relationship between heading and path for (A) traveling on a straight path and (B) traveling on a curved path

Source: Li, L., Chen, J., & Peng, X. (2009). Influence of visual path information on human heading perception during rotation. *Journal of Vision, 9*(3), 1–14. Copyright © 2009 by the Association for Research in Vision and Ophthalmology. Reused with permission.

or path rotation. However, up to now very few studies have examined how these cues are used for the perception of path trajectory.

For the relationship between heading and path perception, given that heading is the tangent to the curved path (Figure 2) and observers can infer heading as soon as they perceive path, recent studies from Li's lab have found that while heading and path perception are two separate processes, path does help heading perception when the display does not contain sufficient optic flow information for accurate heading estimation. Furthermore, accurate perception of path but not heading from optic flow depends on where we are looking, thus supporting the claim that heading is a more reliable cue for the online control of locomotion.

Neural Basis

Many species have neural pathways that selectively respond to optic flow patterns. The neurophysiological basis of heading perception includes several cortical areas. Earlier single-neuron studies by Charles Duffy, Robert Wurtz, and others report that neurons in macaque dorsal medial superior temporal cortex (MSTd) selectively respond to radial, lamellar, and spiral patterns of optic flow. More recent functional magnetic resonance imaging (fMRI) studies on macaque and human brains by Frank Bremmer, Andrew Smith, David Burr, and others reveal that the ventral intraparietal area (VIP) is also involved in heading perception as well as a human homologue of primate MST, the MT complex (MT+).

For the cortical areas involved in path perception, recent brain-imaging work on humans by David Field and others reports that the presence of road markers, which clearly defined the path trajectory, activates the superior parietal lobe (SPL) bilaterally in addition to the MT+ area. Presenting observers with distant road markers during heading judgment reproduces the SPL activation, whereas presenting observers with near road markers results in activation only in the MT+ area.

Control of Self-Motion

Gibson proposes that we use the information that we perceive from optic flow to guide our movement in the world. The main research findings on optic flow cues used for visual feedback-driven control of self-motion are summarized below.

Walking Toward a Target

James Gibson states that to steer toward a target, we move in such way to keep the FOE in optic flow (i.e., heading) on the target. However, work by Simon Rushton and others has challenged this claim. They find that when observers wearing a prism are asked to walk toward a target, they walk on a curved rather than a straight path. The prism deflects the visual direction of the target from the observer, but it does not deflect the FOE in the optic flow pattern from the target. The results thus support the idea that observers rely on the visual direction of the target but not the FOE in optic flow to walk toward the target. Nevertheless, testing people in a virtual environment in which optic flow information can be rigorously controlled, recent work by William Warren and others finds that both the FOE in optic flow and the visual direction of the target contribute to control of locomotion on foot. The FOE appears to increasingly dominate control as more flow and motion parallax information is added to the scene.

Braking

The rate of expansion in optic flow specifies the time-to-contact with objects and can thus be used for the control of braking during driving. David Lee proposes that by adjusting deceleration so that the rate of change in time-to-contact is near the margin value of −0.5, one would stop at the moment of contact. Several naturalistic studies by Lee and others report that hummingbirds indeed follow this strategy in docking on feeding tubes. A behavioral study from William Warren's lab also confirms that observers adopt this strategy to control the direction and magnitude of braking for a linear brake with no higher order control dynamics during simulated driving. However, recent work by Brett Fajen shows that observers do not rely on a single optical variable for braking control during driving. As the dynamics of the controlled system influences the visual cues observers see in the display due to their control actions, observers rely on different optic flow cues (such as global flow rate) to modulate deceleration during braking depending on the dynamics of the braking system (i.e., the mapping between brake position and deceleration).

Lane Keeping

Another commonly experienced control of self-motion task is lane keeping on a straight path during driving, riding a bicycle, or walking down a path. There are at least three types of cues from optic flow that we can use for lane keeping. The first one is, again, the FOE in radial optic flow. Lane keeping can be achieved by keeping the FOE (i.e., heading) centered on the far end of the lane. The lane edges provide two other cues for lane keeping: bearing and splay angle. Bearing refers to the direction from the observer to a reference point on the lane edge, measured with respect to a reference direction such as the gaze direction or meridian, and splay angle refers to the angle between the optical projection of the lane edge and a vertical line on the image plane. To maintain traveling in the center of a lane, observers can adopt the strategy of keeping the left and the right bearing or splay angle equal. The further away the reference point on the lane edge, the less useful bearing information because the harder it becomes for the observer to detect a change of bearing. On the other hand, as the near and the far parts of the lane edges provide the same splay angles, unlike bearing, splay angle information is a property of the whole image plane, independent of distance.

The FOE in the radial flow, bearing, and splay angle strategies for lane keeping in the real world are usually redundant and lead to the same lane-keeping behavior. Early research in human factors has reported that human operators use heading more than the vehicle's lateral position (which defines bearing and splay angle) for lane keeping. Later work by Andrew Beall and Jack Loomis has found that people rely mainly on the splay angle for lane keeping. Recent work by Li Li challenges this finding and shows that heading from optic flow is used for lane keeping regardless of the presence of splay angle information. Several other studies reveal that equating the speed of radial flow in the left and right lateral field of view also contributes to maintaining a centered position in the lane.

In summary, in support of Gibson's proposal that optic flow contains cues for the perception and control of self-motion, research in cognitive psychology and neuroscience over the last four decades has not only identified the cues in optic flow that we use to perceive and control our self-motion in the world but also the underlying neural mechanisms responsible for the detection of these cues. As our detection of information in optic flow puts us in direct contact with the world without the need of mediating representations, optic flow provides the key supporting evidence for the concept of direct perception.

Li Li

See also Common Coding; Depth Perception; Motor System, Development of

Further Readings

Fajen, B. R. (2008). Learning novel mappings from optic flow to the control of action. *Journal of Vision, 8*(11), 1–12. doi:10.1167/8.11.12

Gibson, J. J. (1979). *The ecological approach to visual perception*. Boston, MA: Houghton Mifflin.

Li, L., Chen, J., & Peng, X. (2009). Influence of visual path information on human heading perception during rotation. *Journal of Vision, 9*(3), 1–14. doi:10.1167/9.3.29

Rushton, S., Harris, J., Lloyd, M., & Wann, J. (1998). Guidance of locomotion on foot uses perceived target location rather than optic flow. *Current Biology, 8,* 1191–1194.

Wall, M. B., & Smith, A. T. (2008). The representation of egomotion in the human brain. *Current Biology, 18,* 191–194.

Warren, W. H. (2008). Optic flow. In A. I. Bashaum, A. Kaneko, G. M. Shepherd, & G. Westheimer (Eds.), *The senses: A comprehensive reference: Vol. 2. Vision* (T. D. Albright & R. Masland [Vol. Eds.]) (pp. 219–230). Oxford, UK: Academic Press.

Warren, W. H., Kay, B. A., Zosh, W. D., Duchon, A. P., & Sahuc, S. (2001). Optic flow is used to control human walking. *Nature Neuroscience, 4,* 213–216.

PERCEPTUAL CONSCIOUSNESS AND ATTENTION

The topic of perceptual consciousness has been of great interest to researchers in recent years, ever since the surge of research on what is called *implicit perception*—that is, perception without awareness. Prior to that, most researchers would have considered the term *perceptual consciousness* redundant since the term *perception* was generally defined as the awareness of objects and events through the medium of our senses. Defined in this way, there simply was no perception without awareness. It was only when evidence began to accumulate that we could, in some sense, perceive objects and events without being aware of them—in other words, implicitly perceive them—that serious interest in perceptual consciousness emerged. The primary evidence for implicit perception derives from evidence of what is called *priming*—that is, that an object or event present in our environment can affect our subsequent behavior. For example, if a picture of a corn stalk is flashed in front of us so quickly that we do not see it, if we now are shown the word *stalk* and asked to define it, the first definition we are likely to give is "something on which corn grows" rather than "the act of following someone obsessively." This is so even though the latter is the more frequent use of the word and is the definition most frequently given by observers who have not been primed by the flashed picture of the corn stalk. Evidence of perceptual priming forces us to distinguish between

perception that is implicit and perception that is explicit—that is, which entails awareness and which is referred to as *perceptual consciousness*.

The Relationship Between Perceptual Consciousness and Attention

If perceptual consciousness refers to those perceptions we are aware of, what is the contribution of attention to these kinds of perceptions? One frequently given answer, supported by a very large body of experimental evidence, is that attention is necessary for perceptual awareness. In fact, there are a number of perceptual phenomena that strongly suggest this. One of them is *inattentional blindness*, a phenomenon first reported by Arien Mack and Irvin Rock, which refers to the failure to consciously perceive an unexpected object that may appear exactly where one's eyes are focused when attention is engaged in some other task. As shown by Daniel Simons and Christopher Chabris, this can occur even when the unseen event would seem to be highly salient—for example, a man dressed in a gorilla suit walking across a room in which people are passing around a basketball. The gorilla may not be seen when the observers are busy counting the number of passes among the players wearing either the white or the black uniforms. Another closely related phenomenon is that of *change blindness,* which refers to the frequent failure to perceive a change in a scene that you are viewing and monitoring for changes. The standard technique for demonstrating this phenomenon in a laboratory, devised by Ronald Rensink and his colleagues, involves presenting an alternating pair of real life scenes separated by gray, blank fields. (The interleaved blank fields serve to eliminate the motion transients that otherwise would signal the presence of a change.) The scenes are identical except that one or more elements are removed or changed in one of the pictures. Change blindness frequently occurs unless the change(s) is central to the gist of the scene. Another closely related phenomenon is the *attentional blink,* which is normally demonstrated by experiments in which observers are asked to search for two sequentially occurring targets embedded in a series of rapidly presented other items. If the second target appears between 200 and 500 milliseconds of the first, it is very likely not to be perceived.

Sighted Blindness

The above phenomena, which can be considered instances of *sighted blindness,* that is, blindness that occurs in normally sighted observers looking at above threshold stimuli, are thought to be causally related to the absence of attention. In the case of inattentional blindness, the observer is engaged in some task that requires attention when an unexpected stimulus appears that, because it is not the object of attention, is not seen. Change blindness also is attributed to an absence of attention although it involves more processing steps than inattentional blindness. In change blindness the relevant elements in one array must be encoded in memory and remain there long enough so that they can be compared with the comparable elements in the other array, while inattentional blindness simply involves detecting the presence of a new object. The fact that changes which affect gist are likely to be detected is consistent with the failure-to-attend account of change blindness since the meaning of the scene is what we are most likely to pay attention to. Finally, in the case of the attentional blink, the second target is missed because attention is still engaged in processing the first one and so is unavailable for the processing of the second one, which is therefore not seen. In each of these instances, it is the absence of attention that leads to the failure to see something that is completely visible. It therefore would seem to follow that attention is a necessary condition for perceptual awareness.

Visual Neglect

At least one other phenomenon also lends support to this conclusion, but unlike the three already mentioned, this additional phenomenon only occurs in people who have suffered cortical damage (usually to the right cerebral hemisphere, more specifically to the right posterior parietal lobe). This disorder is called either *unilateral, hemispatial,* or *visual* neglect. It is characterized by the failure to see (i.e., to consciously perceive) objects on the left, located opposite the side of the lesion despite the fact that if the objects were located on the right, they would be seen. All explanations of this failure to see point to inattention—that is, the inability to attend to objects on the left. So here again, inattention is invoked to account for the failure to consciously perceive objects that are otherwise visible.

Attentional Load and Perceptual Consciousness

Additional evidence of the centrality of attention for conscious perception comes from evidence, primarily gathered by Nilli Lavie and her colleagues, relating conscious perception to attentional load. This evidence suggests that the greater the attentional load, where *load* refers to the amount of attentional capacity required by a task, the less likely are stimuli that are irrelevant to the perceptual task to be seen. This again testifies to the importance of attention for conscious perception.

Is Attention Either a Necessary or a Sufficient Condition for Perceptual Consciousness?

There are a series of difficult questions that arise from the linking of conscious perception to attention. If attention is necessary for conscious perception, then it must follow that there are *no* instances of perceiving that do not entail attention. Furthermore, if it is necessary, then where in the processing stream leading to conscious perception does it operate? Is paying attention also a sufficient condition for seeing? That is, does attending always entail seeing, which, if true, would make visual awareness and attention indistinguishable?

It is difficult if not impossible to find an instance in which conscious perception is independent of attention. One example, suggested by Victor Lamme, comes from the study of binocular rivalry, which arises when the images viewed by the left and right eyes are different. It has been suggested that what we see under these conditions is not a function of attention. There is, however, considerable evidence that attention does influence which of the two rivalrous images is seen, so this does not seem to qualify as a persuasive example of conscious perceiving without attention. In the absence of such evidence, the hypothesis that attention is necessary for conscious perception stands.

While it is difficult, if not impossible, to come up with instances in which conscious perception occurs in the absence of attention, it is not at all difficult to come up with instances of attending and not seeing anything. For example, paying attention to a location in space where there is nothing to see, or if what there is to see is not visible either because it is presented too briefly or is of too low contrast, does not result in a conscious percept. This therefore must mean that while attention is necessary for conscious perception, it is not sufficient for it, although in 2008 Robert Kentridge and his colleagues presented evidence that attending to below threshold or masked stimuli increases their capacity to act as primes. This latter kind of evidence does indicate that attention affects processing even when no conscious percept occurs.

How Does Attention Enable Conscious Perception?

Assuming that attention is necessary for conscious perception, at what point does it operate and how? These are large questions but brief descriptions of suggested answers are possible. The first question has led to two competing accounts of where attention operates in the processing of visual input. In one account (early selection theory), attentional selection occurs early in the processing of inputs, while in the other (late selection theory) it occurs late. In a third account (see above), the level at which attention operates is a function of the attentional load, such that the lower the load, the later the filtering and consequently the more input that is consciously perceived. The preponderance of current evidence suggests that the attentional filter occurs late, after meaning has been analyzed. This evidence is seen in findings showing that highly meaningful stimuli, such as one's own name, are seen even when viewed under conditions of inattention, which normally cause inattentional blindness or the attentional blink. Moreover, Arien Mack and her colleagues have reported evidence that such stimuli are even seen with a high attentional load.

Attention Amplifies the Input

The most common answer to the second question about what attention adds that causes a stimulus which is the object of attention to be perceived is that attention amplifies the neuronal responses. In other words, it enhances the level of activation produced by the stimulus, making it more salient. This is thought to be analogous to the way in which increasing stimulus contrast increases stimulus salience. This view is consistent with evidence showing that variations in the direction of attention lead to qualitative differences in performance comparable to those found when stimulus quality is varied. It is also consistent with the proposal made by Petra Stoerig and Alan Cowey in 1997 that the cortical damage that produces visual neglect leads to degradation in the quality of the representation of the contralesional input of the sort generally associated with the absence of attention.

Does Attention Foster Conscious Perception or Memory?

If attention acts as an amplifier of input, does this make the representation of the stimulus more salient, which is why we are aware of it, or does attention only enable the encoding of the attended input into working memory so that we are able to report it? The difference here is whether the amplification of the neural response to the stimulus, which is said to be a function of attention, increases the likelihood of our perceiving it or only of our reporting it. If it were the latter, then our failure to report a stimulus to which we are inattentive would not be due to our failure to see it but only to our failure to consciously remember and report it. It would be what Jeremy Wolfe has called *inattentional amnesia*. If it were the former, then it would be a true failure of perception and rightly termed *sighted blindness* or *inattentional blindness*. There is some disagreement over which of these two accounts is correct.

Priming

As mentioned at the outset, there is considerable evidence that stimuli we do not see because they are flashed too quickly or because we have not attended to them, as is the case in inattentional blindness, the attentional blink, and unilateral neglect, are capable of priming. It is not clear, however, which account this kind of evidence supports. What is clear from this evidence, however, is that the unseen stimuli are processed and encoded to some extent by the perceptual system in the absence of attention; otherwise they could not act as primes.

Arien Mack

See also Attention and Consciousness; Attentional Blink Effect; Blindsight; Change Blindness; Inattentional Blindness; Psychological Refractory Period; Visual Masking

Further Readings

Kentridge, R. W., Nijboer, T. C., & Heywood, C. A. (2008). Attended but unseen: Visual attention is not sufficient for awareness. *Neuropsychologia, 46,* 864–869.

Lamme, V. A. (2003). Why visual attention and awareness are different. *Trends in Cognitive Science, 7,* 12–17.

Lavie, N., & Tsal, Y. (1994). Perceptual load as a major determinant of the locus of selective attention. *Perception and Psychophysics, 56,* 183–197.

Mack, A., & Rock, I. (1998). *Inattentional blindness.* Cambridge, MA: MIT Press.

Rensink, R. A. (2002). Change detection. *Annual Review of Psychology, 53,* 245–277.

Shapiro, K., Driver, J., Ward, R., & Sorenson, R. B. (1997). Priming from the attentional blink: A failure to abstract visual tokens but not visual types. *Psychological Science, 8,* 95–100.

Simons, D. J., & Chabris, C. F. (1999). Gorillas in our midst: Sustained inattentional blindness for dynamic events. *Perception, 28,* 1059–1074.

Wolfe, J. M. (1999). Inattentional amnesia. In V. Coltheart (Ed.), *Fleeting memories: Cognition of brief visual stimuli* (pp. 71–94). Cambridge, MA: MIT Press.

PERCEPTUAL CONSTANCY

Perception concerns the relationship between physical properties of the world and our conscious experience of them. One area of great interest to perceptual psychologists is *perceptual constancy*. Perceptual constancy concerns the degree to which a perception remains the same under varying conditions. Research in this area typically involves keeping some characteristic of a stimulus physically constant and asking observers to make judgments concerning that characteristic under varying contextual conditions.

Researchers have studied color constancy as a function of illumination, color surround, chromatic adaptation to prolonged exposure to a color, and off-color objects known to have a specific color (such as an orange-colored cherry). Others have examined lightness constancy as a function of overall illumination, shadows, and brightness of the surround. Another area of interest is shape constancy where researchers have examined perceived shape as a function of object orientation and distance from the observer to the object. Others have looked at slant constancy as a function of object shape and configuration. Space is too limited to fully describe all aspects of perceptual constancy here, so this entry focuses in detail on the oldest and most thoroughly researched area of perceptual constancy research: *size constancy*.

Size Constancy

In the typical size constancy experiment, a comparison stimulus of adjustable size is located near the observer, and a standard stimulus of constant size is located at several distances from the observer. The observer's task is to adjust the comparison stimulus until its size matches each standard. As one would expect, observers accurately reproduce the standard when it is close to the observer (at the same distance away as the comparison). However, adjustments can become increasingly erroneous as the standard grows more distant from the observer.

If the observer accurately adjusts the near comparison to match the standard at all distances, the data are said to show constancy. On the other hand, if the observer sees distant standards as being smaller than they really are and adjusts the comparison to be physically smaller than the standard, the data are said to show underconstancy. Conversely, if distant standards dispose the observer to make the comparison too large, the data are said to show overconstancy.

Historical Review

Scholars have been interested in size constancy since ancient times. Euclid (c. 300 BCE), Ptolemy (2nd century CE), Plotinus (c. 300 CE), Ibn al-Haytham (c. 1030), René Descartes (1637), and Leonardo da Vinci (c. 1500) all described their observations concerning size constancy and offered explanations for the phenomenon.

Empirical work on size constancy began in earnest during the late 1920s. Egon Brunswik supervised much of this research and provided the first theoretical account for size constancy. Brunswik believed that size judgments reflect a compromise between an objective attitude, where the observer attempts to adjust the comparison to accurately reflect the physical size of the standard, and a subjective attitude, where the observer defines size as an artist would and attempts to adjust the comparison so that its visual angle matches the visual angle of the standard. Here, the visual angle refers to the percentage or proportion of the field of vision taken up by the standard, not its physical size.

Since all size judgments should reflect some combination of these two attitudes, Brunswik suggested that all size judgments should vary between constancy, when the objective attitude predominates, and strong underconstancy, when the subjective attitude does. Overconstancy is theoretically impossible, and any data that show overconstancy must result from experimental error.

Unfortunately, empirical research of this period often was at odds with this theoretical formulation. First of all, observers seemed incapable of fully assuming the subjective attitude. When asked to assume a subjective attitude, observers adjusted the comparison to be much larger than it should have been to correctly match the visual angle of the standard. Brunswik described this phenomenon as a "regression to the real," and it showed that observers are incapable of fully assuming a subjective attitude and ignoring physical size. Trained, intelligent, or artistic subjects were better at assuming the subjective attitude, but even these subjects could not fully overcome regression to the real. Second, a number of empirical studies of this era resulted in theoretically impossible results indicating overconstancy.

Early research analyzed each standard separately. Size constancy methodology changed significantly after Alfred Holway and Edwin Boring introduced a new research paradigm in 1941. They asked five observers to judge the apparent size of circular standards located between 10 and 120 feet from the observer by adjusting a variable comparison located 10 feet away under four viewing conditions. Under binocular conditions, they found a slight overconstancy (the comparison was made too large for distant standards), monocular viewing resulted in constancy, monocular viewing through a small window showed strong underconstancy, and monocular viewing through a dark tube displayed very strong underconstancy that almost (but not quite) achieved a projective match, where the visual angle of the comparison would actually be equal to the visual angle of the standard. Subsequent research followed their multiple standard methodology.

Summary of Empirical Research

In 2006, Mark Wagner conducted a meta-analysis of size constancy research (totaling 118 data sets) from the time of Brunswik to the present, the majority from the post-Holway and Boring period. A number of factors were found to influence size constancy data.

For frontally oriented targets under full-cue conditions, objective instructions (which require the observer to adjust the comparison to physically equal the standard) show overconstancy, the most distant standard was seen as being +28% too large. On the other hand, apparent instructions (which ask the observer to adjust the comparison to look or appear equal to the standard) approximate constancy, on average displaying a slight underconstancy of –2%. Projective instructions (which ask observers to match the visual angle of the standard) show marked underconstancy, averaging –37% for the most distant standard.

Reduced conditions (such as viewing in a darkened room or through a small window) are associated with underconstancy for both objective and apparent instruction. When cues to depth are completely eliminated by controlling for the illumination of nearby objects, judgments approach a visual angle match.

Flat stimuli (oriented parallel to the ground) under full-cue conditions also show strong underconstancy, averaging –30%. For projective instructions, this overconstancy averages –70%.

Another factor that appears to influence size judgments is age. Young children usually display underconstancy with an increasing tendency toward overconstancy with increasing age.

Explanations for Size Constancy Phenomena

The standard explanation for most size constancy research is William Epstein's *size-distance invariance hypothesis* (SDIH). The great majority of studies support the SDIH and find that perceived size (s') is related to perceived distance (d') and the visual angle subtended by the object (θ) by the equation

$$s' = d' \tan\theta$$

However, other explanations for size constancy phenomenon have been offered, including V. R. Carlson's *perspective size hypothesis*. According to this theory, observers are aware that in some sense objects appear to shrink as they get farther from them observer. Objective instructions incline the observer to overcompensate for this effect, while apparent and projective instructions cause observers to embrace this effect in differing degrees. Suzanne McKee and Harvey Smallman propose the *dual calculation hypothesis,* which suggests that perceived size not only depends on perceived distance but also on surface texture and the inclusion of objects of known size. Instructions can alter the relative weights given to these different sources of information. John Baird and Mark Wagner are able to successfully mathematically model past size constancy research with their *transformation theory.* In this theory, the physical sizes of stimuli are transformed into visual angles at the retina. To recover perceived size, the visual system must engage in an inverse transformation. However, this inverse transformation can lead to errors in perceived size if the visual system does not register the correct distance to and orientation of the stimulus. Instructions, cue conditions, stimulus orientation, and age can influence one or the other of these factors.

Mark Wagner

See also Depth Perception; Stereopsis; Visuospatial Reasoning

Further Readings

Carlson, V. R. (1977). Instructions and perceptual constancy judgments. In W. Epstein (Ed.), *Stability and constancy in visual perception: Mechanisms and processes* (pp. 217–254). New York, NY: Wiley-Interscience.

Epstein, W., Park, J., & Casey, A. (1961). The current status of the size–distance hypothesis. *Psychological Bulletin, 58,* 491–514.

McKee, S. P., & Smallman, H. S. (1998). Size and speed constancy. In V. Walsh & J. Kulikowski (Eds.), *Perceptual constancy: Why things look as they do* (pp. 373–408). Cambridge, UK: Cambridge University Press.

Ross, H. E., & Plug, C. (1998). The history of size constancy and size illusions. In V. Walsh & J. Kulikowski (Eds.), *Perceptual constancy: Why things look as they do* (pp. 499–528). Cambridge, UK: Cambridge University Press.

Wagner, M. (2006). *The geometries of visual space.* Mahwah, NJ: Erlbaum.

PERSONAL IDENTITY

This entry is concerned with the concepts of *a person* and of *personal identity* and with various theories of persons and their identity. A paradox is unearthed: We have strong reasons for thinking that any (human) person is identical to a human being yet equally strong reasons to deny this. Our concept of a person thus harbors a contradiction.

Some Terminology

The phrase *personal identity* means different things in philosophy, psychology, and everyday life. Our concern here is with the phrase as it has been understood by philosophers. Typically what philosophers who discuss personal identity want to know is what makes it the case that a person at one time is the same as a person at some later time. Though less frequently discussed, philosophers have also wanted to know under what conditions a single body houses one person or two (as in, e.g., cases of split personality).

Since the phrase personal identity derives from *person* and *identity*, these two notions are conceptually prior to that of personal identity. However, this doesn't mean that they are prior in every sense. Certainly, if we know what a person is, then we know what it is for the same person to persist through time. Still, it may be that the best way to discover the nature of persons is by sifting through competing theories of what it is for a person to persist through time. If we know what changes a person may or may not survive, we will have more idea of what kind of thing is a person. This is what motivates and justifies the methodology of *thought experiments.*

Some comments on *identity* and *person*: In this discussion, we mean identity in the sense of strict numerical identity, not in the sense of qualitative identity. So we are not concerned with the sense of *identical* as it appears in identical twins. Twins may be very similar (qualitatively identical), but numerically they are two people, not one. Note also that in talking of identity our concern is metaphysical not epistemic. That is, we are not asking about the kind of evidence we typically rely on in making judgments of personal identity (e.g., physical appearance). Our concern is with what, if anything, constitutes personal identity. What makes it the case that a person at one time is the same (numerically) as a person at some later time? The answer to this constitutive question will not be the same as the answer to the evidential question, since evidence such as appearance, or even fingerprints, is never a logical guarantee of personal identity.

What of the term *person*? Why do we have such a term? What distinctive work does it do? It would not be too controversial to maintain that we use person to delineate a certain kind of mental being—namely, a self-conscious mental being. This definition puts no restriction on the kind of entity that can be a person. As far as the definition goes, persons could be bodies, brains, nonphysical souls, robots, Martians, parrots, dolphins, or creatures yet to be encountered. This liberality is a strength but also a weakness. For one might have hoped that an answer to the question "What is a person?" would tell us what ontological category (or category of being) we belong to; that is, it would answer the question "What are we?"

What Is a Person?

Here then are some ontologically committing answers to the question "What are we?" We are the union of a nonphysical soul and a physical body (René Descartes's answer); we are animals, specifically human beings (the answer of contemporary Animalists such as Paul Snowdon and Eric Olson); we are not substances (psychic or biological), rather we are "bundles of perceptions" with no substantial self to bind or unify members of the bundle (David Hume's answer). Hume famously compared the self to a republic, an idea endorsed recently by Derek Parfit and called by him "reductionism about persons."

Clearly these answers would also answer the question of personal identity. If persons are souls, then what it is for that person to persist is for that soul to persist; if persons are human beings, then

what it is for that person to persist is for that human being to persist; if persons are bundles of perceptions, then what it is for that person to persist is for that bundle to persist (though, unlike the persistence of a substance, the persistence of a bundle is a largely conventional matter). In this sense, the question "What are we?" is prior to the question "What is it for the same person to exist through time?" Let's examine various answers to the first question.

Dualism

Many modern philosophers are dissatisfied with Descartes' answer, for a variety of reasons. First, Descartes' dualism of soul and body may have seemed reasonable when mentality admitted of no other explanation. But now that we increasingly understand mental activity in terms of brain activity, the need to postulate a nonphysical soul as the bearer of mental states has vanished. Charles Darwin's discovery, two centuries after Descartes, further reinforced this effect. Second, many philosophers have claimed not to understand how a nonphysical soul and its nonphysical mental states are supposed to interact with the physical realm. For interact they plainly do: Stick a pin in your leg and you cause a sensation of pain. Descartes tried to address this worry, but few find his response plausible.

Hume's Answer

What of the Humean answer? In Derek Parfit's version of it the key idea is this: Just as the people and land that make up a republic can be understood without reference to the concept of a republic, so a person's body and mental states (elements of the bundle) can be understood without reference to the concept of a person. (Only so can we think of the self as reducible to the bundle.) However, Parfit's Humean view faces serious problems. First, it is hard to make sense of simple mental states, such as pains and tickles, other than as had by a subject or person. We can make little sense of an unowned or free-floating tickle. Second, a special problem is posed by more sophisticated mental states such as memory and intention. These states seem to have reference to persons built into their content. My memory of tasting coffee yesterday not only requires a current bearer but appears to implicate me in its content: I remember that *I* tasted coffee yesterday. Parfit is aware of these problems and has an ingenious response, but it is fair to say that the view that mental states can be understood without reference to a person stands in need of considerable defense.

Animalism

What of the animalists' answer? Let us be clear what that answer does and does not involve. Animalists do not hold that it is a necessary truth that all persons are human beings. Perhaps dolphins or chimpanzees qualify as persons. Perhaps there are nonhuman persons on other planets. What animalists do hold is that we (human persons) are human beings. That is, you are numerically identical to the human animal in your shoes.

A human being can survive in a coma, irretrievably devoid of mentality. According to animalism, if this fate befell me, I would continue to exist, but no person would then occupy my body. So I can exist without being a person, and hence, person (unlike human being) is not the concept of a fundamental kind of thing. Contrary to traditional views, the question of personal identity is not the same as the question of our identity, since we are not essentially persons.

The Case for Animalism

The animalist view strikes many as the merest common sense. Are we not flesh and blood creatures, members of the animal kingdom? Moreover, animalists have recently offered a compelling argument for their view. The form of the argument is this: Suppose animalism to be false and we end up with an absurdity, so animalism must be true.

Let us set up a version of the argument. *Garrett* is my name, the name of a person. We need a name of the human being in my shoes—call him *Alf*. The animalists' claim is simple: Garrett = Alf. (Analogous identity claims hold for everyone else.) Suppose it is denied that Garrett = Alf. Then the following question arises: Garrett has mental states, but does Alf? Either answer to this question faces a significant obstacle. Suppose we say, "*No*, Garrett is a person and he has mental states, but Alf is just an animal, so he has no mental states only physical ones." The trouble with this answer is that Alf has all my physical attributes, including all my brain states. It is now generally accepted that mental states, if not identical to brain states, are causally dependent on them.

We have the mental states we have because of the brain states we are in. But in that case it seems unfair to deny mentality to Alf. He has a complex human brain (indeed the very brain I have), so why is he not the bearer of mental states?

Suppose we say, "Yes, fair enough, Alf does have mental states and is a person as much as Garrett." But remember that the question we're answering arose on the assumption that Garrett is not identical to Alf. So if Garrett is a person and it is now conceded that Alf is a person, then it follows that there are two people in my shoes! Generalizing from my case, it follows that the population of the planet is twice what we thought it was. But this is absurd. So to deny that Garrett = Alf leads to one of two absurdities: Either we are forced to fly in the face of the well-established thesis that mental states depend on, and are generated by, brain states or we are forced into a bizarre exercise in double counting. Hence, concludes the animalist, we should accept that Garrett = Alf.

The Case Against Animalism

This is a powerful argument. It is unclear exactly where it goes wrong, but go wrong it must, for its conclusion is manifestly false. If I were identical to Alf, then there could be no possible circumstance in which I survive but Alf does not or in which Alf survives but I do not. Yet there are such circumstances. Many would argue that, in the irreversible coma example, Alf survives but I do not.

There are more fanciful examples in which I survive yet Alf does not. As a highly trained athlete, I am naturally invited to be part of the first mission to Mars. The mission is a success and after a few months on Mars we return to Earth. After a routine checkup, doctors discover, despite no change to my appearance or mental life, that all my biological matter has been transformed into a hitherto unknown silicon-based life form. There is no animal (human or otherwise) in my shoes anymore! Alf is an animal, and essentially so: He could not survive without being an animal. Hence, Alf no longer exists. But I continue to exist. So I cannot be identical to Alf, contrary to animalism.

This reasoning might be thought sophistical. How can some bizarre and merely possible scenario in which I exist but Alf doesn't have any bearing on whether I, here and now, am identical to Alf?

But here we must appreciate the logic of numerical identity. If $A = B$ then everything true of A is true of B and vice versa. So if Garrett = Alf, then every possibility for Garrett must be a possibility for Alf and vice versa. Hence, if there is a possible scenario in which Garrett exists but Alf doesn't (or vice versa) it follows that Garrett is not identical (here and now) with Alf.

Concluding Remarks

Our space travel thought experiment has done two things. It has undermined the animalists' central claim: We are not identical with animals. It has also pointed us in the direction of a more promising theory of personal identity: the psychological view. Our thought experiment has made plausible the thesis that a continuing line of psychological continuity is sufficient for the continued existence of a person (whatever physical transformations he or she may have undergone). But there is a massive problem for this view. What if my stream of psychological continuity was to divide into two (e.g., if each of my brain hemispheres was transplanted into a new body)? The psychological view implies that I would be identical to the two resulting people, which is absurd.

Whether the psychological view can be defended against this worry, whether animalists can reply to the space travel objection, and whether Parfit can defend his Humean theory of the self are among the deepest contemporary questions in the metaphysics of persons.

Brian Garrett

See also Consciousness and Embodiment; Mind-Body Problem; Self-Consciousness

Further Readings

Garrett, B. (1998). *Personal identity and self-consciousness* (see esp. pp. 1–70). New York, NY: Routledge.

Garrett, B. (2006). *What is this thing called metaphysics?* (see esp. pp. 90–100). New York, NY: Routledge.

Noonan, H. (2003). *Personal identity.* New York, NY: Routledge.

Olson, E. (1997). *The human animal.* Oxford, UK: Oxford University Press.

Parfit, D. (1984). *Reasons and persons* (see esp. pp. 199–306). Oxford, UK: Oxford University Press.

PERSONAL IDENTITY, DEVELOPMENT OF

Personal identity development has been defined in many ways over the past 50 years of social science history. Most social writers would agree, however, that one's personal identity development is that which gives one a sense of purpose, meaning, continuity, and coherence in life. In the act of personal identity development, one finds expression for one's own life meanings within a social context, and that context, in turn, provides recognition and mutual regulation of the individual and society. As Erik Erikson said in 1963, "For, indeed, in the social jungle of human existence there is no feeling of being alive without a sense of identity" (p. 130). This entry reviews key personal identity development concepts of Erikson and James Marcia. It also mentions four additional general approaches to understanding the development of personal identity.

Views of Erik Erikson

The concept of identity was first used and elaborated by psychoanalyst Erikson to describe a central disturbance among some young veterans returning from World War II. These men seemed to have lost a sense of inner sameness and continuity in their lives. Erikson thus began to refer to the concept of *ego identity* to describe a psychological entity that enables one to retain a sense of inner organization, sameness, and continuity across time and place—an entity under threat among his soldier patients. The psychoanalyst also stressed that one's sense of ego identity development is dependent on the recognition and support that individuals receive from contexts meaningful to them—the immediate family, community, nation, and culture. The formation of an ego identity is thus dependent on the ways in which parents, teachers, social service providers in the immediate community, and representatives of the larger social structure meet and confirm individuals in their charge.

Ego identity is a product of the interaction between biological givens, psychological needs, and social forces according to Erikson. Thus, ego identity development is determined in part by one's gender, physical attributes, strengths and limitations, in part by one's conscious as well as unconscious needs, wishes, interests, and talents, and in part by the roles and opportunities afforded one by the community. One's ego identity is, however, distinct from one's social roles. While the well-functioning individual may have many social roles in life, he or she has only one ego identity (unless there is serious psychopathology). The foundations of personal identity development begin in infancy through the images of and experiences with significant others whom one internalizes. Identity evolves during childhood based on the significant others with whom one emulates and tries to identify. However, in Erikson's view, identity formation is more than the summation of all significant identifications of childhood; rather, identity formation is the sifting, sorting, and synthesizing of earlier important identifications into a new structure, greater than the sum of its parts.

Initial identity resolutions are generally undertaken during late adolescence, though identity formation and reformation remain lifelong processes, according to Erikson. It is during adolescence that the biological changes of puberty, alongside one's growing capacities for pursuing psychological interests and values, in combination with societal demands for the assumption of adult roles and values that personal identity concerns, often first come to a head. He described the main psychosocial undertaking of adolescence to be that of finding an optimal resolution to the *identity versus role confusion* task. A time of identity exploration and experimentation are vital to optimal identity formation. Failure to undergo this identity formation process will leave the individual either drifting and centerless, an uninvolved spectator in life, or oppositional and antagonistic, devising an identity based all those values that parents would hate most, according to Erikson. Optimal identity formation serves as the cornerstone to the eventual expression of intimacy, both with friends as well as a life partner.

The Identity Statuses

Since Erikson's original writings on ego identity, many writers have either extended his work or reformulated the meaning of identity from a somewhat different perspective. One of the writers most noted for elaborating and extending Erikson's concept of identity has been James Marcia. Marcia suggested that ego identity is better conceptualized according to one of four basic styles (or identity statuses) by which individuals seek (or not) resolutions

to questions of personal identity. There are two styles of commitment: *identity achievement* and *foreclosure*. The identity achieved individual, as per Erikson's definition, has undergone a period of exploration and experimentation prior to making meaningful identity-defining commitments on his or her own terms. The foreclosed individual has also adopted firm, identity-defining commitments but has done so without prior exploration; the identity-defining commitments of the foreclosed are based on identifications with significant others, particularly parents. Similarly, there are two styles of identity noncommitment: *moratorium* and *diffusion*. The moratorium individual is in the process of searching for meaningful identity commitments, while the diffuse individual is uninterested in making such commitments. These four identity statuses have been differentially linked with various attachment styles, patterns of family communication, personality variables, behavioral consequences, and developmental patterns of change.

Additional Theoretical Approaches

Other general approaches to defining personal identity include the following: (a) the narrative approach, in which writers suggest that personal identity does not exist until one constructs and tells a story about the self; (b) the sociocultural approach, wherein writers emphasize the roles of culture, society, and the media as primary forces in defining individual identity; (c) the structural-stage approach, in which intrapsychic elements are emphasized in the individual identity formation process; and (d) an historical perspective, in which changing historical conditions are regarded as primary in regulating personal identity development.

Jane Kroger

See also Moral Development; Relationships, Development of; Self, Development of

Further Readings

Erikson, E. H. (1963). *Childhood and society* (2nd ed.). New York, NY: Norton.

Erikson, E. H. (1968). *Identity: Youth and crisis.* New York, NY: Norton.

Kroger, J. (2007). *Identity development: Adolescence through adulthood* (2nd ed.). Thousand Oaks, CA: Sage.

Marcia, J. E. (1966). Development and validation of ego-identity status. *Journal of Personality and Social Psychology, 3,* 551–558.

Marcia, J. E., Waterman, A. S., Matteson, D. R., Archer, S. L., & Orlofsky, J. L. (Eds.). (1993). *Ego identity: A handbook for psychosocial research.* New York, NY: Springer-Verlag.

PERSONALITY: INDIVIDUAL VERSUS SITUATION DEBATE

The division of responsibility for a given behavior between the individual and the situation is central to much work and debate in psychology. This distinction is the foundation of attribution theory, underlies the division of personality from social psychology, and bears on debates about the consistency of personality across situations. The division in many ways resembles the debate between nature and nurture, though both of these, being aspects of the individual, fall into the personality camp. Also as in that debate, there has been a growing sense of the inadequacy and artificiality of the opposition of person and situation and increased emphasis on an interactionist perspective. This view of the interplay of aspects of the person and the situation in producing behavior is to some extent an empirical issue, based on data on the limited predictive power of pure person and situation accounts, and also partly a theoretical issue, based on a closer examination of what is meant by explanation and causality.

Internal Versus External Attributions

Attribution theory, in its most basic form, provides the rules by which people distinguish, or ought to distinguish, between behaviors that are caused by attributes of the individual versus those that are the result of the situation. When a woman is observed gesturing rudely to another motorist, one can inquire whether that indicates a short-tempered hostility in her or whether instead being cut off on the highway represents an intolerable provocation. In Harold Kelley's classic formulation, one would gather information on whether she consistently gestures in that manner, whether she is alone in behaving that way, and whether, in other situations, she displays such behavior. To the extent that such questions are answered affirmatively, the casual responsibility is attributed to her personality and not to the situation.

The attribution framework not only specifies the process of assigning causality, but it also, more practically, provides a way of formulating predictions. If the attribution is internal, attributed to something about the gesturing driver, then one can predict that he or she is more likely to show that behavior in other settings, while if it is external, attributed to the situation, then one can predict that other people are also likely to exhibit the same behavior in a similar situation. In this way, the distinction between person and situation is connected to two other notions: the stability of individual differences and the power of the situation.

Personality Consistency

Questions of the stability of personality, however, have troubled the study of individual differences for some time. While people are stable across time in the same setting, they appear quite inconsistent across situations. People who are aggressive in one setting will, in another setting, be quite meek, and those who are honest in one domain may be quite duplicitous in another. In fact, such findings led Walter Mischel to suggest, in a controversial book that still frames much of the debate in the field, that personality consistency correlations across situations rarely exceed .3 and that the search for broad predictive traits is unlikely to prove fruitful. Those consistencies that are found are frequently a result of method variance or self-report bias. People who say they are generally honest also report that they do not often lie; it is when specific concrete behaviors are measured that consistency proves elusive.

Efforts to overcome the difficulty of predicting specific behaviors have taken several forms. One approach has been to suggest that it is a matter of reliability and that aggregating over multiple instances of concrete behavior will make prediction possible. Another approach has been to move from nomothetic approaches, which should apply to all people, to more ideographic ones, suggesting that for only a subset of the population—for example, those to whom honesty is an important dimension—will there be consistency from one setting to another. Another approach is to suggest that superficial traits may be unstable, but that central ones, such as the "big five," form a stable core to personality. Such approaches, while they have made some headway, have not come close to establishing a way of characterizing broad consistencies in behavior.

Interactionism

What has been an effective approach is to incorporate the person-by-situation interaction into the model. The critical aspect of this approach is not to expect consistency in behavior across all situations but instead only across ones that share essential features. One might find, for example, that a person is consistently shy in situations involving groups of older people but that this trait is not manifest with peers or one-on-one. In essence, it is a way to find clusters of situations that are psychologically similar and so tap the same aspects of personality. Or viewed another way, it allows one to predict behavior based on consistency over time in what are effectively similar situations.

This limited view of the power of personality in behavior appears to be addressing the same question as that addressed by attribution theory. It also seems consistent with conclusions about the power of the situation from such findings as those of Stanley Milgram's classic experiment. In this work, perfectly normal people are led, by the situation and the instructions of the impassive experimenter, to administer apparently lethal shocks to an innocent stranger, regardless of their own personality. However, the notion of limited generalizability of personality across situations is, in important ways, orthogonal to those issues. The exquisite sensitivity of personality to nuances of the situation makes it hard to predict behavior from personality, but it does not mean that personality plays any smaller a role. Nor does the narrowness of the expression of traits mean that situations are powerful. The variability in behavior from one person to another, in a given situation, is a result of individual differences, regardless of whether they are predictable or stable. That is, if one person cries and another does not at the end of a tragic movie, there is no question of person versus situation as an explanation, and the debate is just about in what other situations he will cry.

This issue is also captured with a closer look at attribution theory. If one asks whether that crying behavior is due to the movie or the situation, one needs first to specify the implied comparison group. His crying more than other people is due to something about him; his crying more during the movie

than while waiting in line for popcorn is a result of the situation. To suggest that either the person or the situation is generally more causally powerful is not a meaningful question. One can view the strength of personality as being the degree to which individual differences in a situation are predictive. The strength of the situation can be viewed as the degree to which the average behavior deviates from what one might intuitively expect in such a situation (as with the Milgram experiment) or from behavior in an apparently similar setting (as is shown in findings of limited generalizability of dispositions). Thus, the strength of either person or situation has no bearing on the weakness of the other. Nonetheless, it does seem to be the case that it is harder to predict from personality than most people, including psychologists, expect and also that small changes in the situation have a more profound effect than most expect, and so there is some meaning, albeit an ambiguous one, to the suggestion that the person is weak and situations strong.

Nicholas J. S. Christenfeld

See also Attitudes and Behavior; Attribution Theory; Character and Personality, Philosophical Perspectives

Further Readings

Kelley, H. H. (1973). The process of causal attribution. *American Psychologist, 28,* 107–128.

Mischel, W. (1968). *Personality and assessment.* New York, NY: Wiley.

Mischel, W., Shoda, Y., & Mendoza-Denton, R. (2002). Situation-behavior profiles as a locus of consistency in personality. *Current Directions in Psychological Science, 11,* 50–54.

PERSPECTIVE TAKING IN LANGUAGE PROCESSING

Perspective taking is the spontaneous consideration of another's mental states—thoughts, beliefs, and goals—to understand how they interpret a given situation. The ability to appreciate similarities and differences in perspective is important whenever it is necessary to coordinate one's own actions with those of other people. Such coordination problems arise in many different social activities, such as in economic games involving cooperation and competition. Perspective taking has thus been studied extensively by cognitive and social psychologists, linguists, anthropologists, computer scientists, and economists.

Participating in a conversation requires coordination of thought and action on many different levels. Language users must coordinate their thoughts and actions because language is ambiguous: There is no one-to-one mapping between what people say and what they mean. A critical question in modern psycholinguistics is the extent to which perspective taking is necessary for coordination to succeed. The *audience design* hypothesis assumes that people speak and understand vis-à-vis their *common ground*: the set of information that they believe to be mutually shared. Under this view, speakers should take their audience's informational needs into account when deciding what to say. Similarly, listeners should consider speakers' knowledge when interpreting what they mean. Many theories of language use assume that perspective taking plays a fundamental role in speaking and understanding. However, psycholinguistic studies suggest that perspective taking may play a more limited role than previously believed.

Perspective Taking by Speakers

Experiments show that speakers include information in their speech that is obviously crucial for understanding. For example, when they identify a building to someone from out of town, they are more likely to use a description than a name. But in numerous cases where speakers could phrase their speech in ways that would reduce ambiguity for the addressee, they often do not. They may call a baseball bat "the bat," even when the listener could think that they are talking about the animal, a bat. They choose among different sentence structures based on what is easy or hard to produce, not on what would be easy or hard for the listener to understand. Although certain sentence structures can be made unambiguous for the listener by using certain forms of phrasing, emphasis, or intonation, the evidence again suggests that speakers do not do so. Similarly, speakers tend to pronounce a word more clearly when it is less predictable, but this depends more on how recently the speaker has produced the word, not on the listener's need to understand.

When speakers do tailor their speech to a listener's needs, it seems to require much conscious attention and active monitoring for potential ambiguities. Consequently, when speakers are cognitively busy, such as when they are multitasking, their ability to tailor their speech to the listener is drastically reduced.

To design what they say for their addressees, speakers also need to be able to interpret their utterances from the perspective of the addressee. But speakers encounter major difficulty doing so. For example, they do not fully take into account the constraints of the medium. Utterances are more ambiguous on email than when spoken, but people expect addressees to understand them to the same degree. Furthermore, when people try to use intonation to disambiguate what they say, knowledge of their own intention makes the utterance seem less ambiguous than it really is. Consequently, when they try to take the perspective of the addressee, they routinely overestimate how well the addressee will understand them. Speakers even have the same difficulty taking the perspective of their future selves, overestimating their own ability to understand what they meant when they listen to a recording of themselves in the future. This idea was foreshadowed in the 16th century by Michel de Montaigne, who wrote that when reading his own writing he could not always find his original thought: "I do not know what I meant to say, and often I get burned by correcting and putting in a new meaning, because I have lost the first one, which was better" (pp. 425–426).

Perspective Taking by Listeners and Readers

Although listeners do consider the perspective of the speaker when they interpret speech, their ability to do so is limited. For instance, when asked for help, listeners interpret the request based on the physical constraints of the speaker. Listeners do expect speakers to design what they say for them, and they attempt to take the speaker's perspective. But it is currently a matter of debate just how completely listeners are able to use this information to constrain how they process what is said. Under some circumstances, listeners appear able to use this information during the early moments of the processing of a word or phrase. Even young children seem to use perspective information in this way. However, experiments that have more closely examined the time course of language processing suggest a different story: Listeners may be able to take the speaker's perspective into account to anticipate what the speaker might refer to, but they cannot immediately integrate this information when they process what the speaker actually says.

Occasionally, listeners show complete disregard of the speaker's perspective. This results in a surprising degree of egocentric-based errors when the perspectives of the listener and the speaker diverge. Such perspective errors are more prevalent in young children but are also present with adults. This suggests a developmental continuum in which listeners learn over time to make better use of the speaker's perspective but not to completely incorporate it into the comprehension process.

Readers of literary works may also adopt the perspective of protagonists when they interpret what the protagonists say or how they would understand language. Yet when studies unconfound the perspective of the reader from the perspective of the protagonist, they discover that readers interpret text from their own perspective. It is later in the process of understanding that attempts are made to allow for the perspective of the protagonist, if it is different from their own.

Perspective Taking and Successful Communication

The idea that perspective taking plays a limited role in the coordination of meaning may be seen as conflicting with the intuition that speakers and listeners are routinely successful in communicating their intentions. Instead, it may indicate that the coordination of meaning proceeds via other mechanisms. For instance, there is evidence that a community of agents can coordinate meaning without a representation of any agent's perspective. To conclude, people sometimes use perspective to coordinate meaning, but they need not do so to successfully communicate. During a conversation people's perspectives typically come into alignment, thereby making the active consideration of the other's perspective superfluous.

Boaz Keysar and Dale J. Barr

See also Conversation and Dialogue; Folk Psychology; Production of Language

Further Readings

Barr, D. J., & Keysar, B. (2007). Perspective taking and the coordination of meaning in language use. In M. J. Traxler & M. A. Gernsbacher (Eds.), *Handbook of psycholinguistics* (2nd ed., pp. 901–938). San Diego, CA: Academic Press.

Clark, H. H., & Murphy, G. L. (1982). Audience design in meaning and reference. In J-F. Le Ny & W. Kintsch (Eds.), *Language and comprehension* (pp. 287–299). Amsterdam, Netherlands: North-Holland.

de Montaigne, M. (1943). *The complete essays of Montaigne* (D. M. Frame, Trans.). Stanford, CA: Stanford University Press.

Pickering, M. J., & Garrod, S. (2004). Toward a mechanistic psychology of dialogue. *Behavioral and Brain Sciences, 27,* 169–226.

PERSUASION

The way people change their attitudes, beliefs, and behavior is often influenced by their experiences and their interactions with others. The mechanism through which people adopt and change their attitudes and behaviors based on contextual factors is called social influence. Robert Cialdini defines *social influence* as a change in one's attitudes, beliefs, or behaviors, which may be due to real or imagined external pressure(s). Typically people are exposed to a number of influence attempts daily, sometimes without being consciously aware of it. On any given day, a person may be prompted to apply for a credit card, buy a product advertised on television or radio, and change his or her opinion about a politician by reading a news article online. Persuasion is one component of social influence. Specifically, persuasion is the process by which an individual is influenced to adopt or change a particular attitude or belief. People can be persuaded through a number of different avenues (other people, advertisements, books, TV, Internet, etc.).

This entry focuses on the influence of persuasive messages on peoples' attitudes and beliefs by reviewing the prevailing theoretical models of persuasion. These dual process models indicate that when forming or changing an attitude, people either think deeply about the content of a persuasive message or make decisions based on surface characteristics associated with the message, such as the attractiveness of the individual trying to persuade them. This entry also reviews general factors that may affect message processing, and the six principles of influence.

Key Definitions

As stated above, social influence refers to the change in one's attitudes, behavior, or beliefs because of external pressure that is real or imagined. There are two general types of social influence: *persuasion* and *compliance*. Compliance research examines changes in behavior resulting from a direct request. For instance, if an individual is asked to sign a petition advocating that the U.S. government adopt a universal health care system and he or she agrees to this request, the individual is complying with this request. Persuasion is focused on the change in a private attitude or belief as a result of receiving a message. So, for instance, if an individual reads a newspaper editorial that contains compelling reasons why the government should adopt a universal health care plan and the individual's opinion on this topic is changed as a result of reading the arguments, the individual has been persuaded.

Additional terms relevant to an understanding of persuasion describe the individuals involved in an influence attempt. First, *influence practitioner, communicator,* or *agent of influence* are terms used to describe the individual who attempts to influence others. For instance, in the example above, the person who made the request to sign the petition to change the health care system and the person who wrote the editorial are the influence practitioners. Next, the target or target of influence refers to the person who has the influence attempt directed at him or her.

Dual Process Models of Persuasion

The prevailing theoretical models of persuasion are the *elaboration likelihood model* (ELM) and the *heuristic systematic model* (HSM). These complimentary models explain how individuals process persuasive information and make predictions about how that information influences an individual's own attitudes or beliefs.

The Elaboration Likelihood Model

Richard Petty and John Cacioppo introduced the ELM in 1981. The ELM proposes that there are two routes through which attitude change occurs: a central route or a peripheral route. Central processing occurs when an individual thinks carefully about a persuasive message. That is, a person will carefully consider the persuasive message to determine how much merit the argument(s) have. In this case, higher elaboration is involved with processing the message and any resulting change in attitudes or beliefs tend

to be long lasting. In other situations, people are more likely to process a persuasive message through the peripheral route. Peripheral processing occurs when an individual pays more attention to nonmessage relevant factors, such as attractiveness of the influence agent or the quantity of his or her persuasive arguments. In this case, any resulting changes in attitudes or beliefs tend to be short term because the influence target is not considering the central theme of the message.

In their 1984 experiment, Petty and Cacioppo found evidence for these two different routes to persuasion. They reported that when an issue under consideration would directly impact the target of persuasion, individuals were more likely to think about and be persuaded by stronger arguments and by larger numbers of arguments, indicating central processing of the message. However, when the issue was not directly relevant to the target of persuasion, arguments were not considered as carefully and the number of arguments rather than the quality was more persuasive. This is because the message was peripherally processed and the number of arguments, rather than argument quality, served as a cue of message validity.

The Heuristic Systematic Model

In 1980, Shelly Chaiken proposed a dual processing model of persuasion known as the HSM. Similar to the ELM, the model proposes two routes to persuasion: systematic processing or heuristic processing. However, unlike the ELM, the HSM proposes that it is possible for message processing to occur simultaneously through both routes. According to the HSM, it can be both the quality of the arguments *and* the quantity that simultaneously provide information relevant to persuasion. When systematically processing a persuasive message, a person engages in more effortful thinking, scrutinizing the message carefully and engaging in more cognitive effort. Heuristic processing is less thoughtful processing in which individuals rely more on cues, such as the likeability of the influence agent to determine the validity of the message.

In one of her 1980 experiments, Chaiken demonstrated the different message processing routes to persuasion. Similar to Petty and Cacioppo, she found that when an individual had more of a personal stake with an issue, they were more likely to systematically process a persuasive message. On the other hand, when issue involvement was low because they had no stake in the issue, influence targets were more likely to use heuristic processing. Under conditions of high issue involvement, people showed more opinion change when there were more arguments, suggesting more thoughtful and systematic processing. However, when an issue was less relevant, persuasion was impacted more by likeability of the influence agent rather than the number of arguments, indicating a reliance on more heuristic processing and use of cues. Furthermore, individuals in the study who were more involved with the issue spent more time thinking about the arguments, recalled more arguments, and generated more message-relevant thoughts.

Additional Factors Impacting Persuasion

Over the years, research on persuasion has examined many different factors that affect which route to persuasion a person will use to process a persuasive message. Some factors that have been consistently found to affect the processing of persuasive messages and the overall effectiveness of the persuasion attempt include issue importance or personal relevance (as noted above), source credibility and attractiveness, motivation and ability, and the strength or quality of the argument(s) in the message.

Specifically, individuals process persuasive messages differently depending on whether the source of the message—the influence agent—is someone they perceive to be credible. For instance, an individual may be persuaded to adopt a more healthy diet based on the advice of his or her doctor but may not have been persuaded based solely on the advice of a friend. This is because doctors are assumed to have more expertise in health-related knowledge. In this case, people rely more on heuristic processing, by using the expertise and status of the communicator to evaluate the message. Similarly, attractiveness is another cue people often use as a peripheral or heuristic cue when evaluating a persuasive message. That is, people may judge a persuasive message to be more valid if the source of the message is attractive because people generally associate positive characteristics with attractive people.

As noted above, when a message has more personal relevance or when people are more highly involved with it (i.e., when it may directly impact them), people are more inclined to process the message centrally or systematically. For example, someone who cares deeply about animal rights may be more inclined to think effortfully about a potential law involving the treatment of animals. Similarly, a person will more carefully consider voting for a law banning after hours operation of an airport if their home is near the airport.

Motivation and ability also play a significant role in determining how a message will be processed and subsequent persuasion. Under certain conditions a person may vary in the cognitive ability or the motivation to carefully process a message. For instance, a person who has spent a week studying hard for a biology exam may not be able or motivated to thoughtfully process a message advocating a new university-wide security policy. Thus, he or she may resort to peripheral or heuristic processing. A person who has had a relatively stress-free week and no exams may be more likely to elaborate carefully on the new security policy, especially if he or she believes the proposed policy will impact his or her life, because both motivation and ability will be high. Finally, the quality and quantity of the persuasive arguments may also influence persuasion. In general, research indicates that stronger, higher quality arguments are more persuasive than weaker, poorer quality arguments.

Overall, there is consensus in the literature on persuasion that a combination of these factors work together to influence the processing of persuasive messages. Generally, when a person has high motivation and ability to process, the argument is strong, and the issue is relevant, more elaboration will occur and this will produce an enduring shift in attitude. On the other hand, if motivation and ability to process are low, people may rely more on cues such as source attractiveness or likeability to make a judgment that will likely produce short-term persuasion.

The Six Principles of Influence

While people are capable of processing persuasive messages using the different routes reviewed above, people tend to be cognitive misers. That is, people process information using heuristics or rules of thumb that help simplify decision making. Robert Cialdini proposes that most influence targets respond to a set of trigger features for persuasion and compliance. Specifically, he argues that there are six common principles—heuristics or short cut rules—that people are likely to use when confronted with a persuasion attempt by an influence agent. Responding heuristically allows individuals to react quickly, saving time and mental energy. Heuristic responding is not only efficient, but it allows individuals to make informative and accurate judgments when mentally overloaded. As a result such automatic processing can often lead individuals to make accurate decisions. These six principles of persuasion are as follows: authority, liking or friendship, scarcity, social validation, reciprocity, and commitment or consistency. This entry will review each of these principles below.

Authority

When relying on heuristics, people tend to be more persuaded by an influence agent if they perceive the source as an authority figure. The authority heuristic indicates that if an expert says it's true, then it must be. One study on the influence of an authority indicated that people were 3.5 times more likely to follow a jaywalker in a suit than one in casual clothing. Other research indicates that people heed the recommendations of experts such as doctors, scientists, or executives because these are authority figures that are assumed to have more knowledge than laypersons. This aspect of the authority heuristic also often appears in advertisements that feature product endorsements from actors who portray doctors on television shows. Thus, targets of influence will be influenced by agents who appear to be authority figures.

Liking and Friendship

Research on the influence of liking on persuasion indicates that under most circumstances, people are more persuaded by individuals that they like or find attractive. This is typically based on a second heuristic involving the reliance on likeable individuals as good sources of information. This liking heuristic indicates that if a likeable person (especially if he or she is also similar) endorses something, it must be good. For instance, dating or wardrobe advice from a friend will likely be more influential than similar advice from an acquaintance or stranger. Specific research on this question indicates that negotiators who find common goals and shared interests with the opposing negotiator will be more successful in finding mutually beneficial outcomes. Additionally,

celebrities make effective agents of persuasion because they tend to be both well liked and also perceived as experts.

Scarcity

Another heuristic cue involves scarcity. The scarcity heuristic states that if it is rare, it must be good. That is, if something is not widely available, then it is perceived as valuable. For example, during the 1990s Beanie Babies became a popular stuffed animal. Many of these stuffed animals were rare and limited in production. This scarcity led to an increase in prices, ultimately leading to a higher demand for the toys. People came to believe that this product was more valuable and increased their desire to have the product. Because of the scarcity of the plush toy, an item that cost around $0.25 to produce sometimes sold for hundreds of dollars.

One study illustrated the importance of scarcity in the context of sales of Australian beef. A company selling beef knew there would be a shortage of a certain type of beef from Australia. To examine the impact of this scarcity, the researchers created 3 different sales scripts. With the standard script, customer service representatives called customers and took their orders as usual with no mention of the upcoming shortage. With the scarcity script, the representatives called customers and took their orders while mentioning the upcoming shortage. With the scarcity and exclusivity of information script, the representatives called customers and took their orders while mentioning the upcoming shortage and made it clear that this information was genuinely not well known in the market. The average amount of beef ordered using each version of the script illustrates the persuasive impact of scarcity. With the standard script, an average of 10 loads of beef was ordered; with the scarcity script, an average of 24 loads of beef was ordered; and with the scarcity and exclusivity of information script, an average of 61 loads of beef was ordered. Thus, these results indicate that scarcity in terms of both product supply and information is very persuasive.

Social Validation

Social validation or *social proof* is the tendency for people to look to others to determine appropriate attitudes or behaviors. Across cultures and situations, people follow social norms or rules for behavior and change their behavior to match the actions of others. This phenomenon is enhanced in ambiguous situations where an individual is unsure of the appropriate response. For example, one study examined the extent to which people are influenced by the actions of others by varying the number of people looking up at nothing and observing the number of passersby who also stopped to look up. The researchers placed either one person or five people on a busy street looking up and staring at nothing. They found that 5% of passersby stopped and looked up too when only one person was looking up but 80% of passersby looked up when it was the group of five.

Reciprocity

The rule of reciprocity states that people are obliged to give back to others what they have given to us. People are more likely to be persuaded if they feel they owe the influence agent a favor. For example, if a person asks some of his or her coworkers to help him or her move, the coworkers that had called on this person to help them move in the past will likely be the ones to volunteer. Reciprocity is influential both within individuals' social networks—research indicates that widowed women who gave and received equal amounts of emotional support were happier than those who either solely gave or received too much—and outside them too—a study that examined charitable donation rates reported that the inclusion of "free" address labels from the charity increased donation rates from 18% to 35%.

Commitment and Consistency

People are creatures of habit. The last principle, commitment and consistency, capitalizes on tendency. Generally, people will look to previous attitudes and behaviors when confronted with an influence attempt. Individuals will act or think in accordance with previous actions or thoughts. For example, if a person was previously gregarious at a party, he or she may act the same way at another party to remain consistent with past behavior. Furthermore, if a person makes a commitment to a certain behavior or idea, he or she will be more likely to be persuaded to commitment to a related request at a later time. A well-studied example of this is called the *foot-in-the door* effect, which was introduced in 1966 by Jonathan Freedman and Scott Fraser. In one experiment, housewives who were contacted via telephone and asked to complete a short survey on household products were more likely to later agree to allow men to come into their house and classify all their household products. Those housewives who were not first asked to participate in the telephone survey were far less likely to comply with the request to classify household products.

Overall, these six principles of influence are widely used cognitive shortcuts that people rely on to efficiently respond to social influence attempts. Since persuasive attempts may be directed at individuals in a quick and unexpected manner, this use of peripheral or heuristic processing can allow an individual to process and respond to the persuasive communication in a timely manner. Such heuristics or cues may lead to changes in one's attitudes and also in one's behaviors. However, relying on cues such as these principles can lead to errors in message processing as well. For instance, by relying on heuristics, one may come to reject a strong and valid argument in favor of one that comes from a well-liked source.

Rosanna E. Guadagno and Nicole L. Muscanell

See also Attitude Change; Attitudes and Behavior; Political Psychology; Social Cognition

Further Readings

Chaiken, S. (1980). Heuristic versus systematic information processing and the use of source versus message cues in persuasion. *Journal of Personality and Social Psychology, 39,* 752–766.

Cialdini, R. B. (2001). *Influence: Science and practice* (4th ed.). Boston, MA: Allyn & Bacon.

Cialdini, R. B., & Trost, M. R. (1998). Social influence: Social norms, conformity, and compliance. In D. Gilbert, S. Fiske, & G. Lindzey (Eds.), *The handbook of social psychology* (4th ed., Vol. 2, pp. 151–192). New York, NY: McGraw-Hill.

Petty, R. E., & Cacioppo, J. T. (1981). *Attitudes and persuasion: Classic and contemporary approaches.* Dubuque, IA: W. C. Brown.

Petty, R. E., & Cacioppo, J. T. (1986). The elaboration likelihood model of persuasion. In L. Berkowitz (Ed.), *Advances in experimental social psychology* (Vol. 19, pp. 123–205). San Diego, CA: Academic Press.

Pratkanis, A. R. (Ed.). (2007). *The science of social influence: Advances and future progress.* New York, NY: Taylor & Francis.

PHENOMENOLOGY OF ACTION

This entry concerns the consciousness or experience subjects have of their own actions. The now burgeoning interest in this phenomenology of agency is a fairly recent development, even more recent than the rediscovery of consciousness in general. This is reflected in the fact that much of the literature, especially the philosophical literature, is concerned with defending or battling viewpoints still skeptical of the significance of a distinctive phenomenology of agency or even of its very existence. One source for such skepticism is the assumption that such a phenomenology would have to take the form of a specific and unitary feeling or sensation of acting. A better conception is that of a family of actional experiences. Consider the following everyday scenario: You plan to write a paper, and after much deliberation, you choose a topic and create a rough outline. Sitting down in front of your computer to write, perceiving its screen as something to be filled and the keyboard as a means to this end, you focus your thoughts on creating a sentence, finally executing typing movements, experiencing yourself as moving your hands and moving the keys through them and perceiving the events of letters appearing on the screen as the result of your movements. These are some of the family of experiences connected to action and its authorship: experiences of deliberating, intending, of active and purposive bodily movement, of perceiving entities as objects for and results of action. They raise a host of questions. This entry focuses on the structure of actional experience in the sense of the experience of active, purposive movement, and its relation to perceptual experience.

The Structure of Actional Experience

Attempts to find some order in action consciousness in recent times have often taken the form of a classification of different kinds of intentions or other action representations. John Searle influentially distinguished "intentions in action" from "prior intentions"—the intentions accompanying action ("I am doing A") from those preceding it ("I will do A"). Other authors have proposed related distinctions, for example, between proximal and distal intentions. But contrary to what these terminologies suggest, the difference between, say, the prior intention of raising one's arm and the experience of actually raising it is not solely temporal. It is also structural: They differ in their representational format. These differences can be fruitfully described using the notion of nonconceptual content found in the theory of perception. The nonconceptual content of actional experience is nonsymbolic and richer, more fine-grained and denser than the symbolic, conceptual content of prior intentions.

The distinctions between these action representations are also closely related to different levels of control and ownership of actions and to the corresponding failures, slips, and pathologies. For example, a person may control and own a habitual action at the nonconceptual bodily level but not at the conceptual, rational level of deliberation. A related pathological phenomenon is *utilization behavior*, in which patients are unable to inhibit certain stereotypical actions such as drinking from a cup placed in front of them.

Actional and Perceptual Experience

Some authors claim that actional experience and perceptual experience are more than just structurally similar. They suggest that actional experience is simply a species of perceptual consciousness, even that there is a sense of agency, as there are senses of touch and sight. Searle defends a contrary view, according to which actional consciousness is diametrically opposed to perceptual consciousness in one fundamental respect. Perceptual experience is essentially passive: In perception, we experience ourselves as achieving fit between mind and world by being receptive to an independently existing world (mind-to-world direction of fit). By contrast, actional experience is active: In action, we experience ourselves as making something happen, as achieving fit by adapting the world to the contents of our action representations (world-to-mind direction of fit). It is a condition of adequacy on the perceptual theory that it must account for this fundamental phenomenological difference between action and perception. If this difference is reconstructed as a difference between two basic kinds of perceptual experience, in which we experience ourselves in an active or, respectively, in a passive causal role, it may end up being merely verbally different from Searle's view.

Another difference between the perceptual account and Searle's account is that Searle treats the representational content of actional experience as constitutive of action itself. Action occurs when the content of actional experience is satisfied, when the bodily movement I experience myself as bringing about actually occurs. In this respect, actional and perceptual experience are treated in exactly parallel fashion despite their fundamental difference, as perception is also constituted by satisfied, veridical, perceptual experience. In contrast, the perceptual account treats action as independent of the experience of acting, which is denied a constitutive role.

Whether actional experience is perceptual or not, there is a wealth of empirical data on the relation between these kinds of experience. It is tempting to think that proprioceptive experience is a prerequisite for the experience of action. But the famous case of Ian Waterman, a patient who lost all sensory input below the neck but still experiences himself as an agent, seems to show that this is not so. Indeed, it has been suggested that the attenuation of proprioceptive experience rather indicates the presence of action. Many studies show that the proprioceptive consequences of one's own actions are attenuated—this is why one can't tickle oneself. By comparison, exteroceptively accessed effects of one's purposive movements are bound together with these movements—for example, a sound and the bodily movement that produces it are experienced to be temporally closer than they actually are.

Michael Schmitz

See also Action and Bodily Movement; Philosophy of Action

Further Readings

Jeannerod, M. (2006). *Motor cognition.* Oxford, UK: Oxford University Press.

Pacherie, E. (2007). The sense of control and the sense of agency. *Psyche, 13*(1). Available at http://www.theassc .org/files/assc/2667.pdf

Roessler, J., & Eilan, N. (Eds.). (2003). *Agency and self-awareness.* Oxford, UK: Clarendon Press.

Searle, J. R. (1983). *Intentionality.* Cambridge, UK: Cambridge University Press.

Sebanz, N., & Prinz, W. (Eds.). (2006). *Disorders of volition.* Cambridge, MA: MIT Press.

PHILOSOPHY OF ACTION

The use of the label *philosophy of action* gained currency roughly in the second half of the 20th century. However, although the label is relatively new, the subject matter is not. At least since Socrates, philosophers have been concerned with the problems and questions now gathered under that label. Essentially, the philosophy of action seeks to offer an account of distinctively human behavior—in particular, of behavior that is characteristic of, to use Aristotle's phrase, "rational animals." This is behavior on the basis of which we make judgments about people's goals, characters, and values, and it is the behavior that grounds ascriptions of causal and sometimes also moral and legal responsibility to people for certain occurrences, outcomes, and states of affairs.

A philosophical account of the behavior just mentioned requires a good understanding of issues such as what exactly actions, and their counterparts—omissions—are; when an action is voluntary and intentional; whether there are genuinely free actions or whether freedom is an illusion; and, if there are free actions, what roles do reasons, intentions, and the will play in such actions (which introduces the problem of *akrasia*—the possibility of acting against one's better judgment because of "weakness of the will"). Other issues include how we should understand the explanation of actions by reference to reasons, the role of emotions and of the unconscious in actions, whether moral responsibility for actions (and omissions and their consequences) requires free agency, how to understand collective agency, and the agency of non-human animals.

One distinctive feature of the philosophy of action is that its boundaries are relatively vague. The reason for this is that the core questions in this area of philosophy cannot be addressed without resolving problems in other areas, such as metaphysics, the philosophy of mind, the philosophy of language, ethics, and legal philosophy. Throughout its history, the agenda of the philosophy of action has been defined by different questions, and, as a result, the central debates have, at different times, been closely tied to different areas in philosophy. This entry provides an overview of some of the central questions and arguments in the philosophy of action, as well as an indication of which issues have been at the center of contemporary philosophy of action.

From Aristotle to the 20th Century

Aristotle is probably the philosopher who dealt most thoroughly with the various issues in the philosophy of action. Throughout the centuries, most of the great philosophers grappled with the problems he raised and introduced new ones, but it seems right to say that the 20th century saw a revival of interest in this area of philosophy. This was partly due to the publication in 1957 of *Intention*, a deceptively short book by Elizabeth Anscombe, a disciple of Ludwig Wittgenstein's, who was also much influenced by Aristotle and by St. Thomas Aquinas. *Intention* was greatly influential, and although many of the views she defended there have been forgotten or were never embraced, many of the contemporary debates on action are framed in relation to her treatment of the subject. Among other things, her discussion placed questions about intentional actions, which she characterized, roughly, as actions done for a reason, center stage—displacing questions about voluntary actions, which the tradition she was writing against had characterized as actions caused by *volitions* (acts of will) and which had been the staple of earlier discussions. In the years following the publication of *Intention* and especially after the publication in 1963 of Donald Davidson's paper "Actions, Reasons, and Causes," the theory of action concentrated mainly on questions about the metaphysics of actions and about the relation between actions and reasons in the production and explanation of intentional action. More recent work has focused on debates about free will and moral responsibility, autonomy and control, reasons and rationality, and knowledge and action, among other things.

The Metaphysics and Explanation of Actions

As mentioned above, a central question in this field is what actions are, together with related problems concerning the individuation and spatiotemporal location of actions. In *Intention*, Anscombe emphasizes the fact that agents, whether intentionally or not, often do one thing in, or by, doing another. For instance, I may replenish the water supply of a house by pumping, which I may do by moving my arm up and down. So, in cases when one does one thing by doing another, we need to decide whether we are dealing with one particular action (perhaps amenable to various descriptions) or with many. And if many, we may wonder how these actions are related: As part and whole? As cause and effect? In some other way?

Since the mid-1980s, the dominant doctrine has been that an action is an event (a bodily movement), caused and/or causally explained by a reason (a combination of mental states) that rationalizes the action when the latter is considered under the right description—the description "under which" the action is intentional. An action is also the cause of other events (the action's effects), on account of which new descriptions can be applied to the original (basic) action. Accordingly, when someone does one thing by doing another, there is only one event—an action—amenable to many descriptions. Thus, on this picture, my action of pumping water is an event (the motion of my arm) caused by my desire to replenish the water supply and my belief that pumping water is the way to do so. The basic action, the motion of my arm, is an event that can be redescribed as my pumping water, as my replenishing the water supply, and so on, because that action event causes further events: the motion of the water along the pipes, the filling up of the water tank, and so on.

This doctrine about the relation between actions and reasons, known as the *causal theory of action*, was articulated by Donald Davidson. It is still probably accepted by most philosophers even if some disagree on details and even though its detractors have emphasized its various shortcomings.

One of these shortcomings is that accounts based on this picture tend to deal with omissions mostly as an afterthought. But omissions are an important part of the behavior of agents that falls within the province of the philosophy of action, not least because omissions and their outcomes are susceptible to questions about causal and moral responsibility and also because agents often omit to do things *intentionally* and *for a reason*. A central question relating to the distinction between actions and omissions is whether there is, or there must always be, any morally significant difference between them, or between "making something happen" and "allowing it to happen"—for instance, between killing and letting die. Another is that of the relation between causal and moral responsibility. It is often assumed that direct causal responsibility for an event is a necessary condition for someone to be held morally responsible for that event. But omissions seem to undermine that thought. For it seems that an agent might be morally responsible for an event that she did not contribute to causing if by causing we mean that some motion of her body caused, however indirectly, that event—for example, when the agent failed to prevent the event in question *through an omission*. In other words, it seems that, when certain conditions obtain, just allowing an event to happen could justify an attribution of moral responsibility for that event to the agent that allowed it to happen. (An example might be someone who allows a child to drown, knowing that he could have saved the child without danger to himself, even when he was not causally or morally responsible for the child's predicament.)

Other difficulties associated with Davidson's view concern the idea that actions are events. For instance, the idea that a basic action is to be identified with an event that is a motion of one's body seems to generate problems: To name one, if the causing of the motion (my moving of my arm) and the motion caused (the motion of my arm) are identical, it seems to follow that the causing of an event is identical to the event thus caused, which seems absurd. Moreover, although it seems easy to give some actions a precise location in space and time (e.g., my action of opening a tap), this is not so for other actions: Where and when are we to locate John's action of killing James, when he kills him by shooting him on Monday in the park, but James dies on Tuesday in a hospital? The same does not seem true of ordinary (nonaction) events.

The causal theory also faces the so-called problems of *deviant causal chains* and of the *irrelevancy of the mental* in the causation of action. Davidson himself diagnosed the problem of deviant causal chains, for he realized that invoking causation, if necessary, is certainly not sufficient for a satisfactory account of what it is for an agent to act for a reason. The problem is that an action might be caused by a reason that rationalizes it without its being true that the agent acted *for* that reason. Davidson's own example is of a climber in danger who wants to rid himself of the weight of his companion and believes that he can do so by loosening his grip on the rope, and where these very considerations so unnerve him that they cause him to loosen his grip. So his belief and desire cause him to loosen his grip and yet he does not loosen it *for* the reason he had for doing so: He doesn't loosen his grip *for any* reason. This suggests that a reason must not just cause the action but must cause it *in the right way*. However, there is no widely accepted account of what this right way is.

The difficulty generated by the threat of the irrelevancy of mental can be expressed as a dilemma: In the causal theory, either actions are causally overdetermined, or the mental is irrelevant or *epiphenomenal*. According to the standard causal theory, actions are events caused by reasons, which are mental events (or states). But actions are typically conceived of as motions of the body and hence as physiological events, and if so, these motions are, we are told by neurophysiologists, caused by other physiological and neural events. So either reasons are identical to the neurophysiological events and states that cause actions—in which case *reason* explanation (and causation) seem superfluous, or they are not identical to them—but this has the consequence that every action is causal *both* by a reason *and* by the corresponding neurophysiological events and states. Most philosophers reject the possibility of this sort of causal overdetermination. But then, any sense in which *reasons* causally explain actions becomes obscure. This conclusion has been expressed differently (e.g., as the claim that the mental is causally irrelevant or epiphenomenal or that mental properties have no causal role or that they are inert).

Another reason for dissatisfaction with the causal theory is a sense that, on examination, it appears to leave the agent out of the picture. The causal theory, this objection goes, makes the agent appear, at most, as the locus for the causal transactions between events (or states) that constitute her reasons and her actions. Thus, on this picture, the agent herself turns out to be passive where her actions are concerned! This would be an ironic consequence for the causal theory to have since it was introduced supposedly to explain what it is for *someone to act* for a reason. Thus, unless it can bring the agent back into the picture, the causal theory does not explain why agents should be thought to act at all, let alone to act freely or with moral responsibility. This objection has led some to revisit the traditional concept of *agent causation*—that is, the view that there is an irreducible relation between an agent and her actions, while others have sought to revise this concept to free it from its traditional problems. But most contemporary philosophers tend to be skeptical of the very idea of agent causation, because, they claim, agent causation is not an explanatory notion and it is reducible to event causation: To say that an agent causes an event, they would claim, is just to say that an action of the agent (an event) does. Part of what is at issue in these problems is how to specify the conditions under which an agent can be said to have performed a *free action*—an action for which he can be held morally responsible. This brings us to the much-debated old issue of the compatibility or incompatibility of free will and moral responsibility with determinism.

Agency, Freedom, and Moral Responsibility

The traditional debate on these issues assumed that moral responsibility requires freedom and that freedom requires *alternative possibilities*—the ability to act otherwise. The question then was whether, if determinism is true, freedom and hence moral responsibility are possible and justified, respectively. That is, if actions have causes and if all causes necessitate their effects, then actions seem to be determined and agents, it would seem, are not free to act (or to refrain from acting) and hence should not be held to be morally responsible for their behavior. (The causal theory would face this problem because it says explicitly that actions are events caused by reasons, but anyone who accepts that the events that agents are said to cause could be necessitated faces similar difficulties.)

The abundant recent literature on the topic has a distinctive flavor for several related reasons. One is that in the mid-1960s, Harry Frankfurt published a paper challenging the idea that moral responsibility does indeed require the ability to act otherwise. In that paper, Frankfurt claims to offer an example where people on both sides of the debate about the compatibility of free will and determinism would intuitively agree that the agent *is* morally responsible for his action even though he *could not* have done otherwise. Much ink has been spilled on whether Frankfurt's challenge succeeds, whether it begs the question against incompatibilists (who hold that free will and determinism are incompatible), and indeed whether the thought experiments on which his arguments depend are cogent. Be that as it may, this has led to a revision of the concept of an agent (or a person). Frankfurt, for example, argues that agents (or persons) are characterized by their capacity for second-order mental states (that is, attitudes one has toward first-order attitudes, such as my belief that I want to be liked by all or my desire not to act according to that desire), and he has developed an account of agency in terms of *identification*. In this view, an action is properly an agent's only if the latter identifies with the "springs" or sources of his

or her action—that is, has second-order attitudes (roughly, of endorsement) toward the first order attitudes of desire, which are said to be the origins of his actions. Since then, many philosophers have tried to develop accounts along these lines, which are characterized by the prominence they give to the concepts of control and autonomy.

A related feature of current debates on free will is that they are often informed by the thought that free action must be, in some substantial sense, action that comes about as a result of agents' *responsiveness* to reasons: That is, agents must be acting for the reasons they take themselves to have. This of course raises the issue what *reasons* for action are.

Actions and Reasons for Acting

A recent development in the philosophy of action can be traced to work on practical reasoning (reasoning about how to act) and normativity (a much used but underdefined term that concerns, roughly, the kinds of requirement that norms, reasons, and/or values place on agents). This has resulted in a reexamination of the previously prevalent conception of reasons for action. Since the 1960s, most philosophers of action conceived of an agent's reason for acting, called the agent's *motivating* (or explanatory) reason, as a combination of a belief and a desire. Beliefs and desires were usually thought of as *propositional attitudes*: mental states of agents that consist in the agent's taking a certain attitude to a proposition (to the *content* of the attitude). Thus, a motivating reason was typically construed as a mental state with a content, which could (perhaps via a triggering event) cause events (actions, or intentions that in turn cause actions). But this conception of reasons for action has come under pressure in recent years.

This pressure has largely come from considerations about the relation between motivating reasons (the reasons for which agents *actually* act) and normative reasons (the reasons there are for agents to act in certain ways, regardless of whether they recognize these reasons)—considerations that seem to support the conclusion that motivating reasons cannot be mental states or indeed psychological entities of any type. The arguments for this conclusion vary but its defenders tend to agree that what motivates an agent is not *that he believed* something but rather *what he believed*. We are motivated, say, by what we believe (e.g., that the food is poisoned) and not by our believing it. And what we believe (i.e., that the food is poisoned) is not a mental state. To put the point differently, the reasons that motivate agents are not their own mental states but rather aspects of reality (as some would say, not mental states but *facts*). And while, traditionally, the response might have been that this rests on a confusion between normative and motivating reasons, the insight that normative and motivating reasons must be closer in character than they have traditionally been supposed to be undermines this response.

Thus, considerations about normativity have put pressure on the traditional view of motivating reasons as mental states with causal powers. However, it should be noted that the attempt to bring together normative and explanatory reasons calls for an explanation of the connection between motivation by reasons, which are not mental states, and psychological explanations that seem to refer to mental states. In short, reflection about normative and motivating reasons suggests that we need to think afresh the connection between deliberation, normativity, motivation, and reason explanation.

This brief overview of the philosophy of action leaves out many important issues, such as the problem of akrasia, the role of emotion and the unconscious in human action, the topics of collective or social action, rationality and rational choice, and the rise of so-called *experimental* theory of action. But both what is included and what is left out show how rich, interesting, and relevant this field of philosophy is.

Maria Alvarez

See also Action and Bodily Movement; Collective Action; Explanation of Action; Freedom of Action; Mental Action; Phenomenology of Action

Further Readings

Alvarez, M. (2010). *Kinds of reasons*. Oxford, UK: Oxford University Press.

Alvarez, M., & Hyman, J. (1998). Agents and their actions. *Philosophy, 73*, 219–245.

Anscombe, G. E. M. (1957). *Intention*. Oxford, UK: Basil Blackwell.

Dancy, J. (2000). *Practical reality*. Oxford, UK: Oxford University Press.

Davidson, D. (1980). *Essays on actions and events*. Oxford, UK: Oxford University Press.

Fischer, J. M. (1994). *The metaphysics of free will: An essay on control*. Oxford, UK: Basil Blackwell.

Frankfurt, H. (1969). Alternate possibilities and moral responsibility. *Journal of Philosophy, 66*, 829–839.

Kenny, A. J. P. (1975). *Will, freedom and power*. Oxford, UK: Basil Blackwell.

O'Connor, T., & Sandis, C. (Eds.). (2010). *A companion to the philosophy of action*. Oxford, UK: Basil Blackwell.

Raz, J. (1999). *Engaging reason: On the theory of value and action*. Oxford, UK: Oxford University Press.

von Wright, G. H. (1963). *Norm and action*. New York, NY: Routledge.

von Wright, G. H. (1971). *Understanding and explanation*. New York, NY: Routledge.

Williams, B. (1995). *Making sense of humanity*. Cambridge, UK: Cambridge University Press.

PHYSICALISM

Physicalism is the claim that everything in the universe is physical. That doesn't mean that there is nothing living or mental; otherwise, physicalism would attract few believers. Instead, physicalists hold that the living and the mental are types of physical things. Physicalism is viewed as the default assumption for scientific approaches to the understanding of mental life. The first main section of this entry focuses on what makes something physical and refines our understanding of the claim that everything is physical. The second focuses on the main argument for this position, while the third considers the main problem with physicalism.

The Nature of Physicalism

Earlier physicalists—such as Thomas Hobbes—provided a substantive characterization of the nature of the physical as, for example, occupying space and/or possessing mass. With the development of physics, the emphasis changed. The objects and properties characterized by modern physics seemed very different from our everyday understanding of physical objects, yet it seemed a mistake to take developments in modern physics to prove that physicalism was incorrect. Thus modern day physicalists, such as J. J. C. Smart, sought to define physicalism in terms of physics. They recognized that physics may conceivably develop in ways that would recognize nonphysical entities and that not everything physical is identified by physics.

For example, the properties of being a mammal or of being a chair seem to be physical but aren't identified by physics. So they eventually came up with a characterization on the following lines: A property is a broadly physical property if and only if either it is identified by a physics that sufficiently resembles our own current physics (where by this they mean the postulates of that body of physical theory broadly accepted in the late 20th and early 21st century, including the special and general theory of relativity and quantum mechanics) or it *supervenes* on those properties identified by physics (supervenience will be described below). The basic idea is that a physics that postulated nonphysical entities would be a significant departure from, and hence not resemble, current physics as just understood. Physical objects and events are those that only have physical properties in the specified sense. *Narrowly* physical properties are just those identified by physics of the type indicated.

Great energy was then devoted to identifying what kind of supervenience was involved. Supervenience is a type of covariation between members of specified families of properties, for example, between properties of arrangements of bricks and properties of being brick constructions such as walls. Although identity between properties is a limiting case of supervenience, supervenience does not require identity between them; otherwise, it would be ill-suited to the task at hand since it would require that all properties are identified by physics. Nor can this kind of supervenience be simply a lawful relationship between properties. Those who deny that physicalism is true don't have to deny that there is such a relationship between physical and nonphysical properties. For example, suppose you believed in ghosts and that, in the presence of ghosts, there would be a drop in temperature. Then there would be a lawful relationship between ghostly properties and physical ones but this, alone, would not make ghosts physical. Thus, many philosophers appealed to a metaphysically necessary relationship, for example, the kind that holds between having angles adding up to 180° and being three sided. No matter how things might otherwise might be, the thought ran, if two universes were identical in their arrangement of the properties identified by physics (and no other properties were added), then the distribution of all other properties, including, specifically, mental properties, would be fixed.

However, although this kind of supervenience labeled an intimate connection between types of properties, the nature of the relationship remained mysterious. When there is identity between those properties identified by physics and properties identified by other means, then no further explanation is needed. When there is no identity, the need for some kind of explanatory connection is far more pressing. Talk of the properties identified by physics constituting all the other properties provided one kind of popular answer—just as the arrangement of pieces of cardboard can constitute a box or the arrangements of bricks make up a wall. The desire for an explanatory connection, and attendant talk of constitution, was popular for another reason. Many felt that physicalism must involve the idea that the properties identified by physics determined the presence of all the other properties and were, in some sense, the fundamental properties of the universe. As a way of cashing this out, the laws identified by physics were taken to be the fundamental laws of the universe.

While these additional features (the presence of an explanatory connection, constitution, physical laws being fundamental) certainly capture the kind of physicalism that many find attractive, it is doubtful whether they should be taken to be definitive of physicalism for, at least, two reasons. The first is that this type of characterization of physicalism rests on a highly ordered conception of reality in which everything ultimately is based on physics. Physics may be important in characterizing the nature of the physical but it is by no means clear that reality does have such an ordered character. Instead, physics could be seen as one of a range of sciences each with its own subject matter and various kinds of relations between the subject matters. If physics was just the science of the very small, then it is easy to see how the universe might be thought to be based on physics, but the subject matter of physics is broader than that with its own emergent phenomena—such as quantum superposition and entanglement—reaching across wide areas of space. The second reason for being dubious is that this type of characterization of physicalism ignores the possibility of emergent physicalism. Emergent physicalism rests on the possibility that other sciences—psychology, biology, chemistry—may identify emergent causal powers of arrangements of narrowly physical properties that cannot be understood in terms of the kind of arrangements of properties that have been of interest to physicists.

The Main Argument for Physicalism

The main arguments for physicalism have derived from causality. Often, it has been put, especially in the past, as a worry about whether something nonphysical—ethereal, or outside space and time, or the like—could influence the passage of physical events. So formulated, it has little real bite as there is no reason to expect that fundamental causal relations should be readily intelligible and so no reason to deny that the nonphysical could influence the physical. More recently, systematic causal considerations have been advanced that trade on no such assumption. These are laid out in what is generally dubbed the overdetermination argument with its focus, invariably, on mental properties that are taken to be the main candidates for being nonphysical.

Consider the feeling of awful pain you have (P) after having just put your hand in a flame and, putting it neutrally, the neural state in the brain that neuroscientists have identified as concerned with pain (N). Suppose that P is not identical to N (or anything else physical) but is correlated, perhaps, lawfully with it. The supposition that P is not identical to N might be tempting because it can seem that, while neuroscience can explain why we feel pain, its descriptions cannot exhaust how pain feels to us. As a result of being in pain, you withdraw your hand from the flame. What's the cause of this withdrawal? If you say P or N + P, then you must accept that there is something identified by physics (some component[s] of the arm) that is partly caused by something nonphysical: P. But then, either this conflicts with the apparently plausible thesis that the world described by physics is causally complete—only those things identified by physics are required in the causal explanation of other things identified by physics—or we have overdetermination (which promises to be systematic and extensive because the argument can be run for many mental properties and their neural associates), or P is epiphenomenal. We would have overdetermination if both P and N individually were sufficient to explain the activity in the arm—just as somebody might be killed by two assassins' bullets each of which, individually, would have been enough to kill him or her. P would be epiphenomenal if it had no effect on the arm, in roughly the way that the color of a piece of fruit has no effect on how much it weighs.

The unattractiveness of these consequences has been questioned. Perhaps the causal influence of P is hidden or revealed in systematic ways that need not conflict with the apparent causal completeness of physics. Maybe systematic and extensive overdetermination is not so bad because it can be explained by psychophysical laws. It may not be a central component of our understanding of our mental lives that P has an influence. Instead, epiphenomenalism may be true.

There has also been substantial debate over whether those physicalists who deny that all properties are identical to those identified by physics are in a better position to avoid the argument. After all, they too allow that P is not identical to N and P is a cause of the behavior. Responses to this latter worry center around taking causation between events not identified by physics as constituted in some way from causation between events that are identified by physics, in much the same way that broadly physical properties are taken to be constituted from narrowly physical properties.

Whatever the success of the argument from overdetermination and its ramifications for physicalism, physicalism remains an independently attractive position because it is seen as acknowledging the importance of scientific investigation into the nature of the mental and other phenomena and the central importance that physics can play in such investigation.

Problems for Physicalism

Although challenges to physicalism have been derived from the nature of life, freewill, and intentionality (the power of thoughts to represent the world), the main challenge is generally agreed to be consciousness and phenomenal consciousness—the *what it's likeness* of consciousness—in particular. Physical descriptions of the character of phenomenal consciousness have been felt to be inadequate by many philosophers. The point has been put in various ways, for instance, being unable to imagine what an alien creature's experience is like (such as a bat) even if we have a full physical description of it or being unable to know what it is like to experience a red tomato if color blind. Each of these ways involves additional factors such as the limits of imagination or the nature of knowledge, which can obscure the point. The clearest way to present the challenge is to observe that there seems to be an explanatory gap between the nature of the physical properties of the brain (and its surroundings) and the nature of color experience (say). We can't understand why color experience supervenes on these other properties whereas, in contrast, we can understand why liquidity supervenes on the relatively weak forces between layers of molecules.

The obvious explanation of an explanatory gap is that, in fact, we are talking of two wholly distinct types of properties: physical properties and the properties of experience. This is an answer that physicalists cannot give. So their basic response has been to argue that it only appears to us that there are radically different properties because the concepts we have concerning the nature of our own experiences—often dubbed phenomenal concepts—have distinctive features not shared by concepts of either the entities identified by science or everyday objects in the world. Nevertheless, it has proved to be very difficult to identify the precise features of phenomenal concepts that explain why there seems to be an explanatory gap.

According to one line of thought, phenomenal concepts share with demonstrative and indexical concepts (e.g., *that*, *I*) the feature of being applicable without appeal to description. With an indexical, we don't need to describe ourselves in any particular way in order to refer to ourselves by the pronoun *I*. Likewise, with a demonstrative, we don't need to, indeed find it hard to, describe our experience in any way in recognizing it as feeling like *that*. Unfortunately, while "I am Paul Noordhof" and "A-delta firing [one type of pain] feels like *that*" may both be informative, the latter remains additionally puzzling. Why should it feel like *that*? Lack of a satisfactory response has seen physicalism moving from being apparently irresistible to being a default hypothesis that remains to be fully justified.

Paul Noordhof

See also Access Consciousness; Emergence; Explanatory Gap; Mind-Body Problem; Reductive Physicalism

Further Readings

Chalmers D. (1996). *The conscious mind*. Oxford, UK: Oxford University Press.

Crane T., & Mellor D. H. (1990). There is no question of physicalism. *Mind, 99*, 185–206.

Jackson, F. (1998). *Mind, method and conditionals: Selected essays*. New York, NY: Routledge.

Kim, J. (2005). *Physicalism, or something near enough*. Princeton, NJ: Princeton University Press.

Levine J. (2001). *Purple haze: The puzzle of consciousness*. Oxford, UK: Oxford University Press.

Nagel, T. (1979). *Mortal questions*. Cambridge, UK: Cambridge University Press.

Noordhof, P. (2003). Not old . . . but not that new either: Explicability, emergence and the characterisation of materialism. In S. Walter & H.-D. Heckman (Eds.), *Physicalism and mental causation: The metaphysics of mind and action* (pp. 85–108). Charlottesville, VA: Imprint Academic.

Papineau D. (2002). *Thinking about consciousness*. Oxford, UK: Oxford University Press.

PLACEBO EFFECT

The placebo effect is a change produced by the administration of a substance or physical procedure that is not produced by the physical properties of that substance or procedure. It is, instead, an effect produced by the psychological effects of administering the treatment. A placebo is a substance or procedure that cannot produce a particular effect by virtue of its physical properties. This entry describes the history of the placebo concept, its use in clinical trials, factors affecting the magnitude of the placebo effect, and theoretical accounts of how placebo effects are produced.

The word *placebo* comes from the Latin word placebo meaning "I shall please," and for centuries, it was assumed that placebos could placate troubled patients but not produce any real changes. It was not until the mid 20th century that researchers began to appreciate that placebos might produce changes in symptoms. Once that realization became widespread, placebos became commonplace in the process of approving new drugs. Randomized controlled trials (RCTs) soon became the gold standard for testing new medications.

In an RCT, subjects are randomly assigned to at least two groups, an active treatment group and a placebo group. Some trials may include three or more groups. For example, two different drugs may be compared to each other and to a placebo, or subjects might be randomized to receive different doses of the same drug. Assignment to treatment condition is double-blind, which means that neither the physician nor the patient is told to which group the patient has been assigned. The placebo is made so as to be indistinguishable from the real drug. It is the same color, size, and shape. The idea is to keep all psychological variables constant between the active and placebo treatment conditions so that any differences in the effects obtained can be unequivocally ascribed to the active physical properties of the treatment.

Usually, placebos are physically inert, but active placebos are sometimes used. An active placebo is an active substance that can produce side effects but that should have no physical effect on the condition being treated. The purpose of using an active placebo is to prevent patients from *breaking blind*. Breaking blind occurs when patients are able to figure out which group they have been assigned to, perhaps because of the side effects that the real drug produces.

Magnitude of the Placebo Effect

In 1955, Henry Beecher, a pioneer researcher of the placebo effect, wrote an article titled "The Powerful Placebo," in which he asserted that one third of all patients respond to placebos. In fact, this turns out to be wrong. The strength of the placebo effect depends on a number of factors. Depending on these factors, a placebo might have no effect at all, or it might affect 100% of participants. Most important, the strength of the placebo effect depends on the condition being treated. For example, placebos can duplicate more than 80% of the effect of antidepressant drugs and 50% of the effect of painkillers, but they do not seem to have any effect at all on blood sugar levels in the treatment of diabetes. In general, placebo effects are more likely to occur in responses that are consciously experienced than in those that are not. Other factors affecting the placebo response include the color of the placebo, its price and name, the apparent dose, the strength of the drug for which the placebo is a substitute, and the mode of administration.

Color

The color of a placebo can influence its effects. When administered without information about whether they are stimulants or tranquilizers, blue placebo pills produce tranquilizing effects, whereas red placebos induce stimulant effects. Patients report falling asleep more quickly after taking a blue capsule than after taking an orange capsule, and red placebos seem to be more effective pain relievers than white, blue, or green placebos.

Price and Name

Placebos with a recognizable brand name are more effective than placebos described as generic drugs, and more expensive placebos are more effective than cheaper ones. Perhaps this is why pharmaceutical companies can successfully market their brand-name products even when less expensive, generic equivalents are available.

Dose

There are two ways in which dose can make a difference in the effects of placebo treatment. One is the number of placebos given. In one study, placebos prescribed for the treatment of ulcers were more effective when the patients were asked to take four pills per day than when patients were asked to take two pills per day. Another way in which dose can make a difference is in the degree to which factors deemed to be responsible for the placebo effect are involved in its administration. For example, the placebo effect is thought to be dependent on the presence of a supportive therapeutic relationship with the health care provider and on the confidence that the provider communicates about the effectiveness of treatment. One study showed that placebo treatment of irritable bowel syndrome was substantially more effective when the initial interview with the patient was longer and when the clinician was warm and supportive and expressed confidence in the treatment.

Strength of the Active Drug

A placebo given in the guise of a more potent drug is more effective than one given in the guise of a less potent drug. Recall that placebo painkillers are about half as effective as real analgesic medication. What that means is that placebo aspirin is half as effective as real aspirin, and placebo morphine is half as effective as real morphine. Since morphine is more potent than aspirin, placebo morphine is more effective than placebo aspirin.

Mode of Administration

Placebo injections are more effective than placebo pills, and sham surgery is more effective than either injections or pills. Placebo surgery involves cutting patients open and then sewing them up again but not performing the surgical intervention. Sham operations have been used as control procedures in clinical trials evaluating the effectiveness of mammary ligation in the treatment of angina and arthroscopic surgery in the treatment of osteoarthritis of the knee. In both of these applications, the sham surgery was found to be as effective as the real surgery. Mammary ligation is no longer used as a treatment for angina. Although arthroscopic surgery for osteoarthritis of the knee is still performed, it has become controversial because of the research showing placebo surgery to be equally effective.

Individual Differences

In any given clinical trial, some people will respond to a placebo and some will not. This finding has led researchers to search for the characteristics of placebo responders. The question is, how do placebo responders differ from nonresponders? Many believe that if this question could be answered, placebo responders could be screened out from clinical trials, thereby making it easier to detect the effects of real drugs.

The search for personality characteristics of placebo responders has been largely unsuccessful. Most studies have failed to find significant differences in the traits that were measured. Exceptions include studies indicating that placebo responsiveness might be linked to an acquiescent response set (i.e., a tendency to say yes) and to dispositional optimism. Optimists seem more likely to experience beneficial effects from placebos, whereas pessimists are more likely to experience negative effects. This latter effect is often called the *nocebo effect*. The nocebo effect occurs when negative expectancies produce unwanted consequences. One example is the occurrence of placebo-induced side effects consistent with the known side effects of the active drug. Another example of the placebo effect is mass psychogenic illness (a.k.a. mass hysteria), in which symptoms are spread via psychological contagion.

It is not clear whether particular personality types are consistently related to placebo responding. In fact, it is not clear that there are consistent placebo responders or consistent placebo nonresponders. In one study, people who responded to a placebo were later more likely to respond to the same placebo, but changing the name of the placebo disrupted this consistency. When the name of the placebo was changed, response to the first placebo did not predict response to the second placebo.

Theories of Placebo Effects

There are two main psychological theories of placebo effects: *classical conditioning* and *response expectancy*.

Classical Conditioning

Classical conditioning was discovered by the Russian physiologist Ivan Pavlov at the end of the 19th century. The most famous example of classical conditioning is that in which the presentation of food to a dog is paired repeatedly with the sound of a bell. After a number of such pairings, the bell acquires the ability to cause the dog to salivate even when food is not presented. In this example, the food is termed an *unconditional stimulus* (US), salivation in response to the food is termed an *unconditional response* (UR), the bell is a *conditional stimulus* (CS), and salivation in response to the bell is called a *conditional response* (CR).

The classical conditioning model of placebo effects is based on the observation that active treatments are always administered in some type of vehicle (e.g., a pill, capsule, or injection). Thus, the active treatment (the US) is paired with the vehicle in which it is administered (the CS). As a result of these pairings, the effect of the treatment (the UR) comes to be administered by the vehicle alone as a conditional response. Evidence supporting the classical conditioning model of placebo effects comes from studies in which a placebo cream was used to lower the feelings of pain produced by an experimental pain stimulus. Conditioning is accomplished by surreptitiously lowering the intensity of the pain stimulus when it is applied to the part of the body that to which the placebo cream has been applied. Repeated conditioning trials of this sort result in an enhanced placebo effect when the pain stimulus is later administered at full intensity.

Response Expectancy

Response expectancies are anticipations of subjective experiences and other automatic, unintentional responses. A wealth of research indicates that response expectancies tend to produce the expected responses in the form of self-fulfilling prophecies. For example, the expectancy that one will experience a panic attack seems capable of inducing one, and expected pain reduction leads to experienced pain reduction.

According to expectancy theory, placebos produce placebo effects by altering response expectancies. For example, placebo analgesics produce expectancies of reduced pain, placebo antidepressants lead one to expect to feel less depressed, and placebo caffeine produces expectations of feeling aroused. These response expectancies then elicit the expected responses in the form of placebo effects. Expectancy theory seems to do a particularly good job of explaining some of the factors that affect the strength of the placebo effect. People expect brand name medications to be more effective than generic equivalents, for example, and they know that morphine is more potent than aspirin.

Conditioning and Expectancy

Although conditioning theory and expectancy theory are sometimes pitted against each other as alternatives, modern forms of conditioning theory are compatible with response expectancy theory. According to these formulations, conditioning is not an automatic, unconscious process. Instead, it works by producing expectancies, which in turn elicit conditional responses. In the example of Pavlov's dogs, conditioning trials lead the animal to anticipate food whenever the bell is rung. It is the anticipation of the food that then produces the salivation.

As applied to placebo effects, the integration of conditioning theory and expectancy theory holds that conditioning trials are one means—perhaps the most effective—of producing the expectancies that then elicit placebo effects. Consistent with this approach, studies have shown that conditioning procedures aimed at enhancing placebo pain reduction produce expectancies for reduced pain and that the expectancies are correlated with the amount of pain subsequently reported.

Future Directions

The importance of the placebo effect is now widely accepted. Besides its use as a means of distinguishing between drug effects and psychological effects in clinical trials, the placebo effect is increasingly recognized as a component of active treatments. For that reason, the task of harnessing the placebo effect so that it can be used clinically is important. Hindering this effort is the ethical problem of deceiving patients and the general assumption that deception may be necessary for effective use of the placebo effect in clinical practice. This has led to an ongoing debate about whether deception might be justified when it is likely to benefit the patients who are being deceived.

Irving Kirsch

See also Behaviorism; Reinforcement Learning, Psychological Perspectives

Further Readings

Beecher, H. K. (1955). The powerful placebo. *Journal of the American Medical Association, 159*(17), 1602–1606.

Benedetti, F., Pollo, A., Lopiano, L., Lanotte, M., Vighetti, S., & Rainero, I. (2003). Conscious expectation and unconscious conditioning in analgesic, motor, and hormonal placebo/nocebo responses. *Journal of Neuroscience, 23*(10), 4315–4323.

Harrington, A. (Ed.). (1997). *The placebo effect: An interdisciplinary exploration.* Cambridge, MA: Harvard University Press.

Kaptchuk, T. J. (1998). Intentional ignorance: A history of blind assessment and placebo controls in medicine. *Bulletin of the History of Medicine, 72*(3), 389–433.

Kaptchuk, T. J., Kelley, J. M., Conboy, L. A., Davis, R. B., Kerr, C. E., Jacobson, E. E., . . . Lembo, A. J. (2008). Components of the placebo effect: A randomized controlled trial in irritable bowel syndrome. *British Medical Journal, 336,* 998–1003.

Kirsch, I. (1985). Response expectancy as a determinant of experience and behavior. *American Psychologist, 40*(11), 1189–1202.

Kirsch, I. (2006). Placebo: The role of expectancies in the generation and alleviation of illness. In P. Halligan & A. Mansel (Eds.), *The power of belief: Psychosocial influence on illness, disability and medicine* (pp. 55–67). Oxford, UK: Oxford University Press.

Kirsch, I. (2010). *The emperor's new drugs: Exploding the antidepressant myth.* New York, NY: Basic Books.

Moerman, D. E. (2006). The meaning response: Thinking about placebos. *Pain Practice, 6*(4), 233–236.

Montgomery, G. H., & Kirsch, I. (1997). Classical conditioning and the placebo effect. *Pain, 72*(1–2), 107–113.

Stewart-Williams, S., & Podd, J. (2004). The placebo effect: Dissolving the expectancy versus conditioning debate. *Psychological Bulletin, 130*(2), 324–340.

Voudouris, N. J., Peck, C. L., & Coleman, G. (1985). Conditioned placebo responses. *Journal of Personality and Social Psychology, 48,* 47–53.

PLANNING IN LANGUAGE PRODUCTION

The planning and articulation of speech often overlap in time, much as the downloading and playing of video content overlap when streamed over the Internet. Specifically, while speakers articulate the initial words of an utterance, they plan its subsequent parts. Research has focused on the production of novel, isolated picture descriptions such as "green cat" and "a turtle is squirting a mouse." Little work has addressed the planning of utterances for purposes other than description, narration, or sentence completion, such as utterances with primarily social functions and those containing conventional phrases, such as "How are you?" This entry summarizes the research on the time course of utterance planning for adult, unimpaired, proficient, native speakers of (primarily) Indo-European languages.

Scope

Speakers appear capable of planning and storing in memory (i.e., *buffering*) a representation containing the sounds of an entire utterance prior to articulating it, but for multiword utterances they do not do so spontaneously. Just as pauses in playback and slow connection warnings indicate that downloading has not stayed ahead of playback, the prevalence of disfluencies (e.g., silent pauses and delay signals such as *um* and *uh*) suggests a limited scope of planning and buffering. Moreover, buffering material is resource demanding and feedback from listeners may often make buffered material irrelevant, similar to downloading a whole movie that a viewer cancels after a few minutes.

Message

The preverbal message for a descriptive utterance contains a topic (what an utterance is about) and information that the speaker wishes to express about the topic. As the topic is usually the first thing mentioned, its message representation is probably fully specified and the words and sounds used to express it retrieved before any part of the utterance is articulated. Suggesting that speakers outline a message prior to utterance onset, initial pitch varies with sentence length, while sentence length is largely a function of message content and complexity. Also, having outlined preverbal messages allows speakers to order simple content before complicated content in languages structured like English (e.g., "The philanthropist donated to a charity a wide array of products and services that would prove to be very useful") and complex content before simple in languages such as Japanese. Patterns of spontaneous word anticipations, exchanges, and subject-verb agreement errors suggest that speakers rarely plan or simultaneously consider messages beyond the clause that they are currently articulating.

Speakers need to simultaneously represent and maintain message representations that correspond to entire noun phrases to fluently produce prenominal modifiers (e.g., *the long, brown hair*) and conjoined noun phrases (*dog and cup*). Speakers can modify the content of a noun phrase while articulating its initial parts, but this leads to disfluencies when there is insufficient time to encode the new content. For example, a speaker may fluently utter, "the alien with the small spots," and only decide to mention the size of the spots around the time he or she starts articulating *alien*. However, if the speaker wants to say "the small alien" fluently, he or she needs to consider size at least a half second before the onset of *the*.

Structure and Order of Mention

Message representations are not thought to contain any intrinsic order but primarily relationships between concepts that differ in availability. Some theories posit that bits of grammatical structure are accessed via selection of content words (e.g., nouns, verbs) and then combined. Other theories see the structure of an utterance as emerging from a sequence of decisions about what part of a message to put into words next, constrained by what the speaker has already planned and the language spoken (e.g., in English a direct object follows its verb rather than precedes it).

Words

In spontaneous speech, speakers often hesitate before articulating words that have many near synonyms to choose among. Even in fluent speech, experiments suggest that nouns are selected shortly before or during articulation of their encompassing noun phrase.

However, it is less clear when speakers select verbs, but speakers need not select them before encoding other parts of an utterance. Disagreement centers on whether speakers can select words from the same grammatical class within a phrase (i.e., two adjectives or two nouns) simultaneously or if they select them one at a time with selection affected by such composite message representations.

Closed-class, functional elements such as articles (*a, the*) and verb tense markers (*-ed, -ing*) appear to be selected via a different process than content words are. The extremely high frequency of use for functional elements should make their retrieval very fast and accurate. Indeed, they appear to take relatively little time to plan. However, these elements are acquired later than content words in language acquisition and may be selectively impaired with brain damage. Perhaps contributing to their difficulty in acquisition and planning is the abstractness of their meanings (e.g., *I walked* vs. *I was walking*). Theories of language production tend to link the retrieval of functional elements to the same mechanism that determines grammatical structure.

The selection of a word and retrieval of its sounds appear separable although they nearly always occur in immediate succession. For example, speech errors often involve selecting an unintended semantically related word but retrieving its sounds perfectly (e.g., substituting *bike* for *car*) or selecting the intended word but then flubbing its sounds (saying *urvan* for *urban*). Sometimes speakers are able to select a word successfully but then fail to retrieve most of its sounds, resulting in a feeling of having a word on the tip of the tongue.

Sounds and Movement

Theories often distinguish between retrieving the individual sounds of a word, organizing them into syllables or other rhythmic patterns, and computing the movements needed to articulate them. Sound-related processing appears to have a scope of about one second or up to two content words. Brain-damaged patients who have severe deficits in short-term memory for phonological information nonetheless tend to converse normally, suggesting that there is little need to retrieve sounds more than one message element or phrase in advance.

Current issues in planning concern the role of working memory beyond maintaining messages or phonological plans, the generalizability of results from simple descriptions of objects, variation in planning scope with speech rate, effects in articulation durations, similarities with other forms of action planning, and developing theories that are less dependent on discrete symbolic representations.

Zenzi M. Griffin

See also Aphasia; Language Production, Incremental Processing in; Production of Language; Prosody in Production

Further Readings

Brown-Schmidt, S., & Tanenhaus, M. K. (2006). Watching the eyes when talking about size: An investigation of message formulation and utterance planning. *Journal of Memory and Language, 54*(4), 592–609.

Chang, F., Dell, G. S., & Bock, K. (2006). Becoming syntactic. *Psychological Review, 113*(2), 234–272.

Dell, G. S., Oppenheim, G. M., & Kittredge, A. K. (2008). Saying the right word at the right time: Syntagmatic and paradigmatic interference in sentence production. *Language and Cognitive Processes, 23*(4), 583–608.

Griffin, Z. M., & Ferreira, V. S. (2006). Properties of spoken language production. In M. J. Traxler & M. A. Gernsbacher (Eds.), *Handbook of psycholinguistics* (2nd ed., pp. 21–59). London, UK: Elsevier.

Levelt, W. J. M., Roelofs, A., & Meyer, A. S. (1999). A theory of lexical access in speech production. *Behavioral and Brain Science, 22*(1), 1–45.

Martin, R. C., Crowther, J. E., Knight, M., Tamborello, F. P., II, & Yang, C.-L. (2010). Planning in sentence production: Evidence for the phrase as a default planning scope. *Cognition, 116*(2), 177–192.

POLITICAL PSYCHOLOGY

In its broadest sense, political psychology addresses how human nature shapes political life. Philosophers have been investigating this question for a very long time, dating at least to the ancient Greeks: Plato's *Republic* and Aristotle's *Politics* are both concerned with the limitations of human nature and the implications for the design of political systems. Later, European philosophers such as Thomas Hobbes and Jean-Jacques Rousseau differed sharply in their assumptions about human nature and, hence, in the political conclusions they drew (with Hobbes taking the view that people's inherent tendencies to aggress required a strong state and Rousseau contending that people are naturally inclined toward peaceful coexistence). This entry describes modern political psychology, beginning with Theodor Adorno and colleagues' *The Authoritarian Personality*. It then covers critiques of Adorno's approach, the "rediscovery" of ideology in the 1980s, and modern research on ideology and personality as well as on incidental factors that affect policy preferences and voting behavior. Finally, charges of ideological bias among political psychologists are discussed.

Ideology and Personality

Political psychology in its current sense emerged as a discipline following World War II. Shocked by the ease with which prewar Germany had turned to authoritarianism, researchers sought to understand the personality factors that predisposed individuals to support authoritarian leaders and regimes. Generally, they adopted a Freudian model that regarded early childhood as determinative of adult personality. The most influential work in this tradition was Adorno and colleagues' *The Authoritarian Personality*. Published in 1950, it was an ambitious attempt to link personality characteristics (and the childhood experiences that were thought to have produced these characteristics) with political ideology, and it exerted a singular influence on the nascent field of political psychology. Adorno and colleagues were interested in the psychological underpinnings of anti-Semitism and, more broadly, in support for authoritarian regimes. As such, their research focused mainly on the personality characteristics of authoritarians, specifically authoritarian *submissives*—the followers rather than the leaders in authoritarian regimes. A particular concern was the emergence of authoritarianism in a democracy, and so Adorno and colleagues studied U.S. citizens rather than citizens of actual authoritarian regimes. The ultimate goal was to understand the personalities of supporters of authoritarianism and thus to understand how authoritarian regimes can arise and rapidly gain support, as was the case in prewar Weimar Germany.

The Authoritarian Personality drew on questionnaire measures (the most well known is the potentiality for fascism, or F, scale), semistructured interviews, and projective tests such as the Thematic Apperception Test (TAT). Adorno and colleagues argued that these diverse methods revealed a coherent portrait of potential authoritarians: Unrealistically positive about themselves and about parental figures, they redirect hostility toward socially marginalized outgroups. They value status and material success. Mentally, they are rigid, inflexible, and intolerant of ambiguity, preferring to see the world in black and white.

In the wake of *The Authoritarian Personality*, there was a flurry of interest in personality correlates of ideology and in the validity of the specific methods used by Adorno and his team. Although there were numerous criticisms of Adorno and colleagues' methods, especially of the reliance on subjectively scored tests and interviews, the most lasting damage was inflicted by political psychology's increasing skepticism about whether people (or, at any rate, U.S. citizens) possessed coherent ideologies to begin with.

The most damning critique, advanced by Philip Converse in "The Nature of Belief Systems in Mass Publics," was that most people showed little or no evidence of a coherent ideology. With the exception of the roughly 10% of the population who were, in Converse's terminology, ideologues or near ideologues, survey respondents showed little evidence of a coherent ideological belief system—just because people took a liberal (or conservative) stance on an issue did not mean that they would take similar positions on related issues. Furthermore, the temporal stability of attitudes was quite low: If a respondent was for, say, affirmative action in 1974, odds were little better than chance that he or she would still hold that position in 1976. Even awareness of ideological terms was strikingly low—very few respondents could correctly assign the terms *liberal* and *conservative* to the Democratic and Republican parties and explain what each meant. Converse's argument was extremely influential, and until the early 1980s, researchers made few serious attempts to study ideology. Rather, survey researchers of the 1960s and 1970s attempted to predict political attitudes and voting behavior on the basis of other factors, most notably demographics and party identification.

The Rediscovery of Ideology

Possibly because of increasingly sharp partisan divides in the United States, the 1980s saw a resurgence of interest in ideology, especially conservative ideology. Instruments such as Robert Altemeyer's right-wing authoritarianism (RWA) scale, James Sidanius and colleagues' social dominance orientation (SDO) scale, and John Jost and Erik Thompson's economic system justification scale were intended to measure broad attitudes toward authoritarian government and social and economic inequality.

Recently, John Jost and his colleagues have argued that conservative ideology—which they define as a resistance to change and a tolerance of inequality between social groups—is motivated by the psychological need to control uncertainty and threat. In its conception of conservatism as a product of deep psychological needs, this model is akin to Adorno and colleagues' view of support for authoritarianism as the result of people's refusal to acknowledge negative feelings toward the self, parents, and authority figures. However, there are important differences: Adorno and colleagues took a Freudian perspective that treated the authoritarian personality as the product of an overly punitive parenting style. In contrast, Jost and colleagues see conservatism as a way of imposing order on an unpredictable, dangerous world. In "Political Conservatism as Motivated Social Cognition," they summarize a great deal of research in the last 50 years showing a relationship between conservatism and personality constructs relevant to needs for safety and order: Conservatism correlates positively with measures of anxiety, positively with aversion to ambiguity and uncertainty, and negatively with sensation seeking and openness to new experiences. Although Jost and colleagues' conclusions (and Jost's focus on conservatism in particular) have been vigorously debated, it seems clear that the study of ideology and the psychological motives that underlie it are once again central to political psychology.

This is not to say that political psychologists see people as having completely coherent political views. In fact, a robust stream of research has examined the effect of normatively irrelevant factors on people's policy evaluations and voting behavior. For example, Geoffrey Cohen has shown that people often attend to the political party advocating a policy, rather than to the policy's actual content, when deciding whether to support or oppose it. Even more startling is the effect of completely irrelevant contextual factors on people's actual voting behavior. Candidates who were listed first on the ballot gained an average advantage of 2.5 percentage points across 118 Ohio races, and Arizonans who voted in a school (as opposed to those whose polling place was in another location) were more likely (by about 2 percentage points) to support an increase in the sales tax to increase school funding.

Is Political Psychology Biased?

It is probably fair to say that most political psychologists are personally politically liberal. Throughout the history of modern political psychology, this has led critics to contend that the field is prone to political bias. One kind of critique has focused on how political psychologists formulate research questions. *The Authoritarian Personality* was criticized for focusing on political conservatives as an *other* to be explained; similarly, Jost and colleagues' view of conservatism as motivated cognition has been criticized for assuming that the political views of conservatives, not of liberals, demand explanation in terms of underlying psychological needs and motives. A second type of critique deals with how key concepts are defined—for example, Philip Tetlock has argued that the concept of *modern racism* (as advanced by David Sears and colleagues) is inherently politically biased in that it labels people who are opposed to income redistribution and school busing as modern racists by definition. The validity of these critiques has been hotly debated, but recent work in political psychology has been influenced by them, at least implicitly. One recent example is the work of Jon Haidt and colleagues on the moral foundations underlying the political views of liberals and conservatives, which argues that the two groups rely on divergent but equally valid moral intuitions.

Conclusion

Political psychology—the study of how human nature shapes political life—has attracted the interest of philosophers dating back to the ancient Greeks. More recently, empirical researchers have sought to apply the tools and paradigms of modern psychology to the study of political beliefs and behavior. Political psychology emerged as a discipline following World War II with Theodor Adorno and colleagues' studies of the "authoritarian personality." Although interest in ideology waned for a time as researchers focused on nonideological predictors of voting behavior, personality-driven research into political ideology, especially conservative ideology, has enjoyed a recent revival. This focus on conservative ideology has been criticized as ideologically biased, and some recent research has sought to explain the moral intuitions underlying both liberal and conservative ideologies. Complementary research has examined the effects of incidental factors, such as ballot position or polling place, on voters' choices.

Yoel Inbar and David A. Pizarro

See also Intergroup Conflict; Intergroup Conflict, Models of; Motivated Thinking; Persuasion

Further Readings

Adorno, T. W., Frenkel-Brunswik, E., Levinson, D. J., & Sanford, R. N. (1950). *The authoritarian personality.* New York, NY: Harper.

Altemeyer, R. A. (1981). *Right-wing authoritarianism.* Winnipeg, Manitoba, Canada: University of Manitoba Press.

Berger, J., Meredith, M., & Wheeler, S. C. (2008). Contextual priming: Where people vote affects how they vote. *Proceedings of the National Academy of Sciences, 105*(26), 8846.

Converse, P. E. (1964). The nature of belief systems in mass publics. In D. Apter (Ed.), *Ideology and discontent* (pp. 206–261). New York, NY: Free Press.

Graham, J., Haidt, J., & Nosek, B. (2009). Liberals and conservatives use different sets of moral foundations. *Journal of Personality and Social Psychology, 96,* 1029–1046.

Jost, J. T., Glaser, J., Kruglanski, A. W., & Sulloway, F. J. (2003). Political conservatism as motivated social cognition. *Psychological Bulletin, 129,* 339–375.

Miller, J. M., & Krosnick, J. A. (1998). The impact of candidate name order on election outcomes. *Public Opinion Quarterly, 62*(3), 291.

Sidanius, J., & Pratto, F. (1999). *Social dominance: An intergroup theory of social hierarchy and oppression.* New York, NY: Cambridge University Press.

Tetlock, P. E. (1994). Political psychology or politicized psychology: Is the road to scientific hell paved with good moral intentions? *Political Psychology, 15,* 509–529.

PRECONSCIOUS FREE WILL

This entry presents scientific evidence that the conscious feelings of wishing and deciding that we usually think of as determining our voluntary acts are not themselves responsible for those acts, although they may roughly but accurately represent preconscious mental processes that are responsible for such acts.

How Free Will Is Normally Experienced

Within philosophy, *free will* is commonly thought of as "free" to the extent that its operations are not entirely determined by physical causal laws. However, freely willed actions are not usually experienced as being entirely free of determining factors. Rather, choices, decisions, and actions are normally experienced as operating, with some degrees of freedom, within complex mental, physical, and social constraints. Consequently, psychologists have typically focused their interest on the systems that enable humans to have the freedom to choose, decide, and act that they actually *experience* themselves to have—a form of *constrained* free will. Studies of voluntary action in humans have made it clear that such systems need to include inner needs and goals, a global knowledge store (based on previous interactions with the world), processes for modeling current inner and external states of affairs, alternative strategies for action, methods for assessing the likely success of alternative strategies in the light of existing physical and social constraints, and the ability to learn from experience. Although such systems follow deterministic principles, their operation can be partly self-organizing and flexible, and their complexity can allow sufficient degrees of freedom to accurately model the ability to make choices and decisions, within the available alternatives, that humans actually experience. Given this, there is nothing within current psychological understanding of the mind, viewed as a complex system, which rules out a form of constrained free will—a position known in philosophy of mind as *compatibilism*.

Distinguishing Free Will From Conscious Free Will

Free will does, however, have to be distinguished from *conscious* free will, because in principle, the operations of such decision-making systems do not have to be conscious. If the detailed information processing involved could be sufficiently well specified, it could, for example, operate equally well in a nonconscious robot. Neuropsychological findings have also cast doubt on the role of the conscious experiences associated with willing and deciding in the operation of the volitional processes themselves.

It has been known for over 40 years that voluntary acts are preceded by a slow negative shift in electrical potential recorded at the scalp known as the readiness potential (RP) and that this shift can precede the act by up to one second or more. More significantly, the neurophysiologist Benjamin Libet found that, for simple spontaneous acts such as flexing the wrist or fingers, RP even preceded the experienced wish to flex the wrist or fingers by around 350 milliseconds, suggesting that the brain is preparing to act even before the conscious wish to act appears!

Given its radical consequences, this finding and the experimental methods used to obtain it have been the subject of considerable discussion and debate. The broad consensus, however, is that the findings are not just artifacts. They were confirmed, for example, by Patrick Haggard and Martin Eimer who went on to investigate the preparedness of the brain to act with either the left or right hand, indexed by the lateralized readiness potential (LRP), a negative shift in electrical potential in the cerebral hemisphere on the opposite side to the active hand, when compared to the electrical potential in the one on the same side. Again, as with RP, LRP occurred before the conscious wish to move a given hand, although in this case by around 100 milliseconds (ms).

In an attempt to find a role for the conscious experiences of willing themselves, Libet pointed out that although conscious wishes follow the RP by around 350 ms, they precede the act by around 150 ms, time enough to veto the wish. So he suggested that the ability to veto the wish is the function of conscious volition (rather like a conscious Freudian ego controlling the unconscious id). However, a decision not to act (after a readiness to do so) can be shown to have its own antecedents. Using go or no-go tasks where subjects were given a signal to either press a button or withhold pressing that button, Gethin Hughes found that response inhibition could be preconsciously influenced in various ways. For example, he found that a signal *not* to press the button presented 100 ms before the conscious no-go signal, produced earlier response inhibition, even when the preconscious signal was prevented from entering consciousness by a masking signal that obscured it. To solve the problem that there is no overt behavior in the no-go condition, the onset of response inhibition was determined from the onset of the *no-go N2*, a negative going cortical potential measured over frontally placed electrodes that acts as an index of response inhibition, occurring about 200 ms after a conscious cue *not* to act appears.

Where Free Will Fits Into Mental Processing

Given such findings, is conscious free will an illusion? In assessing this, it is important to note that free will is not a special case. As Max Velmans has pointed out, just as conscious wishes and decisions follow the neural processing required to generate them, conscious percepts follow the perceptual processing required to produce them, conscious thoughts follow the cognitive processing required to produce them and so on. In these cases, the conscious phenomenology that results from brain processing represents the outcome of that processing without itself being that processing—and it is indeed illusory to confuse the products of mental processing with the processing itself. Such conscious experiences can nevertheless give useful information about their mental antecedents. Visual experiences give useful information about the visual features of the world that have been processed; thoughts in the form of inner speech provide useful information about the nature of prior cognitive processing and so on. Similarly, feelings of being able to choose among alternatives can accurately reflect the operation of preconscious decision-making processes constrained by inner goals and needs, social and physical constraints, and so on—supporting a form of what Velmans refers to as "preconscious free will."

Max Velmans

See also Consciousness and the Unconscious; Freedom of Action; Voluntary Action, Illusion of

Further Readings

Banks, W., & Pockett, S. (2007). Benjamin Libet's work on the neuroscience of free will. In M. Velmans & S. Schneider (Eds.), *The Blackwell companion to consciousness* (pp. 657–670). Malden, MA: Basil Blackwell.

Hughes, G. (2008). *Is consciousness required to inhibit an impending action? Evidence from event-related brain potentials* (Doctoral thesis, Goldsmiths, University of London).

Velmans, M. (2002). How could conscious experiences affect brains? *Journal of Consciousness Studies,* 9(11), 3–29.

Velmans, M. (2003). Preconscious free will. *Journal of Consciousness Studies, 10*(12), 42–61.

Wegner, D. (2002). *The illusion of conscious will.* Cambridge, MA: MIT Press.

PREDICTION, CLINICAL VERSUS ACTUARIAL

Successful prediction is an essential activity in scientific and lay life, and this entry traces the nature and lessons of successful prediction. Suppose you have to make a prediction about some target property (e.g., a child's adult height or whether a prisoner will recidivate) on the basis of *n* lines of evidence (e.g., the child's height at 3 years of age, the heights of the child's parents). It doesn't matter how those lines of evidence were acquired—whether via a clinician's judgment or a mechanical procedure (e.g., a computer-graded aptitude test). To arrive at a prediction, one must weigh and combine those lines of evidence and come to a judgment. Clinical prediction is any prediction in which the weighing and combining of evidence is done by an expert human. Actuarial prediction is a purely mechanical procedure in which the weighing and combining of evidence is done algorithmically, via a transparent formula that could be applied equally well by a trained clinician or by a clerical worker.

The literature comparing clinical and actuarial prediction begins with Paul Meehl's 1954 classic, *Clinical Versus Statistical Prediction: A Theoretical Analysis and a Review of the Evidence.* Meehl reports on 20 studies in which actuarial predictions, based on very simple actuarial rules, were more accurate than clinical predictions. Since the publication of what Meehl called his "disturbing little book," psychologists have developed many successful actuarial models or statistical prediction rules (SPRs).

The Golden Rule of Predictive Modeling

There is now overwhelming evidence for "the golden rule of predictive modeling": When given identical evidence, well-constructed SPRs predict at least as reliably, and typically more reliably, than human experts. The most decisive case for the golden rule has been made by William Grove and Paul Meehl, who reported on an exhaustive search for studies comparing SPR predictions to human predictions in which (a) the humans and SPRs made predictions about the same specific cases and (b) the SPRs never had more information than the humans (although the humans often had more information than the SPRs). Their research yielded 136 studies comprising 617 distinct comparisons between SPR and human predictions. These studies covered a wide range of predictive efforts, including medical and mental health diagnoses; treatment prognoses, recommendations, and outcomes; descriptions of personality; adjustment to institutional life in both the military and correctional facilities; success in training or employment; socially relevant aggregate behaviors such as business performance; and many others. Of the 136 studies Grove and Meehl analyzed, 64 clearly favored the SPR, 64 showed approximately equivalent accuracy, and eight clearly favored the human predictor. The eight studies in which the human clinician outperformed the SPR appeared to have no common characteristics and therefore are not indicative of a unique domain in which expert prediction reliably beats statistical prediction; they are simply outliers (given 136 chances, the better reasoning strategy is bound to lose sometimes, after all).

What Explains the Golden Rule?

There are many sophisticated prediction models on the market (e.g., neural networks, naïve Bayes classifiers, classification and regression trees, support vector machines). The most sophisticated of these are optimizing models: They begin with a data set that consists of various lines of evidence that are correlated with the target property and then they employ sophisticated mathematical techniques with the aim of weighing those different lines of evidence so as to best predict new data. Perhaps the most common optimizing model is the proper linear (or regression) model. An intuitive way to understand proper linear models is to suppose we are trying to predict a target property (a person's weight) on the basis of a single line of evidence (the person's height). Suppose we take a set of data (for example, the heights and weights of a large number of people) and plot them on a graph. When doing so, a proper linear model will draw a straight line on the graph that comes closest to all the data points. This line can be described by the formula, $y = k + cx$, where y stands for weight, x stands for height, k is the y-intercept, and c is the slope of the line. In most real-life cases, however, we will have more than just one predictor cue, and so we need a multiple regression equation. The trick to building a *proper* (optimizing) linear model given complex data involves choosing the coefficients (c_n—in the above example, the weights) so that the model best fits the data in the training set. Such equations have the form

$$y = k + c_1x_1 + c_2x_2 + c_3x_3$$

What explanation can be given for the reliability of the golden rule? The obvious answer seems to be that unaided experts cannot possibly hope to be as accurate as optimizing models. On this explanation, unaided experts simply cannot construct and implement an optimizing model in their heads because they can't absorb and process all the available evidence, and even if they could, they can't assign optimal weights to the different lines of evidence, and even if they could do *that*, they cannot solve the model's complex formula to arrive at the model's prediction. However, this explanation can't be right because, in practice, some fairly simple nonoptimizing models are *also* more accurate than human experts. Consider three such models:

1. *Bootstrapping models:* The bootstrapping model is a proper linear model of a person's judgments about a target property but an improper linear model (a model that does not best fit the available data) of the target property itself. The bootstrapping model is built to, in essence, predict the human expert's prediction. And it will, from time to time, be wrong about what the expert will predict. But when it is wrong about the expert, it's more likely to be right about the target property!

2. *Unit weight models:* The unit weight model assigns equal weights to standardized predictor cues so that each input has an equal bearing on the final prediction. Given the success of unit weight models, an unweighted sum of a few of the most predictive variables will tend to be preferable to more complicated regressions equations. What is so surprising is how simply these formulas can be calculated: All you need is knowledge of what those most relevant variables are and then be able to add them all up.

3. *Randomized models:* The bootstrapping models discussed above can also be altered to produce a random linear model. In random linear models, there is no attempt to assign optimum weights to variables. Instead, variables are given random weights—with one important qualification: All the cues are defined so they are positively correlated with the target property. Even given this stipulation, random linear models are still as reliable as the proper models and more reliable than human experts.

A fascinating principle underlies these seemingly counterintuitive findings: The *flat maximum principle* says that for a certain class of prediction problems, as long as the signs of the coefficients are right, any one linear model will predict about as well as any other. It is important to recognize that the flat maximum principle is restricted to certain kinds of problems in which the following conditions obtain:

1. The judgment problem must be difficult and one in which no proper model will be especially reliable, because the world is messy.

2. The evidential cues in the problem must be reasonably predictive. For example, the best cues for predicting academic performance (GPA, test scores) are reasonably predictive. Certainly, a reasonably predictive cue is one that is at least more reliable than chance.

3. The evidential cues must be somewhat redundant. For example, people with higher GPAs tend to have higher test scores.

Given how common these circumstances are, it is in fact not uncommon for the improper unit weight models to be more reliable than the proper models.

The Golden Rule in Practice

The best way to get a sense of the power of actuarial prediction is to consider some examples.

1. Given a patient's marital status, length of psychotic distress, and the patient's insight into his or her condition, an SPR was more reliable at predicting the success of electroshock therapy than medical and psychological staff.

2. Criminologists were less reliable in predicting criminal recidivism than an SPR based on criminal and prison records.

3. An SPR was more reliable than clinical psychologists in diagnosing patients as either neurotic or psychotic, initially using the basis of a Minnesota Multiphasic Personality Inventory (MMPI) profile and then assessing diagnostic accuracy on follow-up. Even when psychologists were given the SPR's results before they made their predictions, they were still less accurate than the SPR.

4. SPRs predict academic performance (in terms of graduation rates and GPA at graduation) better than admissions officers at selective colleges, law schools, medical schools, and graduate school in psychology. This discrepancy holds even when the admissions officers have access to considerably more evidence than the models.

5. SPRs predict loan and credit risk better than bankers. SPRs, not human experts, are now standardly used by banks to make loans and by credit card companies to approve and set credit limits for new customers.

6. SPRs predict newborns at risk for sudden infant death syndrome (SIDS) with much greater accuracy than human experts.

7. An SPR predicts the quality of the vintage of a red Bordeaux wine better than expert wine tasters who are able to swirl, smell, and taste the young wine.

8. An SPR correctly diagnosed 83% of cases of progressive brain dysfunction on the basis of input cues in the form of intellectual tests, while clinicians working from the same data did no better than 63%. When given the results of the actuarial formula, clinicians still did worse than the model, scoring no better than 75%.

9. An SPR outperformed experienced clinicians as well as a nationally renowned neuropsychologist in predicting the presence, location, and cause of brain damage.

10. When predicting violence in a legal setting, one will actually be more reliable than forensic psychologists simply by predicting that people will not be violent. In addition, SPRs are more reliable than forensic psychologists in predicting relative likelihoods of violence.

As these examples suggest, actuarial prediction remains the province of specialized domains such as criminal recidivism or credit risk executed by professionals trained in predictive modeling. If actuarial methods are to actualize their potential to improve clinical and lay judgment, they will have to be made more widely available, easier to use, and applicable to a broader range of problems.

Michael A Bishop and J. D. Trout

See also Decision Improvement Technologies; Modeling Causal Learning; Scientific Reasoning; Thinking

Further Readings

Arkes, H. (2003). The nonuse of psychological research at two federal agencies. *Psychological Science, 14,* 1–6.

Bishop, M., & Trout, J. D. (2002). 50 years of successful predictive modeling should be enough: Lessons for philosophy of science. *Philosophy of Science: PSA 2000 Symposium Papers, 69*(Suppl.), S197–S208.

Bishop, M., & Trout, J. D. (2005). *Epistemology and the psychology of human judgment.* New York, NY: Oxford University Press.

Bootz, B., & Bishop, M. (2007). Goodbye justification. Hello world. *Croatian Journal of Philosophy, 7,* 269–285.

Dawes, R. (1994). *House of cards.* New York, NY: Free Press.

Faust, D., & Meehl, P. (1992). Using scientific methods to resolve enduring questions within the history and philosophy of science: Some illustrations. *Behavior Therapy, 23,* 195–211.

Grove, W., & Meehl, P. (1996). Comparative efficiency of informal (subjective, impressionistic) and formal (mechanical, algorithmic) prediction procedures: The clinical-statistical controversy. *Psychology, Public Policy, and Law, 2,* 292–323.

Meehl, P. (1954). *Clinical versus statistical prediction: A theoretical analysis and a review of the evidence.* Minneapolis: University of Minnesota Press.

PRODUCTION OF LANGUAGE

Producing a linguistic expression involves retrieving a set of words, arranged in a grammatical hierarchically organized sequence so as to convey speakers' intended thoughts. This is accomplished through a series of processing steps. A speaker begins an act of language production by deciding what to say: *message formulation.* For example, a cat owner might want to tell you his or her pet happened to eat an unspecified arachnid. Then a speaker must decide which words to use to express that message, *lexical selection,* and then retrieve those words, *lexical retrieval.* The cat owner might choose the words *my cat, ate,* and *a spider.* A speaker must also assign these words to roles that convey who did what to whom, *function assignment.* The cat owner might assign "my cat" to the subject function and "a spider" to the object function. At least in spoken languages such as English, words can only be produced one after another, so a speaker must then use the principles of the grammar of the speaker's language to order the role-assigned words, *constituent assembly.* In English, the subject goes before the verb and the object after, so the cat owner's sentence will use the sequence "my cat ate a spider." With words and their order (at least partly) determined, a speaker can send a plan off to *phonological encoding* so that the sound of an utterance can be formulated, followed by articulation so that a signal is actually generated for an audience. Additionally, most approaches to language production allow *monitoring*—that is, assessing formulated speech (before or after articulation) for adequacy and accuracy.

To be precise, though it is convenient to present these processing components as operating in a strictly sequenced or staged fashion, it is not clear that the language system works this way. Certainly, it is not the case that each component must finish its tasks completely for an entire sentence before the next stage can start. Rather, production is incremental in the sense that once some initial part of an utterance has been formulated at one level of processing, that part can be sent for processing at the next level of processing as upcoming parts of the utterance are formulated at the first level. For example, once a speaker has retrieved the words *my* and *cat,* they can be sent off for phonological encoding as the word *ate* is selected. Such incrementality allows speakers to start their utterances sooner and, more generally, permits some parallel processing so as to make production more efficient. A more controversial aspect of production planning, whether processing is strictly staged or is more free-flowing, is discussed below where lexical selection and retrieval are detailed further.

Each of these processing components is discussed in turn.

Message Formulation

The first step a speaker must take to produce a linguistic expression is to formulate a message. Based on logical analysis, message formulation is seen as proceeding through *macroplanning* and *microplanning.* Macroplanning involves determining a goal for an utterance and choosing the information needed to express it. Microplanning involves taking a particular perspective on the meaning to be expressed and determining the more versus less important elements of that meaning. The point of all these steps is to formulate a complete, dynamic representation of the information a speaker aims to convey in words and phrases.

One aspect of message formulation that has been heavily studied concerns how we adopt the perspective of our addressees to choose the right bits of meaning to linguistically encode. Specifically, any informative utterance includes some information a speaker's addressee does not yet know—what the speaker wants to convey—described in terms of information the addressee already knows. An utterance out of the blue such as "Steve ran the Boilermaker" will likely be uninformative, but an utterance such as "My friend Steve ran a 15 kilometer race in upstate New York called the *Boilermaker*" will likely be more informative. The reason is the latter utterance describes new information (Steve, the Boilermaker) by using information the addressee will know (social relationships, common knowledge about running events, and geography). Information speakers know their addressees already know is called *common ground,* and speakers' ability to use it properly is critical for successful communication.

Common ground is not easy to determine, however. Information is common ground for a particular speaker and addressee if the speaker knows it, the addressee knows it, the speaker knows the addressee knows it, the addressee knows the speaker knows the addressee knows it, and so forth. Given this infinite regress, speakers must use heuristics and strategies to determine whether some bit of information is in common ground.

These heuristics are of two general types. One type helps determine what sort of information speakers might use when trying to determine common ground. The other type describes the processing strategies speakers might use to compute common ground. Of the first type, speakers might assume that if a fact had been mentioned in the presence of some interlocutors then that fact should be ascribed to common ground. Similarly, if some noticeable feature is in the immediate environment of interlocutors, it could be ascribed to common ground. Of the second type, speakers might track the statistical reliability of different sorts of cues to common ground (e.g., whether a partner's visual perspective tends to indicate that they do or do not know about some element of the environment), or they might assume that their addressees know everything they themselves know except for explicitly excluded privileged information, or they might specifically track relatively simple bits of information that can be used to ascribe knowledge to specific addressees. In all these cases, the point is to be able to know what knowledge speakers and addressees share so that it can be relied on to successfully convey new knowledge.

Lexical Selection and Retrieval

Given a message, speakers must retrieve a set of content words—words describing entities, states, and actions—that can convey the meaning specified in the message. This is typically thought to proceed through two steps: First, speakers must find and select the words that convey the intended meaning; then speakers must retrieve the phonological features that represent the sounds of the words.

Given a particular meaning to convey, multiple lexical forms similar in meaning to the to-be-expressed meaning are accessed. Each of these becomes accessible in proportion to its degree of meaning similarity to the to-be-expressed meaning. This can be thought of as a kind of search: Given that a given to-be-expressed meaning will not necessarily correspond neatly to an individual word, a process of accessing a range of candidates to varying degrees allows an appropriate word to be found. This also allows other factors to influence the selection process, possibly including the accessibility or suitability of the phonological properties of the potential word.

According to most (though not all) approaches to word production, a competitive process then operates to select the to-be-produced word. This will make it so that if many possible words are relatively more accessible, the selection of a target will happen more slowly, but if only one word is highly accessible, selection will be quicker. For example, a speaker might want to name an unusual bug she or he saw. Visualizing the bug will cause its meaning features to become represented in the speaker's message, which in turn will lead the words that can express those meaning features to be accessed. If the bug looked much like a beetle but also somewhat like a tick or a roach, then the lexical representation of *beetle* will be accessed to a greater degree and the lexical representations of *tick* and *roach* to lesser degrees. The more (the speaker represents that) the bug looked like the beetle and the tick and the roach, the closer these accessibility levels will be and (if selection is competitive) the longer it will take for selection to occur. If the bug looked more like a beetle and less like a tick or roach, then the accessibility level of *beetle* will be much greater than the accessibility levels of *roach* and *tick*, and so selection will happen more quickly.

It is important to note that this selection process (competitive or otherwise) is restricted. For example, when speakers make speech errors where they select a wrong word, an intended noun is very often replaced with another noun, a verb with another verb, and so forth. This suggests that lexical selection operates within syntactic category; for example, only nouns are considered if a noun is to be selected. It may be that other sorts of categories similarly restrict lexical selection (e.g., whether a word is at an intended level of abstraction; for bilingual speakers, what language a word is in).

Production processing may be discrete, if selection must complete before retrieval begins, or cascaded, if retrieval can begin for accessible forms even before they are selected. Also, if lexical selection and retrieval is cascaded, it may allow feedback, if the retrieval of phonological properties can affect lexical selection. There are good reasons to allow cascading (it presumably speeds retrieval if it is begun sooner) or to forbid it (there is no point retrieving the phonological features of forms that will not be selected), and there are good reasons to allow feedback (it may be good to allow sound properties to affect selection) or to forbid it (it may be bad to allow sound properties to affect selection). A range of evidence suggests that lexical selection and retrieval is indeed cascaded; whether lexical selection and retrieval allows feedback is less certain.

According to some views, lexical retrieval begins with the retrieval of a whole word (or more precisely, whole morpheme—the atomic unit of meaning in language) representation. Then individual speech sounds—*phonemes* or *segments*—are retrieved. Phonemes are arranged into *syllables* (a unit of sound including a vowel and some of its immediately surrounding consonants), which in turn are specified for *metrical* properties such as whether they should be pronounced with more stress (louder, longer) or less (e.g., different metrical patterns need to be retrieved to produce the noun or verb forms of a word such as *record*: REcord vs. reCORD). At this point, language production processes have completed their lexical job, and speech and motor processing begins.

Function Assignment and Constituent Assembly

Utterances do not just convey the individual bits of content that words express. Utterances also convey the relationships among those bits of content—the "who did what to whom" of language. To do this, to-be-produced content words must be assigned to grammatical roles that indicate what relationship they bear to some event. This is the job of function assignment: to assign content words to grammatical functions such as *subject* and *object* so that their role with respect to an event can be expressed.

Words and their grammatical functions must somehow be outwardly encoded in the to-be-produced utterance. Spoken languages use different strategies for expressing grammatical functions such as subject and object. Languages such as English largely use the relative positions of words in utterances to convey grammatical functions; these languages are thus termed *word order* (or more precisely, *fixed word order*) languages. In contrast, languages such as Japanese largely use special morphemes (usually suffixes) to convey grammatical functions; these languages are sometimes called case-marking languages. So in English, most sentences require that the subject precedes the verb and the object (if present) follows it. So "Steve ran the Boilermaker" conveys that *Steve* is the subject and the *Boilermaker* the object, because of the position of those words with respect to the verb. In Japanese, this is conveyed with "Steve-ga Boilermaker-o hasitta," where the *-ga* and *-o* suffixes convey subject and object, respectively.

The complex task of determining the relative order of words is carried out by constituent assembly processes. This is made complex by the fact that multiple relationships can be embedded in a to-be-expressed thought, and all these must be encoded in a simple linear sequence of words (possibly with case markers, in a case-marking language). For example, "My friend Steve ran the Boilermaker" conveys a relationship between running, Steve, and the Boilermaker but also between friend and Steve, and all these must be appropriately nested with respect to one another. To determine the right way to convey such nestings, constituent assembly processes in some cases must consult representations of the principles of the speaker's grammar to determine what the linear sequence of words should be so that (in English) the adjective ends up preceding the noun, the subject preceding the verb, and so forth. But the grammar does not determine all ordering of words. As noted, case-marking languages such as Japanese do not use word order to indicate subject and object roles, and so constituent assembly is free to order subjects and objects without regard to grammatical principles (and because of this, case marking languages are sometimes called *free word order* languages). So "Steve-ga Boilermaker-o hasitta," and "Boilermaker-o Steve-ga hasitta" both convey the same (overall) meaning. And even in English, the order of nouns in a conjunction is not grammatically determined ("Steve and Kim" or "Kim and Steve" are both grammatical). In these cases, other factors will influence relative ordering, such as the prominence or personal importance of the to-be-ordered items or how easily the sentence material can be retrieved from memory.

Different factors affect function assignment and constituent assembly, revealing the nature of these processes. Speakers tend to repeat the hierarchical structures of sentences they recently heard or said, a phenomenon termed *structural* or *syntactic* priming. Structural priming has been profitably used to determine the representational nature of the hierarchical frames that are enlisted for production. Speakers also will tend to produce sentence structures that allow easily accessed material to be produced sooner and harder to access material later. These are often termed *accessibility* effects and may be motivated by efficiency (saying words as they are retrieved reduces memory demands). *Agreement,* whereby different parts of a sentence must systematically covary (e.g., the subject and verb in English agree in number), has been heavily investigated. Research on agreement has shown that sentence production processes enlist formal, abstract representations that underlie the relevant agreement properties (e.g., singular vs. plural in English).

Phonological Encoding

Above, the processes involved in retrieving the phonological properties of individual words were described. But words are of course produced as parts of longer utterances, and those utterances have their own phonological properties. Most prominently, extended utterances have *prosody*—the melody and rhythm of an utterance that conveys different sorts of information. Specifically, prosody can convey syntactic information, including where phrase boundaries are between words in a sentence; whether a sentence is a declarative, an interrogative, or something else; emotional information, such as whether a speaker is excited or sullen; and so forth. Consequently, the mechanisms responsible for formulating prosody must take into account all these sorts of information.

An important aspect of prosody that must be computed concerns how long the words and pauses should be in an utterance. Production research suggests that prosodic production mechanisms specify at least some of the duration properties of the "slots" words are to be spoken in, and this is done relatively independently of the content of the words themselves. This implies that when a word is shorter, speakers will compensate by producing a longer pause after it and vice versa. This is an elegant demonstration of the relative independence of different production mechanisms, here, between prosodic formulation and lexical retrieval mechanisms.

Monitoring

The task of language production is not completed when an utterance is fully formulated and ready for articulation. Production mechanisms also engage in monitoring, whereby the adequacy and accuracy of a formulated expression is checked. Formulated utterances are monitored both before they begin to be articulated, based on some form of inner speech, and after they are articulated, through standard language comprehension mechanisms. Evidence for the former is that speakers will sometimes halt the articulation of an erroneous utterance quickly—so quickly that it is not possible that the speaker heard

the error (externally) and halted production on that basis. Monitoring based on external speech is evident whenever speakers notice that they have produced some utterance they did not intend or when they realize an utterance did not "come across right."

Different mechanisms might be responsible for carrying out monitoring. One common proposal, the *perceptual loop* hypothesis, is that formulated speech (both inner and external) is monitored with the same comprehension mechanisms we use to comprehend others' (external) speech. The idea is that formulated speech is comprehended to the level of meaning and then the comprehended and to-be-expressed meanings compared; if they differ in any important way, the speaker can stop and reformulate. But other monitoring mechanisms (and more generally, error-detecting mechanisms) may operate in addition to or instead of the perceptual loop. For example, one strategy for monitoring for errors is to detect when some representation at a later level of processing has been selected even though its antecedent representation has not. If a speaker intends to say "cat" but formulates "lat" instead, production mechanisms can detect the error if they are sensitive to the fact that the *l* segment was accessed for production even though no word including an *l* was selected during lexical selection and retrieval.

Conclusions

The ease with which we produce speech belies the complexity of the cognitive mechanisms underlying this ability. This allows us to convey our thoughts to other members of our species with a level of detail and breadth that would not otherwise be possible. This ability, one of only a handful unique to humans, is critical to our survival and success as a species.

Victor S. Ferreira

See also Conversation and Dialogue; Language Production, Agreement in; Language Production, Incremental Processing in; Natural Language Generation; Perspective Taking in Language Processing; Planning in Language Production; Prosody in Production

Further Readings

Bock, J. K. (1982). Toward a cognitive psychology of syntax: Information processing contributions to sentence formulation. *Psychological Review, 89,* 1–47.

Clark, H. H., & Marshall, C. (1981). Definite reference and mutual knowledge. In A. Joshi, B. Webber, & I. Sag (Eds.), *Elements of discourse understanding* (pp. 10–63). Cambridge, UK: Cambridge University Press.

Dell, G. S. (1986). A spreading-activation theory of retrieval in sentence production. *Psychological Review, 93*, 283–321.

Eberhard, K. M., Cutting, J. C., & Bock, K. (2005). Making syntax of sense: Number agreement in sentence production. *Psychological Review, 112*(3), 531–559.

Ferreira, F. (1993). The creation of prosody during sentence production. *Psychological Review, 100*, 233–253.

Ferreira, V. S., & Slevc, L. R. (2007). Grammatical encoding. In M. G. Gaskell (Ed.), *The Oxford handbook of psycholinguistics* (pp. 453–469). Oxford, UK: Oxford University Press.

Garrett, M. F. (1975). The analysis of sentence production. In G. H. Bower (Ed.), *The psychology of learning and motivation* (Vol. 9, pp. 133–177). New York, NY: Academic Press.

Griffin, Z. M., & Ferreira, V. S. (2006). Properties of spoken language production. In M. J. Traxler & M. A. Gernsbacher (Eds.), *Handbook of psycholinguistics* (2nd ed., pp. 21–60). New York, NY: Elsevier.

Levelt, W. J. M. (1989). *Speaking: From intention to articulation.* Cambridge, MA: MIT Press.

Levelt, W. J. M., Roelofs, A., & Meyer, A. S. (1999). A theory of lexical access in speech production. *Behavioral & Brain Sciences, 22*, 1–75.

Pickering, M. J., & Ferreira, V. S. (2008). Structural priming: A critical review. *Psychological Bulletin, 134*, 427–459.

Postma, A. (2000). Detection of errors during speech production: A review of speech monitoring models. *Cognition, 77*, 97–131.

Rapp, B., & Goldrick, M. (2000). Discreteness and interactivity in spoken word production. *Psychological Review, 107*, 460–499.

PROSODY IN PRODUCTION

Although the term *prosody* has been used to describe a wide variety of linguistic and extralinguistic phenomenon, it can, roughly, be defined as the acoustic aspects of an utterance that vary independently of the phonology of the utterance's words. Prosody plays a clear role in conveying information about discourse, syntax, and pragmatics to listeners. However, prosody is also linked to processes related to language production. This entry discusses what prosody is and how it is related to speech production.

Prosodic Structure

Prosody includes acoustic information associated with rhythm, intonation, pausing, and accents (emphasis). Prosodic information is typically conveyed through changes in fundamental frequency ($f0$), which correlates with the perception of pitch, and changes in intensity, which correlates with the perception of loudness. It is also linked to pausing and the lengthening and reduction of individual words.

Prosody can vary between otherwise identical utterances in ways that influence the interpretation of a sentence. For example, consider (1), where capitalization indicates an accent and "//" indicates a break in the speech stream.

(1a) Ketchup is a vegetable.

(1b) Ketchup is a vegetable?

(1c) KETCHUP is a vegetable.

(1d) Ketchup is a VEGETABLE.

(1e) The cop saw // the spy with the telescope.

(1f) The cop saw the spy // with the telescope.

The sentence in (1a) will sound like an assertion if it is produced with a fall in $f0$ across the sentence, but it will sound like a question if it is produced with a rise (1b). These two productions convey different speaker attitudes about the truth of the utterance. In (1c), accenting *ketchup* conveys that it and not, say, mustard is a vegetable. Similarly, (1d) implies that ketchup is a vegetable and not a fruit. Breaks in the speech stream, which are also called prosodic boundaries, can be signaled by a pause, a change in $f0$, or lengthening of the preboundary word. A prosodic boundary after the verb *saw* in (1e) biases the listener toward an interpretation in which the spy has a telescope whereas a break after *spy* biases the listener toward an interpretation in which the cop has the telescope. These examples illustrate that prosody can influence the interpretation of an utterance even if the words in the utterance do not vary.

Prosodic features such as prosodic boundaries, accents, rhythm, and pitch contours are represented at an abstract phonological level of representation called prosodic structure. There is a great deal of controversy over the nature of this representation. There is disagreement over whether there are different types of prosodic phrases and how they might differ, whether and how these phrases are represented hierarchically, whether accents differ in form and meaning, how intonational contours are structured, and the nature of the interface between prosodic structure and other aspects of language.

Production

Traditionally, it has been assumed that the role of prosody is to convey pragmatic, discourse, and syntactic information to listeners. However, a growing body of evidence suggests that there might also be a link between speaker internal production processes and prosody: Speakers are more likely to produce prosodic boundaries and accents at points of production difficulty.

For example, the likelihood of producing a prosodic boundary either before or after a syntactic constituent such as the subject of a sentence is directly correlated with the constituent's length.

(2a) The judge who the reporter for the
      newspaper ignored // fired the secretary.

(2b) The judge who the reporter ignored (//)
      fired the secretary.

In (2), a boundary is more likely to follow the subject of the sentence in (a) than (b) because the subject in (a) is longer. Boundaries may provide speakers with time to plan upcoming structure or recover after encountering production difficulty.

A question of much debate in this literature is whether speakers purposely produce boundaries in locations that are helpful to listeners, particularly ambiguous sentences such as the ones in (1e) and (1f), or whether they produce boundaries to help themselves. While some researchers have found that speakers do not use boundaries to consistently disambiguate syntactically ambiguous sentences for listeners, others have found that they do. Many of the experiments investigating this question have used tasks in which a speaker must instruct a listener to manipulate a set of objects.

(3) Tap (a) the frog (b) with the flower.

(4) Put the dog (a) in the basket (b) on the star.

Jesse Snedeker and John Trueswell have found that in sentences such as (3), speakers disambiguate the sentence using boundaries at positions (a) or (b) only if they are aware of the ambiguity. However, Tanya Kraljic and Susan Brennan have found that in sentences like (4), speakers disambiguate the sentence whether they are aware of the ambiguity or not. One critical difference between (3) and (4) is utterance length: Sentence (4) is longer. If prosodic boundary placement is partly influenced by production constraints, then one would expect boundaries to occur more often in long, difficult sentences than short, easy sentences, independent of the needs of the listener, and this appears to be the case. However, the extent to which boundary placement is speaker or listener centered is currently under debate.

This debate also extends to the literature on accents. Word lengthening, a correlate of accenting, co-occurs with disfluencies and boundaries, suggesting that production difficulty may underlie both. Words that are unpredictable, informative, and low frequency are more likely to be accented than those that are not. These words are likely to be difficult to produce although it is unclear whether prominence in these cases is the result of production difficulty or whether speakers mark words that might be difficult for the listener in order to facilitate comprehension. This question is one that researchers are currently wrestling with.

Overall, it is clear that prosody can signal information about syntax, discourse, and pragmatics, and recent work suggests that prosody may also play an important role in language production.

Duane G. Watson

See also Planning in Language Production; Production of
    Language; Speech Perception

Further Readings

Kraljic, T., & Brennan, S. E. (2005). Prosodic
    disambiguation of syntactic structure: For the speaker or
    for the addressee? *Cognitive Psychology, 50,* 194–231.

Shattuck-Hufnagel, S., & Turk, A. E. (1996). A prosody
    tutorial for investigators of auditory sentence processing.
    Journal of Psycholinguistic Research, 25, 193–247.

Snedeker, J., & Trueswell, J. (2003). Using prosody to
    avoid ambiguity: Effects of speaker awareness and
    referential context. *Journal of Memory and Language,
    48,* 103–130.

Watson, D. G., & Gibson, E. (2004). The relationship
    between intonational phrasing and syntactic structure in
    language production. *Language and Cognitive
    Processes, 19,* 713–755.

PSYCHOLOGICAL REFRACTORY PERIOD

After a neuron fires, it becomes temporarily unable to fire again, no matter how great the excitation. In 1931, Charles Telford wondered whether higher level cognitive processes might be subject to an analogous limitation. That is, after one act of cognition, cognitive-processing mechanisms might become much less excitable during a prolonged recovery phase, leading to slow responses. To test this conjecture, Telford asked his subjects (psychology graduate students) to press a telegraph key as fast as possible whenever they heard a sound. The time between consecutive sounds was either 0.5, 1, 2, or 4 seconds, determined randomly on each trial. Although the task was remarkably simple, response times increased from 0.241 sec to 0.335 sec as the time between tones decreased from 1 sec to 0.5 sec (see Figure 1). These findings appeared to directly support Telford's refractory period hypothesis.

The phenomenon Telford discovered—which became known as the psychological refractory period effect—has been extremely influential. It is of great practical interest, because it bears on the multitasking difficulties faced by human operators of complex systems (which today would appear to include virtually the entire human adult population). His discovery is also of great theoretical interest, because it points to a fundamental limitation in the human ability to process information. An enormous amount of research has been devoted to uncovering the nature of that fundamental limitation.

In addition, his experimental paradigm has been adopted in many hundreds of subsequent experiments and is, in fact, still quite popular today (albeit using far more sophisticated equipment for presenting stimuli and measuring responses).

Although Telford's paradigm and empirical findings were extremely influential, his specific theory has long since been abandoned. A refractory period suggests that cognitive mechanisms are temporarily sluggish—or less responsive—immediately following an act of cognition. Research has revealed no evidence for sluggishness. Although the analogy with the neuronal refractory period seems misguided, the misleading label *psychological refractory period* (PRP for short) became securely attached to this effect. This entry describes modern theoretical accounts of the PRP effect, efforts to test between them, and implications for dual tasking in the real world.

Theories of the Psychological Refractory Period Effect

Instead of a refractory period, contemporary theories propose that cognitive mechanisms are continuously and fully engaged yet have difficulty serving more than one task at a time. The two most prominent accounts of the PRP effect are capacity-sharing models and bottleneck models.

Capacity-Sharing Models

According to capacity-sharing models, humans have a limited pool of capacity to divide between concurrent tasks. An analogy would be a general that divides one large force into two smaller forces, each simultaneously pursuing a different objective. On this view, tasks can operate in parallel. But because they receive only a fraction of the available capacity, they will operate more slowly than is possible under single-task conditions.

Which mental operations require a share of the limited pool of resources? The evidence suggests that multiple perceptual processes can operate in parallel, at least under favorable circumstances (imagine a loud tone presented at the same time as a letter on the computer screen). It also seems clear that people can generally execute simple responses in parallel, as in walking and talking. These considerations suggest that the processes requiring capacity lie somewhere in between perception and response execution, in

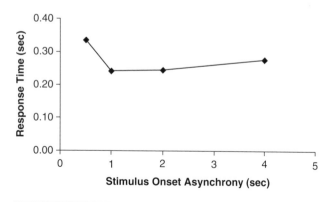

Figure 1 Response time as a function of stimulus onset asynchrony, based on data from Telford (1931)

what is referred to as *central processing*. A clear-cut example of a central process is response selection—deciding what response is warranted given the stimuli in the environment.

Bottleneck Models

Bottleneck models take the rather extreme view that certain mental processes simply cannot operate on more than one task at a time. As an analogy, a bank teller can usually serve only one customer at a time. If two customers arrive at the same time, one of them will need to wait for the other to finish.

Alan Welford, in 1952, was the first to specifically attribute the PRP effect to a bottleneck in central mental operations (see Figure 2). In other words, while any central operation for the task arriving first (Task 1) is underway, all central operations for the second task (Task 2) must necessarily wait. Again, central operations involve deciding how to respond (or not respond) to a given stimulus. Welford showed that this model could account for a wide range of data from the PRP paradigm.

A few decades later, Harold Pashler revived interest in the central bottleneck model by demonstrating that it makes several specific and counterintuitive predictions. For example, the effects of degrading the Task 2 stimulus should actually be much smaller under dual-task conditions than single-task conditions. Consider the concrete example of a Task 2 that involves classifying a letter presented on a computer screen. Dimming this Task 2 letter might prolong perceptual processes by about 50 milliseconds (ms), which should in turn increase single-task response times by 50 ms. But surprisingly, this same 50-ms perceptual delay should have little or no effect on response time in a PRP experiment with a short delay between the Task 1 and Task 2 stimulus onsets. The reason is that Task 2 perceptual operations have ample time to finish while Task 2 central operations wait for Task 1 central operations

to finish. As an analogy, a delay in completing a deposit slip will delay your departure from the bank when there are no other customers (single task). But if you must wait for the teller to first help another customer (dual task for the bank teller), any delay in completing the deposit slip will likely be inconsequential. You can simply complete the deposit slip while waiting in line.

This prediction is counterintuitive because one would normally expect that the negative consequence of increasing task difficulty would be magnified under dual-task conditions. Nevertheless, many experiments have confirmed this prediction of the central bottleneck model. The effects of dimming a Task 2 stimulus or superimposing a noise mask are virtually absent when the delay between the Task 1 and Task 2 stimulus onsets is short. The successful predictions of the central bottleneck model support the hypothesis that central stages often do operate serially (one at a time) in the PRP paradigm.

Data from many PRP experiments are consistent with serial central processing—that is, allocation of attention entirely to Task 1 central operations then entirely to Task 2 central operations. It has been argued, however, that simultaneous sharing of capacity is possible when the conditions favor it (e.g., when tasks are assigned equal priority). Although this debate has not yet been resolved, both sides of the debate appear to agree that PRP effects stem mainly from a limited capacity to carry out central mental operations.

Are There Exceptions to the Psychology Refractory Period Effect?

PRP effects are surprisingly robust. They have been reported with a wide variety of different judgments, even very simple ones. Importantly, they have been reported even when the two tasks are maximally different, with distinct inputs (seeing vs. hearing) and distinct outputs (speaking vs. moving the hands). These findings hint at a pervasive problem that could only worsen with more complex, real-world tasks. Driving a car, for example, is vastly more complicated than Telford's task of pushing a key in response to a sound.

But is there no way to eliminate the PRP effect? Many investigators have attempted to eliminate the PRP effect by using extremely natural tasks, such as repeating a spoken word or moving a joystick in

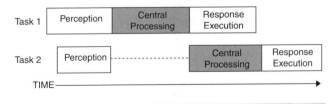

Figure 2   The central bottleneck model

the direction of an arrow. In such cases, the stimulus might strongly activate the corresponding response without any assistance from central mental resources. Perhaps not surprisingly, PRP effects are reduced with such tasks. However, stubborn residual PRP effects have often been reported, hinting that even these tasks might be subject to resource limitations.

Other investigators have taken a different approach. Instead of using inherently easy tasks, they have used somewhat more difficult tasks but allowed subjects the opportunity to master them. Obviously, tasks are performed faster with practice, so the PRP effect should inevitably decrease. The critical question is whether practice can eliminate the PRP effect altogether and, more to the point, whether practice eliminates competition for mental resources. This type of automaticity with practice has in fact been clearly documented in a few recent studies. Most of these demonstrations, however, have thus far involved relatively trivial tasks, involving a very small number of stimuli and responses.

What about highly practiced real-world tasks, for which the array of possible stimuli is essentially infinite? Consider, for example, driving while talking on a cell phone. Despite being extremely well practiced, these tasks nevertheless interfere with each other. Such interference has been documented both in analyses of actual accident reports and in numerous experiments with simulated driving tasks. It has been estimated that cell phone use quadruples the frequency of accidents and is as detrimental to driving as a blood-alcohol level of .08 (considered legally intoxicated in some states). Interestingly, this interference is not ameliorated by using hands-free phones rather than handheld phones. This finding hints that the problem lies in interference between central processes (i.e., cognitive distraction) rather than in competition between tasks for the hands. Ignoring these consistent research findings, lawmakers typically outlaw the use of handheld cell phones while driving yet permit the use of hands-free cell phones.

Another interesting exception to the PRP effect occurs when the second task merely requires moving the eyes (whose position is monitored using special equipment) to a specified type of stimulus, such as any red object. Eye movements might evade the PRP effect because they are quasi-reflexive, supported by special neural circuitry. An alternative view is that fixating one's eyes on a target is a highly practiced action, and it is the unusually high levels of practice that enabled subjects to escape the PRP effect.

Central Bottlenecks: Structural Limitation or a Strategic Choice?

The central bottleneck model implies that people cannot perform central operations on more than one task at a time because of some cognitive resource limitation. This limitation is often described as a single-channel cognitive mechanism that can process only one task at a time. Strictly, speaking, however, most data merely show that people do not perform central operations at the same time. Perhaps people are entirely capable of parallel central processing but typically choose serial processing as a matter of strategy.

This issue remains controversial. At low levels of practice, attempts to induce subjects to choose a parallel processing strategy, and eliminate the PRP effect, have not been very successful. Parallel processing does seem to be possible at higher practice levels, as noted above, although it is not clear that the transition reflects a voluntary choice, per se. Ultimately, the strategic versus structural debate might not have a simple answer. For instance, a structural limitation in central mechanisms might lead to a strategic choice to perform central operations serially (one at a time). Computer simulation of possible cognitive architectures has shown that serial central processing might be the optimal strategy even if parallel central processing were possible.

Conclusion

The PRP effect refers to a kind of dual-task interference, wherein it is difficult to simultaneously perform two tasks presented in close succession. One of the tasks (usually the one presented second) is performed quite slowly. The PRP effect is remarkably robust, with only rare exceptions, such as when tasks are simple and highly practiced or merely involve movements of the eyes. The primary source of the interference appears to be that central mental processes, such as response selection, must compete for access to limited mental resources. In many cases, there is compelling evidence that central mental operations take place strictly serially—one task a time. These findings might shed light on the persistent interference that occurs in many real-world situations, such as driving while talking on a cell phone.

Eric Ruthruff

See also Attention, Resource Models; Attention and Action; Automaticity; Divided Attention and Memory; Multitasking and Human Performance

Further Readings

Lien, M.-C., Ruthruff, E., & Johnston, J. C. (2006). Attentional limitations in doing two tasks at once: The search for exceptions. *Current Directions in Psychological Science, 15,* 89–93.

McCann, R. S., & Johnston, J. C. (1992). Locus of the single-channel bottleneck in dual-task interference. *Journal of Experimental Psychology: Human Perception and Performance, 18,* 471–484.

Meyer, D. E., & Kieras, D. E. (1997). A computational theory of executive cognitive processes and multiple-task performance: Part 2. Accounts of psychological refractory phenomena. *Psychological Review, 107,* 749–791.

Navon, D., & Miller, J. O. (2002). Queuing or sharing? A critical evaluation of the single-bottleneck notion. *Cognitive Psychology, 44,* 193–251.

Pashler, H. (1984). Processing stages in overlapping tasks: Evidence for a central bottleneck. *Journal of Experimental Psychology: Human Perception and Performance, 10,* 358–377.

Strayer, D. L., & Johnston, W. A. (2001). Driven to distraction: Dual-task studies of simulated driving and conversing on a cellular telephone. *Psychological Science, 12,* 462–466.

Telford, C. W. (1931). Refractory phase of voluntary and associative responses. *Journal of Experimental Psychology, 14,* 1–35.

Tombu, M., & Jolicoeur, P. (2003). A central capacity sharing model of dual-task performance. *Journal of Experimental Psychology: Human Perception and Performance, 29,* 3–18.

Welford, A. T. (1952). The "psychological refractory period" and the timing of high-speed performance: A review and a theory. *British Journal of Psychology, 43,* 2–19.

RATIONALITY OF EMOTION

It is sometimes said that emotions in general are irrational or that they cannot be judged in terms of reason: that they are somehow beyond the reach of reason. Yet in particular cases we often deem someone irrational for feeling some specific emotion: "Your anger is unreasonable," we might say, or "You should be glad that your friend got the job." The grounds for such judgments, however, remain disputed. Rationality has been exhaustively studied in belief and action. Emotions are causally and conceptually linked to both, but they are not reducible to either belief or action tendencies. If there are canons of emotional rationality as such, they cannot therefore be simply imported from epistemic and practical rationality. This entry explores how far standards of rationality that are derived from the relatively clear cases of belief and action might apply to emotions. Emotions are seen to pose some special problems, particularly in regard to the evaluation of the future or the past and to the elaboration of a relevant concept of consistency. Their rationality is also seen to be significantly affected by social context.

Standard Constraints on Rationality

The criteria of rationality commonly accepted for thought and action suggest four abstract constraints on rationality in general. These provide a starting point for any discussion of emotional rationality.

1. *Norms of success.* No entity can be assessed for rationality unless it is liable to success and failure. Rationality is not equivalent to success, nor can it ever guarantee success, but X can be said to be *more rational* than an alternative Y, insofar as X has the greater likelihood of success. Truth is the norm of success for a belief; hence, *B1* is more rational than *B2* if it is more likely to be true. Similarly, of two alternative actions, the more rational is the more likely to achieve a given goal.

2. *Intentionality.* The existence of a norm of success implies that whatever can be rational is susceptible of teleological explanation—that is, explanation in terms of some function or purpose. But the converse does not hold. Biological processes typically call for teleological explanations, but only those that are intentional can be said literally to be rational. Intentionality is informally characterized as "aboutness" and is widely thought to be an essential property of mental states. One could speak metaphorically of ants, plants, cells, or even genes as communicating and as choosing alternative strategies of survival or mating. But it would be eccentric to ascribe mentality literally to all biological organisms. Only intentional states can be rational.

3. *Origins.* Rationality is systematically related to future success, but ascriptions of rationality do not await the verdict of success. On the contrary, rationality hangs on provenance: It depends in part on the origin of the action or belief. If one belief derives from the consultation of astrological signs,

while another is soundly inferred from scientific evidence, the latter is the more rational regardless of its truth.

4. *Context dependency.* If origin determines rationality, how do we identify the appropriate antecedents? In statistical reasoning, it may be rational to believe *p* relative to one set of facts and *not-p* relative to another, though both sets are equally correct and relevant. Beliefs and actions may be fairly judged both rational and irrational, depending on the extent of the background circumstances taken into account. This context dependency may be illustrated in terms of the tragic real-life case of Andrea Yates, who was induced by voices she heard to drown her five children. At her first trial, the insanity defense was disallowed, on the ground that her careful planning and execution of the drownings proved her rationality. But if one zooms out from its methodical implementation to the project of drowning one's five children, in obedience to the voice of God, to "save" them, one is bound to see that project itself as irrational. Yet while both Agamemnon and Abraham formed, in obedience to divine command, the project of killing their child, neither is usually thought to have been insane. Unlike truth, a verdict of rationality is never definitive. The framework of its assessment can in principle be extended or modified in an indefinite number of defensible ways.

Applying Standard Constraints to Emotional Rationality

To apply these constraints to emotion, we must first make any sense of the notion of emotional "success." One approach to this is in terms of biological function: Emotions appraise typical life situations and prime the organism for appropriate response; any given emotion is successful if it fulfils that function. This *evolutionary psychological* approach has yielded many insights. But it doesn't quite get at a notion of success that would be relevant to the question of rationality, for not all functional processes or states are intentional. The intentionality requirement disqualifies even some of the states we loosely refer to as emotions: Moods, insofar as they lack intentionality, also lack conditions of success of the relevant sort. Any emotion that is clearly *about* something, by contrast, intrinsically defines what must be true of its target—the thing, person or situation *at* which it is directed—for the emotion to be appropriate. That feature is what many philosophers refer to as the emotion's *formal object.* Truth is the formal object of belief: "Because it's true" gives a trivial answer to the question "Why do you believe *p*?" Similarly, one can give gives a trivial answer to the question "Why are you *E*-ing?" for any given emotion *E*. But there is no global answer for all emotions: Each emotion has its own formal object. Some have obvious names: for fearing, the fearsome; being sad, loss; loving, lovable; being disgusted, the disgusting. Others call for awkward explanatory phrases. Just as the formal object of the sense of touch has no single name but relates to hardness, texture, and relative heat, so the formal object of anger has no single name but is awkwardly describable in terms of unjust harm or insult to oneself or others. Whether or not a formal object has a handy name doesn't seem to correlate with how easily we can tell whether it applies in a particular case. To find something *fearsome*, for example, is to perceive it as *dangerous*: an arguably objective, albeit probabilistic property. By contrast, shame is successful if its object is shameful, but the appropriateness of *shameful*, unlike *dangerous*, does not yield easily to objective confirmation.

Social Context

The reason for the difference relates to the third and fourth constraints. While success depends on a match between formal object and target, rationality is determined by an emotion's origin. If a particular case of fear is caused by factors independent of objective danger, the fear is irrational. Other cases are less clear: There are few objective constraints, for instance, on appropriate origins for love. To be sure, I love him *because he is lovable,* but that places virtually no constraints on the causes of my devotion. Whether he is *really* lovable is a question that barely makes sense, because there is little consensus about the properties that constitute being lovable. Indignation, guilt, and embarrassment, like shame, lie somewhere in between the objectivity of rational fear and the indeterminacy of rational love, but for all of these and many other emotions, what determines rationality are mostly social facts relating to the norms endorsed by members of a given group in historical context.

Where social norms rule, one pertinent dimension of evaluation is *intensity,* a factor generally absent from appraisals of action or belief. In the case of fear, we have seen that an ascription of irrationality rests in part on the objective absence of danger, but it is also based on an assessment of the intensity of the emotion itself. It seems the intensity of fear should be proportional to the extent of the danger (which in turn consists in both the importance and the probability of the undesirable outcome). The intensity of anger, guilt, or shame is deemed irrational if it is disproportional to the seriousness of the offense inflicted or defect contemplated. Here again, actual social norms and expectations are more important than any other objective facts, and the word *rational* is interchangeable with *reasonable*, used to mean something like "I'd feel the same way under the circumstances."

A good illustration of the interaction of biological origins and social expectations is provided by jealousy, which Jesse Prinz has plausibly characterized as "an acquired blend of anger, fear, sadness and disgust [that] . . . arise in the context of infidelity" (p. 280). If that is right, conditions of appropriateness for jealousy will be highly complex and depend heavily on prevalent social mores in the spheres of sexual orientation and behavior on relations between unmarried persons of the same or opposite sexes, on conventions and expectations governing spouses and sexual exclusiveness, and so forth.

In a different way, the importance of context to assessments of rationality is also illustrated by depth psychology. Recent psychology has confirmed Freud's observation that our understanding of our own motives is riddled with ignorance and confabulation. The fact that we can be ruled by unconscious motives can turn the rational into the irrational and vice versa. For when we construe an apparently rational act as motivated by an unconscious motive, we expose its irrationality. Conversely, the bearing of an unconscious motive on an *acte manqué*, or Freudian slip, brings previously inexplicable behavior under the aegis of the belief-desire explanation typical of rational agency.

The Regulation of Emotion

A case frequently discussed is that of *recalcitrant emotions*, where the judgmental component of an emotion contradicts the agent's own belief. Such emotions are comparable to visual illusions such as the Mueller-Lyer lines, in that the agent is aware of the failure of fit between target and formal object. It

has seemed puzzling, however, that recalcitrant emotions are regarded as irrational, whereas visual illusions are not. Michael Brady has suggested that this is explained by the role of emotions in monopolizing our attention so as to "enhance emotional stimuli." Where the emotion embodies an evaluation that we know to be incorrect, this is counterproductive. A related but more general explanation is suggested by the long history of disciplines aimed at mastering emotion. From Stoicism through Buddhism and Christianity to René Descartes, David Hume, and William James, it has been assumed that techniques can be devised to correct, redirect, and tame emotion. There is no need, and therefore no comparable set of techniques, for the correction of sensory perception.

Rationality in Memory and Expectation

Worries about emotional rationality range more widely than is accounted for by the framework described so far. What makes for the rationality of emotions toward the past or future is obscure. Is he who regrets always "twice unhappy or twice impotent," as Benedict de Spinoza (in his Proposition 54) claimed? When evaluating a past experience, should we realistically rate every sequence of moments as the sum of their hedonic value weighted by their duration? Or should we ignore, as Daniel Kahneman has shown we actually do, most of the past moments except for a *peak* and an *end* one? As for the future, at what rate is it rational to discount it? Sometimes a fervently desired experience proves to be "dust and ashes"; if I predict that I will be disappointed—that I won't feel as intensely happy when it happens as I now feel I should—should I maximize utility by enjoying the prospect anyway or reduce my anticipation to fit the way I will eventually feel?

Consistency and Constancy

Many puzzles remain concerning both the standards that bear on verdicts of irrationality and the scope of such verdicts. The examples mentioned so far have been of single emotions experienced at some particular time. But one can also ask whether there are constraints on sets of simultaneous emotions and on emotional change through time.

The former question is about emotional *consistency*. Consistency is not compatibility: If two states are incompatible, they cannot coexist in a single agent; to say they are inconsistent, by contrast, is to say that they *ought* not to coexist, which presupposes that they *can* do so. Whether two emotions are compatible is likely to have to do with the physiological mechanisms that underlie them: If one involves excitation while the other entails inhibition of a certain neurohormonal system, for example, they cannot take place together for mechanical reasons. Genuine inconsistency would derive from the logical conditions on their formal objects. But just what those might be remains obscure.

Questions about the rationality of emotional change through time concern not consistency but constancy. When is it irrational to stop loving someone? How long is it irrational to grieve? The importance of social conventions is particularly obvious in those cases. What remains puzzling, and worthy of investigation, is the extent to which the conventions in question and the variance among them are themselves dependent on biological factors.

Ronald de Sousa

See also Emotion, Cultural Perspectives; Emotion, Structural Approaches; Emotion and Moral Judgment; Emotions and Consciousness; Intentionality of Emotion

Further Readings

Ainslie, G. (1992). *Picoeconomics: The strategic interaction of successive motivational states within the person.* Cambridge, UK: Cambridge University Press.

Brady, M. (2008). Recalcitrant emotions and visual illusions. *American Philosophical Quarterly, 44*(3), 273–284.

Cosmides, L., & Tooby, J. (2000). Evolutionary psychology and the emotions. In M. Lewis & J. M. Haviland-Jones (Eds.), *Handbook of emotions* (pp. 91–115). New York, NY: Guilford.

de Sousa, R. (1987). *The rationality of emotion.* Cambridge, MA: MIT Press.

de Sousa, R. (2003). Paradoxical emotions. In S. Stroud & C. Tappolet (Eds.), *Weakness of will and practical irrationality* (pp. 274–297). New York, NY: Oxford University Press.

Kahneman, D. (2000). Evaluation by moments: Past and future. In D. Kahneman & A. Tversky (Eds.), *Choices, values, and frames* (pp. 693–708). New York, NY: Cambridge University Press-Russell Sage.

Nussbaum, M. (1994). *The therapy of desire: Theory and practice in Hellenistic ethics.* Princeton, NJ: Princeton University Press.

Prinz, J. (2007). *The emotional construction of morals.* New York, NY: Oxford University Press.

Spinoza, B. D. (1985). Ethics. *The collected works of Spinoza* (E. Curley Ed. & Trans; Vol. 4). Princeton, NJ: Princeton University Press. (Original published 1677)

Wilson, T. D. (2002). *Strangers to ourselves: Discovering the adaptive unconscious.* Cambridge, MA: Harvard University Press.

REACTION TIME

Reaction time, sometimes referred to as response time or latency, is measured as the time that elapses between the onset of a stimulus and a person's response to that stimulus. Reaction times (RTs) are widely used in the study of human performance, from testing models of cognitive processing in cognitive psychology to evaluating the design of human-machine interfaces and assisting in diagnoses of such conditions as schizophrenia, learning disorders, and other psychological disorders. This entry presents a brief history of the use of RT, a survey of different kinds of RT experiments, and a summary of how RTs are influenced by other variables.

History

Some of the earliest recorded attempts to evaluate human performance with RT were made by 17th-century astronomers. They worried about the *personal equation*, which is simply the fact that different observers vary in their estimates of the transit times of stars as the stars moved across the visual field. These astronomers were not as interested in why observers had different personal equations as they were in how much they needed to recalibrate their equipment so that transit times were as accurate as possible. The first serious attempt to explain why RTs varied under different conditions—the first use of RT to determine how people's brains perform mental tasks—was made by F. C. Donders (1818–1889).

Donders's idea, called the *method of subtraction*, was to estimate the time taken by different components of a mental task. The tasks he used are now called simple reactions, go/no go reactions, and choice reactions. These tasks, he reasoned, could be broken down into smaller *stages* of processing: perceptual encoding, stimulus identification, response selection, and response execution.

Consider, for example, a task where an observer must respond to the presentation of red and green lights by pressing a button. For a simple reaction, an observer presses a button as soon as he sees any light, no matter what color it is. Donders reasoned that this task could be performed only with perceptual encoding and response execution. For a go/no go reaction, however, the observer presses the button only when the light is green. This requires not only the perceptual encoding and response execution stages but also stimulus identification. For a choice reaction, the observer presses one button for a green light and a different button for a red light. The task now requires response selection, by requiring an observer to determine which of the two possible buttons are appropriate for a presented stimulus.

Donders measured his observers' RTs in the simple, go/no go, and choice reaction tasks. To estimate the duration of the stimulus identification stage, he subtracted the simple RT from the go/no go RT. To estimate the duration of the response selection stage, he subtracted the go/no go RT from the choice RT. This method of subtraction assumed that the task stages were arranged in serial order (so no two stages could be operating at the same time) and that the stages were independent from each other (so if one stage took a very long time to complete, that would not affect how long it took any other stage to complete).

Long after Donders's seminal work, Saul Sternberg began an investigation of the serial order and independence assumptions. Using a memory search task, in which observers were asked to determine whether a numeral had been previously presented in a small set of numerals, he observed that (choice) RT to respond "yes" or "no" increased as a linear function of the size of the set. He argued for a serial process, in which the target numeral is compared to each numeral in the memory set one at a time. He then extended this logic to task stages in his *additive factors* method.

The additive factors approach examines the difference between RTs in different experimental conditions. In particular, the method requires that the experimenter identify experimental factors that selectively influence different independent stages of processing. For example, the memory search task presumably requires at least two stages: perceptual encoding and memory search. Making the stimuli difficult to see will prolong the encoding stage but should not influence the search stage. Similarly, increasing the set size should prolong the search stage but not the encoding stage. A factorial design should, therefore, produce additive effects of encoding difficulty and search set size—that is, there should be no interaction between these factors—if perceptual encoding and memory search are serial processes.

Sternberg's additive factors method is still very influential, even though it can be demonstrated that other kinds of mental architectures can produce RTs that are indistinguishable from those produced by a serial process. Donders's and Sternberg's methods use measures of mean RT, and many researchers still rely on mean RT to explore hypotheses about mental processing. However, many researchers now work with models of the cognitive system that can predict the entire distribution of RTs, as well as the accuracy of different responses. These models have led to the development of new experimental designs as well as new methods of analysis.

RT Experiments

RT experiments can be categorized according to the extent to which information provided by the stimulus is compressed in the response. Many RT experiments have fewer possible responses than the number of stimuli that can be presented. Simple RT tasks can present any number of different stimuli, but only a single response is required to all of them. Choice RT tasks have more than a single response but usually fewer possible responses than possible stimuli. Two-choice RT tasks are by far the most common, in which observers are asked to respond "yes" or "no" to a potentially very large number of stimuli. Word recognition memory experiments, for example, ask observers to respond "yes" (old) to studied words and "no" (new) to novel words. The number of studied and novel words can number in the hundreds, but the number of responses is only two.

Choice RT tasks may have more than two possible responses, in which case they are called N-choice RT tasks. For example, a word recognition memory experiment may ask observers to rate their confidence that a word was previously studied or not by using an N-point scale (e.g., 1 = *confident old*, 2 = *probably old*, 3 = *maybe old*, . . . 6 = *confident new*). Such a task is sometimes called a judgment task. Categorization tasks, where objects are to be classified as members of N different groups, are also N-choice RT tasks. When the number of possible responses is equal to the number of possible stimuli, the choice-RT task becomes an identification task—each stimulus is identified by one and only one correct response.

The go/no go task can be viewed as a choice-RT task where one of the possible responses is not to respond at all. Related to the go/no go task are *stop-signal tasks*. These are choice-RT tasks in which, for some trials, a stop signal is presented at some time after the stimulus, indicating that the observer should not respond. Stop-signal tasks are used to explore the dynamics of response preparation. As the stop-signal delay increases, observers are less able to inhibit their responses, which suggests that the choice process has components that are gradual and build up over time.

The stop-signal task asks observers to do two things at the same time: Select a response to a stimulus and also prepare to stop that response. Two other kinds of RT experiments that are closely related to the stop-signal task are *dual-task* and *task-switching* experiments. These are used to explore mechanisms of response inhibition and automaticity of processing. Results from these kinds of experiments inform our understanding of executive processing, or how people are able to control their behaviors, starting and stopping them at appropriate times, and also of the factors that contribute to uncontrollable (automatic) behaviors.

Influences on RT

Apart from any independent variables an experimenter chooses to manipulate in an experiment, there are a number of other variables that influence RT in simple, choice, and identification tasks. If these other variables are not controlled, they may confound the independent variables. Some variables that influence RT are arousal, age, intelligence, and fatigue. Other variables are more specific to the kind of task the observer is asked to perform.

In simple-RT tasks, RT is positively related to stimulus intensity (e.g., brightness or loudness); as stimuli become easier to detect, simple responses to them can be made more quickly. This relationship is captured by Piéron's law, which states that mean RT is equal to $a + bI^{-c}$, where a, b, and c are parameters, all greater than zero, to be estimated from the data, and I is stimulus intensity. Modality is also very important in simple-RT tasks: Auditory stimuli evoke faster RTs than visual stimuli, for example.

Choice-RT will increase as both the number of stimuli and responses increases. This is the Hick-Hyman law of mean RT: RT is a linear function of the amount of uncertainty in the task. Uncertainty is a dimensionless quantity that depends on the number of possible outcomes in an experiment and their probability. It can be used to describe many things, but in this context it refers to the amount of information provided by the occurrence of an event. For example, if there is only one possible response, observing that response does not tell you very much. If there are n equally likely responses, observing one of them is very informative.

Both choice-RT and identification tasks may be influenced by *stimulus-response compatibility*. Compatibility refers to the ease with which stimuli can be associated to different responses. Compatibility experiments have often focused on the spatial features of stimuli and responses or on where the stimuli appear relative to the location of the responses to be made to them. Highly compatible spatial relationships (e.g., responding with a right button to the stimulus that appears on the right) result in faster RTs than less compatible spatial relationships. Compatibility effects can also occur when the spatial stimulus dimension is task irrelevant and for nonspatial stimulus dimensions such as positive-negative affect of stimuli and verbal responses.

Perhaps the most important issue that arises in choice-RT experiments is the correlation between accuracy and RT: The faster an observer responds, the more errors she makes. Earlier studies such as those of Sternberg and Donders assumed that if the error rate were small then error responses could be safely ignored. While in general this is true, it is also true that very small changes in error rate may reflect a very large change in processing strategy and hence RT.

For this reason, there has been much attention paid to the speed-accuracy trade-off in RT experiments. Much of our current understanding about how people make simple decisions has come from models of RT designed to explain the speed-accuracy trade-off. These models assume that responses arise from a process of information accumulation. Observers sample evidence toward alternative responses from a display, and when that evidence reaches a threshold, a response can be initiated. The speed-accuracy trade-off arises naturally as subjects raise and lower their thresholds for responding. If thresholds are low, it will require less evidence and therefore less time to reach them, but it will be easier for an inappropriate response to accumulate evidence enough to reach a lower threshold. If the thresholds are higher, RTs will be slower, but inappropriate responses will be less likely to reach the threshold.

Evidence accumulation models, sometimes called sequential sampling models, now are applied to problems across the spectrum of brain sciences, including neuroscience aging, developmental disorders, and clinical psychology. We now have good evidence suggesting that at least some parts of the brain function control decisions through groups of neurons that act as evidence accumulators.

Conclusion

It has always seemed incredible so simple a dependent variable as RT could ever tell us anything really important about how the brain works. As R. Duncan Luce described in 1986, this endeavor is similar to trying to reverse engineer the motherboard of a computer by measuring how long it takes to run different programs. In fact, using RT alone, it will not be possible to learn anything of the brain's intricacies. However, by linking measurements of RT to other behavioral variables and to neural data such as single-cell recordings or functional magnetic resonance imaging, we have learned a great deal about how simple choices are made, including how people control their behaviors and attend to different features of their environments. Understanding these simple choices is fundamental to understanding more complex human behavior.

Trisha Van Zandt

See also Aging, Memory, and Information Processing Speed; Automaticity; Decision Making and Reward, Computational Perspectives; Divided Attention and Memory; Multitasking and Human Performance; Psychological Refractory Period; Stroop Effect

Further Readings

Duncombe, R. L. (1945). Personal equation in astronomy. *Popular Astronomy, 53,* 2–13, 63–76, 110–121.

Logan, G. D. (2003). Executive control of thought and action: In search of the wild homunculus. *Current Directions in Psychological Science, 12,* 45–48.

Luce, R. D. (1986). *Response times: Their role in inferring elementary mental organization.* New York, NY: Oxford University Press.

Proctor, R. W., & Vu, K.-P. L. (2006). *Stimulus-response compatibility principles: Data, theory, and application.* Boca Raton, FL: CRC Press.

Ratcliff, R., & McKoon, G. (2008). The diffusion decision model: Theory and data for two-choice decision tasks. *Neural Computation, 20,* 873–922.

Schall, J. D. (2003). Neural correlates of decision processes: Neural and mental chronometry. *Current Opinion in Neurobiology, 12,* 182–186.

Sternberg, S. (1969). The discovery of processing stages: Extensions of Donders' method. In W. G. Koster (Ed.), *Attention and performance* (Vol. 2, pp. 276–315). Amsterdam, Netherlands: North-Holland.

Townsend, J. T., & Ashby, F. G. (1983). *Stochastic modeling of elementary psychological processes.* New York, NY: Cambridge University Press.

Van Zandt, T. (2002). Analysis of response time distributions. In H. Pashler & J. Wixted (Eds.), *Stevens' handbook of experimental psychology* (3rd ed., pp. 461–516). New York, NY: John Wiley.

Welford, A. T., & Brebner, J. (Eds.). (1980). *Reaction times.* New York, NY: Academic Press.

REALISM AND INSTRUMENTALISM

The choice between realism and instrumentalism is at the core of concerns about how our scientific models relate to reality: Do our models aim to be literally true descriptions of reality, or is their role only to be useful instruments for generating predictions? Realism about X, roughly speaking, is the claim that X exists and has its nature independent of our interests, attitudes, and beliefs. An instrumentalist about X denies this. He or she claims that talk of X should be understood as no more than a locution for generating predictions; such talk should not be understood as taking on a commitment to the existence of X. According to an instrumentalist, we should either flatly not believe that X is out there or else should suspend judgment about the existence of X. The most we need acknowledge is that talk of X is useful in making predictions.

The question of realism versus instrumentalism can be asked about almost any theoretical entity in science. It is likely, and seems reasonable, that different answers will be given in different cases. Someone may wish to be a realist about certain theoretical entities (e.g., *electrons*) but an instrumentalist about others (e.g., *centers of gravity*). Not every noun phrase in a scientific theory should be taken as expressing an ontological commitment. Psychological theories are no exception. Almost every theoretical entity posited by psychology has been questioned as to whether it is *really out there* or just a *useful theoretical fiction*. This entry focuses on two such major theoretical entities: (a) *propositional attitudes* (e.g., beliefs, desires) and (b) *conscious states* (qualia).

Propositional Attitudes

Psychological theories, both in science and our folk conceptions, often use propositional attitudes (beliefs, desires, hopes, assumptions, fears, etc.) to explain and predict how people think. These mental representations seem to figure as causal agents in our best explanations of how agents behave and reason (e.g., "If one believes *x* and desires *y*, that causes one to *z*"). Should psychological theories using propositional attitude terms be taken at face value as referring to concrete entities that have an objective existence, that cause action, combine with one another, are caused by sensation, and so on? Or should talk of propositional attitudes be understood as no more than a theoretical fiction that allows our psychological theories to achieve their predictive success but does not correspond to entities that are really out there?

Jerry Fodor argues for a robust form of realism about propositional attitudes. His reasoning is based on the empirical success of psychological theories that employ propositional attitude terms. We do astonishingly well at predicting how people behave if we are allowed to talk in terms of beliefs, desires, and other propositional attitudes. There are no rival accounts of human psychology that enjoy similar predictive success and that do not make use of propositional attitudes. According to Fodor, there is therefore at least a presumptive inference that talk of beliefs and desires latches onto real entities that pull the strings behind our behavior. Just as the success of our physical theories gives us reason to infer that their theoretical terms refer to real entities (e.g., electrons), so the success of our psychological theories gives us reason to infer that their propositional attitude terms latch onto objective features of the world.

If propositional attitudes are real, what sort of entities are they? According to Fodor, in order adequately to account for the explanatory success of psychology, one has to understand propositional attitudes as having a sentence-like structure. Fodor consequently posits a language of thought in which beliefs, desires, and so on appear as sentences. Just as expressions in a computer's machine code control a machine's behavior and cause the occurrence of further expressions of machine code inside the machine, so sentences in our language of thought enter into causal relations, control our behavior, and cause the occurrence of new sentences in our language of thought (new beliefs, desires, etc.). Like a computer's machine code, sentences in our language of thought exist as a pattern of physical activity inside our heads. Hence, propositional attitudes such as beliefs and desires are discrete, reoccurring, entities with causal powers. They are the causal agents behind our behavior, just as patterns of electrical activity instantiating a computer's machine code instructions are the causal agents behind a computer's behavior.

In contrast, Paul Churchland argues for a robust form of instrumentalism about propositional attitudes. According to Churchland, *belief* and *desire* terms fail to latch onto any entities in the world and at best serve as a useful way of talking for ordinary folk. Churchland concedes that psychological theories employing propositional attitudes enjoy some predictive success; however, he thinks that Fodor overestimates the degree of that success in light of the potential of future neuroscientific theories to explain behavior without reliance on propositional attitudes. Churchland points out that many theories are instrumentally useful yet false. Ptolemaic astronomy, which posited celestial spheres, makes many true predictions but is nevertheless false. Churchland claims that beliefs and desires will go the way of celestial spheres. Churchland's main argument for the nonexistence of propositional attitudes can be broken into two steps. The first step is to argue that folk psychology is a theory and that the meaning of propositional attitude terms (expressions such as *belief* and *desire*) is fixed by their role in that theory. What *belief* and *desire* mean is wholly, and exclusively, specified by folk psychology: What it means to be a *desire* is to be something that combines with beliefs and causes action in precisely the way described by folk psychology. Churchland's second step is to argue that folk psychology is false. If the folk psychology theory is false, then *nothing* satisfies the role ascribed to beliefs and desires, and consequently, beliefs and desires, as traditionally conceived, do not exist. Both steps in Churchland's argument have been questioned. Against the first, Ronald Mallon and colleagues have argued that it is far from clear the extent to which the meaning of propositional attitude terms such as *belief* and *desire* ride on the fortunes of folk psychology. It is not obvious how much, or indeed if any, of folk psychology needs to be true in order to fix the meanings of propositional attitude terms. Against the second step, Terence Horgan and James Woodward have argued that Churchland underestimates the success of folk psychology and overestimates the demands we should place in order to be justified in believing it is true.

There are many ways of developing the instrumentalist thought. Daniel Dennett offers a milder form of instrumentalism about propositional attitudes than Churchland. On Dennett's view (unlike Churchland's), talk of beliefs and desires is *true*, but (unlike Fodor's) such talk does not succeed in referring to entities that have an objective existence or representational content independent of our interests. According to Dennett, what is involved in an agent having a belief or desire is not that there is a discrete entity inside the agent—*the belief that p*—with causal powers pulling the strings behind the agent's behavior but merely that there is a predictive payoff in describing the agent *as if* it were controlled by such an entity. To describe an agent in terms of propositional attitudes is to adopt what Dennett calls the "intentional stance": a mode of explanation that attributes to the agent the beliefs and desires that a rational being placed in its shoes *ought* to have. According to Dennett, if the intentional stance is reliable as a method of predicting the behavior of a system *S*, then ipso facto system *S* has those beliefs and desires. All that is required for a system to have a belief is for it to be useful in predicting the behavior of that system to assume that it has that belief. A consequence of Dennett's instrumentalism is that beliefs are easy to achieve. It is often helpful to predict the behavior of cats, robots, washing machines, computers, plants, bacteria, cars, and thermostats by treating them *as if* they have beliefs and desires. According to Dennett, there is no difference between this *as if* and genuine possession of beliefs. It also becomes harder for some systems to achieve beliefs on Dennett's view. Patients suffering from mental illness often cannot be profitably viewed as rational agents when it comes to predicting their behavior. Therefore, on Dennett's view those patients lack beliefs and desires. Their behavior would have to be explained in some other way than intentional psychology—for example, by dropping down to the level of their neurophysiology.

Dennett's instrumentalism about propositional attitudes raises questions about exactly how one should draw the line between realism and instrumentalism. The simple characterization of realism and instrumentalism given at the beginning of this entry fragments into a number of different theses that can, in principle, be affirmed or denied separately. Dennett denies two key realist theses about propositional attitudes: (a) *Mind-independence*—propositional attitudes of an agent have their existence and nature independent of the interpreting interests of observers; (b) *discrete causal powers*—propositional attitudes are discrete, reoccurring, entities inside the head with the causal powers to produce behavior. However, in contrast to Churchland, Dennett affirms a realist intuition about propositional attitudes: (c) *existence*—propositional attitudes exist—they are really out there, unlike celestial spheres. According to Dennett, propositional attitudes exist as patterns that are available to an interpreter to be used for prediction. These patterns are "real" and "objective" in the sense that there are objective facts about what is and what is not predictively successful to assume within the intentional stance. In other words, some belief and desire attributions pay off in that they yield successful predictions of behavior, and others do not. These real patterns of predictive success and failure are the facts in the world that make claims about propositional attitudes true or false.

Qualia

We often report that there is a phenomenal aspect to our experience: Seeing red feels a certain way, having a mouse cupped in one's hand feels a certain way, and the qualitative aspects of different experiences are different. Distinctive qualitative experiences accompany large parts of our mental life. Do our reports of qualitative experiences describe really existing entities (phenomenal properties or states inside our head), or do they serve some other purpose? Are qualia real, or does talk of qualia fail to refer to anything in the world?

An immediate problem that realism and instrumentalism about qualia face is that it is hard even to describe what qualia *are*, and hence, hard to say what one is or is not being a realist about. Often, the best one can do is point to examples of qualia, such as those above. Daniel Dennett develops a strong instrumentalist line against qualia. His target is the widespread assumption that qualia have certain special properties: They are ineffable, intrinsic properties of experience, private and directly accessible to the experiencer. Dennett argues that nothing satisfies this specification, and hence, there are no such things as qualia. Dennett's position is similar to Churchland's strong line against propositional attitudes: Just as the falsity of Ptolemaic astronomy justifies the inference that there are no celestial spheres, so the falsity of philosophical claims about qualia justifies the inference that there are no qualia. Talk of qualia still serves a purpose according to Dennett in that it provides a shorthand summarizing our ability to detect certain properties in the world, such as color properties, that lack a compact description in any other terms.

Dennett's instrumentalism has drawn heavy criticism, not least because it runs up against the robust impression that there *are* real qualitative properties of our mental states that have at least some of the properties mentioned above. However, realism comes at a price. If one grants realism about qualia, then the question arises of what kinds of entities qualia are. Are qualia represented features of the world encoded by our nervous system, similar to our unconscious encoding of features of the world such as position, size, and shape information? If so, what makes conscious "felt" representations different from unconscious representations? Or are qualia intrinsic physical properties of our nervous system, independent of our ability to represent? Or are qualia something different entirely, requiring properties that float free from the physical world and any representations it encodes? No consensus currently exists to the question: the hard question of consciousness—the nature of qualia under a realist understanding.

Mark Sprevak

See also Access Consciousness; Eliminative Materialism; Folk Psychology; Mind-Body Problem; Naïve Realism; Representational Theory of Mind; Smell, Philosophical Perspectives

Further Readings

Chalmers, D. J. (1996). *The conscious mind*. Oxford, UK: Oxford University Press.

Churchland, P. M. (1981). Eliminative materialism and the propositional attitudes. *Journal of Philosophy, 78,* 67–90.

Dennett, D. C. (1987). *The intentional stance*. Cambridge, MA: MIT Press.

Dennett, D. C. (1991). Real patterns. *Journal of Philosophy, 88,* 27–51.

Dennett, D. C. (2002). Quining qualia. In D. J. Chalmers (Ed.), *Philosophy of mind: Classical and contemporary readings* (pp. 226–246). Oxford, UK: Oxford University Press.

Fodor, J. A. (1975). *The language of thought*. Sussex, UK: Harvester.

Fodor, J. A. (1987). *Psychosemantics*. Cambridge, MA: MIT Press.

Horgan, T., & Woodward, J. (1985). Folk psychology is here to stay. *Philosophical Review, 94,* 197–226.

Mallon, R., Machery, E., Nichols, S., & Stich, S. P. (2009). Against arguments from reference. *Philosophy and Phenomenological Research, 79,* 332–356.

Tye, M. (1995). *Ten problems of consciousness*. Cambridge, MA: MIT Press.

REDUCTIVE PHYSICALISM

One way in which something utterly mysterious can be unraveled is to reduce it to something we can understand. Not surprisingly, then, philosophy, which often tries to understand mysteries, takes reduction as one of its tools. Is knowledge reducible to true, justified belief? Are moral codes reducible to personal preferences? Are meaningful statements reducible to constructions of immediate experience? And is the mind reducible to the brain? This entry provides an introduction to the concept of reduction, as it is used in philosophy of mind, and an overview of the various reductive accounts of the mind posited by philosophers, culminating with a brief discussion of the relative merit of these views and of reduction in general.

Reduction

What is reduction? What does it mean to say that the mind is or is not reducible to the brain? Like many terms, both in and out of philosophy, the word *reduction* is used in a variety of ways. In everyday language, we often understand reduction, quite naturally, to mean lessening or reducing in size. You might go on a reducing diet—for example, by eliminating those luscious French sauces that require reduction when cooking. In philosophy, the word reduction is sometimes used with this ordinary meaning, as philosophers often take it to mean simplification. When we reduce one ontological category to another, by showing the one category to be nothing but the other, we simplify our ontology by cutting down the number of kinds of things that exist in the world. However, the philosophical notion of reduction can also encompass an explanatory element. One category reduces to another, in this sense, if can be explained in terms of the other.

In philosophy of mind, these two notions of reduction—the *nothing but* notion and the *explanatory* notion—often (though, as we'll see, not always) overlap. For example, one way in which the mind can be understood as nothing but the brain (or, more accurately, certain parts of the brain) is by reductively explaining mental processes entirely in terms of the neural processes. Not all explanations of one thing in terms of something else are reductive explanations. I might explain the reason for the spill on the floor in terms of why it happened: My cat jumped on the table. But reductive explanations are not like this, they do not tell us the cause of something; rather, they aim to tell us what something is. For example, genetic material is reductively explained in terms of DNA, water in terms of H_2O, temperature in a gas in terms of mean molecular momentum, and if the mental is reductively explainable in terms of neural processes, mental processes in terms of neural ones. For example, one version of reductive physicalism holds that pain is reducible to C-fiber activity (or, more accurately, to whatever neural process that is found to be perfectly correlated with pain). Such a reduction aims to explain pain by showing that it is nothing but C-fiber activity. If pain could be entirely explained in terms of processes in the brain, such as C-fiber activity, we would have both simplified our ontology and found out what pain really is.

Physicalism

What makes reductive physicalism a form of physicalism? Physicalism holds, roughly, that everything is physical. Reductive physicalism is simply the view that the mind is reducible—in one of the various senses to be specified below—to either neural processes or behavior. Assuming that neural processes and behavior are both entirely physical, such a view deems physicalism's primary nemesis, the mental, to be physical.

Eliminative Physicalism

The explanatory and simplifying elements of reduction sometimes come apart. For example, some see neuroscience as paving the way toward an "eliminative reduction" of at least some of what we currently think of as mental processes. Those who uphold such a view, eliminativists, as they are called, think that we should not expect to explain the mental in terms of any other more fundamental theory. But this is not because they hold, as does the dualist, that mental processes are distinct from physical ones. Rather, they hold that much of what we currently think of as mental is just a made–up fiction. Correlations between the mental and neural, they believe, will not be found. Thus the mind, they think, should go the way of witches and phlogiston. Although it was once commonly thought that witches existed, we now simply deny their existence; although it was once thought that when wood burns or metal rusts phlogiston is released, we now deny that phlogiston exists. The mind, according to eliminativists, is more like phlogiston than like the gene. Eliminativism is reductive in as much as is simplifies our ontology (reduces it in the ordinary sense of the term), but rather than explaining the mental in neurological terms, it explains it away.

Eliminativism, apart from being reductive in one sense, is also most definitely a case of physicalism since it posits only physical processes. Although dualism is not a reductive theory, other antiphysicalist positions can be thought of as reductive. For example, phenomenalists hold that physical objects are nothing but sense data; the tomato on your plate, on this view, is something like a concatenation of mental images. Idealists are also reductivists of an antiphysicalistic stripe. For the idealist, physical objects are reducible to ideas. The reductive physicalist, however, turns this theory on its head: Ideas (and everything else mental) are reducible to physical objects.

Eliminative reduction is a version of reductive physicalism, but it is not the most common one. Many physicalists are optimistic that we will find robust correlations between mental and physical processes. And among these some accept that what we think of as mental can, at least in principle, be explained by physical processes, while others think that although mental processes, such as twinges of pain and showers of tickles, will never be explained in terms of physical processes, mental processes are identical to physical processes nonetheless. These two groups of reductive physicalists do not advocate eliminative reduction, as they maintain that all or nearly all that we know and love about the

638 Reductive Physicalism

mental exists. Rather, they advocate what is sometimes called retentive reduction; eliminative reduction eliminates the mental from our ontology, while retentive reduction involves explaining it or at least identifying it in terms of the brain.

Explanatory Mind-Brain Identity Theory

One form of retentive reduction in philosophy of mind is the mind-brain identity theory, also called the type identity theory or sometimes just the identity theory. Philosophers who accept the identity theory think that mental processes are one and the same thing as neural states. For example, the type of thing we call pain, according to this view, is nothing more than the type of thing we call C-fiber stimulation (or, rather, the type of thing we call P, where P refers to the neural state that is perfectly correlated with experiences of pain). Pain exists, claims the identity theorist, and it is reducible to activity in the brain. Just as the uncanny connection between Dr. Jekyll and Mr. Hyde led the London lawyer Utterson to eventually conclude that the misanthropic Hyde was none other than his dear old friend Dr. Jekyll, those who uphold the identity theory think that a correlation between pain and C-fiber stimulation might lead us to conclude that pain and C-fiber stimulation are one and the same thing as well.

Mysterianism

As some see it, the mind-brain identity theory is explanatory in the sense that it provides what some see as a simple answer to the question of why pain is correlated with C-fiber stimulation: The correlation holds because pain is C-fiber stimulation. If pain is just C-fiber stimulation, if *pain* and *C-fiber stimulation* are just two names for the same thing, there is no more question about why every time people are in pain their C-fibers are firing than there is a question about why every time I shut the door I also close it.

Other reductive physicalists, however, although they accept the identities, deny that identities of this form provide explanations; they still think that there is a question of how the activity of C-fibers could be pain or, to use another example, how the activity of pyramidal cells could be consciousness. Pain, in their view, is reducible to neural processes in the sense of it being nothing but something going on in the brain, but as they see it, we lack an explanation of how this could be so.

Behaviorism

So we have two different sorts of reductive accounts of the mind: eliminativism and the type identity theory. And the latter can be divided into explanatory type identity and what is sometimes called *mysterianism*. Another form of reductive physicalism is behaviorism. On the most basic understanding of this view, the mind is nothing over and above behavior. Pain, for example, is just the bodily movements you make when you are in pain. The desire for carrots is just the bodily movements you make when you desire carrots. An obvious problem with this view is that sometimes one deliberately suppresses such movements. If it's not mealtime, for example, you'll need to suppress your urge to open the fridge. However, more sophisticated forms of behaviorism claim not to reduce pain to certain forms of behavior, per se, but rather to the *disposition* to behave in certain ways. To be fragile, for example, is to have the disposition to break if dropped on a hard surface. A glass has this disposition even when it is not dropped. Similarly, the behaviorist will say, to be in pain is to have the disposition to wince, say "ouch," and so forth.

Cost-Benefit Analysis

Are there reasons to accept one reductive view over the others? All have at least some apparent flaws. Eliminativism is criticized for being too pessimistic about the prospects for mind-brain correlations. Neuroscience, the argument goes, is in its infancy and it may be that what seems utterly inexplicable neuroscientifically now will be understood later. And behaviorists are criticized for not being able to spell out the relevant dispositions. What, exactly, are the relevant background conditions under which you would say that you are in pain? What, exactly, are the relevant mitigating circumstances? It is not at all clear how to answer these questions. Moreover, there are some mental states, such as the belief that seven is a prime number, that do not even have any standard associated behaviors. What does one typically do when one believes that seven is a prime number? The question is rather absurd.

The mind-brain identity theory, according to which mental process M is necessarily physical processes *P,* is more widely held than either eliminativism or behaviorism. However, it is open to criticism as well, the central one being that it is chauvinistic since it does not allow for *M* to be anything other than *P.* Going back to pain and C-fiber stimulation, if there were a creature from another planet who behaved as if it were in pain yet did not have C-fibers, the classic mind-brain identity theory implies that this creature would not feel pain. No matter how similar its behavior and outward appearance to ours when we are hurt, the creature's lack of C-fibers would imply, according to the classic mind-brain identity theory, that crushing the creature's foot would not cause it to feel pain. Thus just as John Smith, the CEO at a high-powered accounting firm, is chauvinistic because he refuses to hire women merely because they are women, the proponents of the classic identity theory are chauvinistic because they hold that extraterrestrials cannot feel pain merely because they are extraterrestrials.

There are two further rather subtle objections to the view. The first is that, as some see it, it falls into eliminativism. If the mind is nothing but the brain, then the mind, according to this objection, does not really exist. There are certain neural processes that are being labeled mental processes as well, but as for real feelings, emotions, thoughts, or perceptions, goes the objection, this view leaves them out. A complementary objection is that mind-brain identity theory makes the brain something nonphysical. If the mind is identical to the brain, then the brain is identical to the mind, and if this is so, according to this objection, the brain is, itself, something mental; it is made out of something like tiny experiences and thus is not physical.

There are various responses to these criticisms. But there are also alternatives. Dualism is one alternative. However, a physicalistic alternative is nonreductive physicalism. The nonreductive physicalist finds fault in reductionism in general. Guided by the idea, as Bishop Butler put it in 1736, that everything is what it is and not another thing, the nonreductivist accepts the reality of the mental and does not think that it is something other than it is, such as the neural. For the nonreductive physicalist the world is composed of levels, which roughly mirror the disciplines: physics, chemistry, biology, neurology, psychology. The objects of psychology, according to the nonreductive physicalists, are just as real as the objects of neurology but are not identical to them.

Which view is preferable: reductive physicalism or nonreductive physicalism? As with many questions in philosophy, the jury is still out.

Barbara Montero

See also Anomalous Monism; Eliminative Materialism; Emergence; Explanatory Gap; Idealism; Mind-Body Problem; Physicalism

Further Readings

Butler, J. (1736). *Analogy of religion, natural and revealed, to the constitution and nature.* London, UK: Knapton.

Feigl, H. (1967). *The mental and the physical: The essay and a postscript.* Minneapolis: University of Minnesota Press.

Kim, J. (1999). *Mind in a physical world: An essay on the mind-body problem and mental causation.* Cambridge, MA: MIT Press.

Kripke, S. (1980). *Naming and necessity.* Cambridge, MA: Harvard University Press.

Lewis, D. (1966). An argument for the identity theory. *Journal of Philosophy, 63,* 17–25.

Lewis, D. (1980). Mad pain and Martian pain. In N. Block (Ed.), *Readings in the philosophy of psychology* (Vol. 1, pp. 216–222). Cambridge, MA: Harvard University Press.

Montero, B. (2009). *On the philosophy of mind.* Belmont, CA: Wadsworth Press.

Place, U. T. (1956). Is consciousness a brain process? *British Journal of Psychology, 47,* 44–50.

Smart, J. J. C. (1959). Sensations and brain processes. *Philosophical Review, 68,* 141–156.

REGRET

We feel regret when realizing or imagining that our present situation would have been better had we decided differently. This entry addresses how regret is experienced, whether we regret actions more than inactions, how regret relates to counterfactual thinking and decision making, and how regret influences behavior.

The Experience of Regret

Regret stems from a comparison between outcomes of chosen and nonchosen alternatives in which the latter outperform the former. It is a painful emotion that reflects on our own causal role in the current, suboptimal situation. The emotion regret is accompanied by feelings that one should have known better and having a sinking feeling, by thoughts about the mistake one has made and the opportunities lost, by tendencies to kick oneself and to correct one's mistake, by desires to undo the event and get a second chance, and by actually doing this if given the opportunity. It is a cognitively based emotion that motivates one to think about how the current negative event came about and how one could change it or how one could prevent its future occurrence.

Action and Inaction Regret

We may regret sins of omission and sins of commission. Early regret research indicated that people tend to regret their actions (commissions) more than their inactions (omissions). Later research showed that time plays a crucial role here. In the short run, people tend to feel more regret over their actions (the stupid things they did or bought), but in the long run, they tend to feel more regret over their inactions (the school they never finished, the career or romance never pursued). This temporal pattern to regret is due to a number of factors that decrease the regret for action over time (e.g., we take more reparative action and engage in more psychological repair work for action regrets than for inaction regrets) and to factors that increase the regret for inaction over time (e.g., over time we may forget why we did not act on opportunities, making the inaction inexplicable).

Another factor determining the intensity of regret is the justifiability of the decision. People feel most regret over decisions that are difficult to justify. Decisions that are based on solid reasons produce less regret than decisions that are not well thought through. This justifiability may also explain when actions are more regretted than inactions and when the reverse is true.

Regret, Decision Making and Counterfactual Thinking

Regret is unique in its relation to decision making. One only experiences regret over a bad outcome when at some point in time one could have prevented the outcome from happening. Other emotions can also be the result of decisions; for example, one may be disappointed with a decision outcome or happy about the process by which one made a choice. But these emotions can also be experienced in nonchoice situations. For example, one can be disappointed in the weather and happy with a birthday present, but one cannot regret these instances (unless, of course, if the disappointing present was suggested by oneself).

The relation between regret and decision making is also apparent in regret's connection to counterfactual thinking. Counterfactual thoughts are thoughts about what might have been. Note that not all counterfactual thoughts produce regret but only those that change a bad outcome into a good one by changing a prior choice or decision. Thus, when it rains on the way home from work and I get wet, I feel regret when I generate a counterfactual thought in which I brought an umbrella but not when I generate a counterfactual in which it would be a beautiful day. In the latter case, counterfactual thoughts about better weather that could have been would result in disappointment but not in regret (I could not change the weather, so there is nothing to regret).

Experienced and Anticipated Regret

Psychologists became interested in studying regret partly because it is not only a passive emotional reaction to bad decisions but also a major influence our day-to-day decision making. This influence can take two forms. First, the experience of regret may produce a behavioral inclination to reverse one's decision or undo the consequences. Second, decision makers may anticipate possible future regret when making decisions and choose in such a way that this future regret will be minimal.

The influence of retrospective regret on behavior can be functional. The aversive experience prompts us to undo the cause of the regret. For example, after buying a product that proves to be suboptimal, regret can motivate us to ask for our money back, or it may result in apologies in the case of interpersonal regrets. In both instances, regret can help us to satisfy our needs. It protects us from wasting money and helps us maintain good social relationships. Additionally, regret can be functional in the sense that the painful self-reflective nature of the experience is one of various ways by which we learn. The feeling of regret over bad decisions and wrong choices makes them stand out in our memory and helps us make better decisions in the future.

The idea that people, when making decisions, might take into account future emotional reactions to possible decision outcomes has some history in research on decision making, starting with economists studying rational choice in the early 1980s. We now know that the influence of anticipated future regret on current decision making can take several forms. First, people may avoid deciding in order to avoid making the wrong decision. However, this inactive attitude may result in regret as well, since we know that in the long run inactions produce most regret. People may also avoid or delay their decisions because they want to gather more information in order to make a better decision. Research has shown that these anticipations of regret can influence many real-life decisions, among others, stock market investments, salary negotiations, lottery play, prenatal screening decisions, and condom use.

Taken together, regret is an aversive emotional state that is related to counterfactual thoughts about how the present situation would have been better had one chosen or acted differently. Therefore, people are motivated to avoid or minimize postdecisional regret. This has several implications for decision making since people may employ different strategies in order to prevent regret from happening or to cope with regret when it is experienced. In principle, the effects of regret can be considered rational, because they protect the decision maker from the aversive consequences of the experience of regret. There might be cases, however, in which an aversion to regret leads one to avoid counterfactual feedback (i.e., any knowledge about what the outcome would have been had they chosen differently) and hence results in reduced learning from experience. This might be considered irrational. But irrespective of this rationality question, regret has shown to be a fundamental emotion in the behavior decisions of most, if not all of us.

Marcel Zeelenberg

See also Decision Making, Neural Underpinnings; Decision Theory, Philosophical Perspectives; Emotion Regulation; Rationality of Emotion

Further Readings

Gilovich, T., & Medvec, V. H. (1995). The experience of regret: What, when, and why. *Psychological Review, 102,* 379–395.

Landman, J. (1993). *Regret: The persistence of the possible.* New York, NY: Oxford University Press.

Loomes, G., & Sugden, R. (1982). Regret theory: An alternative theory of rational choice under uncertainty. *Economic Journal, 92,* 805–824.

Roese, N. J. (2005). *If only.* New York, NY: Broadway Books.

Zeelenberg, M., & Pieters, R. (2007). A theory of regret regulation 1.0. *Journal of Consumer Psychology, 17,* 3–18.

REHEARSAL AND MEMORY

Rehearsal refers to the overt or subvocal recitation of to-be-remembered (TBR) verbal material during encoding, storage, or retrieval from memory. This entry reviews the considerable evidence that rehearsal is a major determinant of memory performance in many situations, involving both short-term and long-term retention. Rehearsal has played an explanatory role in otherwise highly diverse theories of memory, for example that of Alan Baddeley. In recognition of the potential circularity of an unobservable explanatory construct (e.g., whenever memory performance is good, there must have been effective rehearsal, and whenever performance is poor, rehearsal must have been absent), much effort has focused on the identification, operationalization, and experimental control of rehearsal.

Elaborative Versus Maintenance Rehearsal

One influential proposal involved the distinction between *elaborative* rehearsal (also known as Type II rehearsal) and *maintenance* (Type I) rehearsal advanced by Fergus Craik: During elaborative rehearsal, new material is meaningfully related to other information—for example, by deciding whether a TBR word fits into a sentence. Maintenance rehearsal, by contrast, involves rote repetition of items without relational processing, usually with the express purpose to maintain already encoded information in awareness.

There is consensus that increasing elaboration of TBR material leads to better long-term retention; for example, judgments involving the meaning of the TBR material lead to better subsequent recall than judgments of its sound, which in turn yields better memory than judgments of surface structure (e.g., reporting the number of letters). By contrast, the effect of maintenance rehearsal is more ambiguous:

On the one hand, when people are led to believe that long-term retention of the material is unimportant, the number of overt recitations of TBR words is often unrelated to subsequent surprise recall performance. On the other hand, when memory is tested by recognition, the duration of maintenance rehearsal is usually correlated with performance, as shown by Robert Greene in an extensive review. The distinction between maintenance and elaborative rehearsal might therefore be best considered as a *continuum* involving the amount of attention that is paid to rehearsal. When attention is minimal, then the number of rehearsals may fail to correlate with measures of memory. In all other situations, the number of articulations of TBR material is correlated with enhanced performance.

Linking Rehearsal to Performance

Going beyond mere correlation, support for a causal link between rehearsal patterns and memory performance has been adduced both empirically and theoretically. Lydia Tan and Geoff Ward provided a detailed analysis of rehearse-out-loud protocols in free-recall experiments. In immediate free recall, performance at all list positions was primarily a function of the recency of an item's last rehearsal, to the exclusion of other experimental variables (e.g., presentation rate, list length, and participants' age) that affect recall when rehearsal patterns are ignored. It follows that those other variables exert their effect on performance only indirectly, via modulation of people's rehearsal patterns. It is noteworthy that the recency-of-rehearsal analysis accommodated the primacy effect (better recall for items that were presented early in the list), because early items tended to be rehearsed again much later in the list. In delayed recall, other factors such as the number and spacing of rehearsals become relatively more important than recency, and those factors may also explain why maintenance rehearsal is sometimes ineffective.

Intriguingly, Tan and Ward found no additional advantage for spontaneous self-generation of the rehearsal schedule in comparison to articulation of an identical protocol that was generated by a different participant. The process of choosing items for rehearsal thus appears less important than their effective re-presentation by articulation.

David Laming presented a detailed mathematical model that predicts entire sequences of recall from the pattern of overt rehearsals and item presentations during study. Laming's theory emphasizes the importance of considering subject-generated events (rehearsal) on par with experimenter-controlled events (presentation of study items). Overall, rehearsal patterns indubitably are a major determinant of long-term memory performance, and the success of recall can be predicted from preceding rehearsals with quantitative precision. To a first approximation, the data warrant the conclusion that an item's probability of recall is determined by the recency of its last rehearsal.

Rehearsal in Memory Over the Short Term

Turning to memory over the short term, relevant models have frequently invoked rehearsal as an explanatory construct. In contrast to long-term memory research, the imputed role of rehearsal in short-term memory has focused less on encoding and more on the protection of information against loss, often presumed to occur through temporal decay—that is, the inexorable decline in memory strength over the passage of time.

Accordingly, research in short-term memory has often focused on the effects of wholesale manipulations that prevent rehearsal altogether. Rehearsal is commonly thought to be abolished by *articulatory suppression* (AS from here on)—that is, the repeated articulation of an irrelevant word. AS is particularly diagnostic because, if it successfully suppresses rehearsal, then the effects of temporal decay should become observable. Contrary to that expectation of decay-based models, Stephen Lewandowsky and colleagues have shown in 2004 and 2008 that performance is unaffected when AS-filled retention intervals are extended. The hitherto tight coupling between a presumed mechanism of forgetting—namely, decay—and rehearsal therefore appears unnecessary.

Tan and Ward in 2008 reported the only analysis to date of (spontaneous) overt rehearsal protocols involving short lists and immediate serial recall (i.e., the recall of list items immediately upon presentation in their original order). Performance was found to be strongly associated with the length of the longest forward-rehearsal sequence; that is, a person who rehearsed the first five items in sequence performed better than a person who rehearsed only two items in sequence.

Further evidence for the role of rehearsal over the short term has evolved from research in working memory. A popular working-memory paradigm interleaves the TBR material with unrelated processing stimuli (e.g., by presenting arithmetic tasks in between list items). Recent models of this "complex-span" task proposed by Pierre Barrouillet and colleagues in 2004 have again coupled rehearsal with decay as two opposing processes. This coupling is based on the finding that memory performance is a function of the *proportion* of time—rather than its absolute duration—in between TBR items that is taken up by the processing task. Memory is presumed to decay during the processing but is restored during brief intervening pauses by a rehearsal process. Although the work by Lewandowsky and colleagues provides reasons to question the presence of decay, there is little doubt that even brief pauses in between processing episodes can be used to restore memory traces; notably, this form of rehearsal appears to be *attentional* rather than articulatory.

Direct behavioral evidence for the presence of attentional refreshing consists of the fact that it can occur concurrently with overt recitation of verbal material. It is known that different brain regions are involved in attentional and articulatory rehearsal and that the two forms of rehearsal make separate but additive contributions in a complex-span task.

Stephan Lewandowsky

See also Memory Recall, Dynamics; Working Memory

Further Readings

Baddeley, A. D. (1986). *Working memory.* New York, NY: Oxford University Press.

Barrouillet, P., Bernardin, S., & Camos, V. (2004). Time constraints and resource sharing in adults' working memory spans. *Journal of Experimental Psychology: General, 133,* 83–100.

Laming, D. (2010). Serial position curves in free recall. *Psychological Review, 117,* 93–133.

Lewandowsky, S., Duncan, M., & Brown, G. D. A. (2004). Time does not cause forgetting in short-term serial recall. *Psychonomic Bulletin & Review, 11,* 771–790.

Oberauer, K., & Lewandowsky, S. (2008). Forgetting in immediate serial recall: Decay, temporal distinctiveness, or interference? *Psychological Review, 115,* 544–576.

REINFORCEMENT LEARNING, PSYCHOLOGICAL PERSPECTIVES

Reinforcement is the process by which experience changes both overt behavior and that more subtle behavior called cognition. The ability of individual experience to change behavior is arguably the most important contribution of natural selection by the ancestral environment. Whereas natural selection adapts the species of which the individual is a member to the more constant contingencies of the ancestral environment, selection by reinforcement adapts the individual to the variable contingencies of his or her personal environment. In natural selection, the environment selects for structural and functional characteristics that favor reproductive fitness—the survival of offspring. In selection by reinforcement, the environment—including interactions with others—selects behavior that adapts organisms to the specific events encountered in their lives.

The entry summarizes experimental research that identifies the factors that select for changes in individual behavior. The entry then indicates some of the neural mechanisms that implement selection by reinforcement. A core belief of many learning theorists is that reinforcement will ultimately play a central role in understanding the origins of complex behavior that is analogous to the role played by natural selection in understanding the evolution of complex species. That is, the cumulative effects of selection by reinforcement will prove competent to produce the complexity and diversity of individual behavior. The entry concludes with a discussion of methods to explore the implications of reinforcement for complex behavior.

Behavioral Analysis of Reinforcement

Experimental research on the factors necessary for selection by reinforcement began around the turn of the previous century in the laboratories of Ivan Pavlov in Russia and Edward Thorndike in the United States. Both sought to control their experiments through the use of nonhuman animals in the belief that natural selection would exploit largely common learning processes that exist in a wide range of species. In Pavlov's procedure, called *classical conditioning,* a neutral stimulus (such as the sound of a tone) occurs before another stimulus (such as taste stimulated by food in the mouth) that already evokes behavior (such as salivation). After several occurrences of this sequence of events, the formerly neutral stimulus begins to evoke salivation when it is occasionally presented by itself. Evoking salivation after the tone allowed the tone to acquire control of the salivary response. The stimulus that evoked behavior at the beginning of the procedure (food in the example) functioned as a reinforcing stimulus, or *reinforcer*. Reinforcers change and strengthen the ability of stimuli to guide behavior. Pavlov's procedure enabled an arbitrary stimulus (the tone) to guide a response (salivation) that was originally evoked by another stimulus (food). In Thorndike's procedure, called *operant conditioning*, a response (such as pressing a lever) occurs before a stimulus (such as food) that already evokes behavior (such as salivation). After several such sequences of events, lever pressing and salivating both become more likely when the learner sees the lever. Thus, the operant procedure enables the environment to guide two sets of responses—the relatively arbitrary response that preceded the reinforcing stimulus (lever pressing) as well as the response evoked by the reinforcer (salivating). B. F. Skinner most clearly appreciated that the operant procedure allowed the full behavioral capabilities of the learner to be modified by experience, not just those responses that could already be elicited by some stimulus. As experience accumulated—thus expanding the behavioral repertoire of the learner—the potential increased for the selection by reinforcement of ever more complex behavior. The change in the guidance of behavior produced by both the classical and operant procedures is called *conditioning* because the change is conditional on (that is, dependent on) events in the individual experience—a stimulus-reinforcer sequence in Pavlov's case and a response-reinforcer sequence in Thorndike's case.

Research with both the classical and operant procedures indicates that the events in the sequence must occur very close together in time for conditioning to occur. In the classical procedure, the neutral stimulus must precede the reinforcing stimulus by no more than a few seconds if the neutral stimulus is to acquire control of the reinforcer-elicited response. Similarly, in the operant procedure the arbitrary response must immediately precede the reinforcing

stimulus if the environment is to acquire control of the arbitrary response as well as the reinforcer-elicited response. Together, findings from these procedures identified the first factor that is necessary for selection by reinforcement—*temporal contiguity* between the events.

The second factor necessary for selection by reinforcement was discovered through an elaboration of the basic classical procedure: A response was first conditioned to one stimulus (S1) by presenting it in temporal contiguity with a reinforcer until conditioning had become strong. Then, a second stimulus (S2) was introduced at the same time as S1 and the reinforcer now followed both stimuli in the same temporal relation as before. For example, a tone would first precede food until salivation had been conditioned. Then, a light would be introduced and the tone and a light together would both precede food. Note that in this procedure, S2 stands in the same temporal relation to the reinforcer as S1, a temporal relation known to permit conditioning. If temporal contiguity were all that was required for conditioning, then S2 should also acquire control of the reinforcer-elicited response. However, tests showed that when S2 was presented by itself conditioning had not occurred. In terms of the previous example, the tone evoked salivation but the light did not. Prior conditioning to the tone blocked conditioning to the light even though the light had occurred in temporal contiguity with the food. This basic result was first clearly identified with the classical procedure but was soon replicated with the operant procedure. Various control procedures eliminated alternative interpretations of the blocking effect. The conclusion from this work was that a second factor in addition to temporal contiguity was required for selection by reinforcement. That factor is typically called *discrepancy*. For conditioning to occur, a reinforcer must not only appear close in time to the stimulus in Pavlov's procedure or to the response in Thorndike's procedure, but the reinforcer must also evoke a change in behavior. Returning to the example, salivation already occurred when the light was first introduced because the accompanying tone had already been paired with food. As a result, the introduction of food after the light did not produce a change in behavior that was large enough to produce selection by reinforcement. The discrepancy requirement may be stated as follows:

$$\Delta R = \alpha \ f(Rmax - Rcurrent),$$

where ΔR is a change in the strength of conditioning between the environmental and behavioral events, α is the proportion of the total possible change that can occur as a result of one contiguous sequence of events, $Rmax$ is the maximum strength of the response to the reinforcing stimulus (e.g., food), and $Rcurrent$ is the present strength of the reinforcer-elicited response to the prevailing stimuli (e.g., the sight of the bar). In short, a change in behavior is some function (f) of the reinforcer-related discrepancy that accompanies contiguous events. Learning theorists differ somewhat among themselves as to how best to characterize the nature of the discrepancy, but almost all agree that both discrepancy and temporal contiguity are required for conditioning. The first formal statement of the discrepancy requirement was proposed by Robert Rescorla and Allan Wagner.

Biological Analysis of Reinforcement

Although additional research on reinforcement is needed at the behavioral level of analysis, enough is now known to warrant an effort to identify its biological mechanisms. The motivation for identifying the biological mechanisms of reinforcement is not only to understand the reinforcement process more completely but also to promote acceptance of reinforcement as the central process in the origins of complex human behavior: The account of evolution through natural selection was not generally accepted until its biological mechanisms (genetics) had been discovered some 70 years after Darwin's initial proposal. If the parallel holds, the acceptance of selectionist accounts of individual behavior awaits the discovery of its biological mechanisms.

Events that initially function as reinforcers, such as food-evoked salivation, do so primarily as the result of natural selection. Such events are called *unconditioned reinforcers* because their reinforcing ability is not dependent on experience. Unconditioned reinforcers stimulate receptors that ultimately activate nerve cells (neurons) in the midbrain that diffusely liberate the neuromodulator dopamine. Axons from these midbrain neurons project widely to frontal cortex and other regions that are involved in the emission of behavior. Thus, the release of dopamine is in a position to affect the strengths of connections (that is, *synaptic efficacies*) between many neurons. Moreover, dopamine is known to facilitate long-lasting increases in synaptic efficacies between simultaneously active pre- and postsynaptic neurons. This facilitation is known as *long-term potentiation,* or LTP. LTP is believed to provide the neural basis of conditioning and was first identified by Timothy Bliss and Terje Lomø.

An experiment by Wolfram Schultz and his colleagues illustrates the role of dopamine in conditioning. A restrained monkey was presented with a light followed closely by a squirt of orange juice into its mouth while monitoring the activity of dopamine-liberating neurons in the midbrain. At first, these dopamine neurons were activated only by the juice, but after a number of light-juice sequences the light began to activate them as well. Once the light activated the dopamine neurons, the juice no longer did. The failure of juice to activate the dopamine-releasing neurons once the light had acquired this ability is the neural basis of blocking. The acquired ability of light to activate dopamine neurons also indicates that the light could now serve as a reinforcing stimulus. Stimuli that acquire the ability to serve as reinforcers after being paired with other reinforcers are known as *conditioned reinforcers*. The cumulative effect of experience establishes many stimuli as conditioned reinforcers. In this way, learning in experienced organisms becomes increasingly independent of unconditioned reinforcers.

Reinforcement and the Emergence of Complex Behavior

The acceptance of natural selection as the primary insight into evolution was also dependent on the development of quantitative methods to trace the cumulative effects of natural selection. Using the computational methods of population genetics, natural selection was shown to be competent to produce the complexity and diversity of species found in nature. Convincing demonstrations that selection by reinforcement provides similarly powerful insights into the origins of complex individual behavior require analogous methods. Among the more promising computational methods are *artificial neural networks*. Artificial neural networks are interconnected sets of units that simulate the interconnected neurons that make up the nervous system. A goal of neural network research is to demonstrate that when the inputs to the network are activated in sequences that mimic the experience of an organism, the outputs of the network simulate the behavior observed in experienced organisms. The strengths of connections between units in artificial neural networks are modified by computational procedures that simulate the action of reinforcement and other experimentally identified processes on synaptic efficacies. Neural networks of interest to experimental science are those that are informed and constrained by findings from behavioral and biological research. Other fields that exploit neural networks, such as artificial intelligence, need not honor these constraints but are primarily concerned with whether the outputs of the network are effective for the task at hand. Exploring the implications of reinforcement by means of neural networks is in a relatively early stage of development but already shows promise with such complex behavior as language acquisition, concept formation, and memory. The work of James McClelland and David Rumelhart has been pioneering in this effort.

John W. Donahoe

See also Behaviorism; Decision Making and Reward, Computational Perspectives; Discrimination Learning, Training Methods; Distributed Cognition; Human Classification Learning; Memory, Neural Basis; Natural Action Selection, Modeling

Further Readings

Bliss, T. V., & Lomø, T. (1973). Long-lasting potentiation of synaptic transmission in the dentate area of the anaesthetized rabbit following stimulation of the perforant path. *Journal of Physiology, 232,* 331–356.

Donahoe, J. W. (2003). Selectionism. In K. A. Lattal & P. N. Chase (Eds.), *Behavior theory and philosophy* (pp. 103–128). Dordrecht, Netherlands: Kluwer Academic.

Donahoe, J. W., & Dorsel, V. P. (Eds.). (1997). *Neural-network models of cognition: Biobehavioral foundations.* New York, NY: Elsevier Science Press.

Donahoe, J. W., & Palmer, D. C (2005). *Learning and complex behavior* (V. Dorsel, Ed.). Richmond, MA: Ledgetop.

Gormezano, I., & Kehoe, E. J. (1981). Classical conditioning and the law of contiguity. In P. Harzem & M. D. Zeiler (Eds.), *Predictability, correlation, and contiguity* (pp. 1–45). New York, NY: Wiley.

McClelland, J. L., Rumelhart, D. E., & PDP Research Group. (1986). *Parallel distributed processing: Explorations in the microstructure of cognition: Psychological and biological models* (Vol. 2). Cambridge, MA: MIT Press.

Rescorla, R. A., & Wagner, A. R. (1972). A theory of Pavlovian conditioning: Variations in the effectiveness of reinforcement and nonreinforcement. In A. H. Black & W. F. Prokasy (Eds.), *Classical conditioning* (Vol. 2, pp. 64–99). New York, NY: Appleton-Century-Crofts.

Rogers, T. T., & McClelland, J. L. (2004). *Semantic cognition: A parallel distributed processing approach.* Cambridge, MA: MIT Press.

Waelti, P., Dickinson, A., & Schultz, W. (2001). Dopamine responses comply with basic assumptions of formal learning theory. *Nature, 412,* 43–48.

RELATIONSHIPS, DEVELOPMENT OF

The development of relationships with significant others is one of the most important tasks that an individual encounters in his or her lifetime. Relationships, according to Robert Hinde, are ongoing patterns of interaction between two individuals who acknowledge some connection with each other. In the case of children and adolescents, the social partners with whom interaction is most frequently experienced include parents, peers, and teachers. From Hinde's perspective, individuals bring to social exchanges reasonably stable social orientations (temperament; personality) that dispose them to be more or less sociable and a repertoire of social skills for understanding the thoughts, emotions, and intentions of others and for interpersonal problem solving. Over the short term, a child's or adolescent's interactions with others will vary in form and function in response to fluctuations in the parameters of the social situation, such as the parent's or peer's characteristics, overtures, and responses. Often, social interactions are embedded in longer term relationships and thus are influenced by past and anticipated future interactions. For example, the nature of any given relationship is defined partly by the characteristics of its members and by its constituent interactions. Over the long term, the kind of relationship that any two individuals form with one another depends largely on the history of their interactions and relationships, not only with each other but also with other members of their personal social community. Consequently, the first dyadic relationships that children experience are embedded within a group—the *family*. Significantly, families help define the type and range of relationships and interactions that are likely or permissible.

Many theories of human development (e.g., Sigmund Freud, Erik Erikson) suggest that relationships with others are important to healthy social and emotional development. This entry reviews the development of relationships with caregivers or parents, peers, friends, and romantic partners. The central argument presented herein is that the earliest relationships children form with their primary caregivers help shape the formation of internalized, mental representations of relationships, which, in turn, subsequently affect the development of other significant relationships.

Attachment Relationships

John Bowlby proposed that the attachment relationship between the child and his or her primary caregiver (most often, the mother) derives from a biologically rooted behavioral system that is marked by the infant's natural proximity seeking to caregivers for safety, security, and support. The attachment system regulates both physical and psychological safety in the context of close relationships. Perceived danger, stress, and threats to the accessibility of attachment figures activate attachment responses. When children with secure attachments are threatened, they tend to seek out those with whom they have formed attachments, and in this way, these figures serve as "safe havens." In novel environments, attachment figures also serve as "secure bases" from which children explore their environment. Herein we briefly review important concepts about attachment and internal working models.

Infant attachment to caregivers is typically assessed through a laboratory paradigm developed by Mary Ainsworth and colleagues. Ainsworth's *strange situation* comprises several episodes during which caregivers and strangers enter and leave an unfamiliar room within which the child is present. The task is designed to mimic how familiar and unfamiliar adults flow in and out of a child's daily life. The quality of the attachment relationship is assessed by observing how the child explores the unfamiliar environment when the caregiver is present and how the child reacts to the departure and subsequent return of the caregiver. Questionnaires, interviews, and other observational paradigms have been developed to assess attachment in alternative settings and with older children and adults.

Secure attachments result from sensitive and responsive caregiving. The sensitive and responsive parent interprets signals correctly and responds effectively and appropriately to the child's behaviors and needs. Sensitive and responsive parents do not direct anger or hostility to their young children, even when they are feeling irritated or annoyed. In the strange situation, infants who explore the environment freely, engage with strangers while the caregiver is present, and seek proximity to caregivers when under stress are classified as *securely attached*. When the caregiver leaves, securely attached infants are visibly upset, but on reunion, they are relieved to see the caregiver and easily soothed. Secure infants become children who express their emotions to others and actively seek help when they are unable to help themselves. These behaviors help them learn to regulate their emotions, adapt to new challenges, and develop healthy relationships with others during their lifetime.

When parents are insensitive and unresponsive, their infants develop insecure attachments to them. There are three types of insecure attachments: *anxious-avoidant, anxious-ambivalent,* and *disorganized*. In the strange situation, children who do not seek caregivers in times of stress and/ or ignore caregivers after separation are classified as anxious-avoidant. Anxious-avoidant children often have caregivers who ignore or reject them in times of need. These children show limited affective engagement with caregivers, learning to inhibit their negative emotions and avoid emotional interactions. Anxious-avoidant children have difficulty controlling their anger in social company and thus have difficulty developing positive peer relationships and friendships.

Children who are unusually clingy with caregivers in the strange situation and need more reassurance than other infants, even in only mildly stressing situations, are typically classified as anxious-ambivalent. These children have more difficulty separating from parents, and during reunion they are more difficult to comfort. Anxious-ambivalent children have caregivers who are inconsistent in their availability and sensitivity. Thus, these children display vigilance for caregiver actions and show inflated distress in order to elicit caregiver attention. In social interactions, these children are easily frustrated, impulsive, and overly anxious. They are less likely to explore in novel situations and have heightened personal fears. With peers, some of these children may act aggressively, whereas others act more passively and are prone to social reticence and withdrawal.

Last, children who develop disorganized attachment relationships are likely to have parents who are emotionally or physically abusive. These children show no clear pattern of behavior in the strange situation. They are at greater risk than other attachment groups to be aggressive and are more likely to develop oppositional defiant disorder, a persistent pattern of uncooperative, hostile behavior that interferes with a child's basic functioning.

Note that the cross-cultural universality of attachment theory has been questioned. Critics argue that attachment theory emphasizes autonomy, independence, and individuation as defining competence, all of which are rooted in Western ideals. They also emphasize that caregiver sensitivity may be culturally defined and thus differ among societies. Consequently, traditional measures of attachment, such as the strange situation, may not be relevant in all cultures. For instance, in Eastern cultures, such as Japan, dependence and accommodation are encouraged in children. Furthermore, babies in those cultures generally experience less separation from their caregivers and subsequently may be more stressed by the strange situation than American babies. These cultural differences may explain, in part, why Japanese babies are more likely to be classified as insecure-ambivalent than are babies from the United States. However, with the acknowledgment that sensitive parenting, the secure base, and competence may differ in expressed form across cultures, attachment theory is still useful in understanding the power of parent-child relationships in later significant relationships.

Internal Working Models

Central to attachment theory is the proposition that early attachment relationships provide a basis for representations of self and others in social relationships beyond the parent-child dyad. These *internal working models* (IWMs) are hypothesized to

become so deeply ingrained that they influence feelings, thoughts, and behaviors with significant others at both the conscious and unconscious level. For example, if the caregiver is consistently responsive to the child's needs, she or he will feel confident, secure, and self-assured when introduced to novel settings. In contrast, if the caregiver is unresponsive to or rejecting of the child, she or he may develop an IWM about the self as being unworthy of care; interpersonal relationships are expected to be rejecting or neglectful, and the social world is viewed as hostile and unwelcoming. Thus, early relationships affect a child's "felt security," a significant developmental phenomenon that provides the child with sufficient emotional and cognitive sustenance to allow for the active exploration of the social environment.

In accord with their internalized expectations about the social world, children act in ways that confirm these beliefs. For example, if a child has negative expectations of peers, he or she is likely to think that an ambiguously intended harmful event was intentionally caused. The child is also more likely to choose to react in aggressive ways toward the perceived provocateur, increasing the likelihood that the peer will respond in a hostile manner in return. Like a self-fulfilling prophecy, IWMs cause individuals to behave in ways in which others fulfill their expectations, strengthening and reinforcing their original schemas. Consequently, IWMs become more difficult to modify with increasing age.

Friendships

Consistent with the assumption that IWMs are carried forward from relationship to relationship, significant associations exist between security of attachment in the parent-child relationships and the quality of children's close dyadic friendships. Friendships typically comprise the first significant nonfamilial relationship that children develop with others. Friendships may be defined as reciprocal, egalitarian relationships in which both partners acknowledge the relationship and treat each other as equals. Friendships are typically characterized by companionship, a shared history, and mutual affection.

Children with secure attachments to parents have more friends and their friendships are of better quality than those of insecurely attached children. Indeed, interactions between friendship dyads comprising two securely attached members are more positive, fair, intimate, and responsive than interactions within dyads comprising only one securely attached member. Moreover, securely attached adolescents are viewed by their best friends as being more altruistic and more conciliatory after conflict; also, they are more satisfied with their friendships than the friends of anxious-avoidant or anxious-ambivalent adolescents. While there generally are associations between parent-child attachments and later peer and friend relationships, a child's attachment relationship to parents is not absolutely deterministic of their later relationships with friends. There are children who are insecurely attached to parents and yet form high-quality friendships. In this way, a good friendship may compensate for the child's insecure attachment to parents.

Wyndol Furman has interviewed young adolescents to explore their IWMs of friendship. Adolescents classified as having secure working models of friendship, or who recounted their relationships in a coherent way and reported that their friendships were influential and valuable, reported more warmth and support in their relationships. Adolescents who were categorized as having dismissing IWMs of friendship, or who had little interest in caregiving and support seeking from friends, also reported that their friendships were unsupportive and lacked warmth; individuals with preoccupied IWMs of friendship who described overconcern for their friends' problems and were vague, angry, or passive in their descriptions of their friendships were more likely than the other groups to be in relationships that had power imbalances.

Finally, the quality of early parent-child attachment relationships predicts the quality of relationships with friends; this association is stronger for older children and adolescents than for younger children who may still rely on parents as their primary attachment figures. As Ainsworth suggested, attachment working models seem to be more influential for friendship development and maintenance as children enter adolescence, when intimacy and social support become more central features of friendship.

Peer Relationships

Given an IWM that the parent is available and responsive, the young child feels confident, secure, and self-assured when introduced to novel settings.

Thus, felt security provides the child with sufficient emotional and cognitive sustenance to allow the active exploration of the social environment. Exploration results in active and interactive play, which, in turn, leads to the development of social competence and interpersonal problem-solving skills. From this perspective, there is a clear association between security of attachment in infancy and the quality of children's social skills and competencies. Indeed, because they demonstrate socially skilled behavior, securely attached children are generally accepted and liked by their peers.

Alternatively, the development of an insecure infant-parent attachment relationship appears to result in the child's developing an IWM that interpersonal relationships are rejecting or neglectful. In turn, the social world is perceived as a battleground that must either be attacked or escaped from. For the insecure and angry child, opportunities for peer play and interaction are nullified by displays of hostility and aggression in the peer group. Such behavior, in turn, results in the child's forced (by the peer group) lack of opportunities to benefit from the communication, negotiation, and perspective-taking experiences that will typically lead to the development of a normal and adaptive childhood. For the insecure and wary or anxious child, opportunities for peer play and interaction are nullified by the child herself or himself. Consequently, social and emotional fearfulness prevail to the point at which the benefits of peer interaction are practically impossible to obtain. Thus, because they demonstrate socially unskilled aggressive or fearful behavior, insecurely attached children are often rejected by the peer group.

Romantic Relationships

Like friendship, romantic relationships are voluntary, reciprocal, and egalitarian associations that provide partners with companionship, intimacy, and support. Unique to romantic relationships, partners are attracted to one another, share feelings of love, and engage in sexual behaviors. Romantic relationships also differ from friendships in that they become more obligatory and exclusive over time, especially if the relationship is publically formalized.

Empirical links between security of attachment in infancy and early childhood and subsequent romantic relationships are beginning to emerge. Preliminary evidence suggests that early secure attachment predicts more positive feelings, felt security, and support, and less negative behavior in romantic relationships over 20 years later. These associations are often indirect, being explained, in part, by social competence and peer acceptance during childhood and secure friendships in adolescence. Additional research has indicated that securely attached adolescents interact positively with romantic partners, even if they were *not* securely attached to mothers as infants.

In summary, researchers have revealed stability between individuals' attachment representations with caregivers in infancy and childhood, their friendships in childhood and adolescence, and their romantic relationships in adulthood. Empirical examinations of these representations suggest that individuals have both a general working model of others as well as domain-specific representations of relationships (e.g., parent-child relationships, friendships, and romantic relationships).

Kenneth H. Rubin and Kristina L. McDonald

See also Love; Personal Identity, Development of; Self, Development of; Social Cognition

Further Readings

Ainsworth, M., Blehar, M., Waters, E., & Wall, S. (1978). *Patterns of attachment.* Hillsdale, NJ: Erlbaum.

Booth-LaForce, C., & Kerns, K. A. (2009). Child-parent attachment relationships, peer relationships, and peer-group functioning. In K. H. Rubin, W. M. Bukowski, & B. Laursen (Eds.), *Handbook of peer interactions, relationships, and groups* (pp. 490–507). New York, NY: Guilford.

Bowlby, J. (1969). *Attachment and loss: Attachment* (Vol. 1). New York, NY: Basic Books.

Cassidy, J., & Shaver, P. R. (Eds.). (2008). *Handbook of attachment: Theory, research, and clinical applications* (2nd ed.). New York, NY: Guilford.

Furman, W. (2001). Working models of friendships. *Journal of Social and Personal Relationships, 18,* 583–602.

Hinde, R. A. (1987). *Individuals, relationships and culture.* Cambridge, UK: Cambridge University Press.

Rothbaum, F., Weisz, J., Pott, M., Miyake, K., & Morelli, G. (2000). Attachment and culture: Security in the United States and Japan. *American Psychologist, 55,* 1093–1104.

Youngblade, L. M., & Belsky, J. (1992). Parent-child antecedents of 5-year-olds' close friendships: A longitudinal analysis. *Developmental Psychology, 28,* 700–713.

RELIGION AND PSYCHIATRY

Religion is an organized system of beliefs, practices, and rituals designed to facilitate closeness to the sacred or transcendent—whether that be God or a higher power (in Western traditions) or ultimate truth or reality (in Eastern traditions). Religion includes specific beliefs and personal commitment to those beliefs, which reflects their overall religiousness and religious motivation (the degree to which religious beliefs and goals are the person's ultimate concern in life). Another essential aspect of religion is its emphasis on one's relationship with and responsibility to others living together in a community that shares common beliefs, rituals, and practices. Besides attending religious services and other forms of involvement in religious community activities, the religious person may also be involved in private religious activities such as prayer, the reading of sacred scriptures, and forms of worship and ritual that are performed when alone.

Psychiatry is the specialty of physicians who receive special training to treat the many forms of mental illness that disrupt a person's sense of peacefulness, hope, and meaning in life. That disruption is often so severe that the person is no longer able to function in healthy ways in their social interactions, work, or recreational activities. Although psychiatry is mainly concerned with the negative or dysfunctional aspects of mental health (depression, mania, anxiety, psychosis, personality disorders, substance abuse, etc.), it also seeks to enhance the positive side of mental, emotional, and behavioral health. Positive mental health has to do with happiness and well-being, being satisfied with life, and having joy, peace, hope, optimism, meaning, and purpose as one pursues life's goals. It also involves having satisfying long-term social relationships and engaging in work that is productive and meaningful. Psychiatry is also concerned with mental states that fall in between positive mental health and mental disorder. This includes helping people deal with a life that, while not dysfunctional, has become unsatisfying, boring, meaningless, or hopeless. This entry focuses on the relationship of religion to mental illness, mental health, and well-being.

Historical Background

For the last 100 years or so, religion has been viewed within psychiatry as related to neurosis and unhealthy functioning. Indeed, Sigmund Freud described religion as an "obsessional neurosis" and psychologist Albert Ellis suggested that the less religious that people are the more emotionally healthy they will be. Other psychiatrists have emphasized that religion is incompatible with mental health, adversely affects self-esteem, self-actualization, and mastery and disrupts healthy sexual functioning. Such opinions, however, are not derived from systematic research but rather from personal experiences and clinical exposure to patients with mental illness who often express their religion in pathological ways.

Recent Research

Within the past two decades, however, systematic research has begun to examine the relationship between religious involvement and mental health in surveys of community populations and persons with physical rather than mental illness. It has been discovered that religion is often used to cope with stresses involving loss of health, loss of loved ones, or other traumatic losses. Harold Koenig and his colleagues have summarized this research in a number of books and articles. These reviews have uncovered over 1,000 studies that have examined relationships between religion and both negative mental health (depression, anxiety, etc.) and positive mental health (happiness, well-being, hope, meaning and purpose, etc.). Nearly two thirds of these studies have found that the religious person on average experiences better mental health, fewer negative emotions, greater social support and is less likely to be engaged in substance abuse. Most of this research has come from the United States, but studies reporting similar findings have been conducted around the world, including Canada, South and Central America, the United Kingdom, Europe, the Middle East, and other continents. While most of these studies are epidemiological in design (cross-sectional or prospective observational studies), a number of randomized clinical trials have been conducted in patients with depression and anxiety disorders, finding that religious interventions often result in faster improvement compared to traditional secular psychotherapy or no treatment. These studies include interventions from a variety of faith perspectives, including Christian, Muslim, and Buddhist approaches.

Besides studies showing lower rates of depression, faster recovery from depression, and faster response to religious therapies, an even larger research base

shows relationships between religious involvement and positive emotions. Of the more than 350 studies that have now examined relationships between well-being or happiness and religious involvement, over three quarters report that the religious person experiences significantly more of these positive emotions than the less religious or nonreligious person. With regard to substance abuse, the results are similar. In the over 375 studies that have now been done, over 80% indicate that the religious person is less likely to drink, use drugs, or smoke cigarettes. These studies have often been done in young persons whose entire lives are ahead of them. Better mental health and healthier lifestyles translates into better physical health as well, which itself influences mental health.

Explanations

Why is this so? How might religion enhance mental health? First, religion can provide a positive, optimistic worldview that gives life meaning and purpose and provides hope. Second, religion often provides rules and regulations to help guide behavior. Third, religion may enhance social interactions by its emphasis on forgiveness, thankfulness, gratitude, generosity, and other attitudes and activities that foster healthy interpersonal relationships. As a result, religion not only helps people to cope but may also reduce the amount of stress that they must cope with.

Not Always Positive

Despite the many contributions that religion makes to mental health, this does not mean that the religious person will always be healthier and happier than the less religious or secular person. Religion can be at times associated with excessive guilt, anxious ruminations, obsessions, prejudice, and can therefore lead to a restricted and limited life, rather than a fuller and freer one. People with psychological problems often turn to religion for comfort, and while religion helps them cope, it may not always eliminate the personality disturbances or the inherited genetic vulnerabilities to mental illness that continue to persist, although moderated to some extent by religion. Religion, then, can be used in neurotic or mentally unhealthy ways to justify actions, judge others, or become the object of ruminations and obsessions. Pastoral counselors—that is, those who are counselors at the master's or PhD level who also have religious education (seminary, divinity school, or clinical pastoral education)—are trained to address these issues. Pastoral counselors are different from community clergy, who may have little or no training in dealing with mental health issues.

Conclusion

In the balance, though, religion is an important resource for mental health, a resource that most mental health professionals—including psychiatrists—have ignored for a long time. In this day and age with research accumulating, that is no longer possible.

Harold G. Koenig

See also Behavioral Therapy; Emotion and Psychopathology; Happiness

Further Readings

Koenig, H. G. (2005). *Faith and mental health: Religious resources for healing*. Philadelphia, PA: Templeton Foundation Press.

Koenig, H. G. (2008). *Medicine, religion, and health: Where science & spirituality meet*. Philadelphia, PA: Templeton Foundation Press.

Koenig, H. G. (2009). Research on religion, spirituality, and mental health: A review. *Canadian Journal of Psychiatry, 54*(5), 283–291.

Koenig, H. G., King, D. E., & Meador, K. G. (2011). *Handbook of religion and health* (2nd ed.). New York, NY: Oxford University Press.

Koenig, H. G., McCullough, M. E., & Larson, D. B. (2001). *Handbook of religion and health*. New York, NY: Oxford University Press.

REPRESENTATIONAL THEORY OF MIND

According to the *representational theory of mind* (RTM), mental representations are often involved when we have a mental state or engage in a mental process. Mental representations are symbols that exist in the mind. Being symbols, they have semantic properties; that is, they have meaning or content and so are about particular things or states of affairs. This entry provides a description of the most prominent historical and contemporary versions of RTM along with a description of the key debates surrounding RTM.

Historical Versions of RTM

RTM was prominent in the modern period of philosophy of the 17th and 18th centuries, being associated with such philosophers as René Descartes, John Locke, David Hume, and Immanuel Kant. Advocates of the theory in this period tended to advance RTM as a theory about such familiar mental states as beliefs, desires, intentions, and so on (mental states generally known as propositional attitudes), and about mental processes of thinking involving such states. They were also prone to regard mental representations as being images that are introspectable, private, and immaterial.

The Return of RTM

With the rise of behaviorist views of the mind in both philosophy and psychology, traditional versions of RTM fell out of favor in the early decades of the 20th century, particularly in the English speaking world. However, as the limitations of behaviorism became apparent a new version of RTM was developed that came to dominate the newly emerging field of cognitive science in the 1960s and 1970s. Such a view has been given its clearest articulation and most thoroughgoing defense by the American philosopher Jerry Fodor. For Fodor, the representations involved in having a propositional attitude such as a belief or a desire are language-like rather than imagistic so that, for example, believing that dogs bark involves having a sentence in one's mind that means *dogs bark*. Fodor labels the language that the mind employs the *language of thought* (LOT). LOT is a nonnatural language that will be shared by all members of the human species regardless of what language they speak. Being a language, LOT has a finite number of basic symbols and a finite number of syntactic rules for combining those symbols to create larger complex structures such as sentences. The meaning of a sentence of LOT is a product of the meaning of its component words and its syntactic structure.

Fodor is a physicalist in the respect that he thinks that the mind is ultimately a physical thing whose mental properties are determined by its physical properties. Consequently, he thinks that the symbols of LOT are physically embodied in the brain. However, any given LOT sentence is multiply realizable in the sense that its instances can take a variety of different physical forms in the brain of distinct individuals. For Fodor, whether or not an instance of a particular sentence of LOT in one's mind expresses a belief, a desire, or whatever, depends on how it is processed by the mental mechanisms that have access to it. Sentences that express beliefs are processed in the distinctive way that is characteristic of the belief relation and so on for all the other types of propositional attitude relations. This idea is often figuratively expressed by saying that when one has a particular belief, one has a relevant sentence of LOT in one's belief box; that when one has a particular desire, one has the relevant sentence of LOT in one's desire box; and so on.

Fodor supplements his theory about propositional attitudes with a theory about mental processes. According to this theory, mental processing involves the manipulation of symbols of LOT by means of computation. Hence, the mind is a computer. A computer, on Fodor's conception, is a symbol manipulating system that takes syntactically structured symbols as input and generates syntactically structured symbols as output by means of the application of symbol manipulating rules. Although the symbols have semantic properties so that a computer's activity can be characterized in semantic terms (as processing information or solving problems), the computer will have no access to those semantic properties.

Fodor argues that his version of RTM, unlike its competitors, explains several salient facts about the mind. Prominent among these is that thought is systematic in that anyone capable of believing that object *a* stands in relation *R* to object *b* (for example, that John loves Jill) is also capable of thinking that *b* stands in relation *R* to *a* (for example that Jill loves John). Fodor has also argued that his version of RTM has scientific support in that it underlies most mainstream work in cognitive science. This claim was perhaps true when first made by Fodor in the 1970s and reflects the fact that the theory can be extended (as it was by many cognitive scientists) to apply to mental states and processes not recognized by commonsense psychology, including those that reside at the unconscious or subpersonal level. However, the 1980s witnessed the rise of an alternative connectionist approach that is widely adopted within contemporary cognitive science.

The Connectionist Challenge

According to connectionism, mental processing is supported by the activity of neural networks consisting of simple units that are connected to one another so that the activation of one unit can be communicated to other units in the network, so pushing them toward a state of activation. In this way, a typical connectionist network serves to transform patterns of activation at an input layer of units into patterns of activation at an output layer. Because the patterns of activation represent things or states of affairs, the network, just like an orthodox computer, processes information or solves problems. Hence, connectionism can be viewed as a version of RTM, although many connectionists would resist such a characterization as they are keen to emphasize their opposition to traditional versions of RTM such as Fodor's. The representations processed by a connectionist network do not typically have syntactic properties. Moreover, because the network's "knowledge" is stored en masse over the connections between its constituent units, it does not store information by means of syntactically structured symbols. For his part, Fodor has objected to this new version of RTM by arguing that it cannot explain the systematicity of thought.

The Chinese Room Argument

One of the most widely discussed philosophical objections to Fodor's version of RTM is the Chinese room argument devised by John Searle. Searle, who has no grasp of Chinese, imagines himself trapped in a room containing batches of sheets of paper with Chinese symbols written on them. The room also contains a book written in English instructing Searle how to correlate symbols of Chinese with symbols of Chinese. Further sheets with Chinese symbols written on them are posted into the room. Searle responds to this input by executing the English instructions that involve considering the syntactic properties of the input symbols and correlating them with symbols written on the batch of sheets. These symbols are then copied onto blank sheets that are in turn posted out of the room. The input symbols are actually questions written in Chinese and the output symbols are sensible answers to those questions so that Searle's symbol processing behavior mimics that of a competent speaker of Chinese. Searle's point is that he does exactly what a computer does, yet he doesn't understand Chinese. Hence, he concludes, no computer, however it is programmed, is capable of understanding Chinese or any other language, a conclusion that he generalizes to all cognitive capacities.

Searle's argument has been widely discussed but no general consensus as to its power has emerged. A common response made on behalf of RTM is the so-called systems reply, a version of which can be described in the following terms. Advocates of RTM are not committed to the claim that computation is sufficient for cognition, only that computation plays a fundamental role in our mental lives. If we should accept that Searle in the room does not understand Chinese, this is because he simulates only a limited element of the behavior of a Chinese speaker. In particular, he does not respond to nonsymbolic input. For example, if a ferocious dog were let into the room Searle wouldn't produce the Chinese equivalent of *help* or *get me out of here*. Moreover, Searle does not respond to Chinese symbols by engaging in relevant nonsymbolic behavior. For example, if a note were posted into the room saying, "There is a bomb under your chair, and to defuse it you need to invert your chair" in Chinese, he would not respond by inverting the chair. Now suppose we built a robot containing a powerful computer. The computer is fed information from a video camera attached to the robot and issues instructions that cause the robot to move around its environment and manipulate objects. In short, the computer is hooked up to the robot's perceptual and motor systems. Also suppose that the computer is programmed in such a way that it responds to Chinese symbols in a way that is coherently related to their meaning and that this sometimes involves engaging in nonsymbolic behavior. Moreover, suppose that it sometimes produces appropriate symbols of Chinese in response to nonsymbolic impingements. Then perhaps the robot as a whole (as opposed to any of its internal subsystems) would understand Chinese. And its ability to understand Chinese would be a product of its computational activity so that that activity would have to be appealed to in order to explain how the robot understands.

Conclusion

In sum, RTM constitutes an enduring theory as to the nature of mind and cognition. Its contemporary versions, particularly as developed and defended by Fodor, are currently both prominent and popular. However, they are subject to potentially powerful philosophical and empirical challenges.

Mark John Cain

See also Atomism About Concepts; Concepts, Philosophical Issues; Concepts and Language; Conscious Thinking; Folk Psychology; Realism and Instrumentalism; Thinking

Further Readings

Cain, M. J. (2002). *Fodor: Language, mind and philosophy.* Cambridge, UK: Polity Press.

Crane, T. (2003). *The mechanical mind* (2nd ed.). London, UK: Routledge.

Fodor, J. A. (2008). *LOT 2: The language of thought revisited.* Oxford, UK: Oxford University Press.

Haugeland, J. (1997). *Mind design II.* Cambridge, MA: MIT Press.

Searle, J. (1980). Mind, brains, and programs. *Behavioral and Brain Sciences, 3,* 417–424.

REPRESENTATIONS, DEVELOPMENT OF

The main focus of this entry is the development of conceptual representations, in particular the representation of objects, spatial relations, and events. A secondary focus is the differentiation of conceptual from perceptual representations. By conceptual representation is meant the construal or meaningful interpretation of perceptual and linguistic information. A common assumption in the field is that such interpretations are explicit (i.e., have the potential to be brought to conscious awareness), whereas it is known that many aspects of perceptual representations are implicit (i.e., cannot be brought to awareness). In the mature organism, perception is suffused with conceptual interpretation, and it is difficult to disentangle the two, but the two kinds of representation follow somewhat different developmental courses. Infants come with few, if any, interpretations of the world but rapidly form perceptual categories of what objects look, sound, and feel like and the kinds of movements they make or are made with them. In some cases, quite detailed perceptual categories appear by 3 months of age. It is not known exactly when conceptual interpretation begins, but it is in evidence at least by 6 months and possibly considerably earlier. In contrast to perceptual categories of objects, early object concepts tend to be global or general in nature. They slowly differentiate into finer grained concepts, but the initial concepts form the bedrock of the conceptual system and remain throughout life.

Early Object and Event Concepts

The traditional view of concept formation, that of Jean Piaget, was that the first 1½ years of life are a period of exclusively sensorimotor development, in which infants learn to recognize objects and the daily events of life and to respond appropriately to them. Conceptualization was said to develop slowly from these perceptual and motor routines, eventually allowing infants to think about objects or events in their absence, to recall the past, to solve problems mentally, and to imagine the future. However, experimental findings in the last two decades have shown that conceptual activity begins much earlier in life, perhaps as early as a few months of age. Infants do learn to recognize and respond appropriately to objects and events in the first 2 years, often in quite a detailed way. For example, they can perceptually differentiate dogs from cats as early as 3 months. However, they also begin to conceptually interpret objects and events quite early in this period, albeit in a more global, less detailed fashion.

A matter of controversy in the field is what, if any, innate proclivities may be required to begin interpreting perceptual input. One proposal is that certain core knowledge is innate, such as that objects move on continuous paths and are solid in the sense that two objects cannot occupy the same space. A somewhat different proposal is that core concepts need not be built in but various aspects of perception, particularly motion through space, are preferentially attended from birth and are redescribed in simplified format to create the first conceptual representations. Still another proposal, often associated with connectionist learning models, is that conceptual knowledge can be derived through perception itself without any innate biases or redescription into another format.

By around 6 months of age, conceptualization is shown by infants beginning to recall absent objects and events. Evidence for conceptual representation of events is shown by deferred imitation, a form of nonverbal recall in which observed events are reproduced after a delay. Recall of a past event requires that a conceptualization of it be brought to awareness. Around the same age, evidence for global object concepts such as *animal* and *vehicle* is shown by familiarization-dishabituation studies, in which infants are given several little models of animals to handle and then are given a new animal or a vehicle. By 7 months, infants show global object concepts by dishabituating to (increasing their interactions with) any vehicle after interacting with animals (and vice versa). Visual similarity of shape aids global conceptualization but is not essential, as

shown by 9-month-olds differentiating little models of birds and airplanes, all of which are quite similar in appearance. Around this age infants also broadly generalize from one instance of a class to another, as shown by their being willing to substitute new members from the same conceptual class when imitating. For example, after seeing an event in which a little model of a dog is given a drink, infants as young as 9 months will haphazardly choose a little model of another dog or any other animal to imitate this event but will not choose a vehicle or other artifact.

Because of the prevalence of Piagetian theory, experimental study of infant conceptual representations began relatively recently. However, research findings such as those just described indicate that the course of the development of object concepts over the first 2 years tends to begin at a global or superordinate-like level, such as animal, vehicle, furniture, and plant and then gradually differentiates to more detailed concepts, such as dog, car, chair, and flower. The onset of language understanding near the end of the first year contributes to this differentiation, because the language children hear is more differentiated than the sketchy concepts they first bring to the language-learning task and thus emphasizes details that previously may be unattended. The initial global concepts, however, organize the further learning that conceptually differentiates one animal or artifact from another, thus leading to a hierarchical system of object concepts. This organization lasts throughout life, barring brain damage. The way the conceptual system breaks down in semantic dementia testifies to the foundational nature of global concepts such as animal; detailed information is lost first and global information is the longest lasting.

The first object and event concepts appear to be heavily influenced by spatial information, especially motion through space. From birth, infants are attracted to motion and in the early months are more apt to notice that something moves and even the kind of path that it takes than what it looks like. Hence, differences in motion, as well as contingent interactions between objects (as in peekaboo games or goal-directed actions), are likely bases for the initial concepts of *animal* and *nonanimal*. One view is that a first conceptualization of animal is a thing that starts motion by itself and interacts with other objects from a distance, whereas a nonanimal either doesn't move at all or, if it does, doesn't start motion by itself and doesn't interact with other objects from a distance. Again, simple notions such as these remain with us throughout life, even when sometimes contradicted by more detailed biological knowledge.

Early Relational Concepts

It is more difficult to differentiate early concepts of spatial relations from perception of them. However, extensive research on relations such as containment, support, and occlusion suggests that at least by 3 to 4 months of age infants are beginning to conceptually interpret these relations. For example, 3-month-olds act as if they expect that when an object goes behind a screen or other occluder it will be hidden; hence, they dishabituate (look longer) if there is a window in the occluder and the object comes into view as it passes the window. Similarly, infants this age look longer at a wide object moving behind a thin occluder when it sticks out of either side than if it is completely hidden. It does not seem plausible that such expectations could be taught by perception alone but instead seem to require some interpretation of what is perceived. The conceptualization of spatial relations, like that of objects, begins in a general or global fashion and gradually becomes more detailed. For example, a concept of containment appears to begin without any quantitative understanding of the relationship between height or width of a container and what it can contain. Such variables are gradually learned over the course of the first year.

Spatial relational concepts are somewhat more subject to linguistic restructuring than are object concepts. Language helps differentiate global object concepts (e.g., children hear the words *dog* and *cat* more often than *animal,* and *car* and *truck* more often than *vehicle*) but rarely restructures object domains. In contrast, spatial relational concepts may be at least partially restructured by language. For example, Korean distinguishes degree of fit (tight versus loose), whether the fit is of a containment or support relation; for example, the same word is used to describe a ring on a finger as a finger in a ring. Thus, the Korean language carves up the spatial domain in a somewhat different way than does English, and Korean-speaking children begin to differ in their spatial categorizations from English-speaking children by the end of the second year. In spite of the fact that both cultures have concepts of containment, support, and tight fit, these differences

in the way they are accustomed to think about them remain in adulthood.

The Developmental Course of Conceptual and Perceptual Representations

In the sense of developing appropriate expectations and actions vis-à-vis objects, young children typically know more about objects and events than they can express, and this is only partly due to limited vocabulary. Although even young infants develop many expectations about how objects behave in the world and also learn how to interact with them successfully, this does not necessarily imply conceptual understanding of that behavior. This divergence between growth of perceptual knowledge and conceptualization is at least partly responsible for what are known as U-shaped developmental curves, in which infants are successful at some tasks while toddlers fail and older children are once again successful. For example, if infants are shown an object dropping to the floor and then a shelf is placed between the object and the floor and a screen placed in front so they cannot see the actual landing place, they expect the object to remain on the shelf rather than continue down to the floor. However, in similar situations 2-year-olds will search for the object on the floor rather than on the shelf. Prediction as a task requirement is a conceptual task, requiring activation of a conceptual representation of the physical world, which is different from perceptual expectations of how the objects behave in the world. Discrepancies between the two kinds of representation often continue into adulthood, indicating that these two forms of representation can exist throughout life without one always influencing the other.

Jean M. Mandler

See also Concepts, Development of; Event Memory, Development; Knowledge Acquisition in Development

Further Readings

Choi, S. (2006). Influence of language-specific input on spatial cognition: Categories of containment. *First Language, 26,* 207–232.

Hodges, J. R., Graham, N., & Patterson, K. (1995). Charting the progression of semantic dementia: Implications for the organisation of semantic memory. *Memory, 3,* 463–495.

Hood, B., Carey, S., & Prasada, S. (2000). Predicting the outcomes of physical events: Two-year-olds fail to reveal knowledge of solidity and support. *Child Development, 71,* 1540–1554.

Luo, Y., & Baillargeon, R. (2005). When the ordinary seems unexpected: Evidence for incremental physical knowledge in young infants. *Cognition, 95,* 297–328.

Mandler, J. M. (2004). *The foundations of mind: Origins of conceptual thought.* New York, NY: Oxford University Press.

Mandler, J. M., & McDonough, L. (1996). Drinking and driving don't mix: Inductive generalization in infancy. *Cognition, 50,* 307–335.

McCloskey, M., & Kohl, D. (1983). Naive physics: The curvilinear impetus principle and its role in interactions with moving objects. *Journal of Experimental Psychology: Learning, Memory, & Cognition, 9,* 146–156.

Piaget, J. (1952). *The origins of intelligence in the child.* New York, NY: International Universities Press.

Quinn, P. C., Eimas, P. D., & Rosenkrantz, S. L. (1993). Evidence for representations of perceptually similar natural categories by 3-month-old and 4-month-old infants. *Perception, 22,* 463–475.

Rogers, T. T., & McClelland, J. L. (2004). *Semantic cognition: A parallel distributed processing approach.* Cambridge, MA: MIT Press.

Spelke, E. S., Breinlinger, K., Macomber, J., & Jacobson, K. (1992). Origins of knowledge. *Psychological Review, 99,* 605–632.

REPRESENTATIVENESS HEURISTIC

This entry provides a brief explanation and background for the *representativeness heuristic*, a cognitive process hypothesized to underlie people's intuitive judgments of probability.

Heuristics and Biases

The representativeness heuristic is a theoretical construct that forms part of the influential *heuristics and biases framework* for explaining intuitive judgment in humans pioneered by Daniel Kahneman and Amos Tversky in the 1970s. From this perspective, because of their limited time, knowledge, and computational ability, in general people cannot make judgments according to the often complex normative rules of logic, probability theory, and statistics. Instead, they have to resort to simpler judgment heuristics that exploit *natural assessments*. Natural assessments benefit from naturally existing propensities of memory and perception that are conveniently available and easily assessed. These judgmental heuristics are often useful, but sometimes they lead to systematic and serious cognitive biases.

In regard to confidence (probability) judgment, the key notion has been variable substitution, according to which the complex judgment of probability is substituted with a simpler natural assessment. Assessment of probability in the sense implied by probability theory and statistics involves consideration of all possible outcomes and their frequencies of occurrence. In the face of this complexity it is proposed that people substitute probability with a subjective variable that is conveniently available and easier to assess. The representativeness heuristic suggests that the degree to which an instance or event is representative of a category is used as a proxy for the probability that the instance or event belongs to the category, as when you assess the probability that a person is a lawyer by assessing how similar he or she is to your stereotype for a typical lawyer.

Although representativeness is a useful guide to probability in many real-life circumstances, because it does not obey the rules of probability theory, use of the heuristic is claimed to produce a number of biases, or cognitive illusions, in probability judgment. Two classical demonstrations of such biases are *base-rate neglect* and the *conjunction fallacy*.

Base-Rate Neglect

If you are in Florida and encounter a male with a short haircut driving a Chevrolet Corvette, you may consider the probability that he is an astronaut (assuming that a clean-cut male driving a sports car close to Cape Canaveral fits your stereotype for an astronaut). In this case, probability theory implies that you should take into account the base rate of astronauts, which presumably is low also in Florida, and the modest reliability of hairstyle and car make as predictors of profession (per the celebrated Bayes's theorem of probability theory). Because people use the representativeness heuristic when they assess the probability that the person is an astronaut, it is proposed that they only take into account the similarity between the person and their stereotype for an astronaut, while neglecting the base-rate of astronauts. Because of this base-rate neglect, they get too captivated by the representativeness of the evidence. Likewise, even physicians tend to be too captivated by a positive result of a medical diagnosis test (e.g., for HIV), neglecting the often low prevalence (base-rate) of the disease in the population, thereby overestimating the probability that the patient actually has the disease.

The Conjunction Fallacy

Another classic judgment bias that is claimed to derive from use of the representativeness heuristic is the conjunction fallacy. Consider the following person description:

> Linda is 31 years old, single, outspoken, and very bright. She majored in philosophy. As a student, she was deeply concerned with issues of discrimination and social justice and also participated in antinuclear demonstrations.

What is the probability of each of the following?

1. Linda is a bank teller.
2. Linda is a bank teller and is active in the feminist movement.

As noted by Tversky and Kahneman in 1983, most people assess the conjunction that Linda is a bank teller and a feminist (B&F) to be more likely than one of its constituents, that Linda is a bank teller (B). This violates a basic rule of logic and probability theory, which states that a conjunction can never be more probable than one of its constituents. More prosaically, it can never be more probable that a person is both a bank teller and a feminist than that the person is a bank teller per se, because the former set (B&F) is a subset of the latter (B), and any person who is a member of the B&F is necessarily also a member of B, but the reverse does not hold. The account proposed by the representativeness heuristic is that Linda is perceived as very unrepresentative of the category bank tellers and very representative of the category feminists, while the conjunction is perceived to be of intermediate representativeness. People will therefore assess a high probability that Linda is a feminist, a low probability that she is a bank teller. The probability of the conjunction falls in between these two constituent probabilities, leading to a violation of probability theory, in essence because similarity judgments do not obey the rules of probability theory.

It is clear that people's probability judgments are often affected by perceived similarity relations and that people robustly produce these and a number of other cognitive biases, relative to the rules of probability theory. However, throughout the years, the heuristic has also been criticized, for instance, for being a too vague construct, and its exact role in producing these judgment biases is still an area of active research in psychology.

Peter Juslin

See also Availability Heuristic; Belief and Judgment; Debiasing; Similarity

Further Readings

Gilovich, T., Griffin, D., & Kahneman, D. (2002). *Heuristics and biases: The psychology of intuitive judgment*. Cambridge, UK: Cambridge University Press.
Kahneman, D., & Frederick, S. (2002). Representativeness revisited: Attribute substitution in intuitive judgment. In T. Gilovich, D. W. Griffin, & D. Kahneman (Eds.), *Heuristics and biases: The psychology of intuitive judgment* (pp. 49–81). New York, NY: Cambridge University Press.
Tversky, A., & Kahneman, D. (1983). Extensional versus intuitive reasoning: The conjunction fallacy in probability judgment. *Psychological Review, 91,* 293–315.

RESENTMENT

This entry defines the emotion of resentment, contrasts it with envy and *ressentiment*, links it with research on relative deprivation, and discusses its consequences. Resentment is an emotion we feel when we suffer a perceived wrong. It can be a powerful, motivating state, characterized by a blend of anger, bitterness, and indignation. The hallmark of resentment is that people feeling it believe that they have a justified moral complaint against another person or general state of affairs. They believe they have suffered undeservedly. Consequently, they feel resentment.

Resentment Contrasted With Other Emotions

It is useful to contrast resentment with envy. Envy involves a painful awareness of another person's desired advantage and the blend of discontent, ill will, and resentment that this awareness can produce. Thus, some sense of resentment or sense of injustice seems to be a common ingredient of envy. However, scholars emphasize that the resentment found in envy is highly subjective because it lacks social approval. Furthermore, it often results from a need to rationalize the ill will associated with the emotion. In its purest form, resentment follows a clearer-cut, seemingly objective, injustice and enjoys greater social approval. In some cases of objective injustice, resentment can appear as moral outrage or righteous indignation as was the case in the race riots of the 1960s and 1970s in the United States. Like envy, resentment can be fueled and exaggerated by rationalization. The wrong may even be imagined. In some cases, it may have originated from envy. But compared to envy, it is less likely to spring from a questionable starting premise.

Another important distinguishing feature of resentment is that, unlike envy, it need not arise from a social comparison. Much of the social science research on resentment focuses on people's reactions to disadvantage, but the range of situations that cause resentment is actually much more than disadvantage. We can resent being ignored when we are entitled to have a say in a group decision, for example. We can resent an insult or injury. We can resent tax rates or university parking policies. In other words, we can resent both unfair procedures as well as unfair distributions. Envy, however, is nonsensical without an explicit social comparison.

Finally, the action tendencies associated with resentment are more evident than with envy. When people feel resentment, because they perceive that they have been unfairly treated, they are liable to take action to remedy the wrong. Examples of open political violence have been explained by noting the resentment caused by group members being deprived of something to which they feel entitled and deserving. Envy can lead to actions, but because the emotion is socially repugnant and unsanctioned, these actions are more likely to be covert.

It is also useful to distinguish resentment from ressentiment, an emotion derived from Nietzschean ideas and further developed by another German philosopher, Max Scheler, in the early 20th century. *Ressentiment* refers to a state of mind resulting from chronic impotence and inferiority. It entails a devaluing of what one secretly craves but cannot obtain. It is like resentment in that it is a negative emotion often containing anger and frequently linked to deprivation. However, unlike resentment, it is passive rather than active. Ressentiment, generally, leads to self-debilitating inaction as a means of numbing the pain of inferiority. In contrast, resentment often leads to action to redress the perceived wrong.

Relative Deprivation

In social science research, resentment is closely linked with the broad topic of relative deprivation. People feel relatively deprived when another person (egoistic relative deprivation) or group (fraternalistic relative deprivation) enjoys a relative advantage, especially an advantage that prompts rising expectations for oneself or one's group. Resentment occurs when people feel entitled to and deserving of this advantage. An example of egoistic relative deprivation would be resentment because a fellow employee receives a promotion to which one also feels entitled. An example of fraternalistic relative deprivation would be resentment because a member of another racial group gains unfair admission into a professional program, thereby taking the place potentially enjoyed by a member of one's own group. Research on relative deprivation, with resentment often being the signature response, has a long and rich history in psychology, sociology, politics, and economics.

Consequences of Resentment

Recent studies link deservingness with resentment and then to subsequent *schadenfreude*, or pleasure derived from another person's suffering. For example, people find misfortunes suffered by high status individuals to be pleasing. This pleasure seems largely explained by the initial resentment felt because the high status is often perceived as undeserved.

Additional research links the resentment felt toward hypocrites and the special pleasure that arises when they are exposed for their hypocrisy. It may be that hypocrites, by their moralizing statements and "holier than thou" demeanor, amount to moral reproaches from the perspective of those around them. This creates a penetrating form of resentment because the moral core of the observers is threatened. By the same token, when hypocrites suffer exposure, the moral table is turn upside down. A self-threatening "upward comparison" is transformed into a pleasing, self-boosting "downward comparison." Initial feelings of resentment in observers seem to enliven the subsequent *schaden-freude*, even producing a sense of poetic justice.

Resentment is often intense and can lead to extreme, sometimes violent actions. Because people feeling resentment believe they have been unjustly treated and wronged, they can correspondingly feel justified in redressing the wrong. However, the possibility of biased, exaggerated, construals of the wrong mean that the redressing actions are themselves wrong. Spiraling retaliatory actions can then ensue. Scholars speculate that many intergroup conflicts mirror this pattern. Clearly, resentment is an important human emotion that deserves careful and sustained study.

Richard H. Smith and David Ryan Schurtz

See also Emotion, Cultural Perspectives; Envy; Intergroup Conflict; Jealousy

Further Readings

Feather, N. T. (2006). Deservingness and emotions: Applying the structural model of deservingness to the analysis of affective reactions to outcomes. *European Review of Social Psychology, 17*, 38–73.

Monin, B., Sawyer, P., & Marquez, M. (2008). The rejection of moral rebels: Resenting those who do the right thing. *Journal of Personality and Social Psychology, 95*(1), 76–93.

Walker, I., & Smith, H. J. (Eds.). (2002). *Relative deprivation: Specification, development and integration.* Cambridge, UK: Cambridge University Press.

Retrieval Practice (Testing) Effect

The *testing effect* is a term used to describe the finding that taking a test on previously studied material leads to better long-term retention relative to restudying the material or not taking a test. Testing is often conceptualized as a neutral event in which the contents of memory are examined but left unchanged. However, the act of retrieving information from memory actually alters the retrieved memory by elaborating on the existing memory trace and/or creating additional retrieval routes. One consequence of these changes is that the probability of successful retrieval in the future is increased, making testing a potent mechanism for enhancing long-term retention. This entry provides a brief history

of testing effect research followed by a discussion of the generalizability of the effect, potential theoretical explanations, and factors that increase its efficacy.

History of Research on the Testing Effect

The idea that retrieving information from memory can increase retention has a long history. Philosophers and other scholars have long recognized the mnemonic benefits of retrieval practice: Aristotle, Francis Galton, and William James, among others, all described how repeatedly recalling information from memory improves its retention. Some early studies in the 1900s confirmed their pronouncements, but only recently have researchers investigated this phenomenon systematically. The early studies were conducted with students in classroom settings and to demonstrate that testing improved retention of course material. In the following decades, research on the testing effect was sporadic. Most studies during this period were part of the verbal learning tradition and investigated the memorial consequences of retrieval in laboratory settings using discrete verbal materials, such as lists of individual words or word pairs. Since the start of the 21st century, a resurgence of interest in the testing effect has arisen, leading to the publication of many studies that explored various theoretical explanations for the phenomenon as well as applications to educational contexts.

Generalizability of the Testing Effect

The testing effect is a robust phenomenon: The basic finding has been replicated over a hundred times and its generalizability is well established. Retrieval practice has been found to promote superior retention of many different types of information, both verbal and nonverbal. These types of information include nonsense syllables, word lists, foreign language vocabulary, general knowledge facts, scientific articles, textbook chapters, pictures, maps, and Chinese characters (among others). In addition, many studies have shown strong, positive effects of testing in a variety of real-world educational contexts, such as after-school programs for elementary school children, middle school classes, college courses, and medical education of residents and nurses. Although for practical reasons, most testing effect studies have used relatively short retention intervals (i.e., a few minutes to a few days), a number of studies have shown that testing produces superior long-term retention using much longer retention intervals of up to six months. Overall, much evidence exists to support the conclusion that retrieval practice promotes long-term retention of many different types of materials across a variety of different contexts.

Potential Theoretical Explanations

Several theoretical explanations have been proposed to account for the testing effect. One of the first proposed that taking a test after studying resulted in additional exposure to the material (i.e., relative to a control condition in which no test was taken) and this additional exposure produced the superior retention. However, this so-called total time hypothesis (also referred to as the amount-of-processing hypothesis) was disproved by subsequent studies that showed that taking a test led to better retention relative to restudying the material for an equivalent amount of time. Another possible explanation is that the effort involved in retrieval is responsible for the testing effect. One piece of evidence that supports the retrieval effort hypothesis is the finding that production tests (e.g., cued recall, fill-in-the-blank), which require greater retrieval effort, often produce better retention than recognition tests (e.g., multiple-choice, true or false). Yet another idea that helps explain the testing effect is *transfer-appropriate processing*, which holds that memory performance is enhanced to the extent that the processes during encoding match the processes required during retrieval. Thus, retrieving information while taking an initial test may lead to better performance on a subsequent test because the processes engaged on an initial test (i.e., retrieval practice) better match the processes required by the final test (relative to restudying or not taking a test). Finally, the idea of encoding variability provides one more possible explanation. Studying and taking a test represent distinct encoding events, and thus testing after studying may increase encoding variability. Increased encoding variability should result in the elaboration of the existing memory trace and/or the creation of additional retrieval routes to that trace. Although no single theory can explain all the extant findings, the last four theories are not mutually exclusive and can be considered complementary.

Factors That Increase the Efficacy of Retrieval Practice

The critical mechanism in learning from tests is successful retrieval. However, two other factors can increase the efficacy of testing: feedback and repetition. Testing often produces better retention than restudying even when feedback is not provided (provided performance on the initial test is reasonably high). Nevertheless, feedback can enhance learning from tests by enabling test takers to correct errors and maintain low-confidence correct responses, thereby increasing the probability of successful retrieval in the future. Repetition can also enhance learning from tests: A single test confers a substantial mnemonic benefit, but repeated testing leads to even better retention. Repeated testing is particularly effective if it is distributed or spaced out over time rather than massed together. Generally speaking, spaced practice usually leads to superior long-term retention relative to massed practice, a finding that has been termed the spacing effect.

Henry L. Roediger III and Andrew C. Butler

See also Desirable Difficulties Perspective on Learning; Rehearsal and Memory; Spacing Effect; Spacing Effect, Practical Applications

Further Readings

Butler, A. C., & Roediger, H. L., III. (2008). Feedback enhances the positive effects and reduces the negative effects of multiple-choice testing. *Memory & Cognition, 36,* 604–616.

Carrier, M., & Pashler, H. (1992). The influence of retrieval on retention. *Memory & Cognition, 20,* 633–642.

Karpicke, J. D., & Roediger, H. L., III. (2008). The critical importance of retrieval for learning. *Science, 15,* 966–968.

McDaniel, M. A., Roediger, H. L., III, & McDermott, K. B. (2007). Generalizing test-enhanced learning from the laboratory to the classroom. *Psychonomic Bulletin & Review, 14,* 200–206.

Roediger, H. L., III, & Karpicke, J. D. (2006). The power of testing memory: Basic research and implications for educational practice. *Perspectives on Psychological Science, 1,* 181–210.

S

SCHIZOPHRENIA

Schizophrenia is a severe, chronic, psychiatric syndrome affecting about 1% of the world's population. In 1911, psychiatrist Paul Eugen Bleuler first coined the term, and since then, a large body of research has been amassed. Research has primarily focused on better understanding the etiology and progression of schizophrenia, while attempting to improve the lives of those with the disorder. As discussed in this entry, contemporary views of schizophrenia involve a syndrome with characteristic clusters of symptoms very similar to those first described by Bleuler and attributes those symptoms to a neurodevelopmental process, by which early and late risk factors contribute to the onset and expression of the disorder. The entry then examines cognitive and neurobehavioral impairments observed in the disorder as well as approaches to treatment.

Clinical Symptomatology of Schizophrenia

Characteristic clinical features of schizophrenia are classified into positive, negative, and disorganized symptoms. Positive symptoms include hallucinations (e.g., hearing voices that others cannot) and delusions (e.g., a persecutory delusion, involving the belief that others intend to harm the individual). Individuals with a diagnosis of schizophrenia also exhibit negative symptoms, which are defined by profound disruption of emotional expression and/or experience and motivation, often resulting in social withdrawal and a drop in day-to-day functioning.

The third category, disorganization symptoms, refers to bizarre behavior, tangential and disorganized speech, and illogical thought patterns. Schizophrenia is commonly associated with a heterogeneous presentation, with individuals exhibiting different combinations of these symptoms. In addition, a wide range of outcomes is observed. For example, some individuals show improved functioning between episodes of psychosis, whereas others display a more chronic course, with the continued presence of one or more of the above symptoms.

Neurodevelopmental Model of Schizophrenia

In its earliest clinical descriptions, schizophrenia was considered a deteriorating brain disorder with a course similar to Alzheimer's disease but an onset in young adulthood. Thus, the neurodegenerative hypothesis of schizophrenia initially prevailed. However, after nearly 3 decades of research, the neurodevelopmental model of schizophrenia is now prominent. This theoretical framework holds that the disorder's neural origins arise primarily during early development, with full emergence of recognizable symptoms typically occurring during late adolescence or early adulthood. By identifying associations between prenatal and perinatal complications and elevated risk for schizophrenia, studies have implicated that adverse events during early life may contribute to the development of the disorder. Furthermore, longitudinal studies have found that subtle deficits in cognition, emotional expression, and behavior are present during early childhood among individuals who ultimately develop schizophrenia as adults. These findings suggest that signs of brain compromise are present long before illness onset. Finally, the majority of postmortem neuropathology studies have failed to detect evidence of a neuronal degenerative process in schizophrenia. Although debate persists regarding the details of this aberrant neurodevelopmental course, when taken together, these findings provide compelling evidence that processes comprising neuronal development are fundamental to the pathophysiology of schizophrenia.

Early Risk Factors

Schizophrenia is a highly heritable illness, with approximately 80% of an individual's likelihood of developing schizophrenia attributable to their genetic makeup. There are now numerous studies demonstrating that unaffected biological relatives of patients with schizophrenia display qualitatively similar, but quantitatively milder, neuropsychological and neuroanatomic deficits, relative to healthy controls. Such findings support the view that these deficits reflect a genetic origin rather than secondary effects of the disease process or chronic medication use. Despite this strong genetic component, however, efforts to identify the precise risk genes involved have been challenging. In fact, not only is our understanding of which genes may be involved constantly being revised, so is our set of possible routes by which any given gene may result in phenotypic variation.

For instance, a major shift in our understanding of schizophrenia genetics comes from new studies of chromosomal structural variation, which indicate that rare mutations (copy number variants, or CNVs) may play a greater role in the etiology of schizophrenia than previously realized. CNVs likely comprise about 12% of the human genome and may be highly relevant for the expression of complex diseases. One particularly compelling example is the 22q11.2 deletion syndrome (22qDS), which represents the greatest known recurrent genetic risk factor to date for the development of schizophrenia. The cause of 22qDS is a deletion of one of an individual's two copies of a particular section of chromosome 22q11.2, a locus that encompasses approximately 40 genes, including some known to play a key role in brain development. A well-defined neurogenetic syndrome like 22qDS can serve as a

compelling model to help us understand how abnormal neurodevelopmental processes, which lead to brain dysfunction, can manifest in disturbances such as the clinical symptoms associated with schizophrenia. Furthermore, it suggests that while schizophrenia is a relatively common illness, it may represent the end product of a number of distinct developmental pathways.

While genetics are clearly a major risk factor, the fact that identical twins only show about 50% concordance for the illness (i.e., that both twins have a diagnosis of schizophrenia) indicates that environmental factors must also play a role. Prenatal and perinatal complications, particularly those associated with fetal hypoxia, or transient oxygen deprivation, appear to be among the environmental factors most robustly associated with increased risk. Furthermore, fetal oxygen deprivation offers a plausible mechanism for much of the structural brain pathology—such as hippocampal volume reduction—detected in neuroimaging studies of adult patients with schizophrenia. Other forms of pregnancy complications, such as prenatal viral exposure, also are associated with increased disease risk but to a lesser extent.

Late Risk Factors

Nevertheless, if risk factors for schizophrenia are at work during early brain development, why is it that the formal diagnostic symptoms and signs of the disorder do not typically manifest until late adolescence and early adulthood? The remarkable consistency in age-at-onset distributions for schizophrenia from around the world implicates late adolescence /early adulthood as the peak period of risk. According to the neurodevelopmental hypothesis of schizophrenia, the typical onset during late adolescence is likely related to widespread brain maturational changes occurring during this time period. As the typical brain matures through adolescence, there is an increase in prefrontal cortical white matter, which is crucial for efficient information transmission between brain regions. Concomitantly, there is a decrease in gray matter volume, likely as a result of synaptic pruning processes, which reduces the overall number of neurons in the brain, thereby retaining more efficient neural configurations.

Evidence from magnetic resonance imaging (MRI) studies suggests that those who go on to develop psychosis show an exaggerated pattern of gray matter loss during this period. In comparison to those who do not develop a psychotic disorder, individuals who convert to psychosis show differential volume decreases in superior temporal and prefrontal regions, cortical regions important for high-order cognitive functions (e.g., planning, memory).

While the reasons for this dysregulation of typical brain maturation are still unknown, diathesis-stress models of schizophrenia suggest that environmental stressors may interact with genetic vulnerability in triggering symptom onset. While life stress is believed to exacerbate psychiatric symptoms across a variety of mental disorders, its role in precipitating illness onset in schizophrenia is controversial. Given the role of hormones in mediating stress response and in adolescent brain maturation, one possible biological mechanism by which rising hormone levels in adolescence may trigger expression of a latent genetic predisposition to schizophrenia is through dysregulation of the hypothalamic-pituitary-adrenal (HPA) axis. However, longitudinal studies are needed to determine causal relationships between early environmental insults, gonadal hormone expression, and the effects of chronic stress on HPA axis functioning and symptom expression in schizophrenia.

Neurobiological changes are likely to map onto behaviors that change during adolescence, such as social cognition. Social cognition, which broadly refers to the mental processes used to recognize, interpret, and respond to others' social behavior, has been highlighted as one area of particular importance in schizophrenia. Deficits in emotion processing, the capacity to identify or discriminate between different emotions, and theory of mind (ToM), which refers to one's ability to comprehend the intentions of others, are present prior to illness onset and appear to be relatively stable across phases of illness.

Because of the major changes that occur in one's social environment during adolescence, it is likely that the development of social cognition in at-risk youth is detrimentally affected during this time. Efforts to understand this hypothesis are currently underway, particularly given an increasing emphasis on early identification and intervention for schizophrenia. The burgeoning area of *clinical high risk* (CHR) research aims to ascertain individuals initially showing symptoms indicating high risk for imminent onset of psychosis and follow them over time in order to characterize the course of neurobiological change among those who develop full-blown psychosis and to elucidate predictors of this outcome. These studies offer the unique opportunity to identify risk markers most predictive of schizophrenia outcome and, by extension, to develop interventions that may be implemented prior to onset of the full-blown disorder.

Results to date from CHR studies have identified several baseline clinical variables that appear to be predictive of conversion to psychosis over and above high-risk criteria alone. Approximately 30% of individuals considered at high risk for developing psychosis develop a full-blown psychotic disorder within 1 to 2 years after ascertainment. In the largest longitudinal study of CHR youth to date, poorer social functioning and a history of substance abuse increased one's likelihood of conversion to psychosis. Neurocognitive studies have additionally identified verbal memory, processing speed, and working memory deficits as significant predictors of psychosis outcome.

Pathology of Schizophrenia

Developmental changes in brain structure may contribute to cognitive deficits seen in patients with established schizophrenia. Though subtle cognitive deficits are present long before the development of overt psychotic symptoms, it is likely that additional cognitive decline occurs right before or at illness onset. In schizophrenia patients, robust cognitive deficits have been observed in a variety of domains, including working and declarative memory, processing speed, and language production. It has been hypothesized that the wide array of observed cognitive impairments reflects global brain dysfunction or "dysconnectivity."

Substantial evidence for cortical dysconnectivity in schizophrenia comes from electroencephalography (EEG), a means of examining the fluctuations in electrical field activity generated by synchronized activity of thousands of neurons. Disrupted synchronization of neurons results in abnormal electrical activity as well as disruption in the information-processing tasks associated with the observed brain activity. Decades of EEG research have demonstrated that patients with schizophrenia process information atypically, even when information-processing demands are very rapid and patients' overt behavior does not appear to be abnormal. For example, measurement of the earliest electrical oscillations measureable within 200 milliseconds after visual stimuli appear has shown that individuals with schizophrenia show an impaired neural response selectively to low-contrast objects, despite normal performance on a routine vision examination. A similar pattern of findings applies to rapid changes in auditory information, and dramatic abnormalities persist during the assessment of more complex cognitive tasks as well. These diverse, characteristic aberrations in the brain's electrical activity are all thought to be signs that the coordinated activity within and between neural circuits is disrupted.

As is the case with behavioral and MRI-based measures, there is rapid change in large-scale electrical brain activity right before and immediately after onset of full symptoms of schizophrenia, which then remains relatively stable over the course of illness.

Treatment of Schizophrenia

Currently, the first line of treatment in schizophrenia is pharmacological intervention, which typically involves administration of antipsychotic medication. First-generation, or typical, antipsychotics (e.g., chlorpromazine, haloperidol) were first introduced in the 1950s. These drugs are thought to work by blocking dopamine receptors, and they are effective in decreasing the severity of positive psychotic symptoms, particularly hallucinations. However, first-generation antipsychotics carry significant side effects, particularly extrapyramidal motor symptoms (e.g., rigid body tremors). In the 1990s, second-generation or "atypical" antipsychotics (e.g., risperidone, ziprasidone, olanzapine) were introduced as an alternative; these medications were associated with fewer extrapyramidal symptoms than the typical antipsychotics. However, it is controversial whether atypical antipsychotics are actually safer; side effects associated with atypical antipsychotics include weight gain and increased risk for diabetes and stroke. Furthermore, although antipsychotic medications attenuate the presence of positive symptoms, the negative symptoms and cognitive dysfunction associated with schizophrenia often remain and continue to substantially impact functioning.

Given these challenges, many psychosocial interventions have been developed for schizophrenia.

Early results indicate that cognitive-behavioral therapy, which focuses on learning to implement more adaptive behavioral responses to one's thoughts and emotions, has shown to reduce positive and negative symptoms of schizophrenia and prevent relapse. Studies have also examined the effectiveness of social skills training programs, which are designed to address the social cognition dysfunction seen in schizophrenia. These studies have shown that after participating in a social skills training program, individuals with schizophrenia show improvements in their ability to recognize emotions and report having more social relationships. Many other psychosocial interventions, including vocational training and family psychoeducation, have been established and have demonstrated improved outcomes in schizophrenia. However, perhaps most important, research has shown that these psychosocial interventions are only effective when used in conjunction with medication and that timing of both pharmacological and psychosocial intervention is key, with reduced severity in the course of illness seen in earlier intervention.

Conclusions

Schizophrenia is a chronic and highly debilitating brain disorder. Currently, available treatments are palliative in nature; thus, there is an increasing emphasis in the field on early identification and early intervention. The case for involvement of early neurodevelopmental influences in the pathogenesis of schizophrenia is compelling, including evidence from human epidemiological studies, prospective studies of birth cohorts and at-risk populations, and postmortem neuropathology studies. The case for involvement of later neurodevelopmental processes is still largely circumstantial, but abnormalities of synaptic pruning processes during adolescence are likely relevant for symptom onset. A better understanding of the developmental trajectory of neurobiological processes in schizophrenia will inform early intervention strategies as to the most vulnerable brain structures and functions, as well as the stages of the illness most amenable to treatment.

Maria Jalbrzikowski, Peter Bachman, and Carrie E. Bearden

See also Behavioral Therapy; Delusions; Emotion and Psychopathology; Social Cognition

Further Readings

Andreasen, N. C., Arndt, S., Alliger, R., Miller, D., & Flaum, M. (1995). Symptoms of schizophrenia. Methods, meanings, and mechanisms. *Archives of General Psychiatry, 52*(5), 341–351.

Cannon, T. D., Cadenhead, K., Cornblatt, B., Woods, S. W., Addington, J., Walker, E., . . . Heinssen, R. (2008). Prediction of psychosis in youth at high clinical risk: A multisite longitudinal study in North America. *Archives of General Psychiatry, 65*(1), 28–37.

Insel, T. R. (2010). Rethinking schizophrenia. *Nature, 468*(7321), 187–193. doi:10.1038/nature09552

Javitt, D. C. (2009). When doors of perception close: Bottom-up models of disrupted cognition in schizophrenia. *Annual Review of Clinical Psychology, 5*, 249–275.

Murphy, K. C., Jones, L. A., & Owen, M. J. (1999). High rates of schizophrenia in adults with velo-cardio-facial syndrome. *Archives of General Psychiatry, 56*(10), 940–945.

Penn, D. L., Sanna, L. J., & Roberts, D. L. (2008). Social cognition in schizophrenia: An overview. *Schizophrenia Bulletin, 34*(3), 408–411.

Selemon, L. D., & Goldman-Rakic, P. S. (1999). The reduced neuropil hypothesis: A circuit based model of schizophrenia. *Biological Psychiatry, 45*(1), 17–25.

Walsh, T., McClellan, J. M., McCarthy, S. E, Addington, A. M., Pierce, S. B., Cooper, G. M., . . . Sebat, J. (2008). Rare structural variants disrupt multiple genes in neurodevelopmental pathways in schizophrenia. *Science, 320*(5875), 539–543.

SCIENTIFIC REASONING

Scientific reasoning, like science itself, is a constantly changing and inherently fascinating system of interrelated concepts, practices, and theoretical approaches to conducting science. This entry discusses the philosophical and empirical approaches used to understand the scientific process and how those approaches have coevolved with it. Early research on scientific thinking offered conclusions that were potentially universal for all sciences about the formation of hypotheses, optimizing scientific research, and the implications of these conclusions for science education. Modern research on scientific thinking has become much more specific to individual scientific disciplines (such as molecular biology), and it studies the way science is conducted in the real world by observing scientists as they work or by analyzing their diaries and research notes. The new field of educational neuroscience has outlined the brain structures involved in such reasoning as well. This entry also explains the importance of viewing science in its appropriate historical context and examines how modern scientific thinking has been influenced by the vast capabilities of robotics and computers.

Just 20 years ago the field was dominated by a small set of questions regarding the best ways to conduct science, the relationship between hypotheses and experiments, what scientific reasoning strategies should be taught, and whether there could be a unified science of science. Much cognitive and philosophical work focused on when and whether scientists should attempt to confirm or disconfirm their hypotheses. Many researchers followed the view of Karl Popper that scientists should attempt to disconfirm their hypotheses. However, more fine-grained research demonstrated that many scientists seek to confirm their hypotheses early on in a research project and seek disconfirmation at later stages of research. Researchers also focused on whether science is primarily inductive (inferring general rules from a finite number of observations), deductive (generating specific conclusions from known, general rules), or abductive (inferring a cause that would best explain a given effect) and found that these different forms of reasoning are all used in science, rather than science being one form of reasoning exclusively.

Understanding Science by Modeling Real Life Situations

The reasoning strategies of renowned scientists and their discoveries have been examined in historical analyses, often using computer simulations of scientific discovery. Historical and computational approaches have revealed that specific scientific reasoning strategies such as following up unexpected results, using analogies to formulate hypotheses, and assessing the coherence of a scientific concept are key features of scientific thinking. Furthermore, investigations of students reasoning scientifically and children reasoning about scientific concepts have demonstrated that search in different types of problem spaces is central to understanding the development of scientific thinking. A problem space includes the current state of knowledge, the goal state (which may not be defined), and all knowledge states in between, as well as the cognitive operators that allow one to move from one knowledge state to the next. Many researchers have adopted a more detailed approach to the development of scientific thinking and have moved away from Jean Piaget's stagelike view of the development of scientific thinking skills to an investigation of scientific thinking strategies that can be taught in the classroom, such as designing experiments, formulating hypotheses, and learning how to assess the adequacy of particular experimental designs.

Putting Science in Its Historical Context

Another strand in research on scientific thinking over the past 50 years has been to investigate the historical context of particular scientific concepts. The genesis of this view of scientific thinking was undoubtedly Thomas Kuhn's *Structure of Scientific Revolutions*, in which Kuhn demonstrated that science moves in ways reminiscent of a political revolution rather than by a steady accrual of knowledge. This realization that science is not the strict accumulation of logical facts, findings, and methods led to many socially grounded theories of scientific thinking. According to this approach, the adoption or abandonment of a scientific theory may be due to many factors and not just whether a theory explains a set of "facts." Consequently, many recent historical analyses of scientific thinking have demonstrated that conceptual change and theory change in science occur for a wide variety of both nonscientific and scientific reasons.

Modern Approaches to Scientific Thinking

Much research in science education and scientific thinking has concentrated on the mechanisms of conceptual change for specific scientific concepts. Research on scientific thinking has moved away from domain-general experiments (studies that can be applied to any number of different scientific disciplines) on how people test simple hypotheses, to more complex domains with complex histories such as molecular biology, physics, evolution, and chemistry. Researchers now routinely investigate the scientific thinking strategies that scientists themselves use in their own labs to understand both the cognitive and social factors involved in scientific thinking.

In the early 2000s, cognitive neuroscientists began to explore the neural underpinnings of scientific thinking, demonstrating the roles of the anterior cingulate and parahippocampal gyrus when students ignore evidence that disconfirms their favored hypothesis, the role of the frontal poles when generating scientific analogies, and the role of the left dorsolateral prefrontal cortex and precuneus in causal scientific thinking. This approach to the brain, education, and cognition has helped lead to the development of the new field of educational neuroscience, in which educationally important questions are addressed using a variety of populations, neuroimaging techniques, and educationally rich contexts to produce more effective teaching, robust learning, and in-depth understanding.

A New Scientific Possibility: The Hypothesis-Optional Experiment

Around the same time as the development of educational neuroscience, major changes began to take place in the ways that scientists use hypotheses and conduct experiments: Many biologists started conducting massive, catchall projects in which millions of experiments—essentially all possible experiments that could be conducted within a particular problem space—could be conducted in a short space of time by automating the process with robotics and supercomputers. These high throughput experiments (conducted by computational devices, robots, and machines) are now routine in the pharmaceutical and genetics industries, and many researchers have argued that this approach obviates the need for hypotheses at all. If this approach endures, it fundamentally changes the nature of scientific thinking. This radical shift in some of the basic assumptions of scientific thinking will be a central focus of research for the next few decades as more of the high throughput technologies are used in all branches of science ranging from astrophysics to zoology. This shift will undoubtedly lead to the proposal of many new types of scientific thinking and will change scientific practice as much as Sir Francis Bacon's introduction of inductive methods in the 1600s changed the nature of science in the subsequent centuries.

Kevin N. Dunbar and Evelyn A. Forster

See also Analogical Mapping and Reasoning; Deductive Reasoning; Distributed Cognition

Further Readings

Chi, M. T. H., Kristensen, A. K., & Roscoe, R. (2012). Misunderstanding emergent causal mechanism in natural selection. In K. S. Rosengren, S. K. Brem, E. M. Evans, & G. M. Sinatra (Eds.), *Evolution challenges: Integrating research and practice in teaching and learning about evolution* (pp. 145–173). New York, NY: Oxford University Press.

Dunbar, K., Fugelsang, J., & Stein, C. (2007). Do naïve theories ever go away? In M. Lovett & P. Shah (Eds.), *Thinking with data: 33rd Carnegie symposium on cognition* (pp. 193–206). Mahwah, NJ: Erlbaum.

Kuhn, T. (1962). *The structure of scientific revolutions.* Chicago, IL: University of Chicago Press.

Langley, P. W., Simon, H. A., Bradshaw, G. L., & Zytkow, J. M. (1987). *Scientific discovery: Computational explorations of the creative process.* Cambridge, MA: MIT Press.

Tweney, R. D., Doherty, M. E., & Mynatt, C. R. (1981). *On scientific thinking.* New York, NY: Columbia University Press.

SELF, DEVELOPMENT OF

"Am I Me?" a thoughtful 2-year-old queried of his parents. Beginning in the second year of life, toddlers begin to talk about themselves. They master self-relevant *personal* pronouns (I and me) that distinguish themselves from others. With development, they come to understand that they possess various characteristics, some of which may be positive ("I'm smart)" and some of which may be negative ("I'm unpopular"). Of particular interest is how the very nature of such self-evaluations changes with development as well as how self-evaluations differ among individual children and adolescents across two basic evaluative categories. The first category is (a) *domain-specific self-concepts*—namely, how one judges one's attributes in particular arenas—for example, scholastic competence, social acceptance, physical competence, and so forth. A given individual may vary tremendously in how they feel across these domains, creating a meaningful *profile* of scores. One typically does not feel equally adequate across all domains. The second evaluative category is (b) *global self-esteem*—namely, how much they value their overall worth as a person. (For a complete treatment of self-development in childhood and adolescents, see Susan Harter's work.)

Developmental shifts in the nature of self-evaluations are driven by changes in the child's *cognitive* capabilities. Cognitive-developmental theory and findings by Jean Piaget and Kurt Fischer alert us to the fact that the young child is limited to very specific, concrete representations of self and others, for example, "I know my A, B, Cs." In middle to later childhood, a child develops the ability to form higher order concepts about his or her attributes and abilities (e.g., "I'm smart"). There are further cognitive advances at adolescence, allowing the teenager to form *abstract* concepts about the self that transcend concrete behavioral manifestations and higher order generalizations (e.g., "I'm intelligent").

Developmental Differences in Domain-Specific Self-Concepts

Domain-specific self-concepts are observed at every developmental level. However, the precise nature of these judgments varies with age. There are five common domains in which children and adolescents make evaluative judgments about the self: scholastic competence, physical competence, social competence, behavioral conduct, and physical appearance. The types of statements vary, however, across three age periods—early childhood, later childhood, and adolescence—in keeping with the cognitive abilities and limitations of each age period.

Early Childhood

Young children provide very concrete accounts of their capabilities, evaluating specific behaviors. Thus, they communicate how they can count, how they can run very fast, how they are nice to a particular friend, how they don't hit their sister, and how they possess a specific physical feature such as pretty blond hair. Of particular interest in such accounts is the fact that the young child typically provides a litany of virtues, touting their positive skills and attributes. One cognitive limitation of this age period is that young children cannot distinguish the *wish* to be competent from reality. As a result, they typically overestimate their abilities because they do not yet have the skills to evaluate themselves realistically. Another cognitive characteristic that contributes to potential distortions is the pervasiveness of *all-or-none* thinking. That is, evaluations are either all positive or all negative. With regard to self-evaluations, they are typically all positive. (Exceptions to this positivity bias can be observed in children who are chronically abused, since severe maltreatment is often accompanied by parental messages that make the child feel inadequate, incompetent, and unlovable. Such children will also engage in all-or-none thinking but conclude that they are all *bad*.)

Middle to Later Childhood

As the child grows older, the ability to make higher order *generalizations* in evaluating his or her abilities and attributes emerges. Thus, in addition to describing his or her prowess at a particular activity, the child will also observe that he or she is good at *sports,* in general. This inference can further be justified in that the child can describe his or her talent at several sports (e.g., good at soccer, basketball, and baseball). Thus, the higher order generalization represents a more developmentally advanced cognitive construction in which an overarching evaluation (e.g., "I am good at sports") is defined in terms of specific examples that justify this conclusion. Similar processes allow the older child to conclude that he or she is *smart* (e.g., does well in math, science, and history). The structure of a higher order generalization about being *well behaved* could include such components as obeying parents, not getting into trouble, and trying to do what is right. A generalization concerning one's *popularity* may subsume accounts of having friends at school, making friends easily at camp, and developing friendships readily when moving into a new neighborhood. The perception that one is *good looking* may be based on one's positive evaluation of one's face, hair, and body.

During middle childhood, all-or-none thinking diminishes and the aura of positivity fades. Thus, children do not typically think that they are all virtuous in every domain. The more common pattern is for them to feel more adequate in some domains than others. For example, one child may feel that he or she is good at schoolwork and is well behaved, whereas he or she is not that good at sports, does not think that he or she is good-looking, and reports that it is hard to make friends. Another child may report the opposite pattern.

There are numerous combinations of positive and negative evaluations across these domains that children can and do report. Moreover, they may report both positive and negative judgments within a given domain—for example, they are smart in some school subjects (math and science) but dumb in others (English and social studies). Such evaluations may be accompanied by *self-affects*—namely, emotions about the self that emerge in later childhood—for example, feeling proud of one's accomplishments but ashamed of one's perceived failures, as Susan Harter's work documents. The ability to consider both positive and negative characteristics is a major cognitive-developmental acquisition. Thus, beginning in middle to later childhood, these distinctions result in a *profile* of self-evaluations across domains.

Contributing to this advance is the ability to engage in *social comparison.* Beginning in middle childhood one can utilize comparisons with others as a barometer of the skills and attributes of the self. In contrast, the young child cannot simultaneously compare his or her attributes to the characteristics of another in order to detect similarities or differences that have implications for the self. Although the ability to utilize social comparison information for the purpose of self-evaluation represents a cognitive-developmental advance, it also ushers in new, potential liabilities. With the emergence of the ability to rank order the performance of other children, all but the most capable children will necessarily fall short of excellence. Thus, the very ability and penchant to compare oneself with others makes the self vulnerable, particularly if one does not measure up in domains that are highly valued. The more general effects of social comparison can be observed in findings revealing that domain-specific self-concepts become more negative during middle and later childhood compared to early childhood.

Adolescence

For the adolescent, there are further cognitive-developmental advances that alter the nature of domain-specific self-evaluations. Adolescence brings with it the ability to create more abstract judgments about one's attributes and abilities. Thus, one no longer merely considers oneself to be good at sports but to be *athletically talented.* One is no longer merely smart but views the self more generally as *intelligent,* where successful academic performance, general problem-solving ability, and creativity might all be subsumed under the abstraction of intelligence. Abstractions may be similarly constructed in the other domains. For example, in the domain of behavioral conduct, there will be a shift from the perception that one is well behaved to a sense that one is a *moral* or principled person. In the domains of social competence and appearance, abstractions may take the form of perceptions that one is popular and physically *attractive*.

These illustrative examples all represent positive self-evaluations. However, during adolescence (as well as in later childhood), judgments about one's attributes will also involve negative self-evaluations. Thus, certain individuals may judge the self to be unattractive, unpopular, unprincipled, and so forth. Of particular interest is the fact that when abstractions emerge, the adolescent typically does not have total *control* over these new acquisitions, just as when one is acquiring a new athletic skill (e.g., swinging a bat, throwing a ball, maneuvering skis), one lacks a certain level of control. In the cognitive realm, such lack of control often leads to overgeneralizations that can shift dramatically across situations or time. For example, the adolescent may conclude at one point in time that he or she is exceedingly popular but then, in the face of a minor social rebuff, may conclude that he or she is extremely unpopular. This typically leads to exasperation by parents and other adults in the adolescent's life since they do not understand that such shifts are inevitable and quite typical in our culture. The shifts stem from new cognitive advances that also reflect liabilities. Plus, recent work reveals that immature brain structures contribute, structures that preclude the more integrated thought that helps control such vacillations. Gradually, adolescents gain control over these self-relevant abstractions so that they become capable of more balanced and accurate self-evaluations, as research by Fischer and by Harter reveals.

Global Self-Esteem

The ability to evaluate one's worth as a person and to make inferences about one's self-esteem also undergoes developmental change. The young child simply is incapable, cognitively, of developing the verbal concept of his or her value as a person. This ability emerges at the approximate age of 8. However, young children *exude* a sense of personal worth in their behavior. The primary behavioral manifestations involve displays of confidence, independence, mastery attempts, and exploration, as Susan Harter's work documents. Thus, behaviors that communicate to others that children are sure of themselves reflect high self-esteem in early childhood. In contrast, behavior indicative of lack of confidence, mastery attempts, curiosity, or exploration, plus excessive dependence on others, reflects a constellation that is predictive of low self-esteem in others' eyes, such as teachers or parents.

At about the third grade, children begin to develop the concept that they like or don't like the kind of person they are, as the writings of Susan Harter and Morris Rosenberg indicate. Thus, they can respond to general items asking them to rate the extent to which they are pleased with themselves, like who they are, and think they are fine as a person. Here, the shift reflects the emergence of an ability to construct a higher order generalization about the self. This type of concept can be built on perceptions that one has a number of specific qualities—for example, that one is competent, well behaved, attractive, and so forth. Self-esteem can also be built on the observation that significant others—for example, parents, peers, and teachers—think highly of themselves. This process is greatly influenced by advances in the child's ability to take the perspective of significant others. During adolescence, one's evaluation of one's global worth as a person may be further elaborated, drawing on more domains and sources of approval, and will also become more abstract. Thus, adolescents can directly acknowledge that they have high or low self-esteem as a general abstraction about the self; that is, they understand the term *self-esteem*.

Individual Differences in Domain-Specific Self-Concepts as Well as Global Self-Esteem

Although there are predictable cognitively based developmental changes in the nature of how most children and adolescents describe and evaluate themselves, there are striking individual differences in how positively or negatively the self is evaluated. Moreover, one observes different profiles of children's perceptions of their competence or adequacy across the various self-concept domains, in that children evaluate themselves differently across domains.

Consider two profiles exemplified by Child A and Child B, neither of whom feels good about the self scholastically or athletically. They evaluate themselves much more positively in the domains of social acceptance, conduct, and physical appearance. In fact, their profiles are quite similar to each other across the five specific domains. However, judgments of their self-esteem are extremely different. Child A has very high self-esteem whereas Child B has very low self-esteem. This raises a puzzling question: How can two children look so similar with regard to their domain-specific self-concepts but evaluate their global self-esteem so differently? We turn to this issue next, in examining the causes of global self-esteem.

The Causes of Children's Level of Self-Esteem

Our understanding of the antecedents of global self-esteem has been greatly aided by the formulations of two historical scholars of the self, William James and Charles Horton Cooley. Each suggested rather different pathways to self-esteem, defined as an overall evaluation of one's worth as a person. William James focused on how the individual assessed his or her competence in domains where one had aspirations to succeed. Charles Horton Cooley focused on the salience of the opinions that others held about the self, opinions that one incorporated into one's global sense of self.

Competence/Adequacy in Domains of Importance

For William James, global self-esteem derived from the evaluations of one's sense of competence or adequacy in the various domains of one's life relative to how important it was to be successful in these domains. Thus, if one feels one is successful in domains deemed important, high self-esteem will result. Conversely, if one falls short of one's goal in domains where one has aspirations to be successful, one will experience low self-esteem. One does not, therefore, have to be a superstar in every domain to have high self-esteem. Rather, one only needs to feel adequate or competent in those areas judged to be important to the self. Thus, children may evaluate themselves as unathletic; however, if athletic prowess is not an aspiration, then self-esteem will not be negatively affected. That is, the high self-esteem individual can discount the importance of areas in which one does not feel successful.

This analysis can be applied to the profiles of Child A and Child B. In fact, Susan Harter has directly examined this explanation by asking children to rate how important it is for them to be successful. The findings reveal that high self-esteem individuals feel competent in domains they rate as important. Low self-esteem individuals report that areas in which they are unsuccessful are still very important to them. Thus, Child A represents an example of an individual who feels that social acceptance, conduct, and appearance, domains in which she evaluates herself positively, are very important but that the two domains where she is less successful, scholastic competence and athletic competence, are not that important. In contrast, Child B rates *all* domains as important, including the two domains where he is not successful, scholastic competence and athletic competence. Thus, the discrepancy between high importance coupled with perceptions of inadequacy contributes to low self-esteem.

Incorporation of the Opinions of Significant Others

Another important factor influencing self-esteem can be derived from the writings of Charles Horton Cooley, who metaphorically made reference to the "looking-glass self." According to this formulation, significant others (e.g., parents and peers) are social mirrors into which one gazes to determine their opinion of the self. Thus, in evaluating the self, one would adopt what one felt were the judgments of these others whose opinions are considered important. Thus, the approval, support, or positive regard from significant others becomes a critical source of one's own sense of worth as a person. For example, children who receive approval from parents and peers will report much higher self-esteem than children who experience disapproval from parents and peers.

Findings reveal that both of these factors, competence in domains of importance and the perceived support of significant others, combine to influence a child's or adolescent's self-esteem. Those who feel competent in domains of importance *and* who report high support rate themselves as having the highest self-esteem. Those who feel inadequate in domains deemed important *and* who report low levels of support rate themselves as having the lowest self-esteem. Other combinations fall in between.

Conclusions

Two types of self-evaluations that can be observed in children and adolescents were distinguished:

(a) evaluative judgments of competence or adequacy in specific domains (*domain-specific self-concepts*) and (b) the global evaluation of one's worth as a person—namely, overall self-esteem. Each of these undergoes developmental change based on age-related cognitive advances. In addition, older children and adolescents vary tremendously with regard to whether self-evaluations are positive or negative. Within a given individual, there will be a profile of self-evaluations, some of which are more positive and some that are more negative. More positive self-concepts in domains considered important as well as approval from significant others will lead to high self-esteem. Conversely, negative self-concepts in domains considered important coupled with lack of approval from significant others will result in low self-esteem.

Why Should We Care About Self-Concepts and Self-Esteem?

Self-esteem is particularly important since it is associated with very critical outcomes or consequences. Perhaps the most well-documented consequence of low self-esteem is depression. Children and adolescents (as well as adults) who display the constellation of low perceived adequacy in domains of importance coupled with low approval support from significant others invariably report low self-esteem. Low self-esteem, in turn, is highly associated with perceived depression and hopelessness about the future. The most seriously depressed consider suicide. Thus, it is critical that we intervene for those experiencing low self-esteem. Our model of the causes of self-esteem suggests strategies that may be fruitful—for example, improving skills, helping individuals discount the importance of domains in which it is unlikely that they can improve, and providing support in the form of approval for who they are as people. It is also clear that there are different pathways to low and high self-esteem. For example, for one child, the sense of inadequacy in particular domains may be the pathway to low self-esteem. For another child, lack of support from parents or peers may represent the primary cause. These different pathways are important to identify because they have critical implications for intervention efforts to enhance feelings of worth for those children with low self-esteem in educational settings, clinical settings, peer groups, the community, and

within the family. Susan Harter's work delineates multiple strategies for promoting realistically high self-esteem. If evaluations are accurate, positive self-esteem is clearly a psychological commodity, a resource that is important for us to foster in our children and adolescents if we want them to lead productive and happy lives.

Susan Harter

See also Concepts, Development of; Personal Identity, Development of; Relationships, Development of

Further Readings

Cooley, C. H. (1902). *Human nature and the social order.* New York, NY: Scribner.

Damon, W., & Hart, D. (1988). *Self-understanding in childhood and adolescence.* New York, NY: Cambridge University Press.

Fischer, K. W. (1980). A theory of cognitive development: The control and construction of hierarchies of skills. *Psychological Review, 87,* 477–531.

Harter, S. (1993). Causes and consequences of low self-esteem in children and adolescents. In R. F. Baumeister (Ed.), *Self-esteem: The puzzle of low self-regard* (pp. 87–116). New York, NY: Plenum.

Harter, S. (1999). *The construction of the self: A developmental perspective.* New York, NY: Guilford.

Harter, S. (2011). *The construction of the self: A developmental perspective* (2nd ed.). New York, NY: Guilford.

James, W. (1892). *Psychology: The briefer course.* New York, NY: Henry Holt.

Oosterwegel, A., & Oppenheimer, L. (1993). *The self-system: Developmental changes between and within self-concepts.* Hillsdale, NJ: Erlbaum.

Piaget, J. (1960). *The psychology of intelligence.* Patterson, NJ: Littlefield-Adams.

Rosenberg, M. (1979). *Conceiving the self.* New York, NY: Basic Books.

Self-Consciousness

The term *self-consciousness* has several often conflated usages in the philosophy of mind and the cognitive sciences. This entry distinguishes the three major common usages and their general philosophical and scientific contexts, with an emphasis on their place in cognitive neuroscience.

Three Usages of *Self-Consciousness*

1. *Core self-consciousness.* According to this usage, self-consciousness is an essential structural property of consciousness that conditions all other forms of awareness. The controversial claim presupposed by the usage (sometimes referred to as the "self-awareness thesis" or SAT) is that all conscious beings possess this type of self-consciousness irrespective of their conceptual sophistication or their capacities for introspection. According to the SAT, consciousness is *necessarily* aware of *itself* in all its streams or episodes. The SAT has been held, in one form or another, over millennia by a variety of philosophers, psychologists, neuroscientists, and other investigators of consciousness, including, notably, Aristotle, René Descartes, John Locke, Immanuel Kant, Franz Brentano, Sigmund Freud, Edmund Husserl, and the phenomenologists who followed Husserl. The SAT has had few supporters in Anglo-American philosophy of mind, but this has recently changed. In the cognitive neuroscience literature, the most notable proponent of the SAT is Antonio Damasio, with his distinction between core and extended consciousness and his focus on the primordial experience of the body and emotion. In the artificial intelligence-inspired literature, it is Douglas Hofstadter. The qualifier "core" derives from the work of Damasio; in the literature, one will find many qualifiers used to designate this form of self-consciousness (e.g., prereflective, nonpositional, nonthetic, marginal, inattentive, peripheral, tacit).

2. *Introspective self-consciousness.* The second usage refers to the exercise of the ability to attend to, conceptualize, and report on one's mental states. This form of self-consciousness is also sometimes marked by the qualifiers "reflective" and "attentive." This form of self-consciousness plays a crucial role in normal mental life: in self-orienting and ongoing inner dialogue, in reconceptualization of personality traits and goals, and in sharing intentions, feelings, and so forth with others. Presumably, animals and infants could be self-conscious in the first sense of the term but have limited or no introspective self-consciousness. Introspective self-consciousness plays a critical role in the practice of cognitive psychology and neuroscience, both in the scientists' own heuristic introspection and in the self-reports of experimental subjects, a crucial source of data in many experimental paradigms. However, it remains subject to multiple sources: "noise" fatigue, distraction, failure to communicate or understand instructions, personality and emotional biases, social conformity, and confabulation. Researchers have called for the development of rigorous experimental methods of cross validation to minimize errors stemming from such limitations and to allow for the better correlation of ongoing experiences with spontaneous brain activity.

3. *Extended self-consciousness.* The third usage is sometimes indicated with the qualifier "autobiographical," and refers to the conscious access to and projection of the memory-laden information necessary for conceptualizing and situating oneself as an ego, self, person, or responsible agent with a culturally and socially mediated history and anticipated future. It is closely related to the notion of the "self-concept." Extended self-consciousness may be the most derivative of the three as it seems to depend on the former two. It requires an extended degree of conceptualization of space, time, dispositions, causal relations, and moral notions, and is likely most developed in adults. Its accuracy depends on the time and resource-consuming cognitive ability to reflectively notice and integrate one's stream of experiences, patterns of behaviors, affective reactions, interests, and motivations. It can be biased by various motives, personality traits, and coping mechanisms. The self-concept tends to undergo development during childhood, adolescence, and midlife and can be modified by positive or negative experiences (e.g., love, loss, depression, and treatment). Finally, the self-concept can be eroded by degenerative disease (e.g., Alzheimer's disease [AD]) or strongly affected by other forms of brain damage, while the subject can remain otherwise self-conscious in senses one and two. Extended self-consciousness is thus a far more dynamic property than the other two types. During the progression of AD, extended self-consciousness is among the first cognitive functions to be affected, followed by introspective self-consciousness, while core self-consciousness is among the last functions to disappear. Core, introspective, and even some extended self-consciousness appear to remain largely preserved in neuropsychological cases of patients with profound retrograde and anterograde amnesia.

Many authors cite experiences of complete absorption during activities in which one seems to lose track of oneself as evidence that there can be consciousness without any self-consciousness whatsoever. Beyond the potential paradox of such a position, which seems to imply the possibility of experiences (e.g., pain) with no owner or subject of the experience, it seems generally to assume that self-consciousness is to be taken in senses two or three. While it is true that one is not introspecting all the time and that one ceases to think about oneself as an autobiographical ego in times of complete absorption, it also does not seem entirely implausible that animals, infants, and sufferers of degenerative disease could be self-conscious without introspective capacity and without having much of an autobiographical self.

Neural Bases of Self-Consciousness

The study of the neural basis of self-consciousness has grown over the past decade. Three classes of hypotheses can be distinguished.

1. The first class refers to specific regions of the brain as underlying self-consciousness or its components, including the following: (a) the insular cortex—for all forms of self-consciousness; (b) the anterior cingulate cortex—for interoceptive and emotional self-consciousness, the conscious monitoring of conflict, and introspective self-consciousness; (c) the medial prefrontal cortex—for self-referential processing in general, and (d) the brain stem, which has recently been hypothesized to be the neural basis for the "primordial feelings" of the living body.

2. The second class of hypotheses focus on more distributed and integrated networks, including the following: (a) the default mode network that has been hypothesized to constitute an essential basis for introspection, the retrieval of autobiographical memory, and the projection of the self into the future; (b) a network of subcortical-cortical midline structures in which cortical midline components subserve introspective self-consciousness and core self-consciousness is implemented by subcortical components; (c) a posterior network relying on interactions between brain stem nuclei, the thalamus, and the posteromedial cortex, which has been hypothesized to constitute an integrative

basis for "subjectivity"—that is, essentially core and introspective self-consciousness.

3. A third class of hypotheses considers self-consciousness as potentially "multiply realizable." It would function like the implementation of an abstractly characterizable computational algorithm capable of exploiting different brain regions in an equipotent manner, similar to the way a computer's virtual machine can flexibly occupy variable hardware resources.

Compatible with the second and third classes of hypotheses, neurological evidence supports the idea that self-consciousness is an extremely robust, flexible, and resilient process. Neurological studies suggest that, beyond coma caused by brain stem and thalamic damage, self-consciousness may disappear only when extensive bilateral damage affects most of the thalamocortical system. Even in such circumstances, as in some persistent vegetative state patients, there is evidence that residual self-consciousness can be present. Moreover, while genetic and environmental factors can result in aberrant brain development, there is often a preservation of basic mental abilities, including self-consciousness. Developmental cases suggest that extremely different brains across individuals can support similar forms of self-consciousness.

Understanding the structure and mechanisms underlying core self-consciousness will represent a key theoretical and methodological challenge for the cognitive sciences. Likewise, uncovering the neural implementation of self-consciousness will represent a tremendous challenge if the "multiple realizability" hypothesis turns out to be true, as the standard anatomo-functional approach of cognitive neuroscience would be of limited help.

Kenneth Williford, David Rudrauf,
and Carissa L. Philippi

See also Anosognosia; Consciousness, Comparative Perspectives; Event Memory, Development; Introspection; Self, Development of; Self-Knowledge

Further Readings

Buckner, R. L., Andrews-Hanna, J. R., & Schacter, D. (2008). The brain's default network, anatomy, function, and relevance to disease. *Annals of the New York Academy of Sciences, 1124,* 1–38.

Craig, A. D. (2010). The sentient self. *Brain Structure and Function*, 214(5–6), 563–577.

Damasio, A. (1999). *The feeling of what happens: Body and emotion in the making of consciousness*. Orlando, FL: Harvest Books.

Damasio, A. (2010). *Self comes to mind: Constructing the conscious brain*. New York, NY: Pantheon.

Dennett, D. C. (1991). *Consciousness explained*. Boston, MA: Little, Brown.

Hofstadter, D. (2007). *I am a strange loop*. New York, NY: Basic Books.

Kriegel, U., & Williford, K. (Eds.). (2006). *Self-representational approaches to consciousness*. Cambridge, MA: MIT Press.

Northoff, G., & Bermpohl, F. (2004). Cortical midline structures and the self. *Trends in Cognitive Science*, 8, 102–107.

Owen, A., Schiff, N., & Laureys, S. (2009). The assessment of conscious awareness in the vegetative state. In S. Laureys & G. Tononi (Eds.), *The neurology of consciousness* (pp. 163–172). London, UK: Academic Press.

Panksepp, J., & Northoff, G. (2009). The trans-species core SELF: The emergence of active cultural and neuro-ecological agents through self-related processing within subcortical-cortical midline networks. *Consciousness and Cognition*, 18, 193–215.

Rosenberg, M. (1965). *Society and the adolescent self-image*. Princeton, NJ: Princeton University Press.

Shewmon, D. A., Holmes, G. L., & Byrne, P. A. (1999). Consciousness in congenitally decorticate children: Developmental vegetative state as self-fulfilling prophecy. *Developmental Medicine & Child Neurology*, 41, 364–374.

Varela, F. J., & Shear, J. (1999). First-person methodologies: What, why, how? *Journal of Consciousness Studies*, 6, 1–14.

SELF-KNOWLEDGE

Self-knowledge is the characteristically human ability of knowing one's own mental states—such as sensations, perceptions, emotions, and propositional attitudes. The following will survey the main philosophical and psychological accounts of self-knowledge proposed in recent years.

The Introspective Model

According to the Cartesian conception, all mental states are like objects presented in one's own mental arena we are introspectively aware of. In particular, they are *transparent* to their subjects; that is, if a subject has them, he is immediately aware of them and in a position to judge that he has them. Moreover, a subject is *authoritative* with respect to them—if sincere, if he judges to be in a mental state *M*, he is.

The Cartesian model has been widely criticized. First, since Sigmund Freud's discovery of the unconscious, the transparency of mental states has been questioned. Second, it has been noted that animals and infants have mental states yet can't self-ascribe them. Third, the discovery of self-deception, whereby subjects self-ascribe mental states they don't actually have, makes authority founder. Fourth, the Cartesian model would introduce a cognitive faculty—namely, introspection—modeled after sight, which, however, appears difficult to characterize in relation to mental states that aren't physical entities. Finally, Ludwig Wittgenstein pointed out how the Cartesian model would entail the view that psychological language is private to each subject. On the one hand, one could know only one's own mental states and may merely surmise those of others. On the other, if only I can know my current mental states, the reference of my psychological vocabulary will be known to myself only. Hence, whenever it will seem correct to me to apply a given term *t* to a current mental state *M*, my use of *t* will be correct. According to Wittgenstein's argument against the possibility of a private language (either in speech or in thought), this would entail that the distinction between correct and incorrect uses of *t* would collapse and, with it, the very idea that *t* could mean anything at all.

David Armstrong has proposed a refined version of the introspective model. In this view, through the operation of an inner subpersonal mechanism, subjects would become immediately aware of their mental states. Working reliably, such a mechanism would also ensure that subjects be authoritative about them.

Armstrong's model has been criticized for considering both transparency and authority to be the result of the correct operation of the inner subpersonal mechanism. These characteristics should be subject to perfectly acceptable exceptions in case the mechanism broke down. Authority and transparency, however, are traditionally considered constitutive traits of self-knowledge and their failure either implies a lack of conceptual competence or rationality or else is a sign that the mental state one fails to have knowledge of is unconscious. Yet—to contrast this view with how we usually think of subpersonal mechanisms—we would never think of blind subjects, whose visual mechanism is impaired and can't therefore see objects presented to them, that they either lack the relevant concepts or are being irrational or else are unconsciously seeing the objects.

The Inferential Model

The inferential model, somewhat traceable to behaviorism, has been proposed by the psychologist Alison Gopnik as part of her *theory theory* conception of knowledge of the mind. Accordingly, subjects at the ages of 3 to 4 would know their own mental states in the same way as they know other people's—namely, by making inferences from their overt behavior to their likely mental causes. Transparency and authority, therefore, aren't constitutive features of self-knowledge but are mere illusions. "Authority" is due to the fact that, being continuously around ourselves, we become reliable at recognizing our own mental states. The illusion of transparency, in contrast, can be explained by means of an analogy: Just as trained physicists can immediately see electrons in a cloud chamber because they have acquired a theory and can immediately and reliably apply it, so human beings can self-ascribe mental states without going through explicit inferences because they quickly and reliably apply their own theory of mind.

The theory theory account of self-knowledge has been criticized on various grounds. Like Armstrong's model, this account would turn transparency and authority into contingent rather than constitutive features of self-knowledge. In addition, it would deny the intuitive asymmetry between knowledge of our own and of other minds.

Constitutive Accounts

Constitutive accounts, developed by philosophers such as Sydney Shoemaker, Crispin Wright, and Akeel Bilgrami, reject the view that self-knowledge be based either on introspection or on inference. Furthermore, they consider transparency and authority to be constitutive features of self-knowledge. They therefore turn them into two conceptual truths, captured by the following thesis:

> Given conditions C, a subject believes/judges that he is in mental state M if and only if he is.

Conditions C restrict the universal applicability of the thesis so as to counter the objections already raised against the introspective account of transparency and authority—that is, the arguments from unconscious mental states, from the mental states of animals and infants, and from self-deception. This restricted thesis holds only for subjects who are conceptually endowed and for specific kinds of mental states, like conscious beliefs, desires, and intentions. Moreover, according to Bilgrami, self-deceived subjects do not make wrong self-ascriptions but rather have two contrasting mental states—only one of which is conscious and correctly ascribed—that explain their conflicting and irrational behavior. Hence, the authority over their self-ascriptions is compatible with their being self-deceived.

Constitutive accounts have been criticized for failing to accommodate two intuitions: that first- and second-order mental states—that is, beliefs, desires and intentions, on the one hand, and our own beliefs about them, on the other—have separate existence, and that self-knowledge is due to some sort of cognitive accomplishment.

Recent Epistemic Accounts

Richard Moran and Christopher Peacocke have claimed that self-knowledge consists in making judgments about one's own beliefs, desires, and intentions on the basis of having them and for the *reason* that one has them. Self-knowledge is thus a modest yet genuinely cognitive accomplishment consisting in immediate, nonobservational judgment about one's own mental states, rationally grounded in their obtaining.

Epistemic accounts, however, are problematic. In particular, awareness of one's beliefs, desires, and intentions must avoid presupposing the very knowledge of them, which should be explained and yet be such that their self-ascription be rational—that is to say, consciously motivated by the occurrence of these mental states rather than simply caused by them. As a matter of fact, however, it is very difficult to see what conception of awareness of one's own mental states could serve this purpose. For, on the one hand, so-called phenomenal awareness—that is, awareness of what it is like to have a given belief, desire, or intention—would arguably fail to provide subjects with reasons for their self-ascriptions. "Propositional" (or "higher order") awareness, on the other, would in fact presuppose self-knowledge as it would consist in judging of being in the relevant mental states.

Annalisa Coliva

See also Behaviorism; Belief and Judgment; Consciousness and the Unconscious; Folk Psychology; Introspection

Further Readings

Armstrong, D. (1968). *A materialist theory of the mind.* London, UK: Routledge.
Bilgrami, A. (2006). *Self-knowledge and resentment.* Cambridge, MA: Harvard University Press.
Gopnik, A. (1993). How we know our own minds: The illusion of first-person knowledge of intentionality. *Behavioral and Brain Sciences, 16,* 1–15, 90–101.
Moran, R. (2001). *Authority and estrangement.* Princeton, NJ: Princeton University Press.
Peacocke, C. (1999). *Being known.* Oxford, UK: Clarendon Press.
Shoemaker, S. (1996). *The first person perspective and other essays.* Cambridge, MA: Cambridge University Press.

SEMANTIC DEMENTIA

Semantic dementia is a brain disorder characterized by progressive loss of world knowledge and conceptual understanding, which results from degeneration of the temporal lobes of the brain. The disorder typically affects people in the 6th to 8th decade of life. It is part of a spectrum of focal dementia syndromes affecting the frontotemporal lobes and is pathologically distinct from the more common degenerative dementia, Alzheimer's disease. This entry describes the clinical symptoms of semantic dementia and discusses factors that influence semantic loss, the capacity for relearning, and people's awareness of their semantic impairment.

The earliest symptoms are typically in the realm of language. People have difficulty remembering the names of things and understanding words. In conversation, they may make semantic errors, such as referring to a sheep as a dog, and use words overinclusively (e.g., *water* to refer to a wide range of liquids). Incorrect word usage reflects a loss of conceptual discrimination between related terms.

On hearing some words (e.g., *sheep*), people with semantic dementia may ask what they mean, indicating that the problem is not simply one of word retrieval but a progressive loss in the person's knowledge of vocabulary. Ultimately, only a few stereotyped words or phrases remain. Nevertheless, people speak fluently and effortlessly within the confines of their increasingly restricted vocabulary. There is no effortful word search because words are no longer available to be sought.

The conceptual loss is not limited to words but encompasses the person's fund of knowledge relating to all sensory modalities. It affects the ability to recognize objects, faces, nonverbal environmental sounds, tactile, olfactory, and gustatory stimuli. Thus, people may no longer recognize fruits and vegetables in the supermarket, understand the significance of the sound of rain on the windowpane, or recognize the smell of coffee or taste of a lemon. These difficulties do not reflect a problem in sensory perception: People perceive and discriminate sensory stimuli entirely normally. The problem is in ascribing meaning to those percepts. They have lost their semantic associations. In contrast to the profound breakdown in semantic memory, day-to-day autobiographical memory is relatively well preserved, providing a striking contrast to the picture in classical amnesia.

What Is Lost and Retained?

Semantic loss is not all-or-none. During the course of the illness the person will know some things and not others and may have partial, degraded knowledge of a concept. Understanding the factors affecting what is lost and retained potentially informs understanding of the cerebral representation of semantic knowledge.

Modality Effects

If conceptual loss is multimodal, does this mean that information relating to different modalities degrades in parallel? The evidence is controversial. It is common for a person still to recognize the meaning of an object (e.g., a cup) while failing to recognize its verbal label (*cup*). This might be taken as evidence for dissociations between knowledge in different modalities, yet it also might simply reflect differences in task difficulty. Visual stimuli provide clues to meaning that are not available in the word.

A picture of a cup suggests a form of container that can be handled; a picture of a dog suggests an animal by virtue of the presence of legs, ears, and tail. Nevertheless, dissociations have also been detected in the recognition of people's faces and names; people with more left temporal lobe atrophy have more difficulty recognizing names than faces, and those with more right temporal lobe degeneration have the reverse. Name-face dissociations are less easy to explain in terms of inherent difficulty, a phenomenon that has been interpreted as evidence for different contributions to semantic knowledge from the two cerebral hemispheres.

Frequency, Familiarity, Typicality

The frequency of a word, the familiarity of objects, and the typicality of features in defining a category are strong predictors of performance. Thus, people with semantic dementia are more likely to recognize the common word *dog* than the uncommon word *antelope*. They are more likely to recognize the typical feature *legs* as being an attribute of an animal than the atypical feature *hump*. Nevertheless, generic measures of frequency, familiarity, and typicality are not sufficient to explain what a person knows. There is also a strong effect of *personal* familiarity. People show better retention of concepts (words, objects, ideas) relevant to their daily life experience than those that have no personal relevance. This finding suggests a much closer relationship between a person's semantic knowledge of the world and their autobiographical (episodic) memory than is often acknowledged. What the person experiences has a strong influence on what that person knows.

Learning in Semantic Dementia

People with semantic dementia are able to learn. They can reacquire lost words and relearn the function of objects. However, that knowledge is tenuous and depends on constant rehearsal and applicability to the person's daily life. Moreover, reacquired knowledge (e.g., that a particular animal is a *dog*) does not mean that the person's concept is normal. There is poor generalization to other instances and contexts (e.g., other dogs).

Awareness and Insight

People with semantic dementia are aware that there is something wrong and typically complain that they "cannot remember things." Nevertheless, they tend to underplay difficulties and typically do not show the great frustration and distress sometimes seen in aphasic patients with severe word finding difficulties. People with semantic dementia are unable to appreciate the magnitude of what has been lost because they no longer have available their prior world knowledge as a comparator.

Conclusion

People with semantic dementia inhabit a shrinking conceptual world. Their understanding becomes progressively narrowed and personalized, limited to the particular instances encountered in their daily life. Semantic dementia provides important insights into how concepts are represented and the relationship between knowledge and experience.

Julie Snowden

See also Aphasia; Memory, Neural Basis; Semantic Memory; Semantic Memory, Computational Perspectives

Further Readings

Hodges, J. R., & Patterson, K. (2007). Semantic dementia: A unique clinicopathological syndrome. *Lancet Neurology, 6,* 1004–1014.

Patterson, K., Nestor, P. J., & Rogers, T. T. (2007). Where do you know what you know? The representation of semantic knowledge in the human brain. *Nature, 8,* 976–987.

Snowden, J. S. (2005). Semantic dementia. In J. O'Brien, D. Ames & A. Burns (Eds.), *Dementia* (3rd ed., pp. 702–712). London, UK: Hodder Arnold.

Snowden, J. S., Kindell, J., & Neary, D. (2006). Diagnosing semantic dementia and managing communication difficulties. In K. Bryan & J. Maxim (Eds.), *Communication disability in the dementias* (pp. 125–146). Chichester, UK: Wiley.

SEMANTIC MEMORY

Semantic memory refers to the reservoir of concepts and propositions that you know and that are not tied to any particular time or place. So, for instance, you know that 2 + 2 = 4, or that carrots are orange, or that there are 50 states in the United States, but you probably don't remember the specific occasion on which you learned those facts. Similarly, there are things that you probably don't know like the 43rd element of the periodic table or the air speed velocity of an unladen European swallow—and when you don't know something you can often determine that you don't know it very quickly.

Semantic knowledge can be divided into two main kinds: concepts and propositions. A concept is a mental representation of something—like a dog, or a book, or running, or the color red. Propositions link concepts in statements that are either true or false, such as "The dog was running," or "The book is red."

During the 1960s and 1970s, a series of models were developed to explain how semantic memory is organized. In this entry, the three most influential of these models—the hierarchical model, the feature overlap model, and the spreading activation model—will be described.

The Hierarchical Model

According to the hierarchical model, concepts are organized into tree structures. So the class of animals is divided into birds, fish, and so forth. The bird concept is divided into canary, ostrich, and so forth, and the fish concept into shark, salmon, and so forth. Propositions defining the characteristics of a concept are stored with those concepts in such a way as to minimize duplication (a principle called cognitive economy). For instance, the proposition "can sing" would be stored at the canary node in the tree structure but not at the ostrich node. The proposition "can fly," however, would be stored at the bird concept, because most birds can fly, so by storing it further up the tree, one could avoid duplicating the "can fly" proposition for all the individual birds. Of course, then there is a problem for the ostrich, which cannot fly, and so the proposition "cannot fly" must be stored with the ostrich. As there are very few birds that cannot fly, it is still more efficient to store these exceptions separately than to duplicate the "can fly" proposition for all birds.

To access a memory, the model proposes that people identify the critical concept (e.g., canary) and then traverse the tree to find the concept or proposition that they need. So, for instance, to verify that "a canary can fly" one would first locate the canary node, note that no flying proposition is connected to that concept, traverse up the tree to the bird node and note that the "can fly" proposition is connected to the bird node, and then make a response. Researchers found that regardless of where the concept was in the tree it took about the same amount of time to go up a level and about the same amount of time to access a proposition—compelling evidence for the hierarchical structure of semantic memory.

However, there is a critical problem. For false statements that are explicitly encoded in semantic memory—that ostriches don't fly, for instance—one can access the ostrich node, find the relevant proposition, and make a rapid response. However, many false statements are unlikely to be encoded explicitly in semantic memory. For instance, it is unlikely that you have ever had to think about the fact that copper is not an animal, so you would have no opportunity to encode that fact. The only way to deduce that statements like this are false is to search the tree and discover that there is no animal concept above the copper concept. That implies that verifying false statements should, in general, be very slow, but this is not the case.

The Feature Overlap Model

To address this and other problems, the feature overlap model was proposed. According to this account, concepts consist of collections of features. So the concept of a robin might consist of the features, *is biped*, *has wings*, *has red breast*, and *not domesticated*. When trying to verify statements like "a robin is a bird," the features of the concept robin are compared to the features of the concept bird. Because there is a lot of overlap, one can quickly conclude that a robin is a bird. "A robin is an animal" is verified a little more slowly because there are fewer features in common. Furthermore, if there are very few features in common, people can make a fast *no* response. So, the statement "copper is an animal" is rejected quickly because copper and animal do not share many features, whereas "a tree is an animal" is rejected a little more slowly because trees and animals are both living things.

The feature overlap model proposes that features come in two types—defining features that all instances of a concept have and characteristic features typical of the concept but which are not present in all cases. However, generating defining features can be problematic. Try to name one feature that all games have and you will see the difficulty—there always seems to be an exception.

The Spreading Activation Model

The spreading activation model was designed to address the weaknesses of the earlier models. It is similar to the hierarchical model in that it consists of concepts connected together. However, in the spreading activation model these concepts are not organized into a tree but rather any two concepts that are related can be connected. Furthermore, rather than traversing the tree to find relevant information, in the spreading activation model, activation spreads through all connections simultaneously. If two concepts are strongly related more activation flows between them and if a concept has many connections emanating from it then the activation is divided between these paths—as if activation were a liquid flowing through pipes of different sizes connected in a web.

The spreading activation model was able to account for fast false judgments and did not require any distinction between defining and characteristic features. Although thinking about semantic memory today tends to focus on new computational algorithms, the spreading activation model still plays a significant role in our understanding of the semantic memory system.

In all the models discussed in this entry, it is left up to the theorist to determine the content of the representations employed. Starting in the late 1980s, attention turned toward automatically constructing representations from large text corpora using computational methods. Today, these models play a role not only in theorizing but in real world applications such as Internet searches and automatic essay grading.

Simon Dennis

See also Categorization, Neural Basis; Categorization, Psychological Perspectives; Classical Theory of Concepts; Concepts, Development of; Representations, Development of; Semantic Memory, Computational Perspectives

Further Readings

Collins, A. M., & Loftus, E. F. (1975). A spreading activation theory of semantic processing. *Psychological Review*, 82, 407–428.

Collins, A. M., & Quillian, M. R. (1969). Retrieval time from semantic memory. *Journal of Verbal Learning and Verbal Behavior*, 8, 240–247.

Rips, L. J., Shoben, E. J., & Smith, F. E. (1973). Semantic distance and the verification of semantic relations. *Journal of Verbal Learning and Verbal Behavior*, 14, 665–681.

SEMANTIC MEMORY, COMPUTATIONAL PERSPECTIVES

Semantic memory refers to factual or conceptual knowledge that is not related to any given personal episode. For instance, the fact that Ottawa is the capital of Canada is a piece of knowledge that you may retain, without necessarily being able to identify when and where you learned it. Similarly, you may know that a poodle and a terrier are similar to each other without ever having been told that they are but rather by virtue of the fact that they fit together in a conceptual representation of the world because they are both small dogs.

The examples given above illustrate the two main kinds of semantic information—conceptual and propositional. A concept is a mental representation of something. So one might have the concept of a dog that becomes active when one sees a poodle, smells a Labrador, is licked by a terrier, or talks about greyhounds. Concepts can also include actions such as running and properties such as red or quickly. Propositions join concepts together into units of mental representation that are capable of having a truth-value. So the concept of a dog is neither true nor false. But the proposition that *dogs have legs* is typically true in our world, although one could imagine a world of legless dogs in which it was not true. Similarly, Ottawa is the capital of Canada, but it is easy to imagine a world in which Toronto was instead.

Early models of semantic memory relied on representations of conceptual and propositional knowledge that were supplied by the theorists. Starting in the late 1980s, however, attention turned to how knowledge could be extracted automatically from exposure to a corpus representing human experience. We will focus on these models starting with those that extract conceptual knowledge and then considering those that extract propositional knowledge.

Conceptual Knowledge

The earliest and most prominent of the models that extract conceptual knowledge is latent semantic analysis (LSA). Introduced by Scott Deerwester, Susan Dumais, George Furnas, Thomas Landauer, and Richard Harshman, LSA derives meaning using statistical computations applied to a large corpus of text. Semantically similar words tend to appear in similar documents. By observing which words appear in which documents in the corpus, LSA defines a set of mutual constraints. These constraints can be solved using singular value decomposition—producing vector representations of both words and documents. The similarity of these vectors is then used to predict semantic similarity.

LSA has been shown to reflect human knowledge in a variety of ways. For example, LSA measures correlate highly with humans' scores on vocabulary tests, mimic human category judgments, predict how rapidly people are able to access words, and estimate passage coherence. In applied domains, LSA has been used to aid information retrieval, guide discussion forums, provide feedback to pilots on landing technique, diagnose mental disorders, select candidates for jobs, and allow automated tutors to understand the input they receive from students. The most surprising and controversial application of LSA has been its use in automated essay grading. Using the semantic vectors provided by LSA, it is possible to compare novel student essays to essays that have already been graded. If the new essay is most similar to the A essays it is awarded an A, and so forth. The accuracy of LSA at this task is remarkable. It has been consistently shown to correlate with human markers at rates equivalent to the agreement between humans.

While LSA is the best studied of statistical semantics models, a number of other alternatives exist. These include the vector space model, hyperspace analogue to language (HAL) model, the topics model, and sparse nonnegative matrix factorization. Each of these models has its strengths and weaknesses. The topics model has been shown to provide a good account of human free association norms, HAL does a good job of modeling deep dyslexia, while the vector space model, sparse nonnegative matrix factorization, and LSA perform best on document-similarity rating tasks. The topics model and sparse nonnegative matrix factorization have

the advantage that they produce vectors with dimensions that tend to be easily interpretable. As of yet, however, no single system addresses all the phenomena of conceptual semantic memory.

Networks of Concepts

Concepts do not exist in isolation but rather are connected together in a web of relationships. Mark Steyvers and Joshua Tenenbaum showed that semantic networks (e.g., the network of associates that people generate) have a small-world structure characterized by sparse connectivity, short average path lengths between words, and strong local clustering. Furthermore, most words have relatively few connections, while a few have high connectivity. These observations are important because they provide constraints on the nature of the process by which conceptual structures grow. A simple model in which new concepts are preferentially attached to already well-connected concepts—a rich-get-richer approach—is sufficient to generate the kinds of graphs observed in adult data.

Propositional Knowledge

What all automated models of conceptual structure have in common is that they assume that documents are bags of words. That is, they do not take into account the order with which words appear and consequently cannot address the question of how propositional knowledge is extracted. Clearly, the sentence "John loves Mary" is not equivalent to the sentence "Mary loves John." In the first case, John is the lover and, in the second, Mary is. To capture propositional knowledge, one must take into account word order, particularly in languages like English in which word order plays a pivotal role in determining who did what to whom.

Constructing a proposition involves assigning semantic roles (like "lover") to the entities described in a sentence (like "John"). The problem has been studied at least since Panini, an Indian scholar who worked around 500 BCE. Today, the majority of effort in this area assumes that one has an existing set of semantic roles and access to a corpus in which the roles have been identified before attempting to label new sentences. What this does not explain, however, is how people are able to induce the set of semantic roles in the first instance, or how they are able to learn when they are not provided with labeled training data.

Simon Dennis provided an answer to this question that revolves around the distinction between syntagmatic and paradigmatic associations. Syntagmatic associations occur between words that appear together in utterances (e.g., *run fast*). Paradigmatic associations occur between words that appear in similar contexts but not necessarily in the same utterances (e.g., *deep* and *shallow*). To understand the logic of the model, suppose we have the following corpus:

John loves Mary

Todd loves Sarah

Barack loves Michelle

Who loves Sarah? Todd

Who loves Michelle? Barack

and then present it with the question "Who loves Mary? xxx." The job of the model is to fill in the "xxx" slot indicating that it understands that John is the lover. To begin with, the model uses syntagmatic associations to determine that words like *Todd* and *Barack* could appear in the xxx slot. This pattern—{Barack, Todd}—represents the lover role. Note a similar pattern occurs in the *John* slot when the model is processing the sentence "John loves Mary." As a consequence, paradigmatic associations form between the {Barack, Todd} pattern and John. The paradigmatic mechanism in itself, however, would not suffice to predict John, as Barack and Todd are also associated with the lover pattern. Only John has an associative connection to Mary, however, and the additional support afforded by this connection favors John.

The syntagmatic paradigmatic mechanism has been shown to be capable of answering simple questions about tennis matches. Taking naturally occurring text from the Association of Tennis Professionals website, the model was able to complete questions of the form. "Who won the match between Sampras and Agassi? xxx." Particularly interesting was the fact that the model takes advantage of the systematic occurrence of words through the corpus that occurs as a consequence of the causal relationships between events. As a consequence, it can determine results even when they are not explicitly stated. For instance, the model answered the question "Who won the match between Kiefer and Safin?" based on the sentence "Safin, Kafelnikov surge toward hometown showdown," without any explicit knowledge that players can only surge toward a showdown when they win. Rather, it relies on the fact that the pattern of players that surge toward hometown showdowns overlaps with the pattern of players that win matches. This kind of inference may be important in understanding how people acquire the impressive stock of commonsense knowledge necessary for comprehending discourse.

Efforts to create computational models of how propositional information is extracted from language are in their infancy. What is clear, however, is that there is a great deal of information that can be extracted to create large-scale models of semantic memory. Advances in computing power coupled with the development of more sophisticated statistical models are providing a deeper understanding of conceptual and propositional structure and how it is acquired.

Simon Dennis

See also Category Learning, Computational Perspectives; Semantic Memory

Further Readings

Dennis, S. (2005). A memory-based theory of verbal cognition. *Cognitive Science, 29*(2), 145–193.

Griffiths, T. L., Steyvers, M., & Tenenbaum, J. B. (2007). Topics in semantic representation. *Psychological Review, 114*(2), 211–244.

Landauer, T. K., McNamara, D. S., Dennis, S., & Kintsch, W. (Eds.). (2007). *Handbook of latent semantic analysis.* Mahwah, NJ: Erlbaum.

Lund, K., & Burgess, C. (1996). Producing high-dimensional semantic spaces from lexical co-occurrence. *Behavior Research Methods, Instruments, & Computers, 28*(2), 203–208.

Steyvers, M., & Tenenbaum, J. B. (2005). The large-scale structure of semantic networks: Statistical analyses and a model of semantic growth. *Cognitive Science, 29,* 41–78.

Sequential Memory, Computational Perspectives

Sequential memory, also called order memory, refers to the process of remembering a sequence of letters, words, digits, pictures, or sounds (here referred to as items) and reproducing these items in the same order. Sequential memory differs from item memory in that the latter is involved in remembering and reproducing a list of items in any order. Sequential memory is involved in tasks such as reporting back a telephone number and learning to spell a new word. Computational models of sequential memory tackle two questions: How are sequences stored in memory, and how are the items of a sequence selected for output?

Storing Sequences

The earliest view about how the mind stores arbitrary sequences of items is referred to as *chaining*. With chaining, each item is connected with a forward link to the next item. When the sequence has to be retrieved, only the very first item needs to be retrieved and then by following the successive links, the whole sequence is reproduced.

Error patterns seen in data challenge the chaining hypothesis. When performing a task of sequential memory, errors are made that provide insights into how sequences are stored. Imagine that M V F Q S D is the sequence of letters that needs to be remembered by a person. *Omissions* are errors when the person does not report all the items: M V F _ S D. *Transpositions* are items reported in the wrong position: M V F S Q D. *Intrusions* are items that were not presented in the original sequence: M V F P S D. These examples illustrate a problem with the chaining hypothesis, the strong version of which assumes that the cue for the next item to be reported is the just-reported item. With an omission and intrusion, the relevant cue (in the example, Q) is absent and the person should not be able to report the subsequent items (continuing with S), but experiments show that people do continue. As in chaining models, the Q is linked to S, which is linked to D; after incorrectly reporting the S, the model would continue forward with the D and not backward with the Q. However, experiments show that transpositions (reporting Q after incorrectly reporting S) are the most common errors in serial recall.

Computational models that are able to capture the pattern of transposition errors are *compound chaining*, *positional*, and *ordinal* models. Compound chaining models are models that assume that storage of a sequence involves adding the items to an amalgamation of previous items, which then gets chained

to the next item. Positional models are models in which the items are encoded in a gradually changing context representation. This gradual change leads to nearby items being encoded in similar context representations. During retrieval, swaps between nearby items are then possible. Ordinal models are models that assume a gradient over all the items, with the first item being encoded more strongly than the second item, which is encoded more strongly than the third, and so on. During retrieval of items, transpositions will occur for nearby items, as they have similar levels of memory strength.

Two types of errors provide support for the view that the mind stores items relative to (sub)sequence boundaries. When the above sequence is split in two between the third and fourth item, transpositions occur between items that occupy the same intragroup position: M V D—Q S F. This error is called an *interposition*. Similar errors occur across sequences. When reporting the current sequence, an intrusion can occur with an item that was studied in the previous sequence. The intruding item tends to have been studied in that same position in the previous sequence. This error is called a *protrusion*. Computational models can produce these types of errors by resetting the context representation at the beginning of each (sub)sequence.

Reproducing Sequences

One way of producing a sequence is by retrieving from memory one of the items and, if it is the first item, reporting it. After this, the next item is retrieved and output, using a direct (as assumed by chaining models) or indirect link (via the changing context representation) between the first and second item, and so on. The current dominant view is that producing sequences follows a two-stage process. For example, in typing, the time between two consecutive key presses is much shorter than would be expected by a scenario in which the next key press starts when the previous one has completed. Instead, the findings are consistent with a scenario in which several fingers are moving toward the relevant keys, and only one finger is allowed to complete the response. The simultaneous activation of responses (the first stage), together with the selection of one response (the second stage), leads to smooth production of the items (key presses); this two-stage process has been called *competitive queuing*.

In computational models of sequential memory, competitive queuing is central to sequence production. The dynamics are such that after cues activate the target items, the item with the strongest support is selected and output. After output, this item is inhibited so that the next strongest item can be selected and output. As ordinal models have a rank ordering of items from strong to weak, these models produce the items in the forward order. As positional models do not have a gradient that rank orders the items, the context signal is replayed and candidate items activated. The strongest item is the most likely item that was encoded in that position and will be output (unless it was already output erroneously).

Eddy J. Davelaar

See also Natural Action Selection, Modeling; Serial Order Memory, Computational Perspectives

Further Readings

Henson, R. N. A. (1998). Short-term memory for serial order: The start-end model. *Cognitive Psychology*, 36(2), 73–137.

Houghton, G. (1990). The problem of serial order: A neural network model of sequence learning and recall. In R. Dale, C. Mellish, & M. Zock (Eds.), *Current research in natural language generation* (pp. 287–319). London, UK: Academic Press.

Lashley, K. S. (1951). The problem of serial order in behaviour. In L. A. Jeffress (Ed.), *Cerebral mechanisms in behaviour: The Hixon Symposium* (pp. 112–136). New York, NY: John Wiley.

SERIAL ORDER MEMORY, COMPUTATIONAL PERSPECTIVES

Serial recall requires people to accurately remember and recall the order of sequences of information such as letters, digits, and spatial locations over short periods of time. This task is of interest as one of a number of tasks used by both researchers and clinicians to tap short-term memory abilities; when combined with an interleaved processing task (e.g., a choice reaction time task), the combination is a good predictor of higher level cognitive abilities such as reasoning. Serial recall is especially popular given the specific focus on memory for the order of information and has been argued to be fundamentally involved in learning the phonology of new words. Reflecting this interest, a number of models of serial recall have been developed to account for serial recall performance. The theoretical development in this area has been impressive, with models accounting for a comprehensive set of data at a fine level of detail. The key phenomena accounted for by these models include primacy and recency, whereby memory accuracy declines across positions in the sequence with the exception that the last one or two items in a sequence are better remembered; the locality effect, whereby an item recalled in an incorrect position will nonetheless tend to be recalled in a nearby position; and the phonological similarity effect, where verbal materials that rhyme or share a number of phonemes will be less well recalled, particularly because of worse memory for the ordering of those materials in the sequence.

Representing Order

One basic issue addressed by these models is how the order of elements in a sequence is represented. Figure 1 shows three general schemes of representation of order in contemporary models of serial order. In the top scheme, *chaining*, adjacent elements of a sequence are associated in memory. Once an item is recalled, the following item can be accessed by using the recalled item to cue the next item via the pair association. Although Stephan Lewandowsky and Bennet Murdock showed that the chaining model could account for many of the key phenomena described above, later work has challenged this model. A particularly troublesome finding is that alternating rhyming and nonrhyming items in a sequence does not harm—and may even enhance—recall of the dissimilar items. Chaining models predict that confusions of rhyming items should be followed by confusions of nonrhyming items: When a rhyming item is recalled in the wrong position, the following nonrhyming item should move with it and thus be incorrectly ordered.

This led to the development of *primacy gradient* models, in which order is represented as a gradient of activation or encoding strength across items. These models successfully account for many of the key phenomena and can allow nonrhyming items to be protected from confusions between rhyming items by assuming that phonological confusions occur in a stage downstream from the primacy gradient. One challenge to these models is the effect of grouping on serial recall: Temporally grouping a sequence by placing pauses between subsequences produces primacy and recency within subsequences and also leads to specific patterns of confusions in between groups, the most telling of these being that elements that appear at the same position in different subsequences are more likely to be confused. These grouping effects imply some form of factorial or hierarchical representation in short-term memory, taking these data beyond the limits of the unidimensional, strength-based, primacy-gradient models.

Positional tagging models address this shortcoming by explicitly introducing a multidimensional representation of order that is located separately from the item representations. Incoming sequence elements are associated to successive positional tags with proximate tags overlapping to a larger extent than tags separated by a large number of intervening tags. Grouped lists are represented jointly by tags coding the position of an element in a group and some coarser representation of that element in the entire list. One debate is whether these tags code the real-time occurrence of items, whether they instead represent the relative timing of items, or whether these tags are purely ordinal and driven by successive encoding events.

Mechanisms of Encoding and Retrieval

Aspects of serial recall data imply additional mechanisms at play in the encoding and retrieval of sequences. To explain the generation of the primacy gradient, Lewandowsky and Simon Farrell suggested that the strength of encoding of elements is determined by the novelty of each element with respect to those already in memory. Successive elements will be less and less novel, thereby leading to a primacy gradient. Additionally, most models assume some form of response suppression whereby those elements that have already been recalled are reduced in activation or competition to prevent their further recall. This is used to explain the unwillingness of participants to repeat elements in their output even when sequences do actually contain repetitions.

Contemporary models also address the role of serial recall in the long-term learning of sequences. Recent work aims at accounting for the Hebb effect—the improvement in performance following

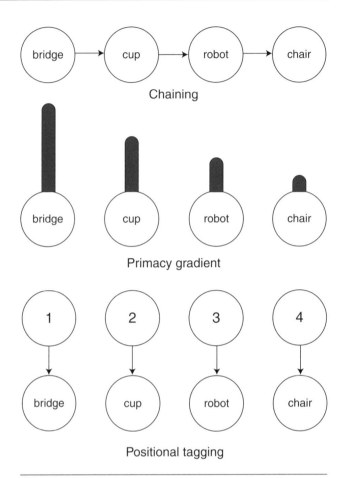

Figure 1   Schemes for representing order in memory

from (nonimmediately) repeated presentations of a list—and relating this to the claimed purpose of verbal short-term memory as a mechanism to learn new words (sequences of phonemes). The model of Neil Burgess and Graham Hitch assumes that the associations between position tags and elements are retained into following sequences and that an incoming sequence is matched to all those previously learned sequences. The Hebb effect results from the fact that repeating a sequence will lead to the continued reuse and strengthening of the specific tag-element associations for that sequence.

Simon Farrell

See also Sequential Memory, Computational Perspectives; Working Memory

Further Readings

Burgess, N., & Hitch, G. J. (2006). A revised model of short-term memory and long-term learning of verbal sequences. *Journal of Memory and Language, 55,* 627–652.

Henson, R. N. A. (1999). Coding position in short-term memory. *International Journal of Psychology, 34,* 403–409.

Lewandowsky, S., & Farrell, S. (2008). Short-term memory: New data and a model. In B. H. Ross (Ed.), *The psychology of learning and motivation* (Vol. 49, pp. 1–48). London, UK: Elsevier.

SIMILARITY

An enormous amount of ink has been spilled in the psychology literature on the topic of similarity. There are two reasons that this seemingly intuitive and prosaic concept has been the subject of such intense scrutiny. First, there is virtually no area of cognitive processing in which similarity does not seem to play a role. William James observed in 1890 that "this sense of Sameness is the very keel and backbone of our thinking" (p. 459). Ivan Pavlov first noted that dogs would generalize their learned salivation response to new sounds as a function of their similarity to the original tone, and this pattern of generalization appears to be ubiquitous across species and stimuli. People group things together based on their similarity, both during visual processing and categorization. Research suggests that memories are retrieved when they involve similar features or similar processing to a current situation. Problem solutions are likely to be retrieved from similar prior problems, inductive inference is largely based on the similarity between the known and unknown cases, and the list goes on and on.

Psychology clearly has an enormous stake in similarity. In fact, the depth of this stake makes it that much more unsettling that similarity can be such a slippery and temperamental construct. Perceived similarity can vary considerably with context. In fact, the act of comparison itself can change people's representations, leading them to construe things as more comparable by reinterpreting the given features or even creating new features. Similarity ratings are often asymmetric; for instance, people view North Korea to be more similar to China than the reverse. Likewise, similarity and difference are not always the inverse of one another. When given a choice between XX and OX, people choose XX as both more similar to and more different from

OO. Similarity can change systematically with temporal distance and physical distance, and there is a growing body of evidence for consistent individual differences in which kinds of features drive a person's similarity judgments. Judgments of similarity can increase with simple association. For example, coffee is judged to be similar to cream because it is contextually associated with cream. In the absence of objective ways to measure psychological similarity, researchers are left to rely on participants' subjective judgments of their own processing, which are potentially unreliable, or on data from tasks in which similarity is proposed to play a role, leading to conclusions that are potentially circular. Thus, it is possible that similarity is both the most essential and the most problematic construct in cognitive science. This entry discusses some of the important findings from the extensive literature on similarity and the ways in which psychologists have attempted to address a topic so critical to our understanding of the mind and yet so elusive.

Theories of Similarity

As one might expect given the importance of similarity for thinking, it is understandable that there have been several attempts to formalize the process of determining similarity. These formal accounts stipulate how similarity is to be empirically measured and provide theoretic accounts of how similarity should be conceptualized. The resulting models have had a large practical impact in knowledge representation, automatic pattern recognition by machines, search engines, data mining, and marketing (e.g., online stores that recommend new products to you based on your similarity to previous buyers). The entry surveys four of the most prominent models of similarity: geometric, feature based, alignment based, and transformational.

Geometric Models and Multidimensional Scaling

Geometric models work under the premise that what it means for two things to be similar is for them to be close to one another in a psychological space. These approaches are exemplified by the statistical modeling technique of multidimensional scaling (MDS). MDS models represent similarity relations between entities as a geometric model that consists of a set of points embedded in a space. The input to MDS routines may be similarity judgments, confusions between entities, patterns of co-occurrence in large samples of text, or any other measure of pairwise proximity. Most straightforwardly, participants may be asked to judge how similar every object in a set is to every other object. The output of an MDS routine is a geometric model of the set of objects with each object represented as a point in an *n*-dimensional space. The similarity between a pair of objects is inversely related to the distance between the objects' points in the space. In MDS, the distance between points *i* and *j* is typically computed by

$$dissimilarity(i,j) = \left[\sum_{k=1}^{n} |X_{ik} - X_{jk}|^r \right]^{\frac{1}{r}}$$

where *n* is the number of dimensions, X_{ik} is the value of dimension *k* for item *i*, and *r* is a parameter that allows different spatial metrics to be used. With *r* = 2, as in standard Euclidean geometry, the distance between two points is the length of the straight line connecting them. If *r* = 1, then distance involves a city-block metric in which the distance between two points is the sum of their distances on each dimension; "short-cut" diagonal paths are not allowed. Empirically, the Euclidean distance measure typically fits human data better when the stimuli being compared consist of perceptual dimensions that are psychologically fused together. For example, brightness is a subjective dimension related to the amount of luminance energy coming off of an object. Saturation is a subjective dimension related to the amount of monochromatic light mixed into a color. Brightness and saturation are psychologically fused in the sense that it is difficult to pay attention to brightness differences between objects without also being influenced by saturation differences. For objects differing on saturation and brightness, their subjective similarity is best measured by a distance calculation that fully integrates saturation and brightness differences together—namely, *r* = 1. Conversely, if objects differ on brightness and size, then their similarity is best measured by computing their distance on brightness and then adding this to their distance on size—namely, *r* = 2.

A classic example of MDS comes from Ed Smith, Edward Shoben, and Lance Rips's study of animal concepts. They asked participants to provide similarity ratings on many pairs of birds or other animals. Submitting these pair-wise similarity ratings to MDS analysis, they obtained the results shown in Figure 1. The MDS algorithm produced this geometric representation by positioning the birds in a two-dimensional space such that birds rated as being highly similar are very close to each other.

One practical limitation of MDS is that obtaining all pairwise similarity ratings among a large set of objects requires a substantial commitment of time and effort. If similarity ratings are used as the input to MDS, then standard N^2 ratings are required for *N* objects. This number is halved if one assumes that the similarity of A to B is the same as the similarity of B to A. Even with this halving, the number of ratings still becomes prohibitively large as *N* increases. Fortunately, automated techniques for analyzing large corpora of text can provide input to MDS models instead of relying on "manually" provided ratings. Using this method, latent semantic analysis is a computational approach to word meaning that has received considerable recent attention. It bases word meanings solely on the patterns of co-occurrence between a large number of words in an extremely large text corpus such as an encyclopedia or thousands of email messages. It employs the mathematical analysis tool of singular value decomposition (SVD) to create vector encodings of words that efficiently capture their co-occurrences; these encodings represent each word by an ordered set of numbers—that is, a vector. The similarities between two words' vectors efficiently capture their co-occurrences. If two words, such as *cocoon* and *butterfly*, frequently co-occur or enter into similar patterns of co-occurrence with other words, their vector representations will be highly similar. The meaning of a word, its vector in a high dimensional space, is completely based on the contextual similarities among words. Within this high dimensional space, Thomas Landauer and Susan Dumais conceive of similarity as the cosine of the angle between two words rather than as their distance. By using these new techniques, it is possible to create geometric spaces with tens of thousands of words.

Featural Models

In the 1970s, it was observed that subjective assessments of similarity do not always satisfy the assumptions of geometric models of similarity:

Minimality: D(A,B) ≥ D(A,A) = 0

Symmetry: D(A,B) = D(B,A)

The Triangle Inequality: D(A,B)
    + D(B,C) ≥ D(A,C)

A   **B**

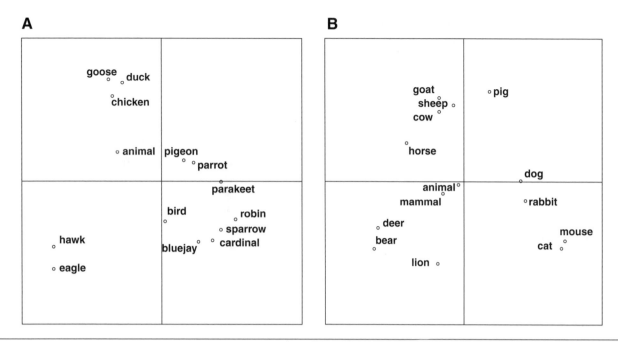

Figure 1   Two multidimensional scaling (MDS) solutions for sets of birds (A) and animals (B)

Source: From Smith, E. E., Shoben, E. J., & Rips, L. J. (1974). Structure and process in semantic memory: A featural model for semantic decisions. *Psychological Review, 81,* 214–241.

Note: The distances between the animals in the space reflect their psychological dissimilarity. Once an MDS solution has been made, psychological interpretations for the dimensions may be possible. In these solutions, the horizontal and vertical dimensions may represent size and domesticity, respectively.

where D(A,B) is interpreted as the dissimilarity between items A and B. Minimality captures the simple ideas that no object should be more dissimilar to itself than it is to another object and that the dissimilarity of an object to itself should be 0. Symmetry captures the notion that the dissimilarity of Object A to B should be the same as the dissimilarity of Object B to A. Whatever Lady Gaga's similarity is to Madonna should be the same as Madonna's similarity to Lady Gaga. The notion behind the triangle inequality is that the length of the direct path from A to C should be no longer than the path from A to B plus the path from B to C. For similarities, this means that if a red square (A) is fairly distant from (dissimilar from) a blue circle (C) then the red square's distance to a red circle (B) and the red circle's distance to the blue circle cannot both be very short, otherwise the two-legged detour route from A to C going through B will be shorter than the direct route from A to C.

In fact, violations of all three assumptions have been empirically obtained. In response to these violations of the geometric model of similarity, some researchers have proposed fixes that allow, for example, the local density of objects in a region to warp the calculation of distance/dissimilarity. More radically, in 1977 Amos Tversky proposed to model similarity according to matching and mismatching features rather than distance on psychological dimensions. In his model, entities are represented as a collection of features and similarity is computed by

$$S(A,B) = \theta f(A \cap B) - \alpha f(A - B) - \beta f(B - A)$$

where S(A,B) is the similarity of Object A to Object B and is expressed as a linear combination of the measure of the common and distinctive features. The term (A ∩ B) represents the features that Objects A and B have in common. (A − B) represents the features that A has but B does not. (B − A) represents the features of B that are not in A. And the θ, α, and β are weights for the common and distinctive components, reflecting how important each component is for determining similarity. For example, in Figure 2 we imagine comparing robots (A) to zombies (B). This would be accomplished by first determining all the features of each of these two objects. Then, their similarity is calculated to be a positive function of their shared features and a negative function of the features possessed by robots but not zombies (A – B) and of the features possessed by zombies but not robots (B – A).

Alignment-Based Models

MDS and featural models make different assumptions about similarity, but they also share a number of similarities. An important commonality between geometric and featural representations is that both use relatively unstructured representations with entities structured as sets of unrelated features or dimensions. However, entities such as objects with parts, real-world scenes, words, sentences, stories, scientific theories, and faces are not simply a "grab bag" of attributes. A dog biting a man is not the same thing as a man biting a dog, even though they both feature a dog, a man, and biting. How these elements are related matters. Partly in response to the problems that geometric and featural models have with structured descriptions, a number of researchers have developed alignment-based models of similarity. In these models, comparison does not just involve matching features but also involves determining how elements correspond to, or align with, one another. Matching features are aligned to

the extent that they play similar roles within their entities. For example, a man wearing a black tie and a woman with black shoes both share the feature *black*, but this matching feature may not increase their similarity much because the man's tie does not correspond to the woman's shoes. Drawing inspiration from a structure-matching model of analogical reasoning by Dedre Gentner, in alignment-based models, matching features influence similarity more if they belong to parts that are in correspondence, and conversely, parts tend to be placed in correspondence if they have many features in common.

Transformational Models

A final approach to similarity maintains that the similarity of two objects is directly related to the number of transformations required to turn one object into the other. An important step for these models is to specify what transformations are possible.

Researchers in artificial intelligence have claimed that objects are recognized by being aligned with memorized pictorial descriptions. An unknown object will be placed in the category that contains the candidate model with which it best aligns. The alignment operations rotate, scale, translate, and topographically warp object descriptions.

According to Ulrike Hahn, Nick Chater, and Lucy Richardson, the similarity between two entities is based on how complex the sequence of transformations is that changes one entity to the other. The simpler the transformation sequence, the more similar the entities are assumed to be. For example, the transformational complexity connecting 1 2 3 4 5 6 7 8 and 2 3 4 5 6 7 8 9 is small because the simple instruction "add 1 to each digit" suffices to transform one into the other. Experiments demonstrate that once reasonable vocabularies of transformation are postulated, transformational complexity does indeed predict subjective similarity ratings. Furthermore, when a new transformation is learned that turns Object A into Object B, A is seen as more similar to B.

Conclusions

It might be argued that all four of the above approaches err on the side of treating similarity as a unitary phenomenon. It could well turn out that calculating similarity is fundamentally different for

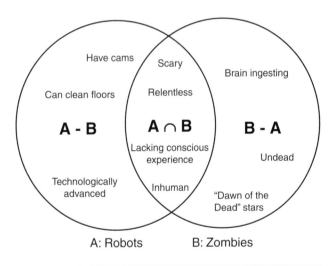

Figure 2 A Venn diagram showing some of the features of robots and zombies

Note: Featural models take the similarity of robots to zombies to be a positive function of the features shared by both and negative functions of the features possessed by one but not the other.

different kinds of entities. Taken to an extreme, this notion raises the possibility that similarity is not a coherent notion at all. Like the terms *bug* or *family values, similarity* may not pick out a consolidated or principled set of things. Consistent with this possibility, it may be that much of the real theoretical work in the future will be achieved by determining what counts as the features and relations that underlie similarity assessments for different kinds of entities and in different situations. Nonetheless, one justification for pursuing general theories of similarity is that if they do exist, a large payoff results. Even if similarity is not a monolithic *entity*, there probably will be common cognitive processes involved in different kinds of comparisons.

Some philosophers have attacked the very notion of similarity as being empty or circular. They have pointed out that the claim that entities A and B are similar is vague and ill defined unless one specifies the aspects under consideration when making the claim. However, part of the power of the notion of similarity is that it integrates over many aspects of entities. All four of the models of similarity can be interpreted as proposals for how the process of integrating across aspects proceeds. By integrating over many aspects, similarity is a powerful tool for cognition because it does not require the cognizer to fully understand exactly what makes entities behave as they do. It only requires that the world is a sufficiently orderly place that similar objects and events tend to behave similarly. This fact of the world is not just a fortunate coincidence. It is *because* objects are similar that they tend to behave similarly in most respects.

Robert L. Goldstone and Samuel B. Day

See also Analogical Mapping and Reasoning; Categorization, Psychological Perspectives; Category Learning, Computational perspectives; Concepts, Development of; Concepts, Philosophical Issues; Semantic Memory; Semantic Memory, Computational Perspectives

Further Readings

Gentner, D. (1983). Structure-mapping: A theoretical framework for analogy. *Cognitive Science, 7,* 155–170.

Goldstone, R. L. (1994). Similarity, interactive activation, and mapping. *Journal of Experimental Psychology: Learning, Memory, and Cognition, 20,* 3–28.

Hahn, U., Chater, N., & Richardson, L. B. (2003). Similarity as transformation. *Cognition, 87,* 1–32.

Holyoak, K. J., & Thagard, P. (1995). *Mental leaps: Analogy in creative thought.* Cambridge, MA: MIT Press.

James, W. (1950). *The principles of psychology.* New York, NY: Dover. (Original work published 1890)

Landauer, T. K., & Dumais, S. T. (1997). A solution to Plato's problem: The latent semantic analysis theory of the acquisition, induction, and representation of knowledge. *Psychological Review, 104,* 211–240.

Medin, D. L., Goldstone, R. L., & Gentner, D. (1993). Respects for similarity. *Psychological Review, 100,* 254–278.

Shepard, R. N. (1962). The analysis of proximities: Multidimensional scaling with an unknown distance function. Part I. *Psychometrika, 27,* 125–140.

Smith, E. E., Shoben, E. J., & Rips, L. J. (1974). Structure and process in semantic memory: A featural model for semantic decisions. *Psychological Review, 81,* 214–241.

Tenenbaum, J. B., & Griffiths, T. L. (2001). Generalization, similarity, and Bayesian inference. *Behavioral & Brain Sciences, 24,* 629–640.

Tversky, A. (1977). Features of similarity. *Psychological Review, 84,* 327–352.

SKILL LEARNING, ENHANCEMENT OF

Skill learning involves experience that leads to improvements in performance. This concept must be distinguished from the similar concept of knowledge acquisition. For skill learning, performance requires attaining procedures, whereas for knowledge acquisition, it requires attaining facts. However, most, if not all, activities involve both procedural information (skill) and declarative information (facts).

To enhance skill learning, three different aspects of the process should be strengthened: acquisition, retention, and transfer. First, training of the skills should be accomplished quickly and efficiently to reduce costs and save time and effort. Second, the skills should be made as durable as possible so that following training they can still be available at a high level even when they have not been used for a long period of time. Third, the skills should be made as flexible as possible so that they can be applied in different contexts and their use is not restricted to the particular situations encountered during training. Research in experimental psychology has led to several principles of training that can enhance the efficiency, durability, and flexibility of skill learning.

Principles of Training

Deliberate Practice

Skill learning usually occurs gradually, with individuals improving their response speed following what is known as the *power law of practice*. According to this law, practice helps most at the beginning, but even after many trials, practice continues to make individuals faster. There is also a complementary power law of forgetting, which accounts for a gradual decline in performance with the passage of time when there is no opportunity to refresh the acquired skills.

Even though the acquisition and retention of skills are well described by these power laws, learning and memory of skills vary depending on multiple factors. One such factor is type of practice. Not all practice is equal in promoting skill learning. Deliberate practice, which requires a high degree of focus and motivation, is required for achieving expert levels of performance, even among individuals who seem to show a natural talent or aptitude for a particular skill.

Procedural Reinstatement

Although acquired knowledge is forgotten very rapidly, learned skills are usually very well retained across periods of disuse. For example, learning a telephone number from a phone book might not survive the 30 seconds it takes to walk from the book to the telephone and dial the number. In contrast, learning how to use a hula hoop might survive years in which no hoop is available so that an individual who learned how to use a hula hoop as a child might be able to use the hoop again perfectly well as an adult, even if there was no intervening practice with the hoop since childhood. However, skill learning is usually not very flexible whereas knowledge acquired in one situation can be easily applied to many other situations. Thus, to continue with the examples, the learned hula hoop skill might not help performance with a hoop that is not the same size as the ones used during childhood, but the knowledge of acquired telephone numbers can be used in many different contexts, including the learning of new sequences of numbers. These observations form the *procedural reinstatement* principle, according to which declarative information shows

poor retention but robust transfer and procedural information shows strong retention but limited transfer.

Evidence supporting this principle comes from experiments showing a high degree of specificity of skill learning. For example, students learned how to use a computer mouse to move a screen cursor from a central location to targets along the screen periphery. The task was made more difficult by changing the relationship between the mouse and the cursor. In one situation the cursor moved left whenever the mouse moved right and vice versa, but the up-down relationship between mouse and cursor movements were intact. Students were able to acquire this skill rapidly and retained it well over a long delay, but in many cases they could not transfer the skill involving one mouse-cursor relationship to that involving another; in fact, sometimes there was interference from learning the first relationship to learning the second. Other experiments show that skills are specific to the context in which they are learned. For instance, students learned how to produce time intervals based on arbitrary units. They were not told how long a given unit was, but they received feedback on their productions, allowing them to become increasingly more accurate. These time intervals were produced in the context of various background tasks, such as the difficult task of repeating the alphabet backward by threes. The difficult tasks lowered performance on time production, but after learning to produce time intervals with one background task, participants could not generalize their skill to producing time intervals with another background task, even when they changed from a difficult background task to no background task at all.

Variability of Practice

Especially given the lack of transfer found for skill learning, it is important to consider whether there are training methods that can be employed to help promote skill transfer. One such method that has proven to be effective is based on *variability of practice*. Training with a variety of tasks usually leads to better transfer performance than training with a single, constant task. This benefit for variable training is sometimes found even when the task used in testing differs from those used during variable practice and is the same as that used during constant practice. For example, practice that varied the target distance at which bean bags were tossed by children (2 or 4 feet) led to better accuracy at test on an intermediate target distance (3 feet) than did practice that was restricted to the same intermediate target distance. This variability of practice principle has been found to apply to both discrete and continuous motor tasks as well as to various cognitive tasks such as learning new concepts or understanding passages of text.

Contextual Interference

Most teachers try to make learning as easy as possible for their students. Indeed students will learn more rapidly under easy conditions than under difficult conditions, and tests of performance immediately after learning will often be better for students who learned under easy conditions than under difficult conditions. However, when testing the same students after a delay or in a new situation, it is often found that performance is better for students who learned under difficult than under easy conditions. In fact, introducing desirable sources of difficulty or interference during training has been shown to be an effective way to promote retention and transfer, following the principle of *contextual interference.*

The most common way to study contextual interference has been to compare mixed and blocked practice schedules. In blocked practice schedules, practice with a given task or with a given set of materials occurs together in the same block of trials, whereas in mixed practice schedules, practice occurs on each task or with each set of materials in every block. Mixing tasks or materials during training produces interference and, thus, retards initial skill learning but often enhances ultimate skill use.

Distribution of Practice

A related way to enhance skill learning concerns the distribution of practice. Practice trials can occur without interruptions or with no time in between trials, in which case they are *massed.* Alternatively, such trials can occur *spaced* apart or distributed in time. It has generally been found that spaced practice is better than massed practice, especially with a long retention interval, or delay between the end of learning and the beginning of testing. In fact, optimal performance at test seems to result when the interval between practice trials is approximately equal in length to the retention interval. This conclusion seems to hold even when practice is distributed across sessions rather than across trials within a session.

Another related question concerns the order in which to train tasks that vary in difficulty. According to one line of research, *errorless learning* should be encouraged. With errorless learning of a motor skill, trainees start with the easiest task and then gradually progress to more difficult tasks. For example, in learning how to putt a golf ball, the trainee might start with the shortest putting distance and then gradually increase the distance. This arrangement of practice trials should be likely to reduce the number of errors made by the trainees relative to other arrangements. It has been argued that when more errors are made during skill learning, performance requires more attention-demanding resources than when errors are minimized, so that distractions and stress cause less performance disruption following errorless learning than following learning that occurs with frequent errors.

Focus of Attention

The demands of attention are also relevant to another training principle that specifically involves the focus of attention. It has been shown for a variety of sport skills, again including golf shots, that an external focus of attention leads to better retention than does an internal focus of attention. With an external focus, attention is given to the results of a movement (e.g., where the ball lands) whereas, with an internal focus, attention is given to the movements of the body (e.g., how the arms move during the swing). The claim has been made that an internal focus requires conscious attention to motor movements and such attention impairs automatic mechanisms in the body underlying skilled performance.

Mental Practice

Whether using an internal or external focus of attention, practice is necessary for skill improvement. However, there are times when it might be inconvenient or even impossible to practice a skill, especially if the skill requires special equipment not readily available. The question arises as to whether mental practice can provide a reasonable substitute for physical practice in those circumstances. In one study involving data entry, participants practiced typing four-digit numbers on a computer, either by actually typing the numbers or by just imagining their typing movements. For both types of practice, participants increased the speed at which they executed the typing responses, showing equivalent improvements in typing skill. When practice involved a key configuration different from that at testing, participants who used physical practice but not those who used mental practice suffered from interference. These results suggest that mental practice supports a more abstract representation of the skill than does physical practice.

Cognitive Antidote

Although practice usually leads to improvements in skill performance, sometimes performance on a task deteriorates with prolonged work on that task. In fact, for the routine data entry skill, lengthy practice led to both improvement and deterioration, depending on the measure used to assess skill performance. For response speed, performance got better and better with practice, but for accuracy, performance got worse and worse. This pattern illustrates an increasing trade-off of accuracy for speed. The faster speed is easily understood in terms of the principles already discussed, whereas the decline in accuracy can be explained in terms of increasing fatigue, boredom, and task disengagement. The drop in accuracy can be overcome, though, by providing feedback about errors, thus increasing motivation. In addition, accuracy can be enhanced and the decline in accuracy eliminated by requiring an extra cognitive task, such as ending the typing response for each number by hitting either a + key or a – key, with the two keys alternating across trials. This cognitive antidote serves to eliminate the speed-accuracy trade-off otherwise observed as a result of prolonged work.

Conclusions

In summary, skill learning can be done efficiently with improved skill performance occurring even following a long delay after practice is completed. However, transferring the skill to new situations is often difficult but can be promoted by following a number of training principles, which recommend employing deliberate practice, increasing the variability of practice, adding sources of contextual interference, using a mixed practice schedule, distributing practice in time, eliminating errors, and using an external focus of attention. Mental practice can substitute for physical practice, and boredom can be overcome by adding a cognitive antidote to routine tasks.

Alice F. Healy

See also Desirable Difficulties Perspective on Learning; Motor Learning, Practical Aspects; Rehearsal and Memory; Spacing Effect; Spacing Effect, Practical Applications

Further Readings

Battig, W. F. (1979). The flexibility of human memory. In L. S. Cermak & F. I. M. Craik (Eds.), *Levels of processing in human memory* (pp. 23–44). Hillsdale, NJ: Erlbaum.

Cepeda, N., Pashler, H., Vul, E., Wixted, J. T., & Rohrer, D. (2006). Distributed practice in verbal recall tasks: A review and quantitative synthesis. *Psychological Bulletin, 132,* 354–380.

Ericsson, K. A., Krampe, R. T., & Tesch-Römer, C. (1993). The role of deliberate practice in the acquisition of expert performance. *Psychological Review, 100,* 363–406.

Healy, A. F. (2007). Transfer: Specificity and generality. In H. L. Roediger, III, Y. Dudai, & S. M. Fitzpatrick (Eds.), *Science of memory: Concepts* (pp. 271–275). New York, NY: Oxford University Press.

Kole, J. A., Healy, A. F., & Bourne, L. E., Jr. (2008). Cognitive complications moderate the speed-accuracy tradeoff in data entry: A cognitive antidote to inhibition. *Applied Cognitive Psychology, 22,* 917–937.

Maxwell, J. P., Masters, R. S. W., Kerr, E., & Weedon, E. (2001). The implicit benefit of learning without errors. *Quarterly Journal of Experimental Psychology: Human Experimental Psychology, 54A,* 1049–1068.

Schmidt, R. A., & Bjork, R. A. (1992). New conceptualizations of practice: Common principles in three paradigms suggest new concepts for training. *Psychological Science, 3,* 207–217.

Wixted, J. T., & Carpenter, S. K. (2007). The Wickelgren power law and the Ebbinghaus savings function. *Psychological Science, 18,* 133–134.

Wohldmann, E. L., Healy, A. F., & Bourne, L. E., Jr. (2008). A mental practice superiority effect: Less retroactive interference and more transfer than physical practice. *Journal of Experimental Psychology: Learning, Memory and Cognition, 34,* 823–833.

Wulf, G. (2007). *Attention and motor skill learning.* Champaign, IL: Human Kinetics.

SLEEP AND DREAMS

Within a day, all animals and humans show recurring periods of immobility, usually in a characteristic posture and environment, and associated with an apparent loss of responsiveness to environmental input—they sleep. In contrast to a comatose state, some sensory discrimination is preserved and sleep is reversible when strong stimulation is applied.

Historically, the views that sleep is simply rest and that dreams convey a special meaning has prevailed in most cultures. Dream contents were assigned a mystical dimension—they were seen as messages sent by a god or as representing states unavailable to waking consciousness and foretelling future events, an attitude still popular. Contrary to these subjective interpretations, but instead based on measurable changes of brain activity and information processing mechanisms, research activities in the past decades have clarified different states within sleep, have unraveled many active processes within sleep, and have highlighted neurobiological processes underlying a multitude of sleep-related phenomena in animals and in humans. Until now, several functions of sleep have been proposed, ranging from energy conservation, thermoregulation, and detoxification to brain plasticity processes resulting in functional or structural changes. Current knowledge substantiates that neuronal assemblies are active, reactivated, or even modified during sleep.

This entry reviews the classic and more recently applied methods to study sleep and sleep-related phenomena. These approaches allow us to describe the substantial changes in the brain's capacities to process external information and brain activation patterns across the different stages of sleep and to investigate the neuronal basis of dream mentation.

Methods

The current understanding of cortical activity across the different stages of waking and sleep mainly derives from surface electroencephalographic (EEG) recordings reflecting cerebral synaptic activity. As a consequence, EEG criteria are generally used to differentiate the increasing depth of sleep on slowing of the EEG rhythms. The formerly held belief of sleep as a cessation of brain activity and annihilation of consciousness was finally overthrown in 1953 when Eugene Aserinsky and Nathaniel Kleitman first described an active brain state recurring in regular intervals within sleep. This state is accompanied by a loss of voluntary muscle control and by rapid eye movements. It is therefore called rapid eye movement (REM) sleep or *paradoxical sleep*, as it shares

many features of neuronal behavior with wakefulness but still represents a sleeping state with high arousal thresholds.

Electrophysiological Sleep Recordings

REM and non-REM (NREM) sleep stages can be differentiated based on recorded EEG, eye movement (electrooculographic [EOG]), and muscle activity (electromyographic [EMG]) criteria. Waking and consciousness rely on activity of neurons in the *formatio reticularis* (reticular formation) of the brain stem, forming the ascending reticular activating system projecting to the thalamus and cortex. Waking EEG recordings are dominated by fast frequency activity in the beta (15–30 Hertz [Hz]) and gamma range (30–80 Hz). The electrophysiological signs of NREM sleep—synchronized low-frequency oscillations with high amplitudes in the EEG recordings—seem to confirm the early notion of NREM sleep as a state of rest with cessation of intense cortical activity.

In contrast to NREM sleep, REM sleep shares many signs with wakefulness such as fast-frequency and low-voltage cortical EEG, including gamma oscillations. Whereas slow-wave sleep depends on thalamocortical synchronization, specialized cells in the brain stem called REM sleep-on cells initiate and generate signs of REM sleep. From an evolutionary point of view, REM sleep is exclusively found in birds and mammals—that is, it is unique to endotherm animals with well-developed brains that also express slow-wave activity, with the exception, for example, of dolphins. During ontogenesis (development of the individual), REM sleep is found in relatively high amounts during early development, and a link to brain maturation in phylo- and ontogenesis was proposed. Because of circadian modulation, REM sleep episodes are longest and REM density is strongest at the time of minimal body temperature, usually in the early morning hours. The concurrent inhibition of spinal motoneurons led to the depiction of REM sleep as a "highly activated brain in a paralyzed body," also lacking proper input processing.

Embedded in circadian and ultradian (occurring more than once in 24 hours) rhythms paced by a circadian clock in the suprachiasmatic nucleus, the sleep stages appear in alternating cycles lasting about 90 minutes in adults, with a predominance of slow-wave sleep in the first and of REM sleep in the second half of the night. About 80% of the sleeping time of adult humans is spent in NREM sleep, characterized also by general slowing of body functions. For clinical purposes, sleep recordings are usually extended to *polysomnographic* recordings with additional measurements of functions such as heart rate, breathing parameters, activity of specific muscle groups, and so forth.

The amount of slow-wave activity as measured by EEG spectral analysis is popular as a measure of NREM sleep intensity, which is sensitive to increased sleep pressure (homeostatic upregulation) after sleep deprivation. Intensity of REM sleep can be quantified in percentage and duration of REM sleep episodes and in REM density as a measure of relative amount of, for example, rapid eye movement activity within REM periods. Quantification of EEG data further encompasses a calculation of coherence between electrode positions as a sign of correlated activity or methods for source localization of the electrical activity recorded at the brain surface.

Event-Related Potentials

In addition to these traditional methods of quantifying sleep, mechanisms of information processing can be studied using event-related potentials (ERPs) on stimulation. Here, surface EEG recordings are separated into individual segments and then averaged time-locked to specific stimulus onset times. The averaging process decreases noisy components and highlights stimulus-locked electrophysiological responses in the range of milliseconds to seconds. The components are described by the polarity (positive-negative) and by the latency (amount of time elapsed from the onset) of the local maximum amplitude. Fast components (up to 50 milliseconds [ms]) reflect early signal transduction pathways preceding higher cortical involvement and show longer latencies throughout sleep. Later potentials (e.g., at 300 ms) reflect higher cortical levels of signal processing and display specific alterations during different sleep stages.

Imaging Methods

In the recent years, major advances in imaging methods have enabled new insights into brain processes during sleep. Positron emission tomography (PET) using radioactive tracers and the noninvasive methods of functional magnetic resonance imaging (fMRI), magnetoencephalography (MEG), and high-density EEG recordings provide maps with localization of neuronal activity. These methods highlight the regional specificity of changes in neuronal assemblies linked to sleep-related phenomena.

Behavioral Assessment and Subjective Reports

Measuring cognitive and neuropsychological aspects in relation to sleep such as pre- and post-sleep performance allows for a more comprehensive understanding of sleep-related functions. Next to objective measures, information on subjective experiences plays a crucial role, especially when studying dreams, which cannot be directly observed. Data can be collected via questionnaires, structured or semistructured interviews, or diaries. Apart from collecting spontaneous memories of dream contents, some sleep laboratory studies provoke awakenings of the participant from specific sleep stages and immediately obtain information on ongoing mentation. This procedure can decrease forgetting, but issues such as self-censorship or difficulties with verbal description may still be present.

Information Processing During Sleep

Missing reactions to environmental changes are a prominent hallmark of sleep. To stay asleep, an organism needs to ignore the disturbing environmental influence. Reactivity decreases during falling asleep and, finally, no reactions can be elicited, which has made sleep appear as an entirely passive state. These changes are paralleled by a fading of consciousness. Thus, the first measurements of sleep depth were based on missing reactions to acoustic stimuli of different loudness. On the contrary, the ability to discriminate stimuli of personal relevance is still preserved, which is very obvious in "mother's sleep," when parents awake to even the slightest sounds of their infants. Not only is sensory processing altered during sleep, but sensory information can also alter the stages of sleep, resulting in a reciprocal interaction of sensory input and vigilance.

Information processing in sleep can be studied using single cell studies in animals or by analyzing EEG, evoked potentials, or imaging data in humans. The main areas of research have been altered reactions during sleep and, more recently, changes in memory or problem-solving capacities following sleep.

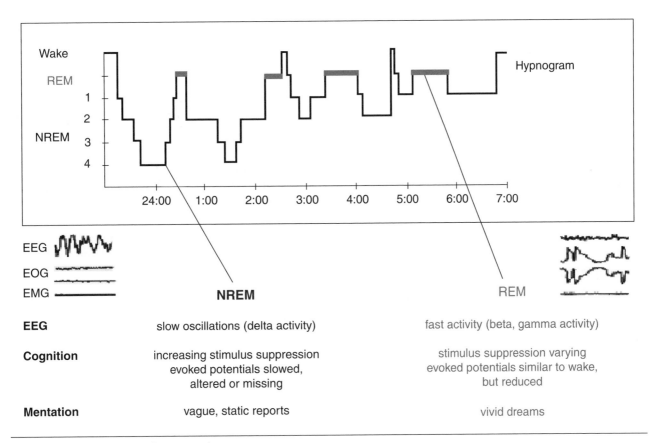

Figure 1   Sleep stages and associated processes

Note: REM = rapid eye movement (sleep); NREM = non-rapid eye movement (sleep).

Mechanisms Underlying Information Processing in Sleep

Studies at the level of single nerve cells have confirmed that during sleep cortical neurons reduce their overall activity compared to wakefulness, switching from continuous, tonic firing to burst-mode pattern (rapid firing followed by silent periods) in NREM sleep as reflected in synchronized EEG delta activity. However, the cerebral cortex is not globally inhibited, and the most striking difference compared to wakefulness is a change to synchronous firing at a low-frequency rhythm. The synchronized burst activity has recently been associated with specific plasticity changes. During the silent periods (hyperpolarized states), less energy is required, similar to an idling motor that needs less energy. It should be noted that many cortical cells fire at high levels also during NREM sleep, confirming active processes within NREM sleep. During REM sleep, cholinergic mediated activation spreads from the pontine structures and activates thalamic, limbic, and cortical areas.

During wakefulness, the thalamus plays a central role in conveying incoming afferent sensory signals—except olfaction—to the corresponding cortical areas, and cortical neurons reciprocally communicate to the thalamus. With increasing depth of sleep, first thalamic and then cortical cells switch to an altered functional state. Prominent graphic elements of NREM sleep EEG in humans with functional significance for information suppression are sleep spindles and K-complexes (KCs). Especially during occurrence of sleep spindles, which are 12 to 15 hertz (Hz) oscillations generated in the thalamic nucleus reticularis, the transfer of sensory signals to the cortex is blocked. However, spindle activity seems to be an autonomous process that even declines with increasing stimulus intensity, in contrast to the cortically generated KCs that can be elicited on all kinds of sensory stimulation.

KCs were first described in 1938 by Alfred Loomis; the name K-complex is derived from "to knock," as an example of an external acoustic stimulation. KCs are a complex of several inhibitory and excitatory evoked potentials, and have been discussed to reflect sleep-protective mechanisms. Finally, during slow-wave sleep, the slow oscillations go along with a strongly reduced excitability of cortical neurons. Thus, even if sensory information is conveyed to the corresponding cortical area, it cannot be properly processed during the long states of hyperpolarization reflecting neuronal silence.

In contrast to the above described gradual loss of reactivity in NREM sleep, the ability to discriminate complex stimuli is restored during REM sleep. Suppression of information processing is not mediated via thalamocortical inhibition in REM sleep but was suggested to lack reasonable integration because of altered activity in frontal, associative, and limbic cortex. Arousal thresholds appear higher during phasic REM periods when bursts of rapid eye movements appear. External stimuli can be kept in REM sleep mentation up to 15 minutes after presentation.

Event-Related Potential and Imaging Studies

By averaging electrophysiological responses, evoked potential studies consistently reveal a decrease of negative and increase of positive cortical potentials as the organism moves from wakefulness to NREM sleep stages, interpreted as reflecting inhibitory action and loss of attentive processes. A very prominent ERP component during wakefulness is the P300, expressed most strongly over parietal areas and linked to the detection of deviant or relevant stimuli. With the first signs of sleep oscillations—the theta rhythm—appearing in the EEG, cortical signal processing is reduced, which is reflected in the discontinuation of cortical potentials. Some authors assume that the cortical P300 component is replaced by a P450 with longer latency, appearing as a sleep-typical component following rare stimuli in NREM sleep. Similarly, cortical components such as the *mismatch negativity* (MMN), related to comparing new sensory stimuli to information in the sensory buffer, are also absent in NREM sleep. Deep, slow-wave sleep is furthermore associated with a lack of a *contingent negative variation* (CNV), which expresses learned expectancy of a second stimulus following a previous cue. Reactivity in sleep depends on stimulus characteristics—rare or strongly deviant stimuli induce K-complexes—whereas frequent or repetitive stimuli lead to a strong decrease or abolishment of most evoked potentials. To conclude, most components typical of information processing in wakefulness are absent in NREM sleep, but the altered mechanisms of processing during sleep still allow for two processes: the detection of strongly deviant stimuli or stimuli of personal relevance, as shown in responses to one's own name during sleep.

During REM sleep, cortical evoked potentials bear more resemblance to wakefulness than to deep NREM sleep. Most late cortical potentials typical for wakefulness reappear in REM sleep, such as a P300 component, an expectancy-related CNV, or the MMN component. This suggests complex processing mechanisms, including reactivation of information stored in long-term memory. Usually these potentials appear with longer latencies than they have in wakefulness, reflecting delayed processing. In addition, the P300 component shifts toward a more parietal origin than during wakefulness, lacking contributions from frontal areas. However, stimuli do not consistently evoke responses in REM sleep, but intermittently during bursts of phasic activity, hardly induce any cortical reaction. Adolfo Llinas and Denis Paré have put forward the notion of the brain acting as a closed loop during REM sleep.

In general, regional metabolic or blood flow activity decreases in cortical areas during NREM sleep, starting at thalamic levels, and with a further prominent focus in frontal areas reflecting the predominance of slow EEG oscillations over frontocentral regions. In contrast, REM sleep is associated with regional increased metabolic or blood flow activity in deeper brain structures such as brain stem or thalamus, and in cingulate, limbic, and some cortical areas. Prefrontal and parietal areas display decreased activity throughout all sleep stages. Decreased reactivity to external stimulation is reflected in decreased activity of the corresponding processing centers during sleep, or even by a transient decrease in wider brain areas that may serve sleep-protective functions.

Dream Mentation

Whereas previous theories of dreaming such as those outlined by Sigmund Freud or Carl Gustav Jung have focused on the interpretation and intention of reported dream contents, a more recent focus lies on formal, neuropsychological aspects and the neurobiological mechanisms underlying the physiology of dreaming, questions that can actually be targeted with hypothesis-based, scientific approaches. The proposal of Freud and psychoanalysts that dreams represent the fulfillment of wishes is challenged by the neurobiological-based conclusion of Allan Hobson, which argues that dream mentation results from brain stem–driven activation during REM sleep. Francis Crick proposed the hypothesis that we "dream to forget" to avoid information overload. Following the notion that dream mentation is not completely random but is modulated by waking experiences, hypotheses of dreaming as stabilization of emotional memory, simulation of threatening events, or individualization by genetic programming have been proposed, but clear empirical support is mainly lacking. Formal and content aspects of dreams are still a focus of research, which frequently tries to establish a link to personality traits of the dreamer.

Dream contents are usually forgotten unless sleepers wake up soon afterward. It can be assumed that dream contents remembered on awakening represent only a limited fraction of the REM mentations in the overall sleep period.

NREM Sleep Mentation

Sleepers, if asked whether "anything was going on in their mind" rather than "if they had been dreaming" will report some mental activity in about 50% of awakenings from NREM sleep. However, these mentations appear rather vague, representing rather a static scene or feeling, and usually lack the vividness found in "classic" dreams. Most research therefore has focused on REM sleep mentation.

REM Sleep Mentation

Sleepers report vivid dreams around 60% to 90% of the time if woken out of REM sleep. These dream mentations usually include actors, incidents, and a storyline. They often contain color and auditory imagery with hyperreal or hallucinatory qualities, whereas touch and taste sensations are rare, pain or smell sensations hardly ever occur, and gravity can sometimes be abolished. Voluntary control and self-awareness in dreams are reduced.

Hobson declared this state to be an enigmatic "third state" of consciousness in which, following his activation-synthesis model, the physiological brain stem–derived activation is synthesized to the—bizarre—dream mentation by sporadically activated higher brain centers in REM sleep. This important neurobiological theory of dream mentation and the ensuing focus on formal properties of dreams contests the so far prevailing interpretation of dream contents as found in psychoanalytical approaches. The vivid imagery of REM sleep-associated dreams is supposedly associated with increased activity in (secondary) visual cortex. Similarly, the intense emotions during dreams probably derive from activity in emotional centers of the brain, whereas the decreased dorsolateral prefrontal activity is held responsible for the bizarreness and incongruities of dream content. The precise role of frontal/prefrontal mechanisms and of neuropharmacology underlying dream mentations is still a matter of investigation. As activation during dreams is not independent of activation during wakefulness, damage to specific brain regions affects the respective characteristics of dreams.

Nightmares

The experience of nightmares, frightening dreams from which the person usually wakes up with recollection of the alarming dream content, is associated with increased heart rate and breathing frequency. Nightmares derive from REM sleep, whereas the similar night terrors occur without dream memories out of NREM sleep. Both are more frequent in early life. The high activity of the limbic system, especially the amygdala, during REM sleep is believed to induce the intense emotions associated with nightmares.

Lucid Dreams

Becoming aware of dreaming while dreaming is called *lucid dreaming*. During ordinary dreams, the sequence of events just happens, whereas in lucid dreams the dreamer can gain control of the course of dreams and can decide on actions. Persons experienced with lucid dreams can signal lucidity by volitional eye movements, enabling investigations of this state.

Renate Wehrle

See also Attention and Consciousness; Electrophysiological Studies of Mind; Neural Correlates of Consciousness

Further Readings

Borbély, A. A. (1986). *Secrets of sleep*. New York, NY: Basic Books.

Bruck, D. (2006). *Teenage sleep*. Retrieved from Wellness Promotion Unit, Victoria University: http://www.vu.edu.au/teenagesleep

Hobson, J. A. (1989). *Sleep*. New York, NY: W. H. Freeman.

Hobson, J. A., & Pace-Schott, E. F. (2002). The cognitive neuroscience of sleep: Neuronal systems, consciousness and learning. *Nature Reviews Neuroscience, 3*, 679–693.

Kryger, M. H., Roth, T., & Dement, W. C. (Eds.). (2005). *Principles and practice of sleep medicine* (4th ed.). Philadelphia, PA: Elsevier Saunders.

Pace-Schott, E. F., Solms, M., Blagrove, M., & Harnad, S. (Eds.). (2000). *Sleep and dreaming: Scientific advances and reconsiderations*. Cambridge, UK: Cambridge University Press.

Nir, Y., & Tononi, G. (2010). Dreaming and the brain: From phenomenology to neurophysiology. *Trends in Cognitive Sciences, 14*, 88–100.

Schwartz, S., & Maquet, P. (2002). Sleep imaging and the neuropsychological assessment of dreams. *Trends in Cognitive Sciences, 6*, 23–30.

SMELL, PHILOSOPHICAL PERSPECTIVES

As far as the philosophical tradition would have us believe, vision is the model from which all theorizing about perception can proceed. Recently, however, philosophers have begun to reexamine tradition by turning their attention to the other modalities and what they, in their own right, have to tell us about the nature of perception. Still, discussions of olfaction are few. This entry introduces three broad areas of inquiry and discusses olfactory experience with respect to each. They are (a) the content of experience, (b) the nature of perceptual objects, and (c) the nature of the perceptual properties. Considering olfactory experience with respect to each presents unique challenges to the traditional visual-based model of theorizing about perception and, as a result, insight into perception unavailable from the visual case alone.

The Content of Olfactory Experience

It is commonplace to suppose that visual experience is world directed and, in particular, that it has representational content. We can think of the content of a perceptual experience as the way the world appears to a subject when she has that experience. If the world is that way, then the experience is accurate, or veridical. If it isn't, then it is inaccurate, or nonveridical.

What must the world be like for an olfactory experience to be veridical? In other words, how does the world appear to be in an olfactory experience? Visual experience is importantly object based, presenting us with ordinary objects like apples and oranges. Perhaps what olfactory experience represents, then, is that there are ordinary objects in our environment with certain olfactory properties. There is no doubt that this view accords with the way we speak. Just as we say that the apple looks red, we say that the lilac smells sweet. According to William Lycan, olfactory experience does represent ordinary objects such as skunks and lilac blooms but only at a secondary level of representation. At a first level of representation, olfactory experience represents odors, or collections of airborne molecules. Lycan's view also accords with everyday thought about the objects of olfactory experience. Not only do we say that the lilac smells, we say that its smell lingers in the garden. And what we suggest when we say the latter is that olfactory experience also presents us with something in the air—a cloud or emanation of sorts.

Despite this, there remains reason to think that we speak more loosely about our olfactory experiences than we do our visual ones, in terms of their presenting ordinary objects as well as individual odors. In each case, the reason for suspicion draws on consideration of the phenomenology of olfactory experience. A characterization of the representational content of olfactory experience should honor the phenomenology of olfactory experience—that is, what olfactory experience is like. (Note that the phenomenological notion of content is not the only notion of content available, though it may be the most common notion at work in the philosophical literature; we will turn briefly to this issue below.) Taking the ordinary objects proposal first, consider a novel smell, one that you have no reason to suppose is the smell of one object as opposed to another. It is only once you know what the source of the smell is that you are able to make remarks such as "I smell the coffee." This fact puts pressure on the view that olfactory experience represents ordinary objects. It would seem that nothing in the olfactory experience itself "says" coffee.

There are further considerations against such a view—ones that avoid the controversial suggestion that kind properties (e.g., coffee) are eligible for representation in experience and that set aside issues of a perceiver's capacity for identification. Many philosophers have held that object perception and, based on that, the ability for thought about individual objects, requires a robust form of spatial differentiation of the properties presented—for example, a figure-ground distinction. Vision achieves this; olfactory experience does not. Consider the experience you have when you indulge yourself in the smell of the breakfast cooking. (Note that *smell* denotes an olfactory property.) You are able to distinguish the coffee smell and the bacon smell, but your experience does not allow you to discriminate the particular objects that bear these properties—whether these are ordinary objects or odors (or both). Unlike visual experience, smells are not packaged together in space in such a way that these packages can be distinguished from one other and from a common ground. At any instant, it seems as if the smells are simply "here." This not only puts pressure on the view that olfactory experience represents ordinary objects but also on the view that it represents individual odors.

Compared to the wealth of detail afforded by visual experience, then, olfactory experience seems a mere smudge. This "smudgy" feature of olfactory experience has prompted some philosophers to suggest that olfactory experience has no representational content. Subjectivist views of perceptual experience maintain that experiences are not world directed—that is, they have no "objective purport." Subjectivist views are also characterized as the view that perceptual experiences are raw feels or "mere sensations." Although discussions of olfaction in the philosophical literature are rare, the subjectivist view is held up as the prima facie view of the nature of olfactory experience.

But a subjectivist view is not inevitable. There is a moderate representational view available that honors the phenomenology of olfactory experience and yet maintains that it is world directed. Recently, discussions of the representational content of visual experience have focused on a debate between the view that visual experience has existentially quantified, or abstract, content and the view that it has object-involving content. To see the difference between these two views, consider the visual experience you have when you look at an orange on the counter. According to the existentially quantified account (from here on, the *abstract account*), your experience has the following content: There is some object x at location L and x is orange, oval, and so on. According to abstract theorists, it is possible that experiences of two qualitatively identical, yet distinct, oranges might be phenomenally indistinguishable. Indeed, a perceiver might hallucinate an orange before her and yet have that experience be phenomenally indistinguishable from a veridical experience of an orange. To preserve this possibility, the abstract theorist proposes that the content of each is content into which no particular object enters. The object-involving theorist, on the other hand, claims that such a view ignores the particularity of visual experience. It's not that *some* object appears to be orange, oval, and so on. *This one* does! The very orange before you, then, must be a part of the content of your experience. Letting o name the actual orange before you, the object-involving account claims that your experience has the content: o is orange, oval, and so on . . . and at L.

This entry will not consider the solution to this debate about visual experience. The debate itself, however, draws attention to the moderate view of olfactory content. Given its phenomenology, an object-involving account is unsuitable for olfactory experience. Unlike visual experience, olfactory experience does not seem to present particular things. As a result, olfactory experience cannot live up to the particularity that such a view demands of experience. However, the abstract account, which requires no such particularity, seems like a natural fit. A version of it can respect that smells are experienced as external to a perceiver and that olfactory experience does not present us with the individual objects that instantiate those smells. Drawing on the considerations of spatial presentation discussed above, the moderate view posits that olfactory experience only ever represents that a single "something or other" is smelly and "here." On this view, the following schema specifies the content of any olfactory experience: There is some x here that is F, G, and so on. If there is nothing in the vicinity that is F and G, then the experience is nonveridical.

There are several reasons to think that any world-directed view is preferable to a subjectivist one.

Despite their difference in phenomenology, we still think of the senses as informational systems. Using the senses, we are able to gather information about the world. Although we might think their phenomenology is impoverished, our olfactory experiences still function to guide behavior and action. If someone smells smoke in the building, they flee. As guides of behavior and grounds of belief, the experiences of the sense modalities form a common kind. A shared world directedness provides a way of accounting for this commonality.

Olfactory Objects

If we accept the abstract view, the next question is, given that some olfactory experiences are veridical, what objects have the properties those experiences present? That is, what are the olfactory objects? As we have seen already, there are several options: Olfactory objects are (1) "source" objects, (2) odors, or (3) both odors and source objects.

Given the traditional, "visuocentric," approach to theorizing about perception, we might feel tempted to say that the properties of which we are aware in olfactory experience are qualities had by regular old objects—lilac blooms, skunks, and pots of coffee. Although olfactory experience is not discriminating enough to report that there are particular objects, on Proposal 1 the bearers of the properties presented in olfactory experience are in fact ordinary objects. We certainly think of lilacs, skunks, and portions of coffee as the sources of smells. But we also speak of them as having a good or bad smell. Consider how, when rooting around in the fridge for the rotten food, you say of the uncovered cabbage, "It's this that stinks." What you direct our attention to is the head of cabbage. Or to take a more pleasant example, we take pride in the roses in our garden, not only because they look beautiful but also because they have wonderful smells. We attribute a property—namely, a smell—to the rose. The same is true of the cabbage. It has a very bad smell, we say.

This might seem a common view, but it is also subject to question. Consider how you can have an olfactory experience even though the object that you think of as responsible for the smell is far away. For example, you might smell the rubbish from your apartment window even though it is outside in the bin. If my olfactory experience represents that properties are instantiated by something or other "here"

then your experience must be nonveridical. The rubbish is not anywhere near you; it is downstairs and outside. The problem with Proposal 1 arises because this kind of circumstance is not rare. If olfactory objects are things like piles of rubbish, many of our olfactory experiences will turn out to be nonveridical. And this is a view that we ought to avoid.

Proposal 2 has it that olfactory objects are collections of airborne molecules given off by the rubbish—that is, odors. On this proposal, the experience you have when you smell the rubbish through the window is a veridical one. The rubbish gives off an odor, that odor is "at" you (indeed, it has gone up your nose), and your experience reports it as such. This is a more plausible result. Experiences we intuitively count as veridical turn out to be so.

Nevertheless, we might feel drawn to the view that the rubbish *also* has the stinky property. After all, the rubbish gives off or emits the odor. If we feel the pull of such a view, there are two ways that we can accommodate it. First, we might hold that the rubbish has the stinky property but that olfactory experience does not present that object (i.e., it presents the rubbish odor only). The second option is more controversial. We do think of ourselves as smelling the rubbish *by* smelling the odor it emits. If we take this proposal seriously, as denoting something about the content of olfactory experience, then we arrive at Proposal 3: Olfactory objects are both odors and source objects.

Lycan's multilayered view of representational content, noted above, is a version of Proposal 3. Both odors *and* ordinary objects are olfactory objects, each definitive of successive levels of representation. According to Lycan, insofar as we might think that there is something both correct and incorrect about a situation in which a rose odor is present when no rose is, his view respects our judgments. On one level, one's experience is veridical; on another, it is nonveridical.

But the view that olfactory objects are (also) things like roses faces a challenge. If ordinary objects are among the olfactory objects, then content cannot be determined by phenomenology alone. As we have seen, the phenomenological notion of content and, in particular, the abstract view applies nicely to Lycan's first level of representation (where the represented objects are odors); it does not, however, fit the second (where the represented objects are ordinary objects). Advocates of such a view, like Lycan, owe us an account of an additional kind of content and an argument for why we ought to think that olfactory experiences have that kind of content. One candidate view is the teleological view of content advocated by both Ruth Millikan and Fred Dretske—in short, the view that the content of an experience depends on its function within the system, or organism, of which it is a part. This, it would seem, is just the approach that Lycan takes—although he endorses it not only for the second level of representation but also for the first.

Olfactory Properties

A final issue to consider is the nature of the smells themselves. Although very little has been written about olfaction in the philosophical literature, the little that there is reveals a contrast in the views favored for the cases of smell and color. For many philosophers, the view that colors can be explained in purely physical terms has seemed very appealing. In the case of smell, this kind of view has seemed less appealing. Those who have discussed olfaction have favored either dispositionalism or projectivism. According to dispositionalism, smells are dispositions to cause certain kinds of experiences in perceivers. Dispositionalists do not deny that smells are properties of objects (we will assume, for the sake of discussion, that these objects are odors), but they do maintain that the nature of these properties cannot be specified without reference to experience. According to dispositionalists, the lilac smell, for example, is the disposition to cause a distinctive kind of experience in suitable perceivers. Unlike dispositionalists, projectivists argue that the lilac smell is a mental property and that something internal to the perceiver (e.g., a sense datum, experience, or portion of the "olfactory field") has that property. Projectivists argue that these properties are then "projected" onto objects in the external world.

Although dispositionalism and projectivism each take into account the "felt character" of olfactory experience, they fall on two sides of one debate over the nature of what John Locke called the secondary qualities—colors, sounds, smells, tastes, and feels. This is the debate between realism and eliminativism. Olfactory realism claims that things in the world have the property ascribed to them by olfactory experience. Dispositionalism is just such a view. Eliminativism, on the other hand, claims that smells are not properties of things in the world. In claiming that smells are properties of experiences, projectivism is a form of eliminativism.

Because it renders all olfactory experience illusory, eliminativism is often regarded as a last resort, a kind of view rendered plausible by the failure of any realist view. Realism, then, is the default position for any view of the secondary qualities. All realist positions fall into one of two camps: relationalism and nonrelationalism. According to relationalism, smells are constituted by relations between objects and perceivers. Dispositionalism is one such view. Nonrelationalism, on the other hand, maintains that smells are properties independent of the perceiver or mind. A natural nonrelationalist position is that smells are molecular properties (also known as physicalism).

There can be significant intersubjective differences between the ways that perceivers smell certain odorants to be and, on these grounds, relationalists can argue against nonrelationalism as follows: Significant intersubjective differences in perceived smell exist. If smells are nonrelational properties of odors, then the smell of an odor does not in any way depend on the experiences that perceivers have when they come into contact with it. So there ought to be a unique smell that an odor has and, as a result, a reason to favor one group of perceivers over any other—that is, those whose experiences present the smell of the odor. But there is no reason to favor one set of perceivers over another. Because it cannot live up to its own demands, nonrelationalism is false.

As it turns out, the issue is not as simple as this argument might make it initially appear. Nonrelationalism is threatened only if these intersubjective differences involve major shifts in perceived quality. If the differences involve minor shifts in perceived quality then the threat is little to none. All sensory systems have limits of resolution. And when a system is pushed to the limits of its resolution, it is bound to make minor mistakes. If shifts in perceived quality are the result of just such a mistake then we do have a reason to favor one group of perceivers over another. One group is simply mistaken—that is, their experiences are nonveridical.

One opportunity for future research on the nature of smells, then, involves determining whether the shifts in perceived quality are major or minor. But we are yet to have a structured quality space for smell and, as a result, lack a model by which to evaluate differences in perceived quality. Many systems have been proposed; none has been found satisfactory. Given the breadth of our olfactory discrimination, each system has been accused of oversimplifying olfactory experience. Obviously some sort of consensus is necessary before we can evaluate claims of perceptual variation. What we can be sure of at this point is that future philosophical work on the olfactory properties will progress with further developments in olfactory psychophysics.

Clare Batty

See also Disjunctive Theory of Perception; Hearing, Philosophical Perspectives; Intentionality of Bodily Sensation; Realism and Instrumentalism; Taste, Philosophical Perspectives

Further Readings

Amoore, J. E. (1971). *Chemical senses.* New York, NY: Springer-Verlag.

Batty, C. (2009). What's that smell? *Southern Journal of Philosophy, 47,* 321–348.

Batty, C. (2010). A representational account of olfactory experience. *Canadian Journal of Philosophy, 40,* 511–538.

Beauchamp, G. K., & Bartoshuk, L. (1997). *Tasting and smelling.* San Diego, CA: Academic Press.

Harper, R., Bate-Smith, E. C., & Lad, D. G. (1968). *Odour description and odour classification: A multidisciplinary examination.* London, UK: Churchill.

Lycan, W. (1996). Peacocke's arguments. In *Consciousness and experience* (pp. 143–160). Cambridge, MA: MIT Press.

Lycan, W. (2000). The slighting of smell. In N. Bhushan & S. Rosenfeld (Ed.), *Of minds and molecules* (pp. 273–290). Oxford, UK: Oxford University Press.

Perkins, M. (1983). *Sensing the world.* Indianapolis, IN: Hackett.

Reid, Thomas. (1764/2000). On smelling. In D. Brookes (Ed.), *An inquiry into the human mind and the principles of common sense* (pp. 25–45). Edinburgh, UK: Edinburgh University Press.

Wilson, D. A., & Stevenson, R. J. (2006). *Learning to smell.* Baltimore, MD: Johns Hopkins University Press.

SOCIAL COGNITION

Although researchers in many different sciences use *social cognition* to refer to a wide range of phenomena, the present entry uses the term to refer to an enormous body of theoretical and empirical work that arguably is the largest and most dominant area within social psychology. But this was not always so, and it is instructive to trace social cognition research back to its beginnings in the late 1970s. At that time, social cognition was a label referring to research conducted by a small group of social psychologists who were interested in how people form impressions of others, or "person memory." Although social psychologists had long been interested in how people form impressions of others, they tended not to focus explicitly on cognitive processes such as how information is encoded, stored, and retrieved from memory. The original social cognition researchers had this explicit focus, thereby distinguishing themselves from other social psychologists, including those who also were interested in impressions of others. The explicit focus on cognitive processes resulted in the development of detailed person memory models that made specific predictions. Additional successes followed, and social cognition became an important area of social psychology.

Person Memory: The Original Social Cognition

Imagine an observer who notices the behaviors of the person who is the target of her observations (i.e., the target person). In addition, suppose the observer has a prior expectancy about the target person and subsequently observes the target person's behaviors that are congruent or incongruent with that prior expectancy. How will the target person's behaviors become represented in the observer's memory? The dominant cognitive view was embodied in the notion of a "schema," which is a cognitive structure that tends to preserve information consistent with the schema and bias recall and judgments in that direction. If prior expectancies act as schemas, then the schema should preserve information that is congruent with it in memory and later recall of the target person's behaviors should be biased in the direction of the schema. For example, if the observer had a prior expectancy that the target person is kind, then the target person's kind behaviors should be better recalled than her unkind ones. In contrast, early social cognition researchers suggested that perhaps incongruent information is more informative than congruent information, and so people form more associations concerning incongruent behaviors than congruent ones. The data supported this reasoning.

As more information accumulated in the early 1980s, person memory theories became more detailed. An important book by Robert Wyer Jr. and Thomas K. Srull titled *Memory and Cognition in Its Social Context* summarizes the theories and empirical findings. In general, the "received view" is that there are two levels at which information about people is represented in the observer's memory, and the representations at both levels are in the form of "nodes" or concepts. The higher level has a "higher order person node," which contains the observer's prior expectation and other general information about the target person. The lower level has congruent and incongruent behavior nodes (as we have already seen) and irrelevant behavior nodes that have nothing to do with the prior expectancy. For example, the target person's eating a sandwich is irrelevant to the observer's prior expectancy concerning the target person's kindness. The three lower nodes representing congruent, incongruent, and irrelevant behaviors are associated with the higher order person node by virtue of the fact that the target person has previously performed these behaviors. The strongest of these three associations is between the higher order person node and the congruent behavior nodes.

But there are other ways in which associations among the behavior nodes are formed (see Figure 1). Because congruent or irrelevant behaviors are easy to understand and do not cause the observer to question her expectancy, they do not stimulate the formation of associations between behavior nodes. In contrast, the performance of an incongruent behavior requires far more processing. To understand the target person's incongruous behavior, the observer compares it to other incongruent or congruent behaviors. Each time the observer makes such a comparison between behaviors, she forms associations between the nodes representing them. Thus, she forms associations between nodes representing incongruent behaviors and other incongruent behaviors, and between incongruent behaviors and congruent ones, but not between nodes representing congruent behaviors and other congruent ones, all while isolating irrelevant item nodes in the network. As a result, there are more associative pathways leading to the recall of incongruent behaviors (from incongruent and congruent ones) than to the recall of congruent behaviors (only from incongruent ones) and fewest leading to the recall of irrelevant behaviors.

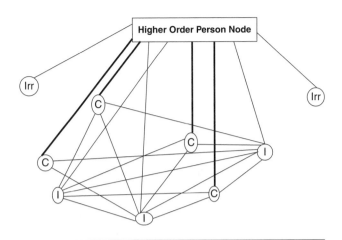

Figure 1   An example of an associative network with irrelevant (Irr), congruent (C), and incongruent (I) items

Note: Thick paths indicate stronger associative pathways.

A number of predictions can be derived from the received view. Most obviously, recall should be greatest for incongruent items and least for irrelevant ones. Less obviously, when an incongruent item is recalled, there are associations leading to both congruent and incongruent items, and so the next item recalled is likely to be a congruent or an incongruent one. But when a congruent item is recalled, then all the inter-item associations lead to incongruent items, and so the next item recalled is likely to be an incongruent one. When irrelevant items are recalled, they are associated only with the higher order person node, which, in turn, is more highly associated with congruent than incongruent items. Thus, the theory predicts that when people recall an irrelevant item, they should traverse an associative pathway first to the higher order person node and then to a congruent item node, thereby leading to the recall of the congruent item. Experiments confirmed all these predictions as well as some others not mentioned here. It is important to appreciate the emphasis that went into encoding (specifying the process by which associations are formed), storage (the structure actually stored in memory), and retrieval (how people traverse associative pathways based on how they were stored), and how this careful theorizing led to interesting predictions.

Although further work in the person memory area continued, the frequency of these investigations decreased in the 1990s, and person memory research is rare today. Although many researchers currently consider person memory to be a "dead" area, its historical importance should be appreciated. Person memory gave social cognition its initial impetus, and there is no way to know whether social cognition would exist at all, or in what form, had the early researchers chosen to study something else.

Category Accessibility: The Other Early Social Cognition Area

Imagine you had been told about a person named Donald who crossed the Atlantic Ocean in a sailboat. Would you judge Donald to be "adventurous" or "reckless"? Early social cognition theorists suggested that much would depend on what other information was accessible to you. If the category of "adventurous" happened to be accessible then you might be likely to encode the behavior as an exemplar of that category, thereby implying that it was adventurous, but if the category of "reckless" happened to be accessible then you would probably encode the behavior as an exemplar of recklessness, leading you to the judgment that it was reckless. In fact, early research demonstrated that manipulating the categories accessible to participants in experiments (i.e., "priming" these categories) caused them to make judgments in the direction of whatever category was primed.

The notion of priming categories to influence judgments expanded in the 1980s in two important directions. Specifically, it became clear that categories could be primed more or less *recently* (just prior to judgments or well before judgments) or more or less *frequently* (many times or fewer times prior to judgment). The impact of recently (and nonfrequently) primed categories tends to be strong immediately and decrease rapidly over time, whereas the impact of frequently primed categories tends to decrease more slowly over time. Two sorts of theories account for the effects. According to the *bin* model, information is accessed depending both on the number of times it is represented in the bin and where it is represented in the bin. Thus, in the case of a single recent prime, this information is sitting at the top of the bin and has a large probability of influencing judgments. But as time goes by, other information is placed on top of it, and so its likelihood of influencing judgments decreases rapidly. But if the category had been primed frequently and many representations of it are stored in the bin then,

even if the passage of time renders none of them to be at the top of the bin, there nevertheless remains a reasonable probability that one of the category representations will be used for making judgments.

An alternative account invoked the concept of decay of excitation. The more frequently a concept has been primed, the slower the rate of decay of its excitation, which is another way of saying that the concept retains much of its ability to influence judgments over time. As a matter of history, although neither of these general theories is particularly influential today, the notion of category accessibility and the empirical technique of employing priming manipulations have been incorporated by almost every subarea within social cognition. It is probably not an exaggeration to say that category accessibility and priming are so ingrained into the social cognition lore that they currently are considered as givens.

Social Cognition, Amalgamation, and Contemporary Themes

Throughout the 1980s, the person memory and category accessibility domains gained in popularity and academic acclaim. Researchers in other domains began to associate themselves with the increasingly trendy area of social cognition, and areas of social psychology that were not considered originally to be within the social cognition domain became so categorized. For example, although attribution theories had been cognitive from their beginnings, it was not until the mid-1980s that they were considered to be part of social cognition. Likewise, the area of attitudes became associated with social cognition. This expansion of social cognition applied eventually to almost every area of social psychology, to the point where it would be difficult to find a social psychology area that has not been influenced by social cognition theories, methodologies, or both. In addition, this expansion has resulted in theories that assume two processes (dual-process theories) that can be distinguished from theories that do not assume two processes.

Dual-Process Approaches

In contemporary research, there has been a great deal of emphasis on the distinction between mental processes that are *automatic* versus *controlled,* to the point where the vast majority of 21st-century social cognition theories are dual-process theories.

Put simply, these theories posit an automatic process that does not use up cognitive resources and does not involve conscious volition and a controlled process that uses cognitive resources and *does* involve conscious volition. Examples of dual-process theories include that persuasion happens via a peripheral (automatic) or a central (controlled) route, or that behaviors result from habitual (automatic) or non-habitual (controlled) processes, or that the formation of plans for implementing behavioral intentions makes automatic the intentional process that otherwise would be controlled, and so on.

New methodological paradigms have been developed to exploit the distinction between automatic and controlled processes featured in these theories. Researchers often collect reaction time data, under the assumption that if two cognitions are associated, priming one of them should increase the speed with which the other will be accessed. Thus, in a study on prejudice, participants might be primed on some trials with a word toward which they have a positive attitude and some words toward which they have a negative attitude. Either way, after being primed, the participants are asked to respond to the names of black or white persons. Those participants who are prejudiced against black people should respond more quickly to a positive prime followed by the name of a white person or to a negative prime followed by the name of a black person, than to positive-black or negative-white combinations.

Another widely used social cognition paradigm is subliminal priming. The idea is as follows. If a hypothesized social cognition process is automatic and conscious volition is not required then relevant behaviors can be influenced outside of consciousness with subliminal priming. For example, priming people at a subliminal level with pictures of elderly people caused them to walk more slowly than those who had not been so primed.

Notwithstanding the popularity of dual-process approaches, they are not touted by everyone. Although different cognitive processes may use up different pools of resources and be automatic with respect to each other, some would argue that few (if any) of the cognitive processes of interest to social psychologists use up exactly zero resources. If so, there would be very few (if any) absolutely automatic processes; on the contrary, one would expect a continuum of resource utilization, and so the notion of separating social psychology phenomena into dichotomous automatic versus controlled groupings would not make sense.

Other Social Cognition Approaches

A substantial amount of social cognition work does not use dual-process theories. An example is the work of cross-cultural psychologists who have distinguished between people in individualist cultures who emphasize private self-cognitions (i.e., their traits and states), as opposed to people in collectivist cultures who emphasize collective self-cognitions (i.e., their group memberships). Social cognition thinking suggested two opposing ways in which self-cognitions might be organized. One possibility is that there is only one self-concept but that culture influences the relative proportions of different types of cognitions associated with it; individualists have more private self-cognitions than do collectivists and collectivists have more collective self-cognitions than do individualists. A second possibility is that there are different cognitive structures for storing different kinds of self-cognitions; private self-cognitions are stored in the private self and collective self-cognitions are stored in the collective self. If so, culture would influence the relative accessibility of these two cognitive structures.

The different possibilities make opposing predictions that can be tested empirically. According to the two-selves theory, priming the private self should increase the retrieval of private self-cognitions, whereas priming the collective self should increase the retrieval of collective self-cognitions. But if there is only one self-concept with no internal organization (if there is internal organization, then this turns into a multiple self-theory), priming to differentially influence the retrieval of private versus collective self-cognitions should make no difference. A second prediction concerns the order in which self-cognitions are retrieved. The two-selves theory indicates that private self-cognitions are associated with each other but not with collective ones, and collective self-cognitions are associated with each other but not with private ones. If so, then the retrieval of private self-cognitions should be likely to be preceded by the recall of private ones, and the recall of collective self-cognitions should be likely to be preceded by the recall of collective ones. But if the one self-theory is true, retrieval should be random. Findings concerning both predictions came out in favor of the theory that there are at least two self-concepts. More recent research has expanded this theorizing to assert that priming different self-concepts influences the process of thinking as well as the content of the thoughts.

Social cognition also has been used to test for the internal structure of attitudes—whether attitudes have both cognitive and affective components. In one experiment, participants wrote down their attitudinal beliefs, and blind coders rated them as mostly cognitive or mostly affective. The researchers hypothesized that during the process of forming an attitude, cognitive beliefs are compared to each other to form the cognitive component, and affective beliefs are compared to each other to form the affective component, but there is little reason for participants to compare cognitive and affective beliefs. Consequently, the attitude formation process should cause stored associations between cognitive beliefs and other cognitive beliefs, between affective beliefs and other affective beliefs, but not between cognitive and affective beliefs. During retrieval, participants should have been able to traverse associative pathways between cognitive beliefs and other cognitive beliefs, between affective beliefs and other affective beliefs, but not between cognitive and affective beliefs. This led to a prediction that retrieval would be clustered by belief type (cognitive beliefs retrieved adjacently to each other and affective beliefs retrieved adjacently to each other). Experimental confirmation of this prediction supported the hypothesis that attitudes have separate cognitive and affective components.

Conclusion

Social cognition has been a major force in social psychology and continues to expand, both theoretically and methodologically. It is very different today than it was at its conception, and it may metamorphose into new forms that would be unrecognizable to its originators. There is no way to predict which new areas of psychology social cognition will influence, but social cognition researchers can look forward to exciting research yet to come.

David Trafimow

See also Attitudes and Behavior; Attribution Theory; Persuasion; Two System Models of Reasoning

Further Readings

Bargh, J. A., Chen, M., & Burrows, L. (1996). Automaticity of social behavior: Direct effects of trait construct and stereotype activation on action. *Journal of Personality and Social Psychology, 71,* 230–244.

Greenwald, A. G., McGhee, D. E., & Schwartz, J. L. K. (1998). Measuring individual differences in implicit cognition: The implicit association test. *Journal of Personality and Social Psychology, 74,* 1464–1480.

Hastie, R., & Kumar, P. A. (1979). Person memory: Personality traits as organizing principles in memory for behaviors. *Journal of Personality and Social Psychology, 37,* 25–38.

Higgins, E. T., Bargh, J. A., & Lombardi, W. (1985). The nature of priming effects on categorization. *Journal of Experimental Psychology: Learning, Memory, and Cognition, 11,* 59–69.

Srull, T. K., Lichtenstein, M., & Rothbart, M. (1985). Associative storage and retrieval processes in person memory. *Journal of Experimental Psychology: Learning, Memory, and Cognition, 11,* 316–345.

Srull, T. K., & Wyer, R. S. (1979). The role of category accessibility in the interpretation of information about persons: Some determinants and implications. *Journal of Personality and Social Psychology, 37,* 1660–1672.

Trafimow, D., & Sheeran, P. (1998). Some tests of the distinction between cognitive and affective beliefs. *Journal of Experimental Social Psychology, 34,* 378–397.

Trafimow, D., Triandis, H. C., & Goto, S. G. (1991). Some tests of the distinction between the private self and the collective self. *Journal of Personality and Social Psychology, 60,* 649–655.

SOCIAL LOAFING

Many notable accomplishments in human history, from erecting the pyramids of Egypt to placing a man on the moon, required that people work as a group, combining their efforts toward a common goal. Yet a common feature of groups is social loafing—a reduction in motivation and effort when people pool their contributions. People tend to be less productive, generating less output when their efforts are combined than when they work individually. This entry summarizes current thinking on social loafing by describing it in the context of related phenomena, providing research illustrations, and reviewing causes of and solutions to social loafing.

Social loafing is a broad construct that includes the free rider effect and the sucker effect. The *free rider effect* refers to the decline in contributions observed when people perceive their contributions as redundant with the contributions of others. The *sucker effect* is the tendency for people to withhold contributions when they perceive or anticipate that other people are loafing at their expense. That is, people sometimes contribute less to avoid being exploited by others who are loafing. Social loafing is distinct from these other effects in that social loafing is a broader term referring to any reduction in effort or motivation when contributions are pooled. The free rider effect and the sucker effect are narrower terms that refer to specific causes of social loafing.

Researchers have documented social loafing in a variety of tasks, including clapping and cheering, swimming in a relay race, solving mazes, wrapping gum, pulling a tug-of-war rope, and generating uses for objects. In a typical study, groups of participants receive instructions to generate uses for an object (e.g., uses for a knife) and believe that their individual contributions are or are not identifiable. Participants reliably generate more uses when they believe the number of uses they generate can be identified by the experimenter than when they believe the uses cannot be identified.

Causes of Social Loafing

Group performance tasks can be regarded as having three components: (a) an effort expectancy component (i.e., expectations regarding the contributions group members make), (b) a performance expectancy component (i.e., expectations regarding the product of those contributions), and (c) an outcome value component (the consequences such as the reward or punishment that result from the performance). Research links social loafing to each component. Regarding effort expectancy, people are more likely to loaf if they perceive that their individual contributions are irrelevant to achieve a good group performance. For example, if a man assembling widgets in a factory believes that he and his coworkers will meet the day's production quota regardless of whether he personally works hard or loafs, he is likely to loaf. Similarly, if the man believes that the group will not meet the day's quota regardless of how hard he works, then he also is likely to

loaf. In both cases, reaching (or not reaching) the quota is irrelevant to the man's individual efforts. Research documenting the role of effort expectancy in social loafing comes from studies that manipulate the redundancy of individual efforts. These studies show that people are more likely to loaf when they perceive their efforts to be redundant with the contributions of other group members than when they perceive their efforts as unique.

Regarding performance expectancy, people are more likely to loaf if they perceive that the quality or quantity of the group's performance is unrelated to the outcome. For example, if the factory worker believes that his work group will receive the same bonus regardless of whether the group meets the production quota, he will loaf. Similarly, if the worker believes that his work group will receive no bonus (and no punishment) regardless of whether the group meets the quota, he will loaf. In short, people in a group will work hard when they believe rewards and punishments are linked to the group's performance and will loaf when they perceive no such link. Evidence linking social loafing to the performance expectancy comes from studies showing that people loaf when they perceive that there is a low likelihood that a good group performance will be rewarded. In addition, the finding that people loaf when group member contributions cannot be identified supports the role of the performance stage in social loafing. When contributions cannot be identified, group members receive no personal reward for working hard or punishment for loafing.

Regarding outcome, people are likely to loaf to the extent that the value of a good group performance is low. Value is low when there is no reward for achieving a good group performance, when the reward is not valued, or when there are overriding costs. For example, the factory worker may perceive that the bonus for making the day's production quota is too small to justify working hard. That is, the cost of working hard exceeds the benefits. Research on outcome value demonstrates that offering powerful incentives for a good group performance reduces social loafing. For example, one study showed that participants wrapping gum in groups wrapped more if they believe the gum they wrapped would be donated to a worthy cause (an intrinsic benefit) than if they believed it would not.

Reducing Social Loafing

According to theorists, effort expectancy, performance expectancy, and outcome value must all be high or people will loaf. That is, if any one of these factors is low then people will reduce their contributions to the group. Yet social loafing is not inevitable. People who depend on groups to accomplish tasks as well as the group members themselves can reduce social loafing by making sure three conditions are met. First, group members must perceive that a good group performance depends on their individual contribution. That is, group members must perceive that if they personally withhold contributions, the group performance will suffer. Second, group members must perceive that a good group performance will be rewarded and that a poor group performance will not. The surest way to create this condition is to make individual contributions identifiable. Third, there must be an adequate reward or incentive for achieving a good group performance, one that exceeds the cost of contributing.

James A. Shepperd and Darya Melnyk

See also Collective Action; Group Decision Making

Further Readings

Karau, S. J., & Williams, K. D. (1993). Social loafing: A meta-analytic review and theoretical integration. *Journal of Personality and Social Psychology, 65,* 681–706.

Shepperd, J. A. (1993). Productivity loss in groups: A motivation analysis. *Psychological Bulletin, 113,* 67–81.

SPACING EFFECT

Practice that is distributed over time rather than massed together within a shorter period has been shown to have a stronger effect on later performance. This spacing effect is an improvement in future memory retrieval performance caused by more widely spaced practice (where repeated learning events are distributed temporally rather than massed at a single time). Research has shown that this effect is very robust for the learning of factual information such as words, images, definitions, or artificial stimuli such as random letter strings and that this benefit persists over delays as long as several years. The spacing effect was first recognized by Hermann Ebbinghaus in his study of the learning of serially ordered lists of words. He found that the massing of study on a single day resulted in poor performance when attempting to relearn items as compared to faster relearning when the study of the word lists was distributed over a 3-day period. This entry briefly describes the spacing effect and discusses three types of theories that attempt to explain it.

Features of the Spacing Effect

The spacing effect is well established in memory-dependent learning tasks and has been demonstrated most frequently using paired-associate and free-recall memory tasks. In a paired-associate spacing-effect experiment, pairs of words or other stimuli are associated over repeated practices that are spaced in time by practicing other item pairs during spacing intervals. Recall in paired-associate memory tasks may be tested at the conclusion of practice by prompting with one member of each pair to cue recall of the other pair member, but many experiments include a buffer task or a short-term or long-term interval (typically at least a day) between learning and retention, since a paired-associate spacing effect seems to require a significant retention interval to become apparent.

In a free-recall task, participants learn a word list in which some of the words repeat, again with spacing defined by the number of intervening items between repetitions. The effect of spaced practice of items in a list is determined with testing after the conclusion of practice, either immediately or with some retention delay interval. Spacing effects in free-recall lists are often apparent without the need for a significant retention interval.

While the spacing effect has been most thoroughly studied in memory tasks and might be expected to occur in any task with a memory component, it has also been reported in motor skill tasks. However, there has been much less research on the spacing effect in motor skill tasks, and it is still unclear to what extent spacing effects are universal to all types of learning. In fact, many researchers have proposed multiple mechanisms for spacing effects, and it is possible that spacing effects occur because of different mechanisms depending on the task.

The spacing effect often shows strong interactions with the amount of practice and the duration of the retention interval. The practice by spacing interaction is characterized by an increasing benefit from spacing as practices accumulate. This interaction means that additional spaced practices beyond the second trial will continue to contribute more learning if the practices are widely spaced. The spacing by retention interval interaction, which can only be detected using experiments with multiple retention intervals, is a tendency for much more rapid forgetting following practice that is narrowly spaced (i.e., the effect of spacing is greater after longer retention intervals).

Theories of the Spacing Effect

The history of spacing-effect research is rich with suggested explanations for the effect.

Fluctuation Theories

Fluctuation theories propose that each repetition of an item to be memorized results in a sample of the item and its context features (stimulus components) being committed to memory. Learning occurs through the accumulation of these samples, and retrieval is determined by how well the components of a later cue match the stimulus components learned. In a fluctuation theory, the stimulus components are supposed to fluctuate with the passage of time. Because of this fluctuation, more widely spaced practice may create an overall encoding that includes a broader share of the possible stimulus components, while narrow spacing results in a rather redundant encoding because very little fluctuation of the available components can happen between repetitions. Two main varieties of fluctuation theory have been proposed: contextual variability, which focuses on the importance of the entire context in building a broad representation, and encoding variability, which focuses on the central importance of fluctuations in the sampling of the items rather than the broader context.

Accessibility Theories

Typically considered as an alternative to fluctuation theories, another class of theory focuses on how the current memory accessibility at the time of repetition results in different effects for each repetition. These "accessibility" theories describe how narrow spacing results in memories that are more accessible at the time of repetition, but they propose that it is this accessibility at repetition that reduces further learning when the repetitions are narrowly spaced. Earlier versions of accessibility theories described how priming or habituation from narrow spacing might block learning; these explanations are similar to the idea of "desirable difficulty" popularized by Robert Bjork because wider spacing increases difficulty by reducing accessibility. Later versions of accessibility theories have elaborated this theory by describing how increased accessibility at repetition may lead to learning that is forgotten more quickly as opposed to learned more slowly. Like fluctuation theories, the newer accessibility theories explain the spacing by retention-interval interaction (the increased benefit from spacing after long retention intervals), which older accessibility theories did not attempt to explain. These newer accessibility theories map well to neurophysiology research, which shows that neurons exhibit this same tendency to show reduced long-term effects from narrowly spaced stimulation. Similar to accessibility theory, the study phase retrieval theory of spacing effects says that when a narrow repetition occurs before the previous repetition has left working memory, learning will be very poor.

Strategic Theories

Though paired-associate spacing effects are usually explained with one of the theories above, strategic processes such as differential rehearsal (rehearsing spaced items more) and rehearsal organization (rehearsing clusters of items) have also been shown to produce spacing effects in free-recall list-learning experiments. Strategic explanations are typically proposed only for list-learning spacing results.

Philip I. Pavlik Jr.

See also Desirable Difficulties Perspective on Learning; Rehearsal and Memory; Skill Learning, Enhancement of; Spacing Effect, Practical Applications; Working Memory

Further Readings

Cepeda, N. J., Pashler, H., Vul, E., Wixted, J. T., & Rohrer, D. (2006). Distributed practice in verbal recall tasks: A review and quantitative synthesis. *Psychological Bulletin, 132*(3), 354–380.

Glenberg, A. M. (1979). Component-levels theory of the effects of spacing of repetitions on recall and recognition. *Memory & Cognition, 7*(2), 95–112.

Hintzman, D. L. (1974). Theoretical implications of the spacing effect. In R. L. Solso (Ed.), *Theories in cognitive psychology: The Loyola symposium* (pp. 77–99). Hillsdale, NJ: Erlbaum.

Pavlik, P. I., Jr., & Anderson, J. R. (2005). Practice and forgetting effects on vocabulary memory: An activation-based model of the spacing effect. *Cognitive Science*, 29(4), 559–586.

SPACING EFFECT, PRACTICAL APPLICATIONS

Placing a temporal gap between study sessions increases the amount of information remembered in the future, a phenomenon called the *spacing effect*. The spacing effect allows students and teachers to efficiently allocate a fixed amount of study time to maximize later retention of a set of facts or a new skill. Educational environments that may benefit from spacing include completion of homework assignments, learning within a classroom setting, studying for exams, business training courses, computer-aided learning, and language-learning courses. Real-world tutors that implement spaced study include SuperMemo, the Mnemosyne project, and the Pimsleur language learning system.

Since the spacing effect was first described in 1885 by Hermann Ebbinghaus, hundreds of studies have examined its effects using materials with classroom and real-life utility. Related to school curriculum, this includes vocabulary, fact, and prose memorization; related to work and leisure activities, it includes typing, tossing balls, and playing video games. From these studies, a set of concrete recommendations for applying the spacing effect to real-world learning can be made.

Practical Techniques

In general, a long temporal gap between learning sessions increases the level of future recall. While very long gaps of at least a month are necessary to produce long-lasting benefits to retention for both verbal materials and motor tasks, relearning on a daily basis is more effective if the learner cares solely about performance on an upcoming exam or performance. Taking a few minutes break between each study session is always preferable to learning material within a single, massed study period. In general, too little spacing between study sessions is quite harmful to retention while too much spacing only leads to small decreases in later recall. An optimal level of spacing can more than double later recall.

The use of cumulative exams is perhaps the simplest technique teachers can implement in their classroom if they wish to promote durable memory for the material being taught. Cumulative exams encourage students to learn the same set of material on at least two separate occasions, providing the essential temporal gap between each learning episode. Other useful instructional design choices include systematic quizzes on previous topics, use of classroom time to review key curriculum content, and homework assignments that emphasize the primary points to be learned. Homework assignments and quizzes that mix, shuffle, or interleave different topics, such as addition and subtraction, have been shown to improve later performance.

Because testing with feedback is more beneficial than restudy alone, students should learn using flashcards rather than merely by (re)reading textbook chapters. When testing with feedback is used during study sessions rather than restudy alone, benefit from study episode spacing is substantially increased. After an exam, teachers should provide delayed feedback about the correct answers, which provides a form of spaced learning. Ideally, this should involve sequentially presenting a frequently missed test item, asking students to generate an answer to that item, and then providing feedback about the correct answer. Unless feedback is provided, students are quite unlikely to fix misconceptions about the correct answer. Tests and exams should emphasize key points rather than minor details so that students retain the most important material being taught. More key material will be remembered if fewer superfluous details are presented within textbook chapters and during classroom lectures. This instructional design choice allows educators to devote more time to spaced restudy of key points.

Areas Needing Further Study

While spacing effects are robust for most forms of verbal and skill learning, using both recall and recognition memory measures, such effects have not been found consistently for all types of learning. Category induction, such as learning to identify whether a novel skin lesion is benign or cancerous, showed spacing benefits in one study while another study failed to find a spacing advantage. Virtually all research has used accuracy rather than speed as an outcome variable. Thus, effects of spacing on speed of task performance are unknown. Likewise, effects on higher level, critical-thinking skills, such as synthesis of material and creation of novel ideas, are unknown.

Some research has addressed the use of increasing gaps between a series of several study sessions, instead of a fixed gap, and this increasing-gap approach is used in most commercial-tutorial software. However, research that examines effects of fixed versus increasing gaps is inconclusive. While spacing benefits have been demonstrated from infancy through older adulthood and across a wide variety of ethnic groups, it remains unknown whether different age groups require different spacing intervals to optimize retention.

Nonintuitive Aspects

Because short gaps between study episodes lead to higher immediate recall, teachers and students may incorrectly feel they should dispense with recommendations to implement spacing in their classroom or in their study habits. Because the goal of education is to provide students with a body of knowledge and a set of skills that follows them throughout life, this intuition is misguided. It is easy for students to be misled into thinking they are learning efficiently and mastering a set of material, when in fact they are not. Educators and students should remain cognizant of the fact that worse immediate recall can mean better long-term recall.

Nicholas J. Cepeda

See also Desirable Difficulties Perspective on Learning; Rehearsal and Memory; Retrieval Practice (Testing) Effect; Skill Learning, Enhancement of; Spacing Effect

Further Readings

Cepeda, N. J., Vul, E., Rohrer, D., Wixted, J. T., & Pashler, H. (2008). Spacing effects in learning: A temporal ridgeline of optimal retention. *Psychological Science, 19,* 1095–1102.

Dempster, F. N. (1989). Spacing effects and their implications for theory and practice. *Educational Psychology Review, 1,* 309–330.

Pashler, H., Rohrer, D., Cepeda, N. J., & Carpenter, S. K. (2007). Enhancing learning and retarding forgetting: Choices and consequences. *Psychonomic Bulletin and Review, 14,* 187–193.

SPATIAL COGNITION, DEVELOPMENT OF

Spatial ability is necessary to much of human activity. Human adults are highly skilled at many forms of spatial skills. We can all find our car in the vast parking lot and find our way home after the game, but where does this powerful and essential skill come from? How do we develop the ability to explore our world and still find our way home? This entry discusses the development of spatial cognition, first by discussing some of the theoretical issues that frame current debates in the research. Next, it presents an overview of the spatial system that emerges and, lastly, it provides a brief sketch of the changes in spatial ability over developmental time.

Theoretical Issues

Spatial ability has been an area of fierce debate in regard to the nature and course of cognitive development. Data-driven arguments are made from diverse perspectives as we gain information about the specifics of the changes in the spatial system over developmental time. Although much of the current research can trace its roots to the writing of Jean Piaget, the actual claims of a Piagetian view have come under increasing fire. There are a number of competing views vying to offer a new view of the development of spatial cognition. The first of these perspectives comes out of the repeated finding that Piaget underestimated the abilities of young infants. This view espouses a nativism (the claim that most if not all cognitive ability is inborn) that puts much emphasis on early ability and infant competence and less stress on later developments. A second view comes out of an interest in Vygotskian social learning (a view that most ability emerges from social experience and active tutoring) and puts emphasis on spatial language and the cultural milieu surrounding spatial development. The third view is an interactionist perspective that represents an attempt to integrate nativism and constructivism (the Piagetian view that children construct their own cognitive structures through active exploration) into a theory that accounts for early competence and subsequent developmental change. Interactionist models generally embrace the idea that cultural issues and environmental influences as well as early starting points and maturation all combine to produce an individual's developmental trajectory.

The Spatial Coding System

The development of spatial cognition starts out with a set of primitive responses that rapidly become the complex system that makes a toddler able to help us find our keys in the morning. Spatial coding has two possible frames of reference, both of which are important to solving our everyday spatial tasks. Within each of these two frames of reference there are two available spatial systems, one simple and the other complex. The first frame of reference is viewer centered. In this format the individual is the focus and their task is about remembering how to do something—that is, which movements in space will achieve the goal. The simplest use of a viewer-centered spatial ability is called *response learning*. This is the system that is functioning when you reach for your coffee cup on the desk while you are writing. The cup is in the same place every day and you do not need to do more than execute a movement of the arm and hand to achieve the goal. Response learning is powerful and successful when the position of the viewer has not changed; however, it cannot account for movement. If my chair has been moved 6 inches to the right, my reach does not encounter the coffee cup anymore. A more complex use of the viewer-centered system is called *dead reckoning* or *inertial navigation*. In this system the location and direction of the viewer movement is tracked in spatial memory, providing a continuously updating sense of location and direction. This system can be best seen when we are navigating in the dark. The weakness in this system is that it is susceptible to small errors in calculation that are compounded over time. A misjudgment of distance or turn angle is updated and used in all subsequent estimations. This accumulation of error leads to larger and larger inaccuracies over time.

The other reference system is an external framework. There is a simple and complex way to use external information. The simple system, called *cue learning*, is the kind of navigation that allows us to use a landmark as a beacon to guide our search for the goal location. In this case, the landmark has to be at the desired location—for example, the keys are in the bowl. This system runs into difficulty when the landmark is not directly marking the desired location. In many cases, a number of landmarks as well as cues such as the shape of the environment provide a collection of pieces of information that when combined specify the desired location. This complex use of multiple sources of external information is called *place learning*.

These four systems have different starting points and developmental trajectories in humans. In general, infants were long thought to move from an egocentric (viewer centered) frame to an allocentric (external) frame. This view, first espoused by Jean Piaget, has the infant start out with response learning (if I look to my left when I hear door open I can see who is coming into my room), then moves to cue learning (if I look at the door when I hear the door open I can see who is coming). Cue learning is more accurate because it can account for any rolling around in the crib.

Research since Piaget has found this shift from the viewer-referenced systems to externally referenced systems to be less absolute than previously thought—that is, younger infants can show the externally referenced systems under supportive conditions far earlier than an absolute shift could be seen. These data indicate that the externally based spatial systems may be available much earlier than previously supposed. That they are not used under strenuous conditions may be related to the effort necessary to use them early in development or the weighting of the different systems across situations.

The adaptive combination model offers an account that can accommodate the finding of early capability. According to adaptive combination models, the four sources of spatial information are weighted such that the requirements of the situation can dictate which of the spatial abilities is most advantageous. In this way of looking at spatial cognition, the use of response learning to get coffee while typing requires minimal interruption of the concurrent task and thus is the best choice for the task at hand.

In development, the adaptive combination model allows for the idea that there may be some spatial abilities that are available but not used by the infant or young child because it is the weighting and reweighting of the spatial systems that is responsible for much of the developmental change through infancy and childhood. By this approach, infants have the ability to use several different spatial strategies from early on, and the task of infancy, instead of the shift from viewer-referenced to externally referenced systems, would be figuring out the advantageous weighting of the available systems. The weighting of navigation systems changes dramatically when the child begins to locomote independently. The advent of crawling is associated with large cognitive change in several areas, including spatial cognition. The infant's ability to move around space provides a new form of feedback, which changes the weighting of the spatial coding systems by providing new information about which system reliably gets the infant to a goal location.

In addition to the spatial systems available to the child and the weighting of those systems, there is also a developmental progression in the sophistication of the use and subdivision of otherwise unmarked spaces. Adults divide up unmarked spaces into a grid that allows them to search for a lost object in a smaller area. In effect, instead of remembering the car keys are on the football field, we divide the field into categories (between the goal line and the 10-yard line), which allows a smaller search area than if we did not divide the field. The hierarchical coding model indicates that estimations of spatial location are influenced by categorical spatial information as well as by a fine-grained estimation of location. Adults divide space into categories that, over a series of estimations, increase their accuracy by systematically biasing them toward the center of the category, thus allowing adult estimates of location to cluster in smaller subareas of a large space, instead of the whole space (e.g., between the 10-yard line and the goal line instead of the whole football field). This bias works with the adult's tendency to subdivide spaces into small categories to result in overall accuracy. This categorical bias increases when the fine-grained estimate is uncertain.

Developmental Change in Spatial Ability

Infants are sensitive to a large amount of spatial information very early in development. Infants as young as 3 months are sensitive to some spatial stimuli. They evidence longer looking times to objects that move from one spatial category to another. Five-month-old infants are sensitive to changes in object location but not to changes in shape or color of an object that remains stationary. At 9 months, infants show the A not B error. This occurs in an experimental paradigm in which the infant sees an object hidden in Location A and, usually after a short delay, is permitted to search Location A several times. Following several sequences of hiding at Location A, hiding the object at Location B in full view of the infant leads to another search at Location A. The A not B error has been intensively researched, and research indicates that the error can be seen earlier and later when delay between hiding at Location B and search is manipulated. At 16 months, children show a categorical bias in their estimates of location in a continuous space, particularly when their estimations are uncertain. At 21 months, infants show evidence of place learning, the most complex of the spatial systems.

Early childhood is a time of leaps in spatial ability. Young children become able to use basic spatial language early in the preschool years. Children also show that they are beginning to understand representations of spatial information, such as simple models and maps, and gradually they extend the number of situations in which they can use symbolic representations of spatial information. By the end of the preschool years, children show spatial perspective taking as long as they do not need to shift frames of reference. A child can now understand that the layout of the table will look different from someone else's seat as long as they can maintain the same reference points.

Search patterns in children become more sophisticated through middle childhood. While 5-year-olds have difficulty with tasks that require them to use landmarks to accurately find a distal object (place learning) this ability improves through middle childhood. In a place learning task that allowed children to search a large-scale space presented on a desktop computer, 5-year-olds' searches were very inefficient, generally relying on distance from the wall of the space, but the 6-year-olds used a single landmark. Neither of these strategies is very successful, but the addition of one landmark is a step toward the triangulation using multiple landmarks that is the hallmark of sophisticated place learning. As they move toward the end of middle childhood, children became more and more sophisticated in their landmark use with 8- and 9-year-olds using two distal landmarks to guide their search for an object that was distal from all the available landmarks. By the age of 12, the children use spatial strategies very similar to those seen in adults.

Map use also becomes more sophisticated during middle childhood, with children becoming able to understand mapping conventions and perspectives as well as dealing with more and more complex maps. Middle childhood is when their ability to use spatial language moves beyond basic spatial terms to a more complex ability to account for the perspective of a listener and understand what a listener needs to know. By the end of middle childhood (10 years or so), children show mature hierarchical coding. They use the same categories as adults and their adjustment to the fine-grained estimates can occur along two dimensions at once.

Amy E. Learmonth

See also Representations, Development of; Visual Imagery; Visuospatial Reasoning

Further Readings

Gallistel, C. R. (1990). *The organization of learning.* Cambridge, MA: MIT Press.

Hermer, L., & Spelke, E. S. (1994). A geometric process for spatial reorientation in young children. *Nature, 370*(6484), 57–59.

Laurance, H. E., Learmonth, A. E., Nadel, L., & Jacobs, W. J. (2003). Maturation of spatial navigation strategies: Convergent findings from computerized spatial environments and self-report. *Journal of Cognition & Development, 4*(2), 211–238.

Majid, A., Bowerman, M., Kita, S., Haun, D. B. M., & Levinson, S. C. (2004). Can language restructure cognition? The case for space. *Trends in Cognitive Sciences, 8*(3), 108–114.

Newcombe, N. S., & Huttenlocher, J. (2000). *Making space: The development of spatial representation and reasoning.* Cambridge, MA: MIT Press.

Newcombe, N. S., & Huttenlocher, J. (2006). Development of spatial cognition. In W. Damon & R. M. Lerner (Eds.), *Handbook of child psychology: Vol. 2. Cognition, perception, and language* (6th ed., pp. 734–776). Hoboken, NJ: Wiley.

Newcombe, N. S., & Learmonth, A. E. (2005). Development of spatial competence. In P. Shah & A. Miyake (Eds.), *The Cambridge handbook of visuospatial thinking* (pp. 213–256). New York, NY: Cambridge University Press.

Piaget, J., & Inhelder, B. (1967). *The child's conception of space.* New York, NY: Norton. (Original work published 1948)

Quinn, P. C. (2004). Spatial representation by young infants: Categorization of spatial relations or sensitivity to a crossing primitive? *Memory and Cognition, 32,* 852–861.

Shettleworth, S. J. (1998). *Cognition, evolution, and behavior.* London, UK: Oxford University Press.

Speech Perception

The primary form of human communication is based on a speaker producing a series of words with a listener understanding the speaker's message. Speech perception is the process that allows the listener to decode the complex acoustic signal that the speaker has produced, ultimately resulting in the listener (usually) understanding what the speaker intended. A full description of speech perception begins with the signal (i.e., what the speaker has produced) and involves both perceptual and cognitive processes. The signal can be considered at many levels: It is a sound, it contains vowels and consonants, it is made up of words, and the words are syntactically arranged to convey the desired semantic content. Speech perception research has examined all these levels.

The Speech Signal

There is a good understanding of the way that the speech signal comes to be the way that it is. The standard theory of speech production is called *source-filter* theory. The idea is that there are certain sources of sound within the vocal tract, and that these sources are then filtered by the changing shape of the vocal tract. The most important source of sound for speech is called "voicing," a kind of a buzzing sound that is produced when air from the lungs is forced upward, through the vocal cords. There are other sources of sound as well, such as the noise produced when air slips through a narrow opening (e.g., the sound of /s/, or of /f/).

The filtering of these sources is due to a physical property called resonance: Each physical object resonates at particular frequencies that depend on its size, shape, and material. As the tongue, lips, and jaw move, the shape of the air spaces within the mouth changes, producing different resonant properties.

Speech can be thought of as alternating between relatively open positions of the mouth and relatively closed positions; the more open positions correspond to vowels, and the more closed positions correspond to consonants. This is the signal that speech perception process must decode—patterns of energy that reflect the articulation patterns for each vowel and consonant in a given language. Linguists have characterized thousands of human languages in terms of the vowels and consonants that each uses. Across all human languages, about 100 different such *phonemes* have been identified. Each language uses a subset of these, with some variation in the number across languages. English is a fairly typical language from this perspective, with about 42 different phonemes.

It has proven useful to think about each phoneme as being made up of a set of phonetic features. For example, it is possible to characterize each of the consonants in English in terms of three features: voicing, place of articulation, and manner of articulation. Voicing specifies whether or not the vocal cords are active during the consonant's production—they are active when producing a sound like /z/ but not when producing /s/. The place of articulation is based on where in the vocal tract the airflow is most constricted. For example, the air is completely stopped by the lips when saying /b/, whereas the restriction is in the middle of the mouth when saying /d/. Manner of articulation refers to how the air flow is restricted: For sounds like /b/ and /d/ (called *stops*) the air is fully stopped momentarily, whereas for sounds like /s/ and /z/ the air is only mostly restricted, with a bit slipping through; the noisy sound of the air escaping is called *frication*, and the manner is *fricative*.

The results of many experiments can most clearly be explained by considering the featural properties of the speech sounds. For example, if syllables are played to listeners under noisy conditions, and the listeners are asked to write down what they hear, the more features that two sounds share the more likely it is that one will be erroneously reported for the other.

Factors That Make Speech Perception Difficult

A number of factors complicate speech perception. One problem is a result of the way that consonants and vowels are produced. The position of the articulators for an intended vowel or consonant will be affected by the sounds that precede or follow that sound. This results in *coarticulation*—the acoustic properties of each vowel or consonant will not be the same each time, because the surrounding sounds are different.

The coarticulation problem is just one version of the general problem of *phonetic variation*: Each

vowel, consonant, syllable, and word will potentially be different each time it is produced. Many factors influence such variation, including the particular individual who is speaking, the rate of speech, the semantic context, and so forth. Thus, there is no simple "template" that can be used that will consistently match the input.

An additional complication is that each word blends directly into the next word. That is, unlike this text, there are no "blank" spaces to separate words in speech. Any gaps in the speech stream are more likely to be due to producing a particular sound like a stop consonant than to breaks between words. This creates the *segmentation* problem— how does the listener know that a speaker said "two lips" rather than "tulips"?

Possible Solutions to the Difficulties

The coarticulation problem is quite fundamental, and some solutions to it are similarly fundamental. For example, in some theories listeners are not assumed to extract individual phonemes (which undergo the most extreme coarticulation). Instead, the basic recognition units are larger, such as combinations of consonants and vowels, or even whole syllables. These larger units are generally more constant in their form than the smaller pieces that make them up. There is also considerable evidence for *compensation for coarticulation*: If coarticulation shifts the acoustics of a phoneme in a particular direction, then listeners essentially shift perception back in the opposite direction, compensating for the coarticulation-induced changes.

The more general problem of phonetic variation seems to require a number of perceptual responses. The most general solution has been to use various *normalization* routines to make the (varying) input a better match to stored representations ("phonetic prototypes" or "perceptual magnets"). A second solution is to store all previously heard tokens of a given word. In such *episodic* models, a word can potentially be matched to hundreds or thousands of stored versions, increasing the chances of a successful match. Recently, a third approach has generated a good deal of research. Work on *perceptual learning* or *recalibration* has shown that, when listeners hear a variant of a speech sound that is far from the normal pronunciation, there is a tendency to expand the speech sound's category to encompass such variation. For example, if a listener hears "alphabet" with a /b/ that is acoustically rather like a /d/, then the /b/ category expands to include more /d/-like sounds than before.

Listeners use several different methods to solve the segmentation problem. For example, certain sounds are produced differently at the beginning of a word than in the middle of a word; hearing such a variant provides an *allophonic* clue for the listener to a word onset. In some languages, the *stress pattern* of a word provides a clue for segmentation. For example, in English, about 80% of the time, a multisyllable word will begin with a stressed syllable (e.g., *donkey*) rather than with an unstressed syllable (e.g., *delay*). Listeners can also use word recognition itself to help segmentation: Recognizing a word in the speech stream provides segmentation information (i.e., there is a word break just before and just after this recognized word). Recent studies have shown that under good listening conditions, this *lexically based segmentation* strategy plays a major role, whereas some of the lower level cues are more important under noisier listening conditions.

Notable Speech Phenomena

Research on speech perception has revealed a number of interesting phenomena. When scientists first began to study speech using relatively modern techniques, they observed two apparently related phenomena: *categorical perception* and the *right-ear advantage*. Researchers created sets of syllables in which a particular acoustic parameter was varied in such a way that the syllable at one end of the continuum was heard in one way (e.g., /ba/), and the syllable at the other end in a different way (e.g., /pa/). For simple nonspeech stimuli, varying a parameter this way leads to relatively continuous changes in perception. For example, if one end of the continuum is a 100-hertz (Hz) tone and the other end is a 200-Hz tone, with the intermediate items changing in frequency in a systematic way (e.g., 120 Hz, 140 Hz, 160 Hz, 180 Hz), listeners typically hear a gradual change across the continuum; each tone is a bit higher pitch than the one before it. For many speech continua, in contrast, perception seemed categorical: Listeners heard a few items as one category (e.g., /ba/), and then things abruptly changed, with the remaining items heard as the other category (e.g., /pa/). This categorical tendency in perception was strongest for stop consonants, somewhat weaker for other consonants (e.g., fricatives), and weaker still for vowels.

This same ordering was found in *dichotic listening* experiments, studies in which headphones were used to play one speech sound to the right ear and a different speech sound to the left ear. Listeners showed a reporting advantage for speech played to the right ear; as noted, the strength of this advantage mirrored the ordering in categorical perception studies. Since the right ear has stronger connections to the left hemisphere of the brain and language is generally processed on the left side, the right ear advantage was taken as an index of specialized language processing.

Another phenomenon that was discovered relatively early was *phonemic restoration*. To produce this effect, a small piece of speech (typically, one phoneme) was cut out of a word, and a sound, such as a cough or white noise, replaced the missing speech. Listeners consistently fail to notice that speech is missing—they seem to perceptually restore the missing speech. Similar effects have also been reported for other complex sounds, such as music. These effects suggest that the perceptual system can use higher order information to help repair degraded speech input, a valuable adaptation in the noisy world in which speech must be heard.

When the speech input is ambiguous, listeners have a strong bias to interpret it in a way that yields real words rather than nonwords. Consider, for example, a sound that has been designed to be acoustically intermediate between /d/ and /t/. If this ambiguous sound is followed by "ask," listeners generally report hearing "task" (a real word) rather than "dask." If the same sound is followed by "ash," listeners instead hear the sound as /d/ in "dash." This lexical bias is called the Ganong effect.

A final widely known speech phenomenon is the McGurk effect, which is generated using audiovisual presentation. The procedure involves showing a headshot of someone producing a short utterance; the audio track is dubbed to create a mismatch between what the video shows and the sound that is presented. For example, a video of the face producing /ga/ can be paired with an audio recording of /ba/. Under these circumstances, listeners often hear /da/, a kind of compromise between the visual and auditory input streams. Many studies have explored how these two sources of speech information get combined.

Summary

Scientists have been studying speech perception for approximately 60 years. They have clarified the acoustic properties of the speech signal and identified several challenges that the signal potentially might pose for perception. Several solutions to these challenges have been identified. In addition, a number of interesting perceptual phenomena have been discovered, with these phenomena having the potential to constrain theories of how speech perception is accomplished.

Arthur G. Samuel

See also Hearing; Hearing, Philosophical Perspectives; Language Production, Incremental Processing in; Machine Speech Recognition; Word Recognition, Auditory

Further Readings

Liberman, A., Cooper, F., Shankweiler, D., & Studdert-Kennedy, M. (1967). Perception of the speech code. *Psychological Review, 74*, 431–461.

Mattys, S. L., White, L., & Melhorn, J. F. (2005). Integration of multiple speech segmentation cues: A hierarchical framework. *Journal of Experimental Psychology: General, 134*, 477–500.

McGurk, H., & MacDonald, J. (1976). Hearing lips and seeing voices. *Nature, 264*, 746–748.

Norris, D., McQueen, J. M., & Cutler, A. (2003). Perceptual learning in speech. *Cognitive Psychology, 47*, 204–238.

Pitt, M. A., & Samuel, A. G. (1993). An empirical and meta-analytic evaluation of the phoneme identification task. *Journal of Experimental Psychology: Human Perception and Performance, 19*, 1–27.

Repp, B. H. (1984). Categorical perception: Issues, methods, and findings. In N. Lass (Ed.), *Speech and Language: Vol. 10. Advances in basic research and practice* (pp. 243–335). Orlando, FL: Academic Press.

Warren, R. M. (1970). Perceptual restoration of missing speech sounds. *Science, 167*, 392–393.

STEREOPSIS

As illustrated by the number and variety of topics covered in this encyclopedia, the human brain is a highly complex system. One of the true wonders is that it performs these feats simultaneously, and in most cases, without conscious effort. One such ability is that of stereoscopic depth perception. As described below, stereopsis is based on binocular disparity, one of many sources of depth information available in the environment. Other depth cues, such as perspective, shading, texture gradients, and occlusion, also provide clues as to the relative distances of objects in the environment, but none of these comes close to the quality and precision of depth percepts provided by stereopsis. The subsequent sections will review some of the defining features of stereopsis in humans and animals and its associated neural mechanisms.

Stereopsis is a cue to depth based on the fact that we have two eyes, which are laterally separated (in humans by about 6.5 cm). This positional difference in the two eyes results in each eye receiving a slightly different image of the world. So the image of one object will fall on slightly different or *disparate* retinal locations. This difference in location is referred to as *binocular disparity* and is the key information used by the stereoscopic system. Imagine that you have two cameras positioned side by side that take a picture of the same scene. While the resulting images will be very similar, there will be subtle differences, as illustrated in Figure 1.

In Figure 1 the observer fixates object F and another object M is positioned closer to the observer. If we trace the lines of sight from the objects to the back of the eye, we can see this positional difference (as illustrated at the bottom of the figure). Note that this binocular disparity information is generated in the same manner for objects in front of fixation (crossed) and beyond fixation (uncrossed). That is, the geometry of these arrangements is the same, but the position of the retinal images relative to the fixation point is reversed.

An important aspect of stereoscopic depth perception is that retinal disparity is generated between the object or point fixated and another object in the scene. Thus the perceived depth is relative to where one is looking, and if a third object is introduced at the same distance as the fixation point it will have zero disparity. In turn, zero binocular disparity indicates that an object lies on the plane of fixation. The set of points that are equidistant with a given fixation location define the *horopter* (e.g., the dashed line and point P in Figure 1).

The preceding description defines the theoretical horopter; however, when observers are asked

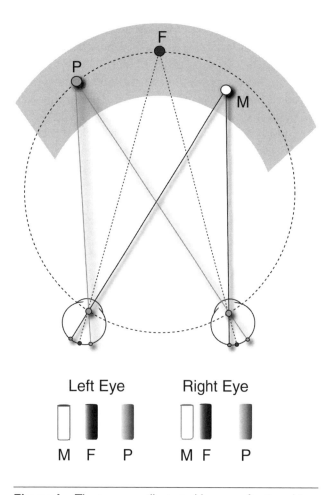

Figure I   The two eyes illustrated here are fixating object F, as seen from above

Note: The views of the three objects as seen in the two eyes are shown at the bottom of the figure. Object M is positioned closer to the observer and has a different lateral position in the two eyes relative to F. The greater the distance an object is from fixation the larger this difference in position, or binocular disparity. Any object (such as P) lying along the circle that passes through F and the nodal point (optical center) of each eye will have zero binocular disparity. This circle is referred to as the *horopter*. Accordingly, the distance between F and P is equivalent in the two eye's views. Object M is inside Panum's fusional area (highlighted in grey) and will appear fused. Objects with large disparities that fall outside this region will appear diplopic.

to set stimuli to be equidistant with fixation, the shape of the horopter is not circular and instead is somewhat flattened. This is known as the empirical horopter. As retinal disparity is increased, there is a corresponding increase in perceived relative depth. Interestingly, over a large range of retinal disparities,

the disparate images appear single, or fused. This region has been referred to as Panum's fusional area. Beyond this range, the images are no longer fused but appear double or diplopic.

An important but often overlooked aspect of stereoscopic vision is that the upper limit for fusion, or Panum's limit (the grey region in Figure 1), does not correspond to the upper limit for depth percepts from stereopsis. Instead, as documented by Armin Tschermak in the early 1900s, observers can reliably discriminate the relative depth of diplopic stimuli. It has been argued subsequently that fine (small) and coarse (large) retinal disparities are processed by different mechanisms. Current research supports such a distinction, though it remains possible that, while the quality of stereoscopic percepts changes at large disparities, the underlying mechanisms represent a continuum.

While binocular vision has been studied for centuries, since the time of Euclid (323–285 BCE), the link between retinal disparity and depth perception was not made until 1838. In a presentation to the Royal Society of London, Sir Charles Wheatstone revealed that the small differences in the views seen by the two eyes are directly responsible for three-dimensional (3-D) vision. Further he showed that it is easy to "deceive" the visual system and recreate the 3-D percept by separately presenting stereoscopic images to the two eyes (see Figure 2). This discovery initiated a new field of study in which investigators could measure the limits of stereopsis and the effect of a range of stimulus attributes on performance. Also, his invention led to the proliferation of handheld stereoscopes, which were used to view stereoscopic images of distant peoples and places. The current advancements in digital technology have lead to a resurgence in popularity of stereoscopic entertainment in the form of 3-D movies.

Stereoacuity

Since Wheatstone's discovery, our understanding of stereoscopic vision has grown exponentially. We now know that humans are able to discriminate the relative depth between two objects based on disparities as small as 30 arc sec (an arc sec [or second of arc] is one sixtieth of one degree). For highly trained observers this threshold can be as small as 4 to 8 arc sec. Such disparities are equivalent to (or smaller

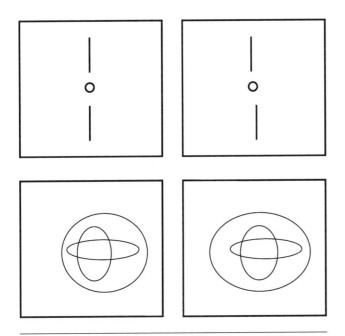

Figure 2   Two pairs of stereoscopic images that can be fused to create 3-D percepts

Note: To view each pair of images, first cross the eyes to align the dark frames that surround the images. When they align in the center (you will see three images now), slowly focus your attention on the center image. It will, eventually, appear in depth. Once fused, the two lines in the upper panel will be displaced in depth with the top line behind fixation and the bottom line in front. The three ellipses in the lower panel will appear slanted in different directions in depth.

than) a hair's width separation between two needles viewed at arm's length! Psychophysical studies have shown that these low thresholds depend on a number of stimulus attributes. For instance, the smallest amount of disparity required to reliably discern that two points are separated in depth (stereoacuity) decreases with increasing image contrast and viewing time. Stereoacuity is degraded by factors such as blur and, in some instances, size.

The Neural Substrate of Stereopsis

In the 1960s, Horace Barlow and John Pettigrew were the first to identify binocular neurons tuned to particular retinal disparities, the possible neural substrate for stereopsis. Subsequent experiments in other laboratories showed that these disparity-selective neurons could be classified as tuned-excitatory, tuned-inhibitory, near, or far neurons. The excitatory

and inhibitory cells responded to small, near-zero, retinal disparities, either with excitation or inhibition. The near and far cells preferred larger disparities and signaled only the direction of the depth offset relative to fixation. This discovery maps onto psychophysical results, which distinguish between the properties of disparity percepts in the small (fine) and large (coarse) range.

The critical link between the disparity-sensitive cells and stereoscopic-depth percepts was made by Randolph Blake and Joy Hirsch. They showed that kittens reared with one eye patched were stereoblind and had only monocular neurons in the primary visual cortex. Subsequent experiments of this type have shown that while the binocular neurons necessary for stereopsis are present at birth, concordant-binocular experience is necessary for the development of stereopsis. That is, the two eyes must move together so that the same region of the visual environment is seen at all times. This line of research has had important implications for the treatment of binocular disorders such as strabismus (misaligned eyes) and amblyopia (reduced vision in one eye).

More recent electrophysiological studies of stereopsis in primates have shown that the encoding of retinal disparity begins in area V1, but neural responses that correspond to perceived depth are found in area V2 and in higher cortical areas. Further, as one moves along the processing pathways, the complexity of the information encoded increases. One of the interesting aspects of ongoing research into the neural basis for stereopsis is the presence of disparity selectivity throughout many visual processing areas. It seems that there is no stereoscopic "center," and even areas believed to specialize in other image properties such as the motion-processing region—the medial temporal region (MT)—have a high percentage of disparity-selective units. Recent investigations of human stereopsis using brain scan technology such as functional magnetic resonance imaging (fMRI) have largely echoed the main results seen in the electrophysiology literature. One of the key topics in current electrophysiological and imaging studies is the possible division of stereoscopic processing into streams that map onto the dorsal/ventral categorization. In a recent study, Tim Preston and colleagues found that dorsal areas encode disparity magnitude, while the ventral stream encodes disparity sign or direction. This is an intriguing result that corroborates the proposed dissociation of coarse and fine disparity processing.

Conclusion

Since Wheatstone's discovery of the link between retinal disparity and depth perception, much progress has been made in our understanding of human stereopsis, and, in particular, its neural substrate. Many questions remain, including the role of distinct dorsal and ventral processing streams in stereopsis, the extent of neural plasticity in disparity selective neurons, and how complex 3-D surfaces and structures are encoded. Answers to these and other open questions will require multidisciplinary approaches that combine rigorous psychophysical methods with brain scanning and electrophysiological techniques.

Laurie M. Wilcox and Debi Stransky

See also Depth Perception; Optic Flow; Perceptual Constancy

Further Readings

DeAngelis, G. C., Cumming, B. G., & Newsome, W. T. (1998). Cortical area MT and the perception of stereoscopic depth. *Nature, 394,* 677–680.

Howard, I. P., & Rogers, B. J. (2002). *Seeing in depth* (Vol. 2). Toronto, Ontario, Canada: I. Porteous Press.

Julesz, B. (2006). *Foundations of cyclopean perception.* Cambridge, MA: MIT Press. (Original work published 1971)

Sacks, O. (2006, June 19). Stereo Sue. *The New Yorker,* 64–73.

Von Noorden, G., & Campos, E. (2002). *Binocular vision and ocular motility.* St. Louis, MO: Mosby.

STROOP EFFECT

The Stroop effect (also called Stroop interference) is the phenomenon in which people are slow and error prone in naming the print colors of incompatible color words (e.g., when seeing the word *yellow* printed in red ink, people are to say "red"). Have you ever tried to remember the title of one song while another song is playing on the radio? You cannot seem to ignore the song on the radio, and so it interferes. Such interference is the bane of attention. Indeed, successfully attending in a world full of stimulation requires that we constantly ignore irrelevant stimuli so as to overcome interference with what is relevant. How might we study the phenomenon of interference, which so clearly influences our ability to process the world around us?

At the dawn of psychology, James McKeen Cattell documented that we are considerably slower to name objects or their properties than to read the corresponding words: Saying "table" to a picture or "yellow" to a color patch is slower than reading *table* or *yellow* aloud. Cattell saw this difference as evidence that word reading becomes *automatic* via extensive practice. Half a century later, John Ridley Stroop combined colors and words into a single task. When the task was to read the word aloud, ignoring the color, people had no difficulty compared to reading words in standard black ink. But when the task was to name the ink color aloud, ignoring the word, people had great difficulty compared to naming the colors of color patches.

In line with Cattell, word reading is taken to be so practiced that it has become automated, and hence words cannot be ignored—even when they should be. This indicates that we do not have absolute control over our attention: Attention can be attracted by the world (exogenous control), not just directed by oneself (endogenous control). The Stroop effect is the best-known evidence of this fact: It is one of the most robust phenomena in all of psychology and the basis of thousands of published studies.

What Causes Interference?

For 40 years, Stroop interference was explained as a kind of "horse race" with the wrong horse (the word) beating the right one (the color) to the stage where a response was prepared—a serial/sequential processing explanation. Thirty to 40 years ago, investigators began to suggest that interference results from performing a controlled process (color naming) simultaneously with an automatic process (word reading)—a parallel processing explanation. Then, about 20 years ago, with the advent of neural network (connectionist) models, emphasis shifted to the idea that learning occurred via changes in stimulus-response connection strength. In the last 10 years, theories have integrated the Stroop effect into larger scale models of perceptual processing or language processing, situating interference in broader cognitive perspective. These increasingly sophisticated models successfully encompass the many published results that constitute the empirical database for the Stroop effect.

Features of the Stroop Effect

After 75 years, we know a very considerable amount about the Stroop effect and, consequently, about the interference that arises when attention is not entirely successful—when ignoring fails. Critically, we know that interference is most likely to occur when there is disparity in practice on the two dimensions. Yet in studies where the color information has been presented sufficiently before the word to give the color response a head start, the Stroop effect does not "flip over," such that the color begins to interfere with reading the word. So relative speed of processing each dimension (word and color) is not the whole story. But there are also empirical challenges to the automaticity explanation, such as the finding that introducing an additional word—not a color word—into the display reduces the interference. If reading is automatic, why should adding another word dilute the interference?

For decades, the Stroop task has been used as a hallmark index of attention; in fact, it is often part of neuropsychology test batteries. Six-year-olds are even familiar with it from the "Brain Age" series of handheld computer games! Moreover, there are many variations on the theme; for example, there is the picture-word task, where the object is to name a simple picture (e.g., a table) when an incompatible word (e.g., *tree*) is printed inside the picture. Interference can also be caused by noncolor words when they are activated—either acutely by recent encounter, or chronically by long-term exposure. This has led to numerous studies, most notably the *emotional Stroop effect,* where time to name print colors is greater for words related to an individual's anxiety (e.g., *crawly* for a spider phobic; *grade* for a test-anxious person) than for neutral words (e.g., *pencil*), thought to result from chronic activation of the anxiety-related concepts and words. The emotional Stroop effect is used to diagnose anxiety disorders and even to measure the success of their treatment.

In the past 20 years, brain imaging techniques have been developed that provide information about the localization of cognitive activity, techniques such as functional magnetic resonance imaging (fMRI). When applied to the Stroop effect, such techniques have shown activity especially in the anterior cingulate cortex and the prefrontal cortex, areas now associated with cognitive control and, in the case of the Stroop task, the failure of that control. This control is viewed as implemented by the prefrontal cortex with the assistance of conflict monitoring done by the anterior cingulate cortex.

What is impressive is that such a superficially simple task, having been used for 75 years, still is useful in our exploration of how attention works. Attention is vulnerable to interference, and the Stroop task demonstrates this beautifully while also providing us with a way to understand that vulnerability better. With the ever-increasing research on the fundamental, cognitive mechanisms of attention, especially on their neural underpinnings, this venerable task will continue to be studied and may even become a more important tool in our cognitive toolkit.

Colin M. MacLeod

See also Attention, Neuroimaging Studies of; Attention and Action; Attention and Consciousness; Attention and Emotion; Automaticity

Further Readings

Cattell, J. M. (1886). The time it takes to see and name objects. *Mind, 11,* 63–65.

MacLeod, C. M. (1991a). Half a century of research on the Stroop effect: An integrative review. *Psychological Bulletin, 109,* 163–203.

MacLeod, C. M. (1991b). John Ridley Stroop: Creator of a landmark cognitive task. *Canadian Psychology, 32,* 521–524.

MacLeod, C. M., & MacDonald, P. A. (2000). Interdimensional interference in the Stroop effect: Uncovering the cognitive and neural anatomy of attention. *Trends in Cognitive Sciences 4,* 383–391.

Stroop, J. R. (1992). Studies of interference in serial verbal reactions. *Journal of Experimental Psychology: General, 121,* 15–23. (Reprinted from the *Journal of Experimental Psychology, 18,* 643–662, 1935)

Williams, J. M. G., Mathews, A., & MacLeod, C. (1996). The emotional Stroop task and psychopathology. *Psychological Bulletin, 120,* 3–24.

SUBLIMINAL PERCEPTION

This entry first provides a definition and overview of the issue of subliminal perception. It then gives a brief history of this issue followed by a discussion of the scientific debate surrounding it. Finally, more recent trends related to subliminal perception are presented.

Definition and Overview

The term *subliminal perception* refers to one's ability to perceive stimulation below the *limen*. The limen refers to the amount of intensity at which the stimulus can be noticed half the time. That is, our sensory systems are not capable of detecting all the stimulation present in the environment. The stimulation has to reach some intensity before it can be noticed. Subliminal stimulation refers to situations in which a stimulus is presented at an intensity below the limen; hence, the stimulus is seldom, if ever, perceived with awareness.

The *American Heritage Dictionary* provides two definitions for *perceive*. The first is "to become aware of directly through any of the senses, especially sight or hearing." The second is "to achieve understanding of; apprehend." The implication is that when sensory information is perceived, one may become aware of the stimulus provoking perception (i.e., supraliminal perception), or one may gain some understanding of the stimulus even in the absence of awareness (i.e., subliminal perception). This latter possibility has intrigued researchers for over a century: Is it possible for one to perceive information that somehow alters our understanding of the world without our awareness of said perception occurring?

Brief History

This question of whether stimuli presented in a subliminal manner can be perceived despite the absence of awareness was the focus of the first published article from a psychology laboratory in North America. In 1884, Charles Pierce and Joseph Jastrow asked participants to guess whether cards contained letters or digits after first establishing a presentation distance wherein participants claimed to be unaware of what was on the cards. Guessing performance was above chance, which the authors attributed to some entity other than the "primary waking self," perception in the absence of awareness.

This issue became of interest to the general public in 1957 when an unemployed market researcher named James Vicary claimed to have subliminally presented the words "Drink Coca Cola," and "Eat popcorn," during a movie, resulting in an increase of product sales. Later, Vicary admitted his study was a marketing stunt with the intent of increasing the number of movie goers. However, the report spawned the worry that it might be possible to influence human behavior without their awareness, a worry reinforced by subsequent books such as Wilson Bryan Key's *Subliminal Seduction; Ad Media's Manipulation of a Not So Innocent America.*

The Scientific Debate

Given the public interest, psychological researchers began attempts to scientifically document, or refute, the existence of subliminal perception. Some argued there was clear evidence for subliminal perception, but critics countered that the methodologies employed were insufficiently rigorous to sustain such claims. The crux of these disagreements centered on the procedure that was used to document subliminal perception.

To demonstrate perception of a stimulus presented at energy levels low enough to preclude awareness, one must first devise a scientific way of measuring awareness and then find an energy level at which this measure indicates null sensitivity. Once established, if some other measure indicates the stimulus is being processed, then subliminal perception has been demonstrated. This methodological approach is termed the *dissociation paradigm*, as the goal is to dissociate some general measure of perception from a more specific measure of perception leading to awareness. The study by Pierce and Jastrow highlighted previously provides such an example in the sense that participants' claims were used to indicate awareness, and their guessing performance provided the more general measure of perception. When guessing performance remained above chance despite claimed unawareness, the general measure of perception was dissociated from the specific measure of perception resulting in awareness.

The controversy with respect to subliminal perception centers primarily on the extent to which researchers accept certain definitions and measurements of awareness. If one allows the participant to indicate when they are and are not aware of some stimulus (a "subjective" index of awareness), then it is relatively easy to demonstrate the perception of a stimulus that participants claim to be unaware of it. However, if one insists on an "objective" index of awareness and further insists that this measure indicate true null sensitivity, the evidence is less compelling.

An objective index of awareness is one that does not rely on the subject telling the researcher what they are and are not aware of but, rather, indexes awareness through a behavioral result. For example, Tony Marcel described a two-part experiment. In the first part, each trial consisted of either a stimulus or nothing being briefly presented prior to a visual mask (e.g., a set of random letters). Subjects were asked to say whether they thought a stimulus had or had not been presented, and a stimulus duration was found at which their performance was roughly at chance levels. Thus presence/absence discrimination was used as an index of awareness, suggesting a lack of awareness when performance was at chance levels; this provided an objective approach to defining and nullifying awareness. Once this duration was established, Marcel demonstrated that stimuli presented at this duration speeded subsequent decisions to stimuli that were semantically related (i.e., a subliminally presented WOLF could "prime" a decision to DOG, such as whether or not it constitutes a correctly spelled word).

This type of finding seemed to provide strong evidence for subliminal perception. However, critics countered these findings as well because Marcel defined "chance" performance as 60% accuracy, leaving open the possibility that the observed priming was due to a small amount of residual awareness. Given the difficulties inherent in both objectively measuring awareness and identifying conditions in which no residual awareness is possible, studies relying on the dissociation paradigm have remained controversial.

Current Trends Related to Subliminal Perception

Although some researchers have suggested more complex versions of the dissociation paradigm to provide clearer evidence of subliminal perception, most subsequent work has relied on methodologies focused on the more general question of how unconscious and conscious perceptual processes interact. There is general agreement that subliminal perception is possible, although it remains unclear how much of a behavioral effect such perception could produce given the extent of stimulus degradation employed. The influence of perception without awareness is likely stronger under less-degraded conditions, with the lack of awareness for "strong" stimuli prevented by factors like divided attention or mental load.

Steve Joordens

See also Attention and Consciousness; Consciousness and the Unconscious; Perceptual Consciousness and Attention; Unconscious Perception

Further Readings

Cohen, J. D., & Schooler, J. W. (Eds.). (1997). *Scientific approaches to consciousness*. Mahwah, NJ: Erlbaum.

Dixon, N. F. (1971). *Subliminal perception: The nature of a controversy*. London, UK: McGraw-Hill.

Key, W. B. (1973). *Subliminal seduction: Ad media's manipulation of a not so innocent America*. New York, NY: Prentice Hall Trade.

Marcel, A. (1983). Conscious and unconscious perception: Experiments on visual masking and word recognition. *Cognitive Psychology*, 15, 197–237.

Merikle, P. M., & Joordens, S. (1997). Parallels between perception without attention and perception without awareness. *Consciousness & Cognition*, 6, 219–236.

Pierce, C. S., & Jastrow, J. (1884). On small differences in sensation. *Memoirs of the National Academy of Science*, 3, 75–83.

SYNESTHESIA

Synesthesia is a neurological condition in which stimulation of one sensory modality or cognitive pathway leads to automatic, conscious experiences in a second, unstimulated pathway. For example, in music → color synesthesia, auditory inputs cause synesthetes to see colors, which typically include movement and texture. In one of the most extensively studied forms of synesthesia, grapheme → color synesthesia, letters and numbers are experienced with a colored overlay. Synesthesia research has expanded dramatically in the past 20 years. This research has demonstrated that synesthesia is a real phenomenon, explored its neural basis, and begun to uncover the genetic mechanisms that might lead to synesthesia. Studies of synesthesia are relevant not only to understanding how individual differences in neural structure lead to unique perceptual experiences but also to understanding universal processes of cross-modal integration and the philosophical riddle of qualia, or the raw subjective feels of sensory experience.

Although synesthesia was a topic of intensive scientific, artistic, and cultural interest in the late 1800s and early 1900s, it was largely forgotten until the late 20th century when research into individual differences and subjective internal experiences once again became widespread. Renewed scientific interest in synesthesia also arose as new behavioral and neuroimaging methods demonstrated the reality of synesthetic experiences. In the past 20 years, there have been more published studies on synesthesia than in the entire preceding century of research.

Behavioral Studies

Behavioral studies have demonstrated that synesthetic associations within an individual are present from childhood and are stable over long periods of time, with synesthetes being greater than 90% consistent in the associations they report, even after years, compared to 30% to 40% consistency after just a month in nonsynesthetes, even when participants are warned they will be retested. Interference paradigms, including modified versions of the Stroop effect, demonstrate that synesthesia occurs automatically. For example, when a grapheme → color synesthete who experiences the digit 5 as green is presented a 5 in red ink, she is slower to name the ink color than if it were printed in green ink. Similar paradigms have been used to demonstrate the automaticity of numerous other forms of synesthesia.

Visual search and segregation paradigms have demonstrated that synesthetic colors can improve performance for synesthetes. In one early test, Vilayanur Ramachandran and Edward Hubbard presented synesthetes and nonsynesthetes with a matrix of 5s in which a number of 2s were embedded to form a hidden shape: a square, diamond, rectangle, or triangle. For a synesthete for whom 2s are red and 5s are green, for example, the display appears as a red triangle on a green background, which improves synesthetes' ability to identify which shape was embedded in the display. Numerous other studies have demonstrated that while synesthesia is elicited early in perceptual processing, it does not occur prior to attention. Additionally, there are substantial individual differences in the intensity of the colors experienced by different synesthetes.

Neural Mechanisms

The neural mechanisms of synesthesia are still debated. Some researchers have suggested that synesthesia arises as a result of decreased synaptic pruning between adjacent brain regions, while others argue that synesthesia is a result of decreased cortical inhibition. Functional neuroimaging studies (including positron emission tomography and functional magnetic resonance imaging) have demonstrated increased activation in color-selective areas including V4 when both music → color and grapheme → color synesthetes are presented with synesthetic triggers. Additionally, neuroimaging studies using methods that focus on brain structure, including diffusion-tensor imaging and voxel-based morphometry, have demonstrated anatomical differences in brain regions involved in eliciting different forms of synesthesia. Grapheme → color synesthetes show increased connectivity in regions of the inferior temporal lobe associated with visual processing, while a unique synesthete who experiences tastes in response to different musical intervals (e.g., she reported that a major third was sweet, while a minor sixth tasted of cream) showed increased connectivity in brain regions associated with auditory and taste processing. These studies showing anatomical differences in synesthetes' brains are consistent with the pruning hypothesis but could also arise because of plastic changes as a result of decreased inhibition. Multiple, neural mechanisms may be involved in synesthesia, and different forms may depend on different mechanisms.

Prevalence and Familiality

Recent estimates of the prevalence of synesthesia suggest that it may be as common as one in 23 people across all its forms. Early studies suggested that synesthesia was more common in women than in men, leading to the suggestion that synesthesia might be inherited through an X-linked mechanism. However, subsequent random sampling has demonstrated that synesthesia occurs equally commonly in men and women, arguing against the X-linked mode of inheritance. Although Francis Galton recognized that synesthesia runs in families in the 1880s, the first candidate genes for synesthesia have only recently been identified. Future research will be required to confirm these findings and to better understand their roles in brain development.

page: Syntactic Production, Agreement in 727

Broader Implications

Although different synesthetes report different associations, large-scale studies have identified trends in synesthetes' experiences. For example, the letter *A* is more likely to be associated with red, smaller numbers and higher pitches are associated with brighter colors, and words tend to share tastes with the phonemes that make up the food names. Such systematic mappings are also found in nonsynesthetes but do not reach conscious awareness, suggesting that some of the same mechanisms underlie synesthetic and nonsynesthetic associations. In addition to its inherent interest as a perceptual variant, synesthesia is of interest to philosophers because it may shed light on the question of qualia: Synesthetes experience additional qualia evoked through nonstandard pathways. The implications of the existence of synesthesia are still debated by philosophers.

Edward Michael Hubbard

See also Music Perception; Stroop Effect; Word Recognition, Visual

Further Readings

Baron-Cohen, S., & Harrison, J. E. (Eds.). (1997). *Synaesthesia: Classic and contemporary readings.* Malden, MA: Blackwell.

Cytowic, R. E., & Eagleman, D. M. (2009). *Wednesday is indigo blue: Discovering the brain of synesthesia.* Cambridge, MA: MIT Press.

Hubbard, E. M., & Ramachandran, V. S. (2005). Neurocognitive mechanisms of synesthesia. *Neuron, 48*(3), 509–520.

Simner, J. (2007). Beyond perception: Synaesthesia as a psycholinguistic phenomenon. *Trends in Cognitive Sciences, 11*(1), 23–29.

SYNTACTIC PRODUCTION, AGREEMENT IN

In linguistics, agreement refers to the correspondence of some formal feature (person, gender, number) between an agreement controller (e.g., the subject noun) and syntactically related words in the sentence (e.g., the verb). Experimental psycholinguistics capitalized on "attraction" errors resulting from interference of an intervening element in agreement production to shed light on the internal dynamics of syntactic constraints in language production. For example, in Sentence 1 the verb *are* erroneously agrees with the plural intervening noun *cabinets*.

1. *The key-S to the cabinets-P are-P on the table.

(S = Singular, P = Plural, * = ungrammatical sentence)

This entry summarizes the major findings about the structural conditions determining interference effects in agreement and their theoretical implications for models of syntactic production.

Interference by Syntactic Features

The first major observation is that, by and large, only syntactic features of the intervening element (like its number or gender features) have the potential to trigger interference. Features on the noun may also be represented conceptually (e.g., plurality) and morphophonologically (i.e., in the word form, like the final *s* on most plural nouns in English). However, it was found that the representation of agreement features at these levels, when manipulated on the intervening noun, play no role in interference (although they were found to influence agreement when manipulated on the agreement controller). For example, conceptually plural but syntactically singular interveners (e.g., The coach of the *team* . . .) fail to trigger plural agreement on the following verb. Similarly, no interference arises with syntactically singular pseudo-plurals that carry typical morphemes of plurality (like the final phoneme /z/, e.g., the color of the *rose*). In contrast, the recurrent finding that syntactically plural interveners (e.g., the daughter of the *neighbors*) generate stronger interference than singular interveners (e.g., the daughters of the *neighbor*) was used to support the claim that plural nouns possess a syntactic feature (marked) capable of triggering interference, whereas singular nouns lack any such feature (default).

Interference Within Hierarchical Structures

The second major empirical finding is that interference occurs within the hierarchical structure and not on the surface word order. The hierarchical structure of the sentence reflects its internal organization: Words combine into phrasal units (e.g., the noun phrase combines the determiner and the noun), which themselves combine to form higher order constituent units (e.g., the prepositional phrase combines the preposition and the noun phrase). The treelike representation is illustrated in Figure 1.

In the marking and morphing model of agreement developed by Kathleen Eberhard and colleagues, interference arises as features from the intervening element are incorrectly transmitted onto the agreement target during the morphing stage. The process of feature transmission is assumed to operate at a stage of language production where elements are organized hierarchically. A first line of evidence comes from the cross-linguistic observation that elements situated higher in the hierarchy intervene more than those situated lower. For example, when two elements intervene in the surface order between the agreement controller and target, the element situated higher interferes with agreement (*programs* in "*The computer with the *programs* for the experiment are broken"), not the element situated lower (*experiments* in "The computer with the program for the *experiments* is broken"), although the latter is linearly closer to the verb. Interference was also found to be stronger with prepositional phrase modifiers (e.g., "The editor of the history *books*") than with relative clauses (e.g., "The editor who rejected the *books*"), the former being situated hierarchically

higher than the latter. Nevertheless, when hierarchical height is kept constant as in disjunctive constructions (e.g., "The boy or the girls"), interference is strongest with the element linearly closer to the verb, showing that linear proximity may also play a role.

Fine-Grained Syntactic Modulation of Interference

Evidence for the role of more fine-grained aspects of the hierarchical structure in interference comes from the observation that the interference occurs in the absence of any intervention in agreement in the surface word order. For example, interference was reported with prepositional phrase modifiers in interrogative sentences involving verb movement (e.g., "*Are-P the helicopter-S for the *flights*-P safe?") and with objects in cleft or relative constructions involving object movement in French (e.g., "*John speaks to the *patients*-P who(m) the medicine-S cure-P"). In such sentences, the object has moved from its postverbal position to a frontal position, which does not intervene between the subject and the verb on the surface. These effects contrast with the absence of interference found in constructions that have exactly the same surface orders but different underlying hierarchical structures (free

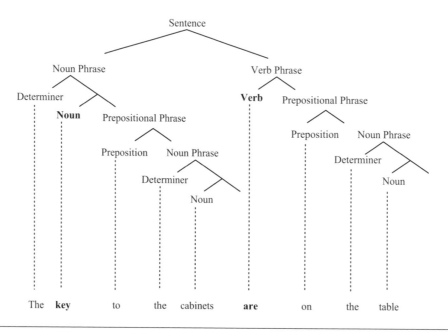

Figure 1   Tree illustration of the hierarchical structure of Sentence 1

Note: In bold, the subject head noun (*key*) occupying the highest position in the tree and the target verb (*are*). Lower down, the intervening noun (*cabinets*) that triggered interference in agreement.

inversion in Italian declarative sentences, e.g., literally, "Phones-S the friend-S of the *neighbors*-P," and complement clauses in French, e.g., literally, "John tells the *patients*-P that the medicine-S cures-S"). Critically, these latter constructions, in contrast to interrogative or relative clauses, fail to involve syntactic movement. The finding that interference effects occur specifically in structures with moved objects was argued to provide evidence for the role, in language production, of the construct of syntactic movement developed in linguistic theory.

In sum, experimental research on interference in agreement strongly argues for a model of syntactic production in which operations like agreement are realized under the guidance of syntactic features over structurally defined hierarchical configurations.

Julie Franck

See also Language Production, Agreement in; Planning in Language Production; Production of Language

Further Readings

Bock, J. K., & Eberhard, K. M. (1993). Meaning, sound and syntax in English number agreement. *Language and Cognitive Processes*, 8, 57–99.

Chomsky, N. (1995). *The minimalist program*. Cambridge, MA: MIT Press.

Franck, J., Lassi, G., Frauenfelder, U., & Rizzi, L. (2006). Agreement and movement: A syntactic analysis of attraction. *Cognition*, *101*, 173–216.

Franck, J., Soare, G., Frauenfelder, U. H., & Rizzi, L. (2009). Object interference: The role of intermediate traces of movement. *Journal of Memory and Language*, *62*(2), 166–182.

Franck, J., Vigliocco, G., & Nicol, J. L. (2002). Subject-verb agreement errors in French and English: The role of syntactic hierarchy. *Journal of Language and Cognitive Processes*, *17*(4), 371–404.

Vigliocco, G., & Nicol, J. (1998). Separating hierarchical relations and word order in language production. Is proximity concord syntactic or linear? *Cognition*, *68(1)*, 13–29.

Taste, Philosophical Perspectives

Taste has been unjustly neglected in the philosophy of perception, largely as the result of the failure to recognize the complexity of tasting experiences. This complexity has been brought to light through research by sensory scientists, which offers philosophers the opportunity to reexamine traditional thinking. This entry will consider traditional views of tastes and tasting, review key empirical findings, and examine the consequences of such research for philosophical views of tastes as subjective or objective.

Tastes as Sensations or Properties of Substances?

Taste has received little attention in the philosophical study of the senses, partly because it has traditionally been considered one of the lower bodily senses, doing little more than producing sensations in us when we eat and drink. On this view, taste is not a perceptual sense like vision or audition, which gives us information about the external environment; it is an inner sense giving us information only about ourselves and our subjective responses to foods or liquids. Although we taste something when we bite into an apple or sip a cup of coffee, such tastes are thought to be no more than pleasant or unpleasant experiences, something immediately known on the basis of sensations on the tongue, and

these sensations are often thought to be too fleeting, too variable, and too subjective to be revelatory of anything beyond themselves.

However, we need not equate tastes with individual responses in the taster. A more objectivist view would see tastes as properties foods or liquids have and that we are able to perceive by tasting. This view seems closer to common sense than the traditional philosophical picture, for we appear to rely on taste to give us knowledge of the flavors of things we eat and drink, to tell us whether a strawberry is ripe and whether our coffee has sugar in it, and to distinguish between the taste of an apple and the taste of an onion. It is hard to imagine how we could come to have this knowledge by any other means.

Those who defend the subjectivity of taste think of tastes as sensations in us whereas defenders of the objectivity of tastes think of the tastes as properties of a food or liquid. How we adjudicate between subjectivist and objectivist positions depends on how we characterize *tastes* and *tasting*. In the traditional picture, the experience of tasting is relatively simple, amounting to no more than having sensations on the tongue in response to the items we consume. However, this view is questionable in its supposition that a tasting experience is due to the workings of a single sense. The case for objectivity requires a more detailed account of our tasting experiences. Such an account is to be found in cognitive psychology and neuroscience where, far from being peripheral to our understanding of the senses, the experience of tasting is thought to provide key insights into the nature of perception.

The Psychology and Neuroscience of Tasting

A growing body of evidence indicates that the senses do not operate in isolation but typically interact to produce integrated multisensory experiences. Tasting is no exception, and contrary to what we commonly assume, the experiences we have when tasting foods are not produced by the single sense of taste alone but by the integration of information from touch, taste, smell, and perhaps other sense modalities. Touch gives us information about the texture of what we consume. We can describe a sauce as creamy or a wine as viscous. The remainder of what we ordinarily call taste is actually a mixture of taste and smell, though subjects are not able to consciously separate these components in their experience. Smell provides the largest part of what we call taste, which is why people who lose their sense of smell often think they cannot taste anything. When questioned, patients will admit they can taste basic gustatory qualities like salt, sweet, sour, bitter, savory, and metallic, but everything else that is missing from their taste experiences is due to smell.

The coming together of information from different sensory streams produces the unified experiences we have when eating a peach or drinking wine. So although we are right to think of tasting as giving us a distinctive kind of sensory experience, we fail to recognize such experiences as involving several sensory components, of which taste is just one. These multimodal experiences of the qualities of foods and liquids have become the focus of intense scientific research, providing as they do clues to the understanding of the cross-modal influence of one sense on another and the multisensory integration of inputs from different senses. The integration of taste, touch, and smell is known as *flavor* to distinguish it from the purely gustatory taste component, which we seldom, if ever, experience in isolation. Flavor describes the sapid and odorous properties of a substance, including its temperature and texture, as well as its power to irritate the trigeminal nerve—the nerve whose activation is responsible for our finding chili "hot" and menthol "cool" despite there being no change of heat in the mouth. So when speaking about the taste of a food, we are actually speaking about its flavor. This point is often missed because we fail to notice the components of our tasting experiences and because we are unaware of the large role smell plays in sustaining them.

Taste and Retronasal Olfaction

It is easy to dispute the claim that what we taste depends on smell when focusing on *orthonasal* olfaction, the external part of smell where we inhale odors and gain information about the environment. The internal part of smell is *retronasal* olfaction, experienced as we exhale, giving us information about what we have just eaten on the basis of odors traveling from the mouth or gullet through the nasopharynx to receptors in the olfactory epithelium at the top of the nose. The odors we sense orthonasally by inhaling may be experienced quite differently when they are sensed retronasally as we exhale. Pungent cheeses, for example, can be much more palatable in the mouth than would have been predicted when smelling them orthonasally. The integration of taste and retronasal olfaction along with touch produces the characteristic experiences of flavor. If we block retronasal olfaction by preventing odors in the mouth from reaching receptors in the nose, blindfolded subjects cannot distinguish the taste of an apple from that of a raw potato.

Taste and Orthonasal Olfaction

The ability to distinguish the components that contribute to an experience of something's flavor depends, to some extent, on the taster's powers of discrimination. However, some smell and taste components of flavor are experientially inseparable. The fusing (or confusing) of smell and taste can be demonstrated by purely odor-induced tastes, where subjects experience a tasteless liquid as sweet or a sweetened liquid as sweeter when it is accompanied by an aroma of vanilla presented orthonasally. Such odor-induced sweetness can even suppress the sourness of a liquid as real sweetness does, leading some sensory scientists to consider such aromas as tastes. This "sweetness enhancement" effect is highly robust and persists even when subjects are asked to attend to each sensory component separately. The inability to distinguish sensations of taste and *retronasally* sensed aromas is understandable, but in this case subjects fail to discriminate between tastes and *orthonasally* sensed aromas presented simultaneously.

Cross-Modal Effects in Tasting

Tasting provides several examples of the cross-modal effects of one sense on another. Certain retronasal aromas can make substances taste creamier. The colors liquids have can influence the perception of flavor. The high-frequency sound of our own crunching, when boosted, can make stale potato chips "taste" fresher. Low temperatures can accentuate bitterness as we notice when coffee goes cold. The greater a liquid's viscosity the greater its perceived sweetness. Should we treat such cross-modal effects as illusions or just routine aspects of human tasting experiences? (Notice that cross-modal effects leave a trace in our language, such as when we describe vanilla as "sweet-smelling" even though sweet is detected only by taste receptors and vanilla is not itself sweet.)

Aftertastes provide further evidence of the conflation of taste and smell. We experience aftertastes as being in the mouth even though they are retronasally sensed odors. Purely olfactory stimuli can be experienced as tastes and not smells, as is easily demonstrated by putting a tasteless aqueous jelly with olfactory properties into the mouth, which will cause subjects to report that they are having sensations of taste on the tongue even when the experimental conditions are known to them. Such cases illustrate what is known as the location illusion, where we relocate or refer olfactory sensations to the mouth. The retronasal detection of odors, when accompanied by sensations of touch from the tongue, leads to the referral of sensations of smell to the mouth where they are interpreted as tastes.

The Temporal Dimension of Tasting

A further dimension to flavor experience is its dynamic time course. Tasting is not a simple occurrence but an unfolding process with a separate series of stages. Different flavors are detected at different places in the mouth, thus tasting experience's dynamic time course affects what we can pick out when. Sensory characteristics will change across time depending on where they are experienced. This complex sequence allows us to build up a profile of the food we consume by attaching different hedonic responses to the different aspects discerned and to the experience as a whole. It is an activity by which we assess the things we eat and drink. Expert wine tasters, for example, pay particular attention to what happens at each stage, which gives them clues about the qualities of a wine. Novices, by contrast, taste in a different way and are unlikely to be

aware of different stages, thereby missing much of the detail. In this way, *how* we taste affects *what* we taste. When assessing food and drink there is room for individual variation, not only because people differ in what they like and dislike but because they may have different experiences as a result of the different thresholds they have for the basic taste qualities of sweet, salt, sour, bitter, savory, and metallic. So-called supertasters have heightened sensitivity to some of these qualities and frequently find unpleasant what the rest of us enjoy.

The Subjectivity and Objectivity of Tasting

How does this newly revealed complexity in our tasting experiences bear on the issue of whether tastes are subjective or objective? At first, it appears to put pressure on the subjectivist view of taste. The subjectivist supposes that tastes are personal experiences had by individuals in response to what they ingest or imbibe and immediately knowable on the basis of gustatory sensations alone. The initial appeal of this view is due to the failure to recognize the underlying complexity of our tasting experiences. But how do matters stand for the objectivist about taste? The objectivist can point out that there is more to what is call taste than we notice at first. We can miss or be in error about features of our experience, thus showing that in the domain of tasting, how things appear to us is not always how they are. This gap between appearance and reality opens up space for a more objectivist view of tastes and the experience of tasting.

However, the subjectivist can reply that the gap just exposed is between experience and how we think about it, not between our experience of tasting and what it is experience of. The reply is telling for both parties. On the one hand, the concession about the often unnoticed gap between our experience and the immediate assumptions we make about it seems to undermine the subjectivist's unproblematic entitlement to the materials she relies on to make out her case. On the other hand, the objectivist needs to do more to show that foods and wines genuinely possess the flavors that we are better able to recognize by improving our perceptual acuity.

The objectivist can point out that since overall flavor perception depends on touch, itself a perceptual sense, flavor perception must be a perceptual sense. Subjectivists may reply that while the products of touch accompany the products of taste (and smell), they are not part of what we call taste. This reply would be unconvincing since tactile experiences do seem to make an essential contribution to our tasting foods. We describe 2-day-old potato chips as tasting stale, when the only difference in flavor between the fresh and the stale crisps is a difference in texture. Texture appears to play a constitutive role in flavor perception.

Is Flavor a Psychological Construct?

But what of the *flavors* perceived? Are they really aspects of the external environment or just psychological constructs? The latter view amounts to a scientifically informed version of subjectivism about taste. Flavors could be an amalgam of sensations produced by different sense modalities united into a single percept. Such a view is still wedded to the idea that all we recognize are properties of our own sensory experiences. However, the texture properties of foods we describe as creamy, crunchy, or viscous are not properties of our sensations but properties of the foods in our mouths.

The objectivist about taste can point out that flavors are not traditional secondary qualities, like sounds or colors, which can only be detected by one sense. It takes at least three senses to pick out flavors. This does not make them common sensibles, like shape, detectable by more than one sense, since none of the contributing senses detects flavors on its own.

A frequent objection to objectivism about taste is the individual variation in subjects' judgments about foods and wines. However, care is needed in pressing this objection. First, the complexity of tasting experiences provides the objectivist with reasons to expect, and the resources to explain, the variety of reactions. Second, talk of variation is often exaggerated. Milk that has soured tastes disgusting to all, and a banana could not taste like an orange to some people without there being something wrong with such people or with the banana. Disagreements about how things taste usually concern complex flavors. Third, we must distinguish between how something tastes and whether it is *to* someone's taste. Individual preferences may vary a lot but it does not follow that the particular flavors people like or dislike vary similarly. Of course, we cannot rule out that the wine you like and that I dislike tastes differently to you and to me. But this may be due to a number of factors, including how skilled we are as tasters and whether we have vastly different thresholds for certain compounds. Thus, variation may be due to something other than that individuals simply have different responses to the *same* tastes.

Flavor Perception: One Sense or Many?

Why suppose that the unified experience of tasting misleads us about its multisensory nature? It could be argued that what we call taste *is* a single sense and that the complexity revealed by neuroscience simply concerns neural mechanisms that subserve given sensory modalities. This view would incorporate retronasal olfaction into taste, even though it makes use of the same olfactory receptors as smell, thus dividing it from orthonasal olfaction, which would now be taken to exhaust the sense of smell. This strategy faces many problems. Not least, it fails to capture generalizations about the interaction between taste and smell. Why, for instance, do individuals with a poor sense of smell have a poor sense of taste? And why do people who lose their sense of smell report losing their ability to taste? Finally, what explanation can be given of the sweetness enhancement effects?

A very different approach is to ask whether there is a single flavor sense, over and above its component senses. This approach treats the sense of flavor as a perceptual system that guides successful food selection by picking out flavors as multidimensional properties of things in our environment.

Conclusion

Tasting may yet prove one of the most illuminating experiences for philosophers of perception to work on, revealing as it does a hidden complexity to our experience. Work in this area will require knowledge of the empirical findings of sensory scientists and an account of how information from separate sensory streams are integrated into a single, unified percept. It is an important area of interdisciplinary research and more work is needed.

Barry C. Smith

See also Smell, Philosophical Perspectives

Further Readings

Auvray, M., & Spence, C. (2008). The multisensory perception of flavor. *Consciousness and Cognition,* *17*(3), 1016–1031.

Korsmeyer, C. (2002). *Making sense of taste: Food and philosophy.* Ithaca, NY: Cornell University Press.

Korsmeyer, C. (Ed.). (2005). *The taste culture reader: Experiencing food and drink (sensory formations).* London, UK: Berg.

Smith, B. C. (2007). *Questions of taste: The philosophy of wine.* New York, NY: Oxford University Press.

Stevenson, R. J. (2009). *The psychology of flavor.* Oxford, UK: Oxford University Press.

TELEOLOGY

Teleology is the study of purposes, goals, or ends; a teleological explanation explains a process or behavior by stating the goal toward which it was directed. This is especially relevant to the study of mind, because part of what it is to be a creature with a mind is to act for purposes, goals, or reasons. To act for reasons is to exhibit *goal-directed* behavior; it is to have one's behavior be teleologically explicable. This entry explores the role of teleology in the explanation of human behavior, contrasting teleological and causal accounts of action explanation and closing with a discussion of attempts to reduce teleological explanation to other forms of explanation.

Explaining Human Action

Typical teleological explanations take forms like the following:

A did *B* in order to *G*.

A did *B* for the sake of *G*.

A did *B* for the purpose of achieving *G*.

A did *B* to *G*.

So, for example, we might say that Kristen went to the kitchen in order to get a beer; this means that the agent (Kristen) directed her behavior (her going to the kitchen) toward the state of affairs in which she has a beer.

When we explain the behavior of persons by citing their reasons, our explanations are often in explicitly teleological form. However, we also sometimes give reason-based explanations where the explanations are not in this form. For example, if we say, "Kristen went to the kitchen because she wanted a beer," then it appears that we have explained the behavior by citing an antecedently existing mental state (her desire for a beer) rather than by citing some goal state toward which her behavior was directed.

The Causalist View

There is an active dispute among philosophers of mind concerning the nature of these different forms of explanation of human action, and the dispute can serve as the dividing wedge between very different views of mind and agency. On the one side are the *causalists*, who maintain that explanation of action in terms of reasons is a species of *causal* explanation. Thus, when we say that Kristen went to the kitchen because she wanted a beer, we are saying that Kristen's desire for beer caused her behavior of going to the kitchen. The causal account of action explanation then becomes the cornerstone of broadly reductionist accounts of mind, according to which facts about the mind are ultimately reducible to physical facts.

The causalist position is generally dominant within contemporary philosophy of mind, but it is less obvious than it might appear. For starters, even if we say that the agent went to the kitchen *because* she wanted beer, this does not by itself imply that the explanation is causal. Other uses of the word *because* are clearly not causal—for example, "the argument does not work because it equivocates on the key term." In this example, the point is that we are *justified* in saying that the argument does not work on the basis of the fact that there is an equivocation; we are not claiming that the equivocation is a cause of invalidity in the way that germs are a cause of disease. So analogously, from the fact that we might say that Kristen went to the kitchen because she wanted a beer, we should not automatically conclude that her desire for beer is being cited as a cause of her behavior, at least not if *cause* is being used in the normal sense associated with the physical sciences.

Moreover, other commonsense explanations of behavior are in explicitly teleological form; for example, "Kristen went to the kitchen in order to get a beer," and such explanations do not even cite an antecedent mental state at all. The causalist must say that such teleological explanations are nonetheless best construed as or reduce to causal explanations. However, there have been persistent problems in getting any such causalist reduction to work, and it is by no means clear that the problems here are merely technical. This will be further discussed below.

The Teleological View

Opposing the causalists are those who take teleological explanations of action to be basic and irreducible to other forms of explanation. In the teleological view, *goal direction* is an ineliminable phenomenon. On this view, explanations such as, "Kristen went to the kitchen because she wanted a beer," are construed as teleological explanations. The reference to her desire for beer serves to specify the goal—namely, that of getting a beer in the way she desires. We need not deny that Kristen's behavior had a cause, and it seems exceedingly probable that the causal chain leading to her behavior crucially involved various states of her brain. However, on the teleological account, our commonsense, reason-based explanation is not aiming to identify the cause of the behavior. The teleological explanation is simply answering a different question: not "What was the antecedent cause of the behavior?" but "Toward what end was Kristen directing her behavior?" Both of these questions might be put in the words, "Why did Kristen go to the kitchen?" but the questions are nonetheless distinct.

Moreover, these distinct questions likewise arguably involve distinct methods of inquiry. When answering the teleological question about an agent's purpose in acting, we take a broadly interpretive approach. We attempt to make as much *sense* of the person as we can. We try for a theory of the agent on which she is, broadly speaking, as rational as possible, meaning that she believes what she ought to believe and values what she ought to value. Accordingly, ascertaining the goal toward which the behavior was directed, we seek candidate explanations on which two things are true: First, the hypothesized goal is such that the agent's behavior is appropriate for achieving that goal, and second, the hypothesized goal is of comprehensible value for the agent. When making these judgments, we naturally take into account facts about the agent's circumstances and epistemic situation. For example, it might be that there is no beer to be found in the kitchen, and thus Kristen's behavior of walking to the kitchen is bound to fail at the supposed goal of getting a beer. However, her behavior can still be appropriate for that goal if Kristen reasonably *believed* that there was beer in the kitchen.

In routine cases, it is often quite obvious which goal to cite in teleological explanation. If Kristen has just been told that there is beer in the kitchen, and she says, "Oh, good, just what I want," then it is clear that her subsequent behavior of going to the kitchen would be appropriate for obtaining a beer, and it is clear enough that having a beer would have value from Kristen's perspective. Of course, things might not be so simple. If an annoying relative just entered the room, then Kristen's real goal might have been to avoid the relative, and the beer could be just an excuse. Or perhaps her behavior was genuinely directed toward both states of affairs—getting a beer and getting away from the relative. Further data about her behavior, including what she says and thinks to herself, will help us in making the most rational sense of the behavior.

On this approach to teleology, there is an irreducibly normative element that makes teleological explanation quite different from causal explanation. When investigating the motions of a rock or of a planet, we are not constrained by the normative requirement that we make the planet or rock's behavior be as rational as possible. Or to put it the other way around, if we were to try to make rational sense of a planet's behavior, we would fail. We might say that the planet had the goal of following the laws of physics, and then its behaviors would be appropriate for the goal, but it would be hard to see why following the laws of physics would have value for a planet or anything else. In a teleological account, being an agent requires a complex set of goals or a life. We cannot successfully attribute anything of the sort to the planet. So we conclude that the planet is not an agent at all, and no teleological explanation of its behavior will be true.

Reductive Accounts of Teleology

The teleological account of action explanation is quite contentious. Some philosophers claim that teleological explanations can be reduced to causal explanations. For example, one might suggest that *A* did *B* in order to *G* is true if and only if

> *A* had a desire for *G* and a belief that by *B*ing she could *G*, and this belief and desire *caused A's Ging*.

However, this analysis appears to be inadequate. To borrow an example from Alfred Mele, a nervous philosopher at a conference desires to distract her commentator and believes that she could distract the commentator by knocking over the pitcher of water on the table. The very fact that she finds herself with this desire and belief unnerves her to the point that her hand shakes uncontrollably and her shaking hand knocks over the pitcher of water. Here, it seems that the belief and desire play the causal role required in the analysis above, but we would not in fact conclude that she actually knocked over the water *in order to* distract her commentator; the behavior was involuntary and not directed at anything. There can and have been ingenious attempts to patch up the causal analysis, but these attempts themselves seem to run into similar problems.

Other philosophers try to reduce teleological explanations, not in a straightforward causal way but by noting their similarity to evolutionary or selectional explanations. Many biological explanations appear to be in teleological form:

Birds have wings in order to fly.

Pandas have a "thumb" in order to strip the leaves off of bamboo.

In cases like this, the form of explanation is species *K* has trait *T* for purpose *G*. Behind such an explanation lies an evolutionary story: Creatures of species *K* had ancestors who developed trait *T* through mutation, and this trait allowed those ancestors to accomplish *G*, which in turn led to higher differential reproduction by members of the species with trait *T*. Thus *T* came to dominate the population. One can put this by saying that *K*s have *T* in order to *G*, but the teleological form is clearly shorthand for the evolutionary story. Clearly, there need be no *agent* involved, and this is not a case of irreducible teleology. One might then try to see teleological explanation of human action along similar reductive lines.

There will, however, be substantial obstacles to this sort of reduction of teleology. First, the explanatory pattern above concerns the relative frequency of *traits*, and the reductionist would need to apply this model in some way to individual items of behavior. Presumably, one can give evolutionary explanations for *dispositions* to behave certain ways in certain circumstances—for example a cat's disposition to arch its back in the presence of perceived threats. However, there will be obstacles to a complete reductive account of rational behavior along these lines. The basic problem is that all evolutionary explanations come back to items being naturally

selected because of their tendency to lead to greater differential reproduction of genes, whereas it is not the case that all *rational* goals that are of conceivable value come down to this one aim. Rational animals can do all sorts of perfectly reasonable things that do not benefit the reproduction of our genes. Indeed, some seemingly quite rational actions are inimical to that end—for example, using birth control.

The debate concerning teleology in mind is still quite active, and there is no consensus on whether teleological explanations can be reduced to more naturalistic causal or selectional explanations. If the nonreductionists are right, then within the realm of creatures with rational minds, purpose is an ineliminable feature of the world, and facts about mind will not reduce to physical facts.

Scott Sehon

See also Action and Bodily Movement; Explanation of Action; Mental Causation; Philosophy of Action

Further Readings

Davidson, D. (1963). Actions, reasons and causes. *Journal of Philosophy, 60*, 685–699.

Mele, A. (1992). *Springs of action: Understanding intentional behavior.* New York, NY: Oxford University Press.

Millikan, R. G. (1984). *Language, thought, and other biological categories: New foundations for realism.* Cambridge, MA: MIT Press.

Okrent, M. (2007). *Rational animals: The teleological roots of intentionality.* Athens: Ohio University Press.

Schueler, G. F. (2003). *Reasons and purposes: Human rationality and the teleological explanation of action.* Oxford, UK: Clarendon Press.

Sehon, S. (2005). *Teleological realism: Mind, agency, and explanation.* Cambridge, MA: MIT Press.

Wilson, G. (1989). *The intentionality of human action.* Stanford, CA: Stanford University Press.

Wright, L. (1976). *Teleological explanations: An etiological analysis of goals and functions.* Berkeley: University of California Press.

THEORY OF APPEARING

When we open our eyes or employ any of our other senses, physical objects in the world appear to us. The *theory of appearing* is a theory of what it is for a physical object to appear to a conscious subject. Preliminarily, we may say that when a physical object appears to a conscious subject, it is *related* to that subject in a certain way, so we can speak here of the appearing relation. The theory of appearing holds that the appearing relation is a unique relation, a relation fundamentally different from all other kinds of relations. Consequently, it is committed to the view that the appearing relation is not a causal relation. The theory of appearing is controversial because one might think that the appearing relation has to be a causal relation. This entry describes and motivates both the theory of appearing and the opposing theory that the appearing relation is a causal relation, the *causal theory of appearing*.

The Causal Theory of Appearing

One might think that there are only a limited number of ways in which distinct entities can be related to each other: They can stand in spatial relations to each other, temporal relations, and/or causal relations. Consider now the appearing relation. Suppose I open my eyes and see a tomato; in virtue of seeing the tomato, the tomato visually appears to me. A tomato cannot appear to me unless it exists at the same time as myself and is situated within my field of vision. But surely to say that the tomato appears to me is to say more than that the tomato is temporally and spatially related to me in a certain appropriate way. So the appearing relation must be at least in part a causal relation. According to the causal theory of appearing, what it is for a physical object to appear to a conscious subject is for the physical object to cause the conscious subject to undergo a certain kind of conscious state: a perceptual experience. Consider again the tomato that is appearing to me. Note that the tomato does not merely appear to me in some general manner; it appears to me in virtue of appearing to me in particular ways: It appears red to me, for example. According to the causal theory of appearing, the tomato appearing red to me is a matter of the tomato causing me to have a certain kind of visual experience, a visual experience somehow characterized by redness. Science gives us many details about the nature of this causal process (the tomato reflects light into my eyes, the light stimulates receptor neurons in my retinas, etc.), but we need not be concerned with these details here. What is relevant here is that according to the causal

theory of appearing, all there is to a physical object appearing to a conscious subject is the object causing the subject to have a certain kind of experience. The experience itself is merely a state of the subject; the subject is related to the physical object only in that the physical object causes the subject to have the experience.

The Theory of Appearing: Response

The advocate of the theory of appearing opposes the causal theory of appearing because she opposes the idea that experiences are merely states of conscious subjects. According to the theory of appearing, these experiences are themselves relations between physical objects and conscious subjects, and it is these experiential relations that constitute the appearance relations. On this view, there are relations other than spatial, temporal, and causal relations. What motivates the advocate of the theory of appearing is the commonsense idea that our experiences encompass the physical objects we perceive. Here I am, looking at the tomato that appears red to me and having a visual experience. As noted earlier, the visual experience is characterized in part by redness. Part of what is involved in my having this visual experience is my being aware in some sense of this redness. But this redness, although an element of my experience, also strikes me as being a feature of the tomato itself; the tomato itself seems to be included in my experience (this is the commonsense idea to which I previously referred). The tomato is appearing to me in virtue of the fact that one of its features is present in my consciousness. Specifically, the tomato is appearing to me in virtue of appearing red to me, and it is appearing red to me in virtue of its redness being present in my consciousness. I am related to the tomato via its redness; the redness of which I am aware is itself a relation between the tomato and myself, and it is this relation that constitutes the appearance relation between the tomato and myself. Some will find it strange to speak of redness as a relation; surely there are no color relations in the same sense as there are spatial relations. But note that a physical object cannot appear red without appearing red *to a* subject; for a physical object to appear red is for it to be related in a certain way to a subject. And the theory of appearing holds that all there is to a physical object appearing red is its presenting its redness in a subject's consciousness, so this redness itself must be of such a nature as to relate the physical object to a conscious subject.

We can now characterize the theory of appearing more generally as the view that what it is for a physical object to appear to a conscious subject is for the physical object to present one or more of its sensory features in the subject's consciousness. The challenge for the theory of appearing is to show that it is compatible with a scientifically informed picture of the world. This challenge is taken up in the readings listed below.

Harold Langsam

See also Disjunctive Theory of Perception

Further Readings

Alston, W. (1999). Back to the theory of appearing. In J. Tomberlin (Ed.), *Philosophical Perspectives: Vol. 13. Epistemology* (pp. 181–203). Malden, MA: Blackwell.

Langsam, H. (1997). The theory of appearing defended. *Philosophical Studies, 87*, 33–59.

Martin, M. G. F. (2004). The limits of self-awareness. *Philosophical Studies, 120*, 37–89.

THINKING

Thinking refers to the process of reasoning in order to reach a goal. In humans, this process typically involves combining externally derived information and prior knowledge so as to formulate and evaluate implications that may provide an answer to a question or a solution to a problem. It is the goal-directed nature of thinking that sets it apart from mere associative processing, where one idea links to another in a nonpurposive manner akin to what takes place when daydreaming. Thinking is a core topic of empirical inquiry and theoretical analysis in cognitive science and subsumes a multitude of inter-related concepts, including reasoning, categorization, judgment, decision making, hypothesis testing, problem solving, and creativity. Of all these inter-connected concepts, however, reasoning is arguably most central to understanding what thinking entails.

This entry begins by summarizing key historical antecedents to research on thinking and reasoning and then progresses to consider important theoretical insights deriving from contemporary research in this field. These insights are discussed with reference to a major paradigm that has been deployed over several decades in researching thinking processes: the four-card selection task developed in the 1960s by Peter Wason. The entry concludes by considering some important trends in current thinking research.

Historical Antecedents to Contemporary Thinking Research

The study of thinking extends back over 2,000 years to Aristotle, who believed that it was the conscious activity of the mind, with thoughts being composed of images. Aristotle also pioneered the method of *introspection* to study thinking, a technique that was dominant in philosophy and psychology until the late 19th century. Aristotle's view that images are the foundation of thinking was central to the associationist accounts of the British Empiricist School of philosophy in the 17th and 18th centuries. This view only became discredited when psychologists at the University of Wurzburg in the early 20th century demonstrated that image-based thoughts did not characterize the thinking of many participants, with some describing no discernible thoughts at all and others claiming their thoughts were indescribable and seemingly nonconscious.

Research in the 20th century further undermined the notion that thinking relates to conscious processing. Freudian theory advanced the idea of unconscious thinking as an essential determinant of behavior, while behaviorists such as J. B. Watson and B. F. Skinner contended that all behavior, including thought, could be explained in terms of individuals learning to associate particular responses with particular stimuli when a reward was present that reinforced such links. From a behaviorist perspective, analyzing the conscious, "mentalistic" correlates of thinking was an irrelevance, with thinking instead being described as reflecting acquired habits and conditioned responses operating at a tacit level.

In the 1960s, the field of cognitive psychology emerged, with its basis in a new computational metaphor for the mind and a resurgence of interest in the mental processes underpinning thinking—an interest that continues unabated. Although the cognitive revolution meant that the study of thinking was back on the agenda as a legitimate area of inquiry, this approach made no commitment to the view that thinking is necessarily conscious and available for introspective access. Indeed, there has long been recognition amongst cognitive psychologists that implicit processes may dominate thinking, with only surface features emerging in the stream of consciousness. The cognitive perspective on thinking additionally avoids limiting such activity to humans, such that certain machines (e.g., artificial intelligence systems) can be viewed as engaging in thinking, as can certain animal species (e.g., higher order primates). Cognitive researchers have also tended to avoid treating human thinking as synonymous with notions of rationality, given abundant evidence that thinking often appears to be irrational and suboptimal. Finally, the cognitive approach brought with it a renewed interest in the mental representations underpinning thinking. Although the concept of images has featured in cognitive theorizing, a rather different concept has burgeoned over the past 30 years, which is the idea espoused by Philip Johnson-Laird that thinking is based on the construction and manipulation of abstract "mental models" of possible situations.

Thinking: An Example Paradigm and Findings

The previous definition of thinking describes it as involving goal-directed reasoning. Reasoning, or *inference*, has a long tradition in philosophy in the fields of logic and probability and emphasizes the process of drawing implications or conclusions from given information (premises). A valid *deductive* inference is one that produces a conclusion that must be true given the truth of its premises. Deduction is closely related to formal logic, which provides a *normative* model against which deductive thought can be assessed. While deductive reasoning is truth preserving, *inductive* reasoning is not, instead providing only plausible conclusions that may or may not be true. The strength of induction resides in its capacity to enable the formulation of conjectures that go beyond the available information, allowing, for example, the generation of generalizations or laws based on repeated observations of events.

The Wason Selection Task

The four-card selection task developed by Peter Wason in 1966 is certainly the most investigated paradigm in the history of thinking research, perhaps because it has all the hallmarks of a useful task for studying thinking, including a stated goal and a need for hypothesis testing, deductive inference, and decision making. In its standard, abstract form (Figure 1) the task involves presenting participants with four cards that are described as each having a letter on one side and a number on the other side. The presented cards display the facing sides A, J, 3, and 7. Participants are also given a conditional sentence, "If there is an A on one side of a card, then there is a 3 on the other side," and are asked to decide which card or cards need to be turned over to determine the truth or falsity of the sentence. Common choices are A or A and 3. The logically correct choice (which few participants make) is A and 7, since only a card with an A on one side that does not have a 3 on the other side would disprove the sentence; hence, selecting the A and the 7 is necessary to reveal such a potentially falsifying combination.

Pioneering research by Jonathan Evans established that responses on this task primarily reflect a "matching bias," a tendency to select cards named in the presented sentence. This was corroborated using sentences involving negated terms (e.g., "If there is *not* an A on one side of a card, then there is *not* a 3 on the other side"). Although negations change the logic of the task, thereby altering the cards that should be selected, participants still tend to select A and 3, in line with matching. These selection task results are curious since they suggest that human thinking may be rather superficial in nature, showing limited sensitivity to logical principles of sound inference. Evans proposes that matching bias dominates our "intuitive" reasoning on the selection task by directing attention in a highly selective way toward aspects of the presented information. However, Evans and Linden Ball also present evidence

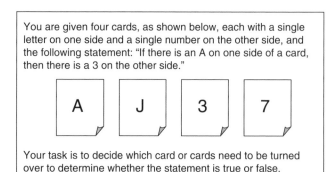

You are given four cards, as shown below, each with a single letter on one side and a single number on the other side, and the following statement: "If there is an A on one side of a card, then there is a 3 on the other side."

A   J   3   7

Your task is to decide which card or cards need to be turned over to determine whether the statement is true or false.

Figure I   An abstract form of the Wason selection task

indicating that more conscious, analytic processes are still engaged on the task but primarily function to enable people to find good reasons to justify the selection of cards cued through intuitive processes. The influence of matching bias on the selection task is so powerful that few participants (typically less that 10% of undergraduates) are able to overcome it so as to choose the logically correct cards. Those individuals who do choose correctly have superior intelligence and an apparent ability to override intuitive processing by the application of what Evans refers to as the "reflective mind"—that is, the capacity to think in an abstract and hypothetical manner that is not merely dominated by the specific content and context of the task at hand.

Keith Stanovich has presented his own concept of the reflective mind, which is different in important ways from the notion discussed by Evans. Stanovich views the reflective mind as being the "disposition" to engage in explicit, analytic reasoning—that is, a person's *preference* for careful, analytic deliberation over quick, intuitive judgment. Furthermore, he views the disposition to engage in analytic thinking as being distinct from the actual "capacity" to execute analytic thinking in an effective manner, what he refers to as the "algorithmic mind." Presumably then, the high level of intelligence needed to reason logically on the abstract selection task is a manifestation of the joint activity of both the reflective and algorithmic minds.

The selection task can be made much easier if it is recast in a real-world format. One variant (Figure 2) involves giving people a social rule, "If a person is drinking beer then he or she must be over 18 years of age," and presenting cards representing four drinkers. One side of each card depicts what the person is drinking; the other side depicts that person's age. The presented cards have facing sides showing Beer, Coke, 22 years of age and 16 years of age. Participants have to decide which card or cards need to be turned over to discover whether the rule has been violated. The majority correctly chooses the person drinking beer and the person under the age of 18. Intriguingly, success on this version has little association with intellectual ability. Evans argues that on the standard selection task the intuitive mind is prompting the wrong answer and hindering the efforts of the reflective mind to apply logical reasoning. In contrast, on the realistic problem, the intuitive mind is cueing the correct answer, taking the pressure

off the reflective mind. Indeed, most people will have previously encountered something similar to the drinking-age rule and will know from experience that rule breakers are those who drink alcohol when underage. As such, little thought is required to select the correct cards, which is why individuals of higher intelligence have no advantage over those with lower ability on this version.

Current Trends in Thinking Research

Research on thinking and reasoning has produced considerable evidence for so-called *dual-process* theories, such as the one sketched out above in relation to the abstract selection task, where implicit, intuitive processes interact with explicit, reflective processes in controlling responding. Evans describes his own dual-process theory as the "two minds hypothesis." He conjectures that the intuitive mind is old in evolutionary terms, sharing features with animal cognition, whereas the reflective mind is recently evolved and distinctly human. The intuitive mind is also claimed to be the source of emotions and intuitions, capturing adaptive behaviors acquired over evolutionary history as well as habits acquired experientially. In contrast, the reflective mind enables abstract thinking so as to facilitate reasoning about hypothetical possibilities.

Critically, dual-process theorists propose that intuitive and reflective processes will frequently come into conflict, and when this happens it is the intuitive mind that often wins out, with the reflective mind seemingly rationalizing the conflict such that people appear to be unaware of the fact that their intuitions are dominating their thinking. This phenomenon is not only seen in the abstract selection task but in many other thinking and reasoning

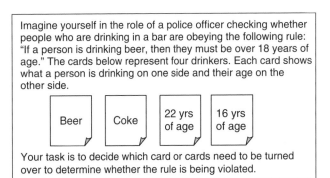

Imagine yourself in the role of a police officer checking whether people who are drinking in a bar are obeying the following rule: "If a person is drinking beer, then they must be over 18 years of age." The cards below represent four drinkers. Each card shows what a person is drinking on one side and their age on the other side.

| Beer | Coke | 22 yrs of age | 16 yrs of age |

Your task is to decide which card or cards need to be turned over to determine whether the rule is being violated.

Figure 2   A realistic form of the Wason selection task

paradigms where intuitive/reflective conflicts can arise. One particularly good example concerns the study of "belief bias" in deductive reasoning, where people frequently make intuitive judgments about presented arguments in accord with the believability status of given conclusions rather than making reflective, analytic judgments in accord with the underlying logic of the arguments. A recent demonstration of this comes from a study by Edward Stupple and colleagues. They showed that the incorrect tendency for people to endorse *believable* conclusions to *invalid* arguments is primarily associated with individuals of moderate or low analytic ability, who engage in less reflective thought (as indicated by relatively rapid response latencies) compared to those of high analytic ability, who take more time over their reasoning in an attempt to resolve validity/believability conflicts.

Dual-process theories of thinking are currently widespread, with key areas of investigation relating to understanding the complex interplay between intuitive and reflective processes in determining how we reason when working toward goals. Dual-process notions are not, however, universally accepted, with some theorists arguing for a more unitary view of thinking processes. Especially dominant in this vein is the *Bayesian rationality* approach of Mike Oaksford and Nick Chater, which proposes that thinking involves implicit, probabilistic calculations that have no relation to deductive logic. Such research has been gaining popularity in its attempt to provide a comprehensive account of all human thinking, including the dominant pattern of card choices on both standard and realistic selection tasks. It is difficult, however, to see how probabilistic theorizing can be reconciled with data indicating that participants often do make an effort at deductive thinking. Another dominant trend in thinking research relates to the examination of the neural underpinnings of reasoning using brain-imaging techniques. Interestingly, current neuroscientific evidence supports the existence of competition between distinct brain systems during many aspects of thinking, thereby further corroborating dual-process ideas.

Linden J. Ball

See also Deductive Reasoning; Two System Models of Reasoning

Further Readings

Evans, J. St. B. T. (2010). *Thinking twice: Two minds in one brain.* Oxford, UK: Oxford University Press.

Evans, J. St. B. T., & Ball, L. J. (2010). Do people reason on the Wason selection task? A new look at the data of Ball et al. (2003). *Quarterly Journal of Experimental Psychology, 63*(3), 434–441.

Holyoak, K. J., & Morrison, R. G. (2005). *The Cambridge handbook of thinking and reasoning.* Cambridge, UK: Cambridge University Press.

Johnson-Laird, P. N. (2006). *How we reason.* New York, NY: Oxford University Press.

Manktelow, K. (2011). *Reasoning and thinking* (2nd ed.). Hove, UK: Psychology Press.

Oaksford, M., & Chater, N. (2007). *Bayesian rationality: The probabilistic approach to human reasoning.* Oxford, UK: Oxford University Press.

Stanovich, K. E. (2011). *Rationality and the reflective mind.* New York, NY: Oxford University Press.

Stupple, E. J. N., Ball, L. J., Evans, J. St. B. T., & Kamal-Smith, E. (2011). When logic and belief collide: Individual differences in reasoning times support a selective processing model. *Journal of Cognitive Psychology, 23,* 931–941.

Vartanian, O., & Mandel, D. R. (2011). *Neuroscience of decision making.* Hove, UK: Psychology Press.

Time Perception

Time perception refers to the subjective experience of the duration or temporal organization of events within a given period of time. In this entry, a brief overview of time perception is provided, including the main phenomena and models used to interpret them. The main neurobiological substrates of timing identified in recent studies are then presented.

Various types of temporal experience can be distinguished: the main types being perception of duration of events or stimuli, perception of order (which between a and b came first or second), and perception of temporal regularity or rhythm. These phenomena can take place on different time scales, varying from a few milliseconds to seconds, hours, days, and even years. For example, musical rhythm is perceived with a series of tones separated by temporal intervals shorter than about 2 seconds, and natural rhythms are perceived in succession of days, months, or years. Perceiving duration, order, and temporal regularity is fundamental in most activities for organisms evolving in a changing environment. Classical Pavlovian conditioning experiments as well as later experiments on animal timing demonstrated that pigeons, rats, and many other nonhuman species adapt remarkably to temporal contingencies of the environment, displaying highly developed abilities in interval timing and revealing a key role of temporal associations in learning. Things that are judged to be close in time tend to be associated, and this link constitutes the basis of learning in humans and other animals. Estimating time and processing temporal order are also essential in performing complex activities requiring coordination in movements or action, anticipation of times of occurrence in a dynamic environment, or remembering ordered elements like digits in phone numbers or words in sentences. In addition to being intimately related to most common activities involving planning, coordination, and memory, the ability to estimate time is also essential in rhythmic activities such as playing music or dancing.

A stopwatch is an efficient mechanism for estimating duration: It starts and ends at distinct moments, and the amount of temporal information accumulated between these two points constitutes an objective assessment of the interval bounded by the two points. Humans can quite accurately perform that kind of interval timing without any external time-keeping device. Interval timing is flexible in that it can start and stop any time in response to the demands of the environment, in contrast to rhythmic timing, such as in circadian rhythms, which is often determined by rather rigid constraints and shows relatively small variability. The phenomena, methods, and models described below mostly concern human interval timing in the few hundred milliseconds to minutes range.

Interval Timing in Humans: The Main Phenomena

Our subjective experience of time does not correspond necessarily to objective time, as measured by an accurate clock. The first experimental studies on the relationship between perceived and objective time were performed in the 19th century by psychophysicists such as Gustav Fechner, Wilhelm Wundt, and Ernst Weber. One issue considered important by these scientists was whether time perception shared common features with perception of other dimensions, such as visual perception or auditory perception. Even though time perception cannot be related to a specific sensory system like visual or auditory perception, some principles indeed seem to apply to time perception as well as to perception of visual or auditory features of stimuli. One major principle is *Weber's law*, which states that the *just noticeable difference* (jnd) between two stimulus values (e.g., line length, light brightness, or tone duration) is a constant proportion of the smaller of the two values. It will be easier to notice the 1-second (s) difference between 1 s and 2 s than the same difference between 50 s and 51 s. Although the jnd appeared to be an increasing function of the smaller duration values, in more recent studies on time perception the relationship is not exactly linear over all values (especially when shorter than .25 s or longer than 2 s) and is better described by a generalized form of Weber's law.

Differences between judgments of very short and longer intervals (e.g., shorter than .25 s and longer than 2 s) suggest that different mechanisms may be responsible for estimating intervals of various ranges. Perception of short time intervals is influenced by their sensory content. One example is the filled-duration illusion: A filled interval is usually perceived as longer than the same empty interval. For example, a .25 s tone will be judged longer than a silent .25 s interval between two brief markers. There are also some differences in judgments of short stimuli of different modalities. One difference is that people judge an auditory stimulus to be longer than a visual stimulus of the same duration. However, although judgments of short durations are influenced by the sensory systems used in the timing task, most current models of time perception assume that a common mechanism underlies time perception in the various modalities.

Judgments of longer durations—that is, longer than about 1 s—require storing temporal information relative to the ongoing duration in working memory. Attention is another cognitive process involved in judgments of longer durations. The influence of attention is especially obvious in interference studies, which reveal that when people are estimating the duration of a time interval, performing some attention-demanding task at the same time perturbs considerably the precision of their estimate. The interference usually results in a shortening of the perceived duration, and the longer or the more attention-demanding the concurrent task, the shorter the perceived duration. A related finding is that the mere expectation of a signal interferes with timing. As with concurrent tasks, the longer the duration of expectancy, the shorter the perceived duration. The interference effect is generally attributed to the fact that precise timing requires continuous attention, so if a distracting activity is performed while timing, then some temporal information is lost, resulting in shorter perceived duration.

Methods and Paradigms

The main methods used in human time perception studies are duration comparison or discrimination, production or reproduction of time intervals, and verbal estimation. Duration discrimination involves posing a relative judgment—for example, deciding which is the longer of two tones. In time production or reproduction, a participant may be asked to reproduce the duration of a tone by pressing a key for a duration equal to the presented duration. Most methods can be used in two general paradigms, retrospective and prospective. In the retrospective paradigm, people estimate in retrospect the duration of a past temporal interval; this paradigm may be required if during the stimulus presentation they were not aware that an estimate of its duration would have to be provided. In the prospective paradigm, people estimate the duration of a stimulus during its presentation. Different factors seem to affect performance in the two paradigms: Retrospective judgments are more dependent on the memory of the number of events or perceived changes taking place during the elapsed duration; prospective judgments are strongly influenced by the amount of attention devoted to time during the ongoing duration. This difference corresponds to the paradoxical observation that a past period of time may seem long in retrospect when many things happened during that period but that time flies when we are busy or having fun. Different models thus attempt to explain experimental data obtained in the retrospective and prospective paradigms, respectively.

Models of Prospective Timing

Prospective temporal estimates in humans are approximately related to objective clock time. In "internal-clock models," on which this section mostly focuses, this relationship is explained by assuming the existence of a mechanism similar to an interval timer in humans and other animals. Like a clock, this mechanism would emit temporal units (often named pulses) that are related to real time in an orderly way. The *scalar expectancy theory* (SET) is an influential internal-clock model of time estimation that includes three categories of processes related respectively to the clock, memory, and decision. Although initially developed from experiments with rats and pigeons, this model appears to be very useful in interpreting results of experiments with humans. In this model, the clock level includes a pacemaker emitting pulses that are stored in an accumulator if a switch is closed, permitting accumulation. The content of the accumulator is transferred to working memory if the task requires a memory representation of the current time. The current time value is compared with a remembered criterion time sampled from a reference memory in order to evaluate whether the ratio between the current and remembered values is small enough to decide that they correspond. The decision rule varies according to the particular task requirements. Some experiments in animal timing suggest that the switch permitting accumulation of temporal information may be attention controlled, which would also explain that distracting activities shorten perceived time in humans by preventing accumulation of temporal information. Attention is also central in other internal-clock models of human time estimation, in which the amount of temporal information accumulated is positively related to the amount of attention devoted to temporal processing.

In the first internal-clock models, pulses emitted by the pacemaker were assumed to be the basis of temporal information in humans, but it has been suggested more recently that oscillatory processes constitute this basis. Periodicities related to oscillatory processes—for example, electrical cortical oscillations—are present in the bodies of humans and other animals. These processes present regular phases and would provide the basic information of the internal clock.

Humans and other animals may also use their own behavior to estimate time (finger tapping in humans, wheel running before pressing a lever for rats). Some behavioral models of timing assume that behavior supports time estimation in a pacemaker-based system similar to an internal clock, but there is also a view, in behavioral models as well as in models on the neural basis of time perception, that suggests that an internal clock or dedicated mechanisms are not necessary to explain temporal performance. These models postulate that there is no specialized system in the brain responsible for processing temporal information. In this view, temporal representation linked to a stimulus duration is derived from the state of neural networks when the stimulus is presented as well as from the neural activity occurring during its presentation.

Neurobiological Substrates of Timing

Many brain areas have been identified in studies on the neurobiological substrates of timing; the specific areas often depend on the timing tasks and the range of durations investigated. One challenging issue, especially in studies on timing of intervals longer than a few hundred milliseconds, is to identify brain regions activated specifically by timing functions, independent of associated task demands such as memory or decision making. When humans are asked to perform perceptual and motor timing tasks, the main structures identified in functional magnetic resonance imaging (fMRI), positron emission tomography (PET), and electrophysiological studies include the basal ganglia, prefrontal cortex, cerebellum, supplementary motor area, and some other discrete cortical areas that vary with the specific timing task requirements (stimulus modality, decisional, and response demands). In research with patient populations, perception and production of series of brief time intervals were disturbed in patients with cerebellar lesions, suggesting the involvement of the cerebellum in time estimation. Finally, pharmacological and lesion experiments as well as data from patients such as people with Parkinson's disease also suggest a central role of dopaminergic activity in timing. Drugs facilitating and blocking the synaptic release of dopamine alter temporal performance in such a way that they seem to speed up and slow down the clock, respectively.

Claudette Fortin

See also Attention, Resource Models; Music Perception; Reinforcement Learning, Psychological Perspectives; Working Memory

Further Readings

Brown, S. W. (1997). Attentional resources in timing: Interference effects in concurrent temporal and nontemporal working memory tasks. *Perception & Psychophysics, 59,* 1118–1140.

Buhusi, C. V., & Meck, W. H. (2005). What makes us tick? Functional and neural mechanisms of interval timing. *Nature Reviews Neuroscience, 6,* 755–765.

Fortin, C., & Massé, N. (2000). Expecting a break in time estimation: Attentional timesharing without concurrent processing. *Journal of Experimental Psychology: Human Perception and Performance, 26,* 1788–1796.

Fraisse, P. (1984). Perception and estimation of time. *Annual Review of Psychology, 35,* 1–36.

Gibbon, J., & Church, R. M. (1990). Representation of time. *Cognition, 37,* 23–54.

Ivry, R. B., & Schlerf, J. E. (2008). Dedicated and intrinsic models of time perception. *Trends in Cognitive Sciences, 12,* 273–279.

Killeen, P. R., & Fetterman, J. G. (1988). A behavioral theory of timing. *Psychological Review, 95,* 274–295.

Zakay, D., & Block, R. D. (1997). Temporal cognition. *Current Directions in Cognitive Science, 6,* 12–16.

TWO SYSTEM MODELS OF REASONING

Abundant evidence suggests that there are two distinct systems of human reasoning, which can be referred to as *intuition* and *deliberation*. The evidence comes from studies of deductive and inductive reasoning, decision making, categorization, problem solving, probability and moral judgment, and planning. Most of the evidence is behavioral, although a little comes from cognitive neuroscience. The distinction rests on a set of properties that characterize each system (see Table 1). The intuitive system is designed to make quick and dirty assessments based on similarity and what can be directly retrieved from memory. It relies more on observable properties and well-ingrained schematic knowledge. The deliberative system is slower and more analytic. It depends directly on learned systems of rules, and its information processing is highly selective. We have conscious access not only to its products but also to its inner workings. The intuitive system is likely more evolutionarily primitive than the deliberative system, has more in common with other animals, and includes a greater proportion of older brain structures. This

Table I Properties conventionally used to distinguish the two systems

Intuitive System	Deliberative System
Product is conscious, process is not	Agent is aware of both product and process
Automatic	Effortful and volitional
Driven by similarity and association	Driven by more structured, relational knowledge
Fast and parallel	Slower and sequential
Unrelated to general intelligence and working memory capacity	Related to general intelligence and working memory capacity

entry provides an overview of the evidence for this characterization.

Characterizing the Systems

Deductive Reasoning

The distinction between intuition and deliberation helps characterize how people think in almost every area of cognition that has been studied. To illustrate, deductive inferences such as determining what follows from "if p then q" and "p is true," can be made either way. Deliberation leads to more correct judgments of logical validity, but correct inferences require more processing time and more attention than intuitive inferences. They are thus less likely in the face of attention-demanding secondary tasks. Even without distractions, people are biased when judging the validity of arguments in favor of conclusions they believe to be true; their intuitive beliefs inhibit their ability to analyze whether a conclusion follows logically from an argument's premises. People are sensitive to instructions; for instance, requests to respond deductively versus inductively change which system dominates, but people do not seem able to rely exclusively on deliberation while ignoring their intuitions.

Studies using functional imaging demonstrate that different brain areas become activated depending on whether a task demands associative responses or rule use. Some studies of deductive inference have suggested that a left temporal pathway corresponds to one reasoning system while a bilateral parietal pathway underlies the other. But

other researchers have compared probabilistic reasoning using a task that involves both intuition and deliberation with a deductive reasoning task that relies more heavily on deliberation and found that both activate the medial frontal region bilaterally as well as the cerebellum. Probabilistic reasoning activated the left dorsolateral frontal regions more and deductive reasoning activated right occipital and parietal regions more.

Decision Making

People differ in which system they habitually use to make decisions. Some people are more likely than others to inhibit incorrect intuitive responses in order to make more deliberative decisions. Such people tend to make choices that map more closely onto the expected value of options. In gambles that promise gains, they are more risk seeking than less deliberate people, and in gambles that promise losses, they are more risk averse. But deliberative reasoning can sometimes lead to worse decisions. Because of the limited capacity of working memory, deliberation is only able to consider a few attributes of each option. Therefore, intuition is better equipped to make decisions when there are many relevant attributes and is better at accommodating attributes that are difficult to verbalize or quantify. Some believe that intuition is closely related to affect, although little evidence supports this claim.

Categorization

Categorization can be either rule based or similarity based. Rule-based categorization classifies based on no more than a few dimensions, is easily applied to novel stimuli, and is learned and used explicitly. Similarity-based categorization aggregates over many dimensions, generalizes only with a measure of uncertainty, and cannot be verbalized. People are more likely to use rule-based processes when they need to explain or justify their responses.

Using different methodologies, several brain-imaging studies have found distinct activation patterns for the two types of categorization, though the activated regions corresponding to rule- and similarity-based processing have varied. A study using artificial visual stimuli found activation in the medial temporal lobe for rule-based category learning and in the basal ganglia for similarity-based category learning. Another study used meaningful category labels and found increased activation in frontal areas for rule-based categorization but not for similarity judgments. A study using novel animal-like stimuli showed increased activation in left inferior frontal cortex and anterior cingulate when explicit rules rather than similarity to prototypes were used for classification.

Problem Solving

People solve problems in two ways, using intuition (the "a-ha" experience) or deliberately and analytically. People can predict how long a problem will take to solve but only when it lends itself to analytic and not intuitive processing. Some types of problems, such as math problems, are inherently symbolic and appropriate for rule-based analytic processing. Greater working memory capacity helps solve such problems. Sian Beilock and her colleagues have shown that pressure to perform can impede performance, especially for individuals with more working memory resources.

Judgment

Several phenomena of judgment provide evidence for and help to characterize dual systems of thinking. The most prominent example is the conjunction fallacy of probability judgment, the observation that an event (e.g., that a flood will devastate Manhattan sometime this century) is sometimes judged less probable than a conjunction that includes that event (e.g., that global warming will cause glaciers to melt and a flood will devastate Manhattan sometime this century) even though this contradicts the prescriptions of probability theory. This exemplifies *simultaneous contradictory belief*, a phenomenon in which we are predisposed to believe that the conjunction is more likely even after we have discovered that it is not logically possible. People with lower IQs are more likely to commit the conjunction fallacy as are people engaged in a secondary task, again suggesting that working memory capacity must be available to engage in deliberation.

Moral judgments also have at least two bases, a deliberative one and a more intuitive one. People are only able to justify some of their moral judgments (e.g., committing a bad act is worse than not acting even if the outcome is the same). Other justifications cannot be articulated. For example, moral judgments tend to conform to the principle that harm intended as a means is worse than harm foreseen as a side effect, but people are not able to articulate that principle. This suggests that some moral judgments are made on the basis of intuition, although people have access to a system sometimes capable of generating justifications. Joshua Greene and his colleagues have given people a variety of moral dilemmas while imaging their brain activation using fMRI. Some dilemmas were solved based on simple rules, others based on feelings that people could not justify. The former were associated with areas of the brain usually associated with working memory, the latter with areas usually associated with emotion and social cognition.

Planning

In research on planning and action, the two systems are evident in the difference between novel and routine action plans. Sometimes we break goals down into subgoals, a deliberate process that is verbally accessible and working memory intensive. In contrast, actions that lead to a familiar goal, such as brushing your teeth, involve acting out learned schema. This can happen with very little awareness or cognitive effort while engaged in a parallel task. Such intuitive planning can result in errors. A stimulus in the environment can evoke a familiar action but one that does not achieve the current goal (e.g., eating another cashew when you intended to stop). Such action slips are common in certain frontal lobe patients and occur in healthy individuals when working memory is occupied by another task—for example, when deliberation is unable to intervene.

Factors Governing System Choice

The deliberative system is more resource intensive than the intuitive system, so intuition dominates when resources are scarce. Increases in time pressure or working memory demands increase the proportion of intuitive responses. Decreasing physiological resources such as sugar has the same effect. After an energy-depleting task, people who drank lemonade with sugar made more rule-based decisions than those who drank lemonade with an artificial sweetener.

Mood also influences which system guides behavior. When people are sad, they deliberate more and make more consistent decisions. When people are happy, they integrate more general knowledge into their thinking, are more risk-averse when choosing gambles, and make better intuitive judgments, all suggesting greater intuitive processing.

Work by Danny Oppenheimer and his colleagues has shown that disfluency, the sense that a task is difficult, increases the degree of deliberative processing on that task. Disfluency is a metacognitive signal that a difficult problem requires deliberation. However, it increases deliberative processing even when incidental—for instance, when a reasoning problem is printed in a blurry font or participants are asked to furrow their brows (suggesting cognitive effort).

Conclusion

The distinction between deliberative and intuitive thinking has helped explain phenomena from a vast assortment of cognitive domains. All these explanations refer to a deliberative system that requires effort and working memory, which is selective in the information it uses but can abstract away from specific content, and that provides conscious access to the process in addition to the result of a computation. These explanations also refer to an intuitive system that is automatic and unhampered by concurrent tasks, that integrates information associated with specific content, and that provides only the result of a computation to conscious awareness. Some theorists argue that rather than two distinct systems, reasoning varies on a continuum between intuitive and analytic processes. Others argue that the many distinctions made between two forms of reasoning do not map onto the same two systems.

Magda Osman and Ruth Stavy show that children use some rules without deliberation or effort in ways that conflict with other rules. The rule-based system is not constituted by a consistent logical system. Rather, different rules emerge depending on how problems are framed, what the focus of the question is, and what is most available to the problem solver. Nevertheless, the evidence suggests that there is a single deliberative system. Whether there is a single intuitive system or a class of loosely related intuitive processes is not so clear.

Imaging data suggests that distinct brain mechanisms can be engaged by varying instructions, but the evidence does not clearly support any specific theory of the neuroanatomy underlying deliberation or intuition.

One open question concerns the relation between intuition and emotion. Another concerns how the systems interact. Jonathan Evans has distinguished several models of their interaction. Most of the evidence favors the parallel-competitive model, which proposes that the intuitive and deliberative systems process information in parallel and any conflict is resolved after both processes generate potential responses. But there is also reason to believe the default-interventionist model, which states that the intuitive system always operates first, followed by an optional deliberative intervention and override or elaboration of the intuitive response. Of course, both models might be partially correct because cognitive processing can involve many cycles of interaction.

Steven Sloman and Adam Darlow

See also Automaticity; Categorization, Neural Basis; Decision Making, Neural Underpinnings; Deductive Reasoning; Mental Effort; Representativeness Heuristic; Thinking; Working Memory

Further Readings

Beilock, S. L., & DeCaro, M. S. (2007). From poor performance to success under stress: Working memory, strategy selection, and mathematical problem solving under pressure. *Journal of Experimental Psychology: Learning, Memory, and Cognition, 33*(6), 983–998.

De Neys, W. (2006). Dual processing in reasoning: Two systems but one reasoner. *Psychological Science, 17,* 428–433.

Evans, J. (2007). *Hypothetical thinking: Dual processes in reasoning and judgment.* London, UK: Psychology Press.

Greene, J., Nystrom, L. E., Engell, A. D., Darley, J. M., & Cohen, J. D. (2004). The neural bases of cognitive conflict and control in moral judgment. *Neuron, 44,* 389–400.

Rips, L. J. (1989). Similarity, typicality, and categorization. In S. Vosniadou & A. Ortony (Eds.), *Similarity and analogical reasoning* (pp. 21–59). New York, NY: Cambridge University Press.

Sloman, S. A. (1996). The empirical case for two systems of reasoning. *Psychological Bulletin, 119*(1), 3–22.

Stanovich, K. E., & West, R. F. (2000). Individual differences in reasoning: Implications for the rationality debate. *Behavioral and Brain Sciences, 23,* 645–726.

Unconscious Emotions, Psychological Perspectives

How do you feel right now? Do you feel happy, sad, disgusted, fearful, excited, disappointed, or angry? If so, to what extent? Further, if you indicated that you are indeed in an emotional state, what is the cause of it? What specific event brought it about? Questions like these are being asked in hundreds of psychological studies conducted all over the world. They are also being asked in a similar form by economists and sociologists who assess life satisfaction, doctors who assess patient pain level or the presence of a psychiatric condition, marketing researchers who assess customer satisfaction, and many other professionals. Though the process by which people answer these questions may appear straightforward, it presumes that people actually know (a) that they feel an emotion, (b) what specific emotion they feel, and (c) why they feel it. In contrast, research in psychology reveals that, under some circumstances, people can be wrong about their emotions. Specifically, people can be in an emotional state without having any conscious awareness of being in that state. People can be wrong about the state they are in. And finally, they can be wrong and even unconscious about the causes of their emotional state. In short, the topic of unconscious emotion deals with the fundamental question of conscious access to and self-understanding of one's own emotional life. The remainder of this entry covers the historical background of this idea and gives several examples from modern research.

Historical Background

Historically, interest in the limits of emotional self-understanding and the relation of emotion to consciousness dates back to Sigmund Freud and several of his contemporaries. Freud speculated that people can sometimes be mistaken about what triggers their emotion. For example, a woman may believe that she is attracted to a man because of his professional achievements, but in fact she likes the man's similarity to her father. Freud also speculated about the possibility of confusion about the nature of one's own emotional state. For example, a man may believe that he feels angry at his partner for being late, whereas in fact he feels jealous—a feeling he either cannot identify, name, or perhaps admit. Finally, Freud wondered whether some emotions are sometimes "kept" from consciousnesses, such as son's sexual feelings toward his mother or his homicidal anger toward his father.

Modern Research

Modern psychology has largely rejected Freud's vision of psyche and his dramatic speculations. However, interest in those issues remains high, and empirical research, now armed with tools of psychology and neuroscience, shows that emotion, consciousness, and understanding can dissociate but usually in much less dramatic forms, as shown next. Note, however, that some of the following examples involve mild, undifferentiated emotional states (e.g., moods and changes in general positivity/negativity).

Mistaken Beliefs About Causes and Nature of One's Emotion

Modern research shows that if a newly encountered person is similar to the participant's significant other (e.g., sibling, parent, close friend), the participant will partially transfer (generalize) the traits of the significant other to the new person, without realizing that he or she is doing so. Several classic studies found that mood or arousal because of one source can transfer (spill over) to an irrelevant object. For example, participants aroused from riding an exercise bike rate pictures of members of the opposite sex as more attractive. Men who have just viewed an erotic picture rate a completely unrelated financial gamble as more profitable. In another example, participants called on a sunny day, and thus feeling happy, give higher ratings on a variety of judgments, including life satisfaction.

Emotional States Induced Without Awareness

It is possible to elicit mild emotional states by presenting stimuli completely without awareness. This is often done using subliminal presentations in which stimuli are presented in a way that prevents awareness. The method can involve flashing the stimuli very briefly (e.g., 5 milliseconds [ms]), presenting them outside the focus of attention (e.g., as flashes in the corner of the computer screen), masking (covering) the stimulus with another, more salient object, or typically, a combination of these methods. For example, participants who were subliminally flashed a large number of emotion-related words reported changes in a generalized mood state, without realizing what brought on that change. Further, repeated subliminal presentation of simple geometric figures (polygons) has been shown to lead to subtle mood enhancement, presumably because repeated stimuli elicit a warm feeling of familiarity. Another study showed that negative mood can be enhanced by subliminally presenting images of snakes and spiders to phobic individuals. Finally, many studies showed that very briefly presented emotional stimuli (e.g., faces) can lead to physiological and judgmental manifestations of emotion (e.g., as reflected in the activation of emotional brain systems and their bodily concomitants). Of course, with all these examples, it is important to remember that the stimuli used are very simple. This is important because there is a debate in psychology to what extent novel, complex stimuli can be processed without awareness and how strong and durable are reactions elicited by such stimuli.

Fully Unconscious Emotion

Perhaps the greatest controversy in psychology regarding unconscious emotion surrounds the possibility that people may sometimes not even realize that they are in an emotional state. There is some literature on dissociations between emotion and consciousness in hypnotic states. Some dramatic cases have been reported of people engaging in strong emotional acts while in a state characterized by lack of full consciousness (e.g., cases of "sleep murder," "sleep intercourse"). Empirically, however, this kind of "fully unconscious emotion" has been a difficult topic to study because of the impossibility of completely excluding that a person did not feel something or wasn't somehow aware. There are also limits on generalizing from cases that may involve psychopathology. Still, there are some intriguing results from a series of studies on typical college participants. Those studies unobtrusively exposed participants to several happy or angry subliminal emotional facial expressions. After that emotional induction, participants were asked to perform some emotion-related behavior (e.g., drinking a novel beverage, making a gamble). Participants were also asked to report their emotional state. The emotion state was also monitored using psychophysiology. Interestingly, in those studies the ratings of conscious feelings were unaffected by subliminal faces. Yet participants showed changes in their emotional behavior. For example, they consumed more of the beverage after happy rather than after angry faces. They gambled more after happy than after angry faces. Further, the psychophysiological measures indicated that the emotional faces elicited emotion-appropriate changes in the bodily state (e.g., more smiling and less startling to loud noises, etc.). As such, these results suggest that, at least in some circumstances, one can induce an emotional state that drives a person's physiology and overt behavior without that state giving rise to conscious, reportable feelings. In short, there may indeed be fully unconscious emotion.

Piotr Winkielman

See also Consciousness and the Unconscious; Emotions and Consciousness; Subliminal Perception; Unconscious Perception

Further Readings

Feldman-Barrett, L. F., Niedenthal, P., & Winkielman, P. (Eds.). (2005). *Emotion and consciousness*. New York, NY: Guilford.

Kihlstrom, J. F., Mulvaney, S., Tobias, B. A., & Tobis, I. P. (2000). The emotional unconscious. In E. Eich (Ed.), *Cognition & emotion* (pp. 30–86). New York, NY: Oxford University Press.

Winkielman, P., & Berridge, K. C. (2004). Unconscious emotion. *Current Directions in Psychological Science, 13*, 120–123.

Zajonc, R. B. (2000). Feeling and thinking: Closing the debate over the independence of affect. In J. P. Forgas (Ed.), *Feeling and thinking: The role of affect in social cognition* (pp. 31–58). New York, NY: Cambridge University Press.

UNCONSCIOUS PERCEPTION

If you are reading this, you are probably experiencing conscious perception. Is it possible that you could understand this sentence without conscious awareness? If so, this would constitute unconscious perception. Consciousness per se has been difficult to capture operationally and scientifically, but progress has been made recently, at least in terms of neurological correlates of subjective awareness. Delineating the *absence* of consciousness has been fraught with methodological and theoretical challenges, but subjective unawareness on the part of the human perceiver has become scientifically legitimized. Namely, when there is any measureable change in one's experience, thoughts, or actions as a function of current external events juxtaposed with an absence of awareness of the events, then unconscious perception has occurred.

Different Types of Unconsciousness

Although Sigmund Freud is generally given credit for raising consciousness about unconsciousness, his brand—the psychoanalytic unconscious—is only one aspect. While Freud's conception of the unconscious deals primarily with appetitive urges and motivations, more recent work by researchers including John Bargh, Ap Dijksterhuis, and John Kihlstrom has focused on—and found empirical evidence for—cognitive and social processes that operate at an unconscious level. Many of the cognitive and social processes involved in unconscious

perception have been revealed to be surprisingly sophisticated and complex and are discussed below.

Terminology

A variety of terms have been used to describe perception without awareness: *unconscious perception, nonconscious perception, subception, implicit perception,* and *subliminal perception.* The term *limen* (a root of *subliminal*) implies a threshold for consciousness. Philip Merikle and Jim Cheesman (1986) have most effectively defined this boundary as a *subjective threshold,* or "the level of discriminative responding at which observers claim not to be able to detect perceptual information at better than a chance level of performance" (p. 42). However, since the subjective threshold is based entirely on a perceiver's self-report, it should be combined with an additional criterion—performance that is qualitatively different during aware versus unaware episodes—which in turn permits distinguishing conscious from unconscious processes. Thus, the term implicit perception has recently gained popularity among cognitive neuroscientists, both because it avoids the logical problem created by the term subliminal (i.e., evidence suggests the existence of a continuum along the conscious-subconscious spectrum, not simply a threshold) and, according to John Kihlstrom and others, because subliminal perception is just one subcategory of unconscious perception. In particular, we shall see that unconscious perception covers a much wider range of phenomena than the narrower term subliminal. A PsycINFO search (June 2010) revealed 1,932 citations concerned with unconscious perception, in contrast to only 636 involving subliminal perception.

Unconscious *Processes* Versus Unconscious *Stimuli*

Information can be unavailable to consciousness for many reasons. On the event side, the stimulus can be uninterpretable or not sensed at all because it is too degraded (either optically or aurally distorted), too faint (too dim or too soft), or too brief (e.g., presented for 2 milliseconds). (The preceding are examples of an absolute threshold, a concept in *psychophysical scaling*.) Alternatively, the observer can be the cause of the unconscious processing. A person can be outright unconscious (e.g., asleep or under anesthesia), unaware because of concurrent attentional demands, or suffer from a neurological condition that precludes conscious perception (e.g., *blindsight*, discussed below).

By definition, subliminal phenomena are restricted to stimuli that are either extremely degraded or presented so briefly that nothing meaningful can be perceived. For example, a word flashed on a computer screen for 1 millisecond (ms) is experienced as no more than a flash of light; although there *is* a *sensation*, neither word nor even letters are perceived. Nevertheless, even such stimuli can be shown to have been processed ("perceived") subconsciously.

How can a stimulus be unconscious? It cannot, of course. But a person can be unaware of a stimulus or at least unaware of its identity. For example, in one typical experiment by John Seamon, Richard Marsh, and Nathan Brody (published in 1984), irregular 8-sided polygons were presented for 2, 8, 12, 24, or 28 ms. Polygons presented for 2 to 8 ms were indeed processed, as evidenced by subsequent "correct" affective judgments: Compared to nonpresented items, previously presented items were "liked better." In contrast, conscious recognition (i.e., subjects had to determine which polygons had been presented previously) required presentations of at least 12 ms to achieve above-chance levels of performance. These findings demonstrate two principles: (a) Very briefly presented stimuli *are* (or at least can be) processed unconsciously, but (b) conscious access is available only for stimuli presented for somewhat longer intervals. (In this study, the threshold was presumably somewhere between 8–12 ms.)

Sensation, Perception, and Memory

Although cognitive psychology allots these three processes to separate pigeonholes, of course they are all related. Indeed, the three phenomena normally function seamlessly and often subconsciously. Sensation can be defined as the raw input of external stimuli and involves processes by which sensory receptors and the nervous system receive and represent environmental stimulus energies. Although we are typically aware of sensory inputs, elementary sensation can occur without awareness. For example, the pupil of the eye can respond to light, and galvanic skin responses or event-related potentials in the brain can be recorded independent of concomitant awareness.

In contrast, perception—in its quintessential definition—typically requires some cognizance of meaning. Perception organizes and interprets sensory information, making it possible to understand the meaning of objects and events. A compelling distinction between sensation and perception (and between conscious and unconscious perception) can be illustrated by the case of a rare neurological syndrome, *prosopagnosia* (sometimes referred to as "face blindness"). A person with prosopagnosia can have perfect perception of individual facial features (e.g., eyes, nose, lips), but cannot synthesize those details appropriately to accurately recognize a well-known friend or spouse. It is unclear whether individuals with prosopagnosia have unconscious perception of familiar faces or whether such perception is simply neurally disconnected. (Once a familiar but visually unrecognized person speaks, that person can be identified immediately.) Foreign language provides another example: The spoken phrase *tudo azul* can be heard (sensed) by any normal listener as human speech but only *perceived* as a meaningful phrase by someone who speaks Portuguese.

Memory also affects perception, even (or perhaps especially) when such memory is unconscious (known as *implicit memory*). For example, even though subjects could not consciously remember pictures they had seen 17 years previously (some could not even remember having participated in the experiment!), David Mitchell found that implicit memory enabled perception of the corresponding 17-year-old picture fragments. In our everyday experiences, sensation, perception, and memory blend into a seamless process. However, the remainder of this entry focuses on events in the observer's current perceptual field.

A Brief History of the Unconscious

Within experimental psychology, unconscious perception is one of the most venerable topics. Its primordial status can be traced to 1884, when C. S. Pierce and J. Jastrow published the first empirical report "on small differences in sensation" (without awareness). The concept of unconscious perception, however, predates empirical research. For example, in 1867 Hermann von Helmholtz theorized that that perception was dependent on "unconscious inference."

Unconscious perception has been one of the most controversial topics in experimental psychology (a "checkered past," in John Kihlstrom's words).

Skepticism surrounding its existence (and accompanying methodology) has contributed to its controversial nature. Interest in unconscious phenomena has waxed and waned for over a century, both among scientists and the hoi polloi. The waning of empirical research on subliminal perception in particular may be traced to a famous but highly controversial movie theater "study" by James Vicary in 1957, in which he claimed that popcorn and Coca-Cola sales were increased by subliminal ads. Indeed, the 1960s saw only 8% of the studies in this area, but the number of studies picked up in the last three decades (71% of all subliminal studies). In contrast, the number of studies dealing with the more general concept of unconscious perception (including both cognitive and social processes) has shown a steady rise, with the count nearly doubling since 2000. Indeed, research in unconscious perception has mushroomed recently, and a 2005 volume by Ran Hassin, James Uleman, and John Bargh proclaimed the current era as "the new unconscious."

Controversy

What made the topic of unconscious perception controversial? In spite of earlier empirical research documenting the phenomenon, the publicity surrounding Vicary's hoax coupled with some failures to replicate, along with the behaviorists' demonization of mentalism, made subliminal perception scientifically improper. Even following the "cognitive revolution" spurred by Ulric Neisser's 1976 *Cognition and Reality*—where mental phenomena were restored to scientific legitimacy and intellectual respectability—the emphasis in cognitive psychology remained grounded in *conscious* experience, and the unconscious remained taboo. The zeitgeist subsequently shifted, due in part to John Kihlstrom's 1987 "Cognitive Unconscious" article in *Science,* which restored the respectability of this field. Namely, the unconscious was no longer restricted to Freudian concepts or to pseudoscientific claims about subliminal advertising.

In addition to the controversial (pseudoscientific, cargo cult status) and methodological issues surrounding subliminal perception in particular, were fears foisted on the public by nonscientists claiming that advertising agencies were using subliminal techniques to effectively alter consumer behavior and endanger the American culture via sexual imagery (popular books by Wilson Bryan Key in the 1970s, 1980s, and 1990s, and by August Bullock in 2004). In spite of the negative publicity, however, legitimate research on unconscious phenomena in cognitive and social psychology finally picked up.

Empirical Evidence and Recent Research Topics

Hundreds of studies (nearly 1,300 since 1990 alone) have revealed—according to most researchers—unambiguous evidence for unconscious perception. As John Kihlstrom put it in 2008, the evidence "satisfies all but the most determined critics" (p. 587). Thanks to rigorous methodological developments, even the critics have come around, with only some particular phenomena excepted. For example, Anthony Greenwald and his colleagues demonstrated conclusively that "subliminal message self-help" audio media do nothing for consumers beyond standard expectancy (placebo) effects. For example, while products claiming to promote weight loss or to improve memory or self-esteem produced no such effects, audiotapes that were systematically mislabeled *did* affect consumers' perceptions solely according to what was printed on the label. In a series of studies, John Vokey and Don Read investigated claims about "backmasking"—backward speech presumably embedded in rock music intended to promote evil behaviors—and found no evidence that subjects could process backward speech at any level. (Note that backmasking has no relation to *backward masking,* a rigorous experimental technique for eliminating conscious perception in visual tasks.)

In any case, the predominant current view is that unconscious perception is a viable, replicable, and scientifically respectable phenomenon. According to Sid Kouider and Stanislas Dehaene, the only controversy remaining has to do with the *depth* of processing of "invisible stimuli." In other words, are unconsciously perceived stimuli processed only at a physical level (shapes, letters, or partial components of words) or at a complete and meaningful semantic level? The jury is not yet in on this question; evidence exists for both scenarios.

Stimuli That Are Not Consciously Perceived

Evidence that stimuli blocked from conscious awareness can be perceived comes from process-dissociation procedures, neurological correlates, evaluative and affective effects, semantic priming effects, social judgments, perception under surgical anesthesia, behavior, and neuropsychological dissociations, just to name a few. Work by Anthony Marcel in the 1980s set the standard for rigorous laboratory demonstrations of unconscious perception in word recognition paradigms. Marcel used the technique of pattern masking, in which a mask presented immediately after a briefly presented word prevented observers from seeing the word. Nonetheless, subsequently presented words that were semantically related to the unperceived primes were facilitated. More recent work has employed "sandwich masking," in which patterns are presented both before and after a brief stimulus, making the possibility of conscious perception extremely unlikely. The *mere exposure effect* championed by R. B. Zajonc includes affective preferences for stimuli experienced without awareness—even prenatally—even though the same stimuli cannot be consciously recognized.

Although most of the research on unconscious perception has involved vision, recent work has included unconscious perception in the realms of olfaction and audition. Unconscious auditory perception has been investigated not only in the laboratory, but also in patients under general anesthesia. In the latter studies, the stimuli are presented at an audible level (typically via headphones), but the perceiver is unconscious during input. After an early study by B. W. Levinson in 1965, this field was quiet, but with the advent of work on *implicit memory*, research picked up in the 1990s. In 2007, Jackie Andrade and Catherine Deeprose found at least two-dozen studies that included the Bispectral Index, a rigorous indicator of the "depth of anesthesia" (i.e., is the patient actually unconscious?). They concluded—with careful emphasis on studies that had controlled for "undetected awareness" on the part of patients undergoing surgery—that some degree of unconscious perception occurs during anesthesia. That perception (measured by implicit memory) can occur when patients are unconscious is so accepted that a recent article explored the possibility of "sex differences in memory formation during general anesthesia" (none were found).

Regarding neuropsychological conditions, blindsight (first reported by Lawrence Weiskrantz in 1986) involves a phenomenon wherein individuals with damage to the striate cortex in the brain cannot consciously see objects; however, they can point toward or grasp these objects accurately when encouraged to reach out. A similar dissociation between conscious perception of facial features without corresponding recognition of a familiar person occurs in prosopagnosia.

Unconscious Processes

In very recent research, Ap Dijksterhuis and his colleagues have discovered many advantages of unconscious processes. Complex decisions (e.g., choosing an apartment, playing chess, predicting soccer matches, clinical diagnoses) can be made faster and even more accurately unconsciously than consciously. Dijksterhuis argues that unconscious thought is faster because it is not constrained by the capacity limitations of conscious processes. Some investigators have concluded that the brain "does not care" whether representations are conscious or not—that is, the representation is just there. Such processes have also been found to influence unconscious behaviors such as walking speed. For example, John Bargh and his colleagues have found that people walked more slowly after being exposed to words related to "elderly" concepts implying slowness.

Applications and Conclusions

Regarding advertising, recent work has focused on "using and abusing" subliminal stimulation in this field, showing that under very specific circumstances, it is possible to influence consumer choices. For example, Dijksterhuis and his colleagues found that subjects can be stimulated to increase their subjective ratings of hunger and thirst, can be made to actually eat or drink more, and that even brand choices can be influenced. Some investigators argue that the evidence is strong enough to say that commercial applications of subliminal stimulation can work in principle and that such phenomena should not be treated as a myth unworthy of investigation. On the other hand, there has been abuse of popular belief in subliminal stimulation by marketing self-help audio media ("I feel fantastic," "Let's stay away from pizza," etc.); research has repeatedly failed to find any benefit. However, some research suggests that visual subliminal perception may be more effective than auditory subliminal perception.

If true, a probable explanation is that information processing capacity is magnitudes greater for visual than the auditory modality. However, subliminal auditory stimuli can be processed—even across to the visual modality—but backward speech cannot be perceived at any level.

In conclusion, there are a number of good reasons for continuing to investigate unconscious perception, beyond the purely scientific interest of knowledge for its own sake. There may be potential beneficial use (improving health), and it may be important to know when there is potential for consumer abuse.

David B. Mitchell

Author's Note: Research for and writing of this entry was facilitated by grants from the Foley Family Foundation and the WellStar Foundation.

See also Anesthesia and Awareness; Attention and Consciousness; Blindsight; Consciousness and the Unconscious; Implicit Memory; Neural Correlates of Consciousness; Perceptual Consciousness and Attention; Subliminal Perception

Further Readings

Andrade, J., & Deeprose, C. (2007). Unconscious memory formation during anaesthesia. *Best Practice & Research Clinical Anaesthesiology, 21,* 385–401.

Bargh, J. A., & Morsella, E. (2008). The unconscious mind. *Perspectives on Psychological Science, 3,* 73–79.

Dijksterhuis, A., & Aarts, H. (2010). Goals, attention, and (un)consciousness. *Annual Review of Psychology, 61,* 467–490.

Goodale, M. A., & Milner, A. D. (2004). *Sight unseen: An exploration of conscious and unconscious vision.* New York, NY: Oxford University Press.

Hassin, R. R., Uleman, J. S., & Bargh, J. A. (Eds.). (2005). *The new unconscious.* New York, NY: Oxford University Press.

Kihlstrom, J. F. (2008). The psychological unconscious. In O. P. John, R. W. Robins, & L. A. Pervin (Eds.), *Handbook of personality: Theory and research* (pp. 583–602). New York, NY: Guilford.

Kouider, S., & Dehaene, S. (2007). Levels of processing during non-conscious perception: A critical review of visual masking. *Philosophical Transactions of the Royal Society, 362,* 857–875.

Merikle, P. M., & Cheesman, J. (1986). Consciousness is a "subjective" state. *Behavioral and Brain Sciences, 9,* 42.

Merikle, P. M., Smilek, D., & Eastwood, J. D. (2001). Perception without awareness: Perspectives from cognitive psychology. *Cognition, 79,* 115–134.

Mitchell, D. B. (2006). Nonconscious priming after 17 years: Invulnerable implicit memory? *Psychological Science, 17,* 925–929.

Öğmen, H., & Breitmeyer, B. G. (Eds.). (2006). *The first half second: The microgenesis and temporal dynamics of unconscious and conscious visual processes.* Cambridge, MA: MIT Press.

Seamon, J. G., Marsh, R. L., & Brody, N. (1984). Critical importance of exposure duration for affective discrimination of stimuli that are not recognized. *Journal of Experimental Psychology: Learning, Memory, and Cognition, 10,* 465–469.

Vokey, J. R., & Read, J. D. (1985). Subliminal messages: Between the devil and the media. *American Psychologist, 40,* 1231–1239.

Weiskrantz, L. (2000). Blindsight: Implications for the conscious experience of emotion. In R. D. Lane & L. Nadel (Eds.), *Cognitive neuroscience of emotion* (pp. 277–295). New York, NY: Oxford University Press.

Zajonc, R. B. (2001). Mere exposure: A gateway to the subliminal. *Current Directions in Psychological Science, 10,* 224–228.

V

Visual Imagery

Visual imagery refers to the processes through which people create "mental pictures" that they can inspect with their "mind's eye." These mental representations resemble actual depictions both subjectively and functionally and play an important role in remembering and problem solving. More broadly, they can, by virtue of their content, powerfully guide the flow of thought.

The Subjective Qualities of Visual Images

Visual images can be (and usually are) created in the absence of an actual visual stimulus—and so one can create an image of (or "visualize") an elephant even if none is nearby. One can also create images that *alter* things that are in view (and so one could, for example, imagine this page with all the words printed in green ink). More ambitiously, one can create images of things that do not exist at all (e.g., an image of a unicorn). In some cases, images are created deliberately (and so someone can, if they choose, call up an image of a beautiful sunset); in other cases, the images arise spontaneously (perhaps triggered by someone else's mention of a sunset).

Visual images are not hallucinations—the person experiencing the image can tell that the image is "in their head," and not a real sight. Nonetheless, there is a strong subjective resemblance between visual images and actual sights. This is reflected in the way people commonly talk about their visual images, and references to mental pictures or the mind's eye

have been common at least since Shakespeare's time (e.g., *Hamlet*, Act 1, Scene ii). It is noteworthy that people feel these terms are apt; this is a strong indication that the conscious experience of having an image does resemble the experience of seeing. More specifically, the imaged object or scene seems to be "viewed" from some particular vantage point and is typically "seen" against some background; objects in the image have colors, shapes, and surface textures that are immediately "visible" and so on.

Experimental Studies of Visual Images

Here as elsewhere, though, researchers are cautious in how they interpret these self-reports on conscious experience. However, the self-reports can be corroborated via the appropriate experiments, and the data make it plain that visual images do share many functional properties with actual sights, as one would expect based on the self-report. For example, participants in one study were first asked to memorize a map of an island, including the location of several landmarks on the island. With this done, participants were asked to create a mental image of the map and then to "scan" their image from one landmark named by the experimenter to another. When these scanning times were carefully recorded, they showed a strong linear relationship between the time needed for each scan and the distance between the relevant pair of landmarks on the original map. This result confirms that the image accurately represents all the spatial relations on the map—and so points close together on the map are functionally close on the image; points further apart on the map are far

757

apart on the image. In this fashion, the image seems truly to depict the layout (and thus all the shapes and patterns) in the scene that is being represented.

Experiments also indicate that images function as though they have an identifiable "view point," just as an actual visual scene would. This is evident, for example, in the fact that aspects of the image that depict larger objects or objects that are at the front of the imaged scene are more rapidly accessible. Likewise, participants need time to "zoom in" on an image to inspect small details or to "zoom out" to survey the larger scene, suggesting that again, just like actual scenes, images are inspected from a particular "viewing distance."

Visual images also respect spatial layout in another regard—in the pattern of *transformations* in the image. In many studies, for example, participants have been shown two forms and asked if the forms are the same shape but viewed from different vantage points, or actually different shapes. In these studies, participants seem to imagine one of the forms "rotating" into alignment with the other and then make their decision only after this imagined rotation. The imagined rotation itself seems to take place at a constant velocity, and so the time needed for these judgments is a linear function of the angular distance between the initial orientations of the two forms being compared.

The Imagery Debate

Across the 1970s and 1980s, there was heated debate about the results just described. In part, the argument hinged on a methodological point—namely, the notion that these response-time findings might be attributable to the *demand character* of the experiments (i.e., cues within the experimental setting that signaled to the participants how they were "supposed to" behave). More broadly, there was debate about the meaning of the experimental results. Thinkers such as Zenon Pylyshyn argued that the data were the result of experimental participants seeking to "simulate" the relevant activities, more or less as a mime might seek to simulate some action; this simulation, Pylyshyn argued, was guided by participants' "tacit knowledge" about the relevant events in the world (rotation, straight-line movement, etc.). In response, Stephen Kosslyn and others argued that mental imagery relied on a specialized representation "medium," and that the

experimental data were revealing the properties of this medium.

The narrow concern about experimental demand was easily dealt with by appropriate experimental controls, and indeed, the response-time patterns remain the same when these controls are in place. The larger issue, an explanation in terms of simulation versus one in terms of an imagery medium, required a different type of analysis, and although some scholars regard the issue as still open, most researchers believe that the data reviewed in the next section argue powerfully for the notion of an imagery medium.

Neuroscience Studies of Imagery

What brain mechanisms might lie behind the behavior data described so far? In the view of many researchers, the various parallels between visual imagery and actual vision invite the hypothesis that these two activities rely on similar brain circuits, and several lines of evidence confirm this claim. Neuroimaging results indicate an enormous overlap between the brain sites activated during visual imagery and sites activated during ordinary vision. Likewise, brain damage often has parallel effects on imagery and vision. Thus, patients who (because of stroke) have lost the ability to perceive color often seem to lose the ability to imagine scenes in color. Similarly, if as a result of occipital damage patients have a blind spot in a particular region of visual space or some restriction of the extent of visual space, they are likely to have a corresponding limit on their visual imagery.

Further confirmation comes from studies that use transcranial magnetic stimulation to produce temporary "lesions" in visual cortex. Not surprisingly, this procedure causes a disruption of vision, but crucially, it also causes a parallel disruption in visual imagery.

Differences Between Visual Imagery and Vision

Even acknowledging these important parallels, however, there are also differences between visual imagery and vision and between mental pictures and actual pictures. For example, some discoveries that are easily made from a picture (the reinterpretation of an ambiguous drawing) are enormously difficult if the participant is relying on a mental image of that picture. According to some authors, this is because the image—as a mental representation—is accompanied by a "perceptual reference frame" that organizes the depiction, specifying the figure/ground organization, how the form is parsed, where the form's top is located, and so on. This reference frame guides how the image is interpreted and so can place obstacles on image reinterpretation (or image-based problem solving of any sort). Pictures do not on their own have this sort of reference frame (the frame must be created by the perceiver), and so pictures ("unorganized depictions") are more readily reinterpreted than images ("organized depictions").

A further distinction between images and pictures is suggested by cases in which brain damage has disrupted someone's vision but spared their ability to perform imagery tasks; the reverse pattern (disrupted imagery but intact vision) has also been observed. In addition, studies have often documented normal or near-normal performance on various imagery tasks from individuals who have been blind since birth—individuals who are unlikely to be relying on a picturelike mode of representation. Findings like these have led several researchers to propose a difference between *visual imagery* and *spatial imagery*. The former type of imagery yields a representation that bears a closer resemblance to a picture (and so visual images, but not spatial images, depict an object's color or surface texture), and the processes needed to create visual images rely heavily on brain sites ordinarily used for actual vision. Spatial imagery, in contrast, relies more heavily on brain sites ordinarily used for guiding movements through space (both overt bodily movement and covert movements of attention). Presumably, individuals blind since birth rely on spatial imagery, not visual, and likewise, spatial imagery is what allows patients with disrupted vision (because of brain damage) to perform normally on many imagery tasks.

The distinction between visual and spatial imagery is also valuable in explaining a different point—namely, the ways in which (neurologically intact, sighted) individuals differ from one another in their imagery abilities. Both self-report and behavioral testing indicate that this variation is considerable: Some people report rich, vivid, visual images; some report no visual images at all. Some people perform well on paper-and-pencil tests requiring them to imagine folding pieces of paper or spinning forms; others perform much less well. Recent studies suggest that these individual differences need to be assessed separately for visual and spatial imagery (especially since self-report measures of imagery are powerfully shaped by someone's strengths in visual imagery, while the paper and pencil measures often reflect someone's ability in spatial imagery).

The Role of Visual Imagery in Cognition

Finally, what is imagery's role within the broader context of mental processing? The answer has many elements. For some purposes, imagery is essential for remembering. (Imagine someone trying to describe a previously viewed face; that person may have no choice but to call up an image of the face and attempt to describe the contents of that image.) For other purposes, imagery may not be essential for memory but is nonetheless enormously helpful. We know, for example, that easily imaged words are easier to remember, and that deliberate attempts to form images of the to-be-remembered material usually aid memory. (Indeed, the use of imagery is a frequent component of many deliberate mnemonic strategies.) Imagery also seems to play a role in autobiographical memory, and memories of past episodes often take the form of images of those previous episodes.

In addition, imagery can play a role in problem solving. This is plainly the case when the problem involves spatial arrangement. (Imagine trying to decide whether a sofa, viewed in a store, will fit well in your living room. Most people would try to solve this problem by visualizing the sofa in place to "see" how it looks.) However, imagery also plays a role in other sorts of problems, including a variety of mathematical word problems. Moreover, casting any problem's elements in terms of a visual image can shape the sequence of thoughts that come to mind in thinking through the problem. For example, thinking about your pet cat in terms of an image will make the cat's appearance prominent for you, and this can call to mind other animals with a similar appearance. If you had thought about the cat without an image, the appearance might have been much less prominent so that some other set of ideas would be likely to come to mind. In this way, the mere step of casting the problem in terms of an image can guide the selection of available ideas, and this may have important consequences for the flow of thought.

It should be mentioned, though, that there are contexts in which imagery can be an impediment to problem solving. These include cases in which someone is better served by drawing an overt sketch rather than relying on an image (in part because this helps the person set aside the image's reference frame) and also cases in which someone is better served by relying on some more abstract, perhaps algebraic, mode of representation. Visual images can powerfully shape the flow of thought, but this does not mean that images reliably enhance or improve the flow of thought.

Daniel Reisberg

See also Visual Working Memory; Visuospatial Reasoning

Further Readings

Heuer, F., & Reisberg, D. (2005). Visuospatial imagery. In A. Miyake & P. Shah (Eds.), *Handbook of visuospatial thinking* (pp. 35–80). New York, NY: Cambridge University Press.

Kosslyn, S. M. (1994). *Image and brain: The resolution of the imagery debate.* Cambridge, MA: MIT Press.

Mellet, E., Tzourio-Mazoyer, N., Bricogne, S., Mazoyer, B., Kosslyn, S. M., & Denis, M. (2000). Functional anatomy of high-resolution visual mental imagery. *Journal of Cognitive Neuroscience, 12,* 98–109.

Pylyshyn, Z. (2003). *Seeing and visualizing: It's not what you think.* Cambridge, MA: MIT Press.

Reisberg, D. (2009). *Cognition: Exploring the science of the mind* (4th ed.). New York, NY: W. W. Norton.

Shepard, R. N., & Cooper, L. A. (1982). *Mental images and their transformations.* Cambridge, MA: MIT Press.

Thompson, W. L., & Kosslyn, S. M. (2000). Neural systems activated during visual mental imagery: A review and meta-analyses. In A. W. Toga & J. Mazziotta (Eds.), *Brain mapping II: The systems* (pp. 536–560). San Diego, CA: Academic Press.

Visual Masking

Visual masking refers to the reduced visibility of one stimulus, called the *target*, because of the presence of another stimulus, called the *mask*. As the generality of this definition suggests, visual masking is not a unitary phenomenon. Instead, a broad range of masking effects exists depending on the types of target and mask stimuli as well as their spatial and temporal relationship. This entry provides a classification of different masking types and illustrates their use in the study of vision and cognition.

Typology of Masking

Typically, the target and the mask are briefly presented (e.g., 10 milliseconds [ms]) and three types of masking occur according to their temporal order. Let us denote by stimulus onset asynchrony (SOA) the time delay between the onset of the target and the onset of the mask. When the target is presented before the mask (by convention negative SOAs), we have *forward masking*, and when the opposite holds, we have *backward masking*. The case when the target and mask are presented with SOA = 0 is called *simultaneous masking*.

The most basic form of visual masking, called *masking by light*, occurs when the mask stimulus is a spatially extended uniform field of light. Depending on the type of the target, masking by light can be divided into two subtypes: *masking of light by light* (the target is, like the mask, a spatially uniform stimulus but with much smaller spatial size) and *masking of pattern by light* (the target is a patterned stimulus such as an alphanumeric character). The more interesting types of visual masking occur in *visual pattern masking*, when a patterned target stimulus is masked by a patterned mask stimulus. From a methodological point of view, one can distinguish between three types of pattern masking: When the target and the mask do not overlap spatially, forward pattern masking is called *paracontrast*, and backward pattern masking is called *metacontrast*. When target and mask overlap spatially, if the mask does not contain any structural characteristics of the target, one has *pattern masking by noise*. On the other hand, when the mask has structural similarities to the target, one has *pattern masking by structure*. Figure 1 provides examples of different types of visual pattern masking.

Uses of Masking

Historically, the first formal use of visual masking dates back to the second half of the 19th century. It was mainly used as a tool to investigate the temporal evolution of perceptual processes. For example, researchers wanted to experimentally address questions such as the time it takes for a stimulus to reach the observer's awareness and the phenomenal duration of a stimulus. Today, visual masking continues to be a method of choice in investigating not only

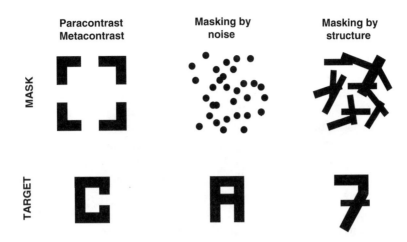

Figure 1   Types of masking according to spatial and informational content of the stimuli. *Left:* paracontrast and metacontrast; *middle:* masking by noise; *right:* masking by structure.

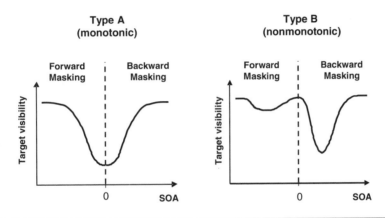

Figure 2   *Left:* Type A forward and backward masking functions. Maximum suppression of target visibility occurs at SOA = 0, that is, when the target and the mask are presented simultaneously. *Right:* Type B forward and backward masking functions. Here maximum suppression of target visibility occurs at SOA values different than zero.

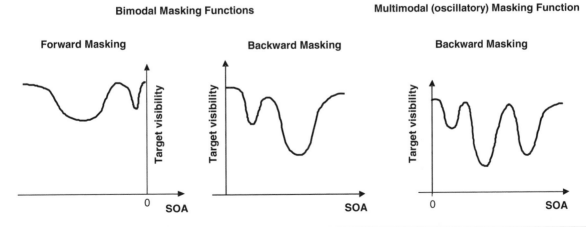

Figure 3   Nonmonotonic masking functions can also exhibit more than one SOA value where target visibility reaches a local minimum. On the left, forward and backward masking functions with two local minima each. These are called bimodal masking functions. When there are more than two local minima, the masking function is multimodal, or oscillatory, as shown on the right.

problems pertaining to the temporal aspects of visual processes but also those related to conscious and unconscious information processing. Furthermore, a large amount of research is devoted to reveal the *mechanisms* of visual masking, and several models and theories have been proposed in the literature. Research in visual masking is voluminous, and the monographs referenced below provide an in-depth review of relevant literature and findings. In the following, a few examples will be presented to illustrate different uses of visual masking.

As mentioned above, one critical parameter in masking is SOA. The function that plots a measure of target visibility (e.g., brightness, edge completeness, shape, identity) as a function of SOA is called the *masking function*. The shape of the masking function depends on stimulus parameters as well as on the task of the observer. Nevertheless, masking functions can be categorized under two generic types: monotonic (also called Type A) and nonmonotonic (also called Type B) functions, as illustrated in Figure 2. Furthermore, the nonmonotonic functions can be classified as unimodal, bimodal, or multimodal (oscillatory) types (Figure 3).

While a complete understanding of neural processes underlying these masking functions remains a fundamental research question, the morphologies of these functions provide valuable insights into the temporal aspects of visual processes. For example, in Type A masking functions, one can interpret the SOA interval where masking effects occur as the "broad temporal window," during which the processing of the target and the mask occurs.

From a practical viewpoint, many researchers use masks as basic components of their experimental design to control the duration or effectiveness of the processes generated by their stimuli: Neural responses to a brief stimulus presented in isolation may persist hundreds of milliseconds and generate ceiling effects in performance. If this brief stimulus is followed by an appropriate mask, the mask-generated activity will interfere with the processing of the target, thereby reducing the effective duration and performance to a desired level. Let us note, however, that the effect of the mask is not a total stopping of the target activity; instead, the mask typically interferes in a selective way with the target. For example, the mask may render the contours of the target invisible, yet observers can report the location of this invisible target without any difficulty.

The selectivity of the mask has been used to infer relative timing of different processes. For example, by comparing metacontrast masking functions obtained by contour and surface-brightness judgments, Bruno Breitmeyer and colleagues suggested that processes computing surface brightness are delayed with respect to those computing boundaries. Visual masking is also a powerful technique to investigate conscious and unconscious information processing. The mask can render the target completely invisible, thereby eliminating it from the visual awareness of the observer. However, as mentioned above, this does not mean that all target-related processes are extinguished; instead, the processing of several attributes of the target continues to take place at unconscious levels. By measuring the effects of the unconscious target stimulus on other stimuli, recent research has shown that a variety of stimulus characteristics, such as form and emotional content, are processed at unconscious levels.

Haluk Öğmen and Bruno G. Breitmeyer

See also Auditory masking; Consciousness and the Unconscious; Subliminal Perception; Unconscious Perception

Further Readings

Bachmann, T. (1994). *The psychophysiology of visual masking: The fine structure of conscious experience.* Commack, NY: Nova Science.

Breitmeyer, B. G., Kafalıgönül, H., Öğmen, H., Mardon, L., Todd, S., & Ziegler, R. (2006). Meta- and paracontrast reveal differences between contour- and brightness-processing mechanisms. *Vision Research*, 46, 2645–2658.

Breitmeyer, B. G., & Öğmen, H. (2006). *Visual masking: Time slices through conscious and unconscious vision.* Oxford, UK: Oxford University Press.

VISUAL SEARCH

Visual search is the act of looking for an item. The *target* of one's search can be defined as an object (such as a person), a feature (such as a color), or an event (such as the sudden appearance of something). Visual search has two roles in the study of the mind: first, as a phenomenon to be understood, and second, as a method for revealing how other aspects of the mind work. The entry describes a typical visual-search experiment and how it is analyzed, reviews aspects of visual search that are of interest in themselves, and discusses the application of visual search to the study of cognition and the mind.

Visual search takes time because more visual information is hitting the retina at any given moment than one can process. Attention is a fundamental cognitive mechanism that enhances the processing of some information at the expense of momentarily irrelevant information. One way to attend to some items is through *overt* attention—that is, eye movements. However, one can attend to a subset of a visual scene with *covert* attention as well, most commonly referred to as "seeing out of the corner of the eye." Researches on visual search and attention thus provide insights about each other.

Method and Analysis

Visual search is a common activity in daily life and in many cognitive activities: looking for a word on a page while reading, trying to find a friend in a crowded room, examining an X-ray for anatomical abnormalities in a hospital, or searching the ground for fossils and artifacts. The scientific study of visual search often examines much simpler tasks that afford greater experimental control. Of primary interest for many scientists interested in visual search is why some search tasks are fast and efficient and others are slow and inefficient.

Figure 1 displays an example of the sort of task a participant in a visual-search study would commonly see. Here the target is the letter *T* among nontarget letter *F*s. A typical experiment would require the participant to look for the target and to press one button if it is present and another if it is absent; half of the trials would have a target and half would not. The items would generally appear to the participant and remain visible until the response. The speed (or *reaction time)* and the accuracy of the search would be recorded for each trial.

The data are summarized commonly in a plot of reaction time as a function of the number of items displayed. Other variables, such as presence or absence of the target, are plotted as different functions or groupings of data points in the graph. Each group of data points can be summarized by a slope and intercept of the linear function that fits those points. The slope provides information about the rate of visual search, and the intercept summarizes the amount of time required for all other aspects of the search task (such as the motor preparation for the response).

Most analyses of the reaction time in a visual-search task assume that accuracy has not been traded off to achieve the speed found. (A speed-accuracy trade-off is common and occurs when speed is increased but accuracy is low and compromised for speed, or when speed is decreased and accuracy is high and improved due to the slower reaction time.) Most reaction time analyses in visual search require high levels of accuracy in all conditions so that a speed-accuracy trade-off does not confound the results. Of course, some scientists examine the effects on accuracy rather than on reaction time, perhaps with a manipulation of how long the display is shown to the participants. Yet others manipulate both speed and accuracy as an analytical method.

The Phenomenon of Visual Search

One of the most fundamental questions about visual search is what makes some tasks efficient and others inefficient. There is no clear dichotomy between efficient and inefficient search tasks; however, there is a great degree of variability in the relative efficiency of search tasks to be explained. As noted in the previous section, the slope is often of primary interest for understanding the relative efficiency of visual search with one set of variables versus another (see Figure 2 for typical, but invented, visual-search data). A slope of zero would occur when the reaction time does not increase as more items are added to the display; this would be considered an efficient search task,

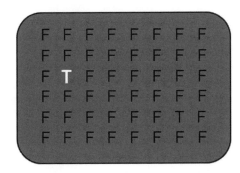

Figure 1   Look for the *T*s among the *F*s. The large, white *T* can be found efficiently; however, the small black one requires an inefficient search.

such as finding the large, white *T* in Figure 1. As the slope increases, then the task is considered inefficient because the number of items in the display slows the search task with each additional item; an example would be finding the black *T* in Figure 1.

A number of variations of the task can be made to observe the effects on speed and accuracy. Common variables that are manipulated include the following: (a) the *set size*—that is, the number of items to search through including the target (Figure 1 displays a set size of 48), (b) the *defining feature of the target* (the letter *T* in Figure 1), (c) the *reported feature of the target* (typically, whether it is present or absent in the display; participants could also be asked to make a judgment about it, such as what color it is or what the orientation of the target is), and (d) the *degree of similarity* between the target and the nontargets and amongst the nontargets (a *T* might be more difficult to find amongst *F*s than *O*s, for example).

A common distinction in many search tasks is whether the defining feature of the target is a single feature (such as a single color, like red) or a conjunction of features (e.g., a combination of color and orientation, such as a red and vertical target among vertical nontargets that are another color, such as green, and red nontargets at the other orientation,

horizontal). However, any search task can be made more or less efficient by manipulating the similarity of the target and nontarget items, independent of the number of features that define the target.

Several models have been developed to describe the mechanisms responsible for the efficiency of a visual-search task. Anne Treisman, in her *feature integration theory*, proposed that items are first processed simultaneously in a preattentive stage as basic features (such as color and orientation). If the target is defined as a single feature, then its presence can be detected at this stage. However, if a target is defined as a conjunction of features, then each item must be attended to have its features bound together and identified, with each item processed successively. Each item is attended in a random order until the target is found or until all items have been attended. Feature integration theory is still highly influential even though some details of this theory came into question after some experiments found that a target defined by a conjunction of features can, under some conditions, be found just as efficiently as a target defined by a single feature. Jeremy Wolfe later proposed a model that is similar to the feature integration theory, called *guided search*. With guided search, Wolfe accounts for these exceptions by not having items attended in a random order but rather

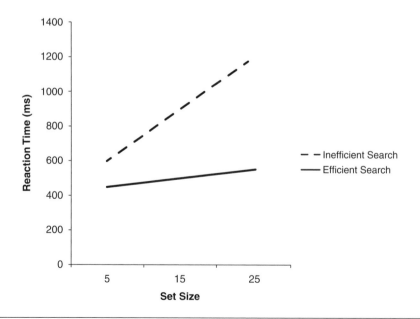

Figure 2   Typical (but invented) data for a visual-search experiment; reaction time (in milliseconds) is plotted as a function of set size.

in order of prioritization based upon the match between the features of the items and the features for which the participant is searching.

Applications: Visual Search as a Window to Cognition

Visual search is a common method used to understand the mechanisms of attention. For visual search to be efficient, some information must be more easily prioritized than other information. Bottom-up and top-down mechanisms guide attention to items of interest. Top-down mechanisms guide attention based on the information that the observer is looking for, such as the color or orientation of the target. Bottom-up mechanisms guide attention based on the information in the scene and the manner in which it is processed in the early visual system of the brain. Unique items—rendered salient due to a contrast in color or orientation when compared to surrounding items—provide strong bottom-up guidance for attention and under some conditions even capture attention. The bottom-up salience of the items and the top-down, target-defining information that the participant uses combine to create an attentional priority map that indexes the locations of items that are likely to be the target. By manipulating the features of the target and nontarget items and the number of items, among other variables, visual search can reveal the mechanisms of attention and the prioritization of information for further processing, such as object identification and memory consolidation. Many studies have examined this both in terms of covert attention (where the eyes remain motionless, fixated at the center of the screen) and overt attention (where eye movements to different items are monitored and analyzed).

Visual search not only reveals how some information is prioritized but also how momentarily irrelevant information is inhibited. For example, in searching for a *T* in Figure 1, it would not be useful to check each nontarget *F* location more than once. Research in visual search provides converging evidence for a mechanism that suppresses attention to previously processed locations (inhibition of return). Visual search thus serves as a model task for how information is prioritized and processed by the mind.

Also of key interest in the study of information processing is that of serial versus parallel mechanisms. The search rate, as revealed by the slope derived from reaction time as a function of set size, provides some indication of whether items can be visually processed in serial (i.e., successively) or in parallel (i.e., simultaneously). Many mathematical models of parallel processing can mimic serial models, however, so visual-search rates provide only partial, converging evidence for this issue.

Although these fundamental issues of the mind can use visual search as a tool, so can many applied tasks. Visual search has been examined in reading, driving, and X-ray examination, just to name a few tasks that depend on fast, accurate visual search. As more is discovered about the basic mechanisms of visual search, the design and training for these real-world tasks can be improved to better suit how the mind processes visual information.

Michael J. Proulx

See also Attention, Neuroimaging Studies of; Inhibition of Return; Neurodynamics of Visual Search; Reaction Time

Further Readings

Desimone, R., & Duncan, J. (1995). Neural mechanisms of selective visual attention. *Annual Review of Neuroscience, 18,* 193–222.

Duncan, J., & Humphreys, G. W. (1989). Visual search and stimulus similarity. *Psychological Review, 96,* 433–458.

Egeth, H. E., & Yantis, S. (1997). Visual attention: Control, representation, and time course. *Annual Review of Psychology, 48,* 269–297.

Pashler, H. (1998). *The psychology of attention.* Cambridge, MA: MIT Press.

Treisman, A., & Gelade, G. (1980). A feature-integration theory of attention. *Cognitive Psychology, 12,* 97–136.

Wolfe, J. M. (1994). Guided Search 2.0: A revised model of visual search. *Psychonomic Bulletin & Review, 1,* 202–238.

Wolfe, J. M., & Horowitz, T. S. (2004). What attributes guide the deployment of visual attention and how do they do it? *Nature Reviews Neuroscience, 5,* 1–7.

VISUAL WORKING MEMORY

To understand visual working memory, it is helpful to consider human memory more generally. Human memory is not a single mental faculty or cognitive system; rather, the cognitive processes that we collectively call memory are composed of a number of independent and specialized cognitive systems that encode and store information in different formats. The various taxonomies of human memory agree on two main distinctions: First, memory may be explicit, or declarative, in the sense that personal knowledge and previous experiences are consciously recollected or recognized, or memory may be implicit, or nondeclarative, in the sense of being expressed indirectly in behavior without accompanying conscious recollections of previous learning episodes. Second, a distinction is drawn between short-term memory, called immediate memory by early memory researchers, which has been proposed as the seat of consciousness and active processing and which is able to store limited quantities of information for limited periods of time—in the range of seconds rather than minutes—and long-term memory, which stores unlimited amounts of information for unlimited periods of time. These distinctions are not completely orthogonal, since short-term memory is coupled to explicit memory.

The theory of *working memory* was proposed 35 years ago by Alan Baddeley and Graham Hitch and later developed in a very influential book by Alan Baddeley, *Working Memory,* published in 1986. According to this theory, short-term memory is not a simple mechanism for passive storage of information; rather, it is a coordinated set of mechanisms that combines incoming information from sensory systems with information retrieved from long-term memory and consists of a central executive operating with the assistance of domain-specific verbal, and visual support systems. Broadly speaking, the concept of *visual working memory* refers to the short-term memory system, which stores information that enters the brain through the eye and is maintained and manipulated by the support system referred to as the *visual-spatial sketchpad.* The definition may be too broad, however, because visual information, such as written words or pictures of naturalistic scenes, is easily recoded and stored in verbal-memory systems. A more restricted definition of visual working memory is *the maintenance and manipulation of information represented as visual codes.* Since performance with complex, meaningful visual stimuli may be supported by both visual and verbal working memory systems operating in concert, much of the research in visual working memory has aimed at isolating the visual component of

memory. This entry considers the scientific evidence for visual memory codes and the organization and capacity limitation of visual working memory.

The Evidence for Visual Memory Codes

The idea of visual representations or memory codes has been challenged by researchers who favor a unitary verbal memory system. There is, however, mounting evidence that verbal and visual information is handled in separate cognitive and neural systems.

Perhaps the strongest evidence for separate visual and verbal memory representations comes from so-called dual-task experiments. In these experiments, subjects are required to carry out two tasks simultaneously. For example, they have to remember a previously presented visual pattern while counting backward or making a spatial judgment. The results of such experimental manipulations show that the performance on visual working memory tasks is not impaired by a parallel verbal task, but it is impaired by a parallel visual task. Thus, concurrent visual processing tasks compete for processing resources, whereas verbal and visual tasks are processed independently. A complementary interference pattern is found for verbal working memory. This pattern of interference strongly suggests the existence of separate, parallel, limited-capacity visual and verbal working memory systems.

Further evidence that the brain stores information in terms of visual representations comes from the study of brain-injured patients. In the neuropsychological syndrome of *visual agnosia* the patient sees, but the visual world is meaningless. There may be nothing wrong with the perceptual process, per se, and the person navigates safely in the geographic environment and may even copy diagrams and drawings. However, there is no visual recognition and no visual memory, although other forms of working memory (and long-term memory) may be completely intact.

Modern brain-imaging techniques, such as functional magnetic resonance imaging (fMRI) that allow fairly local and precise brain activity patterns to be mapped during the execution of cognitive tasks, would appear to offer a unique possibility of isolating the visual versus verbal components of working memory. But isolation of specialized memory systems is not a simple and straightforward procedure, both because cognitive tasks activate many cognitive and brain systems concerned with perceptual, attentional, and memory processing, and because most neural networks in the brain probably perform many processing tasks in parallel. Even if the performance on a specific visual memory task is not assisted by verbal memory, the simple fact that we identify a recognizable pattern that can be verbally classified and later remembered implies activation of verbal memory processes. However, imaging studies have demonstrated distinct areas localized to the occipital and temporal lobes of the brain, specialized for processing particular classes of stimuli such as objects and human faces. These regions are activated in visual memory tasks with these classes of stimuli but not in verbal memory tasks, suggesting that at least certain kinds of information are represented as visual codes. There is also evidence that some visual memory tasks recruit visual-processing regions in the early stages of the processing hierarchy, which indicate a close relationship between visual perception and visual memory.

The Visual-Spatial Sketchpad

The theory of working memory includes two support systems for manipulation and maintenance of sensory information. The verbal support system, referred to as the phonological loop, is easily understood; it may be thought of as the process of repeating information in silent (subvocal) speech. The second support system, the visual-spatial sketchpad, is less intuitively understood. It is not a purely visual processing mechanism but thought to combine information from visual, tactile, and haptic sensory channels. To a first approximation the visual-spatial sketchpad may be thought of as largely equivalent to the phenomenon of visual imagery. Visual imagery is the ability to produce "inner" images of previously seen persons, objects, and geographical scenes and to produce images of scenes that are simply imagined. Visual mental imagery tasks require subjects to retrieve information from long-term memory or to maintain visual information that is recently viewed and to perform cognitive operations on or make judgments of this information. The purely visual nature of visual imagery is supported by experiments showing that cognitive operations on visual mental images are governed by the same laws as similar operations performed on online visual images,

and that visual imagery recruits many of the brain regions involved in online perception, even including some of the earliest brain regions in the visual process. This process is quite similar to task of the visual-spatial sketchpad. However, whereas visual imagery is conceived as conscious process of image generation, maintenance in visual working memory is not conceived as a conscious process in the same sense. Differences between the visual imagery and the visual-spatial sketchpad are also suggested by the finding that visual imagery is disrupted by task-irrelevant visual noise whereas maintenance in visual working memory is not disrupted by visual noise. Thus, despite similarities, visual imagery and the visual-spatial sketchpad are not identical.

Fractionation of Visual Working Memory

Recent dual-task experiments indicate that visual working memory may be composed of additional subsystems. It is now claimed that there is one subsystem that is partly specialized for processing objects and object properties such as color, orientation, and shape and a second system that is specialized for processing the spatial characteristics of visual displays. For example, it has been shown that when subjects have to remember information about object color while simultaneously performing a mental task that requires shape recognition, there is substantial interference between the two tasks, whereas no interference is observed between a task requiring memory for spatial position and a second, shape recognition task.

Evidence for a possible third component of visual working memory comes from a parallel line of research, on so-called perceptual memory. In classical visual working memory tasks, participants are required to consciously remember the stimuli to be compared, and the difference between the patterns is easily detected in simultaneous displays. For example, in a typical experiment, one object in the display may change in color, orientation, or shape, and what is varied is the number of objects in the display and/or the number of object features that are changed. This approach is governed by what some cognitive psychologists call a *storehouse* metaphor—how much is retained in memory? Perceptual memory research, on the other hand, is governed by a *correspondence* metaphor, investigating the fidelity of memory. How well are the details of the original display retained, and what distortions of color, texture, and orientation are observed? In these experiments, the memory of elementary attributes of visual images—size, orientation, movement—is measured using psychophysical discrimination tasks where participants are requested to decide, or guess, if a test pattern has a higher or lower value than a previously shown reference pattern on the stimulus dimension in question, and a discrimination threshold is determined, representing the value of 75% correct guessing. The results from these experiments show, somewhat surprisingly, that information about such elementary attributes is not degraded or distorted but maintained with the fidelity of the sensory image during intervals up to two or three minutes. The storage is impaired by a concurrent processing task along the same dimension but not by a concurrent task along another dimension, and there is evidence that at least three stimulus dimensions may be stored in parallel. Thus, the pattern of interference mimics the interference pattern observed in the more traditional visual working memory tasks. However, the performance on this task does not require conscious recollection or recognition; it turns up in forced choice tasks and may be more implicit in nature. It is an open question whether this low-level memory system is part of the visual working memory system or a parallel memory system associated with implicit memory.

Capacity Limitation of Visual Working Memory

The capacity of visual working memory depends upon several factors, such as the type of information tested, the test procedure employed, the time allowed for memory encoding, and the discriminability of the items in the visual display. There are individual differences in working memory capacity, and there are age effects. Visual working memory performance in the adult population starts to decline around 60 years of age and decreases steadily toward older age, a trend observed for most memory tasks involving explicit but not implicit memory.

Until quite recently, most research on visual working memory has been concerned with the spatial aspect of visual displays, and comparatively little was known about memory for the properties of visual objects and visual scenes, such as their color, texture, and orientation.

Experiments investigating the object property aspect of visual working memory suggest that visual-object working memory is a unitary mechanism, with a capacity limitation that is fairly independent of object properties and complexity. To a first approximation, visual working memory may be conceived of as storing integrated objects, thus when remembering objects and their properties, it does not matter if they have different colors and orientations or if they share color and orientation. The capacity limitation is four objects; when the number of objects exceeds this limit, memory suffers. This does not mean that the visual working memory capacity is completely independent of complexity. While the magical number *four* pops up in most experiments, it is clear that several stimulus and encoding parameters determine the capacity of the visual working memory. Thus, if object complexity is high and encoding time is low, the estimated visual working memory capacity decreases, but if object complexity is low and there is unlimited encoding time, capacity increases but never exceeds the magical number four.

In summary, visual working memory consists of a set of limited-capacity, short-term memory mechanisms handling information transmitted through the eyes, operating in concert with other working memory systems. Because visually transmitted information may be coded in both verbal and visual representations, it is likely that few everyday visual short-term memory tasks will be solely reliant on visual working memory.

Svein Magnussen

See also Divided Attention and Memory; Memory, Neural Basis; Visual Imagery; Visuospatial Reasoning; Working Memory; Working Memory, Evolution of

Further Readings

Baddeley, A. (2001). Is working memory still working? *American Psychologist, 56,* 849–864.

Cornoldi, C., & Vecci, T. (2003). *Visuo-spatial working memory and individual differences.* Hove, UK: Psychology Press.

Logie, R. H. (1995). *Visuo-spatial working memory.* Hove, UK: Erlbaum.

Magnussen, S., Greenlee, M. W., Baumann, O., & Endestad, T. (2009). Visual perceptual memory. In L. Bäckman & L. Nyberg (Eds.), *Memory, aging and the brain: A festschrift in honour of Lars-Göran Nilsson* (pp. 58–75). Hove, UK: Psychology Press.

Woodman, G. E., & Vogel, E. K. (2008). Selective storage and maintenance of an object's features in visual working memory. *Psychonomic Bulletin and Review*, *15*, 223–229.

Zimmer, H. D., Magnussen, S., Rudner, M., & Rönnberg, J. (2007). Visuospatial thinking, imagination and remembering. In S. Magnussen & T. Helstrup (Eds.), *Everyday memory* (pp. 27–56). Hove, UK: Psychology Press.

VISUOSPATIAL REASONING

Visuospatial reasoning is essential for survival. If we couldn't find our way home or get food into our mouths, life would be nearly impossible. Visuospatial reasoning occurs whenever we go beyond the information given to make inferences about what we see or where we are, as when we recognize a friend from a glimpse of her face or see a face in the moon or recognize a neighborhood from the architecture. Visuospatial reasoning is involved in more than recognizing things and places, it also is involved in imagining things and places and mental transformations on things and places. Mundane activities, such as catching a fly ball and packing a suitcase, as well as sophisticated ones, such as refining a model of plate tectonics or designing a museum, rely on visuospatial reasoning. More surprising, visuospatial reasoning underlies abstract thought, such as deciding whether a giraffe is more intelligent than a tiger or whether a conclusion follows logically from its premises. Visuospatial reasoning allows inferences about motion in space as well as inferences about things in space. Even small children can distinguish motion paths caused by actions of animate agents from motion paths caused by inanimate agents. Because visuospatial reasoning is mental and therefore not directly observable, research began only after the behaviorist grip on scientific psychology loosened and the cognitive revolution of the 1960s began. It began with work on images, visual mental representations, and mental transformations and then broadened to explore spatial mental transformations and created spaces. This entry follows that history.

Visual Images

Demonstrating the psychological reality of images entailed showing that they preserved visual properties of the objects they represented, such as size, shape, distance, orientation, and color. In that spirit, some studies have shown that the time to mentally detect or compare those properties in images reflects actual differences in size, distance, or orientation. Other studies have shown that judgments of imagined shape or color yield the same similarity spaces as judgments of perceived shape or color. This approach views imagery as internalized perception. That is, having an image is like having a percept, and performing mental transformations on an image is like perceiving changes in the world. Impressive support for the psychological reality of visual images and the transformations performed on them has come from brain studies that have shown that visual imagery relies on some of the same areas of the brain involved in visual perception.

Mental Transformations

It is common in analyses of cognition to distinguish mental *representations* of aspects of the world from mental *transformations* of those representations, a distinction analogous to data and operations performed on data. One of the more remarkable visuospatial mental transformations demonstrated is mental rotation: the time to judge whether a pair of figures at different orientations, such as a configuration of boxes or an asymmetric letter of the alphabet, is the same or whether mirror images increase linearly with the degree of tilt, as if the mind were rotating the figures into congruence at a steady rate. Mental rotation has a real-life role in identifying and imagining objects that are not upright. Mental size and shape transformations also seem to be in the service of object recognition and, like mental rotation, can be appropriated for the kind of creative thought that serves rearranging furniture, understanding how molecules fit together, or designing a building. These are mental transformations of objects in space. Another major class of visuospatial mental transformation is imagining reorientations of one's own body in space, a set of skills that plays roles in tasks such as navigating a crowd or a new neighborhood, dancing, and playing Frisbee.

The two major classes of spatial mental transformations, mental transformations of things in the world and mental transformations of our bodies in the world, are rooted in everyday perceptual experience of the world, consistent with the imagery-as-internalized-perception approach. Interestingly, both classes of mental transformations appear to involve motor as well as spatial reasoning. When participants are engaged in mental rotation while turning a wheel, the fluency of mental rotation is enhanced by turning the wheel in the direction of rotation and hindered by turning the wheel in the opposite direction. Another example comes from recognition of bodies in motion. The stimuli for these studies come from films of participants dressed in black with lights attached to their joints, moving in various ways. Although all that is visible in the films is the movements of the lights, these movements are readily perceived by human observers as walking, dancing, or skipping. People can readily distinguish men from women and friends from strangers. Surprisingly, recognition of bodies in motion is better for our own bodies than for those of friends, even though we have little visual experience of our own bodies in motion. The fact that people recognize themselves better than they recognize friends suggests close interactions between motoric and perceptual processes, interactions thought to underlie speech understanding, motor learning, empathy, and other processes as well. Observing human movement is thought to resonate in the observer's motor system; that is, the observer may mentally simulate the movements while watching them. Observers seem to recognize when the simulated pattern is similar to the pattern evoked by their own movement. Conversely, motor movements affect visual recognition; for example, recognition of graspable objects like cups is facilitated when the hand is held in the appropriate grasping movement.

Spatial Mental Representations

Visual images are one kind of mental representation, but there are other kinds of visuospatial mental representations. Imagery for action has also been discussed and can be used for mental practice of playing the piano or gymnastics. There is also imagery reflecting other senses, such as sound, touch, smell, and taste as well as imagery not based in a particular sense, such as imagery for emotion or space. Spatial mental representations are typically more abstract than a specific sensory system. Congenitally blind people can form rich and full spatial mental representations from other sensory information, especially kinesthetic and auditory. These senses also play a role in spatial mental representations of sighted

people. Spatial mental representations of the world reflect both perceptions of the world and actions in the world. Thus, they differ for the different kinds of spaces that people inhabit. The spaces important for human behavior and interactions are the space of the body, the space around the body, and the space of navigation.

As mental representations, images have been characterized by fidelity to visual attributes of the world. In contrast, mental spatial representations reflect behavioral and hence functional aspects of the world as well as visual aspects. The visual features do not always align with the spatial and behavioral aspects, in ways that will be revealed below.

Space of the Body

In order to accomplish daily or extraordinary tasks, the body moves in the world. For the body, we have both insider and outsider—visual—knowledge. Proprioceptive feedback from our own movements and the responses of the environment is crucial to coordinated movements but also seems to play a role in recognizing movement as well as movers, as was seen in the studies using point-light movers. In other research, people were shown pictures of bodies with parts highlighted and asked to verify whether the highlighted part is the same as a named part. The more functional, important parts—for example, head and hand, are relatively small. However, people verify the small, functionally important body parts faster than the large ones, in sharp contrast to research on imagery.

Space Around the Body

The space around the body is the three-dimensional space surrounding the body in reach of hand or eye. As people—and rats—go about the world, they keep track of the changing positions of the objects around them relative to their own bodies, forming and updating egocentric mental representations. Perceptual and behavioral aspects of the body and the world affect the organization of those representations. The body has three axes: an asymmetric axis from head to feet, an asymmetric front-back axis, and a more-or-less symmetric left-right axis. The encompassing world also has three axes, only one of which is asymmetric, the up-down axis of gravity. These aspects of the body and the world have implications for perception and behavior. Both perception and action are primarily directed forward as the front/back axis separates the world that can be seen and manipulated from the world that is difficult to perceive and manipulate. Gravity affects where we are, hence what we see, and how we can move in and manipulate the world. It also affects how objects in the world look, change, and can be interacted with.

These properties of the body and the world shape the mental representations of the space around them that people form and update. In one research program, people read descriptions of "you" in an opera house or museum. The descriptions placed objects around "you"—above, below, front, back, left, and right—after which a computer repeatedly reoriented "you" to face different objects and queried the participant for the current positions of all the objects. In particular, when the character ("you") was upright, objects located above and below the body—that is, at head and feet—were easiest to retrieve because of the double asymmetries of the body and the world. Objects in front and back were next easiest because of the strong body asymmetry, and objects to right and left were most difficult, because those body asymmetries are weakest. Variations of the experiment established the spatial mental representations from models, diagrams, or real life, yet the consequent mental representations were essentially the same.

Space of Navigation

People (and rats) not only build mental representations of where things are relative to their bodies, they also build representations of where the objects are relative to each other and the world at large, *allocentric mental representations*. Allocentric representations are needed for navigating the larger world from many different directions. These, too, are biased, a consequence of the way spatial scenes are encoded and represented.

Mental representations of large spaces, or *cognitive maps,* are an amazing feat of the mind. Three-dimensional spaces that are too large to be seen from any particular viewpoint can be assembled from navigation with a view from within, from descriptions, and from external maps and then mentally shrunk and turned into a two-dimensional representation with a view from above. Assembling the pieces depends on coordinating common objects

and reference frames, a process that distorts judgment and memory so that geographic bodies are remembered as more aligned with each other and with their reference frames than they actually are. Consequently, people erroneously think that Rome is south of Philadelphia and that Berkeley, in the east bay, is east of Stanford, which is west of the bay but east of Berkeley. Actual navigation is situated in the world, which corrects at least some of these misconceptions.

Created Spaces

Describing Space

Great literature, such as novels and poetry, and small literature, such as tourist guides and instruction manuals, all rely on the power of language to create mental spaces. The studies of the space around the body showed exactly that: From descriptions, people form spatial mental models that can be mentally transformed, allowing inferences and information retrieval. From verbal directions, people can imagine a battle scene, arrive at their desired destinations, or put together a piece of furniture. Spatial descriptions require a perspective. In describing space, people spontaneously adopt either a route (egocentric or intrinsic) perspective, where landmarks are described relative to a traveler from the traveler's right, left, front, or back, or a survey perspective, where landmarks are described relative to each other using an allocentric reference frame such as north, south, east, west. Just as frequently, people mix perspectives, often midsentence and usually without warning. When people learn limited environments from either of these perspectives, they form mental representations that are perspective free—that is, that allow answering questions from either perspective equally quickly and accurately.

Space of Graphics

People have long used their extraordinary visuospatial capacities to create cognitive tools, such as diagrams, pictures, maps, and graphs that increase the power of the mind by augment memory, information processing, and communication. These graphics reflect the spatial metaphors that support abstract thought. For example, proximity in space represents proximity on abstract dimensions, as in graphs and in expressions such as, "We've grown apart." Direction in space also has meaning, especially up and down, going against or with gravity. Going up, against gravity, reflects strength, goodness, and other positive qualities, which are typically plotted upward. These biases are evident in gesture and speech as well in reasoning: "Give me a high 5," "She's at the top of the heap," and "He's fallen into a depression." And with that, we end: "Onward and upward!"

Barbara Tversky

See also Common Coding; Mirror Neurons; Spatial Cognition, Development of; Thinking; Visual Imagery; Visual Working Memory; Working Memory, Evolution of

Further Readings

Farah, M. J. (2004). *Visual agnosia* (2nd ed.). Cambridge, MA: MIT Press.

Johnson-Laird, P. N. (2006). *How we reason.* Oxford, UK: Oxford University Press.

Kosslyn, S. M., Thompson, W. L., & Ganis, G. (2006). *The case for mental imagery.* New York, NY: Oxford University Press.

Shepard, R. N., & Podgorny, P. (1978). Cognitive processes that resemble perceptual processes. In W. K. Estes (Ed.), *Handbook of learning and cognitive processes* (Vol. 5, pp. 189–237). Hillsdale, NJ: Erlbaum.

Tversky, B. (2005). Visuospatial reasoning. In K. Holyoak & R. Morrison (Eds.), *The Cambridge handbook of thinking and reasoning* (pp. 209–240). Cambridge, MA: Cambridge University Press.

VOLUNTARY ACTION, ILLUSION OF

What distinguishes a voluntary action from an involuntary one? That the former may be expressed *at will* does little to answer the question, because "wills" are difficult to observe in others or other species. For instance, whether a monkey looks rightward voluntarily or reflexively is indistinguishable to an observer. (The former may occur when a monkey is trained to look away from an attention-grabbing flash in the *anti-saccade* task; the latter may occur during the *visual grasp* reflex.) Thus, drawing a principled distinction between actions that are voluntary and involuntary is less than straightforward. This entry explains from a cognitive science perspective how voluntary action is intimately related to "sup-

pressibility," the skeletal muscle system, ideomotor processing, and the sense of authorship.

Suppressibility

It has been proposed by Richard Passingham that unlike involuntary actions (e.g., reflexes, automatisms during seizures, and unconscious actions during pathological states), voluntary actions are special in that they can be suppressed. Though involuntary actions may be counteracted, as when the patellar (knee-jerk) reflex is counteracted by contracting the leg muscles, such indirect control is different from the kind of direct suppression that occurs during voluntary action, as when one refrains from making a comment or dropping a hot dish. Hence, suppressibility serves as a useful behavioral index of voluntary action in humans and other species.

Sense of Agency and Ideomotor Processing

With respect to one's subjective experience, however, voluntary and involuntary action could not feel more different from each other. As researched extensively by Daniel Wegner and colleagues, the subjective sense of agency associated with voluntary action is based on several high-level cognitive processes, including the perception of a lawful correspondence between action intentions and action outcomes. If one intends to flex one's index finger and then it happens to flex, one is likely to believe that the movement was voluntary. One is unconscious of the sophisticated motor programs giving rise to the action outcome but is often aware of the perceptual consequences (e.g., perceiving flexing a finger). William James and contemporary "ideomotor" theorists such as Wolfgang Prinz propose that, for voluntary action, the conscious mind then uses such perceptual-like representations to later influence the generation of motor efference (the signals to the muscle fibers), which itself is an unconscious process. From this standpoint, when one deliberately performs an action, one aims to reproduce the same sensations that occurred when a similar action was done in the past. To effect a desired efference to the muscles, all the conscious mind has to do is pay a certain kind of attention to such perceptual-like representations. Then, following some sort of "go" signal and if not curbed or controlled by James's "acts of express fiat" (i.e., exercise of veto), unconscious motor programs take care of the rest by meticulously activating the right muscle fibers at the right time, thus giving rise to the action. John Bargh's classic research demonstrates that incidental stimuli, such as ambient objects in one's environment (e.g., a dartboard) can unconsciously activate processes that then influence one's behavioral dispositions (e.g., making one more competitive).

Matching intentions to outcomes also underlies the sense of agency in the mental realm. If one intends to imagine the *Mona Lisa* and then happens to experience the relevant imagery, one is likely to believe that the imagery arose voluntarily, even when the percept may have been caused by an experimental trick, as in the Perky effect. (In the Perky effect, experimental subjects are fooled into believing that they are imagining an image that is actually presented physically on a screen.) In such a way, experiments on "authorship processing" by Wegner and colleagues have demonstrated that subjects can be fooled into believing that they caused actions that were in fact caused by someone else. Together, the findings indicate that we experience agency when our intentions satisfy the causal principles of *consistency, priority,* and *exclusivity:* Our intentions should be consistent with, and be experienced at an appropriate interval prior to, the relevant action, and there should be no other available explanation for the action. It has been shown that experimentally manipulating these three factors leads to systematic distortions in the sense of agency.

Intentional Binding

In *intentional binding,* investigated by Patrick Haggard and colleagues, the perceived elapsed time between voluntary actions (pressing a button) and their consequences (hearing a tone) is shorter than the actual time elapsed. The action is perceived as occurring later than it did and the outcome as occurring earlier than it did, as if the two events were temporally attracted to each other. In this way, one also binds the actions and outcomes performed by others.

Beyond findings showing the illusory and malleable nature of the sense of agency, there are good arguments a priori that there should be no such thing as an undetermined free will, homunculus, or ghost in the machine: The premise in science is that there cannot be a thing (e.g., a will) that is undetermined by past events. The classic research by Benjamin Libet corroborates this deterministic view. Libet instructed subjects to move their hand at will and to indicate when they experienced the conscious urge to perform the action. Although the consciously reported urge to move came about 200 milliseconds (ms) prior to the movement, detectable neural events began approximately 550 ms before the movement and, importantly, 350 ms before the reported urge to move. In short, unconscious neural activity preceded the onset of the conscious urge in a predictable manner. More recently, the research group led by John-Dylan Haynes discovered that the outcome of a willed decision can be predicted by unconscious brain activity occurring up to 10 seconds before the decision is made.

Skeletal ("Voluntary") Muscle

Another feature of voluntary action is that it is limited to skeletal muscle effectors. Other effectors (e.g., smooth muscle) cannot be influenced by it, at least not directly. It has been proposed that skeletal muscles are "voluntary muscles" because they are directed by actional systems in the brain that, in order to influence skeletomotor action collectively, require conscious states to *crosstalk* with each other. Thus, consciousness is intimately related to voluntary action. Unlike involuntary actions (e.g., reflexive inhaling, the pain-withdrawal reflex), voluntary actions can be construed as a form of *integrated action,* which occurs when multiple action plans that could normally influence behavior on their own (when thus activated) are coactivated and trying to influence the same skeletomotor effector, such as when one holds one's breath, refrains from dropping a hot dish, or makes oneself breathe faster. As Richard Passingham noted, suppression is an archetypal integrated action.

In conclusion, the experience (or illusion) of voluntary action can be indexed by suppressibility and characterized by its temporal properties (e.g., intentional binding), its link to the skeletal muscle effector system, the nature of the representations directing it (the conscious perceptual-like representations described in ideomotor theories), and the causal principles that furnish it with a sense of authorship.

*Ezequiel Morsella, Margaret T. Lynn,
and Travis A. Riddle*

See also Access Consciousness; Action Slips;
    Automaticity; Common Coding; Freedom of Action;
    Phenomenology of Action; Philosophy of Action;
    Preconscious Free Will

Further Readings

Gray, J. (2004). *Consciousness: Creeping up on the hard problem*. New York, NY: Oxford University Press.

Libet, B. (2004). *Mind time: The temporal factor in consciousness*. Cambridge, MA: Harvard University Press.

Morsella, E., Bargh, J. A., & Gollwitzer, P. M. (2009). *Oxford handbook of human action*. New York, NY: Oxford University Press.

Wegner, D. M. (2002). *The illusion of conscious will*. Cambridge, MA: MIT Press.

WILLIAMS SYNDROME

Williams syndrome (WS) is a neurodevelopmental disorder caused by the deletion of some 28 genes on one copy of Chromosome 7. The deletion gives rise to distinctive facial features and affects the developing body, brain, mind, and behavior. WS occurs in roughly 1 in 15,000 live births. Compared to more common disorders, such as Down syndrome, why would such a rare syndrome be of interest not only to psychologists but also to philosophers, neuroscientists, linguists, computer scientists, molecular biologists, and educationists? The reason lies in the promise that WS seemed to hold for substantiating a popular view of the mind/brain, namely, that it is composed of innately specified, independently functioning modules. Indeed, initial reports suggested that, despite low IQs and seriously impaired visuospatial and numerical cognition, individuals with WS had intact language and face processing. Was this not proof that language could develop independently of general intelligence? After more in-depth analyses of the phenotype, it became clear that WS was far more complex than researchers originally thought. In reality, far from illustrating the juxtaposition of intact and impaired modules, WS turned out to be a model of the extreme complexity of genotype/phenotype relations and of how domain-general deficits in infancy could cascade over developmental time to result in seemingly domain-specific outcomes in adulthood. In the following, some of the latest genetic, brain, and cognitive findings on this intriguing syndrome are presented, showing how WS continues to offer insights to all those fascinated by the human mind.

Genotype/Phenotype Relations

Early molecular research identified partial deletion patients (PD) with only two genes missing in the WS critical region: *elastin* (ELN) and *LIM-kinase1* (LIMK1). ELN is important for elasticity of skin, lungs, and blood vessels and seemed to explain the WS arterial problems and facial dysmorphology. The PD patients also presented with visuospatial deficits implicating LIMK1, which is expressed in the brain, in these cognitive impairments. However, studies of other PD patients revealed neither facial dysmorphology nor spatial impairments despite deletions of ELN and LIMK1. Current research on PD patients with larger deletions, as well as animal models, indicates that four genes at the end of the deletion are those critical for the full WS cognitive and physical phenotype. Interestingly, these are all "transcription factors"; that is, they regulate numerous other downstream genes, suggesting that any one-to-one mapping between specific genes and specific cognitive outcomes is highly unlikely.

The Williams Syndrome Brain

The WS brain is clearly not a normal brain with parts intact and parts impaired. Its volume is only 80% of typically developing brains, with widespread differences across brain regions: particularly small cerebrum but average cerebellum; abnormal size and shape of the corpus callosum, the central sulcus, and the orbitofrontal cortex. Parietal regions have reduced gray matter with abnormal neuronal layering, orientation, density, and size. Where normal brains become increasingly lateralized (hemispherically specialized) over time, the WS adult brain continues to process stimuli bilaterally, also revealing abnormal connectivity between the orbitofrontal cortex and the amygdala. Note that our knowledge of the WS brain results from research on adults and not on the *developing* WS brain, which would be informative regarding how differences compound or are compensated for by other networks over developmental time.

The Williams Syndrome Cognitive Profile

Individuals with WS present with an average full IQ of 56, but usually verbal IQ is higher than performance IQ. It is this uneven cognitive profile that has attracted attention. However, even within the domain of language, relative strengths in vocabulary can coexist with serious impairments in pragmatics and complex grammar. Visuospatial abilities also display peaks and troughs, with particular deficits in constructional and strengths in perceptual abilities.

One domain of particular interest is WS face processing, because on standardized tasks scores fall within the normal range. Could this be an example of a preserved function? In fact, brain imaging and cognitive studies have shown that the apparently normal performance stems from different brain processes. Again, a developmental approach is critical. For example, when studying spatial frequency biases in face recognition over development, children with WS demonstrate an adultlike bias much earlier than typically developing children, pointing to a less flexibly developing system. WS adults use more featural than configural strategies when processing faces. WS illustrates how, even when scores fall in the normal range, it is vital to probe the underlying brain and cognitive processes.

Conclusion

What, then, can be learned from the study of Williams syndrome? Not that WS will be a model of direct-gene behavior or cognition-brain region mappings. Rather, WS illustrates the complexities of the human mind/brain. While significant advances have been made in the genetic, brain, and cognitive domains, it will be critical to bring these complementary levels of analysis together. It is also essential to understand

how having a syndrome like WS alters the environment in which a child develops and thus to study disorders within the full context of their developmental trajectories. Cross-syndrome studies will help identify which traits are truly syndrome specific. Williams syndrome provides an ideal model for the developmental study of how gene expression, brain, cognition, and environment are integrated to give rise to both the typical and atypical human mind.

*Hayley C. Leonard and
Annette Karmiloff-Smith*

See also Autism; Face Perception; Language Development; Spatial Cognition, Development of

Further Readings

Bellugi, U., Lichtenberger, I., Jones, W., Lai, Z., & St. George, M. (2000). The neurocognitive profile of Williams syndrome: A complex pattern of strengths and weaknesses. *Journal of Cognitive Neuroscience, 12,* 7–29.

Karmiloff-Smith, A. (2009). Nativism versus neuroconstructivism: Rethinking the study of developmental disorders. *Developmental Psychology, 45,* 56–63.

Karmiloff-Smith, A., Grant, J., Ewing, S., Carette, M. J., Metcalfe, K., Donnai, D., . . . Tassabehji, M. (2003). Using case study comparisons to explore genotype-phenotype correlations in Williams-Beuren syndrome. *Journal of Medical Genetics, 40,* 136–140.

Martens, M. A., Wilson, S. J., & Reutens, D. C. (2008). Williams syndrome: A critical review of the cognitive, behavioral, and neuroanatomical phenotype. *Journal of Child Psychology and Psychiatry, 49,* 576–608.

Meyer-Lindenberg, A., Hariri, A. R., Munoz, K. E., Mervis, C. B., Mattay, V. S., Morris, C. A., & Berman, K. F. (2005). Neural correlates of genetically abnormal social cognition in Williams syndrome. *Nature Neuroscience, 8,* 991–993.

WISDOM OF CROWDS EFFECT

Psychologists have historically conceived of crowds as suppressing individuality. Recently, an alternative vision of crowds has emerged: Each person potentially brings unique insights, which if combined properly can make the crowd a better decision maker than most individuals. This entry will discuss the conditions under which crowds are wise, whether individuals acting alone can mimic the effects of a crowd, as well as psychological biases that may prevent people from taking full advantage of what crowds have to offer.

Published demonstrations of the *wisdom of crowds effect* go back to the early 20th century. In one early study from the 1920s, students estimated the temperature in a classroom. When the estimates were averaged together, the resulting group answer was more accurate than the estimate of a typical member. Although early authors attributed the result to some mysterious group property, the statistical underpinning of the effect is now generally understood: A large sample of imperfect estimates tends to cancel out extreme errors and converge on the truth. Subsequent research demonstrated that simple algorithms that weight people equally, such as averaging, often compare favorably to more sophisticated statistical methods of combination. The literature on aggregation was reviewed by Robert Clemen in a 1989 paper in the *International Journal of Forecasting* and more recently by J. Scott Armstrong in his 2001 book *Principles of Forecasting*. The power and simplicity of averaging was also featured in James Surowiecki's 2004 best-selling book *The Wisdom of Crowds*. The logic of tapping diverse perspectives extends to many tasks, including identifying decision objectives, generating alternatives, and choosing among alternatives.

Conditions for Crowd Wisdom

To take full advantage of collective wisdom, groups should be composed of people with topic-relevant knowledge or expertise. As important, the group needs to hold diverse perspectives and bring different knowledge to bear on a topic. Diversity helps because any given perspective is likely to be wrong. People who share a perspective will all be wrong in the same way (e.g., numerical estimates that all over- or underestimate the truth), in which case there is little benefit gained from a crowd. For numerical estimates, the benefit comes when errors "bracket" the truth and cancel out. Interestingly, diversity is so valuable that one can still benefit from averaging when individuals differ greatly in accuracy. In short, knowledge and diversity are the reasons that crowds are often wise.

Differences in perspective (and bracketing) are created both through who is included in the group—when people have different experiences, training, and judgment models—and through process—when ideas are formed and expressed independently from the ideas of others. The importance of process is illustrated by a result in the brainstorming literature. In the classic approach to brainstorming, people generate ideas face-to-face, and build on one another's ideas. However, these interacting groups perform less well—in quality and quantity of alternatives—than noninteracting groups. Although exposure to others' perspectives benefits individuals, over time it can lead people to think more alike, and diversity of perspective is lost.

Can a Person Be a Crowd?

An intriguing recent area of research has extended the logic of the wisdom of crowds to individuals. It turns out that people can achieve some of the benefit of a crowd by digging deeper into their own minds. The key insight is that people typically rely on only a sample of the evidence available to them at any given time. But what if people had a reset button, so that they could retrieve facts from memory anew or handle the same facts in a new way? Simply asking people to answer again does not work; people will inevitably anchor on their initial opinions. There are at least two effective ways to break this anchoring effect, both illustrated in recent papers in *Psychological Science*. First, Edward Vul and Hal Pashler showed that people can be freed from their original answer by delaying a second answer. With the time delay people may forget their initial perspectives and think about the problem differently. The second approach, developed by Stefan Herzog and Ralph Hertwig, is to ask people to assume that their first answer was wrong and to answer the question again. Overall, averaging two opinions from the same person using either time delay or "assume you're wrong and answer again" improves performance by about half as much as averaging across two people.

Psychological Obstacles to Crowd Wisdom

Given that crowds are often wise (including the crowd in the mind), an important question for psychology is whether people make the best use of knowledge that is distributed across perspectives. In general, one can conceive of people using advice from others in three stages: People first collect opinions, then combine the opinions into a judgment or belief, and finally hold this belief with a certain degree of confidence. When it comes to making the most of diversity, people fall short at all three stages. First, people do not uniformly seek out additional opinions. When they do, they often do not seek diversity. Instead, they collect opinions from relatively homogenous sources that share a common perspective, either because they seek confirmation or because similar others are more proximate. For example, a doctor may talk to a colleague with the same specialty or training, and an economist may discuss a forecast with someone who shares the same theoretical assumptions. Second, people combine fewer opinions than they should. One reason for this is that many people have incorrect intuitions about averaging, believing that it locks in the accuracy of the average judge in a crowd. Another reason is that people are overconfident in their ability to identify expertise and consequently "chase the expert" by selecting the single opinion they believe to be most accurate. Even with a larger group, people may focus on themselves or on just a few judges and miss out on the wisdom of the rest. In a 2009 article in *Management Science,* Albert Mannes showed that neglecting others comes at a high price in large crowds. Third, as shown by David Budescu and his colleagues, people are more confident when opinions are in agreement as opposed to disagreement. Although agreement is a signal of accuracy, it is also a signal of a shared perspective and shared error. People rarely recognize this latter implication of agreement. In fact, Ilan Yaniv, Shoham Choshen-Hillel, and Maxim Milyavsky have shown that confidence increases even when people understand that others' opinions were cherry-picked to agree with their own initial answer.

To tap into the crowd's wisdom, appreciating the roles of both knowledge and diversity are essential. People value the knowledge of individuals, and they often chase the expert to obtain it. But in doing so they may forsake diversity and risk missing out on the combined knowledge of the collective.

Jack B. Soll, Albert E. Mannes, and
Richard P. Larrick

See also Anchoring; Debiasing; Decision Improvement Technologies; Dissent, Effects on Group Decisions; Group Decision Making

Further Readings

Armstrong, J. S. (Ed.). (2001). *Principles of forecasting: A handbook for researchers and practitioners.* Boston, MA: Kluwer Academic.

Mannes, A. E. (2009). Are we wise about the wisdom of crowds? The use of group judgments in belief revision. *Management Science, 55*(8), 1267–1279.

Page, S. E. (2007). *The difference: How the power of diversity creates better groups, firms, schools, and societies.* Princeton, NJ: Princeton University Press.

Soll, J. B., & Larrick, R. P. (2009). Strategies for revising judgment: How (and how well) people use others' opinions. *Journal of Experimental Psychology: Learning Memory and Cognition, 35,* 780–805.

Surowiecki, J. (2004). *The wisdom of crowds: Why the many are smarter than the few and how collective wisdom shapes business, economies, societies, and nations.* New York, NY: Doubleday.

WORD LEARNING

Language learning raises unique problems of learning and memory. This is widely recognized with respect to syntax learning, but it is also true of word learning. Word learning is the process of developing generalized (i.e., abstracted) mental representations to associate a *word form* (e.g., sequence of speech sounds or hand shapes/movements) with a *meaning* (e.g., category of events or objects that the word refers to) and *conditions of use* (e.g., Where in a sentence does this word typically belong? In what social contexts does one use the word?). The remainder of this section describes some unique features and questions about word learning in comparison to other kinds of learning. The next section describes research findings on children's word learning, including the typical course of vocabulary development, individual differences, typical errors, and ecological and cognitive factors that facilitate word learning. Subsequent sections briefly describe the neurological changes associated with word learning, the relation of word learning to reading, the nature of word learning in multilingual individuals, and word learning in adulthood.

Word learning entails special questions because the corpus of words we learn, our *lexicon,* is a unique set of information. It is dynamic and additive: Consider how the compound word *electronic mail*, coined in the 1980s, was quickly reduced to *e-mail*, which has since spawned analogous terms such as *e-commerce*. Adults can rapidly understand such words despite their novelty. This illustrates how we can, throughout life, add new elements (words) to our lexicon. In so doing we establish new, systematic connections (of sound, meaning, syntax, and usage) to other words and other linguistic and conceptual knowledge. Although words are arbitrary in form (e.g., nothing about the sound *dog* is inherently doglike), the lexicon is nonetheless somewhat principled. For example, words are hierarchical in meaning (e.g., *animal* refers to a category that includes all referents of *dog*) and in structure (e.g., an *-ed* verb ending denotes the real or hypothetical completion of an act or state). Also, words are combined in particular ways to express more precise meanings (e.g., *fire truck* and *truck fire* have different meanings). The lexicon is both social and normative (e.g., only our cultural knowledge makes *e-commerce* understandable) *and* internalized (e.g., we use words to facilitate cognitive processes such as explicit memory).

Word learning can be called *symbol learning* because it encompasses not only spoken words but signed words and even pictorial symbols (e.g., brand logos). Several nonhuman species (i.e., apes, parrots, dolphins) can learn small numbers of abstract names and symbols for objects, properties, or actions. There is no evidence that nonhuman animals use the full human range of word meanings (e.g., *not, think, silly, maybe*), word variants (*go, gone, went, had gone*), or word functions (e.g., puns, metaphors, novel compounds such as "climbing wall"). Yet children as young as 2 to 4 years old flexibly adopt such a wide range of forms, meanings, and uses: They can learn words defined by tone variations (e.g., Mandarin; Yoruba), percussive "click" or ingestive noises (Sindhi, Xhosa, Zulu), or gestures (American Sign Language). They learn words that take complex *inflections* (i.e., changes to the forms of a word, such as *run, ran, running*). Such variations are extensive and complex in languages like Turkish and Hungarian. Children also can integrate word meanings with cultural and conceptual knowledge (e.g., American children know that *Pokémon* refers to fictional characters, toys, playing cards, a game, a TV program, DVDs, and a video game, but *Pokémon Diamond* only refers to the last of these). How do children learn all of this?

How Children Learn Words

Vocabulary Development in Childhood

The course of word learning in young children is somewhat predictable. The first 50 to 75 words are acquired slowly, typically by 18 to 24 months of age. These words include proper names (*Mama*), nouns (*bottle*), a few verbs (*give*), descriptive terms (*down, more*), and social routine words (*bye*). Words like *nothing* or *think* are absent. The largest subset of early words is nouns, though it has been argued that this is not true of all languages.

Although first words are acquired slowly, even infants recognize a few words: Their own name sounds familiar by 4 months and by 10 to 12 months they tend to look selectively at an object when they hear its name ("truck!"). Many infants say a few words around 12 months (infants who are learning signed languages gesture their first words around 9 months). Then around 18 to 24 months, toddlers start learning words faster. In Indo-European languages (e.g., English, Italian, Dutch), infants start learning nouns faster, until their total *receptive vocabulary* (i.e., the words they understand) includes 150 to 200 items. Subsequently, the proportion of new verbs and adjectives increases relatively faster. This suggests that children learn nouns until they can and must express more diverse and specific relations between nouns (e.g., "The man petted the dog," vs. "The man fed the dog"). This requires verbs. Fittingly, toddlers start producing two- and three-word sentences around 18 to 24 months. These protosentences are *telegraphic*: They lack articles, prepositions, and inflections. Only after children understand 200 to 400 words (2½–3 years) do they add many such *function morphemes* to their sentences.

From 3 to 5 years of age, vocabulary grows substantially. Although total vocabulary size becomes harder to measure, English-speaking first graders might know an average of 3,000 *root words* (i.e., uninflected terms such as *house, run*), and many more inflected or compound words (e.g., *running, houseboat*). These large gains have spurred folk beliefs that children are uncannily precocious word learners. However, this claim lacks specificity or verification, and adults in controlled tests learn new words faster than preschoolers. Thus, acceleration in word learning around 18 to 24 months and large vocabulary gains from 2 to 5 years do not prove that word learning is a specialized childhood learning ability.

Individual Differences in Children's Vocabulary

Throughout childhood there is great variability in individual vocabulary size. According to parental report data, average English-learning 24-month-olds use about 300 words. However, children in the lowest 10% use only about 50, and those in the highest 10% use about 500: a 10-fold difference. Adults have similar large differences in vocabulary. At the lower extremes, virtually all children with cognitive or language disorders have some sort of restricted vocabulary.

Among children with language impairment but no other cognitive deficits, a common problem is that the auditory system (i.e., brain network that processes sound information) is slow to process the sound information in speech. This will inevitably impair word learning because, for example, it is harder to separate individual words in continuous speech. It now seems that this problem leads to later problems in decoding words while reading.

The Setting for Children's Word Learning

How do children learn words, and what factors influence children's success in word learning? As to "how," the simplest answer could be that children hear words while attending to the referent and form an association between the two. However, this explanation is inadequate. There are so many possible associations that a more specific theory of learning processes is necessary. A traditional associationist account holds that learning requires words and referents to be paired (a) close in time and (b) frequently. Both assumptions are only partly supported. First, in some situations, toddlers associate a novel word with something they saw a few minutes ago, not the last thing they saw. Second, frequency of input does not precisely predict learning. Preschool children sometimes sensibly guess a word's meaning from hearing it only one to two times. Even infants, after hearing a new word only a few times, might remember something of that word's sound for days. However, such *fast mapping* has been documented in simple, unambiguous experimental contexts, where adults use *ostension* (i.e., naming while showing the child a referent). Ostension is used by parents in specific situations, like picture-book reading. It

is unknown how much fast mapping happens in common, everyday situations. Even in moderately complex experimental tasks, young children require many repetitions to learn a word. A correlation has been found between how much parents speak to infants (i.e., variety of words *and* total words) and the infants' vocabularies several years later. Thus, although repetition is not all determining, it usually promotes learning.

Children learn words even when adults are not providing ostensive naming or speaking to them at all. In many cultures, adults speak to infants infrequently or not at all. Perhaps surprisingly, there is no evidence that those infants learn language slower or have smaller lexicons than infants who are spoken to. Thus, the correlation between amount of speech to infants and later vocabulary does not rely on *direct* speech to infants. Infants must learn a lot by overhearing other people talking. Experiments show that toddlers may learn words as effectively from overhearing as from direct ostension.

The Progress of Word Learning: Errors

Children's knowledge of a word does not simply fit into one of two binary states, learned or unlearned. Children, like adults, can know a little about a word (e.g., "It sounds familiar . . . maybe it's a kind of food . . .") or a lot (e.g., can recognize, define, and use it correctly), or anything in between. However, children show a lag from *comprehension* to *production*. That is, they typically understand a word before they will say it. This is partly because of slow development of the fine motor skills for speech production. Nonetheless, children do speak, and this can reveal what they know or do not know about a word's meaning. Children's characteristic errors include *overextending* words (e.g., calling any medium-sized mammal "kitty"). These errors sometimes reflect real confusion about a word's meaning (e.g., *kitty* = any cute, fuzzy pet) and sometimes reflect pragmatic accommodations to their small vocabulary. If your only animal words are *kitty*, *horsey*, and *birdy*, your best option for labeling a rabbit or squirrel is "kitty."

How do children correct errors like these? Occasionally children seek information (e.g., "What dat?"), but children often do not seem to realize they are making errors. However, parents sometimes correct children's overt errors of meaning or word choice. They also use less direct strategies, like expanding and elaborating on their toddlers' telegraphic statements. A 20-month-old might point to a pond and say "duck!" The parent might then expand, "Yes, the duck is swimming, isn't it?" This expansion might teach the child not only about *swimming* but also confirm the correct usage of *duck* and implicate a semantic relation between *duck* and *swim* (i.e., ducks are a sort of thing that swims). Or if the parent elaborates, "Yes, ducks are pretty birds!" this provides semantic information about the class-inclusion relation between the categories *duck* and *bird*. Regarding the individual differences noted above, parents who speak more to their infants (who will later have larger vocabularies) also tend to elaborate. Parents' expansions might therefore provide important input to toddlers about word forms, meanings, and uses.

Children's Readiness to Interpret Words

Young children are not "equal opportunity" learners, assigning any plausible meaning to a new word. Children have certain biases. Some are based on perceptual processes. In general, objects that are novel, bright, and prominent will be associated with a novel word. Also, infants tend to associate a new word with an object if the object is moved in rhythm and synchrony with repetitions of the word. Finally, children tend to map novel words for objects onto whole objects, as opposed to specific parts, colors, or textures. However, more specific information about the word can cause children to override their bias and associate the word with another property.

Other biases in interpreting words seem to reflect human conceptual knowledge and ignorance. For example, children seem to assume that words refer to categories of objects, events, or properties, rather than to individuals. A child hearing "lemur" will associate it with a category of similar animals. Although some of toddlers' first words may be narrowly context specific, this seems to be the exception rather than the rule. Even by their first birthdays, infants tend to generalize new words to classes of similar referents. Also, children, like adults, tend to generalize words for objects at a *basic level* of abstraction; that is, an intermediate-breadth category (e.g., car) rather than a very specific one (Mazda 626) or a very general one (vehicle). More specifically, once toddlers know 50 to 100 words

they begin to assume that novel object words generalize to categories of same-shape objects. However, this is a *learned* bias, and it is contingent on other properties (e.g., is the object an animal or artifact?). Thus, conceptual biases are not freestanding: They rest on other experiences and learned patterns. For this reason, it is no surprise that children's language constrains the specific concepts that they learn and name. Cross-linguistic studies confirm that meaning biases are affected by language experience. For example, English and Korean prepositions denote different spatial relations: English *in* and *on* do not have exact analogs in Korean. Korean 1-year-olds are sensitive to spatial relations denoted by different Korean words, but English-learning 1-year-olds do not discriminate those relations. Thus, toddlers' lexicons influence their sensitivity to specific meanings and patterns in the world.

Children also have social biases that affect how they learn meaning. By 18 months of age, toddlers monitor where adults are looking, so that when the adult says a novel word, the toddler associates it with whatever referent the adult was looking at. This prevents the infants from spuriously associating words with whatever *they* are attending to, if the toddler and adults are attending to different things.

Other biases for inferring word meanings are ambiguous. One claim is that children believe that each nameable category only has one label—a *mutual exclusivity* bias. For example, if the child sees a horse and a tapir, they will assume that an unfamiliar word (*tapir*) refers to the unfamiliar animal. However, evidence does not support that this is children's true bias. They do preferentially associate a novel word with a novel rather than familiar referent, but there are many possible explanations for this. This exemplifies a general pattern: Although children have many biases for interpreting new words, it is not clear which, if any, of these biases are specific to word learning per se.

Words on the Brain

To understand word learning requires understanding how sound patterns of words are processed by the brain and represented by brain networks so that subsequent brain states (caused by, e.g., the sound of the word) will reactivate that word representation. Activation of lexical knowledge involves widely distributed networks in the cortex, but in most healthy adults it persistently (not exclusively) involves left frontal and temporal cortical areas. However, this anatomical specialization is the result of development: Infants show wider distributed and more bilateral activation during word processing. Activation becomes more focused in left temporal and parietal regions from 14 to 20 months, showing that neuroanatomical specialization starts early. Intriguingly, infants who understand at least 150 words show a more focused electrophysiological response to familiar words as early as 200 to 400 milliseconds (ms) after the word begins.

Word Learning and Reading

As children get older, they can *decontextualize* language—see it as separable from the "here and now" (e.g., talk about absent referents, tell stories). Decontextualization of language is maximized in written text, such that we can enjoy the language of "speakers" who are absent, or even deceased.

Learning to read during childhood has a bidirectional relation to word learning: Children with larger vocabularies do better in reading, and children who read a lot learn more words. Throughout school, vocabulary is the best predictor of reading comprehension. During grade school, some nontrivial proportion of vocabulary growth is due to word learning from text. When unfamiliar words arise, we try to use the meaningful content of surrounding text to interpret them. Although a minority of contextually learned words are retained, the consequences are nevertheless substantial: Hypothetically, if a child reads 600,000 words in a summer (e.g., the last three Harry Potter books) and 1% of words are unfamiliar but inferable from context, and if she has only a 5% chance to infer and remember a word from context, her net gain would be 300 words. Thus, reading a lot of grade-level text is important for vocabulary growth. Children at risk for reading failure enter school with a lower level of language skills, read less, and remain below-average readers with smaller vocabularies.

In skilled readers, recognition of written words elicits maximal activation in a specific region in the temporal cortex. Less skilled readers show too widely distributed patterns of activation over many cortical regions, and recent evidence suggests that training these readers' discrimination of sound patterns in words can lead to more focused patterns of brain activation during reading.

Words in Two Languages

Most people in the world are multilingual: Monolingualism is the exception. How do people learn two lexicons, which might overlap in meaning but contain many single-language word forms? One debate is whether two lexicons are initially merged or separate. Although there is great diversity across individuals and situations, toddlers' two languages begin separating very early. Recent brain research suggests that bilinguals show activation of largely but not completely overlapping areas of cerebral cortex for each language.

Word Learning Later in Life

Word learning continues throughout life. There is a general idea that *age of acquisition* matters: Words learned earlier (e.g., as a toddler) are the most strongly represented in neural networks. For example, in *aphasia*, or loss of language due to brain injury, there is usually some degree of *anomia* (i.e., poor production or understanding of words). However, early learned words are more likely to be retained.

Word learning in adulthood can be very robust. Some words learned as a young adult will be retained for decades, even if never heard or used in the interim.

What do we know about the processes of word learning in adults? Like children, adults learn most new words by inferring meaning from context. Adults' rich phonological knowledge helps them efficiently learn new sounds of words. Adult word learning is affected by many general cognitive effects: For example, words at the beginnings or ends of sentences are more likely to be remembered (i.e., primacy and recency effects: the general advantage in remembering items from, respectively, the beginning and end of a list). When learning words over time, *distributed practice* rather than *massed practice* tends to increase retention intervals (i.e., how long words are remembered). Associations of new words are subject to both *proactive* and *retroactive* interference (i.e., confusion caused by prior information or subsequent information, respectively). In all these effects, we see continuity from childhood to adulthood, and substantial overlap of word learning with general processes of learning and memory.

Gedeon Deák

Further Readings

Anglin, J. M. (1993). Vocabulary development: A morphological analysis. *Monographs of the Society for Research in Child Development, 58*(10), 1–165.

Bates, E., & Goodman, J. C. (1999). On the emergence of grammar from the lexicon. In B. MacWhinney (Ed.), *The emergence of language* (pp. 29–79). Mahwah, NJ: Erlbaum.

Benson, D. F. (1988). Anomia in aphasia. *Aphasiology, 2,* 229–235.

Choi, S., McDonough, L., Bowerman, M., & Mandler, J. (1999). Early sensitivity to language-specific spatial categories in English and Korean. *Cognitive Development, 14,* 241–268.

Clark, E. V. (1997). Contextual perspective and lexical choice in acquisition. *Cognition, 64,* 1–37.

Deacon, T. (1997). *The symbolic species.* Cambridge, MA: Harvard University Press.

Deák, G. O. (2000). Chasing the fox of word learning: Why "constraints" fail to capture it. *Developmental Review, 20,* 29–80.

Fenson, L., Dale, P. S., Reznick, J. S., Bates, E., Thal, D. J., & Pethick, S. J. (1994). Variability in early communicative development. *Monographs of the Society for Research in Child Development, 59*(5).

Hart, B., & Risley, T. (1995). *Meaningful differences in the everyday experiences of young children.* Baltimore, MD: Paul H. Brookes.

Jusczyk, P. W. (1997). *The discovery of spoken language.* Cambridge, MA: MIT Press.

Mills, D. L., Coffey-Corina, S., & Neville, H. J. (1997). Language comprehension and cerebral specialization from 13 to 20 months. *Developmental Neuropsychology, 13,* 397–445.

Naigles, L. (1990). Children use syntax to learn verb meanings. *Journal of Child Language, 17,* 357–374.

Smith, L. B., Colunga, E., & Yoshida, H. (2003). Making an ontology: Cross-linguistic evidence. In D. Rakison & L. Oakes (Eds.), *Early category and concept development* (pp. 275–302). Oxford, UK: Oxford University Press.

Tomasello, M. (2001). Perceiving intentions and learning words in the second year of life. In M. Bowerman & S. C. Levinson (Eds.), *Language acquisition and conceptual development* (pp. 132–158). Cambridge, UK: Cambridge University Press.

Werker, J. F., Cohen, L. B., Lloyd, V. L., Casasola, M., & Stager, C. L. (1998). Acquisition of word–object associations by 14-month-old infants. *Developmental Psychology, 34,* 1289–1309.

WORD RECOGNITION, AUDITORY

Language provides humans with the remarkable capacity to express their thoughts through a physical medium to share with others. To do so, we combine elements, words, whose form has been conventionalized within a particular language community. Thus a critical step in the process of retrieving a talker's message consists of identifying these elements in his or her speech. This entry discusses how our knowledge of the auditory forms that words take may be represented in memory, and how listeners decide, based on the auditory stimulus, which words they heard, out of all possible word combinations the talker may have spoken.

What Does Our Knowledge of Words Look Like?

When we listen to someone talk, words seem to pop out of his or her speech effortlessly. This impression is misleading, however. Words are not neatly segregated from one another in speech as they are in print. How many words the utterance contains, and where they begin and end in the speech stream, are properties that the listener must establish. Moreover, the way spoken words sound varies considerably across contexts—for example, when produced by a man or a woman, in the clear speech used in lecture halls, or in the casual speech characteristic of informal conversation. Our knowledge of the form of words must accommodate this variability. Two approaches to this issue can be contrasted.

First, listeners may represent the form of a word as a compilation of the memory traces that correspond to all past exposure with the word. Each instance retains the acoustic properties resulting from the context in which the word was uttered. Such a representation is sometimes described as a cluster of observations in a multidimensional space. A more compact representation may also be postulated, such as one that represents the central tendency derived from past instances of a word, its prototype. These views assume ever-changing word representations because new instances of words are constantly added to the cluster or the set of instances that contribute to the central tendency.

These *exemplar* and *prototype* views are rooted in cognitive theories of categorization and contrast with a second, linguistically grounded, approach where words are represented by the features that distinguish them from other words. The acoustic properties of a spoken word, such as the voice quality of the talker that utters it, are considered irrelevant to this distinction and consequently not part of the representation of the word's form. This approach assumes abstract, context-independent, and immutable representations. Normalization algorithms transform information extracted from the speech to neutralize the influence of contextual variability, in effect treating it as noise, or to model the variation and factor out its influence.

Distinguishing between the two approaches has proven difficult. For instance, some have taken the fact that people recognize words uttered by familiar talkers more readily than the same words from unfamiliar talkers as evidence supporting the instance-based approach because it demonstrates that nondistinctive properties of spoken stimuli are maintained in memory and contribute to recognition. However, the finding is also compatible with the *abstractionist* approach if one assumes that the normalization algorithms can be optimized to reflect past experience with a given talker.

Does Recognizing a Word Require Recognizing Its Parts First?

Another widely discussed issue concerns the internal structure of words. Phonological theories describe words as built out of elements, the phonemes, grouped into larger units, such as syllables. Words' internal structure is known (albeit implicitly) to language users because changes that word forms undergo under the influence of morphology or other linguistic constraints have regularities that depend on the decomposition of word forms into such a structure. The critical question here is whether people, when analyzing speech, decompose the signal into individual elements to establish which word matches the structure best. Recognizing phonemes or other units first, as opposed to analyzing the spoken word as a whole, may offer an advantage because there are fewer phonemes to discriminate than there are

words. However, phoneme recognition itself has proven difficult because the acoustic realization of a given phoneme varies greatly across contexts. Furthermore, listeners can successfully retrieve which of the phonemically identical strings (such as *two lips* and *tulips*) the talker said because they make use of subtle acoustic differences between the strings. This finding is difficult to explain if the speech signal was first translated into its phonemic subcomponents.

Word Recognition as a Perceptual Choice

In contrast to the question of how the form of words is represented, the process by which the perceptual stimulus is compared to these representations is relatively well understood and uncontroversial. Spoken words become available to the listener over time. Because speech is a complex, transient, and rapidly changing signal, and, because sensory memory is limited, speech must be evaluated and interpreted incrementally rather than word by word. But the early portion of a spoken word (e.g., *cap . . .*) is often compatible with many different words (e.g., *cap, captive, capital, captain*). Dominant views posit that all possible interpretations of the spoken word can be simultaneously considered. For example, in William Marslen-Wilson's *cohort theory*, the first sounds of a spoken word determine a cohort of hypotheses compatible with this early information. Subsequent information serves to prune the hypotheses no longer supported by the signal. Although the "propose-then-dispose" aspect of the theory has since been falsified by evidence that words can be successfully recognized even when their first sounds are distorted, the privileged role of the early portion of a word has been maintained by assuming a form of competition among simultaneously considered hypotheses. The more evidence has accumulated in favor of a given hypothesis, the less likely its alternatives. This mechanism, in effect, favors words that match the early portion of the spoken stimulus over those that match a later portion, because the latter will have been largely discounted before the stimulus supports them as possible contenders. Importantly, competition is modulated by the likelihood of encountering each hypothesis, which can be estimated by how often it has been encountered before. Frequent words are recognized more accurately and faster than rarer words, and frequent hypotheses interfere with the recognition of rare words.

Delphine Dahan

See also Cohort Model of Auditory Word Recognition; Frequency Effects in Word Recognition; Speech Perception

Further Readings

Dahan, D., & Magnuson, J. S. (2006). Spoken-word recognition. In M. J. Traxler & M. A. Gernsbacher (Eds.), *Handbook of psycholinguistics* (2nd ed., pp. 249–283). Amsterdam, Netherlands: Elsevier.

Marslen-Wilson, W. (1987). Functional parallelism in spoken word-recognition. *Cognition, 25,* 71–102.

McClelland, J. L., & Elman, J. L. (1986). The TRACE model of speech perception. *Cognitive Psychology, 18,* 1–86.

WORD RECOGNITION, VISUAL

Reading is one of the most remarkable of our cognitive abilities. Skilled readers are able to recognize printed words and compute their associated meanings with astonishing speed and with a great deal of accuracy. This level of performance arises despite the fact that letters frequently appear in an unfamiliar form (e.g., in new fonts) and constitute a limited array that renders individual words highly confusable (e.g., *salt, slat*).

This entry provides an overview of some of the key theoretical claims about the cognitive architectures and processing mechanisms that underlie visual word recognition. These claims were first instantiated in the *interactive activation model* developed by James McClelland and David Rumelhart in 1981, from which many of the more recent theories in the field have been developed. They are supported by evidence from a variety of experimental methods, including observation of word recognition performance in skilled readers (e.g., measuring the time taken to read a word aloud), investigation of the reading behavior of people with acquired or developmental language impairments (e.g., dyslexia, pure alexia), and computational modeling (e.g., testing theories of visual word recognition through computer simulations of human performance).

The Architecture of the Visual Word Recognition System

Though the earliest theories of visual word recognition claimed that words are recognized as wholes on the basis of their shapes, modern theories suggest that words are recognized in a hierarchical manner on the basis of their components. Information from the printed stimulus maps onto stored knowledge about the *visual features* that make up letters (e.g., horizontal bar, left-opening curve), and information from this level then proceeds onto a system of stored *abstract letter representations* that code letter identity as well as letter position (so that anagrams like *top, pot,* and *opt* can be distinguished). These letter representations are abstract in the sense that they can be activated irrespective of surface characteristics such as case, size, font, and retinal location. Information at the letter level of representation then proceeds onto an *orthographic lexicon* (a body of stored knowledge about the written forms of whole words). Units in the orthographic lexicon can then activate information about the meanings and/or sounds of words. Visual word recognition is thought to be achieved when a unit in the orthographic lexicon reaches some critical threshold of activation.

There is widespread agreement that each unit in the orthographic lexicon is coded in terms of an individual's experience with that word. Precisely how lexical experience is best conceptualized is a matter of some debate, however. Until recently, most theories argued that orthographic units are coded in terms of the frequency with which a word occurs in the language, and indeed, word frequency is known to be the most powerful determinant of the time taken to recognize a word (i.e., its latency). However, recent research has suggested that the age at which words are acquired, or perhaps the cumulative frequency with which an individual encounters words over his or her lifetime, may provide a better means of conceptualizing lexical experience. Both age of acquisition and cumulative frequency have also been shown to influence word recognition latencies, though because age of acquisition, cumulative frequency, and word frequency are naturally correlated, it is not yet known which variable provides the optimal index.

Processing Dynamics in Visual Word Recognition

Information is thought to flow through feature, letter, and whole-word orthographic levels of representation in an *interactive* manner, such that information at higher levels of representation can influence processing at lower levels of representation. The finding that provided the initial support for interactive processing is the *word superiority effect*. Participants are better able to decide which of two letters (e.g., *D* or *K*) is in a briefly presented target masked by another stimulus (e.g., immediately followed by hash marks) when that target is a word (e.g., WORK) than when it is a nonword (e.g., OWRK). This finding supports the notion of interactive processing because it suggests that a decision based on activation at the letter level is influenced by higher level information from the orthographic lexicon. More recent research has shown that tests of visual word recognition such as speeded lexical decision (i.e., deciding as quickly as possible whether a stimulus is a known word) show top-down influences of semantic variables such as imageability, number of semantic features, and number of meanings. Similarly, substantial evidence also suggests that the recognition of printed letter strings is influenced at its earliest stages by information about the sounds of words.

It is generally thought that printed letter strings activate multiple candidates in the orthographic lexicon (e.g., the stimulus *cat* activates units for *cat, cab, rat, mat, car, cut*, etc.). The activation of multiple units thus raises the question of how the target unit is ultimately selected. Though theories are divided on this issue, one popular mechanism is competition. Inhibitory connections between units in the orthographic lexicon enable the most active unit (usually the one corresponding to the target) to drive down activation of multiple alternative candidates. One key piece of evidence for competitive processing is that presentation of a high-frequency, masked stimulus (e.g., *able*) tends to inhibit recognition of an orthographically related target (e.g., *axle*). There is also mounting evidence for a processing cost involved in the recognition of words with higher frequency orthographic neighbors (i.e., orthographically similar words), though further research is needed to establish this finding conclusively.

Kathleen Rastle

See also Compound Words, Processing of; Dyslexia, Acquired; Eye Movements During Reading; Frequency Effects in Word Recognition; Word Recognition, Auditory

Further Readings

Coltheart, M., Rastle, K., Perry, C., Langdon, R., & Ziegler, J. (2001). DRC: A dual route cascaded model of visual word recognition and reading aloud. *Psychological Review, 108,* 204–256.

Davis, C. J., & Bowers, J. S. (2006). Contrasting five theories of letter position coding. *Journal of Experimental Psychology: Human Perception & Performance, 32,* 535–557.

Grainger, J., & Jacobs, A. M. (1996). Orthographic processing in visual word recognition: A multiple read-out model. *Psychological Review, 103,* 518–565.

Rastle, K. (2007). Visual word recognition. In M. G. Gaskell (Ed.), *Oxford handbook of psycholinguistics* (pp. 71–89). Oxford, UK: Oxford University Press.

WORKING MEMORY

Working memory is the term used to describe the information one is thinking about at any particular moment. That information keeps changing, and the amount one holds in mind in this way at any moment is quite small compared to the vast amount of information in one's permanent memory storage system in the brain. The concept of working memory has become one of the most important and often-used concepts in the field of psychology, as it helps a great deal in explaining what tasks are easy or hard for individuals to carry out. There are consequently thousands of articles on various aspects of working memory.

The term working memory was suggested in 1960 in a book by George Miller and his colleagues, and the concept was made popular 14 years later in a book chapter by Alan Baddeley and Graham Hitch. The idea behind the term is that there are various kinds of mental work such as thinking, problem solving, reasoning, language comprehension and production, and keeping track of changing events (i.e., while watching a baseball game). To do these kinds of mental work, one must hold in mind certain information relevant to the situation. One might need to hold in mind *data* such as, in baseball, which team is at bat and how many outs there are in the inning or, when doing addition in one's head, the carried digits. One might also need to hold in mind *plans* such as, when solving an arithmetic problem, the steps to follow or, when running errands, the order in which errands are to be accomplished. The key point is that the amount of information that can be held in working memory is limited. This fact in turn puts limits on how well humans can solve problems, formulate plans in their heads, and so on.

Working memory appears to have various components, but they operate together as an integrated system. For example, there appears to be cross talk such that, if the goals are too complex, one can forget not only goals but data; conversely, if there are many data to be kept in mind, one can forget not only data, but goals.

This entry will include a discussion of many important aspects of working memory, including a comparison with similar concepts and terms, the kinds of studies demonstrating working memory, limits on working memory, theories of working memory, individual and group differences in working memory, and some possible neural and evolutionary reasons why working memory capacity is limited.

Similar Concepts and Terms

One of the most common questions asked of researchers of working memory is how it differs from certain other types of memory. Usually, there is a lot of overlap between the different types of memory in question. Here are some of these overlapping concepts and how they subtly differ from the term *working memory*. This discussion is meant to resolve some of the confusion that inevitably comes about when so many terms are used.

Limited-Capacity System

In some of the early work on working memory, a single term was sometimes used for many different types of things that were limited in the mind. We can only attend to a limited number of objects in the visual field at once. We can only keep in mind a small number of randomly arranged letters, numbers, or words at once. We can only fully comprehend one talker at a time. We can only solve math problems in our heads if they are sufficiently simple. A term often used to describe these limits is a *limited-capacity system*. Capacity is the ability to carry out tasks, and this capacity is limited in various ways just described.

Are all these limitations based on the same, single, limited-capacity part of the human mind and brain? It may be, but it would be difficult to prove, and no such proof has emerged as of yet. There are shortcomings of that way of thinking. For example, your memory for just how the final note of a symphony sounded, just after the end of the symphony, may linger at most a few seconds, without interfering with

your ability to carry out a math problem. If you finish the math problem and then turn attention to the sound that has just finished, you may still be able to experience that sound through memory (though you will have missed much of the immediately preceding part of the symphony). If the memory for sound and the math problem activity are indeed separate from one another in your mental processes then they should not both be considered part of a common limited-capacity system.

The math problem is the kind of activity more often considered dependent on a limited-capacity system; it requires attentive thought. Passively remembering a few tones, words, or images, on the other hand, is generally considered to be partly outside of that limited-capacity system because some such memory continues for a short time even when your attention is elsewhere. Yet both the active, attentive and the passive, inattentive types of mental processing typically contribute to performance on tasks considered to be working memory tasks.

Immediate Memory

Immediate memory is memory for a list or array of items that was just presented. There is no delay between the stimulus and the time at which you are supposed to try to recall that stimulus, so it is called immediate. Tasks using immediate memory procedures are probably the most common types of task used to study working memory.

Short-Term Memory

This term is used in different ways by different folks. When many people say "I'm having trouble with my short-term memory" they are saying that they cannot recall things that they did within the last day or so, such as where they parked their car in the morning. That kind of memory clearly cannot be the same as the information currently held in mind, unless one spends the entire day trying to bear in mind where the car was parked.

When psychologists use the term short-term memory, they are contrasting it with the term long-term memory, the vast amount of information that we have learned over a lifetime. In this sense, short-term memory is the same thing as working memory. One difference is that some researchers use the term short-term memory to describe only the passive, effortless storage of information for a few seconds. Some of them reserve the term working memory to refer only to temporarily held information that does require attention, whereas others use the term working memory to refer to all the temporarily held information—both active and passive. For the latter researchers, short-term memory is a part of working memory. (Differences in how researchers use the terms are regrettable, but they are hard to control. Researchers would like to be able to communicate with one another and with other people in a standard manner, but slightly different interpretations of the term are already embedded in a lot of published literature.)

Sensory Memory

The memory for exactly how a sound sounds, how a visual scene looks, how a caress feels, or how a food item smells or tastes is sometimes impossible to put into words. Research shows that our memory for sensory qualities is excellent and can include myriad things in the environment at once. This kind of memory, however, fades within a few seconds. In that time we are able to concentrate on a few items and save them in a more categorical form. In one type of experiment, for example, an array of characters is very briefly presented; perhaps three rows of four randomly chosen letters are presented. Then the array disappears and a tone is presented to indicate whether the top, middle, or bottom row is to be recalled. If the tone comes very soon after the character array, almost all the letters in that row can be recalled. If the tone is delayed, the ability falls off. We can retain only about four of the characters but, if given prompt notice by the tone, we can choose which four characters to draw from a rich but short-lived visual sensory memory and to encode in a verbal form. Visual sensory memories are richer in spatial details, whereas auditory sensory memories are richer in precise details about the timing of the sounds.

Most researchers do not consider sensory memory as part of working memory, but it cannot be denied that sensory memory plays an important role in tasks used to measure working memory. For example, the memory for a spoken list of words is typically better than the memory for the same words presented visually, and this auditory superiority comes from items at the end of the list, where auditory sensory memory preserves vowel sounds in the last word or so and makes these words easier to remember.

Activated Memory

One way to think of working memory is that it consists of the elements of memory that are currently in a heightened state of activation. For example, whereas long-term memories might be preserved in terms of the pattern of synapses between nerve cells that have developed over time, working memory might be represented by the temporary activation of some patterns of neural activity that represent the concepts currently in working memory. Of course, we often perceive things that are different from anything we have perceived before, in which case the information has to be added to long-term memory while it is being activated. For example, have you ever thought of carrots that are purple? That thought has just been added to your long-term memory, and it is also currently active, which may make up your working memory of this novel variety of vegetable.

The Focus of Attention

Often, it is emphasized that attention makes a very important difference in memory. This certainly seems to be true in the field of working memory. Items to which one pays attention can be understood much more completely than items outside one's attention (for example, what people in the room you are in are saying to one another while you are engrossed in a telephone conversation). If you want to form new, strong connections between items or ideas you must pay attention to the ideas. For instance, you cannot memorize directions from a map without intensely attending to the map.

Studies Demonstrating Working Memory

Even though we use working memory to help carry out a variety of problems, researchers often want to measure working memory in a manner as simple as possible so that the measurement will be valid for a range of types of problem to which working memory can be applied. Tests of intelligence have long included tests of *digit span* in which series of digits are presented and span is defined as the longest list that the participant can repeat back without error. Typically, young adults can repeat lists of about six or seven random digits. Other times, lists of letters or words are used and the results are similar. One can present series of shapes that cannot easily be named and the results are similar. People seem to do best at the beginning of the list (called the primacy effect). If they are allowed to recall the items in any order, they do very well also for items at the end of the list (called the recency effect).

Individuals tend to use strategies to remember lists as well as possible, such as trying to group words together or repeating them silently (which is called covert verbal rehearsal). Such strategies can be prevented by requiring that the individual recite a meaningless word (such as *the, the, the*) while the items to be recalled are presented. This typically interferes most with memory for items at the beginning of the list. Some researchers are most interested in the best memory, strategies and all, but other researchers are more interested in understanding how much can be retained even without the use of such strategies.

Instead of lists, other studies have used arrays of characters presented all at once on the computer screen. The results are similar, although rehearsal may be more difficult for arrays than for lists.

Some studies are designed to find out how well people are able to save information while it is being used. The studies may present lists that require both saving information and using it, at the same time. These procedures will not necessarily look the same as tasks in the real world (such as problem solving or language comprehension), because in the real world it is not easy to find out how much the task depends on working memory and how much it depends on other abilities. In some working memory tests, therefore, the storage and processing parts of the task are interleaved rather than integrated. The research participant may have to answer a math problem, memorize a word, answer another math problem, memorize a second word, and so on. The number of words that can be remembered and repeated back, despite the interleaved math, is known as *operation span*.

Limits on Working Memory

Chunk Limits

Humans are, of course, impressive thinkers who often come up with ways around their limitations. It appears that the main limit on the ability to remember information is how many meaningful units must be remembered. These meaningful units are called *chunks*. Most people would have great difficulty in committing to memory a nine-letter series such as BIMICASUA. It is much easier, however, to

remember the series IBMCIAFBI, if one notices that it is composed of three chunks, each a meaningful acronym: IBM, CIA, and FBI. Some individuals have learned to repeat back lists of up to 80 digits, but they do so by having already memorized many series of digits that make up athletic records (like a running time for the mile of 3.86 minutes) and using that information as a chunk when that sequence happens to come up in the list. You probably cannot recall such long strings of digits, but everyone uses chunking a great deal. You could probably recall many, many words if they make up the words of the first verse of *Mary Had a Little Lamb* followed by the first verse of *Twinkle, Twinkle, Little Star*.

A great deal of research—for example, that summarized by Nelson Cowan and his colleagues—shows that adults generally can remember only three of four chunks of information. Sometimes each chunk includes a lot of information, but it is held by a very limited working memory mechanism. This limit may have to do with how much information can be attended at one time.

Time Limits

Baddeley and Hitch showed that chunks are not the only things important for retaining information in working memory. They found that lists of long words cannot be remembered as well as lists of the same number of short words, even if the long words are equally familiar. This difference has to do with the ability to use covert verbal rehearsal to keep words active in memory. It takes longer to rehearse long words and, while some words are being rehearsed, other words in the list can be forgotten.

Pierre Barrouillet and his colleagues have found that what is important for retaining items in working memory is having enough time to use attention between items. Attention, and not just covert verbal rehearsal, may be used to reactivate items in memory before they can be forgotten. What appears to be important for working memory is the ratio of free time to time occupied by distractions. The more free time, the better.

Theories of Working Memory

The theories of working memory are theories of what can and cannot be remembered and why. If we had a complete understanding of what can and cannot be remembered, we probably would know which theory is correct. There are many subtleties, though, and researchers still are investigating this issue.

Central Storage Theory

According to the central storage theory, working memory requires attention (a process that is central in the mind, not specific to one type of stimulus or another). If you add one working memory task, it will interfere with other working memory tasks and with other kinds of effortful thinking. There is some truth to this inasmuch as simply having to remember a series of about seven digits—what is called a *memory load*—can impair one's concurrent ability to reason out problems logically and make good decisions. (Similar to memory load, one reason that too much alcohol results in bad decisions is that it impairs working memory.)

J. Scott Saults and Cowan carried out research on memory for both visual and auditory memory arrays together (colored spots on the screen and spoken digits in different voices from four loudspeakers at once). They found that participants could remember a maximum of about four items. If they were allowed to pay attention only to the colored spots, they were able remember about four of those. If they were required to pay attention to both modalities, they were able to remember still about four items total: about three colored spots and one spoken digit. This suggests that a central storage mechanism exists, though it certainly does not show that this central storage is the only kind. For one thing, sensory memory had to be eliminated using a meaningless audiovisual pattern, or *mask,* after the arrays in order for this fixed capacity of about four items to be observed.

Modular-Stores Theory

Some other theorists, such as Robert Logie, believe that there is no central memory, only separate memories for items stored in visual form and items stored in verbal form, examples of specialized subsystems or *modules*. These theorists attempt to explain results such as the ones using visual and auditory stimuli together by saying that items are thought of in a different way or *recoded*. One can make up a verbal code for a visual stimulus (like naming a colored spot), or one can make up a visual code to go with an acoustic stimulus (like envisioning

how a spoken digit would look in print). We know that stimuli that are similar in their codes interfere with one another in working memory. For example, it is difficult to remember the printed letter series *c, d, v, p, t, z, b* because the letters tend to be mentally recoded into a speech form and they sound similar. This shows how difficult it will be to determine with great certainty whether there is a central store.

Hybrid Theories

Today many researchers believe some sort of hybrid model that includes both (a) a central store that is closely tied to attention and accepts a variety of types of information and (b) some other forms of storage that are more passive and automatic and may be designed to accept only certain specific kinds of information. For example, for attention-related memory, Cowan thinks of the focus of attention as a central storage device in the mind, and Baddeley talks of an *episodic buffer* that contains links between information of different sorts (like an association between a face and a spoken name). In both theoretical views, there is also a *central executive* component that represents the attention-driven control of information as it is transferred from one state or store to another but that presumably does not itself store information.

For passive storage devices, Cowan talks of various sorts of activated elements from long-term memory, and Baddeley talks of visual and phonological storage buffers as separate modules. One difference between these models is that Cowan is unsure whether the types of activated long-term memory are few enough or simple enough to be considered modules, or whether there are instead just a myriad of different kinds of activated memory for different kinds of features of the stimuli (color, spatial location, sound quality, semantic meaning, geographic arrangement, and so on).

Individual and Group Differences in Working Memory

Individuals with lower scores on working memory tests have been shown to do worse on many different kinds of cognitive tests. They remember fewer items in working memory, find it more difficult to inhibit irrelevant thoughts, and find it more difficult to remember the goal of an activity than do individuals with a larger working memory span. Therefore, working memory is of great practical significance. Recent work has suggested that the attention-related part of working memory can be improved through training, and that it improves cognition and helps in the treatment of attention deficit disorder and dementia. If that information holds up, it will be exciting indeed.

Why Is There a Limit in Working Memory Capacity?

Various kinds of explanation have been given for the working memory limit. Saving information in working memory seems to depend on areas in the parietal lobes in the brain, and deciding what information to save and how to use it seems to depend on areas in the frontal lobes. The coding of a stimulus seems to depend on different areas that code different features all firing at once. For example, the representation of a blue circle would include neurons that represent blueness and neurons that represent circles firing at the same time. When several items have to be represented at once, there is the danger that they will corrupt one another. A blue circle and a green square that are parts of a set of items that is slightly too large for memory might get misremembered as a blue square and a green circle.

A few mathematically oriented researchers have argued that groups of three or four items make up an ideal grouping for the retrieval of information from memory. Items within a group of three are easily identifiable inasmuch as there is a beginning, middle, and end of each group. Evolutionary psychologists have argued that working memory is especially important in group interactions. One might have to figure out and bear in mind not only what a friend thinks but also what the friend thinks that he or she thinks, and what other people think that they both think. A good theory of the minds of others can help one be a leader in society. That takes working memory.

Nelson Cowan

See also Aging, Memory, and Information Processing Speed; Emotion and Working Memory; Intelligence and Working Memory; Rehearsal and Memory; Visual Working Memory; Working Memory, Evolution of

Further Readings

Baddeley, A. (2007). *Working memory, thought, and action.* New York, NY: Oxford University Press.

Baddeley, A. D., & Logie, R. H. (1999). Working memory: The multiple-component model. In A. Miyake & P. Shah (Eds.), *Models of working memory: Mechanisms of active maintenance and executive control* (pp. 28–61). Cambridge, UK: Cambridge University Press.

Barrouillet, P., Bernardin, S., & Camos, V. (2004). Time constraints and resource sharing in adults' working memory spans. *Journal of Experimental Psychology: General, 133,* 83–100.

Cowan, N. (2005). *Working memory capacity.* Hove, UK: Psychology Press.

Cowan, N. (2009). Working memory from the trailing edge of consciousness to neurons. *Neuron, 62,* 13–16.

Jonides, J., Lewis, R. L., Nee, D. E., Lustig, C. A., Berman, M. G., & Moore, K. S. (2008). The mind and brain of short-term memory. *Annual Review of Psychology, 59,* 193–224.

Klingberg, T. (2009). *The overflowing brain: Information overload and the limits of working memory* (N. Betteridge Trans.). New York, NY: Oxford University Press.

Miller, G. A., Galanter, E., & Pribram, K. H. (1960). *Plans and the structure of behavior.* New York, NY: Holt.

Miyake, A., & Shah, P. (Eds.). (1999). *Models of working memory: Mechanisms of active maintenance and executive control.* Cambridge, UK: Cambridge University Press.

Saults, J. S., & Cowan, N. (2007). A central capacity limit to the simultaneous storage of visual and auditory arrays in working memory. *Journal of Experimental Psychology: General, 136,* 663–684.

WORKING MEMORY, EVOLUTION OF

This entry discusses a prominent cognitive theory called *working memory* and discusses evidence for its evolution in the archaeological record. Working memory is a theory of cognitive function proposed by experimental psychologists Alan Baddeley and Graham Hitch in 1974. In their original formulation, working memory was conceived to be a multicomponent system that allows an organism to keep task-relevant information in active attention while filtering out task-irrelevant interference. At the core of this system was the central executive, a limited-capacity, attentional controller and decision maker. At its behest were two subsystems, the phonological loop and the visuospatial sketchpad. The phonological loop consisted of two components: a quickly fading phonological store (about 2 seconds in length) and an articulatory rehearsal mechanism, which could be invoked vocally or subvocally. Repeated articulatory rehearsal of verbal stimuli was considered to have obligatory storage in declarative long-term memory. Baddeley and his colleagues found empirical support for the hypothesis that the phonological loop was critical to language comprehension and production. The visuospatial sketchpad maintained visual and spatial information in attention and played an important role in spatial orientation and wayfinding. More recently, Baddeley has proposed a fourth component, the episodic buffer. As originally conceived, the central executive had no storage capacity of its own; it was the analytical component of working memory. Because the phonological loop and visuospatial sketchpad consisted of modality specific, rapidly fading, limited-capacity stores, the model as originally conceived lacked a store that could hold integrated information. He therefore proposed a subsystem for the multimodal integration of verbal and visual information and the temporary maintenance of the resulting information for manipulation by the central executive.

Misconceptions About Working Memory

There is some confusion in the cognitive literature about the term *working memory*. Sometimes, the term working memory is used only in a narrow sense, and it does not imply Baddeley's multi-component model. When it is used in the narrow sense, the term usually refers to the ability to maintain and manipulate thoughts over a brief period of time despite interference. Readers must often discover for themselves whether the term is being used in the narrow sense or the broad, multicomponent sense.

Evolution of Working Memory

Baddeley himself recognizes that evolutionary approaches are currently popular within psychology. His own investigations led him to believe in the selective value of the phonological loop as a powerful aid in the acquisition of language. Baddeley has also pondered the biological, adaptive functions of the other components of working memory. The two working memory subsystems (phonological loop and visuospatial sketchpad) would play a role in an organism's perception of its environment. Baddeley recognized that

because organisms must make decisions regarding their perceptions of the world, the central executive must play a prominent role in deciding on subsequent behavior based on information held in attention and analyzed. Baddeley noted that conditions of rapid change, such as those that would have confronted our early ancestors, would require the organism to be able to learn and learn quickly (i.e., implicit learning). Finally, Baddeley proposed that a successful system would be able to remember previous experiences and use this information in the creation of alternative scenarios (i.e., planning). Baddeley's episodic buffer, described in his 2007 book, plays a central role in this planning function, and working memory would therefore reside at the intersection of cognitive functions, including perception, learning, attention, and action, which he believed enhanced the organism's flexibility and survivability.

Recently, Frederick L. Coolidge and Thomas Wynn have proposed that an enhancement in working memory capacity was an important component in the long evolutionary trajectory of human cognition. Their model of cognitive evolution posits two major evolutionary leaps in cognition, one about 1.8 million years ago with the transition from sometimes living in trees (the *Australopithecines)* to fully terrestrial life (*Homo erectus*), and the second beginning somewhere between 100,000 to 30,000 years ago with the advent of fully modern behavior.

Several developments in cognition can be inferred from the archaeological and fossil evidence that marked the advent of *Homo erectus.* Among them are developments in spatial cognition, fine motor control (praxis), ability to imitate (perhaps driven by the motor neuron system), and a likely change in sleep. The transition from tree to ground sleeping aided in the integrity of a single sleep period, which may have released pressures against the deepest stages of sleep (slow-wave and REM sleep). This in turn may have led to a greater ability to consolidate procedural memories, a greater opportunity for threat rehearsal in dreams, and even creativity. One development in working memory is also evident. *Homo erectus* was able to coordinate visual information from the ventral stream (shape recognition) and dorsal stream (spatial arrangement) in the manufacture of stone tools. This ability was almost certainly deployed via the visuospatial sketchpad of working memory and indicates an advance in cognition over ape abilities.

Coolidge and Wynn's second major leap in cognition was initiated by a transmissible genetic event that enhanced working memory capacity. They have proposed a number of possibilities, including increased phonological storage capacity, greater inhibitory function of the central executive, greater range of speech acts (the reasons why people speak), more powerful theory of mind (being able to understand what someone else is thinking), and/or some heretofore unexamined, domain-specific aspect of working memory. Archaeological support for this enhancement includes evidence for managed foraging systems that planned months and years in advance, age and gender divisions of economic behavior (in which adult men hunted big game, while women and juveniles foraged and hunted small game), depictive artistic traditions that included abstract concepts (e.g., half-animal, half-human figures), and the ability to plan and successfully conduct over-the-horizon colonizing voyages. The timing of this development hinges on the serendipity of archaeological discovery. A strict reading from multiple lines of evidence places enhanced working memory very late in human evolution, sometime after 50,000 years ago. A sanguine interpretation of more scattered evidence (e.g., beads made from shells) would push evidence for modern working memory back to 100,000 years ago.

Frederick L. Coolidge and Thomas Wynn

See also Attention, Evolutionary Perspectives; Visual Working Memory; Working Memory; Working Memory in Language Processing

Further Readings

Baddeley, A. (2007). *Working memory, thought, and action.* Oxford, UK: Oxford University Press.

Coolidge, F. L., & Wynn, T. (2005). Working memory, its executive functions, and the emergence of modern thinking. *Cambridge Archaeological Journal, 15,* 5–26.

Coolidge, F. L., & Wynn, T. (2009). *The rise of* Homo sapiens: *The evolution of modern thinking.* Chichester, UK: Wiley-Blackwell.

Coolidge, F. L., & Wynn, T. (Eds.). (2010). *Working memory: Beyond language and symbolism.* Chicago, IL: University of Chicago Press.

Wynn, T. (2002). Archaeology and cognitive evolution. *Behavioral and Brain Sciences, 25,* 289–438.

Wynn, T., & Coolidge, F. L. (2007). A Stone-Age meeting of minds. *American Scientist, 96,* 44–51.

Working Memory in Language Processing

Adult comprehenders differ in language-specific skills involved in processing words, sentences, and extended discourse. Skilled adult comprehenders also differ in general abilities, such as the ability to flexibly allocate attention, to suppress or inhibit irrelevant or distracting information, in overall processing speed, and in working memory capacity (WMC). Working memory is conceptualized as a cognitive organ in which information is kept in a readily accessible form and manipulated as needed. Some theories of language comprehension claim that working memory is the core ability that determines why some individuals process language more efficiently and effectively than others. This explains why working memory tasks correlate with measures of comprehension ability and overall verbal ability, whereas short-term memory tasks do not. This entry outlines three approaches to working memory that explain why differences in WMC can lead to differences in language comprehension ability. It also reviews evidence suggesting that WMC relates to comprehension ability in skilled adults only by virtue of its relations to other reader characteristics. Because of space limitations, it does not review WMC contributions to language production processes.

How Is WMC Measured?

To understand language, comprehenders must undertake multiple related processes, including lexical access, syntactic parsing, and contextual integration. As these processes are unfolding, readers must maintain their comprehension goals, information extracted from the text, world knowledge, and the partial products of interpretive processes. Working memory supports each of these functions. Working memory resembles short-term memory, which also keeps information temporarily active. Working memory differs from short-term memory because it entails both storage and processing. Working memory also includes executive processes that regulate and control task-relevant information.

Working memory is uncontroversially a limited capacity system, but different theories make different claims about the factors responsible for capacity limitations. These factors may include limitations on the amount of activation, similarity-based interference, processing speed, encoding and retrieval problems, and the ability to inhibit irrelevant information.

Variation in WMC has been shown to correlate with performance on a range of cognitive tasks, including language comprehension. Complex language-processing tasks place the greatest demands on working memory and so offer the opportunity to observe differences in performance across individuals who differ in WMC. Complex tasks involve multiple component processes, however, which complicates the interpretation of any observed correlations between WMC and task performance.

WMC measures assess an individual's ability to keep information activated while undertaking a task that prevents rehearsal. Reading span is often used to measure WMC. In this task, participants read aloud a set of sentences, presented one at a time. They recall the final word of each sentence after reading the entire set. Reading span is the largest set size for which a reader recalls all the sentence-final words. Reading span correlates with the verbal Scholastic Aptitude Test (SAT) (about .5) and the ability to answer questions about a text (about .8). When reading span and text complexity are used to predict reading times, they interact. Differences between high- and low-capacity comprehenders increase as text complexity increases. However, reading span does not correlate with short-term memory tasks, such as digit span.

Other measures of working memory capacity include the following: (a) operation span— participants perform simple arithmetic problems while retaining a set of words; (b) alphabet span— participants repeat a list of words after arranging them in alphabetic order; and (c) minus span— participants repeat a list of numbers after subtracting two from each. These measures correlate highly with each other and with the reading-span measure.

The Relation Between WMC and Language Comprehension

Marcel Just and Pat Carpenter's theory of working memory and language comprehension requires a working memory system that maintains partial products of the comprehension process in an active state while additional input is analyzed. A general purpose working memory system supports both linguistic and nonlinguistic functions. Moreover, the storage and processing functions are fueled by activation, a commodity that maintains knowledge elements in memory and supports computation. Activation is shared among storage and processing functions such that activation-consuming processes limit the amount of activation available to support storage and vice versa. Individual differences in language comprehension depend on differences in capacity, the total amount of activation available to the system. Language places demands on limited working memory resources, and more complex language creates greater demands than less complex language. So, for example, syntactically complex sentences consume more memory resources than simple sentences. As a result, individuals with lower working memory capacities should have greater difficulty with more complex than simple sentences, whereas individuals with large working memory capacities should process complex sentences with about the same efficiency as they process less complex sentences. In some studies, groups of individuals with lower WMC show greater complexity effects than groups with higher WMC. Dual-task paradigms also provide evidence that lower capacity comprehenders are more affected by complexity than are higher capacity comprehenders.

Just and Carpenter's formulation has been challenged by two separate lines of inquiry. First, working memory capacity does not interact with syntactic complexity when appropriate statistical methods are used. Second, groups of patients with scores of zero on working memory tasks are able to parse and interpret sentences containing complex structures and long-distance dependencies. Results such as these have motivated David Caplan and Gloria Waters to propose two separate sources of working memory resources: One is involved in *interpretive* functions (e.g., lexical access, parsing, and the assignment of standard meaning), and the other is involved in *post-interpretive* functions (e.g., contextual integration, and inferencing). Aphasic patients could parse and interpret complex sentences even though they could not remember any words in the reading-span task, perhaps because one source of working memory resources was impaired while the other source was intact. Minimally, theories of WMC must explain how an individual whose reading-span score is zero can comprehend complex sentences.

Other approaches to working memory and language start by noting that scores on working memory tasks depend on (a) the content of the information being held in working memory and (b) the degree to which processes have been automatized. The reorganization of to-be-remembered information by chunking can increase the apparent capacity of working memory, so a single retrieval cue can recover vastly greater information than the standard seven plus or minus two "chunks." Further, automating a process can greatly reduce the demands that processes impose on working memory. To determine the extent to which a task loads working memory, one has to know what information is being manipulated, how that information is organized, and how much practice the individual has had with that specific task. Language interpretation processes such as syntactic parsing are overlearned and automatized; thus, they may place minimal demands on working memory. This account places heavy emphasis on experience—the more often you have encountered a stimulus of a given type, the more automated the interpretive processes should be and the more efficient you should be in processing that stimulus.

A third approach to working memory and language appeals to processes that "clean up" the by-products of automated access and retrieval processes. These approaches argue that differences in working memory capacity are a by-product of the ability to efficiently activate relevant information and suppress or ignore activated but irrelevant information. Two individuals may have equivalent ability to activate and manipulate information, but one individual may overactivate associated information in response to a particular string of words or be unable to reduce or suppress information not directly relevant to the intended meaning. In that case, the individual will behave as though he or she has a small working memory, because the available capacity supports the activation of irrelevant information.

Methodological Advances in Studying WMC and Language

Research on the relation between WMC and language comprehension has been plagued by a set of methodological problems. These involve the psychometric qualities of the instruments used to measure working memory capacity, the nature of the statistical designs used to test the relation between working memory and language comprehension, and the fact that working memory capacity is correlated with a wide variety of other individual differences. Studies often rely on a single measure of working memory capacity. No single measure of capacity has exhibited very high reliability in studies assessing the psychometric properties of working memory tasks. In other words, tests used to assess WMC do not produce the same score for the same individual if the test is taken on two separate occasions. This problem can largely be avoided by using multiple measures of WMC.

The relation between WMC and language comprehension is often studied using quasi-experimental designs. WMC is measured and then people participate in an experiment in which some text variable is manipulated (e.g., word frequency, syntactic complexity). Quasi-experimental designs treat continuous variables (such as WMC) as categorical. This technique can artificially magnify differences between groups and mask variation in performance within each artificially established group. Most of the published quasi-experimental studies of individual differences on WMC and language comprehension also use an extreme-groups design. In such experiments, individuals are selected for analysis because they score very high or very low on some test, such as the reading-span test. Subjects who are closer to average are excluded. This kind of experiment does not allow one to draw conclusions about performance on the language comprehension task across the full range of WMC. Finally, the results of these studies can be difficult to interpret when WMC is the only measure of individual variation examined. Individuals who score low on measures of working memory span tend also to score low on tests of word-recognition ability, vocabulary, print exposure, reasoning ability, and domain knowledge. Is variation in language comprehension because of individual differences in WMC, or is it secondary to abilities that are correlated with capacity?

Some researchers have begun to examine this question using multiple regression and multilevel modeling techniques. For example, Bruce Britton and his colleagues used structural-equation modeling to examine the individual characteristics that affect learning from instructional texts. They assessed the influence of four individual difference factors on text learning: the ability to make inferences, metacognitive ability, working memory capacity, and domain knowledge. Text learning was predicted by a reliable path such that metacognitive ability predicted inference-making ability; inference-making ability predicted domain knowledge, and domain knowledge predicted text learning. Also, metacognitive ability predicted inference ability and inference ability predicted WMC. The relation between WMC and text learning, however, was not significant. Thus, WMC strongly correlated with other individual differences but did not predict text learning when these other variables were entered into the model.

Other studies have also failed to find a relation between language comprehension and working memory capacity when correlated variables have been included in the analyses. Alexandra Gottardo, Linda Siegel, and Keith Stanovich examined the influence of WMC on comprehension in adults with reading disabilities. They found that WMC predicted reading comprehension when it was entered early in a regression equation but failed to predict unique variance when it was entered after other variables.

Debra Long and her colleagues found similar results in a study examining how individual difference variables interact with properties of texts to influence comprehension. They assessed participants' performance on several information processing and language tasks. The individual difference tests included (a) word decoding speed (how quickly a person can pronounce a visually presented word), (b) word decoding accuracy (the number of word-reading errors), and (c) WMC. Sentence-reading times for each participant were analyzed as a function of three text characteristics: (a) number of function words (grammatical markers such as *of* and *although*); (b) number of new argument nouns—how many new concepts a sentence introduces; and (c) number of repeated argument nouns—the number of old concepts. Individual differences in reading times were influenced by different combinations of word-decoding ability, overall verbal ability, and print exposure. When all the individual difference variables were included in the analyses, working memory capacity did not moderate the effect of function words, repeated arguments, or new arguments. When WMC was entered into the model by itself, it did predict the relation between the number of function words and sentence-reading time.

Research examining the shared variance among working memory capacity and other individual-difference variables is still in its infancy. Initial studies suggest that the relation between WMC and language comprehension may be derivative. WMC and language comprehension share variance because WMC is correlated with other variables that have a causal relation with comprehension. More studies are needed before we can definitively say whether WMC plays a direct role in explaining variation in language comprehension ability.

Matthew J. Traxler and Debra L. Long

See also Attention, Resource Models; Automaticity; Discourse Processing, Models of; Working Memory

Further Readings

Baddeley, A. D., & Hitch, G. J. (1974). Working memory. In G. H. Bower (Ed.), *The psychology of learning and motivation: Advances in research and theory* (pp. 47–90). San Diego, CA: Academic Press.

Britton, B. K., Stimson, M., Stennett, B., & Gülgöz, S. (1998). Learning from instructional text: Test of an individual-differences model. *Journal of Educational Psychology, 90,* 476–491.

Caplan, D., & Waters, G. S. (1999). Verbal working memory and sentence comprehension. *Behavioral and Brain Sciences, 22,* 77–126.

Daneman, M., & Carpenter, P. A. (1980). Individual differences in working memory and reading. *Journal of Verbal Learning and Verbal Behavior, 19,* 450–466.

Gottardo, A., Siegel, L. S., & Stanovich, K. E. (1997). The assessment of adults with reading disabilities: What can we learn from experimental tasks? *Journal of Research in Reading, 20,* 42–54.

Just, M. A., & Carpenter, P. A. (1992). The capacity theory of comprehension: New frontiers of evidence and arguments. *Psychological Review, 99,* 122–149.

MacDonald, M. C., & Christiansen, M. H. (1992). Reassessing working memory: Comment on Just and Carpenter (1992) and Waters and Caplan (1996). *Psychological Review, 109,* 35–54.

Masson, M. E., & Miller, J. A. (1983). Working memory and individual differences in comprehension and memory of text. *Journal of Educational Psychology, 75,* 314–318.

Salthouse, T. A. (1996). The processing-speed theory of adult age differences in cognition. *Psychological Review, 103,* 403–428.

Traxler, M. J., Williams, R. S., Blozis, S. A., & Morris, R. K. (2005). Working memory, animacy, and verb class in the processing of relative clauses. *Journal of Memory and Language, 53,* 204–224.

Index